# The Routledge Handbook of Cultural Tourism

*The Routledge Handbook of Cultural Tourism* explores and critically evaluates the debates and controversies in this field of Tourism. It brings together leading specialists from a range of disciplinary backgrounds and geographical regions, to provide state-of-the-art theoretical reflection and empirical research on this significant stream of tourism and its future direction.

The book is divided into seven inter-related sections. Part I looks at the historical, philosophical and theoretical framework for cultural tourism. This section debates tourist autonomy role play, authenticity, imaginaries, cross-cultural issues and inter-disciplinarity. Part II analyses the role that politics takes in cultural tourism. This section also looks at ways in which cultural tourism is used as a policy instrument for economic development. Part III focuses on social patterns and trends, such as the mobilities paradigm, performativity, reflexivity and traditional hospitality, as well as considering sensitive social issues such as dark tourism. Part IV analyses community and development, exploring adaptive forms of cultural tourism, as well as more sustainable models for indigenous tourism development. Part V discusses landscapes and destinations, including the transformation of space into place, issues of authenticity in landscape, the transformation of urban and rural landscapes into tourism products, and conservation versus development dilemmas. Part VI refers to regeneration and planning, especially the creative turn in cultural tourism, which can be used to avoid problems of serial reproduction, standardisation and homogenisation. Part VII deals with the tourist and visitor experience, emphasising the desire of tourists to be more actively and interactively engaged in cultural tourism.

This significant volume offers the reader a comprehensive synthesis of this field, conveying the latest thinking and research. The text is international in focus, encouraging dialogue across disciplinary boundaries and areas of study and will be an invaluable resource for all those with an interest in cultural tourism.

This is essential reading for students, researchers and academics of Tourism as well as those of related studies, in particular Cultural Studies, Leisure, Geography, Sociology, Politics and Economics.

**Melanie Smith** is an Associate Professor and Researcher in Tourism at the Budapest Business School in Hungary.

**Greg Richards** is Professor in Leisure Studies at Tilburg University and Professor in Events at NHTV Breda University of Applied Sciences in the Netherlands.

# The Routledge Handbook of Cultural Tourism

*Edited by*
*Melanie Smith and Greg Richards*

Routledge
Taylor & Francis Group

LONDON AND NEW YORK

First published 2013
by Routledge
2 Park Square, Milton Park, Abingdon, Oxon OX14 4RN

Simultaneously published in the USA and Canada
by Routledge
711 Third Avenue, New York, NY 10017

*Routledge is an imprint of the Taylor & Francis Group, an informa business*

*British Library Cataloguing in Publication Data*
A catalogue record for this book is available from the British Library

*Library of Congress Cataloging in Publication Data*
Smith, Melanie.
The Routledge handbook of cultural tourism / Melanie Smith and Greg Richards.
 p. cm.
Includes bibliographical references and index.
 1. Heritage tourism–Handbooks, manuals, etc. I. Richards, Greg. II. Title.
 G156.5.H47S558 2012
 338.4'791–dc23
  2012019572

ISBN: 978-0-415-52351-6 (hbk)
ISBN: 978-0-203-12095-8 (ebk)

Typeset in Bembo
by Taylor & Francis Books

Printed and bound in Great Britain by
CPI Group (UK) Ltd, Croydon, CR0 4YY

# Contents

Contents

Contents

# Illustrations

## Figures

## Tables

## Boxes

# Contributors

**Paul Barron** is Reader in the School of Marketing, Tourism and Languages, Edinburgh Napier University. Paul's research interests include students' educational experiences and emerging markets in the tourism industry. Paul is currently Hospitality Editor for the *Journal of Hospitality, Leisure, Sport and Tourism Education*.

**Sean Beer**, International Centre for Tourism and Hospitality Research, School of Tourism, Bournemouth University, UK. Originally Sean trained as an agricultural scientist studying at Reading University in the UK and Massey University in New Zealand. Work relating to the food supply and local food increasingly lead to an involvement with the tourism and hospitality industries. This academic work has been backed up with considerable practical experience gained in family and other businesses, locally and internationally. His principle research interests include: the food supply chain, consumer behaviour, rural business, society and development. Currently he is part way through his PhD, a body of work that is looking at human perceptions of the authenticity of food.

**Juan Gabriel Brida** is Associate Professor of Economics at the School of Economics and Management, Free University of Bolzano. His research interests and expertise are in the areas of tourism economics and economic growth. He has a degree in Mathematics from the Universidad de la Republica (Uruguay) and a PhD in Economics from the University of Siena.

**David Macaulay Bruce** is a Visiting Research Fellow in Tourism at University of West of England, Bristol (formerly Principal Lecturer, Bristol Business School, UWE). As Academic Adviser to European Walled Towns (formerly the Walled Towns Friendship Circle), research interests are in and about walled towns – their history, tourism and sustainable development. (See www.walledtownsresearch.org for relevant publications.) Nineteenth-century tourism history associated with Mariana Starke, Baedeker, Murray and other guide books is a further research area. He studied History, Political Economy and Town Planning at St Andrews (MA) and Edinburgh (MPhil) Universities, and is professionally qualified in Town Planning (MRTPI), Transport (MCILT) and Tourism (MTS).

**Karolina Buczkowska** (PhD) is a tourism lecturer at the University School of Physical Education (AWF) in Poznan, Poland. There she is also the tutor of the Cultural Tourism and Tourism Journalism courses and the Departmental Co-ordinator of the LLP/Erasmus Program. She is the Deputy Editor-in-Chief of *Cultural Tourism*, a Polish scientific internet journal (*Turystyka kulturowa*), and a member of the Association for Tourism and Leisure

Education (ATLAS) Cultural Tourism Research Group. She has published three books and over 25 articles concerning cultural tourism.

**Claire Burnill-Maier** studied English and Drama Education at the University of Exeter and, following a three-year period of living, working and extensive travel in Asia, she then returned to the UK. Having developed an interest in the field of Cultural Studies during the course of completing her MSc in Development Studies at the University of Bath, she now lives in Germany and lectures in Cultural Sciences and English in Austria.

**Maria Cândida Pacheco Cadavez** is a Lecturer in English Language and Culture at the Estoril Higher Institute for Hotel and Tourism Studies, in Portugal. She has a Master's degree in English Culture Studies with the thesis *A Room with a View to the World: Tourism, Globalization and Culture*. As a PhD student in Cultural Sciences at Lisbon University, she is currently working on the institutional importance of tourism representations in a nationalist environment. She has participated in several international congresses and published articles about her main academic research interests, which include tourism, culture, nationalism, globalization and visual studies.

**Maria João Carneiro** is an Assistant Professor of Tourism and a researcher at the GOVCOPP Research Unit at the University of Aveiro. Her research interests include competitiveness in tourism, tourism impacts, image and positioning of tourism destinations, consumer behaviour in tourism, and tourism destination marketing. She is co-ordinator of the degree in Tourism at the University of Aveiro.

**Clare Carruthers** is a Lecturer in Tourism and Marketing at the School of Hospitality and Tourism Management, University of Ulster. Her current research interests include culture-led regeneration of post-industrial cities, the role of the European City of Culture in urban tourism, and urban tourism destination marketing.

**Erik Cohen** is the George S. Wise Professor of Sociology (emeritus) at the Hebrew University of Jerusalem, where he taught between 1959 and 2000. He has conducted research in Israel, Peru, the Pacific Islands and, since 1977, in Thailand. He is the author of more than 180 publications. His recent books include *Contemporary Tourism: Diversity and Change* (Elsevier, 2004), and *Explorations in Thai Tourism* (Emerald, 2008). He is a founding member of the International Academy for the Study of Tourism. Erik Cohen presently lives and does research in Thailand.

**David Crouch** is a cultural geographer whose research and writing include critically conceptual and empirically informed work on leisure and tourism, cultural and cultures of tourism. He has written and edited 10 books and authored numerous academic papers and chapters, as well as more popular essays and TV, across geography, culture, landscape and land use, tourism, leisure, art theory and practice. He has also worked with the UK government and regional agencies.

**Lóránt Dávid** was born in Hungary, and graduated in History, Geography, European Studies and Tourism. He is a college professor in Tourism at Károly Róbert College, Gyöngyös, and an Honorary Associate Professor at Szent István University, Gödöllő in Hungary. He has longstanding teaching, publication and research interests in tourism, regional development and environmental studies. More recently he has been undertaking research on tourism management. He is the author and editor of over 10 books as well as over 100 journal articles and book chapters, and has been active in a number of international research and teaching associations.

**Anya Diekmann** is Associate Professor and Head of Tourism (Master de Gestion et Analyse du tourisme) and co-director of the tourism research department LIToTeS (Laboratoire Interdisciplinaire Tourisme, Territoires et Sociétés) at the Université libre de Bruxelles (Belgium). Since her PhD on the relationship between heritage sites and tourist consumption, she has collaborated on numerous national, European and international research projects related to cultural tourism development. Moreover, for several years her research has focused on cultural and slum tourism in India as well as ethnic tourism in Europe. Her publications include work on social tourism and cultural tourism with a particular focus on heritage, urban and ethnic tourism. In 2011 she co-authored with Kevin Hannam *Tourism and India: A Critical Introduction* (Routledge), and she is co-editor with Scott McCabe and Lynn Minnaert of *Social Tourism in Europe: Theory and Practice* (Channel View), and together with Kevin Hannam in 2010 *Beyond Backpacker Tourism: Mobilities and Experiences* (Channel View).

**Celeste Eusébio** is an Assistant Professor of Tourism and a researcher at the GOVCOPP Research Unit at the University of Aveiro. Her research interests include tourism economics, tourism impacts, tourism forecasts and consumer behaviour in tourism. She is vice-coordinator of the degree in Tourism at the University of Aveiro.

**Juan Ignacio Pulido Fernández** is the director of Laboratory of Analysis and Innovation in Tourism (LAInnTUR) at the University of Jaén. He is an Associate Professor in the Department of Economics and his academic background focuses on sustainability of tourism, destination management and economic development, tourism impacts, and innovation. Juan Ignacio has published a number of articles in international peer-reviewed journals and several books, conference papers and book chapters among other prestigious publishing by, among others, Routledge and Springer-Verlag. He has served as main researcher in several national and international research projects. He currently chairs the Spanish Association of Scientific Experts in Tourism (AECIT).

**Sonia Ferrari** has been Associate Professor of Tourism Marketing, Event Marketing and Place Marketing in the University of Calabria, Italy, since 2005. She has been researcher in the same University since 1993. She has also taught Management, Service Management and Tourism Management. She has been the Director of the Tourism Science degree course and Director of the Valorizzazione dei Sistemi Turistico Culturali degree course in University of Calabria since 2007. Her main fields of study and research are quality in services (also in tourism), tourism marketing, place marketing, event marketing and experiential marketing.

**Patrick S. Föhl**, DrPhil in Arts Management and graduate cultural worker, 1978 in Berlin. Since 2005 he has been Head of the Network for Cultural Consulting, Berlin (www.netzwerk-kulturberatung.de), and since 2006 Head of the research group 'Regional Governance in the Cultural Sector' at the Cultural Work Programme at the University of Applied Sciences Potsdam (www.regional-governance-kultur.de). In 2011 – among other projects – together with and on behalf of Prof. Dr Oliver Scheytt, he implemented a strategic process for the Cultural Region Stuttgart. Since 1996 he has worked in different cultural institutions (e.g. Jewish

Museum Berlin, Stiftung Schloss Neuhardenberg, Klassik Stiftung Weimar). Guest lecturer and speaker at various universities, colleges and institutions in Austria, Germany, Poland, Switzerland, USA and Vietnam. Working, publishing and research priorities include strategic arts management, collaborations and mergers, governance, arts marketing, project management, cultural financing, cultural policy and cultural development planning. He publishes extensively in the field of arts management and cultural policy in theory and practice.

**Béla Zsolt Gergely** contributes to shaping and guiding the strategic direction of the Department of Tourism at Edutus College in Budapest as Project Manager in charge of international projects and initiatives. In that capacity he is responsible for the administration of several major international European Union-funded projects, including KnowNet – the European Network of Excellence for Promoting the Competitiveness and Sustainability of Tourism Industry small and medium-sized enterprises. Previously, he worked as Office Manager of the State Science and Technology Institute (SSTI) in Westerville, Ohio, a US non-profit organisation dedicated to improving government-industry programmes that encourage economic growth through the application of science and technology. Prior to joining SSTI, he served as Institute Administrator of the Institute for Theoretical Sciences at the University of Notre Dame. He holds a BA degree in British and American Studies from the Babeş-Bolyai University of Cluj, Romania.

**Monica Gilli** is Assistant Professor at the University of Milano-Bicocca, where she teaches Sociology of Territory and Tourism. Her research interests are the relationship between tourism and identity construction, and tourism as a factor in urban regeneration and community development. Among her recent publications are *Autenticità e interpretazione nell'esperienza turistica* (Authenticity and interpretation in the tourist experience) (Milano, 2009).

**C. Michael Hall** is a Professor in the Department of Management, University of Canterbury, Christchurch; Docent, Department of Geography, University of Oulu, Finland; Research Fellow, Freiburg Institute of Advanced Studies; and a Visiting Professor at Linneaus University, Kalmar, Sweden and the University of Eastern Finland, Savonlinna. He is co-editor of *Current Issues in Tourism*, and he has published widely in tourism, environmental history, and gastronomy.

**Kevin Hannam** is Associate Dean of Research, Head of the Department of Tourism, Hospitality and Events, Professor of Tourism Development and Director of the Centre for Research into the Experience Economy (CREE) at the University of Sunderland, UK, and a visiting Senior Research Fellow at the University of Johannesburg, South Africa. He is a founding co-editor of the Routledge journal *Mobilities*, co-author of *Understanding Tourism* (Sage) and monograph *Tourism and India* (Routledge). He is co-chair of the ATLAS Independent Travel Research Group and chair of the World Leisure Commission on Tourism and the Environment. He has published research on aspects of cultural, heritage and nature-based tourism development in India and Scandinavia. He holds a PhD in geography from the University of Portsmouth.

**Joan C. Henderson** is an Associate Professor at Nanyang Technological University's Business School in Singapore and teaches on the Tourism and Hospitality Management programme. Her research interests encompass different aspects of tourism development in South East Asia, including issues of heritage and culture.

**Michael Hitchcock** is Dean of the Faculty of Hospitality and Tourism Management at the Macau University of Science and Technology. Formerly he was Academic Director of IMI Switzerland and a Deputy Dean for External Relations and Research at the University of Chichester. He was at London Metropolitan University from 1995 to 2008, where he was a Professor and a Research Institute Director. He also taught Southeast Asian Development Sociology at the University of Hull and was Assistant Keeper (Ethnography) at the Horniman Museum, London. Michael Hitchcock took his doctorate (DPhil) in 1983 at the University of Oxford, and has written and edited 14 books, as well as 40 refereed journal papers and numerous other published outputs.

**Keith Hollinshead** is a cross-disciplinary/post-disciplinary (sometimes pungently adisciplinary!) researcher of the representation of culture, heritage and nature. Largely 'Australian' by field experience, he draws on cultural studies/political science/human communications in investigating the iconology of peoples and places. Having a particular interest in primal populations, he frequently probes clashes of cosmology between dominant global practices and longstanding indigenous worldviews. Professor of Public Culture (University of Bedfordshire, England), his current research agendas feature matters of 'Worldmaking', 'Transitionality', and 'Emergent/Hybrid Culture' as revealed through international tourism. He is Distinguished Professor with the International Tourism Studies Association (University of Peking, China).

**Zsuzsanna Horváth** is a Lecturer in Entrepreneurship and International Business at the Budapest Business School and about to complete her PhD studies at Pécs University, Faculty of Economics. Her focus of research is empowerment of students in higher education by teaching them responsible entrepreneurial skills and competencies and thus improving their future expectations. She is the author of several articles on value co-creation in tourism and the nature of tourism experience. She was Founding Secretary-General of the Hungarian Council of Shopping Centres and was instrumental in establishing the industry in Hungary.

**Michael Ireland** is an Associate Lecturer in the School of Geography, Earth and Environmental Science at the University of Plymouth. Before joining the university he was Programme Leader from 1992 to 2006 on the MA in Tourism and Social Responsibility (EXON) at the College of St Mark and St John, Plymouth. His research interests include tourism development and the anthropology of tourism in Cornwall (UK), Scandinavia, the Baltic States and the former republics of the Soviet Union. As part of these research interests he has undertaken field work in the Altai Mountains of Western Siberia on nature tourism. He is a Fellow of the Royal Anthropological Institute and member of ATLAS.

**Milka Ivanova** is a PhD candidate in Tourism Studies at University of Bedfordshire, England. Her main research interests in tourism embrace matters of traditionality vis-à-vis transitionality. Milka's other research interests include the representations of place through tourism and communist/socialist/totalitarian projections of heritage. Her long background in history and in inter-cultural communications informs her current research regimes on national inheritances. She is currently working with Professor Hollinshead on two Special Issues of *Tourism Analysis* – one on 'Worldmaking' and one on 'Foucault and Tourism Studies'.

**Myriam Jansen-Verbeke**, a geographer, is a member of the International Academy for the Study of Tourism and Professor emeritus of the Geo Institute (Tourism Master Program),

University of Leuven, Belgium. During her academic career she has undertaken research on a wide range of topics related to tourism. Her current research interests focus on heritage, culture and tourism. She is now involved in the World Heritage Tourism Research Network (WHTRN) and launching international workshops and projects in this multidisciplinary field. In January 2011 she was appointed Visiting Professor to the CAS-Chinese Academy of Sciences – IGNRSS, in particular to introduce the debate on sustainable tourism development in the GIAHS project, China.

**Elisabeth Kastenholz** is Assistant Professor at the University of Aveiro and a researcher at the GOVCOPP Research Unit, currently coordinating the Master's in Tourism Management and Planning at the University of Aveiro and a research project on the integral rural tourism experience. Holding an MBA and a PhD in Tourism Studies, her research focuses on rural tourism, destination marketing and sustainable destination development.

**James Kennell** is Director of the Economic Development Resource Centre at the University of Greenwich, where he is also Senior Lecturer in Tourism and Regeneration. He carries out research and consultancy in the fields of local economic development, cultural regeneration, tourism development, events management and cultural industries development. Before joining Greenwich, James worked at the British Council and he has managed programmes and projects in the fields of urban regeneration, housing and social care in the south-east of England.

**Anna Leask** is Reader in Tourism at Edinburgh Napier University, UK. Her teaching and research interests combine and lie principally in the areas of visitor attraction management and managing Generation Y as visitors and workers. She has co-edited several textbooks, in addition to publishing a range of journal articles and practitioner papers.

**Willy Legrand** has been lecturing in the Department of Hospitality Management at the International University of Applied Sciences Bad Honnef, Bonn, Germany for the past decade. Prior to this, he held numerous managerial positions in the hospitality industry in Canada and Germany. Willy holds an MBA with a specialisation in Environmental Management. He regularly publishes research articles in leading journals and has published a textbook on the principles of sustainable development and management in the hospitality industry – he is currently working on a second edition. He recently took the lead in the academic support of the United Nations World Tourism Organization (UNWTO) pilot testing of the Hotel Energy Solutions (HES) eToolkit with the City of Bonn, Germany.

**Philip Long**, Associate Dean, Head of Tourism, Bournemouth University. Phil Long's research interests include: festivals, cultural events and their tourism dimensions; connections between international film, television and tourism; diaspora communities, social exclusion and tourism; partnerships and collaboration in tourism development and the relationships between royalty and tourism. Phil is a board member of the Tourism Society (UK), and the International Festivals and Events Association (Europe). He is a Fellow of the Tourism Management Institute. Before embarking on an academic career, Phil worked for 12 years in the tourism industry in the UK and Zimbabwe.

**Donald Macleod** is a Senior Lecturer at the University of Glasgow. He has a DPhil in Social Anthropology (University of Oxford) and has researched in the Caribbean, the Canary

Islands and Scotland. His publications include the books: *Sustainable Tourism in Rural Europe: Approaches to Development* (2011, co-editor); *Tourism, Power and Culture: Anthropological Insights* (2010, co-editor); *Tourism, Globalisation and Cultural Change* (2004); *Niche Tourism in Question* (2003, editor); *Tourists and Tourism* (1997, co-editor). His research interests include: the anthropology of tourism; sustainable tourism development; globalisation; and cultural change, power, cultural heritage and identity.

**Nicola MacLeod** is Principal Lecturer in Tourism in the Business School of the University of Greenwich, London, where she contributes to undergraduate and postgraduate tourism programmes. Her current research interests are cultural landscapes of tourism with specific emphasis on self-guided trails.

**Kevin Meethan** is Associate Professor in Sociology in the School of Social Science and Social Work at Plymouth University. His research interests are broad and interdisciplinary, encompassing tourism, socio-cultural change, and global–local relations, tourism policy, embodiment and performance in tourism and visual research methods. He is an active member of the International Sociological Association and is Vice-President (Publications) of ISA Research Committee 50, International Tourism, and Founding Editor of the *Journal of Tourism Consumption and Practice* (www.tourismconsumption.org).

**Marta Meleddu**, is a Research Fellow at the Economics Department (DiSEA), University of Sassari and CRENoS, Italy. She holds a Master's degree in Economics and Econometrics from the Univerity of Bristol, UK, and a PhD from the University of Sassari. Her research interests include cultural economics, tourism economics, environmental economics, economics of crime, and consumer choice.

**Marjan Melkert**, MA, is a researcher and consultant at the Centre for Cultural Tourism Research and teacher at the Academy of Fine Arts and Design at Zuyd University. She has been a member of the ATLAS Special Interest Group Cultural Tourism since 2004.

**Petr Merta** is a graduate in Economics and Management at the Faculty of Civil Engineering at Brno University of Technology. Currently studying a postgraduate academic programme at the same faculty, working on the topic 'Quantification of values of historic buildings', and co-operating with the Art and Theatre Institute in Prague on an expert study and research project.

**Qingwen Min**, Director of the Institute of Geographic Sciences and Natural Resources Research (IGSNRR), CAS, Project Coordinator GIAHS – China.

**Nigel D. Morpeth** is an academic and artist based in the Carnegie Faculty of Education and Sport, at Leeds Metropolitan University. He is engaged with teaching and research in diverse inter-disciplinary academic groups in Cultural Studies, the Creative Industries, Sport and Tourism. He has published internationally on a wide range of research interests including special interest tourism, sustainable tourism policy, communities and cultural events and festivals. He previously worked for three UK local authorities in the north of England in the field of community-based leisure, events and festival organisation. He combines his role as an academic with artistic work and has previously exhibited in a variety of cultural contexts throughout the UK.

**Wil Munsters** is Director of the Centre for Cultural Tourism Research and Professor of Cultural Tourism at Zuyd University (the Netherlands). He is the author of cultural tourism studies on the Netherlands, Belgium and research methodology. As a member of ATLAS he has been engaged in the international Cultural Tourism Research Project since 1994.

**Can-Seng Ooi** is an Associate Professor at Copenhagen Business School. He is also Director of the Centre for Leisure and Culture Services there, and Editor of the journal *Asia Matters: Business, Culture and Theory*. His research interests include comparative cultural tourism, destination branding and art worlds. Can-Seng has contributed to various tourism studies debates, including in defining the 'versatile tourist', explaining why the accreditation branding strategy makes destinations alike, and showing how personal tourist experiences can be mass produced. He has published extensively, including in *Annals of Tourism Research*, *Tourism*, and *Place Branding and Public Diplomacy*.

**Xerardo Pereiro** is a social anthropologist who works in the University of Trás-os-Montes and Alto Douro (Portugal) as assistant teacher in Anthropology and Cultural Tourism. He is a researcher in CETRAD (Centre for Transdisciplinary Development Studies).

**David Picard** is an anthropologist working at the Centre for Research in Anthropology at New University of Lisbon, Portugal (CRIA-FCSH/UNL). He holds a PhD in anthropology from the University of La Reunion, Indian Ocean (2001). He has co-edited *Festivals, Tourism and Social Change* (Channel View Publications, 2006); *The Framed World: Tourism, Tourists and Photography* (Ashgate, 2009); and *Emotion in Motion: Tourism, Affect and Transformation* (Ashgate, 2012). His first single-authored book, *Tourism, Magic and Modernity: Cultivating the Human Garden* was published by Berghahn in 2011.

**Yvonne Pröbstle**, MA, studied European History and Cultural Management. She is a research assistant at the Institute of Cultural Management in Ludwigsburg. Her research areas include culture tourism, audience development and volunteering. She is currently writing her PhD thesis on the motives and behaviour of culture tourists in Germany. She has written several articles about marketing in cultural tourism and has done feasibility studies for different cultural institutions and destinations. Besides her research activities she works in the field of non-profit marketing and does freelance work.

**László Puczkó** graduated in 1993 as an economist specialising in tourism at Budapest University of Economics. Then, led by his interest in culture and the arts, he completed a dance teaching course at the Hungarian Institute of Culture and Arts (1995), and also graduated from the Art and Design Management department of the Hungarian University of Applied Arts (1996). He successfully completed his PhD studies in 2000. He became a Certified Management Consultant (CMC) in 2003. He is the (co-)author of numerous specialised books, including *Health and Wellness Tourism, Impacts of Tourism* (in English); *From Attractions to Experiences, Tourism in Historic Cities* (in Hungarian), and articles in professional journals. He has been active in experience mapping, cultural interpretation and heritage management.

**Manuela Pulina** is a Lecturer in the Economics Department (DiSEA), University of Sassari and CRENoS, Italy. She holds a PhD from the University of Southampton, UK. Her main research interests include tourism economics, crime economics, growth and consumer behaviour.

**Alan Quaglieri-Domínguez**, born in Locarno, Switzerland, is a PhD candidate in Tourism at the Universitat Rovira i Virgili, Tarragona, Spain. He has a Master's degree in Tourism Management and Planning (2009) from the same university and a previous degree in Economics (2004) from the Università Bocconi, Milan, Italy. He collaborated on several projects in the fields of tourism studies and cultural management both at academic level and for private institutions. His research interest is currently focused on urban tourism, urban populations and mobility, urban and cultural planning.

**Tereza Raabová** is an expert in economy of culture, economic impacts of culture and tourism. She is the founder of the 'Economic Impact' agency, specialising in the elaboration of studies of economic impacts. Tereza is a lecturer at the University of Economics in Prague and she collaborates with the Arts and Theatre Institute in Prague on a number of research projects.

**Yvette Reisinger** is an Adjunct Professor of Business at James Cook University, Singapore. She received her PhD in Tourism Marketing at Victoria University, Melbourne, Australia. Her major research interests are in the area of cultural influences on tourist behaviour and destination marketing. She has a special interest in cross-cultural and behavioural analytical/ quantitative studies. She is the author of three books and 140 papers on cross-cultural behaviour in international tourism. She received research awards for her work on cultural differences among Asian tourist markets. She has a wide spectrum of professional and personal experiences spanning across the four continents of Australia, Europe, North America and Asia.

**Bulcsú Remenyik** is an Associate Professor of Tourism at Károly Róbert College in Gyöngyös, Hungary. He has a long-standing research interest in tourism and regional development, and a lengthy publishing record. He was responsible for the administration of more than 20 regional and local projects and initiatives involving development of tourism destinations along the Hungarian–Croatian border and is currently involved with visitor-based economic development projects in the southern Danubian area of Hungary. He is fluent in German, Russian and English. Mr Remenyik holds a BA in History, Geography and Tourism, and a PhD in Geography, both from the University of Pécs.

**Greg Richards** is Professor in Leisure Studies at Tilburg University and Professor in Events at NHTV Breda University of Applied Sciences in the Netherlands. He has written numerous books and articles on cultural and creative tourism, and directs the ATLAS Cultural Tourism Project.

**Mike Robinson** holds the Chair of Cultural Heritage at the University of Birmingham, UK. He is director of the Ironbridge International Institute for Cultural Heritage, founder of the Centre for Tourism and Cultural Change and Editor of the *Journal of Tourism and Cultural Change*.

**Sujama Roy** studied for her MSc and PhD degrees in tourism at the University of Sunderland. Her PhD degree was entitled *A Cultural Politics of Mobilities: An Analysis of the Darjeeling Himalayan Railway*.

**Antonio Paolo Russo** is Assistant Professor in the Department of Geography, Universitat Rovira i Virgili, Tarragona, and Research Director of the Science and Technology Park of Tourism and Leisure. Previous appointments were with the Erasmus University Rotterdam (where he received his PhD in Economics in 2002), the Universitat Autònoma, Barcelona, and IULM University, Milan. He is author of various publications in academic journals and books. His research interests range from tourism studies to cultural and urban economics and planning. He has been involved as a staff member of university departments and as an independent expert adviser in various research projects on these topics, both in specific local issues and in European Union research networks and other international programmes.

**Jarkko Saarinen** is Professor of Human Geography, Tourism Studies, at the University of Oulu, and Senior Research Fellow at the School of Tourism and Hospitality, University of Johannesburg. His research interests include: tourism development and its management, impacts and sustainability; tourism and climate change; community-based natural resource management and tourism; and the construction of the ideas of nature and local culture in tourism. He is currently Chair of the International Geographical Union's (IGU) Commission on Tourism, Leisure and Global Change, and Associate Editor of the *Journal of Ecotourism*.

**Noel B. Salazar** received his PhD in anthropology from the University of Pennsylvania and is currently Assistant Professor and Senior Researcher of the Research Foundation Flanders at the University of Leuven, Belgium. In addition, he is on the United Nations Educational, Scientific and Cultural Organization's (UNESCO's) and the United Nations World Tourism Organization's (UNWTO's) official roster of consultants and an expert panel member of the National Geographic Society's Centre for Sustainable Destinations. His research interests include mobility and travel, the local–global nexus, imaginaries of Otherness, heritage, and cosmopolitanism. He has published widely about these topics and is the author of *Envisioning Eden: Mobilizing Imaginaries in Tourism and Beyond* (Berghahn, 2010).

**Marcelino Sánchez Rivero** is Lecturer in the Department of Economics at the University of Extremadura, Spain. His research interests include statistical analysis of contingency tables, latent structure models, analysis of tourist behaviour, sustainability, and competitiveness. Marcelino has published articles in international journals such as *Tourism Economics, International Journal of Tourism Research* or *Journal of Travel Research*. Also he publishes book chapters, conference papers, etc. Currently, he is General Secretary of the Spanish Association of Scientific Experts in Tourism (AECIT).

**Tony Seaton** is MacAnally Professor of Travel History and Tourism Behaviour at the University of Limerick. He has an Oxford MA in English Literature, a first class degree in the Social Sciences, an MA in Theology (Lampeter), and a PhD in Tourism Studies from Strathclyde. For 25 years he has researched and consulted on destination marketing and cultural tourism for governments, national tourist offices, academic institutions and libraries in 65 different countries. His best-known work has been on Thanatourism and book town tourism, which led to the setting up of Scotland's book town, Wigtown, and England's book town, Sedbergh.

**Tom Selwyn** is Director of Studies in Anthropology of Travel, Tourism, Hospitality, and Pilgrimage at the School of Oriental and African Studies (SOAS), University of London, where he established a Master's degree in the field in 2011. He became Series Editor (with Dr Parvathi Raman) of Berghahn Books' *Mobile Worlds: Studies in Migration, Travel, and Tourism* in 2012. He is Honorary Librarian of the Royal Anthropological Institute and was recipient of the RAI's Lucy Mair medal in 2009. His geographical research interests include the Mediterranean, and Palestine/Israel. Recent publications include the co-edited volumes *Thinking Through Tourism* (Berg, 2010) and *Contested Mediterranean Spaces* (Berghahn, 2011).

**Stephen Shaw** is Reader in Regeneration and City Management, Cities Institute, London Metropolitan University. His current work focuses on the development of more effective approaches to community engagement in tourism-led regeneration. He chairs the Cultural Tourism Committee of ICOMOS UK (UNESCO World Heritage).

**Claudia Simons-Kaufmann** is Professor at the International University of Applied Sciences in Bad Honnef, Germany. She lectures in Economics and Accounting. From 1998 until 2001 she lectured and did research at the Universidade Católica de Moçambique, in Beira, Africa. Since then she has been doing short-term consultancies and seminars for different development organizations in Mozambique and Ghana in the areas of private-sector promotion, donor co-ordination and social market economy. She was working as a project manager for a private company in Mozambique, developing and structuring new business ideas. Her research interests lie in the area of sustainability, developing countries and models of economic systems.

**Heather Skinner** is a Principal Lecturer in Marketing at the University of Glamorgan's Business School. Her main research interest is the representation of national identity through nation brands, and in particular the role that the cultural output of a nation can play in economic regeneration.

**Philip Sloan**, Head of Hospitality, International University of Applied Sciences Bad Honnef, Bonn, is one of the founding members of the lecturing team that started the Department of Hospitality Management at the IUBH in Bonn, Germany, in September 2000. Philip's earlier career was in the management of London hotels before creating his own small chain of organic restaurants in England and then in Strasbourg, France, where he is now based. He holds a Master's degree in Environmental Management, an MBA and has a long list of peer-reviewed scientific journal articles to his credit, and books. In addition to teaching sustainable hospitality management studies, he is a passionate environmental entrepreneur and is currently working on various sustainable food projects in addition to running a small organic vineyard on the university campus.

**Melanie Smith** is an Associate Professor and Researcher in Tourism at the Budapest Business School in Hungary. She was Director of BA Tourism and MA Cultural Tourism Management Programmes for several years at the University of Greenwich in London, where she undertook extensive curriculum development in cultural tourism. During this time she completed a PhD on the role of culture in urban regeneration, and was involved in research and consultancy work with local authorities and agencies on cultural and creative industries, as well as community involvement in culture-led regeneration. She is author or editor of several books about cultural tourism, including *Issues in Cultural Tourism Studies* (2003, 2009); *Cultural Tourism in a Changing World: Politics, Participation and (Re)presentation* (2006) with Mike Robinson; and *Tourism, Culture and Regeneration* (2006). She has also published many book chapters and journal articles on heritage tourism, urban cultural tourism, World Heritage sites, festivals, culture-led regeneration, and cultural and creative industries. She is currently Chair of ATLAS, which has around 300 members in 70 countries.

**Yehong Sun**, geographer, is a postdoc researcher at the Institute of Geographical Sciences and Natural Resources Research – Chinese Academy of Sciences (IGSNRR, CAS) and Lecturer in Tourism, Institute of Beijing Union University, China. Her research interests are agricultural heritage systems, dynamic conservation, heritage tourism, cultural tourism and tourism planning. She was a visiting scholar at K.U. Leuven, Belgium in 2008 and 2011, guest lectured in the Department of Geography at K.U. Leuven, NHTV Breda, Netherlands, and the International Studies University, China in 2011.

**Anna Thompson–Carr** is a Māori academic whose research interests include visitor experiences, cultural landscapes, community development and ecotourism. She has been co-owner/-operator of two adventure tourism companies and was a director of Te Ana Whakairo Ltd (2007–11).

**Alena Tichá** is a University Lecturer and Associate Professor in the field of Civil Engineering Management at the Faculty of Civil Engineering at the Brno University of Technology. She deals with the economics of the project lifecycle and specializes in costs and prices. She is an author of many specialised texts, and researcher/co-researcher of many research projects.

**Karel Werdler** is the head of External Relations of Tourism and Leisure Management Studies at Inholland University of Applied Sciences in Amsterdam. He is also a guest lecturer at CETT Barcelona and London South Bank University, where he is currently involved in his PhD focusing on the relationship between dark tourism objects and venues and the possible proposition of these in selected European destinations. His other research area is sub-Saharan Africa and as a board member of ATLAS Africa he has published several articles on tourism in this continent. For several years he has also been directing a project aimed at the organisational strengthening and academic capacity development of the Rwanda Tourism University College in Kigali.

**Gernot Wolfram** studied German Philology, Rhetoric and Communication Sciences in Tübingen and Berlin. He has lived in Berlin since 1997 and teaches as Professor of Arts Management at the MHMK University of Berlin and as Professor of Cultural Studies at the FH Kufstein (Tyrol). He has produced numerous publications within the fields of Inter-cultural Exchange, International Arts Management and Discourses of Otherness. Since 2010 he has belonged, as an expert for Cultural Projects, to Team Europe of the European Commission in Germany.

**Simon Woodward** is Senior Research Fellow at Leeds Metropolitan University in the UK, where he teaches and researches on a range of issues around communities, culture and heritage. He has a particular interest in the ways in which values associated with heritage change over time, across and within stakeholder groups, and is currently working on a project investigating these issues within the context of Durham World Heritage site. He sits on the ICOMOS-UK and ICOMOS International Cultural Tourism Committees and on the Dean's Committee at Durham Cathedral, and is a former Advisory Board Member of the International Ecotourism Society.

# Preface

I first 'discovered' cultural tourism around 15 years ago when I decided to focus on this subject for my Master's degree thesis at the University of Surrey. Of course, I then realised that I had been an avid cultural tourist for most of my life, having a specific interest in visual and performing arts, festivals, heritage sites and museums, not to mention being fascinated by the lives of local people in tourism destinations. However, 15 years ago cultural tourism was still something of a niche subject in tourism studies. It was hard to find academic literature or research. Of course, by digging deeper it was possible to find all kinds of literature relating to the impacts of tourism on the cultures of local communities (e.g. the research of anthropologists like Smith, Nash and Graburn from the 1970s). Many researchers had also started to consider issues relating to heritage interpretation from the 1970s (e.g. Tilden); however, the term 'heritage tourism' was not really coined until much later. It was around the mid to late 1990s when the literature relating to arts, heritage and cultural tourism started to flourish. I remember towards the end of my Master's thesis in 1996 discovering the work of Greg Richards on cultural tourism and feeling incredibly excited that someone had already paved the way for this new field of enquiry.

My first academic job was at the University of Greenwich, where I was asked to help establish a Master's course in cultural tourism management. Thanks to the progressive ideas of my then Head of Department Sue Millar, we managed to validate and run this degree fairly successfully for many years. Greg Richards very kindly validated it (the world of cultural tourism was incredibly small at that time!). My first academic conference (Association for Tourism and Leisure Education – ATLAS) in 1998 was focused on cultural tourism and it was again initiated by Greg, who was the founder and then chair of ATLAS. It was an extremely well-attended conference and it seemed that the whole world was suddenly discovering and researching cultural tourism. A couple of years later it emerged that there was enough material to write a whole book on the subject and this was very much needed for our MA cultural tourism students. So this is what I did and my first book, *Issues in Cultural Tourism Studies*, was published in 2003.

I found that there is something quite self-indulgent about writing books on subjects that you love and are passionate about! It is a way of exploring and trying out new ideas and making these accessible to as wide a readership as possible. However, the first edition of *Issues in Cultural Tourism Studies* was a bit over-theorized as I tried to compensate for the lack of theory in the field and drew on numerous disciplines to support my ideas. Multi- or inter-disciplinary approaches have now become the norm in tourism studies, but at that time I felt a bit nervous about the lack of a disciplinary 'home' for cultural tourism. The book somehow found its way onto sociology shelves, which seemed as reasonable a place as any! The second edition (2009) offered less theory and more practice. Somehow cultural tourism had gone from being a niche product in the 1990s to something of a mass activity in the 2000s (for example, for many arts cities, heritage sites or festivals). The second edition was much more global, with less focus on Europe, and it was also more political. The politics of cultural tourism had by then become a major theme, including issues of ownership, interpretation, representation, identity, etc. Experiential approaches to tourism and the development of creative tourism had also become more widespread. Again, Greg Richards was one of the first academics to develop research on creative tourism.

Cultural tourism never really left my life during those years, and there were other publications in between, including work on the relationship between *Tourism, Culture and Regeneration* (Smith, 2006). Also in 2006 a collaboration with Mike Robinson (another academic who was at the forefront of cultural tourism studies) resulted in an edited book which debated many of the major themes in cultural tourism. This was in many ways a shorter version of this *Handbook*, as it included the work of many of the most esteemed and experienced researchers in the field who similarly contributed to the themed sections here.

Over the past few years I had a lot of opportunities to work with Greg Richards, especially as I always had close involvement with the activities of ATLAS. He kindly invited me to teach a workshop on cultural tourism in 1998 for an ATLAS Winter University where I met (for the first time) and taught with my now husband László Puczkó, another cultural tourism expert and enthusiast! However, Greg and I have so far not had the chance to edit a cultural tourism publication together, even though we wrote chapters for each other's publications. So this work is arguably the natural culmination of a relationship that started with my distant admiration of Greg's work, which inspired me to take my own research in cultural tourism further, to a whole range of activities including conferences, workshops, degree programmes, courses and, of course, publications. Cultural tourism is no longer new or niche, but the field is constantly evolving and it has been a privilege to be part of the ever-widening cultural tourism 'community'. This publication contains the work of 'only' 72 authors, but we acknowledge that there are many others and that there will be many more in the future. I want to thank Greg for providing the opportunities and the inspiration for developing cultural tourism research to the extent that he has, and to all the authors who contributed to this book and others for creating one of the most interesting and diverse fields of tourism studies.

Melanie Smith
Budapest Business School, Hungary
April 2012

Cultural travel and travelling cultures have always been an important part of society. Writing this preface in the Pousada at Mong Ha in Macau, now home to the Institute for Tourism Studies (IFT), but formerly the home of the African soldiers protecting the last vestiges of Portuguese colonialism in Asia, the breadth and significance of cultural tourism is all too apparent. If Macau has done a reasonably good job of preserving its physical cultural heritage in the face of overwhelming casino development, the question of what will happen in future as Chinese tourism expands further and the city-state is designated as an international 'leisure and tourism centre' is now a pressing one. Cultural tourism here has taken on the form of a mass market rather than a niche; a flood of tourists and buses that chokes the city centre every day. What will happen when visa restrictions for outbound Chinese tourism are lifted still further and the eager tourism marketeers in other parts of the world are able to welcome a new wave of tourists with a very different view of the 'traditional' cultures they are visiting? Such developments are likely to mean that the face of cultural tourism and the way it is researched will change just as much in the coming years as it has in the previous two or three decades.

What is unlikely to change, however, is the importance of having a context for research. In a seminar with IFT staff we reflected on the main issues in undertaking research, one of the main ones being collaboration. This has been a major part of my own research career, not only through the ATLAS network, but also with a number of key research partners without whom most of my publications would not have seen the light of day. These include Carlos Fernandes, Ilie Rotariu and Wil Munsters, all of whom have made major contributions to the ATLAS Cultural Tourism Research Programme and have helped to enrich my own insights into the relationship between culture and tourism. This book is also a product of my collaboration over many years with Melanie Smith, which has developed through a series of professional and personal encounters that have enriched my own intellectual thinking and my general outlook on life. I would like to thank Melanie for her hard work and perserverence in producing this volume, which has been a mammoth task in view of the vast scope of contributions it contains. I would also like to thank Diane, Benjamin and Eva for providing the inspiration for me to keep working on projects such as this and for reminding me that leisure is also a vital part of life.

Greg Richards
Pousada Mong Ha, Macau
April 2012

# Acknowledgements

We would like to thank Routledge for commissioning this *Handbook*, and Emma Travis, our Editor, for her support and encouragement throughout the writing and editing. Thank you also to Carol Barber for her patience and excellent work on production.

Thank you to all of our authors for meeting their deadlines and for providing us with such rich material for this publication.

Any URLs given were correct at the time of writing and we cannot unfortunately take responsibility for changes or the subsequent disappearance of web addresses.

# Introduction

Cultural tourism is widely seen as being one of the most important segments of global tourism (OECD 2009). This is hardly surprising, given the ubiquity of both tourism and culture these days. In fact, we may well have come full circle, approaching once again the position in which we could legitimately ask if 'all tourism is cultural' (UNWTO 1993), since travel inevitably involves contact with other cultures and the acquisition of knowledge. As Smith (2003) has shown, cultural tourism these days covers a vast range of activities and types of cultural experiences.

However, the reality is that there are still plenty of people who travel without overtly cultural intentions or motivations. It is against this background that 'cultural tourism' has crystallized as a concept related to those who travel in search of culture, in its most general sense. Cultural tourism is the target of a large number of policies and marketing campaigns, launched by destinations eager to attract these allegedly high-spending guests. The idea that cultural tourists benefit the places they visit not only economically but because they are more culturally sensitive and aware is implicit in the positioning of cultural tourism as 'good tourism' against more seemingly frivolous or less lucrative forms of travel.

Even though cultural tourism has become desirable, until recently relatively little was known about the cultural tourist, about why they travel, what they experience, how much they spend, and even if they consider themselves to be 'cultural tourists'. Research has indicated that cultural tourism is often a concept more widely present in the minds of policy makers and academics, rather than in the minds of those who visit cultural attractions or attend cultural events (Richards 2001).

The *Handbook of Cultural Tourism* is an attempt to draw together a broad range of perspectives on the consumption, production and reproduction of culture by and for tourists. This introductory chapter tries to draw together some of the important themes in cultural tourism, concentrating particularly on past and present developments. The concluding chapter in the volume looks towards the future, drawing together major themes identified in the 50 contributions to the present volume and identifying potential areas for research.

## Drawing on the past

As a number of contributions to this volume emphasise, modern cultural tourism has its roots in the origins of contemporary tourism itself, the Grand Tour. In eighteenth- and nineteenth-century

Europe a tour of the 'highlights' of European culture was considered de rigueur for young aristocrats wishing to complete their classical education. The trails blazed at that time, running through France, Italy, Germany, Switzerland and the Netherlands, and still leave an indelible mark on the face of European tourism (Towner 1985). This elite celebration of 'high' culture is still mirrored by the droves of tourists visiting cities such as Rome, Florence or Venice. Even though the Grand Tour itself was gradually democratized by the arrival of the railways and the endeavours of Thomas Cook and his competitors, cultural tourism during the nineteenth and early twentieth centuries retained an upper-class flavour. Even though more and more people were able to enjoy culture on holiday, it was generally the same 'high' culture enjoyed by Ruskin and other luminaries (Bruce, this volume).

One of the mechanisms that reinforced this tendency towards elitism was the institution of the museum. The advent of museums in Europe during the eighteenth and nineteenth centuries was the most physical manifestation of the bourgeois idea of the universality of culture. Museums were organized to demonstrate the progress of human artistic and industrial achievement, the pinnacle of which was represented by the products of Modernity (Richards 1996: 6).

Daniel Boorstin in his classic work *The Image* (1964) also traced the development of the first 'tourist attractions' to the mid-nineteenth century, which was also the period in which nations began showing off their material progress through the World Exhibitions. Such attractions consolidated the market for cultural tourism, strengthened in the first half of the twentieth century though the advent of motorized road travel and growth in domestic tourism.

Cultural tourism was also stimulated by the nation-building activities of many countries in the late nineteenth and early twentieth centuries, as Cadavez (this volume) explains in detail in the case of Portugal. The ability to direct tourists to sites of particular national cultural significance and the opportunity to construct a positive image of the country and its rulers made cultural tourism a popular political tool. This tendency continued with the birth of mass package tourism in Europe after the Second World War, as Franco's Spain developed the first mass tourism resorts as an economic and political support for his regime.

What brought almost all of these early developments in cultural tourism together was their heavy reliance on the past as a source of cultural experiences. The past was conveniently removed from the present; it was quite literally the 'foreign country' (Lowenthal 1985) that tourists sought. This was particularly true in Europe, which had a lot of 'past' to sell to tourists. Not only does Europe still dominate the United Nations Educational, Scientific and Cultural Organization (UNESCO) World Heritage list, but it could boast a wide range of 'cultural tourism' sites of international, national and local significance, as the European Union Inventory of Cultural Tourism Resources (1988, quoted in Richards 1996) was designed to show. The weight of the past is still a problem in major tourist centres in Europe, most notably in Italy. Not only did this heritage have to be conserved, but with the growth of tourism it also needed to be made accessible.

The solution to this problem was to 'turn history into heritage', as Hewison (1987) put it. Heritage was, he argued, commodified history, sanitized and packaged for tourist consumption. This meant that culture, rather than being a burden, became a new source of income for cities and regions across the world. That income could help to pay for the upkeep of the very monuments visited by tourists. In fact, in the case of the Sagrada Familia cathedral in Barcelona, this system has worked so well that the money generated by tourism has speeded up the construction work to the extent that Gaudi's unfinished masterpiece will actually be finished in 2026, decades earlier than previously anticipated.

Tourist spending not only helped to conserve culture, but also injected income into the wider economy. The vast majority of cultural tourism spending goes to hotels, restaurants and transport companies, much to the annoyance of cultural institutions, which see relatively little of the money (Föhl and Pröbstle, this volume). However, this wider multiplier effect of cultural tourism is of great interest to policy makers eager to boost employment (see Brida *et al.*, this volume). A number of studies began to appear in the 1980s and 1990s that underlined the importance of cultural tourism to the economy (e.g. Myerscough 1988).

This connection was also made in the field of events, as major cultural and sporting events were identified as potential catalysts for urban and regional development. In particular the European Capital of Culture became a highly desirable prize for cities keen to boost their economies and polish their image, particularly after the success of Glasgow in hosting the event in 1990. In subsequent years not only did this event become more sought after by European cities, but it also generated copy-cat Capitals in the Americas and Asia, as well as a raft of national Cultural Capital events (e.g. in Russia, Canada and Catalunya).

## Fragmenting the present

The positioning of cultural tourism as a 'good' form of tourism which could deliver significant economic benefits partly explains its emergence as the 'fastest growing' and possibly largest segment of global tourism. Perhaps more significant in recent years, though, has been the postmodern popularization of culture, which effectively led to the culturization of everyday life. With the disintegration of modern structures of taste, education, gender and class since the 1970s, so the automatic coupling of cultural tourism and 'high' culture has also faded.

Today's cultural tourist is just as likely to be in search of 'popular', 'everyday', 'low' or 'street' culture as they are likely to visit a stuffy museum. Peterson (1992) identified a trend towards 'omnivorous' forms of cultural consumption that combine both 'high' and 'popular' or 'mass' culture. These postmodern cultural mixers not only consume different forms of culture, but they also consume lots more of it. In fact, Sullivan and Katz-Gerro (2007) refer to the 'voracious' cultural omnivore. These omnivorous patterns are also found in cultural tourism, as the Association for Tourism and Leisure Education (ATLAS) research project has illustrated (www.tram-research.com/atlas). Cultural tourists who consume a mix of high and popular culture during their leisure time are also more likely to consume different forms of culture on holiday. Rather than seeing holidays as a time of rest, many cultural tourists in fact use them as an extension of their working or professional lives, with museum employees often taking a 'busman's holiday' sniffing around in other museums (Richards 2007).

The de-differentiation of cultural forms has allowed a massive expansion to take place in the scope of cultural tourism. Rather than being restricted to classic museums and monuments, cultural tourism has seeped into every pore and orifice of contemporary society. As Cohen (this volume) shows, this includes using our own bodies as an arena for cultural tourism experience and display, and Werdler (this volume) shows that even death is not immune to cultural tourismification.

As the museum has lost its dominant role as a factory of meaning in postmodern society, so cultural tourists have gone in search of meaning elsewhere. The predominant direction of expansion has been into 'everyday life' (Richards 2011). The authenticity now sought by cultural tourists can quite literally be found on the street, as the graffiti-based cultural tourism attractions of cities such as Bristol attest. The search for everyday life takes cultural tourists into previously unexplored areas, as Russo and Quaglieri-Domínguez (this volume) illustrate in the case of Barcelona.

Culture is increasingly consumed not for its own sake, or as a normative expression of taste, but as a form of relational aesthetics (Bourriaud 2002). The art inside the museum is no longer quite as important as the 'starchitect'-designed building in which it is housed. The important thing is being there, preferably in the presence of like-minded or like-wired individuals who can confirm that this is 'the place to be'. As culture is now a relational good shared by the many rather than the elite few, value is found in with whom it is shared, when and where. This is an important explanation for the rise of the 'eventful city' (Richards and Palmer 2010), which acts as a relational and creative space for contemporary nomads, mobile consumers and residents alike.

In this context the growth of cultural tourism can be seen as a combination of a growing supply of cultural attractions (the symbolic economy), a growing desire for cultural experience (e.g. the cultural omnivore) and a growing culturalization of everyday life (new tourist areas) (Pappalepore *et al.* 2010).

Not only has the volume of cultural tourism increased, but its form has undergone significant change in recent decades. One of the most noticeable trends has been a fragmentation of the cultural tourism market as a whole. Niche products such as gastronomic tourism, architectural tourism, music tourism, film tourism, etc., have appeared as cultural tourism has grown. In fact, one might ask, as several authors in the current volume do, if 'cultural tourism' as such still exists. Cultural tourism, in hindsight, seems to have disappeared at about the same time as it appeared. What has emerged in its place is a rich landscape of interlinking perspectives on the dynamic and fascinating relationship between culture and tourism. As in most fields of scientific endeavour, the most fertile areas for intellectual discovery often exist at such intersections.

## The background to the current volume

When we were asked to produce a *Handbook of Cultural Tourism* it felt as if the subject had somehow 'made it' to the summit of tourism studies! The field of cultural tourism has grown exponentially over the past few years to the point where it is now so diverse and complex that even the smallest sub-sectors are worthy of their own publications. Thus we see numerous works and research emerging on heritage, arts, festivals, gastronomic, religious, film, literary and creative tourism, to mention but a few. It is therefore difficult to do justice to the whole of this field in one publication, even if it is double the length of a standard book. The aim was thus not to be comprehensive or exhaustive, but to illustrate some of the main issues that seem to be pertinent or currently 'cutting edge' in cultural tourism studies.

A *Handbook* is different from an encyclopaedia in the sense that it does not aim to include every term or concept that has ever existed in a subject. There are many themes that have not necessarily been covered in this *Handbook*. However, the aim is that the approaches that are used by authors (e.g. to management, interpretation) could be applied to any field of cultural tourism. It was also not the aim to produce a 'Who's Who' of cultural tourism that includes every author who has ever written about the subject. Unfortunately, there were many excellent researchers and authors who were unable to contribute because of professional or personal constraints. Nevertheless, it is hoped that the ideas of any absent authors are present in many of the chapters included here.

The justification for the structure of the book is partly influenced by past Handbooks in this series, which tend to have a somewhat standardised framework (i.e. themed sections), but also because the proposal reviewers advocated a thematic rather than a disciplinary approach. It has reached the stage in cultural tourism studies where it is indeed inadvisable and perhaps impossible to commission uni-disciplinary research. An exception may be the field of anthropology, where quite focused use of theory and research methods still prevails (see, for example, Macleod and Carrier 2010). However, in other areas of research, multi- or trans-disciplinary approaches are more widespread and in many cases add extreme depth and richness to the work. The authors' chapters were partly commissioned in response to key themes identified by the editors, but the work of the authors also influenced the final struture and thematic sections of the book. This is something like a process of 'co-creation', a major theme in this *Handbook*!

As with all publications, there will only be partial coverage or even omissions of some themes that may seem to be integral to the study of cultural tourism. There is, for example, very little on gastronomic tourism, almost nothing about religious tourism, no focus on literary or film tourism. It was felt by the editors that it was not always necessary to commission work that has been covered in depth elsewhere. For example, one of the authors and her co-authors produced a publication entitled *Key Concepts in Tourist Studies* (Smith *et al.* 2010), which summarised many aspects of cultural tourism including arts tourism, dark tourism, festivals and events, film and TV tourism, gastronomic tourism, heritage tourism, indigenous tourism, literary tourism, and spiritual and religious tourism. More significantly, there are often whole books devoted to these themes, such as Lennon and Foley (2000) on dark tourism; Timothy and Boyd (2003) on heritage tourism; Hall *et al.* (2003) on food tourism; Robinson and Andersen (2004) on literary tourism; Beeton (2005) on film tourism; Leask and Fyall (2006) on World Heritage sites; Timothy and Olsen (2006) on religious and spiritual tourism; Picard and Robinson (2006) on festivals; and Butler and Hinch (2007) on indigenous tourism. There are also all of those books that have focused on cultural tourism more generally, such as Richards (1996, 2007); McKercher and du Cros (2002); Ooi (2002); Smith (2003); Smith and Robinson (2006). Through these books it is possible to trace the evolution of cultural tourism, including its definitions, typologies, products, activities, destinations and markets.

What this book does contain instead is an analysis of key issues, dilemmas, challenges and recommendations, rather than discussions of definitions or typologies of tourism or sub-sectors of cultural tourism. The authors were asked to identify subjects and themes which they had recently researched and which they themselves considered to be unique or cutting edge. In some cases, they built on their previous work; in others, they provided a new theme. A variety of authors were commissioned, ranging from the 'grand old men and women' of cultural tourism who had been at the forefront of the field, to fledging researchers who have recently completed PhDs, but who had something fresh to contribute to existing, ongoing or emergent debates. This blend of old and new, established and novice, traditional and contemporary has helped to create quite a diverse and original publication. Case studies and examples are taken from all over the world, and the authors themselves are from a range of countries.

## References

Beeton, S. (2005) *Film Induced Tourism*, Clevedon: Channel View.

Boorstin, D. (1964) *The Image: A Guide to Pseudo-Events in America*, New York: Vintage.

Bourriaud, N. (2002) *Relational Aesthetics*, Paris: Presses du reel.

Butler, R. and Hinch, T. (eds) (2007) *Tourism and Indigenous Peoples: Issues and Implications*, Oxford: Butterworth-Heinemann.

Hall, C.M., Sharples, L., Mitchell, R., Macionis, N. and Cambourne, B. (eds) (2003) *Food Tourism Around the World: Development, Management and Markets*, Oxford: Butterworth-Heinemann.

Hewison, R. (1987) *The Heritage Industry: Britain in a Climate of Decline*, London: Methuen.

Leask, A. and Fyall, A. (eds) (2006) *Managing World Heritage Sites*, Oxford: Butterworth-Heinemann.

Lennon, J. and Foley, M. (2000) *Dark Tourism: The Attraction of Death and Disaster*, London: Thomson.

Lowenthal, D. (1985) *The Past is a Foreign Country*, Cambridge: Cambridge University Press.

McKercher, B. and du Cros, H. (2002) *Cultural Tourism: The Partnership Between Tourism and Cultural Heritage Management*, New York: Haworth Press.

Macleod, D.V.L. and Carrier, J.G. (eds) (2010) *Tourism, Power and Culture: Anthropological Insights*, Clevedon: Channel View Publications.

Myerscough, J. (1988) *The Economic Importance of the Arts in Britain*, London: Policy Studies Institute.

OECD (2009) *The Impact of Tourism on Culture*, Organisation for Economic Co-operation and Development.

Ooi, C. (2002) *Cultural Tourism and Tourism Cultures*, Copenhagen: Copenhagen Business School Press.

Pappalepore, I., Maitland, R. and Smith, A. (2010) 'Exploring Urban Creativity: Visitor Experiences of Spitalfields, London', *Tourism, Culture and Communication* 10: 217–30.

Peterson, R.A. (1992) 'Understanding Audience Segmentation: From Elite and Mass to Omnivore and Univore', *Poetics* 21: 243–58.

Picard, D. and Robinson, M. (eds) (2006) *Festivals, Tourism and Social Change: Remaking Worlds*, Clevedon: Channel View.

Richards, G. (ed.) (1996) *Cultural Tourism in Europe*, Wallingford: CABI.

——(2001) *Cultural Attractions and European Tourism*, Wallingford: CABI.

——(ed.) (2007) *Cultural Tourism: Global and Local Perspectives*, New York: Haworth.

——(2011) 'Creativity and Tourism: The State of the Art', *Annals of Tourism Research* 38(4): 1225–53.

Richards, G. and Palmer, R. (2010) *Eventful Cities: Cultural Management and Urban Revitalisation*, London: Routledge.

Robinson, M. and Andersen, H. (eds) (2004) *Literature and Tourism: Essays in the Reading and Writing of Tourism*, London: Thomson International.

Smith, M.K. (2003) *Issues in Cultural Tourism Studies*, second edn 2009, London: Routledge.

Smith, M.K., Macleod, N.E. and Robertson, H. (2010) *Key Concepts in Tourist Studies*, London: Sage.

Smith, M.K. and Robinson, M. (eds) (2006) *Cultural Tourism in a Changing World: Politics, Participation and (Re)presentation*, Clevedon: Channel View Publications.

Sullivan, O. and Katz-Gerro, T. (2007) 'The Omnivore Thesis Revisited: Voracious Cultural Consumers', *European Sociological Review* 23(2): 123–37.

Timothy, D. and Boyd, S. (2003) *Heritage Tourism*, London: Prentice Hall.

Timothy, D.J. and Olsen, D.H. (eds) (2006) *Tourism, Religion and Spiritual Journeys*, London: Routledge.

Towner, J. (1985) 'The Grand Tour: A Key Phase in the History of Tourism', *Annals of Tourism Research* 12: 297–333.

UNWTO (1993) *Recommendations on Tourism Statistics*, Madrid: United Nations World Tourism Organization.

# PART I

# History, philosophy and theory

This section provides a framework for the book in the sense that it outlines some of the most important theoretical, philosophical and historical debates that have shaped cultural tourism studies. It is of course by no means exhaustive, but it offers a selection of some key ideas and principles. The histories of tourism have been well documented elsewhere – for example, Walton (2005), who makes the point that history is an essential component in understanding the humanistic and inter-disciplinary nature of tourism studies. For many years now there has been a growing interest in historical representation, heritage and authenticity in the study of cultural tourism. Walton (2005) makes the point that history is constantly being rewritten and reinterpreted by and for present and future generations. Many of the decisions about what should be represented and how it should be done are closely connected to power, a subject that now recurs regularly in the study of cultural tourism, and increasingly in other areas too, e.g. anthropology (see Macleod and Carrier 2010).

History influences debates about national and regional identity, which are central to image making and branding in all forms of tourism, but especially cultural tourism. Much of our understanding of the history of tourism has been based on fairly limited material, such as Towner on the Grand Tour or stories of Thomas Cook, but there is a wealth of historical work that has thus far been relatively hidden or under-researched (Walton 2005). In this section, David Bruce makes the important point that guidebook authors like Marianna Starke have traditionally been overlooked in favour of Murray and Baedeker (probably because she was a woman). Rather than being descriptive, historical research can provide fresh insights into the nature and scope of tourism and the profile and motivation of tourists. For example, Tony Seaton here describes how many tourists simply retrace the steps of significant others from history or re-enact the roles of historical figures. He also emphasises the growing importance of the theme of performance in the study of cultural tourism.

Of course, many aspects of tourism do not change. David Bruce refers to the tendency of most tourists throughout history, aristocratic, bourgeois or otherwise, to defer to guidebooks and other signposts rather than trusting in their own intuition. This theme continues throughout this section, with Mike Robinson's observations about the *angst* engendered in tourists who are forced to go beyond the 'script', especially in the context of cross-cultural encounters. However, he emphasises that it can be liberating for tourists and hosts alike to engage in more spontaneous inter-cultural dialogue. Meaning making in tourism has largely been pre-determined and pre-scripted by historical, social and cultural factors, as well as commercial ones (e.g. marketing and advertising). Noel Salazar focuses on 'imaginaries', which are a combination of all of these influences, many of which are difficult to deviate from or escape. However, like the changing interpretation of history, the representation of destinations is a dynamic process that changes over time; therefore, imaginaries can also play a role in reshaping social and cultural processes on a global scale.

The theme of globalisation is always an important focus in any study of cultural tourism and one that is often closely connected to the theme of identity creation, as well as cross-cultural exchange and inter-cultural dialogue. Some of the authors in this section question the binarisms that have tended to dominate (cultural) tourism studies, such as global and local, homogenisation and heterogenisation, host and guest, work and play, east and west (e.g. Robinson, Reisinger). Yvette Reisinger revisits the globalisation debate and emphasises the positive impacts of globalisation on the differentiation and domestification of cultural tourism destinations and local products. The emphasis in this chapter and in this section more generally tends to be on the continua along which cultural tourism operates, rather than polarised binarisms which are becoming more meaningless in an increasingly mobile and fluid world.

In addition to history and inter-cultural theory, philosophy can be used as a framework for cultural tourism studies. Again, this is not a new subject in tourism and has been discussed quite extensively – for example, Tribe 2010, who mentions in particular the 'perennial questions' in philosophy, which are truth, beauty and virtue. The subject of virtue in tourism studies has become pervasive because of the growing necessity of debates around sustainability, responsibility and ethics. However, he argues that beauty has been relatively under-researched, even though the aesthetics of tourism have always been an important consideration. Most tourists are drawn first and foremost to the beauty of a destination, whether it be the built environment, the landscape or the beach. Beauty also wields power – for example, many value judgements have traditionally been based on beauty (e.g. World Heritage sites).

As mentioned in the context of history, 'truth' is also an important element in cultural tourism, especially when it comes to establishing what really happened in the past. Most of our representations are only partial or reflect the view of certain dominant groups in history. The 'truth' of other phenomena such as authenticity has been questioned extensively, especially by tourism anthropologists. Sean Beer in this section considers the authenticity debate from a philosophical perspective, drawing not only on existentialist philosophers (see also Reisinger and Steiner 2006 in the context of 'existential authenticity'), but places it in the context of much wider philosophical considerations.

Coles *et al.* (in Tribe 2010: 95) consider disciplinary debates as being part of the philosophy of tourism studies and advocate an interdisciplinary approach to transcend the 'restrictive dogma and parochialism of disciplines'. This follows much of John Tribe's own work, which has focused on the disciplinary challenges of tourism studies (Tribe 1997, 2000). Hollinshead and Ivanova in this book follow some of these debates with their own analysis of post-disciplinarity. Cultural tourism has traditionally drawn on a number of disciplines, such as anthropology, sociology, geography and economics. However, the editors recognise the problems of trying to embed each of the chapters in one disciplinary section, as many of the chapters are not uni-disciplinary in their approach. They also acknowledge the limbo status of cultural tourism as a field of enquiry and not yet a discipline. However, the breadth, depth and scope of this book indicates how worthy cultural tourism may soon be of this accolade.

## Summary of the chapters in this section

**David Bruce** begins this section by tracing the history of cultural tourism back to its 'golden age' in the nineteenth century and the transition from 'Grand Tourists' to 'modern' mass tourists. He examines in particular Ruskin's role in constructing the concept of cultural tourism, the guidebooks of Mariana Starke and Murray and Baedeker in informing the routes of cultural tourists, and the role of Thomas Cook in creating cultural tour packages for mass tourists. Wry and witty observations are made about the enduringly prescriptive nature of cultural tours for both aristocrats and bourgeois travellers alike, shifting from Grand Tour to guidebooks to packages. He uses a case study of E.M. Forster's *A Room with a View* to illustrate the comic dependence of most supposedly independent travellers on the guidebooks of Baedeker, even to the point of controlling and regulating their emotional responses. The manipulation, signposting and scripting of tourists is a recurrent theme even in cultural tourism today.

**Tony Seaton** considers the history of travel from a different perspective, namely the phenomena he names metempsychosis and metensomatosis. He suggests that much of tourism and travel is based on historical and cultural patterns, many of which follow in the footsteps of (significant) others. Once again, tourism is considered to be a scripted activity. Metempsychosis refers to repetitions of famous journeys, which may lead to the contrasting of the past and present in space, place and time. Metensomatosis, on the other hand, refers to the multiple roles played by the tourist, sometimes simultaneously. These may be historical, contemporary, real or mythical. Indeed, the study of performance in tourism is becoming the subject of considerable interest (e.g. Edensor 2009). This suggests that tourists cannot be as easily and rigidly typologised as was originally thought, and that modes of being and performance are essentially plural, fluid and transient.

**Mike Robinson** questions the binaries and hierarchies that are so deeply embedded in the study of cultural tourism, many of which are the result of language, an under-researched dimension of tourism. Tourism has a critical role to play in the shaping of inter-cultural dialogue between tourists and host communities in multiple everyday encounters, not just in the context of frontline service. Sometimes the challenge of dealing with 'otherness' and the 'angst' generated can enable tourists to experience a sense of freedom outside the 'script', forcing them to trust in the non-signed world, and liberate them from dependence. Hosts can also reap rewards for their ability to communicate with tourists in different languages, going beyond trading to an enriching cross-cultural human exchange.

**Noel Salazar** considers other factors that serve to shape the world making and meaning making of tourists – namely imaginaries, which are a combination of personal, social, political and commercial representations, images and discourses. Many of these are the result of historical and cultural processes that go way beyond marketing and are perpetuated in literature, arts, film and other forms of global media. Imaginaries are intangible and difficult to measure, let alone tracing their origins. Many local imaginaries have been globalised and embedded in new contexts through tourism, and are now difficult to escape. Some tend to be based on nostalgia, romance or idealisation, but others are a testament to the fact that culture is never static and can be instrumental in political or social reinvention.

**Yvette Reisinger** considers changing perceptions of the concept of globalisation and its consideration within cultural tourism studies. She suggests that it is no longer fruitful to consider globalisation to be a homogenising process dominated mainly by Western (American) culture. Although tourism can seem to represent the 'globalisation of nothing' (Ritzer 2004), staged authenticity and commodification, there is also much evidence to suggest that globalisation can generate conditions that support the local and the unique ('domestification'). Contrary to previous theories, globalisation can actually encourage rather than erode distinctiveness and differentiation. Instead of categorising tourism according to binarisms like global and local, or homogenisation and heterogenisation it is more interesting to think in terms of cultural innovation, recontextualisation or fusion.

**Sean Beer** provides an analysis of the relationship between philosophy and cultural tourism, with particular reference to the concept of authenticity. He traces many of the debates about objective authenticity, questioning the extent to which authenticity ever really existed and whether tourists even want(ed) this. Philosophical enquiry might suggest that tourists are responsible for constructing and experiencing their own sense of authenticity in the present moment. However, this is also influenced by their historical, social and cultural conditioning. Existential authenticity is largely defined from within the individual and draws on the philosophy of Sartre and Heidegger (e.g. Reisinger and Steiner 2006). However, the author suggests that post-structuralist and postmodern theorists and philosophers may offer a more complex, yet playful analysis of the phenomenon of authenticity. Ultimately, it is difficult to judge what is authentic and what is not, even though perceptions of authenticity can be said to exist.

**Keith Hollinshead** and **Milka Ivanova** discuss the theoretical framework for cultural tourism with reference to the complex issue of disciplinarity and how tourism studies should be approached. While questioning the need to fetishise disciplinary boundaries, the authors do not advocate an anti-disciplinary approach. Instead, they explore notions of multi- or pluri-disciplinarity, as well as trans- and post-disciplinarity. The latter implies that tourism is embedded in fluid spaces and intersections, whilst the former potentially embraces all disciplines to gain a holistic understanding of the complex nature of tourism (including not only academia but also industry and social sectors). Post-disciplinarity can embrace multiple truths, including those of sub-cultures and historically suppressed groups. Such an approach is especially important for the study of indigenous and local cultures.

## References

Coles, T., Hall, M. and Duval, D.T. (2010) 'Post-disciplinary Tourism', in Tribe, J. (ed.) *Philosophical Issues in Tourism*, Clevedon: Channel View, 80–100.

Edensor, T. (2009) 'Tourism and Performance', in Jamal, T. and Robinson, M. (eds) *The Sage Handbook of Tourism Studies*, London and California: Sage, 543–57.

Macleod, D.V.L. and Carrier, J.G. (eds) (2010) *Tourism, Power and Culture: Anthropological Insights*, Clevedon: Channel View.

Reisinger, Y. and Steiner, C.J. (2006) 'Reconceptualizing Object Authenticity', *Annals of Tourism Research* 33(1): 65–86.

Ritzer, G. (2004) *The Globalization of Nothing*, London: Sage.

Steiner, C.J. and Reisinger, Y. (2006) 'Understanding Existential Authenticity', *Annals of Tourism Research* 33(2): 299–318.

Tribe, J. (1997) 'The Indiscipline of Tourism', *Annals of Tourism Research* 24(3): 638–57.

——(2000) 'Indisciplined and Unsubstantiated', *Annals of Tourism Research* 27(3): 809–13.

——(ed.) (2010) *Philosophical Issues in Tourism*, Clevedon: Channel View.

Walton, J.K. (ed.) (2005) *Histories of Tourism*, Clevedon: Channel View.

# 1

# The nineteenth-century 'golden age' of cultural tourism

## How the beaten track of the intellectuals became the modern tourist trail

*David M. Bruce*

Ruskin, doubtless to his own distress, can be named the godfather of cultural tourism. His early family travels were modelled on a previous generation's Grand Tour but travelling as a family unit, even if for an educational but also recuperative purpose (Hanley and Walton 2010: 43), was in the spirit of his own times. Much as he disliked them, these were the times of the steam ship, of the spreading industrial revolution and increasingly the early railways. Throughout his multi-journey life, he remained in denial about his own tourism; he saw himself as the cultured aesthete, who just happened to be obsessed with Italy and therefore impelled to visit Venice and Florence repeatedly. His art historical works were summarised, even by himself, to become museum vade-mecums. Perhaps too weighty in their binding to be called or used as 'hand books', they were beautifully designed to be read in the Italian cities where the pictures, sculptures and above all the buildings were to be appreciated. Like some latter day 'green' ecologist, who travels the rainforest to explain the importance of its virginity (for example, *Last Chance to See* – Adams and Carwardine 1990), but is promptly followed by 'explore'-type tour operators and massified treehouse safari resort hotels, Ruskin's *Stones of Venice* (1851–53) paved the way for the Cooks continental tours of the 1850s to 1900s.

The century from 1814 to 1914 was arguably the golden age of cultural tourism because it was the time when bridges were made between the cultural aesthetes and 'Grand Tourists' on the one hand, and the recognisably 'modern' group (mass) tourists on the other; these bridges were the guidebook writers; their independent (middle-class) traveller users were those who crossed over. Ruskin's aestheticism or 'high' culture was mediated by Murray and Baedeker who thereby defined their cultural tourism.

Wynne (1992) and other sociologists in the 1990s dismissed, with some justification, such high culture as bourgeois national or European cultural imperialism (Smith 2003). They expanded the meaning of 'culture' to include the popular. However, in terms of tourism development it was this nineteenth-century cultural travel (from the industrialised and then imperialist countries) that set the parameters for early trans-European tourism. Cultural travel was spawned by the intercourse of 'high' culture and cheaper, more reliable (steam) travel: high culture was moving/had moved from the aristocratic to the bourgeois; tourism from the Grand Tour via the guidebook itinerary towards the early Thomas Cook continental package. For cultural tourism this is one history that it is important to recognise, despite its proper demotion from being the *only* history of tourism (see Towner 1995; and Mackenzie 2005, for the value of other strands of tourism's history).

Buzzard (1993) provides a general discussion of how the 'beaten track' links to literature; Hanley and Walton (2010) develop Ruskin's role in constructing the concept of cultural tourism; Mullen and Monsen's *The Smell of the Continent* (2009) gives the broader tourism history; essays in Koshar's book *Histories of Leisure* (2002) and Walton's *Histories of Tourism* (2005) discuss different aspects of the context. The commercial exploitation of the cultural beaten track which generated the first modern mass tourists of Thomas Cook was hotly contested at the time by the 'anti-tourists' (in Buzzard's 1993 term), with a sharp rather misjudged repost from Thomas Cook himself (Cook 1870). This was discussed later in MacCannell (1976) and developed further in Urry (1990).

This chapter adds to the discussion of the cultural 'beaten track' by using nineteenth-century sources to describe the history and atmosphere of the time, using an Elias figurationist approach (Dunning 1996) to suggest a picture of the fragile 'civilizing process' of the networks or 'figurations' of the middle-class travellers involved. The method stresses quotation from contemporary sources – guidebooks, literary works, journals and biographies of Victorian notables: notables because tourism or any foreign travel other than migration or in the military was the preserve of the well-off. The prices of rail fares were high. For example, the price of a single ticket (rail and boat) from London to Paris taking six and a half hours in 1914 was £2.10s (s is shillings) (first class); £1.5s. 9d (d is pence) (third class) (Bradshaw 1972: viii), compared to a working (UK) wage of around 15/- (or 15 shillings) a week. Equivalents today are a multiple of about 80 for prices but nearly 300 for wages. The price of hotels in Starke for the 1830s, and Baedeker for the 1900s were lower in real terms – one reason to make trips of longer duration than today.

'A golden age' is a concept that is implicitly a criticism of the present (or recent past) state of affairs. It is an era of excellence that has ended some time, even centuries, before but is looked back on both with nostalgia and as a source of inspiration. In the nineteenth century, the golden age idea was contested between the Whig school (or figuration) of history with a belief in progressive improvement, especially in imperialist England and the new *medievalists*, who saw a golden age in the high middle ages before 'modernism' intruded with new ideas in art society and technology around the time of the painter Raphael. This movement (or figuration), calling itself Pre-Raphaelitism, linked literature with art or 'doggerel illustrated by daubing', as the Whig historian dubbed it privately at the time (Macaulay 1851: 145). In 1853 Ruskin established the word *medievalism* and both Ruskin and Macaulay drew on Italy for inspiration. The debate (analysed in Simmons 2009) between the *classicism* (with a modernist belief in progress and empire) epitomised by Rome versus *medievalism* (with a belief in preservation), which Ruskin epitomised by Venice, fanned the flames of the growing cultural tourism.

## Guidebooks for cultural tourists

Nineteenth-century guidebook writers and publishers (a figuration) assumed cultural intent. A major source of inspiration in the English-speaking world, who even influenced German and French guidebooks, was Mariana Starke. Her guidebook, developed over time from her *Letters from Italy* (1800) was translated into German and later editions were published by John Murray II and John Murray III, who used her format closely enough almost to the point of plagiarism. As the *Dictionary of National Biography* (1909: vol. XVIII, 994) puts it, her 'guidebooks are carefully compiled and proved useful forerunners of the labours of Murray and Baedeker'.

Starke's grading of sights (exclamation marks in her guide) were picked up in Murray's and Baedeker's stars (★) and were systematised to Michelin's star system (Bruce 2010).

Maybe because she was a woman, perhaps more because she did not continue to appear in print posthumously as the 'brand' of a namesake publishing house, Mariana Starke has been overlooked compared to John Murray and Karl Baedeker. Born in 1762, she was taken abroad in 1792 with her invalid father (who died in 1794) and as her mother's companion to roam Italy for six years to 1798. There she witnessed Napoleon's invasion of Italy's cities. In 1800 she published her *Letters from Italy*, then one of a number of 'different approaches to describing Italy [including] ... the female perspective ... the valetudinarian approach, such as Mariana Starke' (Sweet 2010). After the end of the Napoleonic Wars, her continual travel to and around Italy spanned a further 25 years; she died in 1838, aged 76, in Milan while travelling home to England (*Dictionary of National Biography* 1909). She often travelled in 'manly garb', even as Jack Starke (Parsons 2007), and surely merits detailed research and a full biography.

Among her many users were Ruskin, Murray and Macaulay, each differently representative of Victorian (high bourgeois) cultural figurations (Macaulay 1838; Murray 1840; Hanley and Walton 2010). When Ruskin travelled with his parents in the 1820s and 1830s in pursuit of culture, his tracks were dictated by a 'Grand Tour' tradition and agenda, but were advised by guidebooks like Starke's. Possibly (suggest Hanley and Walton 2010) after having his early work *Modern Painters* rejected for publication, Ruskin developed a 'radical antagonism to Murray's influential attitudes and practices, which he mocked for embracing and encouraging the haste and superficiality of the railway age' (Hanley and Walton 2010: 29).

Rome as described by Macaulay and Venice as depicted by Ruskin were at opposite poles of Victorian England's tourist enthusiasm for Italy, but both drew on Florence for inspiration. With medievalism came nostalgia and the idyll of the (rural) past from Rousseau's noble savage developed as the contented peasant. Florence was apparently neutral between Venice and Rome, so Tuscany could then provide the contented peasantry. Starke describes them (in 1837) in a 1,000-word digression with anecdotes, *inter alia* 'Considered collectively, [as] pure in their morals, and pastoral in their manner of living; the peculiar comeliness of both sexes is very striking ... Their manners are uncommonly graceful' (Starke 1837: 78–80).

*Figure 1.1* Florence – a watercolour view in the nineteenth century
Source: (Author's collection)

Starke's meticulous detail on personal necessities, baggage requirements, means of travel, hotel recommendations and price expectations made her guidebook indispensable. Dependency could become risible in the case of an 'English historian' lampooned in the pages of Stendhal's *Chartreuse de Parme*: 'In Parma ... to write a history of the Middle Ages ... he refused to pay for the merest bagatelle without looking up the price in the travelguide of a Mrs Starke, which has gone into a twentieth edition because it lists for the prudent Englishman the price of a guinea fowl, an apple, a glass of milk, etc., etc.' (Stendhal 2006: 236).

Possibly it was Ruskin or even Macaulay himself that Stendhal ridiculed: Macaulay's own journal puts him near that part of Italy (researching his *Lays of Ancient Rome*) when Stendhal was thinking about the novel and Macaulay's journal shows his use of Mariana Starke. Macaulay, meanwhile, was reporting how the Italians who feared and despised her made cartoons of the absurd English using her guide:

> I am amused today by seeing in a shop [in Rome] a set of caricatures reflecting on the way in which the English appeal to Mrs Marianne [sic] Starke on every occasion 'Voi volete ingannarmi – Madama Starke ha stabito il prezzo del vino d'Orvieto tre paoli' ('You want to cheat me – Madame Starke has fixed the price of Orvieto wine at three paoli').
>
> *(Macaulay 1838: 57)*

Macaulay is a transitional figure between the 'grand tourist' and the bourgeois independent traveller, who might see himself as a cultural tourist and was again about to be in a Whig Cabinet (another figuration). Author of a best-selling and hugely influential *History of England*, 'in Whig circles Macaulay was a parvenu; among writers he was an aristocrat' (Thomas 2008: xviii). Unlike his younger contemporary, Ruskin, Macaulay embraced steam ships and early rail travel, and even in the year before he died (1859) visited and enjoyed Venice as a tourist.

Culture and tourism were redefined and the popularity of culture among the expanding travelling classes was creating a high plateau of seasonal mobility between northern and southern Europe (and including North Americans).

Baedeker's prefaces show that empowering the independent tourist was a chief objective '... To render him as independent as possible of the services of interested parties ... [and] save him many a trial of temper' (Baedeker 1899: v). Despite the then conventional 'him', this especially helped the increasing number of women from the (upper-) middle classes who became financially able to travel on rentier incomes or as 'companions' to their wealthier relations (Bruce 2010).

## Forster – Baedeker and Tuscany

Cultural tourists in Italy were the people (the figuration) subjected to 'the comic muse' of E.M. Forster in his early novels. After graduating a bit disappointingly from Cambridge in 1901, Forster and his mother (Morgan and Lily) had 'embarked on something more Middle Class and Edwardian than a Grand Tour. Their assault on Italy was ambitious in its thoroughness ... [but] Morgan confessed ... "Baedeker-bestarred Italy ... is all that I have yet seen"' (Moffat 2010: 58). He then specifically used the Baedeker as the symbol of the conventional 'beaten track' cultural tourists. In his first novel, *Where Angels Fear to Tread* (1904) he imaginatively even recreated a page of Baedeker based on that for San Gimignano, a town unmentioned earlier in the century (Starke 1837: 113, mentions Poggibonsi only).

> Mrs. Herriton found *Central Italy*, by Baedeker, and opened it for the first time in her life and read in it as follows ... [see Box 1.1] Mrs. Herriton did not proceed. She was not one to

## Box 1.1 Case study

*Forster using Baedeker: the two full pages of the 1904 edition (16–19) are similarly abbreviated for direct comparison.*

### Forster's Monteriano

**Monteriano** (pop. 4,800). *Hotels:* Stella d'Italia, moderate only; Globo, dirty. *Caffè Garibaldi. Post and Telegraph in Corso Vittorio Emmanuele, next to Theatre. Photographs at Seghena's (cheaper in Florence). Diligence (1 lira) meets principal trains.

*Chief attractions (2–3 hours)*: Santa Deodata, Palazzo Pubblico, Sant' Agostina, Santa Caterina, Sant' Ambrogio, Palazzo Capocchi. Guide (2 lire) unnecessary. A walk round the Walls should on no account be omitted. The view from the Rocca (small gratuity) is finest at sunset.

*History*: Monteriano, the Mons Rianus of Antiquity, whose Ghibelline tendencies are noted by Dante (Purg. xx), definitely emancipated itself from Poggibonsi in 1261. Hence the distich, *'Poggibonizzi, fatti in là, che Monteriano si fa citta!'* till recently inscribed over the Siena gate. It remained independent till 1530 when it was sacked by the Papal troops and became part of the Grand Duchy of Tuscany. It is now of small importance, and seat of the district prison. The inhabitants are still noted for their agreeable manners [more Starke-like then Baedeker].

The traveller will proceed direct from the Siena gate to the COLLEGIATE CHURCH OF SANTA DEODATA, and inspect (5th chapel on right) the charming *frescoes ...

### Baedeker's San Gimignano

**San Gimignano** (1089 ft. pop. 4060) [Hotels] *Albergo Centrale* ... 4–6 fr., well spoken of; *Albergo Leon Bianco* ... (good cuisine) [no reference to Cafe or photographer].

From Poggibonsi ... 7½ m. Carriages may be hired at the station ... An omnibus plies twice daily (in 2hrs., return 1½ hrs.)

[*History*] An ancient and loftily situated town ... In 1353 after having suffered terribly from the dissensions of the leading families ... (Ghibellines) and ... (Guelphs), it became subject to Florence. Its walls, its towers (whence the name 'San Gimignano delle belle torri') and its streets all carry us back the middle ages. Perhaps no other town in Tuscany presents so faithful a picture of Dante's time.

[*Chief attractions* – no time indication] The centre of the town ... [has] several important buildings.

The Gothic PALAZZO COMUNALE ... the cathedral, usually called *LA COLLEGIATA ... contains frescoes ... the church of SANT' AGOSTINO ... containing famous *Frescoes by *Benozzo Gozzoli* ...

Further on ... The *Rocca* (1353), or the highest part of the old fortifications ... (Ascend to the right from La Collegiata) in a private garden, commands a fine view of the town and neighbourhood.

The novelist's imagination used more than just the text of San Gimignano to gain his comic effect and in his hotel critique he was untrammelled by the libel case that had forced Baedeker to withdraw an edition a few years earlier (Boyle 2010: 17) – simple omission was Baedeker's response to a bad hotel.

detect the hidden charms of Baedeker. Some of the information seemed to her unnecessary, all of it was dull. Whereas Philip could never read 'The view from the Rocca (small gratuity) is finest at sunset' without a catching at the heart.

*(Forster 1976: 29–30)*

In Forster's Edwardian masterpiece *A Room with a View* (1908), the significance of the Baedeker in defining the English tourist (or 'Britisher abroad') (Forster 2000: 18), structuring 'her' movements only barely failing to control her experiences and emotions, is blatant. A whole chapter (2) is called 'In Santa Croce with no Baedeker' (Forster 2000: 14). The *Handbook to Northern Italy* is scornfully dismissed as 'but touch[ing] the surface of things' (ibid.: 15) by the 'clever woman', who promptly gets lost rather than use it to find her way, but still contrives to confiscate the Baedeker from heroine Lucy. The subsequent narrative of the novel then depends on Lucy's non-Baedeker-mediated encounters (Bruce 2010).

In Florence, 'the Pensione Simi may have offered a room with a view but was run, improbably, by a Cockney landlady' (Moffat 2010: 38). *Northern Italy* and *Central Italy*, both of which were in up-to-date editions at the time, would have been his vade-mecum. Page 409 of *Northern Italy* 1899 lists his choice of 'Pensions' (boarding houses), including those on the banks of the Arno with, therefore, rooms with views, such as Miss White's. The listings also show a boarding house 'frequented by Americans', with a lift. The guide notes facilities like restaurants, an English pharmacist, bookshops, the British and American consulates, an English doctor, a tobacconist for Havana cigars, to build a picture of the urban scene. Cafés listed were reported in Florence as 'less inviting than in many other Italian towns, a few only with seats in the open air … Visitors … are frequently importuned by hawkers …' (Baedeker 1899: 410).

## Conclusion

'Unless tourism history engages in the theoretical and ideological debate that exists among leisure historians, then it will remain as a superficial preface to contemporary tourism research' (Towner 1995: 341), but to understand contemporary *cultural* tourism, which seeks to broaden its perspective and become more inclusively creative (Richards 2011), its narrow, arguably bourgeois and imperialistic origins and development need to be appreciated through the figurations of the players. The focus has been on the British Continental movement – the beaten track – but parallels may be found elsewhere.

A golden age of cultural tourism should be capable of inspiring culture through travel, not just nostalgia. If nostalgia is a lazy vacant sensation, which passively uses heritage for relaxation, then inspiration is in contrast about breathing life into current activity to create new strands of culture. Nineteenth-century cultural tourism had enjoyed a golden age which itself spawned literature from Byron onto Ruskin and finally Forster, but it ended suddenly on 31 July 1914 with 'the shots fired by the Austro-Hungarian guns at Belgrade [which] reverberate across the English Channel' (*The Times* 1914: 9). Great Britain and its Empire went to war with Germany on 4 August; Italy was lured into the conflict a year later.

The last word goes to the *Venus de Medici* from the Tribuna of Florence's Uffizi. Exiled to Florence from Rome in 1680 for supposedly corrupting young art students, she inspired Byron (1818) to five stanzas (a quantitative accolade?) in *Childe Harold's Pilgrimage*: 'There, too, the goddess loves in stone, and fills/The air around with beauty … ;/We gaze and turn away, and know not where/Dazzled and drunk with beauty …' (Canto IV: xlix/l). She was awarded the ultimate !!!! by Starke (1837: 62), being thought to be by Praxiteles. By 1899, however, Baedeker (p.429) was still giving her a ★ but saying dismissively, 'found at Rome in 16th Cent …; the affectedly held fingers and the inscription on the base are modern'. Dent's *Florence* (Gardner 1924) saw her as 'a typical Graeco-Roman work ... formerly absurdly over praised ... [now,] perhaps, too much depreciated'. Again ★★★ as 'a perfect masterpiece of Greek Sculpture' in Michelin's *Italy* of 1964 (p.102), but downgraded to 'famous ... carved by a Greek sculptor in 3C BC' (Michelin 1988: 90), she is now reckoned to be a mere 'first-century BC copy of the Praxitelean *Aphrodite of Cnidos*', and given only a cursory mention in the *Rough Guide to Tuscany & Umbria* (Jepson *et al.* 2006: 119). The goddess, unmoved, looks back serenely at the tourists' gaze.

# References

Adams, D. and Carwardine, M. (1990) *Last Chance to See*, New York: Ballantine Books.

Baedeker, K. (1899) *Northern Italy including Leghorn, Florence, Ravenna and Routes Through Switzerland, and Austria*, 11th remodelled edn, Leipzig: Baedeker.

——(1904) *Central Italy and Rome*, 14th rev. edn, Leipzig: Baedeker.

Boyle, L. (2010) *A Selection of Baedekers & General Travel Guides, Catalogue of Shaperos*, London: The Travellers' Bookshop.

Bradshaw (1972 [1914]) *August 1914 Continental Guide*, facsimile edn, Newton Abbot: David & Charles.

Bruce, D.M. (2010) 'Baedeker: The Perceived "Inventor" of the Formal Guidebook – A Bible for Travellers in the 19th Century', in Butler R. and Russell R. (eds) *Giants of Tourism*, Wallingford: CABI, 93–110.

Buzzard, J. (1993) *The Beaten Track: European Tourism, Literature, and the Ways to Culture, 1800–1918*, Oxford: Clarendon Press.

Byron, G., Lord (1818) *Childe Harold's Pilgrimage*, London: John Murray.

Cook, T. (1870) *Dr. W.H. Russell and Consul Lever (of Trieste): Letters to His Royal Highness the Prince of Wales and to the Right Honourable the Earl of Clarendon, His Majesty's Secretary of State for Foreign Affairs*, London: Cook's Tourist Office.

*Dictionary of National Biography* (1909) 'Starke, Mariana (1762–1838)' CFS (Miss C. Fell Smith) for *Dictionary of National Biography* Vol. XVIII, Oxford, 994.

Dunning, E. (1996) 'Problems of the Emotions in Sport and Leisure: Critical and Counter Critical Comments on the Conventional and Figurational Sociologies of Sport and Leisure', *Leisure Studies* 15: 185–207.

Forster, E.M. (1976 [1904]) *Where Angels Fear to Tread*, Harmondsworth: Penguin.

——(2000 [1908]) *Room with a View*, Harmondsworth: Penguin.

Gardner, E.G. (1924) *The Story of Florence*, 10th edn, Medieval Towns, London: J.M. Dent.

Hanley, K. and Walton, J.C. (2010) *Constructing Cultural Tourism: John Ruskin and the Tourist Gaze*, Clevedon: Channel View.

Jepson, T., Buckley, J. and Ellingham, M. (2006) *Rough Guide to Tuscany & Umbria*, London: Rough Guides.

Koshar, R. (ed.) (2002) *Histories of Leisure*, Oxford: Berg.

Macaulay, T.B. (1838–39, 1848–59) 'Journals', in Thomas, W. (ed.) *The Journals of Thomas Babington Macaulay*, Vols 1–5, London: Pickering and Chatto.

MacCannell, D. (1976) *The Tourist: A New Theory of the Leisure Class*, Berkeley, CA: University of California Press.

Mackenzie, J.M. (2005) 'Empires of Travel: British Guide Books and Cultural Imperialism in the 19th and 20th Centuries', in Walton, J.K. (ed.) *Histories of Tourism*, Clevedon: Channel View, 19–38.

Michelin (1964) *Italy*, fourth English edition, London: The Dickens Press.

——(1988) *Italy*, London: The Dickens Press.

Moffat, W. (2010) *E.M. Forster: A New Life*, London: Bloomsbury.

Mullen, R. and Monson, J. (2009) *The Smell of the Continent: The British Discover Europe*, London: Macmillan.

Murray, J., III (1840) *Handbook for Travellers on the Continent – North Germany*, London: John Murray.

Parsons, N.T. (2007) *Worth the Detour: A History of the Guidebook*, Stroud: Sutton Publishing.

Richards, G. (2011) 'Creativity and Tourism: The State of the Art', *Annals of Tourism Research* 38(4): 1225–53.

Ruskin, J. (1851–53 [1960]) *The Stones of Venice*, London: Collins.

Simmons, C.A. (2009) 'Macaulay's Rome and the Defense of Classicism', *Prose Studies* 31(2): 102–12.

Smith, M. (2003) *Issues in Cultural Tourism Studies*, London: Routledge.

Starke, M. (1837) *Travels in Europe for the Use of Travellers on the Continent including the Island of Sicily*, 9th edn, London: John Murray.

Stendhal (2006 [1839]) *La Chartreuse de Parme* [The Charterhouse of Parma], trans. Sturrock, J., London: Penguin.

Sweet, R. (2010) 'The Changing View of Rome in the Long Eighteenth Century', *Journal for Eighteenth-Century Studies* 33(2): 274–94.

*The Times* (1914) 'Interests and Duty of Great Britain, The Position Analysed', 31 July, Issue 40590; col. F. London: 9.

Thomas, W. (ed.) (2008) *The Journals of Thomas Babington Macaulay*, Vols 1–5, London: Pickering and Chatto.

Towner, J. (1995) 'Tourism's Histories', *Tourism Management* 16(5): 339–43.

Urry, J. (1990) *The Tourist Gaze*, London: Sage.

Walton, J.K. (ed.) (2005) *Histories of Tourism*, Clevedon: Channel View.

Wynne, D. (1992) *The Culture Industry: The Arts in Urban Regeneration*, Aldershot: Avebury.

## Further reading

In addition to works listed in the *References* above:

Hanley, K. and Dickenson, R. (eds) (2009) 'Nineteenth Century Cultural Travel' special edition *Prose Studies* 31:2. (A well-judged set of articles based on a conference in Venice in 2008.)

Harris, C. and Newall, C. (2010) *The Pre-Raphaelites and Italy*, Ashmolean Museum of Art and Archaeology, University of Oxford. (Finely illustrated catalogue with scholarly articles.)

Ruskin, J. (1895) *The Ruskin Reader: Being Passages from Modern Painters' The Seven Lamps of Architecture and The Stones of Venice*, London: George Allen. (Ruskin's own selection, 'writing beneath the cloudless peace of the snows Chamouni', edited with notes.)

# 2

# Cultivated pursuits

## Cultural tourism as metempsychosis and metensomatosis

*Tony Seaton*

## Introduction

Metempsychosis and Metensomatosis were concepts introduced in two papers on tourism behaviour published a decade ago (Seaton 2001, 2002). The first paper adapted and adopted the word *metempsychosis*, a concept originally found in classical myth and ancient religion, to describe a *form of cultural tourism* in which travellers repeated itineraries made by significant historical others from within their own culture. Such repetitive journeys were taken by people as individual travellers or within packaged tours. Examples included journeys and tours in which subjects followed in the footsteps of James Boswell and Dr Johnson in the Hebrides, William Cobbett on his round-Britain tours, Charles Darwin in the Galapagos Islands, and many other prestigious travellers in history.

The second paper extended the notion of ritual repetition more radically. It proposed that *all tourism forms*, but cultural tourism especially, could be viewed as repeat journeys, but ones made not just in the footsteps of a *single* significant other, but of *many* others, some of whom might be *significant*, while others might be *generalised*. The label it gave to imitation of such multiple role models was *metensomatosis*, another adapted concept from ancient myth and religion.

This chapter sketches out the evolution of the two concepts and illustrates them from two cultural tourism case histories.

## Metempsychosis

The metempsychosis paper focused on the history and socio-cultural significance of repeating famous journeys from the past which, it was argued, had been increasing in literary works, broadcast programming and cultural tourism programmes through the twentieth century. The word came from religious texts (e.g. Buddhist and Hindu), mythology (Eliade 1954), folklore and fairy stories (Propp 1971), found in traditional cultures as far apart as Chile, Japan, Russia and India (Disraeli n.d.: vol. 1, 192–94), and received a chapter in Picart's celebrated work on world religions (Picart 1733: vol. IV, pt 3, 159–87). It named transformational journeys found in these literatures where characters travelled in disguise, switching from one persona to another, sometimes from human to animal forms. Metempsychosis was defined as:

> ... a journey undertaken ... as the replication of, and a comparator to, a previous one made by a historical or mythical figure or group, in which the subject to some extent adopts the persona of the original traveller.
>
> *(Seaton 2001: 122)*

The paper sketched out a history of metempsychotic texts based on more than 100 examples of books, articles and broadcast works, produced in the nineteenth and twentieth centuries, with an analysis of their main generic features; the kind of significant others whose journeys had been repeated; the historical scripts recording them; and the rules of textual presentation and concealment underlying them (Seaton 2001: 128–36).

Metempsychosis, it was argued, offered a solution to the modernistic problem of discovering new places in a world where all the tracks had become beaten. It allowed the modern traveller/ tourist a kind of semiotic recovery of travel virginity in the terra nova of new experiences to be found in revisiting the spaces of travellers from the past, refracted through the social and cultural perspectives of the present.

---

### Box 2.1 Metempsychosis case study: in the footsteps of Dylan Thomas in South Wales, 2003

> ... we get the genuine Dylan Thomas fan ... some of them are from America ... they walk through the door and burst into tears. They can't sort of believe that they are standing on the spot and the environment that Dylan Thomas wrote about and it is all about them ...
>
> *(Lorraine Schofield, Carmarthenshire County Council)*

In 2003 tourism stakeholders in Welsh cultural heritage in South Wales planned and implemented a touristic tribute to the life and work of the poet Dylan Thomas, to coincide with the 50th anniversary of his death.[1] It comprised a programme of exhibitions, plays, festivals and events and the opening of a new Dylan Thomas Centre in Swansea. A key development was a 'Dylan Thomas trail' comprising 17 places associated with Thomas's life, intended as a four-day, metempsychotic itinerary for visitors.

#### The metempsychotic dimension

The visitor guide introducing the trail began with words that evoked following the footsteps of the poet:

> ... 2003 is the fiftieth anniversary of Dylan's death ... The anniversary is the perfect opportunity *to follow in the great man's footsteps* and *explore the places of his life, from his birthplace* in maritime Swansea, on the edge of the Gower Peninsular, through Carmarthenshire's lush rolling countryside, where he spent his most productive adult years, to the verdant landscapes of Pembrokeshire and Ceredigion.
>
> *(Anon 2003a: 3, my italics)*

*Figure 2.1* Literary journeys in South West Wales 2003 – the brochure and compact disc

However, it was the CD that was, from a metempsychotic standpoint, the most novel exhibit. It lasted 40 minutes, used the voices of several speakers, and told the story of Dylan Thomas and his work and life from birth to death. The metempsychotic mode was found primarily in the section that opened and the one that ended the CD. The first speaker was Jeff Towns, owner of Dylan's Bookshop in Swansea, an expert on Thomas and the poet's locality. He took the listener on a trip from his shop, to a tour of the Thomas house opposite:

At present ... if I look down ... we've got a fantastic view of the Mumbles and Swansea ... If I look across the road I can see No 5 Cwmdonkin Drive. It's got a blue plaque on the front door that says, 'Dylan Thomas, was born here' ... [sounds of movement, and voice emerging into outdoors] ... So ... we're going across the road to the house now. It's eh ... a very standard, suburban, semi-detached house, of no grandeur, no great merit ... The front door ... [noise of door opening] ... OK ... We're here ... [pause] *Under Milk Wood* was begun to ... begin at the beginning ... and this is where it began for Dylan Thomas ... This is the house where he was born, grew and [where he] spent the first 20 years of his life ...

*(Anon 2003b)*

What makes this metempsychotic? First the *speed* with which Towns draws in the listener-visitor. The move from his bookshop to the site is accomplished in just six words: 'As *I* look down *we've* got …' That linguistic shift from 'I' to 'we' imperceptibly moves the perspective from his own, to a *shared one* with the listener, which Towns then reveals is also that of Thomas as the house tour begins. The tour is a 'footstep-following' walk around the house ('In the hallway here there are two doors with two rather grand art nouveau panels on it … The front room here takes us into the lounge. We are back out into the hall. The room here at the left is what in earlier days was the study of the house …'). At every turn Towns notes and affirms the authenticity of what *can be seen today* and *what Thomas might have seen and experienced*. It is, of course, a rhetorical construct since the past can never be fully recaptured, but the promise to the imagination is made convincing by Town's detailed and passionate presentation of the minutiae of Dylan's life and work and the geography of the house which are juxtaposed with recordings of Thomas reading descriptions of his domestic circumstances that seem to corroborate the commentary (Anon 2003b: passim).

In the final section, Pat Hughes of the Merlin Theatre Company described Laugherne and the church of St Martin's where Thomas and Caitlin, his wife, were buried, adopting a metempsychotic mode of address:

> … we're heading in the glorious sunshine *along the walk that Dylan probably took every day of his life* at the Boathouse. *Heading towards his favourite pub, Brown's Hotel* …
>
> *(Anon 2003b: passim, my italics)*

Later she leads the listener in another metempsychotic site, which Thomas shared with his writer friend Richard Hughes:

> If we walk on through the entrance into Laugherne Castle … [Richard Hughes leased this castle] … *right on the edge overlooking the estuary is the Gazebo where Richard Hughes and Dylan Thomas would sit on many a day and write* …
>
> *(Anon 2003b: passim, my italics)*

The CD illustrates two essential truths about metempsychosis: first, that it is both *geophysical practice* (in this case, a mapped, physical itinerary of 17 places along a trail intended to be walked in four days); but also, second, a *narrative strategy, a way of telling a story*. Metempsychotic narrative is constructed through *linguistic conventions* and *modes of address* that aim to position readers-tourists within a discursive frame that promotes rapid *personal identification* with the subject through the shared topographical imaginary, created in the language (Anon 2003b). Both CD and printed materials exemplified ways in which these linguistic effects can be achieved (Anon 2003b). The metempsychotic mode of address was a key part of the anniversary planning. Jeff Towns and Pat Hughes consolidated it by developing 10 separate Dylan Thomas trails and training 10 guides to conduct tourists around them.

Metempsychotic values may be so important in cultural narratives that their absence may be experienced as a felt deficit by tourists expecting them. An instance of this was observed in 2011 by the writer in observational research of a different cultural tourism programme, a battlefield tour of the locations of the Duke of Wellington's Peninsular War campaign in Spain. At one of the locations, Ciudad Rodrigo, the tour included a walk around the battlements of the city to view the setting of the siege and examine the point where the wall was breached by the English Army. That night, over dinner, two members of the party criticised what they felt were weaknesses in telling the story:

> I wanted to be told *exactly* how it was both inside and outside the town … I wanted to have somebody standing on the battlements with me pointing out all the features of the surrounding country and giving me the detail …'*You can see from this spot exactly what he would have seen as he led his men … It was over there that they blew that bridge that had cost 200 guineas … and this is where the first soldiers fell …*' … Something like that …
>
> *(Seaton 2012)*

The plea was thus for more detail and greater, metempsychotic address.

## Metensomatosis

A year after the metempsychosis paper was published, a chapter in an edited collection of articles on tourism sociology (Dann 2002) extended the notion of tourism as ritual repetition more radically (Seaton 2002). Where metempsychosis had first been viewed as a specialist kind of cultural tourism in which tourists repeated a journey or journeys made by one *significant other* (e.g. Dylan Thomas), the second proposed that many other types of tourism, including cultural forms, were ritual repetition of travel behaviour by *several or many significant others*, but also *generalised others*, of whose influence tourists were largely unaware. The name given to this was metensomatosis, a word which, like metempsychosis, was adapted from classical religion/ mythology, and meant, 'the migration into one body of many souls' (Webster 1971: 1422). As a tourism concept metensomatosis embodied a view of the tourist as a performer who, through the holiday activities in which s/he engaged, *acted out several implicit roles*. The repertoires supporting the enacted roles were unconscious imitations of precedents set, either by *significant others*, or ones the individual thought represented the *imagined*, exemplary demands of a *generalised other*, both of which had evolved in the value system of the tourist's culture. As a result, cultural tourism was less a quest for the existential authenticity of a single self, than the adoption and orchestration of temporary personæ on holiday, a drama in which the tourists play-acted several roles.

Metensomatosis represented something of a bricolage theoretically, incorporating ideas from the domains of anthropology, structuralism and critical theory, and included discussion of work by Mircea Eliade (1954), Roland Barthes (1973, 1977), Walter Benjamin (1999a, 1999b), and Louis Althusser (1971). In the space available these theoretical discussions cannot, nor need be, repeated, but two additional theoretical connections need to be recognised to clarify what has been said so far.

The first is the debt the papers owed to the symbolic interactionism of G.H. Mead (1934), which sought to explain how individuals achieved selfhood and identity within specific societal constraints. Mead assumed that the self was a social product that derived from each individual's observation and emulation of two kinds of role models or 'others' – 'significant others' and 'generalised others'. 'Significant others' were specific individuals who represented quintessential values and achievements within their community or society, and thus became role models for emulation. The 'generalised other' was not a specific individual but an *imagined* composite of behavioural characteristics and attributes, thought to constitute an exemplary typification of what a person within a community should be (e.g. the 'typical American', 'the British soldier'), and thus an aspirational ideal for its members. It has been defined as '... the organized attitudes of the whole community enabling people thereby to incorporate an overarching sense of community values into their conception of self' (Marshall 1994: 589–90).

Mead assumed that both kinds of 'other' were real and present influences, shaping individual behaviour. Metensomatosis followed Mead's ideas on the importance of emulation, but allowed for the possibility that significant others and generalised tourist others might be *historical* role models as well as contemporary ones, and include both *real* and *mythical* figures. In the 1960s, for instance, the mythic persona of James Bond influenced notions and enactments of male style and travel sophistication.

Metensomatosis also owed something to one of Mead's most creative successors, Erving Goffman (1961), who developed Mead's idea of role-taking and role-making in self-formation, and elaborated it into a dramaturgical model of behaviour in which all social situations were seen as *theatres of performance* in which interactants played out roles that could be minutely analysed. Tourism awaits a new Erving Goffman to apply his kind of theatrically grounded micro-analysis to illuminate tourist repertoires and performances. Edensor has made a start in this direction (Edensor 1998, 2007) and recently reviewed work on tourism and performance that suggests that the wait may not be too long (Edensor 2009).

---

### Box 2.2 Metensomatosis case study: Titan River Cruises and cultural tourism

Permutation of these metensomatosic repertoires are widely in evidence, wholly or in part, in cultural tourism programmes. Titan is a leading cruise specialist that carries 'discerning travellers' on ships described as, 'floating 5 star boutique hotels' on voyages of 'inspiring travel' along the great rivers of the world (Titan 2012: 1, 3). It offers an extensive portfolio of international cruises that can cost up to £8,000–£9,000. The manifold pleasures it offers are set out in a glossy, 100-page brochure.

The cultural agenda is provided through Titan's 'Signature lectures, experts in European history, art, music, architecture', and the daily schedule of stops and activities. Among its principal cruises are included travelling the oldest European mountain railway in Konigswinter; exploring picturesque medieval streets in Brussels; visiting historical palaces and cathedrals; viewing baroque and renaissance architecture in Antwerp, Cologne and Vienna; visiting the Jewish Quarter in Prague and nineteenth-century fishermen's houses in Bomburg; visiting famous gardens and the Floriade, the World Horticultural Expo in Venlo; Belgian beer drinking and European wine tasting in many places, typically in aristocratic palaces and castles (Titan 2012: passim).

The eclectic diversity of these activities offers suggestive insights into the individual and distinct *performance repertoires* that support the constructed persona of the cultural tourist, which are as much about *enacted class position* as knowledge acquisition. The repertoires here include the *metensomatosic roles* of gourmet, wine lover, architectural buff, historian, horticultural student, art critic and religious visitor. Though Titan's cruises are targeted at an upmarket audience (the proverbial 'discerning traveller'), the cultural rituals of metensomatosis have trickled down the social scale so that more and more tourists have been *interpellated*, in Althusser's terms, into enacting repertoires of cultural tourism performance, once confined to a few.

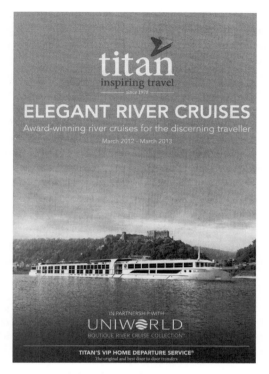

*Figure 2.2* Titan's brochure, 'Elegant River Cruises'

The structuralist/symbolic interactionist approach to tourism behaviour in metensomatosis contrasts with psychological approaches to motivation. Instead of assuming that tourists are driven by relatively stable tourism needs (e.g. sunlust or wanderlust (Gray 1970)), and fall into identifiable, typological categories (e.g. allocentrics, midcentrics or psychocentrics (Plog 1973)), it conceptualises tourists as transient performers of cultural repertoires, acted out with a greater or lesser degree of intensity and commitment for brief periods. Role playing better suggests the theatricality of tourist behaviour as temporary performance, involving short-term emotional and mental investment, different degrees of performing ability, and variations by time and place.

## Problems with metensomatosis as a theory

Metensomatosis may superficially seem to cast the tourist in the role of programmed robot or hopeless copycat, acting out pre-determined roles and blissfully unaware of doing so. Yet in reality the risk for the cultural tourist of appearing to be 'punched to a pattern' may be mitigated by several variables. Performances are not as uniform as theory might suggest. There are differences in both the *degree of scripting* available for the different roles, and tourists' knowledge of them (e.g. the degree of knowledge required to perform as aesthete, or scientific traveller, or gourmet). People may differ in the extent to which they want to play the game of playing roles.

Second, the personæ and required repertoires of tourism performance change. They are modified and augmented by: cultural innovations, through the emergence of new significant and general tourism others; the product innovations of the tourism and leisure industry; and the media coverage travel and tourism attracts which affirms, expands and sometimes undercuts the roles and performance repertoires of tourism. The role of surfer, for example, is one which has emerged comparatively recently in Britain, while the persona of sun worshipper is being undermined by medical propaganda.

Metensomatosis may also seem a problematic construct since it assumes processes of implicit and unconscious emulation that are logically beyond direct observation and thus cannot be explored directly. This is an attribution problem which metensomatosis shares with other social science constructs that hypothesise 'hidden' mainsprings of action – Freud's concept of the unconscious; Jung's assertion of archetypal patterns in culture.

There are no definitive ways of overcoming these difficulties, but one way of exploring implicit cultural repertoires is *historically* by tracing the beginnings of specific cultural tourism discourses and the activities and repertoires associated with them. One source for this is *the literature of tourist instruction*, published intermittently from the early days of modern tourism, designed to induct the novice into different tourist roles (e.g. Kitchiner 1827; Galton 1867; Batsford 1940). Another source is through appraisal of *guidebooks* that helped to elaborate knowledge and understanding of the tourist roles appropriate to specific places. Third, there are *tour memoirs* that reveal feelings of the earliest modern tourists, and suggest the cultural discourses that shaped them – for example, the late eighteenth-century journals of John Byng (1934–38) which reflect uncertainties about role performance – what he should see and do – and where he explicitly references a wide range of literary 'significant others' whose metensomatosic influence he acknowledges when available, and desires when absent.

## Concluding comments

Metempsychosis is a concept that defines and characterises a specific kind of journey found in literary travel, broadcast schedules and cultural tourism, which had previously received little attention. The original paper drew attention to the growth in media representation of metempsychotic journeys, a trend that has since included big budget TV series, featuring quests following celebrity 'significant others' as diverse as Alexander the Great, Daniel Defoe, Thomas Pennant, Charles Darwin and Ernest Hemingway, *by* presenters who are, or have themselves become, celebrities, including Michael Palin, Nicholas Crane and Michael Wood.

Metempsychosis is exclusively and specifically a cultural tourism form, but metensomatosis affects all tourism, though it has particular importance for the cultural tourist, because the acquisition of the discursive repertoires necessary to perform roles successfully (e.g. knowing the right galleries to see, the right artists to praise, the right named architecture to admire, the right food and drink to like) is relatively demanding for anyone who is not raised, as Bourdieu has proposed, within a familial, educational or occupational environment where high culture and the arts are absorbed effortlessly through a kind of cultural osmosis (Bourdieu 1984: passim).

Metempsychosis and metensomatosis both involve transient performances, pulsar role playing that switches on and off during holiday time. The tourist travels not as his or her everyday self, but in part as a quick change artiste, permutating a range of temporary personæ drawn from exemplary, imagined phenotypes within his/her culture. People sometimes say that a holiday has changed them. The illation of metempsychosis and metensomatosis proposed here is that they go off changed, but revert to what they were when they return.

## Note

1 Stakeholders included: South Wales Tourism Partnership, Carmarthenshire County Council, City and County of Swansea, Neath Port Talbot County Borough Council, Pembrokeshire County Council, Cei Dev Ltd, Carmarthenshire Tourist Association, Neath Port Talbot Tourism, Tourism Swansea, Pembrokeshire Tourism, Writers' Routes Consortium, and Wales Cymru.

## References

Althusser, L. (1971) 'Ideology and Ideological State Apparatuses', in *Lenin and Philosophy and Other Essays*, London: New Left Books, 45–67.

Anon (2003a) *Literary Journeys in South West Wales*, Cardiff: Writers' Routes/Wales Tourist Board.

——(2003b) *Literary Journeys in South West Wales. Dylan Thomas*, compact disc, Cardiff: Writers' Routes/ Wales Tourist Board.

Barthes, R. (1973) *Mythologies*, London: Paladin.

——(1977) *Image, Music, Text*, London: Fontana.

Batsford, H. (1940) *How to See the Country*, London: Batsford.

Benjamin, W. (1999a) *The Arcades Project*, trans. H. Eiland and K. McLaughlin, Cambridge, MA: Belknap/ Harvard University Press.

——(1999b) *Selected Writings, Vol. 2, 1927–1934*, Cambridge, MA: Belknap/Harvard University Press.

Bourdieu, P. (1984) *Distinction: A Social Critique of the Judgement of Taste*, London: Routledge, Kegan, Paul.

Byng, Hon. John (1934–38) *The Torrington Diaries*, 4 vols (ed. C. Bruyn Andrews), London: Eyre and Spottiswoode.

Dann, G.S. (2002) *The Tourist as a Metaphor of the Social World*, Wallingford: CABI.

Disraeli, I. (n.d. [1839]) *The Curiosities of Literature*, 3 vols, London: Chandos Classics.

Edensor, T. (1998) *Tourists at the Taj*, London: Routledge.

——(2007) 'Mundane Mobilities, Performances and Spaces of Tourism', *Social and Cultural Geography* 8(2): 199–215.

——(2009) 'Tourism and Performance', in Jamal, T. and Robinson, M. (eds) *The Sage Handbook of Tourism Studies*, London and California: Sage, 543–57.

Eliade, M. (1954) *The Myth of the Eternal Return or, Cosmos and History*, Princeton, NJ: Princeton University Press: Bollingen Series XLVI.

Galton, E. (1867) *The Art of Travel or, Shifts and Contrivances Available in Wild Countries*, London: John Murray.

Goffman, E. (1961) *Encounters*, London: Penguin.

Gray, H.P. (1970) *International Tourism – International Trade*, Lexington, KY: Lexington Books.

Kitchiner, W. (1827) *The Traveler's Oracle or, Maxims for Locomotion: Containing Precepts for Promoting the Pleasures and Hints for Preserving the Health of Travellers*, London: Henry Colburn.

Marshall, G. (1994) *Oxford Dictionary of Sociology*, Oxford: Blackwell.

Mead, G.H. (1934) *Mind, Self and Society*, Chicago, IL: University of Chicago Press.

Merriam-Webster (1971) *Webster's Third New International Dictionary*, Encyclopaedia Britannica.

Picart, B. (1733) 'The Ceremonies and Religious Customs of the Idolatrous Nations', Vol. IV, Part 3, London: William Jackson, for Claude du Boc.

Plog, S. (1973) 'Why Destination Areas Fall and Rise in Popularity', *Cornell Hotel and Restaurant Administrative Quarterly* 15 (Nov.): 13–16.

Propp, V. (1971) *Morphology of the Folk Tale*, Austin: University of Texas.

Seaton, A.V. (2000) 'The Worst of Journeys – The Best of Journeys: Travel and the Concept of the Periphery in European Culture', in Robinson, M., Evans, N. and Callaghan, P. (eds) *Expressions of Culture, Identity and Meaning in Tourism*, Sunderland: Business Education Publishers, 321–46.

——(2001) 'In the Footsteps of Acerbi: Metempsychosis and the Repeated Journey', in Jarva, E., Makivuoti, M. and Sironen, T. (ed.) *Tutkimusmatkalla Pohjoisseen, Acta Universitatis Ouliensis*, Finland: Oulu University Press, B40, 121–38.

——(2002) 'Tourism as Metempsychosis and Metensomatosis: The Personae of Eternal Recurrence', in Dann, G. (ed.) *The Tourist as a Metaphor of the Social World*, Wallingford: CABI, 135–68.

——(2012) *Unpublished Transcript from Notes Kept*, October 2011.

Titan (2012) *Elegant River Cruise*, brochure, Salford, UK.

# 3

# Talking tourists

## The intimacies of inter-cultural dialogue

*Mike Robinson*

The study of tourism is riven with paradoxes, tensions and dilemmas invoking innately moral questions surrounding both the actions of the tourism sector and the practices and behaviours of tourists themselves. The field of critical tourism studies is overflowing with cases that highlight an extensive variety of effects attributed, in part at least, to the 'doing' of tourism. In the main, and indeed what makes such cases worthy of attention, is that they direct us to consider the negative consequences of tourism as a form of social action (exclusion, marginalisation, erosion of identity, disempowerment and various degrees of degradation of the natural and built environment, etc.). Scholarly consideration of such consequences points to a wider recognition of the importance of tourism as a global phenomenon now firmly embedded in the developed and developing worlds as a leisure practice and in the lesser developed world as an important livelihood. It also points to further traits which seem to accompany the study of tourism. First, there is significant attention given to tourism as an agent of negative disturbance rather than positive change in a rather narrow interpretation of the term 'critical'. Second, there is still a tendency to isolate tourism as a discrete category of social activity more than occasionally lapsing into the actions of tourists as being a precise cause for environmental and social impact, despite recent work amongst anthropologists and cultural geographers attempting to locate tourism within life's more complex patterns and processes (see, for instance, Edensor 2001; Crouch 2003; Larsen 2008). Third, often accompanying the above, the study of tourism has tended to be centred upon the destination as the key space of interaction and as a crude signifier of tourist typology (people are cultural tourists because they are in Venice!).

Such characteristics mark out tourism, in operation and study, as decidedly binary, working with generic conventions of 'work and play', 'home and away', 'hosts and guests', along with the more spatially oriented 'East and West', 'developed and developing worlds'. While in a post-structuralist vein the academic community has sought to create ways to break from the narrow intellectualism of these binaries and their 'violent hierarchies' (Derrida 2002) by invoking notions of 'third spaces' and ideals of the cosmopolitan tourist (Swain 2009; Picard this volume). However, it is difficult to ignore the ways in which oppositions do permeate the tourist world and how they are embedded in the meta-narratives that structure tourism. They have a reality precisely because they are essential to how we think of the world and how we communicate the world through language. Language, and how it is used in dialogue, is the under-researched dimension of tourism, partly as we are frequently locked into our own realms of comprehension, which are of course cultural as well as linguistic, and partly because access to moments and meanings of dialogue is often problematic for researchers. Adjusting the label of cultural tourism to the more meaningful 'tourism as cultural' points to the importance of dialogue and the conditions in which it is practised.

## Engaging with otherness

Tourism is emblematic of the liberating and dramatic global mobilities that have marked the past decades. While globalisation is a larger category still, able to operate at more remote levels of represented knowledge and rapidly communicated imagery, tourism is essentially involved with the actual *being there*, providing the opportunities for embodied encounter and engagement with difference and the 'other'. While questions remain regarding the extent to which tourists actively seek to engage with difference, some aspect of direct engagement is embedded in the desire to travel. Material and immaterial differences (buildings, landscapes, artefacts, food, dress, events, behaviours, etc.) are sensed, absorbed, processed, compared and memorised to varying degrees by the tourist. Frameworks of performance and play are helpful in understanding how tourists negotiate the differences with which they are faced, producing rituals of practice and ways of coping that are often extensions of normative social practice exported to 'new' situations. The everyday and the habitual ground the tourist, so that one can make sense of otherness. Edensor (2009: 553) outlines various means by which tourists engage with and perform their encounters with the 'other' in multi-faceted and embodied ways, embracing the senses in 'an interactive and contingent process'. Tourists *learn* competencies for dealing with the alien, which are themselves transmitted to other tourists. An expanse of guides, websites and a vast informal knowledge network are employed to effect ways for the tourist to access the 'other' and it is within such mediation and communication where there are opportunities for hegemonic asymmetries to manifest themselves, consciously and unconsciously. Hollinshead (2009) uses the term 'world-making' to encapsulate a 'normalising' process whereby the authority of tourism is established and implicitly, and often imperceptibly, channelled *through* the tourist. Moreover, scholars such as Jaworski and Pritchard (2005) and Thurlow and Jaworski (2010), amongst others, have pointed to the scripting power of tourism discourse and the 'talk', which filters through to the tourist and which is the currency of representation and the imagined. Notions of a 'contact' or 'border' zone (Pratt 1992; Bruner 2005) help to make sense spatially of where tourists do encounter difference. While we can acknowledge the circulation and imposition of dominant scripts, however, the exercise of power and the ways by which tourists are (often unknowingly) implicated as agents of a sort of temporary colonialism, there still remain questions as to what are the actual *mechanisms* of tourists engaging with the 'other'? Of what does inter-activity consist? What is involved in the face-to-face aspect of 'world-making'?

## Grand narratives and meaningful contact

Tourism, as both a social and cultural practice, and also as a political act, has been recognised as having a critical role to play in facilitating and shaping inter-cultural dialogue (Viard 2001). Facilitation refers to the rather superficial aspect of tourism of encouraging new mobilities across space and cultures rather than considering the detail of any dialogue. Whether this represents any more than a superficial 'aesthetic cosmopolitanism' (Szeszynski and Urry 2006) or 'banal cosmopolitanism' (Haldrup 2009), is debatable. Certainly, at the level of intergovernmental politics, the term 'intercultural dialogue' is seen as a way of exploring complex themes of cultural diversity and plurality and is now central to the humanistic agendas of the United Nations (UN) agencies, most notably the UN Educational, Scientific and Cultural Organization (UNESCO), which since its founding has worked to foster dialogue between cultures in acknowledgement of this being a fundamental basis for a culture of peace. The premise of UNESCO's work relates to concepts such as mankind's 'common heritage', 'shared values' and 'cultural pluralism', and is enshrined in the 2005 Convention on Cultural Diversity (UNESCO 2005). However, whatever the intentions behind grand and worthy projects, there has been limited attention to the micro-realities of dialogue as it exists between tourists and host communities. This is peculiar given that tourism arguably represents the leading opportunity for cultures to come into *direct* contact with one another in any significant way.

Within the world of the 'other', bearing in mind that the 'other' is not solely the exotic, but rather manifests itself in someone else's 'ordinary', the tourist is frequently exposed by the absence of cultural reference points, the most fundamental of which is language. Though as tourists we may journey into otherness armed with pre-tour knowledge and accumulated imaginaries, we often underestimate the extent to which we need to engage in dialogue with our hosts. Following the work of Bakhtin (1981), dialogue is taken to mean discourse that is able to increase our understanding of differing perspectives, create new understandings, and which generates a change in a situation. For Bakhtin, it is dialogue that has the potential to transgress cultural borders. Dialogue refers to a social process of meaning-making through 'language in action'; going beyond the spoken word to include aspects of tone, sound and body language. Dialogue between cultures is a learning process, a form of pedagogy concerned with both actions and values. Accepting the obvious, manufactured locatedness of the tourist, it implies a fundamental form of human exchange which is still relatively spontaneous and exploratory. The goal of dialogue is a deeper understanding of the 'other', bearing in mind that the tourist is also the 'other'. A counter-argument to this invokes the obvious ephemerality of the tourist visit and as a body, passing through a place tourists may not be presented with need, or opportunity, to engage in dialogue outside of their immediate peer group. However, there would always seem to be room for adjustment in understanding and the acquisition of new meanings.

## Context and operations of inter-cultural dialogue

The so-called tourist 'bubble' (Cohen 1972; Jacobsen 2003) is relatively rare in its pure conception. Even enclave destinations and inclusive packaged holidays, despite their attempts to streamline the experience of otherness, nonetheless contain exposed and fragmented insights into cultural difference; waiters and hotel staff retain their foreignness in appearance, accent and behaviours; food and drink concede some attempt to bear the mark of difference; and excursions allow for more direct, if contrived and managed, cross-cultural contact. Accepting the need to contextualise exchanges between tourists and locals, there is generally an expanse of both opportunity and necessity for contact with the 'other'. Indeed, for many tourists the pleasure of being in a non-familiar environment presents itself as a series of experiences always with possibilities for some degree of inter-cultural dialogue; a satisfied sense of communication and a moment of human connection. The foreign holiday is accompanied by distortions of time and space routines so that we may sleep less or longer, eat at different times and so on. The routine tasks of daily life thus take on a new significance. It is instructive to examine the ways that recent holidays are remembered. Increasingly these are publicly reported in great detail through online blogs, complete with photographs and intimate reminiscences. The holiday is recounted as a story, and while we may find reference to gazing at buildings and landscapes, the most discussed aspects relate to encounters with people – local people in ordinary situations. Ordering a coffee, having a meal, buying toothpaste, getting on a bus, all become significant occasions. In part, the significance is a function of having to communicate outside of our own language, thus being forced into a position of directly negotiating and mediating with others. The sense of personal achievement is striking when, as a tourist, you break free of the script and start composing the story yourself. The difficulties of coping with 'otherness' are also sometimes our reward. As Phipps (2007) has argued, learning the language of the 'other', in the most functional of ways, opens up experiences that can sustain and strengthen inter-cultural dialogue.

The reward of inter-cultural dialogue does not just reside with the tourist. Hosts engaging in dialogue with tourists are frequently involved in a learning process – culturally, linguistically – to which otherwise they are never exposed. Within toured societies there is symbolic capital – what Salazar (2010) refers to as 'cosmopolitan capital' – to be gained by entering into dialogue with tourists as a way of temporarily appropriating them, and by association gaining or maintaining status in the community. This manifests itself in opportunities for economic exchange. In the daily markets of Cairo or Istanbul tourists are frequently approached by stall-holders in their native tongue. This linguistic dexterity, which often extends well beyond a common greeting to complicated exchanges and remarkable conversations, is not usually the product of a formal education or firsthand experience of another country, but is, nonetheless, part of daily life. It is easy to dismiss this phenomenon purely as part of the ritual surrounding the need to make a living through trade, but beyond some minor annoyances on both sides, this is also a very humanising form of engagement. To be approached by strangers in your own language offers an invitation, however momentary, into the world of the 'other'.

As a tourist, not speaking the language of the host generates vulnerability and dependence. Tourist guides and interpreters can reduce this sense of exposure, but it seldom leaves the tourist completely. The apparent dominance of the tourist can readily be exposed through his or her inability to read signs, or ask for the most ordinary of items. From the perspective of the host, the tourist becomes the exoticised 'other', different not only in appearance but as a function of a visible insecurity in dealing with difference. As Giddens (1991) notes, this difference itself can become a means of inter-cultural dialogue.

## Smoothing angst

Even within the formalised settings of organised travel, with guides and translators to mediate, and in the relative comfort of a tour bus or resort hotel, tourists rarely fail to engage with the ordinariness of the other and vice versa. Julia Harrison, who has studied the experiences of Western, middle-class tourists, emphasises the moments of contact between tourist and local, however fleeting or unpredictable, and which go toward redefining social relations. In Harrison's (2003: 50) words, 'no matter how brief these touristic encounters were, they left lasting impressions in the tourists' minds. People in places far from home became something other than complete strangers'.

The actuality of *being* a tourist places us in various states of angst which, it is argued, help to drive processes of redefining social relations. The word 'angst' was abstracted from the German language to the English language in the mid-nineteenth century and was used by religious and secular thinkers struggling to articulate feelings associated with the rapidity of change brought about by modernity. For tourists, angst relates to the act of finding the toilet through signs in another language, to ordering a meal from a menu they cannot understand, to worrying about whether the public bus they are on actually goes back to their hotel. In such ways angst is, as Heidegger (1962) used the term, the fear of metaphysical insecurity and testimony to the authenticity of experience.

One of the ways we negotiate our angst is to trust in the immediate. Lingis (2004), in his discussion of trust, suggests that when we travel, particularly within the non-signed world, we are bound to momentarily give over our lives to others. Though we may have read of procedures and practices at some point, we have to let go and allow ourselves to be taken into the differences we seek. Getting into a taxi, taking a turn into an unsigned street, eating outside of the hotel, are all instances of trust; a state of commitment which depends upon inter-subjectivity and which cuts through any binary concepts of 'us and them' and allows true hospitality to flourish. In moments of angst, and in line with notions of trust, tourists fall back on intuition and humanity. Tourists do not just occupy spaces; they create them for the purposes of negotiation, reflection and understanding to overcome their angst. These are the spaces of dialogue and mediation. Cronin (2006: 135) warns that, 'To remove the space of mediation, the intermediary zone of time and difficulty which is the attempt to get to know another culture and another language, is to move from the triangular space of negotiation to the binary space of opposition'. In the context of understanding tourist behaviour, and through dialogue, these are also moments of belonging, when the tourist attains empathy with those around and is able to project his or her own humanity. These may only be instants, but they act as metaphorical roads or bridges (Jackson 1998), allowing the transcendence of worldviews and, at very least, the selective forgetting of binaries. Understanding the conditions, content and mechanisms of inter-cultural dialogue amongst tourists assists with grander objectives to bridge cultures and recognise the joy of difference.

# References

Bakhtin, M. (1981) *The Dialogical Imagination: Four Essays*, Holquist, M. (ed.), Austin: University of Texas Press.

Bruner, E. (2005) *Culture on Tour: Ethnographies of Travel*, Chicago, IL: University of Chicago Press.

Cohen, E. (1972) 'Toward a Sociology of International Tourism', *Social Research* 39: 163–82.

Cronin, M. (2006) *Translation and Identity*, London: Routledge.

Crouch, D. (2003) 'Spacing, Performing, and Becoming: Tangles in the Mundane', *Environment and Planning A* 35: 1945–60.

Derrida, J. (2002) *Of Grammatology*, trans. Chakravorty Spivak, G., Baltimore, MD: Johns Hopkins University Press.

Edensor, T. (2001) 'Performing Tourism, Staging Tourism: (Re)producing Tourist Space and Practice', *Tourist Studies* 1: 59–81.

——(2009) 'Tourism and Performance', in Jamal, T. and Robinson, M. (eds) *The SAGE Handbook of Tourism Studies*, London: Sage, 543–57.

Giddens, A. (1991) *Modernity and Self-Identity: Self and Society in the Late Modern Age*, Stanford, CA: Stanford University Press.

Haldrup, M. (2009) 'Banal Tourism? Between Cosmopolitanism and Orientalism', in Pons, P.O., Crang, M. and Travlou, P. (eds) *Cultures of Mass Tourism: Doing the Mediterranean in the Age of Banal Mobilities*, London: Ashgate, 53–76.

Harrison, J. (2003) *Being a Tourist: Finding Meaning in Pleasure Travel*, Vancouver: University of British Columbia Press.

Heidegger, M. (1962) *Being and Time*, New York: Harper & Row.

Hollinshead, K. (2009) 'The "Worldmaking" Prodigy of Tourism: The Reach and Power of Tourism in the Dynamics of Change and Transformation', *Tourism Analysis* 14(1): 139–52.

Jackson, M. (1998) *Minima Ethnographica: Intersubjectivity and the Anthropological Project*, Chicago, IL: University of Chicago Press.

Jacobsen, J.K.S (2003) 'The Tourist Bubble and the Europeanisation of Holiday Travel', *Journal of Tourism and Cultural Change* 1(1): 71–87.

Jaworski, A. and Pritchard, A. (2005) *Discourse, Communication and Tourism*, Clevedon: Channel View.

Larsen, J. (2008) 'De-exoticizing Tourist Travel: Everyday Life and Sociality on the Move', *Leisure Studies* 27(1): 21–34.

Lingis, A. (2004) *Trust*, Minneapolis: University of Minnesota Press.

Phipps, A. (2007) *Learning the Arts of Linguistic Survival: Languaging, Tourism, Life*, Clevedon: Channel View.

Pratt, M.L. (1992) *Imperial Eyes: Travel Writing and Transmigration*, London: Routledge.

Salazar, N. (2010) 'Tourism and Cosmopolitanism: A View from Below', *International Journal of Tourism Anthropology* 1(1): 55–69.

Swain, M.B. (2009) 'The Cosmopolitan Hope of Tourism: Critical Action and Worldmaking Vistas', *Tourism Geographies* 11(4): 505–25.

Szeszynski, B. and Urry, J. (2006) 'Visuality, Mobility and the Cosmopolitan: Inhabiting the World from Afar', *British Journal of Sociology* 57(1): 113–31.

Thurlow, C. and Jaworski, A. (2010) *Tourism Discourse: Language and Global Mobility*, Basingstoke: Palgrave Macmillan.

UNESCO (2005) *Convention on the Protection and Promotion of the Diversity of Cultural Expressions*, Paris: UNESCO.

Viard, J. (2001) *Court Traité sur les Vacances, les Voyages et l'hospitalité des Lieux*, Paris: Aube.

# 4

# The (im)mobility of tourism imaginaries

*Noel B. Salazar*

As with many other activities – reading novels, playing games, watching movies, telling stories, daydreaming, etc. – planning and going on holidays involve the human capacity to imagine or to enter into the imaginings of others. Seductive images and discourses about peoples and places are so predominant that without them there would be little tourism, if any at all. I conceptualise such imaginaries as socially transmitted representational assemblages that interact with people's personal imaginings and are used as meaning-making and world-shaping devices. In this chapter I discuss the multiple links between cultural tourism and the imaginary, paying particular attention to institutionally grounded imaginaries implying power, hierarchy and hegemony. I focus on how otherwise lived spaces are shaped by and are shaping tourism practices and fantasies (the original Greek word for imaginaries). The Indonesian case study (Box 4.1) illustrates how the critical analysis of cultural tourism imaginaries offers a powerful deconstruction device of ideological, political, and socio-cultural stereotypes and clichés.

## Tourism imaginaries on the move

Cultural tourism is 'the quintessential business of "difference projection" and the interpretive vehicle of "othering" par excellence' (Hollinshead 1998: 121). Stories, images and desires, running the gamut from essentialised, mythologised and exoticised imaginaries of otherness to more realistic frames of reference, often function as the motor setting the tourism machinery in motion (Amirou 1995). Marketers eagerly rely on them to represent and sell dreams of the world's limitless destinations, activities, types of accommodation, and peoples to discover and experience. Prospective tourists are invited to imagine themselves in a paradisiacal environment where the local landscape and population are to be consumed through observation, embodied sensation, and imagination. In tourism, identities of destinations and their inhabitants are endlessly (re)invented, (re)produced, (re)captured and (re)created in a bid to obtain a piece of the lucrative tourism pie. This is especially true of cultural tourism or tourism with cultural elements (Amirou 2000).

For Said (1994) geographic imaginaries refer, literally, to how spaces are imagined, how meanings are ascribed to physical spaces (such that they are perceived, represented, and interpreted in particular ways), how knowledge about these places is produced, and how these representations make various courses of action possible. Tourist ways of 'seeing' places often differ from other representations because places are being fashioned in the image of tourism (Hughes 1992). The Caribbean as 'tropical nature', for example, is mobilised through a range of tourism imaginaries and practices (Sheller 2004: 17). The past is being reworked by naming, designating, and historicising landscapes to enhance their tourism appeal (Gold and Gold 1995; Bacchilega 2007). Who represents what, whom and how are critical and often contested issues for socio-cultural insiders as well as outsiders (Morgan and Pritchard 1998; Adams 2004). There are important bonds between imaginative geographies and imagined communities as peoples and places are constructed in both the imaginative and the material sense (Gregory 1994).

Destination marketers have no monopoly over manufacturing the exotic. Tourism fantasies are always situated within wider socio-cultural frameworks (Hutnyk 1996). They emerge not from the realm of concrete everyday experience but in the circulation of more collectively held images. Critical scholarship reveals how broader cultural and ideological structures create and mediate tourism representations (Selwyn 1996; Morgan and Pritchard 1998; Hall and Tucker 2004; Ateljevic et al. 2007). Images of difference have been (re)constructed over centuries of cross-cultural contact. In the case of Western tourism to developing countries, the circulating representations cater to certain images within Western consciousness about how the Other is imagined to be. Such imaginaries form a 'representational loop' (Sturma 2002: 137) which heavily relies upon the fictional worlds of literature, film and the fine arts to give 'authenticity' to peoples and places (Urbain 1994; Hennig 2002; Robinson and Andersen 2002). At the same time, tourism imaginaries do not exist in a vacuum, but have to contend with other circulating images and ideas. Global media streams overwhelm people with thousands of impressions of the world, in real time.

Studying tourism imaginaries seems as daunting as it is exciting. By their very nature, imaginaries remain intangible, so the only way to study them is by focusing on the multiple conduits through which they pass and become visible in the form of images and discourses. As an anthropologist, I operationalise imaginaries as real (networks of) social practices. Through a combination of historical and ethnographic methods, we can assess how imaginary activities, subjects, social relations, etc. are materialised, enacted and inculcated. Thus, although the precise workings of imaginaries are hidden from view, the operating logic can be inferred from its visible manifestations and from what people say and do. Cultural tourism imaginaries in particular become tangible when they are incarnated in institutions, from archaeological sites, museums, and monuments to hotels, media, and cultural productions (Wynn 2007: 21). Careful empirical study of situated articulations and (dis)connections between tourism imaginaries and their broader context is a fruitful way of analysing tourism in general.

How exactly imaginaries influence a broad public is an ambiguous question that merits grounded ethnographic research on reception and consumption rather than mere ideological critique. Images, discourses and ideas have certain points of origin – in tourism many of them are marked by distinctly Western genealogies – but are now incessantly moving in global 'rounds', reaching new horizons and periodically feeding back to their places of departure. The older the imaginaries and the longer they have been circulating, the harder it becomes to trace where they originated. Imaginaries circulate unevenly, not freely; their spread is shaped by processes that delimit and restrict movement. In order to understand how circulation works, we not only need to study what is on the move but also the socio-cultural structures and mechanisms that make that movement possible or impossible.

Empowered by imagined vistas of mass-mediated master narratives, tourism imaginaries have become global. They are now sent, transferred, received, accumulated, converted, and stored around the world (Crouch et al. 2005). The mobility of images and narratives of otherness signify familiar notions of global difference. Through this continuous circulation, tourism fantasies help in (re)creating peoples and places. Global tourism dis-embeds images and ideas of peoples and places from their original context, making them available through their transformation, legitimisation, institutionalisation and distribution. Tourism imaginaries are easily re-embedded in new contexts by a process that constantly alters both the imaginaries and the contexts, building on local referents to establish their meaning and value.

It is no coincidence that the travel concept is linguistically related to the French word *travail*, which means labour. Tourism involves networked orderings of people, natures, materials, mobilities and cultures. As actor-network theory stresses, everything circulating within such networks is continuously 'translated', deformed and modified (van der Duim *et al.* 2012). In some destinations, tourism imaginaries are so firmly established and all-encompassing that they are difficult to escape. In other places, the tourismifying images and ideas are much more diffuse and open to changes (Picard 1996; Bruner 2005). Indeed, reproduction processes are rarely without negotiation and resignification. The circulation of tourism discourses and imaginaries is, in many respects, a translocally negotiated process involving variously situated actors and their 'glocal' engagements with tourism to (re)produce 'stereotypic images, discredited histories, and romantic fantasies' (Bruner 2005: 76). Rather than mere projections, these transactions are negotiated in various ways and both restrict the lives of people and create new subject positions.

Studying the (im)mobility of imaginaries reveals how cultural representations are mixed together, consumed and interpreted. In his study on contemporary media productions of Tibet, Mercille (2005), for instance, shows the remarkable homogeneity of Shangri-La imaginaries in a movie (*Seven Years in Tibet*), a guidebook (*Lonely Planet*), and a magazine (*National Geographic*). One master image of Tibet seems to circulate by the various representations of it. In a similar vein, Bruner (2005) talks about tourism imaginaries in terms of 'metanarratives', and calls them 'the largest conceptual frame within which tourism operates. They are not attached to any locality or to any particular tour, and they are usually taken for granted, not brought to consciousness' (Bruner 2005: 21).

---

## Box 4.1 Case study: Indonesia

Many Western representations depict Asia in general as exotic and erotic (Prasso 2005), an image that attracts travellers, adventurers and tourists (Michel 2001). The guided tours offered in and around the Water Castle in Yogyakarta, Indonesia, offer a textbook example of how such imaginaries are subtly translated in cultural tourism practices. Tamansari, as it is locally known, was the former pleasure garden of the local Sultan, a complex of enchanting pavilions and mesmerising swimming pools. Many of the on-site guides (all males) enthusiastically enact the role of the Sultan, strolling with an imaginary girl (when possible substituted by a willing female tourist), from the women's swimming pool to the Sultan's private pool and adjacent quarters. They convincingly tell tourists stories about how life was organised 'back in the days'. At the castle's watchtower, the guides invite people to go upstairs and imagine themselves observing the make-believe harem girls around the pool.

The swimming pools of the Water Castle are still there (and have been beautifully restored), but the lovely girls bathing have long disappeared. Yet tourists are invited to participate in an entertaining performance that will bring an imagined past back to life, namely that of the oriental harem. This Islamic institution (etymologically linked to the Arabic *haram*, 'something prohibited') exerted a certain fascination on the Western imagination, especially during the Romantic period

*Figure 4.1* Exciting tourism imaginaries at the Water Castle in Yogyakarta, Indonesia
Source: © Noel B. Salazar.

(due in part to Richard Francis Burton's translation of *One Thousand and One Nights*, which included extensive footnotes on oriental sexual practices). Many people imagined a harem as a brothel with sensual wives and concubines (including abducted Western girls) lying around pools with naked, oiled bodies, with the sole purpose of pleasing the powerful man to whom they had given themselves. Although historically incorrect, much of this imaginary continues circulating through orientalist art and its reproduction and clichés, including in movies.

Making multiple (often playful) references to this harem imaginary, the Water Castle is depicted by tour guides as a Shangri-La or earthly Garden of Eden with guiltless sexuality and freedom from work and want, and the physical structure perfectly lends itself to enact such fantasies (imagination at play). One could see the eroticised representations of this cultural heritage site as a form of nostalgia, a kind of mourning for the destruction of an imagined traditional culture (or a sexualised and eroticised one) by colonial and other imperialist forces. Yet this is not just a sentiment; it is a script, performed and enacted on site. Discourses of the past – orientalism, colonialism and imperialism – seem to be fertile ground for nostalgic and romantic tourism dreams (Edensor 1998; Henderson and Weisgrau 2007). The imagery used in cultural tourism is often about fantasies, and about an ambivalent nostalgia for the past – ambivalent because returning to the past is not what people actually desire (Bissell 2005). This ambivalence is captured in Rosaldo's (1993: 69–70) notion of 'imperialist nostalgia', 'a particular kind of nostalgia, often found under imperialism, where people mourn the passing of what they themselves have transformed'.

## Conclusion

Tourism imaginaries are potent propellers of both socio-cultural and environmental stasis and change, and essential elements in the process of identity formation, the making of place, and the perpetual invention of culture (Adams 2004). We need to retain a clear idea about the chief interest groups behind these processes and avoid the mistake of seeing imaginaries as just a range of possibilities. Tourism imaginaries come to occupy a central position in a complex set of connections among very diverse societies, very dissimilar locales, and very different kinds of relations of production and consumption. They resonate most clearly in destinations, the physical and mental landscapes where the imaginaries of local residents, tourism intermediaries, and tourists meet and, occasionally, clash. As they are grounded in relations of power, they can never be politically neutral. Places across the globe have different images attached to them. A series of social practices, ideologies and behaviours derived from tourism imaginaries and their discourses subtly influence how people engage with the 'Other'. I have focused mainly on Western imaginaries of culture(s) in developing countries, but similar analyses can be made for non-Western imaginaries (e.g. Wynn 2007) or for imaginaries about the Western world by both Westerners and others (Carrier 1995).

The failure of both those studying tourism and those working in tourism to understand how imaginaries are embedded within local, national, regional and global institutions of power restricts their ability to determine the underlying forces that restrict some tourism practices and not others, some imaginings and not others, and which make possible new hegemonies in new fields of power. Cultural tourism imaginaries renegotiate political and social realities. The fierce local (and national) power struggle over globally circulating tourism imaginaries seeking to redefine peoples and places reaffirms that the social construction of place is still partly a process of local meaning-making, territorial specificity, juridical control and economic development, however complexly articulated localities become in transnational economic, political and cultural movements. This chapter offers but a critical introduction to a complex topic that is approached best in a multi-, cross-, inter- or, ideally, trans-disciplinary manner. Finally, the subject of tourism imaginaries has so many practical implications that it offers unique opportunities to open up a constructive dialogue between tourism academics and practitioners.

## References

Adams, K.M. (2004) 'The Genesis of Touristic Imagery: Politics and Poetics in the Creation of a Remote Indonesian Island Destination', *Tourist Studies* 4(2): 115–35.

Amirou, R. (1995) *Imaginaire Touristique et Sociabilités du Voyage*, Paris: Presses Universitaires de France.

——(2000) *Imaginaire du Tourisme Culturel*, Paris: Presses Universitaires de France.

Ateljevic, I., Pritchard, A. and Morgan, N. (eds) (2007) *The Critical Turn in Tourism Studies: Innovative Research Methodologies*, Amsterdam: Elsevier.

Bacchilega, C. (2007) *Legendary Hawai'i and the Politics of Place: Tradition, Translation, and Tourism*, Philadelphia: University of Pennsylvania Press.

Bissell, W.C. (2005) 'Engaging Colonial Nostalgia', *Cultural Anthropology* 20(2): 215–48.

Bruner, E.M. (2005) *Culture on Tour: Ethnographies of Travel*, Chicago, IL: University of Chicago Press.

Carrier, J.G. (ed.) (1995) *Occidentalism: Images of the West*, Oxford: Clarendon Press.

Crouch, D., Jackson, R. and Thompson, F. (eds) (2005) *The Media and the Tourist Imagination: Converging Cultures*, London: Routledge.

Edensor, T. (1998) *Tourists at the Taj: Performance and Meaning at a Symbolic Site*, London: Routledge.

Gold, J.R. and Gold, M.M. (1995) *Imagining Scotland: Tradition, Representation, and Promotion in Scottish Tourism Since 1750*, Aldershot: Scolar Press.

Gregory, D. (1994) *Geographical Imaginations*, Oxford: Blackwell.

Hall, C.M. and Tucker, H. (eds) (2004) *Tourism and Postcolonialism: Contested Discourses, Identities and Representations*, London: Routledge.

Henderson, C.E. and Weisgrau, M.K. (eds) (2007) *Raj Rhapsodies: Tourism, Heritage and the Seduction of History*, Aldershot: Ashgate.

Hennig, C. (2002) 'Tourism: Enacting Modern Myths', in Dann, G.M.S. (ed.) *The Tourist as a Metaphor of the Social World*, Wallingford: CABI, 169–87.

Hollinshead, K. (1998) 'Tourism, Hybridity, and Ambiguity: The Relevance of Bhabha's "Third Space" Cultures', *Journal of Leisure Research* 30(1): 121–56.

Hughes, G. (1992) 'Tourism and the Geographical Imagination', *Leisure Studies* 11: 31–42.

Hutnyk, J. (1996) *The Rumour of Calcutta: Tourism, Charity, and the Poverty of Representation*, London: Zed Books.

Mercille, J. (2005) 'Media Effects on Image: The Case of Tibet', *Annals of Tourism Research* 32(4): 1039–55.

Michel, F. (2001) *En Route Pour l'Asie: Le Rêve Oriental Chez les Colonisateurs, les Aventuriers et les Touristes Occidentaux*, Paris: L'Harmattan.

Morgan, N. and Pritchard, A. (1998) *Tourism Promotion and Power: Creating Images, Creating Identities*, Chichester: John Wiley.

Picard, M. (1996) *Bali: Cultural Tourism and Touristic Culture*, Singapore: Archipelago Press.

Prasso, S. (2005) *The Asian Mystique: Dragon Ladies, Geisha Girls, and Our Fantasies of the Exotic Orient*, New York: Public Affairs.

Robinson, M. and Andersen, H.C. (eds) (2002) *Literature and Tourism*, London: Continuum.

Rosaldo, R. (1993) *Culture and Truth: The Remaking of Social Analysis*, Boston: Beacon.

Said, E.W. (1994) *Orientalism*, New York: Vintage Books.

Selwyn, T. (ed.) (1996) *The Tourist Image: Myths and Myth Making in Tourism*, Chichester: John Wiley.

Sheller, M. (2004) 'Demobilizing and Remobilizing Caribbean Paradise', in Sheller, M. and Urry, J. (eds) *Tourism Mobilities: Places to Play, Places in Play*, London: Routledge, 13–21.

Sturma, M. (2002) *South Sea Maidens: Western Fantasy and Sexual Politics in the South Pacific*, Westport, CT: Greenwood Press.

Urbain, J.-D. (1994) *L'idiot du Voyage: Histoires de Touristes*, Paris: Éditions Payot & Rivages.

van der Duim, R., Jóhannesson, G.T. and Ren, C. (eds) (2012) *Actor Network Theory and Tourism: Ontologies, Methodologies and Performances*, London: Routledge.

Wynn, L.L. (2007) *Pyramids and Nightclubs: A Travel Ethnography of Arab and Western Imaginations of Egypt*, Austin: University of Texas Press.

## Further reading

Anderson, B.R. (1991) *Imagined Communities: Reflections on the Origin and Spread of Nationalism*, New York: Verso. (A classic work on the role of the imagination in identity construction.)

Brann, E.T.H. (1991) *The World of the Imagination: Sum and Substance*, Lanham, MD: Rowman & Littlefield. (A magnum opus discussing theories of the imaginary across the humanities.)

Castoriadis, C. (1987) *The Imaginary Institution of Society*, Cambridge, MA: MIT Press. (A thought-provoking analysis of how imaginaries structure societies.)

Crapanzano, V. (2004) *Imaginative Horizons: An Essay in Literary-philosophical Anthropology*, Chicago, IL: University of Chicago Press. (An in-depth exploration of the roles that creativity and imagination play in our experience of the world.)

Durand, G. (1999) *The Anthropological Structures of the Imaginary*, Brisbane: Boombana Publications. (An anthropological atlas of the human imagination.)

Salazar, N.B. (2010) *Envisioning Eden: Mobilizing Imaginaries in Tourism and Beyond*, Oxford: Berghahn. (An ethnography of tourism imaginaries with empirical material from Indonesia and Tanzania.)

Skinner, J. and Theodossopoulos, D. (eds) (2011) *Great Expectations: Imagination and Anticipation in Tourism*, Oxford: Berghahn. (An edited volume exploring the expectations that fuel tourism.)

Strauss, C. (2006) 'The Imaginary', *Anthropological Theory* 6(3): 322–44. (A review of anthropological takes on the imaginary.)

Taylor, C. (2004) *Modern Social Imaginaries*, Durham, NC: Duke University Press. (A philosophical treatise on the concept of Western imaginaries.)

# 5

# Reflections on globalisation and cultural tourism

*Yvette Reisinger*

## Introduction

National cultures and cultural identities are the foundations of cultural tourism. We can diminish the threats to national cultures and cultural tourism by abandoning the pursuit of a common understanding of globalisation and become genuinely committed to the value of globalisation. Globalisation conventionally understood as an homogenous process is not possible. A conceptualisation of globalisation based on a theory of cultural diversity and uniqueness is desirable because it does not homogenise cultural differences but respects national cultures, cultural differences and identities and thus encourages cultural tourism.

## Globalisation and cultural homogenisation

As a result of cultural homogenisation, the world is moving from being a 'space of places' (unique settings with rich and well-defined culture, history and longstanding traditions), to being 'spaces of flows' (which represent discontinuity, ephemerality, fluidity and lack of stability) (Castells 1996). Global tourism is a good example of this trend (Ritzer 2004). Global tourism can represent the 'globalization of nothing'; it involves the global production of non-places (Disneyland), non-things (mass-manufactured souvenirs) and non-people (clerks at souvenir shops) (Ritzer 2004: 105). Global tourism can be about the production of 'nothing ... and ... devoid of distinctive content' (Ritzer 2004: 3). Flows of people, information, signs and symbols that characterise global tourism delocalise culture, making it difficult to develop meaningful human interactions, or individual and communal identities. Globalised, standardised tourism is characterised by the replacement of real authenticity with a 'staged' authenticity in which local cultures and traditions become manufactured or simulated for tourist consumption (MacCannell 1973, 1992; Cohen 1988). The commodification of local traditions, and a sanitisation of culture that is delocalised from the actual social, political and cultural contexts makes local tourism disappear and is the direct result of cultural homogenisation (for overviews, see Sorkin 1992; Kearns and Philo 1993).

In summary, globalisation defined as a homogenous process threatens the existence of national cultures and local cultural patterns. Global tourism delocalises national cultures and local cultural tourism disappears. Too great a focus is placed on the Western hemisphere and Western/American culture as shaping the rest of the world. The global world is not a culturally homogenised totalitarian world; it is represented by different cultural powers.

## Alternative concepts of globalisation

### Globalisation as acknowledgement of cultural differences

Harvey (1989, 1993) and Lash and Urry (1994) suggest that the more global interrelations become, the more the world's population increasingly clings to place and neighbourhood, to region and ethnicity, to tradition and heritage. Eade (1997) and Scott (2000) note that globalisation does not produce cultural homogeneity and destroy local differences; rather it generates the conditions that allow for local cultural traditions to be preserved and cultural innovations to thrive (see also Cox 1997; Hudson 2001). In the face of globalisation people and organisations use their own 'localness' to maintain and produce unique products, establish locally specific social ties and networks, and build and enhance place distinctiveness by using different symbols and motifs. Becoming global is not about being similar or the same because the context of globalisation is different in different places (e.g. local history, forms and types of community associations, intensity and extensiveness of local networks). The way people make contacts, convey and exchange information and ideals, understand signs and cultural meanings, and symbols embedded in discourses all reinforce place differences, local character, and local uniqueness (Gotham 2005). Tourism destinations also need differentiation. Global forces do not eliminate local cultural standards; rather they force places to produce local cultural elements and promote their distinctiveness. Global forces create conditions for local traditions to survive.

### Globalisation as cultural domestication

The development of local cultural tourism (e.g. local food and wine festivals, arts and crafts festivals or music festivals) represents an important trend of domestication of global tourism and shaping it according to local needs. Since people travel across the globe and become increasingly interconnected and interdependent in order to avoid homogenisation of their touristic experiences they seek local standards; global standards have to be abandoned to cater to tourists' needs. 'Glocalisation', or domestication of global mass tourism and developing local cultural tourism is one of the important means of local culture conservation and preservation and the solution to the deterioration of local culture. Local products are recognised and traditional values enhanced, provided that local communities maintain control over their own products.

### Globalisation as cultural innovation

Eriksen's (2003) and Hannerz's (1992, 1996) work on 'creolisation' suggests that recontextualisation or mixing of different cultural identities and symbols and traditions creates cultural innovations. The persistence of old cultural traditions and the creation of new traditions are not products of global homogenisation or heterogenisation; rather they are part hybrid and reflect local efforts to resist, absorb and change the global processes of commodification and standardisation to produce new and locally distinctive traditions. Cultural tourism is known for production of new products, such as music and dance carnivals, fashion shows, or modern glass expositions, and unique cultural creations in the form of furniture or architectural designs. For example, there are numerous music festivals around the globe ranging from world to local traditional or folk music played by indigenous musicians from various regions of the globe. Ethnic-specific music, through globalisation is expanding its scope; it now often includes world fusion, or ethnic fusion music.

## Are foreign culture elements tools of global domination and a threat to cultural tourism?

Global cultural elements do not necessarily represent tools of domination; instead they depend on interpretation, translation and adjustment according to local rules. By incorporating foreign products and adapting foreign standards in local places consumers create their 'own' globalisation, adjusted to local conditions, purposes and frameworks of meaning. For example, culinary tourism is popular around the world. However, while spicy dishes are popular in Asia, they had to be modified to suit non-Asian tastes. McDonald's offers salads and soups in France, vegetarian hamburgers in India, shrimp and chicken burgers in Japan, and sausages and beer in Germany to accommodate the cultural tastes of locals. Although standardised fast-food proved to be successful in China, where consumers praise short waiting times and fast service, it is criticised in France, where consumers tend to like slow food and fine dining.

Cultural tourism products such as theme parks, special events or cultural festivals also have different purposes, usages and appeals to consumers from different corners of the world. The best example is the theme parks industry. The American Disneyworld theme park was extremely successful in the USA; however, it was not popular in France, where tourists have different entertainment needs and seek different quality.

In summary, the threats of globalisation to national cultures and cultural tourism can be diminished by conceiving globalisation as acknowledgement of cultural differences, cultural domestication, or cultural innovation. Such conceptualised globalisation respects national cultures and cultural identities which are the foundations of the cultural tourism industry. Global tourism is not able to dominate local cultural tourism. Global influences need adjustment to local conditions.

## Implications for cultural tourism

Tourism, on the one hand, is a global industry dominated by global hotel chains, entertainment corporations, casinos and professional sports franchises (Gottdiener 1997, 2000; Hannigan 1998; Hollands and Chatterton 2003) and, on the other hand, it is a localised business 'with place as its raw material' (Molotch 2002: 677). The unique culture of a place is what differentiates and attracts people to it. Locals and the tourism industry resist the global homogenisation process. Local tourism organisations, local arts and cultural facilities, museums and historic preservation groups produce unique local tourist sites and construct place images to attract consumers and investment (Eade 1997; Judd 2003; Sheller and Urry 2004). Place character and its uniqueness is produced via local events and traditions or through interaction and active participation of people within indigenous organisations (Alsayyad 2001). Every place recontextualises whatever it borrows and reworks global influences to create a new work, thus encouraging diversity and variety. In an era of major socioeconomic restructuring, cultural places try hard to differentiate themselves, playing up their cultural distinctiveness and advertising themselves as places to visit (for overviews, see Boissevain 1996; Judd and Fainstein 1999; Meethan 2001; Coleman and Crang 2002; see also Nevarez 2002).

Cultural tourism represents a very unique set of local cultural activities that help frame the unique 'habitus' of local social life through which people perceive, understand and evaluate places (Bourdieu 1977: 78–87). Distinct local cultures and traditions give destinations significance; diverse groups engage in various activities to develop different images of places, use different symbols to enhance local culture and oppose global attempts to commodify local traditions (Molotch *et al.* 2000). The challenge for local tourism institutions and businesses is to develop tourism based on unique local culture to attract tourists and investment while maintaining local character and tradition. It is important to reconfigure global tourism and accompanying trends of standardisation and commodification and focus on local strengths – organisations and people. To resist global influences destinations must incorporate global tourism images into local culture and actively produce new symbols and meanings that emphasise the individuality of the place.

While cultural tourism is affected by a globalised process of commodification and homogenisation their effects and meanings are created and expressed at the local level of the industry. Consequently, despite the fact that international tourism is developed at the macro-level by globalised institutions, cultural tourism is developed at the micro-level by local organisations and people's day-to-day activities. Gotham (2005) distinguished between 'tourism from above' (that is effects of the global economic, technological, media and legal forces on travel) and 'tourism from below' (the ways in which locals resist the homogenising effects of tourism and preserve old traditions and promote the 'invention of tradition') (Hobsbawm 1983: 1). Cultural tourism is the 'tourism from below' because it promotes and maintains local differences, traditions and cultures. Even as global transformation changes traditional cultural forms and forces the place to create new forms of identity these forms will always reflect local self-expression and promote local cultural exclusivity, individuality and uniqueness.

Saying this, developing homogenised global tourism is elusive. The aim of international tourism is to give people the opportunity to learn about differences and value them. Cultural tourism acknowledges and promotes the existence of cultural differences, and it gives an opportunity to appreciate them. By appreciating cultural differences one becomes more 'authentic' as an individual human being. Cultural tourism solves the 'problem' of global tourism as a homogenising force and may also be the solution to cultural polarisation. Cultural tourism is the form of tourism which communities should learn about and which should be promoted to tourists.

## Box 5.1 Case study: globalisation of the didgeridoo

The didgeridoo is an ancient instrument of the Australian Aboriginal people. It is the world's oldest woodwind instrument, traditionally used in the Northern Territory, Western Australia and Queensland. It is an icon of the native Australian culture. The instrument is sold in all the major population centres and tourism destinations in Australia. One can see and buy didgeridoos at airport souvenir shops, city retailers, Aboriginal art galleries and weekend market stalls, ranging from short ones, long ones, plain wood or painted, bamboo, hardwood to plastic. Its short history shows how the didgeridoo progressed from ancient Aboriginal traditions to become a powerful element of contemporary global culture.

Traditionally, the didgeridoo was an integral part of life of Aboriginal groups; it accompanied singers and dancers in cultural ceremonies. It represented the cultural identity of Australian Aboriginal people, which encouraged the maintenance of traditional artistic values. Today, the didgeridoo is played for recreational purposes in both indigenous and non-indigenous Australian communities. Its music inspires thousands of modern domestic and international artists. In the late

1970s and early 1980s didgeridoo music began appearing in a non-traditional context in various Australian bands, including genre-setting groups such as Yothu Yindi. By the late 1980s and continuing through the 1990s, the didgeridoo spread to Europe and the Americas with sufficient popularity to support several bands featuring didgeridoo sounds blended with European instruments, such as piano, guitar, flute, violin and clarinet. The didgeridoo sounds blended with Western music were presented in jazz and rock concerts and folk festivals. A huge variety of CDs available on the market provides good examples of how the didgeridoo is used in contemporary compositions by Aboriginal and non-Aboriginal players, traditional didgeridoo music and songs, and 'one-track wonders'. The recent blend of didgeridoo music with electronic sounds and ethnic or 'world music' broke new musical frontiers.

The popularity of the didgeridoo in the global market has increased since the 1990s and reached an all-time high in recent years. The Internet contains a vast amount of information on the instrument's history, properties, playing techniques, festivals and concerts, and sales. The deep resonance of the instrument is cited as an active treatment for imbalance of the female reproductive system, insomnia, asthma, stress and emotional pain. It is claimed that didgeridoo vibrations facilitate meditation. The mystical and metaphysical properties are used as a magical tool or religious icon for spirituality and shamanism. New Age believers suggest that listening to didgeridoo music allows experiencing connection with nature and the world thus developing a feeling of global harmony and achieving personal transformation. Didgeridoo cultural power is also used as a political tool in the fight for Aborigines' human rights.

The didgeridoo has become a part of world culture. This change took place at the local (used by Aboriginal artists), national (symbol of Australian cultural identity), and global levels (to connect with the world). In the continuous search for artistic innovation one only wonders what new developments there will be.

## Conclusion

Globalisation is not the sole force of standardisation and homogenisation. Although this is a process that involves a set of global forces it attempts to focus on different national cultures, local traditions and distinction. This is the process that reaches far beyond the two borders – the West and the rest. It is about various multiple cultures which function together in the increasingly interdependent and interconnected world. As such, globalisation conceived as standardisation and conformity is impossible. Anyone prepared to settle for that notion of globalisation should consider what life would be like if all we did was to do things similarly, sacrifice individuality and surrender to a conformist vision of the world in which we live. This conformity is inauthentic. Each human being is unique because each human being experiences the world from a unique place in that world.

A conceptualisation of globalisation based on a theory of cultural diversity and uniqueness is desirable because it does not homogenise cultural differences but respects national cultures and identities and encourages localness. Globalisation conceived this way offers the possibilities to become open to distinct cultural experiences. It opposes commodification and calls for authenticity of these experiences. Globalisation conceptualised as acknowledgement of cultural differences, appreciation of human cultural wealth and cultural innovation, the scope and effects of which are of global scale, allows the world to value local difference rather than to obliterate it.

By accepting globalisation as a differentiating process the tourism industry can limit global influences on the local culture. Locals receive the power to respond to and resist global influences, recognise local characteristic peculiarities, and long-standing traditions. Despite the globalised nature of modern tourism, the local cultural tourism industry will always be embedded in specific locations, and depend on local social networks and cultural ties.

The cultural tourism industry ought to reflect on the assumption that globalisation is good and see its value in the opportunity to focus on places' cultural uniqueness, thereby noticing not only differences among them but also the industry's unique capacity to value and save these differences. By seeking and encouraging cultural differences, globalisation offers the possibility of opening places more to cultural diversity that allows the industry to realise its potential.

## References

Alsayyad, N. (2001) 'Global Norms and Urban Forms in the Age of Tourism: Manufacturing Heritage, Consuming Tradition', in Alsayyad, N. (ed.) *Consuming Tradition, Manufacturing Heritage: Global Norms and Urban Forms in the Age of Tourism*, London: Routledge, 1–33.

Boissevain, J. (ed.) (1996) *Coping with Tourists: European Reactions to Mass Tourism*, Providence and Oxford: Berghahn Books.

Bourdieu, P. (1977) *Outline of a Theory of Practice*, London: Cambridge University Press.

Castells, M. (1996) *The Rise of the Network Society*, Oxford: Blackwell.

Cohen, E. (1988) 'Authenticity and Commodification in Tourism', *Annals of Tourism Research* 15: 2371–86.

Coleman, S. and Crang, M. (eds) (2002) *Tourism: Between Place and Performance*, Oxford and New York: Berghahn Books.

Cox, K. (ed.) (1997) *Spaces of Globalization: Reasserting the Power of the Local*, New York: Guilford Press.

Eade, J. (ed.) (1997) *Living the Global City: Globalization as a Local Process*, London and New York: Routledge.

Eriksen, T. (2003) 'Creolization and Creativity', *Global Networks* 3(3): 223–37.

Gotham, K.F. (2005) 'Tourism from Above and Below: Globalization, Localization and New Orleans's Mardi Gras', *International Journal of Urban and Regional Research* 29(2): 309–26.

Gottdiener, M. (1997) *Theming of America: Dreams, Visions, and Commercial Spaces*, Boulder, CO: Westview Press.

——(ed.) (2000) *New Forms of Consumption: Consumers, Culture, and Commodification*, New York: Rowman and Littlefield Publishers.

Hannerz, U. (1992) *Cultural Complexity*, New York: Columbia University Press.

——(1996) *Transnational Connections*, London: Routledge.

Hannigan, J. (1998) *Fantasy City: Pleasure and Profit in the Postmodern Metropolis*, New York: Routledge.

Harvey, D. (1989) *The Condition of Postmodernity: An Enquiry into the Origins of Cultural Change*, New York: Blackwell.

——(1993) 'From Space to Place and Back Again: Reflections on the Condition of Postmodernity', in Bird, J., Curtis, B., Putnam, T., Robertson, G. and Tickner, L. (eds) *Mapping the Futures: Local Cultures, Global Change*, London: Routledge, 3–29.

Hobsbawm, E. (1983) 'Introduction: Inventing Traditions', in Hobsbawm, E. and Ranger, T. (eds) *The Invention of Tradition*, Cambridge: Cambridge University Press, 1–14.

Hollands, R. and Chatterton, P. (2003) 'Producing Nightlife in the New Urban Entertainment Economy: Corporatization, Branding and Market Segmentation', *International Journal of Urban and Regional Research* 27(2): 361–85.

Hudson, R. (2001) *Producing Places*, New York: Guilford Press.

Judd, D. and Fainstein, S. (eds) (1999) *The Tourist City*, New Haven and London: Yale University Press.

Judd, D.R. (ed.) (2003) *The Infrastructure of Play: Building the Tourist City*, New York: M.E. Sharp Armonk.

Kearns, G. and Philo, C. (1993) *Selling Places: The City as Cultural Capital, Past and Present*, Oxford: Pergamon Press.

Lash, S. and Urry, J. (1994) *Economies of Signs and Space*, London: Sage Publications.

Liebes, T. and Katz, E. (1990) *The Export of Meaning: Cross-cultural Readings of Dallas*, New York: Oxford University Press.

MacCannell, D. (1973) 'Staged Authenticity: Arrangements of Social Space in Tourist Settings', *American Journal of Sociology* 79: 589–603.

——(1992) *Empty Meeting Grounds*, New York: Routledge.

Meethan, K. (2001) *Tourism in Global Society: Place, Culture, Consumption*, New York: Palgrave.

Molotch, H. (2002) 'Place in Product', *International Journal of Urban and Regional Research* 26(4): 665–88.

Molotch, H., Freudenberg, W. and Paulsen, K.E. (2000) 'History Repeats Itself, but How? City Character, Urban Tradition, and the Accomplishment of Place', *American Sociological Review* 65(6): 791–823.

Nevarez, L. (2002) *New Money, Nice Town: How Capital Works in the New Urban Economy*, New York and London: Routledge.

Ritzer, G. (2004) *The Globalization of Nothing*, Thousand Oaks, CA: Pine Forge Press.

Scott, A.J. (2000) *The Cultural Economy of Cities: Essays on the Geography of Image Producing Industries*, London: Sage Publications.

Sheller, M. and Urry, J. (eds) (2004) *Tourism Mobilities: Places to Play, Places in Play*, New York: Routledge.

Sorkin, M. (ed.) (1992) *Variations on a Theme Park: The New American City and the End of Public Space*, New York: Hill and Wang.

# 6

# Philosophy and the nature of the authentic

*Sean Beer*

In this reflection I examine the nature of philosophy with particular respect to the concept of authenticity and attempt to develop an analytical framework for the study of authenticity. There is an initial problem with such an undertaking and that is the definition of authenticity. In simple terms we can consider the authentic to be something that conforms to fact, something that can be trusted, believed and relied upon, that is genuine. This argument can, however, prove to be circular. After all, what is a fact? How do we define or construct 'facts'? This analysis looks initially at the development of analytical philosophy with a focus on ideas relating to existence. I conclude that the actual nature of facts/existence is a component of, but does not explain, authenticity. This leads on to a discussion of the nature of more embedded perspectives, a characteristic of what is sometimes called the Continental School of philosophy. This involves an overview of concepts such as existentialism, modernism, structuralism, post-structuralism and post-modernism. I then draw a range of conclusions and propose a way forward.

## The Analytical School of philosophy

What is a fact would seem to be a fairly straightforward question. One way of analysing philosophy as a subject is to consider that it has two perspectives: the scientific and the moral; the concrete and the abstract; quantitative and qualitative; objective and subjective. Bernstein (1983) would add rational and irrational, and realism and antirealism. In his book *The Problems of Philosophy* Russell (1912) spends the opening chapters examining some of these specific questions of fact. For example, Berkeley would have argued that reality consisted of nothing but minds and ideas; there is no such thing as matter and fundamentally everything exists in the mind of God. This perspective is known as idealism. Descartes doubted all things that could not be proved. Ultimately he was left with the conclusion that the only thing that could be proved was the existence of his own mind, hence the expression, *Je pense donc je suis*; *cogito ergo sum*; I think therefore I am.

The discussion of facts and existence can soon become bogged down in the multitude of philosophical perspectives. I have already alluded to idealism. In addition to Berkeley it is also possible to include thinkers such as Plato, Kant, Schelling and Hegel. There is rationalism, where knowledge is based on reason (Descartes, Spinoza, Leibniz, Kant – Kant can be considered as idealist and at times rationalist), rather than empiricism (William of Ockham, Bacon, Locke, Hume and Rousseau), where it is based on experience. The empiricists can be regarded as the predecessors of the positivists, who favour a scientific perspective and considered religion and metaphysics as pre-scientific and something that must give way to the new scientific ideas of a maturing civilisation. Positivists include Comte, Spencer, Haeckel, Mach, Quine and Popper.

Cole (2007) provides a useful observation from the tourism perspective in that she considers that authenticity is a Western cultural notion, with no objective quality, which is socially constructed and therefore negotiable, and that this negotiation often leads into a complex process of potentially positive and negative exploitation. However, the picture is still not coherent, as at the same time she maintains that within the literature there is a notion that there is a primitive other pre-modern world which is considered authentic, either because it is objectively so (cool, after the scientific philosophy of Karl Popper (1934), for example) or because this is socially constructed in some way (hot, after the sociology of Durkheim (1893), for example) (Selwyn 1996). If the former, this would seem to be an objective quality and therefore self-contradictory. There is also a modern world that is inauthentic, and it is the tension between these two worlds that provides the space for the discussion of authenticity. Even when a researcher does discuss this negotiation process, as if from some sort of blank sheet, as in Wang (2007), there seems to be a fall back, such that the tourist does get something that is authentic, but actually it is not, as the authentic thing was not something that they wanted or that the hosts thought they would want.

Wang (2007) and others trace the initial genesis of the discussion of authenticity to MacCannell (1973), which seems to establish a basis for an objective truth upon which authenticity is based, where authenticity is a self-explaining concept that is fully genuine and trustworthy, and a tourist experience of authenticity that is in some way staged. Thus the tourist experiences a performance of authenticity that is put on by the host. This links to Smith's (1977) discussions of the relationship between the self (the tourist) and the other (the host), and was developed further by Cohen (1989) in looking at the way that authenticity might emerge as a result of this interaction, or might actually become negotiated and agreed (Bruner 1994; Hughes 1995). Such arguments might be considered to be constructivist in nature, where individuals co-construct their lives and understandings of life. Still there is an idea of objective authenticity upon which all this is based.

## The Continental School: spectator and embedded perspectives

The so-called Continental School of philosophy approaches ideas from more embedded perspectives. These perspectives may well be considered to be less quantifiable, more qualitative. In terms of authenticity we might consider the approach to be about the relationship that the individual has with the thing being considered; the experience of the thing. This school of thought initially developed as a result of the work of individuals such as Kierkegaard, Nietzsche, Husserl, Heidegger, Gadamer and Sartre.

For many people Kierkegaard is considered to be the first existential philosopher. He identified that human existence was part history, nature and society, and part inner and reflective. In his first major work, *Either/Or*, he sets out two ways of living: the aesthetic and the ethical (Stangroom and Garvey 2005). These were radical ideas that were not appreciated at the time but which formed the basis for existential and phenomenological thought. Nietzsche developed this, principally in terms of existentialism, and the freeing up of the individual. Nietzsche challenged the authority of society, the church and any absolute. For him these structures were redundant, but he did not look forward to abandonment or 'nihilism'; he looked forward to freedom (Nietzsche 1882). Husserl (1900) developed the epistemological base of the phenomenological tradition. His philosophy was founded on the idea that life is based on an individual's experience of things. A second important distinction was that the actual objectivist existence of an object was in many ways irrelevant, or at least of secondary consideration; what mattered were the perceptions of the individual that was engaging with the object.

Heidegger further added to these ideas. The main thrust of Heidegger's thinking centres on the idea of Dasein, which he laid out in *Being and Time* (Heidegger 1962). The focus here is on ontology. Dasein is primarily a theory of existence. It concerns human existence in the world and how individuals relate to it; how they connect to physical reality. The concept of Dasein is based on individuals who are dependent on a past that they can recognise, but over which they now have no control, and a future that is open and undetermined. The final component of what individuals are is the ability to ignore both the past and the future. In other words, individuals live now, at this very moment, at this very time. Thus relationships and experiences of the world are based upon what individuals are experiencing now. In terms of the authenticity of a thing, individuals are able to define their own authenticity, though there is a context within which that decision is made. Heidegger did recognise the importance of the individual's relationship with society and also had his own conception of authenticity. This is based on an individual understanding of their position in the world and taking personal responsibility for it, whilst being engaged with the world.

Gadamer continued to develop ideas that stressed the relationship between the individual and society. In his book *Truth and Method*, Gadamer (1989) argued that there was a need to consider what people do within the context of their history and culture. In effect, Gadamer said that individuals have an 'historically affected consciousness' in that the history and culture of the environment within which individuals exist affects them. This would seem to be fundamental to any understanding of a concept such as authenticity. From the moment an individual is born he or she interacts with society, via the family and also directly. There could be an argument that this interaction actually begins before birth as a result of interaction with the mother or even as a result of some form of genetic memory. Originally the ideas of some form of genetic memory were put forward by Lamarck in the eighteenth century. Jung postulated forms of cultural memory, racial memory, collective unconscious and objective psyche (Jung 1964). More recently there has been a series of discussions surrounding the idea of memetics, or genetic memory, by commentators such as Blackmore (1999).

Sartre is one of existentialism's most potent symbols. He is responsible for laying out its principle tenants. In *Being and Nothingness* (1943) Sartre analyses the nature of consciousness. Sartre divided being into two areas: being for itself or consciousness, and being in itself which is everything else and which he considered was empty or nothingness. In other words we exist, but nothing defines what we are; there is no human essence and we are free to write our own story on this clean sheet of paper. This is existential freedom, but with it comes responsibility. This total freedom can cause *anguish*: on what can the individual rely? Because of this the individual may seek to deny their own freedom and to live a life that is not, in Sartre's terms, authentic or true to the principles of freedom. Instead this would be a life lived in *bad faith*, as would any attempt to transfer responsibility to others. Life is not value free, but individuals are *abandoned* and have to construct their own values. There is only the personal subjective moral sphere; no objective sphere exists. At the same time there is no hope that we can rely on to help us out, which leads to a situation of human despair – indeed, Sartre maintained that 'man is condemned to be free' (Sartre 1943: 631).

Within the tourism literature the existential debate was developed by Wang (1999), who discusses the concept of existential authenticity, where authenticity in terms of experience and actuality is defined from within the individual (see also Brown 1994; Hughes 1995; Crang 1996; McIntosh and Prentice 1999; Wang 1999; Taylor 2001). As such this in part reflects the existential philosophy of writers such as Sartre (1943, 1946) and the existential concept of the authentic life. Reisinger and Steiner (2006), Steiner and Reisinger (2006) and before them Pearce (2005) have indicated that the philosophy of Heidegger might provide a framework for the analysis of authenticity. It was Heidegger's concept of Dasein as outlined in *Being and Time* (1962) that helped foster the existentialist movement and the work of individuals such as Sartre. Consideration of Heidegger in isolation, however, without putting his work into the context of those who came before and after him would seem to me to be somewhat incomplete and unsatisfactory.

## Structuralists, post-structuralists, modernists and post-modernists

Sociologists developed comparative ideas that came under the heading of structuralism, an approach that regards social structure as having priority over social psychology. This was influenced in the mid-to-late twentieth century by Levi-Strauss (structural anthropology), Foucault (history of ideas), Lacan (psychoanalysis), Althusser (structural Marxism), and Saussure (structural linguistics). It is not clear whether post-structuralism is a continuation of or counter-reaction to structuralism. Structuralism is seen as shackled by pseudo-scientific methodology, bereft of more free-thinking and playful analysis. There may be other areas of overlap with the ideas of post-modernism. There are specific problems of definition as post-modernism is a broad and shape-shifting term and those who might be considered to be of the school take great pleasure in rejecting the label and all labels. Some have labelled post-modernist approaches as negative and nihilistic, whereas in many ways they can be seen as a more playful embrace of life's complexity and an acknowledgement of that complexity. Key figures in the movement include many post-structuralists, and in the context of authenticity people like Derrida, Foucault and Baudrillard are of interest.

Derrida had specific things to say on language (Derrida 1997). He argued that it might be considered that speech is a central, natural presence and is superior to writing that is peripheral, unnatural and is characterised by absence. He maintains a binary opposition between speech and writing. He developed the idea of logocentricity in that it might be considered that truth is speech; speech is the cause and origin of truth. Possibly he did not go far enough, for surely experience is also a truth and it should not be a binary opposition but a ternary tension between experience, speech and writing? Derrida extended these ideas, often in a playful way to look at the tensions between opposites and the way that our understandings are not necessarily constrained, but fluid. Foucault and Baudrillard took these ideas further – some would consider to extremes. A Foucaultian perspective might resist all forms of definition; what it is, it is. Baudrillard's (1994) concepts of Simulacra and the hyperreal unpick ideas of fact and truth to a point where everything is constructed fantasy. In terms of the tourism literature Wang (2007) considers that the constructivist arguments are expanded upon by a series of post-structuralist interpretations of authenticity by authors such as Boynton (1986) and Millinger (1994). These are characterised by pessimism with regard to any notion of authenticity and a focus on the experience of the toured object. The state of pessimism with regard to the idea of authenticity is developed further by Reisinger and Steiner (2006).

## Conclusions

What, therefore, can we conclude? The situation is complex. At one end of a continuum it might be considered that object reality is a given. Things exist. Authenticity can be defined.

However, if we follow other arguments we might conclude that object reality cannot be defined. We cannot say that anything exists; all we have is the evidence of our own senses. Applying an existential perspective to this idea of authenticity would seem to be reasonable, but where do we draw the lines with unlimited variation and relativism? With the fantasy world of Baudrillard? There is a point of balance, or praxis as Bernstein (1983) would call it. This can be achieved by recognising that human beings do have concepts of authenticity and the important thing is to see how they arrive at these definitions without being judgemental in terms of what is authentic or not.

In terms of our understanding of cultural tourism surely the question of authenticity is at its centre. Human beings are social and cultural animals. Some would argue that our existence is such that there is no division between us as individuals and the social and cultural world that we inhabit. When we travel as tourists with culture in mind (and even without it in mind) we bring with us our own cultural background and an expectation of the culture of the other: the people and places that we are visiting. Those whom we visit do the same from the perspective of the host. If we are looking for one type of 'pure' authentic experience, to experience the culture of a group of people as they experience it, then as tourists we are unlikely ever to succeed. Our mere presence as observers will change the dynamics of what we experience to one degree or another. If we accept that this is the case then there are many other types of authentic experience that we can have, depending on how we and our hosts view the world. The way in which this is constructed and the resultant satisfaction for the guest and host is surely the basis for our understanding of the dynamics of cultural tourism. Some might argue that all experience is authentic for it is what it is. Others might say that there is a greater truth to living authentically and therefore engaging in authentic experiences, and that rests with the individual's choice to live a life that is true to themselves, and to embrace the consequences whilst still recognising their care for the other.

## References

Baudrillard, J. (1994) *Simulacra and Simulation (The Body in Theory: Histories of Cultural Materialism)*, Ann Arbor: University of Michigan Press.

Bernstein, R.J. (1983) *Beyond Objectivism and Relativism: Science, Hermeneutics, and Praxis*, Philadelphia: University of Pennsylvania Press.

Blackmore, S. (1999) *The Meme Machine*, Oxford: Oxford University Press.

Boynton, L. (1986) 'The Effect of Tourism on Amish Quilt Designs', *Annals of Tourism Research* 13: 451–65.

Brown, D. (1994) 'Genuine Fakes', in Selwyn, T. (ed.) *The Tourist Image: Myths and Myth Making in Tourism*, Chichester: Wiley, 33–47.

Bruner, E. (1994) 'Abraham Lincoln as Authentic Reproduction: A Critique of Postmodernism', *American Anthropologist* 96: 397–415.

Cohen, E. (1989) 'Primitive and Remote: Hill Tribe Trekking in Thailand', *Annals of Tourism Research* 16 (1): 30–61.

Cole, S. (2007) 'Beyond Authenticity and Commodification', *Annals of Tourism Research* 34(4): 943–60.

Crang, M. (1996) 'Magic Kingdom or Quixotic Quest for Authenticity', *Annals of Tourism Research* 23: 415–31.

Derrida, J. (1997) *Of Grammatology*, trans. Spivak, G.C., Baltimore, MD: Johns Hopkins University Press.

Durkheim, E. (1893 [1984]) *The Division of Labour in Society*, Basingstoke: Palgrave Macmillan.

Gadamer, H.G. (1989) *Truth and Method*, London: Continuum.

Heidegger, M. (1962) *Being and Time*, Oxford: Blackwell.

Hughes, G. (1995) 'Authenticity in Tourism', *Annals of Tourism Research* 22(4): 781–803.

Husserl, E. (1900 [1976]) *Logical Investigations*, trans. Findlay, J.N., London: Routledge.

Jung, C.G. (1964) *The Development of Personality (Collected Works of C.G. Jung, Vol. 17)*, Princeton, NJ: Bollingen.

MacCannell, D. (1973) 'Staged Authenticity: Arrangements of Social Space in Tourist Settings', *American Journal of Sociology* 79(3): 589–603.

McIntosh, A. and Prentice, R. (1999) 'Affirming Authenticity: Consuming Cultural Heritage', *Annals of Tourism Research* 26: 589–612.

Millinger, W. (1994) 'Towards a Critical Analysis of Tourism Representations', *Annals of Tourism Research* 21: 756–79.

Nietzsche, F. (1882 [1984]) *The Gay Science: With a Prelude in Rhymes and an Appendix of Songs*, New York: Vintage Books.

Pearce, P.L. (2005) *Tourist Behaviour: Themes and Conceptual Schemes*, Clevedon: Channel View.

Popper, K. (1934 [2002]) *The Logic of Scientific Discovery*, London: Routledge.

Reisinger, Y. and Steiner, C.J. (2006) 'Reconceptualizing Object Authenticity', *Annals of Tourism Research* 33(1): 65–86.

Russell, B. (1912) *The Problems of Philosophy*, Oxford: Oxford University Press.

Sartre, J.P. (1943) *Being and Nothingness*, trans. Barnes, H., London: Routledge.

——(1946) *Existentialism and Humanism*, trans. Mairet, P., Eyre: Methuen.

Selwyn, T. (1996) 'Introduction', in Selwyn, T. (ed.) *The Tourist Image: Myths and Myth Making in Tourism*, Chichester: Wiley, 1–32.

Smith, V. (ed.) (1977) *Hosts and Guests: The Anthropology of Tourism*, Oxford: Blackwell.

Stangroom, J. and Garvey, J. (2005) *The Great Philosophers*, London: Arcturus.

Steiner, C.J. and Reisinger, Y. (2006) 'Understanding Existential Authenticity', *Annals of Tourism Research* 33(2): 299–318.

Taylor, J.P. (2001) 'Authenticity and Sincerity in Tourism', *Annals of Tourism Research* 28(1): 7–26.

Wang, N. (1999) 'Rethinking Authenticity in Tourism Experience', *Annals of Tourism Research* 26(2): 349–70.

Wang, Y. (2007) 'Customised Authenticity Begins at Home', *Annals of Tourism Research* 34(3): 789–804.

## Further reading

Bernstein, R.J. (1983) *Beyond Objectivism and Relativism: Science, Hermeneutics, and Praxis*, Philadelphia: University of Pennsylvania Press. (An interesting of debates about objectivism versus relativism occurring in philosophy of science, literary theory, the social sciences, political science, and elsewhere.)

Russell, B. (1912) *The Problems of Philosophy*, Oxford: Oxford University Press. (An approachable introduction to the theory of philosophical enquiry.)

# 7

# The multilogical imagination

## Tourism studies and the imperative for postdisciplinary knowing

*Keith Hollinshead and Milka Ivanova*

### Introduction: the call for outlooks beyond disciplinarity

In recent decades, an increasing number of social scientists have simply expressed the view that a large range of major social, cultural, economic, political and other problematics – such as poverty reduction, migration/immigration, environmental care, ecological stewardship, neo-colonialism/ neo-imperialism and terrorism – are not really, or easily, understood and dealt with via the outlook of any single discipline (Becher 1989). At the same time, universities are condemned en masse for almost always and inevitably being uni-disciplinary institutions that promote education and understanding of singular academic domains rather than being pluri-disciplinary institutes that decidedly promote education and understanding via the cultivation of different and differing multiple mixes of disciplinary approaches and collaborative structures of learning and knowing across academic domains (Moran 2002: 74). Over three decades, various protagonists have stepped forward to demand (variously) new organised styles of interdisciplinary, multi-disciplinary, transdisciplinary and crossdisciplinary inquiry and education (Repko 2008), and even of pluridisciplinary styles where that beyond-the-discipline co-operation is not so much organised and scaffolded to deal with an emergent problem or issue, but it is associational, occurring almost *naturally* because of the felt compatibility in approach (of say physics, chemistry and geology, or of history, sociology and language – see Max-Neef 2005). According to most of these beyond-the-discipline advocates, the organisation (or rather, the pre-organisation!) of the academy into faculties (within universities) and into strong publication fields (built around prestigious disciplinary journals) holds back the expansion of knowledge into new territories of understanding. While hard scientists increasingly specialise within their own domains and have increasing difficulty communicating to others outside of them, soft scientists increasingly reveal exactly the same sectorial narrowness of vision. Understanding has become over-rationalised within discrete blocks of logic, and specialist scientists of many sorts find it most difficult to build feeling or imagination, for instance, into their ordinary approaches, or otherwise build intuition and 'contemplative looking' (*Anschauung*) into their study regimes (Naydler 2000).

In Nicolescu's (2000) view, both the hard and the soft sciences could benefit from the conduct of much more iterative work, whereby researchers from home disciplines learn how frequently/ regularly to venture into and across other disciplines/fields in order to examine the issues or problems at hand from a litany of perspectives, with the hope of generating new but coherent simplicities of and about the world. Put another way, such simplicities (i.e. such *simplexity*) encourages the researcher to probe for understandings about 'the excluded middle', or about that conceptual territory that is lost between the play of adamantine disciplines and their fixed perspectivities. This call to explore the excluded middle and to probe for 'simplexity' constitutes a demand for much more dialogic awareness, and for *broader sorts of open understanding* at the expense of closed *sorts of entrenched knowing*. What is required, where many, complex and multidimensional issues are keenly investigated, according to Max-Neef – a staunch advocate of transdisciplinary insight – is not so much the development of a super-disciplinary approach, but rather the cultivation of a new and varied spectrum of ways of seeing the world, or rather the generation of the very capacity *to envision the world differently* via the possibilities of more systematic and holistic angles of seeing:

> The knowing has grown exponentially [over recent decades], but only now we begin to suspect that that may not be sufficient; not for quantitative research, but for qualitative research. Knowledge is only one of the roads, only one side of that coin. The other road, the other side of the coin is that of *understanding*.
>
> *(Max-Neef 2005: 15, emphasis added)*

To him, we will constantly fail to take proper and adequate outlooks of inspection on the great problematics of our age (viz. the aforesaid subjects of poverty reduction, migration/immigration, environmental care, etc.) if our starting assumptions and our operating vantage points remain partial, fragmented and limited. Both hard and soft scientists must work with regular alacrity and reflexive decidedness on the effort to generate new options and opportunities for plural vision, and (for him) the endeavour to cultivate new *transdisciplinary* programmes of understanding is still, sadly, a most adolescent exercise.

## Background: the call for beyond-the-field outlooks in tourism studies

Since the turn of the century, a rising coterie of commentators in tourism studies have joined their hard science and soft science colleagues elsewhere by calling for supradisciplinary or extradisciplinary approaches to understanding, and they have tended to reason that much more flexible sorts of knowledge production and conceptual synergy are required because of the width of cultural, social, political, economic and psychic issues that international tourism projects commonly rub up against (Franklin and Crang 2001: 5). To date, perhaps the critique of Coles, Hall and Duval (2006) in *Current Issues in Tourism* is the most informed and penetrative of these within-field statements. In their assault against the commonplace fetishisation of disciplinary boundaries, Coles *et al.* do not set themselves up as anti-disciplinarians, for they note that in many areas of tourism (as for each other industry or applied field) there are many areas of activity and many contemporary issues which justifiably demand highly specialist insight. Coles *et al.* do not want to kill off disciplinarity per se, but they do suggest that it is the very artificiality of boundaries around a 'field' or 'discipline' like tourism studies which so often prevents encountered problematics from being considered from a healthy panoramic width of insights, and they pointedly draw on the early 1990s judgement of Graburn and Jafari (1991) that 'no single discipline alone can accommodate, treat, or understand tourism: it can be studied [roundly and effectively] only if *multidisciplinary* perspectives are sought and formed'. While Graburn and Jafari demanded richer 'multidisciplinary' approaches in this fashion, Coles *et al.* (writing a decade and a half later) call for deeper or more sincere 'postdisciplinary' perspectives. Like Graburn and Jafari, they suggest that the character of disciplinary organisation acts as a significant hindrance to meaningful interdisciplinary or multidisciplinary collaboration, but Coles *et al.* put added weight upon the fact that fields or disciplines like tourism studies have simply failed to keep up with changes in society and with the changing face of the world under globalisation.

Drawing from Klein (1996), Coles *et al.* maintain that the most innovative and creative locations for knowledge cultivation lie at the intersections of disciplines, and they suggest that the postdisciplinary approaches are much more acute at generating such hybrid forms of knowledge production than multidisciplinary or interdisciplinary ones. To them, it is the sheer broad array of new forms of tourism that have (in recent years) been developed around other forms of human movement, mobility and identity-formation which necessitate in many contexts the recognition and development of postdisciplinary approaches to understanding: it is the immense scale and scope of the interactivity of tourism with human, cultural and natural 'systems' (Coles *et al.* 2006: 310) which nowadays brings about the need for sensitivity amongst tourism studies scholars to postdisciplinary ways of seeing and acting in the world. It is thus their considered view that tourism is now embedded in the intersections and fluid spaces of many different areas of being and becoming that it has saliences and importances that are not easy to register and monitor via the techniques and theories housed within a single discipline. Put another way, the new potentialities of tourism in people making, in place making, in past making and in present making around the world oblige tourism studies scholars to be sensible about the traditional and transitional cosmologies of not only many different *established populations* around the world, but many different *emergent populations* in their ever-mobile/much-changing, restless locales (after Bhabha 1994).

## Caveat: knowledge production beyond multidisciplinarity and interdisciplinarity – towards transdisciplinarity

Before attention is turned towards a more fulsome explanation of what constitutes post-disciplinarity, ipso facto, perhaps it is opportune to clarify what transdisciplinarity is, so that felt bona fide differences between transdisciplinarity and postdisciplinarity can be reasonably gauged. In this regard, the definitional work of McGregor (n.d.) is rather helpful. In her rumination about what indeed qualifies as due or proper transdisciplinarity, McGregor – an erstwhile interdisciplinarian – deems it to be made of enquiry that crosses through veils to fresh realities where the researcher learns to take on board different isomorphies, patterns and metaphors, and where s/he learns to honour different imaginal structures, zones of resistance and living adaptive systems (McGregor n.d.: 1). To her, transdisciplinarity will serve for many monodisciplinarians, multidisciplinarians and interdisciplinarians almost as 'a close encounter of the third kind', where the researcher learns how to negotiate the multiple realities of intellectual perimeters and of virtual 'creative commons' (McGregor n.d.: 1). In this light, transdisciplinarity is that effort to generate understanding which criss-crosses disciplines, goes between, beyond and outside of disciplines, thereby traversing the possibilities of understanding from many or all disciplines. In McGregor's view, the term (transdisciplinarity) has several contesting but overlapping meanings:

- drawing from Nicolescu (2001), she suggests that, to many, transdisciplinarity is the effort to understand the present world *in all of its complexities*, in lieu of looking at one part of it;
- drawing from Regeer (2002), she suggests that to many others, transdisciplinarity is that effort to involve *both scientific and non-scientific sources* of insight or practice – or that

effort to encourage mutual co-operation amongst different parts of society (including academia) – in order to yield understanding on and what large and specific challenges face society;

- drawing from Nègre (1999), she suggests that to many yet other advocates, transdisciplinarity is that effort to generate new visions of nature and reality and *new interactions between academia and other sectors of society*.

Taking into account these nuanced interpretations of what transdisciplinarity is, McGregor maintains that transdisciplinary research and practice involves the eclipse of the importance of any single discipline and decidedly involves the formation, or formulation, of a new mental or cerebral 'open space' (i.e. *an intellectual outerspace*) where new concepts, metaphors and patterns of understanding can flower. It is there, in the new conceptual territory of that intellectual outerspace that the complexity of things can be refreshingly probed and different/emergent/ multiple perspectives upon it exercised. To her, the use of transdisciplinary approaches are particularly pertinent when researchers seek to pry into or celebrate our various connections with earth (i.e. the Earth) and with each other (i.e. our perceived others). Thereby – particularly when the world's indigenous populations are confronted/engaged/involved – it is a research effort that is highly demanding of acute listening skills (McGregor n.d.: 10).

## Focus: knowledge beyond colonialism and eurocentrism – postdisciplinarity revealed

The case for postdisciplinary enquiry in tourism studies – following the pioneer groundwork of Coles *et al.* – has been advanced by Hollinshead in two short manuscripts on the subject. In the first, an article in *Tourism Analysis*, Hollinshead (2010) makes the case that postdisciplinary enquiry is a field of scholarship that is notably useful in tourism settings and scenarios where (context one) populations are involved or encountered that exist in *difficult/halfway/halflight situations*; where (context two) *dominant modes of power* have been exercised in ways that ought to be questioned because new/different/emergent sorts of cultural, political, symbolic or other intelligence have rendered that presumed (and normally 'external') power irrelevant or inappropriate for that milieu or that encounter; and where (context three) there is some other demonstrable need for *critical scholarship* of some form or other to be brought in to analyse/synthesise/catalyse what has transpired at the locale under inspection.

In a subsequent, second manuscript – a chapter in the Routledge publication *The Critical Turn in Tourism Studies* – Hollinshead (2012) attempts to show how recent advances in the soft science emporium of qualitative research have enlivened the art and craft of interpretive social science to such a degree since the early 1990s that a host of new critical approaches have been adopted which have helped till or fertilise the conceptual ground upon which postdisciplinary thought operates. In that chapter, Hollinshead (2012: 66–69) attempts to distil the work of the miscellany of recent qualitative researchers across the broad social sciences from Denzin and Lincoln (2005), where these investigators were called upon to substantiate how the soft/interpretive sciences have lately 'developed' in accelerating fashion. He then endeavoured to relate those manifest recent trends in the theory and conduct of social justice practices within qualitative inquiry to the very case for postdisciplinary insight.

Having worked to provide a synthesis of some of the recent advances in critical and pedagogic practice that are consonant with, and which help cultivate the mind towards, postdisciplinary approaches, Hollinshead then provides the following definition, of *postdisciplinarity*, ipso facto, where postdisciplinary studies are:

forms of systematic or exhaustive longitudinal (through time) and latitudinal (through place) critique which utilise scholarly and non-scholarly reasoning to map the multiple truths which exist in a found context or setting, and which pay distinct attention to emic/ local/grounded understandings which have significant communal, public, and/or claimed longstanding inheritances or otherwise upon emergent and dynamic projections of being and becoming. Such forms of critique tend to serve as dialectical open-to-the-future inspections which uncover and account for the plurality of important (i.e., well-supported) outlooks which have been overlooked, ignored, or suppressed either historically (or which are being subjugated in the present) by dominant authorities/dominant cognitions.

*(Hollinshead 2012: 64)*

The rest of Hollinshead's (2012) chapter suggests – in the light of the above definition – that postdisciplinary lines of enquiry might be particularly appropriate in tourism management/ tourism studies settings where an enhanced colonialist or neo-colonialist outlook and the world holds sway, where an individual institution or corporation has seemingly acted with some form of imperial authority or neo-imperial agency over a suppressed/silenced/ignored local population or culture/subculture, or where some other strong unidimensional outlook or universalising truth has been exercised to normalise how culture and heritage is projected or naturalise how nature and space is represented.

Clearly, given the continued North Atlantic weight of influence over contemporary culture (until the Age of the Pacific or the Age of Africa completely envelopes us!?), the implication present in the works of much of the essentialisation and subjugation of peoples, places and pasts will still be *eurocentric*. Hence, the impetus of most current postdisciplinary conceptual shifts will be to recalibrate the world or to re-imagine localities and inheritances vis-à-vis some felt local or indigenous cosmology in settings and situations where the European or North American governance of international tourism has been rather slow or reluctant to identify those local/ indigenous/other ways of seeing or has otherwise not currently appeared to respect them.

In her study of the character and parameters of transdisciplinary research and practice, McGregor provides a number of heuristic statements (i.e. rule-of-thumbs guidelines) to help researchers and practitioners embrace the 'existing, deep mind shift' required if and when an interdisciplinary investigation or operation moves into transdisciplinary thought and action. Currently, Hollinshead and Ivanova (n.d.) are in the process of translating these McGregor heuristics – and other like heuristics – to the issues and concerns that social scientists are encountering these days with the new/emergent and open to the future understandings which are appearing under the call for postdisciplinary vision. In this evolving paper, Hollinshead and Ivanova acknowledge that many of the impulses and imperatives of 'postdisciplinarity' may indeed be seen to lie along the same trajectory/trajectories as those of 'transdisciplinarity'. They are nuanced much more strongly, contextually or critically in their force of application, though. Thus, while Hollinshead and Ivanova argue that postdisciplinarity is a veritable cousin articulation of transdisciplinarity, they deem it to be one that is decidedly more pungent and protean in its emergent, gelling, transcultural or corrective imaginative force. One could thus say, in modern parlance, that it (postdisciplinarity) is transdisciplinarity to the power of 10, or otherwise that it is transdisciplinarity with transgressive attitude. If tourism studies is effectively to understand the different worldviews by and through which the world is seen and not seen, it must be a main part of the conceptual arsenal of the academy there, and not just a bit player for certain 'safe' intellectual settings. During the rest of the twenty-first century, postdisciplinary insight must be cultivated and practised by many more tourism studies scholars and practitioners who (if they are to be informed, relevant and useful in the dynamic world about them) must learn how to trespass well beyond the often stultifying barriers of the disciplines into which they might first conceptually have been spawned. Knowing how and when to think as a well-rehearsed disciplinarian is a vital skill, but so is knowing how not to! If any field needs a bodyweight of scholars and practitioners who can openly see as 'other' and openly 'think' as 'other', it is world-crossing tourism studies!

---

## Box 7.1 Case study

The following case study now seeks to draw attention to the fashions in which postdisciplinary lines of inquiry can help those who work in tourism studies to improve their understanding of and about the emergent and dynamic contestations that so commonly crop up in the projection, programming and performance of international tourism today. The case study is provided by means of Exhibit 1 (Table 7.1), which attests to the sort of multilogical imagination that is increasingly demanded of the culturally engaged researcher, manager or administrator today.

*Table 7.1* Exhibit 1 – The protean character of diasporic self-making: 10 major insights on difficult contemporary inscriptions of diasporic identity

| | |
|---|---|
| 1 = Diasporic outlooks on self and society tend to be CORRECTIVE:<br>Diasporic inscriptions of identity frequently seek to call up old and previously longstanding nations of peoplehood from which a given population has been forcefully ruptured. | Δ e.g. In tourism studies, projections of selfhood may frequently involve declarations of identity and longing for host or travelling populations which seek to challenge dominant colonialist or neocolonialist views as to who they are. |
| 2 = Diasporic outlooks on self and society tend to be ANTI-NATIONAL:<br>Diasporic inscriptions of identity are generally identifications that the territorial order of (and within) nation-states is inclined to sanction, and diasporas themselves are explicitly anti-national groupings of people who adhere collectively – in part in opposition – to the coercive unanimity of 'the nation'. | Δ e.g. A diasporic group or community may have cultivated a zone of resistance in which it now 'lives' – either being strongly resistant to that host nation or otherwise strongly resistant to the authorities that currently govern things in the homeland territory to which it (or members from it) now propose to travel. |
| 3 = Diasporic outlooks on self and society tend to be TRANSGRESSIVE:<br>Diasporic inscriptions of identity may be fruitfully understood to be the particularities of dissident outsiders; that is, of those who are comfortable with 'build block' models of being and with 'conflictual' negotiations of bonding. | Δ e.g. Researchers in tourism studies may have to learn the subtle (spiritual (?), secular (?), symbolic (?), political (?), other (?)) ways in which a diasporic population has trespassed over/against the dominant ways in which that population has been labelled and externally known. |
| 4 = Diasporic outlooks on self and society tend to be DIFFICULT TO READ:<br>Diasporic inscriptions of identity are, as a rule, accretive compounds, constituting a transcultural mix of 'being' which has become divorced from the purity of any special affiliation or allure. | Δ e.g. In a so-called 'first world' country, a national tourism organization may have to recognize an ever-new and varied spectrum of ways of seeing the world as cultivated by the throbbing mix of diasporic populations which now exists within its cosmopolitan cities. |

| | |
|---|---|
| 5 = Diasporic outlooks on self and society tend to be EMERGENT:<br>Diasporic inscriptions of identity may be initially platformed on longstanding cultural, ethic and other ties, but in the face of vicissitudes of contemporary globalizing life they tend to be emanative and incomplete rather then fully formed. | △ e.g. A national tourism organization in a homeland territory may identify the need to educate returning 'relatives' or 'travellers' (who live at some distance abroad) about the ways in which new laws have been developed in that visited home territory. |
| 6 = Diasporic outlooks on self and society tend to be GELLING:<br>Disaporic inscriptions of identity habitually involve ongoing processes of self-making where a population may initially come together in accordance with longstanding or long-illustrious bonds of being, yet also where that population consciously and actively seeks new and refreshing forms of social interactivity to further its own possibilities of economic or spiritual life. | △ e.g. A national tourism organization in a homeland territory may identify the need to inform/interpret returning 'relatives' or 'travellers' (who live at some distance abroad) about important changes in cultural practice … perhaps regarding food consumption/sport/religion/commemoration … which are fast unfolding in that visited home territory. |
| 7 = Diasporic outlooks on self and society tend to be NEGOTIATED:<br>Diasporic inscriptions of identity – particularly for individuals caught up in diasporic cross-currents – are continually being changed, re-shaped and re-defined. | △ e.g. A tourism studies research team may need to engage in much iterative work (going to and fro between a drawcard homeland territory and a removed diasporic population in order to gauge how important aspects of life or aspiration have changed … sometimes in small (to the outsiders), but large (to the homeland population), or vice versa. |
| 8 = Diasporic outlooks on self and society tend to be TRANSCULTURAL:<br>Diasporic inscriptions of identity regularly involve the projection of global networks which have an entreaty that reaches beyond limited and traditional identification with 'roots' and 'common biology'. | △ e.g. A tourism studies research team may need to work quickly with conceptual synergy in order to interpret how the 'original' people of a homeland country or territory have been globalized (or glocalized) at a seemingly distinctly different rate or along a distinctly different trajectory than that of an outlying diasporic population associated with that country/territory. |
| 9 = Diasporic outlooks on self and society tend to be IMAGINATIVE:<br>Diasporic inscriptions of identity are not only inclined to draw on distinctive and cherished icons of yester-year and yester-century, but also tend (in some circumstances) to be productive in terms of the creation of imaginary icons and ancestors. | △ e.g. In order to reveal how a revered 'historic', 'literary', 'natural' or other hallowed site has been formally re-designated or informally de-appreciated, a promotional agency in the tourism/travel industry may need to learn how to decode not only 'academic' knowledge about that space or place, but also cultivate fine-line sensitivity to other local/emic/idiosyncratic notions of being and becoming newly connected with it. |

| 10 = Diasporic outlooks on self and society tend to be PROMISSORY: Disaporic inscriptions of identity ordinarily stand as an invocation to the ancient ritual and myth,but they are just as much promissory vocalizations as primordial ones. It is seldom that diasporic outlooks suddenly become not only highly expressive acts of commemoration, but highly articulated acts of affiance or pledged undertaking. | Δ e.g. An agency charged with the responsibility of promoting a (or to a) particular diasporic population must recognize that all identities tend to be aspirational and thereby open to some envisaged 'better future', and are not necessarily consistent with all aspects of the supposedly adamantine ways in which that homeland population has been labelled/known/othered, historically. |
|---|---|

Notes:
The 10 hard-to-decipher diasporic outlooks are inspired by Gilroy (1997: especially 306–41), and first appeared in Hollinshead (2004: 37–38).
Δ = Examples: the imperatives to interpret these difficult and dynamic 'halfway'/'halflight' ways being and becoming in tourism studies ... via postdisciplinary understandings which currently emanate beyond the field.

The exhibit constitutes an attempt to reveal something of the very difficult matters of identification and counter-identification which nowadays routinely arise in representational matters of international travel in the area of diasporic tourism. The exhibit is a re-scaffolding of a table that first appeared in Hollinshead (2004), and is inspired by the work of Gilroy (1997) on race, ethnicity and colour in cultural studies. While the left-hand side of the exhibit comprises the effort to generally account for some of the principal features of identity claiming and of identity maintenance in which diasporic populations of all sorts engage today, the right-hand column comprises the endeavour to situate (or contextually illustrate) those restless or messy Bhabhian matters of being and becoming in tourism and travel, per se. The protean (or multifarious and fast-changeable) character of diasporic longing and belonging stands tall in the exhibit, as it ranges across Gilroy's ideas on plural vision, on excluded vision, on contested vision and on reflexive vision. Thus, it is implicit from the exhibit that those who work in the often misty and murky realms of diasporic travel need training in or access to fine-hair sensibilities about the many-sidedness of cross-border being and becoming, and about the difficult predictabilities of transitional people-hood under the postcolonial moment. It is not a zone for prescriptive learning. The world of cultural identity, cultural location and cultural aspiration lacks the modernistic certitudes it once had (Hall 1992). As Coles *et al.* (2006) have suggested, few researchers or practitioners in tourism studies/tourism management are rich in their received schooling on the bumpy terrain of cultural connectedness and in the disobediences of emergent group aspiration. Such constant questioning of received notions of being and such often transgressive acts of becoming indeed warrant understandings that are not commonly served up within schooling for tourism studies/tourism management, and demand not only transdisciplinary insight, but postdisciplinary insight into the unfolding articulations of identity which characterise the increasingly shrill voices of the postcolonial world. The world of travel is a fertile space in which all kinds of old inheritances and new cultural projections comingle uncertainly. Indeed, it is conceivably the contemporary world's consciousness industry (Kirshenblatt-Gimblett 1998). However, are those who manage and research in that fertile precinct sufficiently awake in their received education and field-preparedness to really cope with what Gilroy (1997) calls 'the detours of identity' in and of our time and know who is saying what about each where, when and why? In that fertile space, there are indeed many new cultural logics to not only learn, but to imagine. Are you equipped for the contestations of being and becoming that lie ahead, as the world is so regularly re-made and re-projected in accordance with the preferences and privileges of different groups? Are you geared up conceptually for the ways in which proclamations of 'new sense' visions of culture-dom from bold groups and liberated communities trespass over what might formerly have been regarded as steady and secure 'old sense' understandings? Are you decently versed in the messy art and craft of identifying cultural ambiguity and interpreting cultural ambiguity in its many restless, protean protestations? Are you fit for purpose – to serve twenty-first-century tourism studies and twenty-first-century tourism management?

## Acknowledgement

Keith Hollinshead and Milka Ivanova are deeply appreciative of Lisa Schwarzin of the Phoenix Arbor project at the Institute for Transformative Sustainability Education (Wageningen University, the Netherlands) for drawing their attention to a number of articles used in this piece. They also appreciate the regular intellectual prods and pushes from Chunxiao Hou (Dr Hou) at the University of Bedfordshire for never letting them rest secure in their own conceptual euroscopes.

## References

Becher, T. (1989) *Academic Tribes and Territories: Intellectual Enquiry and the Cultures of Disciplines*, Milton Keynes: Open University Press.

Bhabha, H. (1994) *The Location of Culture*, London: Routledge.

Coles, T., Hall, C.M. and Duval, D.T. (2006) 'Tourism and Post-Disciplinary Enquiry', *Current Issues in Tourism* 6 (4–5): 293–319.

Denzin, N.Z. and Lincoln, Y.S. (eds) (2005) *The Sage Handbook of Qualitative Research*, Vol. 3, Los Angeles, CA: Sage.

Franklin, A. and Crang, M. (2001) 'The Trouble with Tourism and Travel Theory?' *Tourist Studies* 1 (1): 5–22.

Gilroy, P. (1997) 'Diaspora and the Detours of Identity', in Woodward, K. (ed.) *Identity and Difference*, London: Sage, 299–346.

Graburn, N. and Jafari, J. (1991) 'Introduction: Tourism Social Science', *Annals of Tourism Research* 18: 1–11.

Hall, S. (1992) 'The Rest and the West: Discourse and Power', in Hall S. and Gieben B. (eds) *Formations of Modernity*, Cambridge: Polity Press, 275–331.

Hollinshead, K. (2004) 'Tourism and Third Space Populations: The Restless Motion of Diaspora Peoples', in Coles T. and Timothy D. (eds) *Tourism, Diaspora, Space*, London: Routledge, 33–49.

——(2010) 'Tourism Studies and Confined Understanding: The Call for "New Sense" Postdisciplinary Imaginary', *Tourism Analysis* 15: 499–512.

——(2012) 'The Under-conceptualisations of Tourism Studies: The Case for Postdisciplinary Knowing', in Ateljevic, I., Morgan, N. and Pritchard, A. (eds) *The Critical Turn in Tourism Studies*, London: Routledge, 55–72.

Hollinshead, K. and Ivanova, M.B. (n.d.) *The Requisite Craft of Postdisciplinarity: Responsible and Responsive Conduct in International Tourism Studies*, unpublished, Luton: University of Bedfordshire.

Kirshenblatt-Gimblett, B. (1998) *Destination Culture: Tourism, Museums, Heritage*, Berkeley: University of California Press.

Klein, J.J. (1996) *Crossing Boundaries: Knowledge, Disciplinarities and Interdisciplinarities*, Charlottesville: University Press of Virginia.

McGregor, S.L.T. (n.d.) *The Nature of Transdisciplinary Research and Practice*, Peace and Conflict Studies Program, unpublished, Halifax, Canada: Mount Saint Vincent University.

Max-Neef, M.A. (2005) 'Foundations of Transdisciplinarity', *Ecological Economics* 53: 5–16.

Moran, J. (2002) *Interdisciplinarity*, London: Routledge.

Naydler, J. (2000) *Goethe on Science*, Edinburgh: Floris Books.

Nègre, A. (1999) *A Transdisciplinary Approach to Science and Astrology*, cura.free.fr/quinq/02negre2.html (accessed 19 October 2012).

Nicolescu, B. (2000) *Transdisciplinarity and Complexity*, Paris: Bulletin Interactif de CIRET.

——(2001) *Manifesto of Transdisciplinarity*, Albany: University of New York Press.

Regeer, B. (2002) *Transdisciplinarity*, www.bio.vu.nl.vakgroepen/kens/HTML/trandisciplin.htm (accessed 19 May 2004).

Repko, A. (2008) *Interdisciplinary Research: Process and Theory*, Los Angeles, CA: Sage.

# PART II

# Politics, policy and economics

---

As cultural tourism has grown in recent decades, it has become an increasingly important vehicle for political narratives, tourism and cultural policy initiatives and local economic development. This section contains a range of contributions that examine the growing integration of policies, economics and cultural tourism from different perspectives.

As the Organisation for Economic Co-operation and Development (OECD) report *The Impact of Culture on Tourism* (2009) has emphasised, culture has come to play a key role in the competitiveness and attractiveness of places worldwide. Culture helps to create distinction in a crowded marketplace and is an 'acceptable' form of tourism development in many cases because it combines economic benefits with cultural and social development. Politically, cultural tourism can also provide the basis for nation building, place making and identity strengthening.

At national level the role of cultural policy has changed as culture has come to be seen as a tool for economic development. The increasingly instrumental approach to culture is reflected in the growth of policies related to the 'cultural industries' and more recently the 'creative industries'. Although these policies have tended to emphasise cultural production, there has been also a recognition that cultural production needs to find markets. Cultural tourism has been identified widely as an important market, particularly because it positions culture as an export product and can provide an external impulse to local economies.

As economic output has become a more important role for culture, so the justification of cultural expenditure by governments has come to rest on the return of culture to the rest of the economy and to the broader society. This shift has been particularly notable in the case of mega events such as the European Capital of Culture, where the justification for staging the event has come to be couched almost exclusively in terms of the economic and image returns to the host city (Richards and Palmer 2010).

This 'economic turn' in the support for culture is not just a reflection of neo-liberal ideologies, but also relates to the growing need to involve a wide range of stakeholders in the decision making and funding process. The decline of traditional welfare state regimes in Western Europe, for example, has seen the growth of public-private partnerships designed to inject private finance into the economy and to increase the flexibility of the application of capital. Politics are therefore increasingly influenced by 'regimes' or coalitions of public and private interests formed to promote a specific agenda (Stone 1989). This pattern has long been evident in the tourism field, where the limited ability of government to influence the production and consumption of tourism has stimulated a high degree of public-private partnership, for example in the development of destination marketing or development organisations.

More recently this mixed economy approach has also penetrated the cultural tourism field, with the rise of event and festival marketing organisations, the 'programming' of cities and regions by cultural production and ticketing organisations and the growth of public-private destination marketing partnerships. As the complexity of partnership, politics and policy making in cultural tourism increases, there is also a growing need for leadership that can take a long-term view of the relationship between tourism and culture and attempt to find a balance between often competing interests (OECD 2009).

The increasingly mixed economy of culture and tourism has also forced cultural organisations in particular to justify the 'value for money' that culture can offer. This has stimulated a battery of economic impact studies for events (e.g. the Edinburgh Festivals – BOP Consulting 2011), cultural attractions, cultural industries and cultural quarters (e.g. Communauté métropolitaine de Montréal 2005). In many of these studies, the single most important source of income for the local economy is tourism. Tourists, in fact, are often the only major group injecting money into the local economy from outside, and in this sense the only source of 'new' money. Not surprisingly, therefore, considerable effort has been directed at calculating the economic impact of tourist visits and modelling how this money flows through the economy.

As Raabová et al. point out in this section, however, obsession with money often forces other impacts of cultural tourism – such as cultural development, local identity or social cohesion – into the background. The reality is that even though economic impacts are difficult to measure (as the chapters in this section show), other impacts are even more difficult to quantify, and are therefore often left out of the story. The economic figures are also easier to communicate to policy makers, who prefer simple messages supported by 'hard' figures to complex issues of community development or individual expression.

## Summary of the chapters in this section

**Can-Seng Ooi** makes the point that tourism policy requires the support of different stakeholders, and that a balanced approach to stakeholder interests is important to maximise the benefits and minimise the negative impacts of tourism. He illustrates this point with examples from Singapore, which adopts a top-down approach to tourism policy, and Denmark, which has a more consultative approach. In Singapore (cultural) tourism is utilised as part of a wider social engineering strategy, whereas in Denmark tourism is viewed as something that should not change society. The Singaporean approach is shown to generate new products and initiatives, which are eventually embraced by locals, whereas Danish tourism policy remains more conservative.

**Patrick Föhl** and **Yvonne Pröbstle** explore the nature of co-operation and collaboration in cultural tourism, arguing that it is a prerequisite for successful cultural tourism development. They provide an analysis of the advantages of co-operation, such as adding value, whilst acknowledging the challenges (e.g. competition). They emphasise the fact that co-operation should be multi-level, integrated and balanced, giving examples of cultural tourism attractions, products and events from the German context. They discuss types of co-operation which can be horizontal, vertical or lateral. If it is well managed, co-operation can be a catalyst for change within and between organisations. This is especially crucial for those that have funding problems or lack strategic direction.

**Heather Skinner** examines the complex inter-relationships between culture, nationalism and the politics of place. She shows how England has been presented for tourists through

'Brand England', which has its roots in the rise of nationalist narratives over the centuries, and the distinction of English heritage from that of Scotland and Wales. She argues that much of the heritage presented to tourists is based on 'fakelore', which raises questions about place authenticity. She asks the key question of what mechanisms are driving the marketing of heritage: the stories tourists want to hear, or the stories that place marketeers want them to hear?

**Maria Cândida Pacheco Cadavez** examines how the Salazar regime in Portugal used tourism in the 1930s to construct cultural narratives about the nation. The officially validated culture of the regime was reflected in the presentation of Portugal as a humble, rural nation that celebrated its long history and independence. At the same time there was also a narrative of modern cosmopolitanism, attached to the Portuguese Riviera. Culture was therefore presented in a way that justified the Portuguese nation and the Salazar regime itself.

In a more recent example of the deployment of cultural tourism to boost national identity, **Monica Gilli** examines the celebrations of the 150th anniversary of the unification of Italy in 2011. She traces the development of heritage tourism as a support for community cohesion and identity, which in Italy is particularly important at local level. She shows how the building of the Italian nation has been subject to discussion and political disputes over the years, complicating the celebration of a 'national' event. The rather low-key celebrations arguably have been successful in underpinning a feeling of national unity, and attracted large crowds in cities such as Turin. The event has underlined the division between the 'traditional' cultural tourism image of Italy, formed during the Grand Tour, and the desire for a new image based on the contemporary culture that is becoming increasingly important for tourism, such as food, architecture and design.

**Tereza Raabová**, **Petr Merta** and **Alena Tichá** investigate the different ways in which the economic impact of cultural tourism can be measured. They distinguish between methods employed before (ex-ante) the start of a project and those used to measure impacts after finalising a project or event (ex-post). They pay particular attention to cost–benefit analysis (usually employed to examine feasibility) and input-output analysis (usually used after a project has finished), including the use of multipliers. They apply these methods to events such as the Bregenz Festspiele in Austria and the Prague Quadrennial in the Czech Republic.

**Juan Gabriel Brida**, **Marta Meleddu** and **Manuela Pulina** look more specifically at microeconomic and macroeconomic impacts of museums as cultural attractions. At the micro level these include the willingness to pay of users and non-users as well as Revealed Preference methods. These techniques are illustrated with case studies from Spain and Italy, and they show how visitor characteristics strongly influence propensity to spend. At the macroeconomic level they examine the use of Input-Output models, particularly in the case of the Guggenheim Museum in Bilbao.

Variations in cultural tourism expenditure is a theme subsequently picked up by **Celeste Eusébio**, **Maria João Carneiro** and **Elisabeth Kastenholz**. They review the literature relating to visitor spending and show how a wide range of factors, including education level, travel motivation, group size and accommodation use, can influence spend levels. These relationships are tested empirically using data from the Association for Tourism and Leisure Education (ATLAS) cultural tourism surveys worldwide. These data are used to produce a regression model to predict expenditure levels.

**Juan Ignacio Pulido Fernández** and **Marcelino Sánchez Rivero** analyse the creation of value in cultural tourism destinations. They examine different techniques for analysing the value chain in cultural destinations, including multi-criteria decision techniques, data envelopment analysis, artificial neural networks and structural equation models. Use of these techniques can address the three key questions relating to the value chain – namely the generation of value in the cultural destination, stakeholders' decision-making processes and the productive efficiency of businesses, and the relationships between the links in the chain.

## References

BOP Consulting (2011) *Edinburgh Festivals Impact Study*, Edinburgh: BOP Consulting.

Communauté métropolitaine de Montréal (2005) Culture Cluster, Montreal: CMM.

OECD (2009) *The Impact of Culture on Tourism*, Paris: Organisation for Economic Co-operation and Development.

Richards, G. and Palmer, R. (2010) *Eventful Cities: Cultural Management and Urban Revitalization*, London: Routledge.

Stone, C.N. (1989) *Regime Politics*, St Lawrence: University Press of Kansas.

# 8

# Tourism policy challenges

## Balancing acts, co-operative stakeholders and maintaining authenticity

*Can-Seng Ooi*

Tourism policy matters in cultural tourism. The starting point of this chapter is the observation that many tourism policy studies draw three inter-related conclusions. One, tourism policy must be inclusive and requires the support of different stakeholders (Baker 2009; Bernhard Jørgensen and Munar 2009). Two, a balanced approach to tourism policy is needed to harness the benefits of tourism while mitigating negative effects (Teo and Yeoh 1997; Budeanu 2009). Three, tourism policies should accentuate and maintain the cultural uniqueness and authenticity of the destination (Morgan *et al.* 2011). Many policy makers will concur with researchers on the need to be inclusive, to find a balanced approach to tourism development, to keep the uniqueness and authenticity of local cultural products. However, it seems that many tourism authorities are ignorant of local interests, unaware of the touristification of local cultures and uninterested in promoting local cultures (see Stevenson *et al.* 2008; Bernhard Jørgensen and Munar 2009; Maria 2010; Farsari *et al.* 2011). The disjuncture between researchers' conclusions and tourism authorities' intentions gives rise to two questions: are tourism authorities not doing the things they say they are doing? Or are tourism researchers ignorant of the complexity and nuances of policy making and they have become too idealistic in their conclusions? This chapter attempts to answer these two questions.

## Tourism policy and co-operative stakeholders

Tourism policies are designed to affect the tourism industry, society and culture. Policies to enhance a destination, for instance, go beyond improving the image of the place: they often aim to attract investments, generate wealth and employment, enhance the local cultural scene and improve infrastructure, among other things. Tourism offers welcome impacts and also undesirable side-effects. Building consensus for policies amongst stakeholders is paramount (Baker 2009; Bernhard Jørgensen and Munar 2009). These stakeholders would include tourism authorities, local government, land control authorities, cultural management agencies, civic groups, politicians and local residents. Without the consultation process, unintended negative consequences on local cultures may result. Besides that, the strategy may not roll out smoothly without the support of various stakeholders. Each set of stakeholders has different interests. So in using Gidden's Third Way, Burns (2004) offers a bipolar view of tourism planning. The first view – 'leftist development first' – focuses 'on sustainable human development goals as defined by local people and local knowledge. The key question driving development is 'What can tourism give us without harming us?' (Burns 2004: 26). The second view – 'rightist tourism first' – aims to 'maximize market spread through familiarity of the product. Undifferentiated, homogenized product depends on a core with a focus on tourism goals set by outside planners and the international tourism industry' (Burns 2004: 26). In trying to bring different local community and industry interests together, the Third Way conceptually bridges the two poles. In practice, how this can work out remains to be seen and tested.

The building of consensus is easier said than done. Different stakeholders should ideally collaborate and co-operate to bring about the common good for society and also enhance their own interests (Baker 2009). There are, however, challenges. First, from the beginning, identifying relevant stakeholders is a difficult exercise (Currie *et al.* 2009). For instance, who should constitute a stakeholder group? Or more specifically, which groups of residents should be consulted when developing a new destination brand? Second, stakeholder groups may not want to co-operate. For example, in a study of the Copenhagen International Film Festival and the promotion of Copenhagen as a tourist destination, Ooi and Strandgaard Pedersen (2010) show that the organisers of the film festival and the tourism promotion agency are not interested in developing closer collaboration because of their different interests. Closer co-operation may have detrimental consequences for the film festival because it may lose its credibility if it is seen as merely a tourism promotion event. Third, consultation also entails co-ordination costs. Building up a broad consensus is time consuming and requires resources. The eventual proposals may not be effective or efficient. These hurdles give rise to the reluctance of stakeholder groups coming together. Fourth, even with inclusive consultation, decision making and leadership are needed in realising policy direction and implementation (Budeanu 2009). Official tourism promotion authorities often take up the leadership, but by doing so, certain groups may remain dissatisfied and will blame the tourism authorities as high-handed, coercive or incompetent (see Frey and George 2010; Teo and Yeoh 1997). So, inclusive consultative processes are also unlikely to prevent future criticism.

So, researchers advocate the need to be inclusive in devising and implementing tourism policies. Practitioners agree. How this principle translates into practice, however, requires a more nuanced understanding of the economic, social and political dynamics of the tourism industry. The stakeholder approach sounds right but the good ideas are often not translated into practice.

## Tourism policy as a balancing act

Good tourism policies take a balanced approach, meaning they bring in the benefits of tourism, while minimising the industry's negative impacts (e.g. Newby 1994; Leheny 1995; Chang 1997; Jenkins 1997; Teo and Yeoh 1997). The negative impacts include problems related to traffic congestion, pollution, wear and tear of heritage sites, and price inflation (van der Borg *et al.* 1996). Aspects of the host society may also be commodified and touristified: 'mass trinketisation', for instance, debases local handicrafts (Cohen 1988). These impacts should be minimised, while its positive economic and social impacts should be welcomed. So, for instance, Newby (1994: 208–15) defines conceptual relationships between heritage and tourism as a continuum with three principal foci: co-existence, exploitation and imaginative reconstruction. Tourism and heritage co-exist when the former does not dominate the local economy. The relationship becomes exploitative when cultural heritage becomes the basis for generating a cash flow. Imaginative reconstruction allows preservation without being swallowed by commercialism. This balanced strategy ensures that the heritage remains 'alive', but the lines separating co-existence, exploitation and creative redevelopment are unclear and subject to disagreement (see Yan and Bramwell 2008; Yang *et al.* 2008; Nyaupane and Timothy 2010).

Tourism policies bring social change and economic development. There are different directions and ways society and culture can change and the economy can develop. The balanced approach sounds reasonable but also ambiguous. Negotiation on the way forward takes place amongst tourism stakeholders, resulting in different destinations coming up with their own versions of 'balanced' tourism development (Yan and Bramwell 2008; Yang *et al.* 2008; Nyaupane and Timothy 2010). Consequently, stakeholders with more economic and institutional resources are more likely to be able to further their own agendas (Ooi 2002). As will be elaborated in the case on Denmark and Singapore later, the formulation and implementation of tourism policies take place within the political economy of the destination.

## Tourism policy as social engineering

Related to the last discussion, tourism policies, by definition, are meant to shape industry, society and culture. In the context of cultural tourism products, issues of authenticity arise; local cultures should not be excessively touristified or commercialised in case they lose their integrity and uniqueness. For example, many destinations are branding themselves and tourism has become a vehicle for tourism authorities selectively to market their destinations and reinvent their destination identities (see Morgan *et al.* 2011). The crystallised public image may also be introduced to the native population for it to recognise itself (Oakes 1993; Lanfant 1995; Leonard 1997; Ooi 2005). The process of crystallising the destination's culture and identity may lead to the process of rediscovering, reinventing and reinterpreting local customs and cultures. Arguably, then, the tourism industry may insidiously destroy the spirit of the place.

On the other hand, tourism also brings about societal change that is appreciated by locals. For instance, Shanghai is no longer a fishing village or a colonial outpost of the 1930s. Today it is a booming metropolis with more than 23 million people. The city is modern (see Figure 8.1). While the city is searching for its soul amidst the tall buildings, highways and shopping malls, the authorities have decided to conserve parts of old Shanghai. The neo-classical colonialist buildings along the Bund have been listed. Yu Gardens – a landscaped traditional Chinese park – and its surrounding area, have been dubbed as 'Chinatown' by locals. Newly built, ancient-looking Chinese houses and shops clutter the area outside Yu Gardens. In this case, the tourism policy of the city, with the support of urban planning, has maintained and reinvented aspects of old Shanghai. Residents shop there and have come to accept the spruced-up Yu Gardens area as quintessentially Shanghai. A new authenticity has emerged.

The social engineering functions of tourism policy are often treated with disdain by researchers, but authenticity emerges (Cohen 1988; Knox 2008; Ooi and Stöber 2010), culture changes and cultural change and social engineering are welcomed at times. Considering that local residents may welcome the changes brought about by tourism, the relationships amongst tourism, host society and policy are more complex and nuanced than keeping past cultures and heritage. Relating to the balanced approach, when is change brought about by tourism activities acceptable?

*Figure 8.1* A modern Shanghai that wows residents and tourists

## Convergence of tourism policy and products

Art biennales (e.g. in Venice, Singapore, Shanghai), processions (e.g. Berlin's Love Parade, Mardi Gras), spectacular physical icons (e.g. Sydney's Opera House, the Eiffel Tower, Beijing's Olympic Stadium), art museums (e.g. New York's Museum of Modern Art, Bilbao's Guggenheim Museum, Doha's Museum of Islamic Art), and the staging of blockbuster musicals (e.g. Mamma Mia, The Lion King) have come to glorify destinations. These tourism and cultural products transform destinations. Many are popular with tourists and locals. It is debatable if such attractions make the places more unique. While tourism authorities try to maintain the uniqueness of their destinations, many of their plans actually make their destinations more similar to one another (Ooi 2011). This arises partly because policy makers and industry players copy ideas from other places.

Policy makers and industry players copy because they want to attract more tourists. Tourists are not necessarily looking just for the unique; they also seek out familiar attractions (Ritzer and Liska 1997; McIntosh and Prentice 1999; Prentice 2004; Weaver 2005). The tourism industry taps into the preconceptions and habits of tourists. Thus, Versace, Disney theme parks, Hilton hotels and the like are welcomed into many destinations, and so are familiar tourist attractions like zoos, observation towers and street bazaars. If new types of attractions prove to be popular (e.g. the London Eye), they will be copied (e.g. Eye on Malaysia, Singapore Flyer, both modelled on the London Eye). So today, many destinations have pedestrian walking malls, gentrified, disused industrial spaces and art in public places. New tourism developments are often part of wider development plans for the host society, and local residents may welcome them. In sum, while each tourist attraction claims to be unique, the cultural offerings and attractions are primarily similar – partly because policy makers and industry players learn from other destinations. It is not true that tourists are only interested in the unique; destinations can be too exotic to attract visitors. So in devising tourism policy, learning from good practices and using tested formulas from other places are just as important as keeping the uniqueness and authenticity of local cultures.

# 9

# Co-operation as a central element of cultural tourism

## A German perspective

*Patrick S. Föhl and Yvonne Pröbstle*

### Culture and tourism: an unequal pair?

Current social challenges and declining public funds are bringing culture practitioners and local communities closer together. The culturally interesting synergy effects of co-operative efforts are increasingly encouraging those working in the culture sector to pull together. The result is an alternating process of competition and co-operation reflected in the term 'co-opetition' (Voesgen 2009). Brandenburger and Nalebuff (2009) even view 'co-operative competition' as the most important success strategy for companies.

Not only are co-operative relations among cultural organisations and cultural projects growing, but there is also more collaboration between culture and industry, culture and social organisations, and teamwork in many other configurations. One field that would be unthinkable without co-operation is cultural tourism (for more detailed analysis see Pröbstle 2011a, 2011b, 2011c).

According to the German Tourist Association (DTV) 'culture is the most important attraction factor' for city tourists (DTV 2006: 13). It is therefore not surprising that the public sector, local tourist organisations and commercial tourist service providers in Germany (such as cultural tourism specialist Studiosus), have recently been relying on the pulling power of cultural tourism. Cultural organisations are also targeting 'cultural tourists'. Cultural tourism can strengthen cultural enterprises both by increasing the number of visitors, and by profiling culture as an image and locality factor (Hausmann 2002: 50; Klein 2007: 284).

The marriage of culture and tourism is seldom smooth, however. Critics argue that private tourist companies and cultural organisations are unable to speak the same language (cf. McKercher and Du Cros 2002: 14; Schwark 1996: 121; Wolber 1999: 140). However, Buri (2009a, 2009b) argues that there is some convergence between these apparently contrasting organisations. Regardless of one's position, it is clear that no form of tourism can exist without co-operation. The need for teamwork in (cultural) tourism is rooted in the nature of tourism products. The tourist does not judge the quality of the individual services consumed, but rather the overall experience. The creation of experiences requires a co-ordinating mechanism (among others Freyer 2007: 96ff.; Steingrube 2003: 441; Stolpmann 2007: 24). However, there are many obstacles to co-operation, including rigid organisation structures and cultures, competing interest groups, and political issues (Steingrube 2003: 451f.).

It is clear that culture and tourism providers often have different aims, attitudes and procedures, although this is not a problem specific to cultural tourism. The tourist system generally constitutes a pot pourri of unequal partners, who have no alternative but to work together owing to the particular quality of tourism as a product.

## Cultural tourism: hype or healer? – a critical comment

Many cultural organisations and local communities see cultural tourism as a panacea. However, they often misjudge the competition prevalent in the sector, originally a seller's market but now a buyer's market. Tourist expectations have risen considerably, and there are multiple cultural niche markets that are increasingly difficult to target (Stolpmann 2007: 8). McKercher and Du Cros (2002) identify increasing product interchangeability, rooted in the fact that many providers are blinded by routine and have a high level of identification with 'their' product and 'their' destination.

In the competition between regions and destinations (Föhl 2009b), cultural practitioners and cultural policies also concentrate too much on projecting a positive external image through cultural tourism and tend to lose sight of the pressing issues of citizen-oriented cultural development. Given that culture is largely publicly funded, one might question what contribution cultural tourism can make to the task of imparting knowledge and awareness? It is therefore important to assess in each case whether the tourist market is attractive, and if so, with whom one should co-operate, and how to create an acceptable balance between local/regional and supra-regional/national orientations (Föhl 2010a).

Before cultural tourism concepts are developed, it is therefore necessary to analyse the potential. This involves not just the attractiveness of the cultural programme, but also the quality of the tourist infrastructure. Visitor surveys conducted in 2004–09 in Vienna show clearly that theatres and concerts are frequented much less often than museums or historical sites (Wien-Tourismus 2009). In Berlin over 30 per cent of visitors to Stiftung Oper in Berlin (Berlin Opera Foundation) and Friedrichstadtpalast (the revue theatre) are cultural tourists. This shows that even in major cities, one has to be realistic about the potential of cultural tourism for different products.

Cultural tourism development in rural areas often depends on linking tourist attractions together. Such opportunities arise, for instance, in the Liebliches Taubertal (Lovely Tauber Valley), a predominantly rural destination in the regions of Franconia and Heilbronn-Franconia, which offers hiking, cycling and wine-growing. These resources are also of advantage to the Kloster Bronnbach (Bronnbach Monastery), which after thorough renovation has become a cultural tourism attraction. In addition to being accessible on cycle paths and hiking routes and possessing parking facilities, the monastery offers guided tours and has its own wine-cellar and shop. A café-restaurant has been installed in the orangery and hotel facilities have been established.

The Bronnbach Monastery shows how important an existing and functioning tourist infrastructure and a variety of co-operative relationships are (Wagner 2009). From a (cultural) tourism viewpoint, a solitary cultural object without integrated catering and hotel facilities is hardly capable of further development. How can a festival, for example, be positioned as a supra-regional attraction if there are no accommodation facilities at the venue capable of meeting visitor demands? The tourist sector as a whole needs to make a general overall examination of visitor requirements and motivation.

A glance at target groups in the cultural tourism sector clarifies the challenges. For the cultural tourism segment the motive 'contributing to one's own culture and education' constitutes the primary reason for travel. Most 'partial cultural tourists', on the other hand, travel first and foremost for non-cultural motives, although having once arrived at their destination, they make use of local cultural tourism facilities. It is thus not unusual for the sports or outdoor tourist to reveal certain cultural tourism tendencies (Pröbstle 2010). An analysis of cultural tourism potential must therefore look not only at the cultural programme on offer, but also examine the tourist infrastructure and necessary co-operation relations in their totality. Satisfying the complex package of tourist expectations and motives is the key to success in the cultural tourism sector.

## Advantages of co-operation

The concept of co-operation is characterised by numerous definitions and interpretations: 'alliance', 'strategic association', 'work group' or 'network' are just a few synonyms for the generic term *co-operation*, but they are partly distinct from one another. Co-operation projects are generally characterised by the following features (Föhl 2008: 2f.):

- Co-operation consists of a collaboration between two or more partners, which as a rule is fixed by contract. Unlike a fusion, however, the two partners remain legally independent.
- The core of their collaboration is the exchange of resources, knowledge and capabilities between the partners.
- In entering into the collaboration, the institutions have the same or compatible goals. The common aim is to improve or maintain the economic, cultural or tourist-trade position of each partner.
- Co-operation provides greater chances of goals being reached. In return, the partners are willing to limit their own individual autonomy, partially giving up their political, cultural or economic independence for the sake of co-operative action.
- Co-operation therefore occurs voluntarily.

In terms of cultural tourism, the common goal of all tourist providers is the successful positioning of the product in the tourist market. Collaboration ensures not only improved chances of success, but it also creates the necessary preconditions for success. A solitary cultural element alone will not generate as much tourism.

The following section gives an overview of a selection of opportunities that can result from co-operation in the cultural tourism sector.

### Concentrating strengths

The exchange of resources is central to co-operation. If each partner contributes what they can best achieve and what is useful to the common goal, then an optimal allocation of resources is created. The choice of partners is accordingly influenced by resources which the partners wish to exchange and which ideally also complement each other.

In the case of cultural tourism these resources are tourist services which are contributed by various providers to supply the product required by the traveller. For instance, in 2009 the Bregenz Festival had a total of 260,000 visitors. This remarkable level of attendance, at 98 per cent occupancy, was achieved through collaboration with various tour operators, who were responsible for selling 40 per cent of the total tickets available. This would not have been feasible without the co-operation of local hoteliers and caterers and the support of many other tourist service providers. This does not mean individual participants have their own areas of competence curtailed. On the contrary, in this way the creative services, for instance, are entirely the domain of the cultural contributors who possess the appropriate competence. Collaboration with tourist service providers and openness to their knowledge and expertise is required to develop and position the cultural tourism product.

## Generating added value

Co-operation in cultural tourism also helps to create added value. Co-operation can make a far more attractive product than a single element alone. Because of their complex travel motivations, contemporary travellers often opt for a complex product, which can increase length of stay and thereby increase tourism income. Surveys have shown that once at their destination, tourists usually participate in a greater number of activities than might be assumed from their main travel motive (e.g. F.U.R. 2005b; ISOE 2005).

Collaborative projects in cultural tourism can also generate added value by using general overall themes linking cultural tourism participants together. This may be particularly useful in rural regions, which can achieve added cultural tourism value through theme collaboration. A successful example is the collaborative product 'Klösterreich' ('The Realm of Monasteries') which links (chiefly in Austria) 22 monasteries, religious houses and other religious foundations. This thematic marketing collaboration has given hitherto less well-known monasteries, religious houses and religious foundations the opportunity to reach the general tourist public within the aura of popular attractions like the Stift Melk (Melk Monastery).

Finally, added value is also generated because co-operative projects can help to restrict (unproductive) competition, for instance by allowing collaborative agreements on opening hours or on combination tickets. Even with regard to funding support, collaborative efforts can achieve greater success than solo attempts, demonstrated currently by the examples of the East Frisia Culture Network or the Roman Road in Rheinland-Pfalz, both of which are co-operative projects supported among others by the European Agricultural Fund for Rural Development.

## Introducing a breath of fresh air

Many cultural institutions have traditional bureaucratic structures. Co-operation with tourist providers can therefore be a catalyst of change. Encounters with new ways of working can help to broaden a narrow focus on one's own traditional forms of organisation. For example, tourist organisations can also learn from the encounter with creative ways of thinking and methods of working. Co-operation can be understood as a mutual process of learning in which new knowledge is continuously generated and flows into the systems of culture and tourism, ensuring long-term quality. This is the principle of Culture Tour Austria, a strategic priority programme for cultural tourism in Austria.

## Helping to secure the future

Cultural institutions are also faced with the challenge of doing more to justify their existence. As public funding crumbles, new partners are needed who can help to anchor cultural life more strongly in society (Klein 2007: 249ff.). Cultural tourism is important as a domain with a multitude of contributors from politics, social fields and the economy. This in turn draws attention to the cultural infrastructure in the region concerned (see on this point also for the concept of *governance* Föhl 2009b: 15ff.). Destinations developing cultural tourism therefore need to support local culture. The importance that cultural tourism is currently taking on in political discussion can be seen in the latest proposal by the German CDU/CSU (Christian Democrat/Christian Socialist) and FDP (Free Democrat) parliamentary parties 'to strengthen cultural tourism in Germany' (Deutscher Bundestag 2010).

## Interim conclusions

Concentrating strength, creating added value, breathing fresh life into cultural institutions and helping to safeguard the future – all these are opportunities that lie in co-operation in cultural tourism, but at the same time are not confined to this field of activity. Particularly the latter two perspectives show that cultural tourism is more than a simple marketing tool, and can be of considerable strategic value for cultural institutions. The following section focuses on con-stellations for cultural tourism co-operation and attempts to systematise them.

# Who with whom? Forms and practical examples

## Co-operation as an intermediate stage between market and hierarchy

Co-operation in the (culture-) tourist market can take on various forms, depending on objectives, content and degree of intensity. Among these are ad hoc types of collaboration (e.g. occasional individual agreements), formal co-operation on individual issues (e.g. a work group), and strategic development planning (e.g. co-operative regional tourist development), extending to joint service units in sales and distribution or production (co-operative resource linking or controlling) (see Figure 9.1).

Co-operation also occupies a hybrid position between purely hierarchical and purely market-based organisational forms (Figure 9.2).

Here the market constitutes an organisational form of economic activities in which market participants exchange services, such as the purchase of a tourist service. The co-ordination takes place here primarily via price and quality. Exchange relations are therefore loose and mainly characterised by direct competition with other providers. Different forms of co-operation can also be identified (Föhl 2008: 5):

- *Horizontal co-operation*: collaboration involving two or more partners who provide an identical or similar product (e.g. a museum region with an appropriate travel route).
- *Vertical co-operation*: an alliance of participants occupying positions on a preceding and/or following net product chain (e.g. co-operation between railway, theatre, catering and hotel trades).

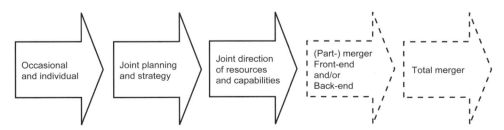

*Figure 9.1* Increase in degree of interconnection with different forms of collaboration
Source: (After Föhl and Huber 2004: 55).

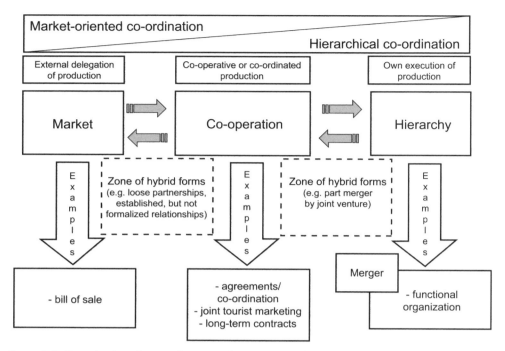

*Figure 9.2* Organisation forms of economic activities of cultural institutions in the cultural tourism field

Source: (Following Sydow 1992: 104; and Föhl 2011).

- *Lateral co-operation*: the products of the partners have little if any direct relationship with one another. The relations are defined through the co-operation (e.g. an umbrella marketing network for all culture and leisure market participants in a particular region).
- Particularly in very broad-based alliances mixtures of these different co-operation types are to be expected.

## Success factors in cultural tourism co-operation

The success factors of co-operation in cultural tourism can be derived and expanded from the stumbling blocks to co-operation reviewed earlier in the chapter (BMWA 1999; MWFK and TMB 2005; Grabow 2006; Föhl 2008, 2009a, 2009b).

- Entry into the field of cultural tourism must occur on the basis of a strategic decision by the partners in favour of co-operation. Cultural tourism cannot be imposed, and requires the basic willingness of the partners to collaborate with each other.
- Partners involved in co-operative systems also need a high degree of empathy, coupled with the openness and willingness to learn from new experience.
- With more intensive co-operation projects there is a basic need to test feasibility regarding strategic and organisational fitness for the tasks at hand (see Föhl 2007).
- All those involved must be aware of the reasons for the co-operation, so that they can also identify with them.

- Clear agreements on objectives must be reached and contracts drawn up. The goals must be compatible with each other.
- An understanding must be reached on keeping to the same norms and standards in carrying out project tasks.
- Procedural steps and their sequences must be defined (regarding time-frame, content, etc.), and tasks distributed in such a way that efficient co-operation can be guaranteed.
- Co-operation undertakings can be conceived of as complex projects and co-ordinated as such.
- To mobilise success potential fully, the collaboration should be carried out in an atmosphere of parity and equal partnership.
- Internal and external communication are important keys to success.

In summary, basic success factors in co-operation are (Scheytt 2005: B1.14):

- jointly saying 'yes' to collaboration (readiness);
- jointly learning one language (understanding);
- jointly defining and pursuing goals and interests (content); and
- jointly celebrating successes (result).

For only when successful results are actually achieved can existing co-operation be continued with the necessary motivation.

## Conclusions

In cautiously uniting the two poles of culture and tourism, cultural managers have the task of weighing the opportunities and risks of cultural tourism alliances (see Föhl *et al.* 2011). They need to mediate between tourism and cultural institutions and connect them professionally in order to bring about a win-win situation. At the same time, however, they should not be afraid to modify or end any kind of co-operation that is unproductive.

There is a considerable need for research and evaluation regarding actual influences and effects of co-operation in cultural tourism, in terms of participant constellations, the material and immaterial processes of exchange and both the hard and soft factors involved in such inter-organisational alliances. This chapter attempts to provide an initial thematic approach and support towards systematising co-operative undertakings in cultural tourism.

## Acknowledgement

Text translated from the German by Peter Fenn.

## References

BMWA (1999) *Handbuch Kultur & Tourismus*, Wien: Bundesministerium für Wirtschaft und Arbeit.
Brandenburger, A. and Nalebuff, B. (2009) *Coopetition. Kooperativ konkurrieren. Mit der Spieltheorie zum Geschäftserfolg*, Eschborn.
Buri, H. (2009a) 'Kultur und Tourismus – zwei notorische Lieblingsfeinde? Über das Verhältnis von Kulturschaffenden und Touristikern', *Politik und kultur* 3: 22f.
——(2009b) 'Tourismus und kulturelles Erbe. Versöhnungsstrategien für zwei Lieblingsfeinde', in Loock, F. and Scheytt, O. (eds) *Handbuch Kulturmanagement und Kulturpolitik*, Berlin u.a.O. 2006ff., Kap. H 2.13.
Deutscher Bundestag (2010) *Kulturtourismus in Deutschland stärken* (Drucksache 17/676), dip21.bundestag.de/dip21/btd/17/006/1700676.pdf (accessed 5 January 2012).

DTV (2006) Grundlagenuntersuchung Städte-und Kulturtourismus in Deutschland (Langfassung), www.deutschertourismusverband.de/fileadmin/Mediendatenbank/PDFs/Staedtestudie_Langfassung.pdf (accessed 5 January 2012).

Föhl, P.S. (2007) 'Die Machbarkeitsstudie im öffentlichen Kulturbereich. "Sorgfaltpflicht" vor der Durchführung von Veränderungsmaßnahmen und Projekten', in Loock, F. and Scheytt, O. (eds) *Handbuch Kulturmanagement und Kulturpolitik*, Berlin u.a.O. 2006ff., Kap. D 1.2.

——(2008) 'Kooperationen im öffentlichen Kulturbereich. Mit Zusammenarbeit Synergien ausschöpfen', in Loock, F. and Scheytt, O. (eds) *Handbuch Kulturmanagement und Kulturpolitik*, Berlin u.a.O. 2006ff., Kap. D 1.5.

——(2009a) 'Potenziale von Kooperationen als Präventiv-und Anpassungsstrategie zur Gestaltung des demografischen Wandels im Kulturbereich', in Hausmann, A. and Körner, J. (eds) *Demografischer Wandel und Kultur. Veränderungen im Kulturangebot und der Kulturnachfrage*, Wiesbaden, S. 203–27.

——(2009b) 'Regionale Kooperationen im Kulturbereich. Begriffe und Systematisierungen', in Föhl, P.S. and Neisener, I. (eds) *Museumsentwicklungskonzeption für die Museen im Kreis Euskirchen*, Potsdam, 15–46.

——(2010a) '(K)ein harmonischer Dreiklang? – Kultur, Kooperation und Tourismus', *Das Orchester* (May): 19–21.

——(2011) *Kooperationen und Fusionen von öffentlichen Theatern. Grundlagen, empirische Untersuchungen, Handlungsempfehlungen*, Wiesbaden.

Föhl, P.S., Glogner-Pilz, P., Lutz, M. and Pröbstle, Y. (eds) (2011) *Nachhaltige Entwicklung in Kulturmanagement und Kulturpolitik. Ausgewählte Grundlagen und strategische Perspektiven*, Wiesbaden.

Föhl, P.S. and Huber, A. (2004) *Fusionen von Kultureinrichtungen. Ursachen, Abläufe, Potenziale, Risiken und Alternativen*, Essen.

Freyer, W. (2007) *Tourismus-Marketing. Marktorientiertes Management im Mikro-und Makrobereich der Tourismuswirtschaft*, 5. überarb. Aufl., München.

F.U.R. (2005a) *Urlaubsmotive*, Kiel.

——(2005b) *Urlaubsarten*, Kiel.

Grabow, B. (2006) 'Stadtmarketing und Regionalisierung – Herausforderungen der Zukunft', in Pechlaner, H., Fischer, E. and Hammann, E.-M. (eds) *Standortwettbewerb und Tourismus. Regionale Erfolgsstrategien*, Berlin, 27–38.

Hausmann, A. (2002) 'Kulturtouristen als wichtiges Besuchersegment im Marketing von Kulturbetrieben', *Tourismus Journal* 1: 49–57.

ISOE (2005) *Urlaubs-und Reisestile – ein Zielgruppenmodell für nachhaltige Tourismusangebote* (ISOE-Studientexte, Nr. 12), Frankfurt am Main.

Klein, A. (2007) *Der exzellente Kulturbetrieb*, Wiesbaden.

McKercher, B. and Du Cros, H. (2002) *Cultural Tourism. The Partnership Between Tourism and Cultural Heritage Management*, New York: Haworth.

MWFK and TMB (2005) *Leitfaden Kulturtourismus in Brandenburg*, www.mwfk.brandenburg.de/sixcms/media.php/4055/leitfaden_kulturtourismus.pdf (accessed 5 January 2012).

Pröbstle, Y. (2010) 'Kulturtouristen: Soll- und Ist-Zustand aus Perspektive der empirischen Kulturforschung', in Glogner, P. and Föhl, P.S. (eds) *Das Kulturpublikum. Fragestellungen und Befunde der empirischen Forschung*, Wiesbaden, 239–78.

——(2011a) 'Kulturtourismus als Handlungsfeld im Kulturbetrieb: eine vermeintliche "Baustelle"?' in Klein, A. (ed.) *Taten.Drang.Kultur. Kulturmanagement in Deutschland 1990–2030*, Wiesbaden, 299–319.

——(2011b) 'Kulturtourismusmarketing', in Klein, A. (ed.) *Kompendium Kulturmarketing. Handbuch für Studium und Praxis*, München, 393–414.

——(2011c) 'Kultur und Tourismus. Entwicklung, Strukturen und Aufgaben einer strategischen Partnerschaft', in Klein, A. (ed.) *Kompendium Kulturmanagement. Handbuch für Studium und Praxis*, 3., Auflage, München, 657–77.

Scheytt, O. (2005) *Kreative Allianzen bilden – Beispiele kommunaler Kulturkooperationen*, Vortrag auf der EUROFORUM-Konferenz 'Interkommunale Kooperationen', Berlin, 20 January, Typoskript.

Schwark, J. (1996) 'Thementourismus – am Beispiel des Lutherjahres', in Dreyer, A. (ed.) *Kulturtourismus*, München, 137–50.

Steingrube, W. (2003) 'Freizeit-und Tourismusdestinationen: Management – Struktur – Politik – Planung', in Becker, C., Hopfinger, H. and Steinecke, A. (eds) *Geographie der Freizeit und des Tourismus*, Bilanz und Ausblick, München; Wien, 441–53.

Stolpmann, M. (2007) *Tourismus-Marketing mit Profil. Reiseziele positionieren – Gäste und Kunden gewinnen*, Landsberg am Lech.

Sydow, J. (1992) *Strategische Netzwerke. Evolution und Organisation*, Wiesbaden.

Voesgen, H. (2009) 'Kooperation und Konkurrenz', *Föhl and Neisener*: 83–102.

Wagner, M. (2009) 'Kloster Bronnbach: ein Ort gelebter Kooperation', *Föhl and Neisener*: 231–40.

Wien-Tourismus (2009) *Wiener Gästebefragung 2004–9*, Kurzbericht, b2b.wien.info/de/statistik/marktforschung/gaestebefragung-2004-2009 (accessed 5 January 2012).

Wolber, T. (1999) 'Die touristische Inwertsetzung des kulturellen Erbes in größeren Städten – Historic Highlights of Germany', in Heinze, T. (ed.) *Kulturtourismus. Grundlagen, Trends und Fallstudien*, München, 103–45.

# 10

# Territory, culture, nationalism, and the politics of place

*Heather Skinner*

Academic interest in the marketing of places can be traced back to two key themes arising in the literature from the 1960s: the place as a geographical locus of production that can exert influence on consumers to purchase goods and services with which the place is associated; and the place as a destination where 'the product is substantially a location and the geographical locus is what is being sold' (Kavaratzis and Ashworth 2008: 153). More recently, it has become increasingly of interest for place marketers to also consider the authenticity of the cultural tourism 'product'. Another focus of recent interest within the extant place marketing and place branding literature is whether it is more appropriate to consider marketable places that transform through the act of experiential consumption, or as entities that confer identity. The latter is especially evident at the national level where it is often 'the utilisation, or creation, of a cultural heritage to create a place brand [that] ... provides the link between the cultural and political aspects of national identity' (Croft *et al.* 2008: 301–2). Thus it is not only the natural and physical environments that contribute to the essence of the place brand, but also the politics, history and culture of a place, along with the 'sensory and symbolic elements that may encompass staged spectacles, and which may or may not be based on authenticity' (Skinner 2011: 289). This chapter therefore explores the link between the issues of authenticity, identity and experiential consumption as they relate to cultural tourism.

Simmel (2007) proposes that boundaries are vital to the human conception and perception of any landscape. Whether that place is a country, region, city, town, village or individual location, each of these places is a boundaried geographical entity. According to Brighenti (2010), the concept of a boundaried territory within which various events, processes and procedures 'take place' has been deemed necessary in order to understand, for example, the political extension of the nation-state and its laws, and the way in which government exerts sovereignty over its peoples; thus territory comprises aspects of geography, behaviour, politics and law, and 'defines spaces through patterns of relations' (Brighenti 2010: 57), whether that territory is physical or indeed metaphorical. The focus on Western Europe as the home of the creation of the nation-state concept (Cobban 1969) has informed the way nations historically have been viewed – either solely as a political entity in line with the thoughts of French political scientists, or solely as a cultural entity in line with German schools of thought – with more recent perspectives reconciling these views, and seeing the nation as both a political and cultural entity (Skinner and

Kubacki 2007). However, there are also two opposing perspectives that consider how a national culture and identity develops over time: the 'primordialist' view that cultural and ethnic attachments evolve naturally within a given society, and the 'instrumentalist' view that such attachments are 'invented and manipulated by elites to construct the nation as a privileged source of a group loyalty' (Biswas 2002: 179). It is in this concept of invention of a cultural heritage that the issue of authenticity becomes of relevance, and starts addressing the issue of what it is that cultural tourists are indeed consuming.

According to Brewer (1994: 6, original emphasis) '*marketable tradition*' is that which is perceived as the '*unique* and *externally presentable* cultural heritage of ... societies, the acceptable face of the past'. When we visit another culture, purchase souvenirs and choose where to rest our camera's gaze, we are expressing our desire not only to see and experience another culture, but also 'to be seen to have seen', and it is this that drives us 'to package our cultures for easy and palatable and fast consumption' (Brewer 1994: 7–8). Goulding (2000) concurs, arguing that any commercially driven analysis of history tends to become sanitised, entertaining and 'inauthentic, in order to appeal to popular tastes'. This chapter proposes that it is not just the packaging of cultural heritage that may lead to it being rendered inauthentic, but that the cultural heritage that is packaged may never have had any authentic base in reality in the first place, resting less on folklore and more on 'fakelore' (Atkinson Wells 1994).

---

## Box 10.1 Case study: Brand England and the power of narrative

The link between sovereignty and government is indeed the territorial relationship *par excellence*. In order to work properly, government needs to territorialize a given population within its own framework of sovereignty.

*(Brighenti 2010: 55)*

Authenticity is also relevant when considering the historical antecedents of the myths and stories upon which the place brand rests, particularly at a national level. The concept of Brand England can be traced back to the Middle Ages. Towards the end of the tenth century, various 'kingdoms' existed across Britain, one of which, Wessex, successfully dominated others, in no little part based on the concerted efforts of the Church and the Abbot Dunstan of Glastonbury Abbey, along with the House of Wessex:

> ... to lay claim to the country as a whole. As Wood (1999, pp. 61–62) summarizes it, 'the creation of a kingdom of England and the elevation of Glastonbury to national shrine had gone hand in hand.' The myth-making, then, obscured something less spiritual, 'the power politics of the Old English State'.
>
> *(Croft et al. 2008: 297)*

This brand creation is also interesting when considering the 'fakelore' associated with both the Abbey and the symbols associated with the nation-state, especially when Glastonbury had become a major destination for pilgrimage tourism. As explained by both Wood (1999) and Croft *et al.* (2008), such myths included: the Abbey's reliquary and range of documents, the authenticity of which has been questioned; the timely 'discovery' of the remains of King Arthur and Queen Guinevere at the Abbey shortly following a fire that destroyed its reliquary and collection of ancient documents; the mythology associated with the Glastonbury Thorn, a bush

---

claimed to have grown from the staff of Joseph of Arimathea when he travelled to the site following the crucifixion of Jesus of Nazareth, burying the *Holy Grail* in what is now known as Glastonbury Abbey's Chalice Well (indeed, more myths have since grown around Joseph, the uncle of Jesus, who, it is also claimed, travelled to the country with Jesus as a boy, a narrative immortalised in the poem Jerusalem by William Blake); and the association with Saint George as England's patron Saint. Saint George, who has associations as patron saint of a number of different nations and cities around the world, was born in what is modern-day Turkey, while his legends tend to be associated with what is modern-day Palestine. Moreover, he almost certainly never set foot in England, and so could not have been present for Joseph of Arimathea to use his own blood to draw the symbolic emblem of the red cross on George's shield (Carley 2001). Nor was Saint George therefore present to slay the (Welsh) dragon.

The concept of differentiation between nations was also evident in the rise of Brand England and differentiation from (and eventual rule over) its neighbour, Wales. The discovery of Arthur's remains at Glastonbury could be seen to be a deliberate attempt by the ruling English elite at putting paid to Welsh hopes that their 'Once and Future King' could return. We even see such attempts at using such instrumental narratives in the fairy tales that have become embedded in British culture, such as that of *Jack the Giant Killer*, where the tale's hero, Jack, is sent 'to Wales to deal with a troublesome giant there. Moreover, Jack's over-sized Welsh adversary is known for his deviousness and stupidity – both supposed characteristics of the Welsh stressed in popular folklore such as nursery rhymes right into the nineteenth century' (Croft *et al.* 2008: 298).

It makes an interesting comparison to consider the way these historic narratives were created instrumentally by the English elite not only to mobilise their subjects to engage with the brand of the new England and its instrumentally constructed mythologies and symbols particularly against warring invaders such as the Danes, and its troublesome Welsh neighbours, with the power of some of more recent narratives, such as the anecdotes underpinning Enoch Powell's 'Rivers of Blood' speech (Powell 1968). Such a comparison highlights the point that negative stories, especially those that fit prejudices, are often deemed to be stronger and more powerful than positive ones.

The Glastonbury myths also had an element of the 'bad' story, mobilising the prejudices of the English court against the Celtic 'others', and which underpinned the creation of the brand of the nation-state of England so much that many of these myths remain embedded in English culture today, and their symbols remain the focus of much merchandise targeted at the cultural tourist.

Authenticity further becomes an issue when considering the political drivers to conserve cultural traditions once they have become embedded within a society. Arantes (2007) believes that globalisation underpins the political imperative to preserve cultural traditions not only to gain the benefits of differentiating one place from another, but also to preserve heritage for future generations. While attempts are made by social policy makers to protect and enhance the cultural heritage of a place (Arantes 2007), as Peñaloza (1998: 347) points out, it is the 'commercialization and privatization of culture' that causes concern to cultural theorists. Yet when considering whether or not authenticity indeed matters to cultural tourists, Mikunda (2004: 10) believes that staged spectacles will be of value because 'those who did not experience these past events themselves can have them conveyed by means of [staged] visible traces of the past', even when these spectacles are based on fakelore or simulated heritage. In many respects, fakelore can be seen to confuse attempts at identifying the essence of the place brand.

Authenticity can also be overlooked when attempts are made to re-position a place for a new, contemporary audience, as, for example, the city of Hull in the UK. In the 1960s Hull was 'Britain's premier fishing port' (Atkinson *et al.* 2002: 26), but its maritime heritage had 'all but been overlooked in the creation of its new post-industrial urban identity' (Skinner 2008: 918). A base in authenticity can also lead to benefits, as explained by Bennison *et al.* (2007: 629), who note, when discussing a town's historic 'quarters', 'the greater the authentic character and sense of place, the more likely it is that there will be greater effort expended in their preservation and revitalisation'.

When based in some level of authenticity, tourist motivations can also be questioned when considering the rise, for example, of niche activity such as 'slum tourism', where in India such tourism rose dramatically following the release of the film *Slumdog Millionaire* (Ma 2010). Yet, as Peñaloza (1998) also points out, it is such non-market forms of cultural spectacle that make researching aspects of cultural production so problematic to marketing theorists.

In conclusion, this exploration of territory, culture, nationalism and the politics of place leads to questions concerning who or what is driving the marketing of heritage; understanding what consumers want from the cultural tourism experience and indeed what it is they are consuming; what stories and whose stories are being told; whether these stories and other elements comprising the essence of the place brand are authentic or inauthentic; and, finally, whether or not this indeed matters and, if so, to which groups of a place's stakeholders.

Some answers to these questions can be found in a critical consideration of the way culture evolves within any given society, whether primordially or instrumentally, as outlined by Biswas (2002), and whether or not the heritage that is being marketed is indeed based in fact or a romanticised version of the past that may never have existed. When based on a wish to view a place 'warts and all', such as with the recent growth of slum tourism, this can be seen to be just as 'exploitative … and imperialistic' (Ma 2010: 4) as those cultural tourists' consumption of the symbols and spectacles originating in historical elites' attempts at dominating subordinate populations to their sovereignty.

# References

Arantes, A.A. (2007) 'Diversity, Heritage and Cultural Politics', *Theory Culture and Society* 24: 290–96.

Atkinson, D., Cooke, S. and Spooner, D. (2002) 'Tales from the Riverbank: Place Marketing and Maritime Heritages', *International Journal of Heritage Studies* 8(1): 25–40.

Atkinson Wells, P. (1994) 'Marketing of Tradition: A New Approach', in Brewer, T. (ed.) *The Marketing of Tradition: Perspectives on Folklore, Tourism and the Heritage Industry*, Chippenham: Antony Rowe Ltd.

Bennison, D., Warnaby, G. and Medway, D. (2007) 'The Role of Quarters in Large City Centres: A Mancunian Case Study', *International Journal of Retail and Distribution Management* 35: 626–38.

Biswas, S. (2002) 'W(h)ither the Nation-state? National and State Identity in the Face of Fragmentation and Globalization', *Global Society* 16: 175–98.

Brewer, T. (ed.) (1994) *The Marketing of Tradition: Perspectives on Folklore, Tourism and the Heritage Industry*, Chippenham: Antony Rowe Ltd.

Brighenti, A.M. (2010) 'On Territorology: Towards a General Science of Territory', *Theory, Culture and Society* 27(1): 52–72.

Carley, James P. (ed.) (2001) *Glastonbury Abbey and the Arthurian Tradition*, Cambridge: D.S. Brewer.

Cobban, A. (1969) *The Nation State and Self-Determination*, London: Fontana.

Croft, R., Hartland, T. and Skinner, H. (2008) 'And *Did* Those Feet? Getting Medieval England On-message', *Journal of Communication Management* 12(4): 294–304.

Goulding, C. (2000) 'The Commodification of the Past, Postmodern Pastiche, and the Search for Authentic Experiences at Contemporary Heritage Attractions', *European Journal of Marketing* 34(7): 835–53.

Kavaratzis, M. and Ashworth, G. (2008) 'Place Marketing: How Did We Get Here and Where Are We Going?' *Journal of Place Management and Development* 1: 150–65.

Ma, B. (2010) 'A Trip into the Controversy: A Study of Slum Tourism Travel Motivations', *2009–2010 Penn Humanities Forum on Connections*, repository.upenn.edu/uhf_2010/12 (accessed 28 December 2011).

Mikunda, C. (2004) *Brand Lands, Hot Spots and Cool Spaces: Welcome to the Third Place and the Total Marketing Experience*, London and Stirling: Kogan Page.

Peñaloza, L. (1998) 'Just Doing It: A Visual Ethnographic Study of Spectacular Consumption Behavior at Nike Town', *Consumption, Markets and Culture* 2: 337–465.

Powell, E. (1968) 'Rivers of Blood', speech given at the Annual General Meeting, West Midlands Conservative Political Centre.

Simmel, G. (2007) 'The Philosophy of Landscape', *Theory Culture and Society* 24: 20–29.

Skinner, H. (2008) 'The Emergence and Development of Place Marketing's Confused Identity', *Journal of Marketing Management* 24(9/10): 915–28.

——(2011) 'In Search of the *genius loci* – The Essence of a Place Brand', *Marketing Review* 11(3): 281–92.

Skinner, H. and Kubacki, K. (2007) 'Unravelling the Complex Relationship Between Nationhood, National and Cultural Identity, and Place Branding', *Place Branding and Public Diplomacy* 3(4): 305–16.

Wood, M. (1999) *In Search of England*, London: Penguin.

## Further reading

Ashworth, G.J. and Kavaratzis, M. (eds) (2010) *Towards Effective Place Brand Management: Branding European Cities and Regions*, Cheltenham: Edward Elgar. (Clarification of issues surrounding application of place branding.)

Bechhofer, F., McCrone, D., Kiely, R. and Stewart, R. (1999) 'Constructing National Identity: Arts and Landed Elites in Scotland', *Sociology* 33(3): 515–34. (Considers identity markers and identity rules as they relate to studies of national identity.)

Brown, S. (2001) *Marketing – The Retro Revolution*, London: Sage. (The rise of retro marketing.)

Fan, Y. (2010) 'Branding the Nation: Towards a Better Understanding', *Place Branding and Public Diplomacy* 6(2): 97–103. (Emphasises the need to shift from 'branding' the nation to nation image management.)

Geary, P.J. (2002) *The Myth of Nations: The Medieval Origins of Europe*, Princeton, NJ: Princeton University Press. (Dismantles the nationalist myths about how the nations of Europe were born.)

Lichrou, M., O'Malley, L. and Patterson, M. (2008) 'Place-product or Place Narrative(s)? Perspectives in the Marketing of Tourism Destinations', *Journal of Strategic Marketing* 16: 27–39. (Examines the role of culture and symbolic meanings in the construction and experience of place and the contested 'realities' involved in the making of a tourism destination.)

Liebich, A. (2007) 'Roma Nation? Competing Narratives of Nationhood', *Nationalism and Ethnic Politics* 13: 539–54. (Considers alternative constructions of contested nationhood.)

Maitland, R. and Ritchie, B. (eds) (2009) *City Tourism: National Capital Perspectives*, Walligford: CABI. (Investigations of tourism in national capitals.)

Tsiotsou, R. and Ratten, V. (2010) 'Future Research Directions in Tourism Marketing', *Marketing Intelligence and Planning* 28(4): 533–44. (Takes a global perspective to compare different international research directions.)

Zake, I. (2007) 'Inventing Culture and Nation: Intellectuals and Early Latvian Nationalism', *National Identities* 9: 307–29. (Investigation of the creation of national identity by intellectual elites.)

# 11

# Cultural lessons

## The case of Portuguese tourism during *Estado Novo*

*Maria Cândida Pacheco Cadavez*

This chapter discusses how during the first years of the Portuguese *Estado Novo* (1926–74) the tourism policies designed by the National Bureau of Propaganda (SPN) created two different national tourist destinations represented by contrasting cultural narratives and experiences. These parallel representations aimed at justifying and publicising the ideology of the regime and were deployed as evidence of the so-called neutrality policy adopted by António de Oliveira Salazar, the president of the Portuguese council for most of *Estado Novo*, and portrayed by António Ferro, the head of Portuguese propaganda for 16 years.

Even while the concept of cultural tourism was hardly ever mentioned by the authorised voices of *Estado Novo*, this chapter argues that whatever tourism practices were allowed and encouraged by Salazar and Ferro, they were but obvious impositions of an officially validated culture. We believe that the main purpose was to force ideological itineraries disguised as cultural and tourist ones and therefore consider they may be labelled as examples of a specific type of cultural tourism.

## Culture and tourism

Raymond Williams argued that culture was one of the most complicated words in the English language (Williams 1983: 87). The understanding of the concept of culture undertaken by tourism professionals and by committed nationalists is exactly the opposite. In fact, when used in tourism or in nationalist discourses *culture* emerges as the clearest and most obvious notion ever. Tourism promotion lives on allegedly authentic narratives supposed to represent the cultural core of destinations and visitors are promised the opportunity of enjoying and living typical and genuine cultural experiences not found anywhere else. Authentic cultural essences can help tourists choose between different destinations. On the other hand, nationalist representations are supported by arguments that are built on cultural truths that justify any national discourse and are meant to represent the very essence of the nation. Whether in tourism representations or in nationalist narratives, culture is presented and displayed as a collective drive that makes sense of and organises the way a community lives.

## The Portuguese scenario

Portugal lived under a nationalist-oriented political regime called *Estado Novo* (New State) from 1926 to 1974. Gradually, from 1928 and right through to the end of the 1960s, Salazar became and remained the face and the head of a regime, which insisted on repeating and reproducing the uniqueness of the nation reflected in a rare and singular (popular) culture.

As happened with similar political paradigms at the time, propaganda mechanisms were a vital instrument for attracting and motivating followers. In 1933 António Ferro, the intellectual who had interviewed Salazar so that the 'Nation' would know who the politician was, was appointed director of the SPN, and many of what are nowadays considered as 'typical Portuguese traditions' were created by this man who always considered tourism a source of poetry and wealth. Six years later, in 1939, the SPN was assigned a new area of intervention: tourism. Henceforth Ferro's monitored tourism actions were of an undeniable importance to implementing and reinforcing narratives that would validate the nation proposed by Salazar.

## The meaning of culture and tourism for *Estado Novo*

As a writer, poet and journalist, António Ferro was a so-called 'man of culture' and expounded much about the concept while in charge of the SPN and the SNI (Board for Information, Popular Culture and Tourism) after 1944. The notion of culture was very much elaborated upon by a regime that considered 'popular culture' as the display of the most authentic and genuine essence of the nation. Non-urban culture was then highlighted and promoted by the regime as a signifier of the pure ancestry of the Portuguese nation. In fact, tourism narratives and representations would emphasise this to the point where even in cities there was a strange need to build semi-detached houses with small front gardens that would somehow reproduce the rural atmosphere of the real nation. History, particularly events related to the birth of Portugal, the discoveries and independence from Spain, were also favourite subjects frequently put forward as evidence of the national essence.

The regime constantly evoked a political neutrality, which enabled the country to stay out of the Second World War. When expanding on this, Ferro would speak about Portugal as the natural sanatorium where other European peoples would relax and heal from the conflicts going on elsewhere. In one of his famous dramatic and eloquent speeches, Ferro suggested that young, rural girls welcome tourists upon their arrival by train. These women would be wearing traditional costumes and their participation was designed to represent a first and clear introduction to the nation and its culture.

Not only António Ferro, but also several other authorised voices of *Estado Novo*, for example the delegates to the First National Tourism Congress in 1936, referred to tourism activities as a precious propaganda tool. It was believed that tourism would help the outside world understand the ideology implemented by Salazar and grasp the peculiarities of a regime engaged in protecting its nationals from all danger and falsehood.

## The importance of tourism for *Estado Novo*

Tourism was of particular interest to the Salazar regime. The National Union, the only authorised political party at the time, held its first major meeting in 1934 with the revalidation of the *Estado Novo* ideology as a major topic on its agenda, specifically through the national and public acknowledgement of its leader. Nevertheless, one cannot help but notice how tourism in Portugal encroached into the debates. In fact, seven presentations commented on the importance of this growing activity as an obvious result of the different political paradigm implemented by Salazar, which was able to maintain the social peace and tranquillity that would encourage tourism to bloom. The fact that tourism practices were a good tool to remind both nationals and foreigners of the past history of the nation, as well as a very good propaganda vehicle, was also praised. Some participants expanded on the need to improve tourism-related infrastructures or to better train all the professionals involved in this activity. Other speakers preferred to point out foreign examples of dealing with the industry, stressing that the Spanish or Italian national tourism organisations would be perfect role models for Portugal to adopt should the nation wish to develop the sector in a clever and beneficial way.

In the 1930s the Portuguese nationalist-oriented regime welcomed a meeting of the Alliance International de Tourisme and promoted the First National Tourism Congress that took place in 1936 and gathered 180 delegates in Lisbon. Never before had the country witnessed the meeting of so many delegates at a single tourism congress. In attendance were the chairs of regional tourist boards and city council delegates in charge of tourism policies. The organising and the honour committees included important *Estado Novo* characters, such as President of the Republic Óscar Carmona, and of course President of the Portuguese Council Salazar. The five-day meeting was widely covered by the press and broadcast by the national radio station, which had been very keen on commenting about the summit immediately after its first announcement one year previously. There were interviews with the most important members of the organising and honour committees, regular updates about the ever increasing number of delegates registered to attend and the subjects they would be presenting, as well as recurrent articles about tourism as an issue certainly representing a national interest. It was almost impossible to ignore the summit, the programme of which included one-day tours to Costa do Sol (sunny coast) and Sintra and a final dinner party at the most luxurious hotel in Estoril, the Palace Hotel.

When considering all the papers presented at the First National Tourism Congress, one notices many similarities with the presentations to the First Congress of the National Union. There comes a point when it is rather difficult to understand whether the speaker was elaborating a position on tourism in Portugal and its priorities, or instead commenting on the benefits of Salazar's ideology and his *Estado Novo*. Most speeches followed the same structure: first, they would begin by acknowledging how appropriate the timing of the congress was as a result of Salazar's intelligent policies and by discussing issues such as the characteristics of the Portuguese race, the glorious history of navigators and colonisers and how they all were reflected in traditions that urgently should be recovered and promoted; second, delegates would comment on tourism activities or destinations and present plans or suggestions for improving them; then the majority of speakers concluded with further praise of President of the Portuguese Council António de Oliveira Salazar, and his fatherly efforts to protect the country.

## Portugal, two different (cultural) destinations

The aforementioned meetings clearly emphasised how important national culture was for publicising the nation and how tourism was a suitable means of achieving this. However, it is important to understand how the regime dealt with this in two completely diverse ways, depending on the target it wanted to reach and on the narrative to be conveyed. These two different paradigms were even more noticeable when it came to the tourism section, which proved a naive pathway for promoting both narratives.

When the target was the Portuguese masses, the official tourism narratives would emphasise the rural and humble features of the country as something endemic and of which everyone had but to feel proud. The limited range targeting Portuguese tourists represented the 'medium-type' of tourism described by Álvaro Viana de Lemos in the First National Tourism Congress when stating that the most appropriate way for lower-income and larger groups would be simple and modest practices as they would create positive tourist routines and also educate the nation (Lemos 1936: 118).

This statement was in accordance with the purposes of an organisation founded one year earlier with the goal of most suitably organising the free time activities of the lower classes. In fact, the 1935 National Foundation for Joy at Work (FNAT) provides clear evidence that *Estado Novo* wanted to take particular care of the population when they were not working. Its main goal was to cater for healthy and cultural activities and was clearly inspired by the German *Kraft durch Freude* and the Italian *Opera Nazionale Dopolavoro* in its attempt to avoid, or at least to control, the 'dangerous' outcomes of unmonitored popular gatherings. FNAT was known both for its summer camps and for organising tourist tours and weekend excursions to places held up as representative of popular and national culture, such as Guimarães, symbolising the birth of the nation. Some other activities were strongly promoted by FNAT as they were deemed important displays of the Portuguese essence. These included watching groups of young, rural dancers wearing 'characteristic' outfits, visiting exhibitions and showing movies as a disguised strategy to remind nationals of the meaning of nationality and to insert them into a context of clearly rooted ideology. Symbolic historical dates, such as 1140 (founding of the nation) and 1640 (independence from Spain), and locations such as Guimarães and Batalha (where a monastery commemorated the defeat of Spanish troops), were favourite themes for FNAT-organised leisure activities.

At least during the first years of the regime, there was another tourism destination that was not, however, a destination for Portuguese visitors. Apart from being an inviting location for different types of refugees during the Second World War, the Costa do Sol, a coastal area including parts of the regions of Lisbon, Oeiras, Estoril and Cascais, was the cosmopolitan site hosting royal families and spies as well as those able to afford sophisticated vacations in a safe location which was later labelled the Portuguese Riviera. Most nationals would not even consider visiting the place where more modern social behaviours brought in by foreigners had become accepted. The Salazar regime acknowledged the differences that existed here and insisted on the need to improve hotel services and infrastructures so as to attract more international visitors to a place described by Ferro (1949: 54) as the sanatorium of a sick Europe. Casinos, hotels and outdoor activities constituted the daily routine of international visitors to the Costa do Sol, which we believe helped Salazar convey and stress the image the regime wanted to publicise of a neutral country. We would also argue that the tourists were aware of the difference they were experiencing and the final image they would build of the country would include this gap between the Costa do Sol and the humble destinations and activities available to nationals.

We believe that these two different tourism destinations were part of the same strategy designed to teach the Portuguese population about past glorious experiences as well as a way to convince them of the privilege of living in a humble but honest and safe place. On the other hand, foreigners would grasp the essence of the Portuguese nation by observing its rural, humble features from afar while themselves embodying clear evidence of a neutral country willing to welcome and host other guests, whose usual social patterns were allowed. At the end of the day both groups were being taught the lessons of Salazar's ideology of the nation.

## Conclusion

Tourism representations and experiences seemed a naive and hidden conveyor of validators for the nationalist regime of Salazar. Without using the expression 'cultural tourism', Portuguese tourism at the time was a vehicle for exhibiting the culture that justified the nation. While looking for stereotyped and essential features identified as characterising this particular tourism (desti)nation, visitors would thus acknowledge and validate the *nationalist* narratives prepared for them.

The guidelines making up the different tourism narratives scripted by António Ferro deployed the interests that tourists have in cultural and national experiences deemed representative of the essence of a destination. The difference between a destination for nationals and another for foreigners is evidence that tourism was a preferential tool for teaching cultural (or should we say political?) lessons. The first group would learn never to forget their humbleness and rurality while simultaneously serving to populate the stage that foreigners would observe from a distance. As for the latter group, we believe that by allowing and welcoming them, the Portuguese *Estado Novo* was proving its neutrality to the world while at the same time hiring conveyors for its propaganda.

Tourism representations are apparently a useful and at first sight a naive arena for easily fostering nationalist- and totalitarian-oriented ideologies, which in turn recalls David Lowenthal when stating that 'tourism seems indeed a privileged arena for celebrating great powers' (Lowenthal 1996: 47).

## References

Ferro, A. (1949) *Turismo, fonte de riqueza e de poesia. Política do Espírito*, Lisbon: Edições SNI.

Lemos, A. (1936) 'Excursionismo Popular – Turismo Médio', *I Congresso Nacional de Turismo*, Lisbon: Relatório do I Congresso Nacional de Turismo.

Lowenthal, D. (1996) 'Identity, Heritage, and History', in Gillis, J. (ed.) *Commemorations: The Politics of National Identity*, Princeton, NJ: Princeton University Press, 41–57.

Williams, R. (1983) *Key Words: A Vocabulary of Culture and Society*, London: Fontana.

## Further reading

Hobsbawm, E.J. (2007) *Nations and Nationalism Since 1780. Programme, Myth, Reality*, Cambridge: Cambridge University Press. (A canonical study on nations and nationalisms.)

Hodgkin, K. and Radstone, S. (eds) (2007) *Memory, History, Nation. Contested Pasts*, New Brunswick, NJ and London: Transaction Publishers. (Several essays on national memory.)

Lasansky, D. (2004) *The Renaissance Perfected. Architecture, Spectacle, and Tourism in Fascist Italy*, Pennsylvania: Pennsylvania State University Press. (National history in fascist tourism narratives.)

Morgan, N. and Pritchard, A. (1998) *Tourism Promotion and Power. Creating Images, Creating Identities*, Chichester: John Wiley & Sons. (The cultural role of tourism imagery.)

Pack, S. (2006) *Tourism and Dictatorship. Europe's Peaceful Invasion of Franco's Spain*, New York: Palgrave Macmillan. (Tourism in Franco's Spain.)

# 12

# The establishment of national heritage tourism

## Celebrations for the 150th anniversary of the unification of Italy

*Monica Gilli*

### Introduction: the international image of Italy for tourists

Starting in the 1980s there was a marked rise in the number of museums and a significant growth in cultural tourism throughout Europe (Ginsburgh and Mairesse 1997; Prentice 2001). These trends have stimulated profound changes in cultural tourism which have also affected Italy, perhaps more than many other countries.

The international image of Italy seems to be unchanged in terms of its typical stereotype: that of a country with a culture that is unique, which is strongly anchored to universally well-known cultural assets, which are masterpieces in the history of European art. In particular, it is the testimony of the Greco-Roman era and of the Renaissance that gives Italy its tourism identity. This identity was formed during centuries of experience of the aristocratic Grand Tour and bourgeois travel in Italy (Brilli 1995, 2006; Savelli 1998). This process has had two consequences: first, the acquisition of a strong, widespread international brand which has become established without any particular communication; and second, the emergence of tourism itineraries, which made it difficult for cities in other areas to emerge on the tourism market. These are cities (such as Milan and Turin) which have little to offer in terms of that classic, renaissance and neo-classical culture which was at the heart of the aesthetic experience of the Grand Tour. The Italian educational system contributed to the creation of this classical sense of aesthetics. Just consider the lack of consideration of the Medieval and Baroque periods up to the 1980s in history of art guides, or in international tourism guides. This has been an obstacle to the creation of aesthetic appreciation and exploitation for tourism purposes of prehistoric art, art of the late antiquity, and of the Medieval and the Baroque ages (Gilli 2009b).

The situation in Italy has changed a lot in the last 30 years. First, the reassessment of entire periods of history by German historians and by the French Annales school, which influenced the teaching of history in schools. Second, museums now represent every segment of Italian history, and no longer only classical periods; third, the tremendous work undertaken by educational departments in museums, thanks to which the museum experience is a part of every school programme; and fourth, the educational departments of museums are no longer seen as a minor part of the tourism offering, but as a segment in which to invest with a view to winning over and retaining customers.

## Historical-artistic assets and cultural assets

The growth of museums in Italy has also entailed great diversification in the offering, to the extent that it is now possible to distinguish between two main categories of assets: historical-artistic assets and assets belonging to tangible and intangible culture. The historical-artistic line refers to traditional historical-artistic objects and monuments, such as museums of painting and sculpture, buildings, archaeological ruins – i.e. assets with a recognised historical or aesthetic value. The list includes universally famous assets, from St Mark's basilica in Venice to the frescoes by Giotto, the Riace bronzes to the ruins of Pompeii. These are places and works of art for which art history provided interpretation and assessment some time ago. To this traditional collection we may then add the fairly well-developed collection of contemporary art which is mainly regulated by art critics and the art market. The growth of cultural assets and museums has mainly involved contemporary art. For example, in 2010 alone Rome saw the opening of two new dedicated locations: MAXXI and MACRO. As for the art of the past, excluding the occasional archaeological find, or the attribution of authorship of a work, cultural assets have not increased, but, nonetheless, museums have increased thanks to the use of multimedia technologies, which have enabled the reconstruction of environments, even with a bare minimum of actual objects, which previously would not have been sufficient to warrant the creation of a new museum (Gilli 2009a). The second macro-category of cultural tourism is that of tangible and intangible culture – in other words objects that have no aesthetic value, but bear witness to everyday life (in the home, at work, etc.), both tangibly (household objects, agricultural equipment, etc.) and intangibly (songs, dances, etc.). Historically in Italy, interest in this segment of culture was the response of anthropologists and museum experts in the mid-1970s, to the risk of rural society falling into oblivion as it became increasingly urbanised and almost indistinguishable from the city (Cavalcanti 1984). Correspondingly numerous museums of rural culture came into being. In a later period (the mid-1990s) eco-museums were created which broadened the reference framework from 'peasant' culture to any culture that was rooted in the local territory, whether that was urban, rural, coastal, or alpine (Maggi and Falletti 2000). Eco-museums are often an expression of the local economy and reveal the community's socioeconomic and cultural changes. Even if a decision-making role is attributable to regional lawmakers, the role of the community involves several levels, so we can state that without the community there cannot be an eco-museum: the local community seems essential for establishment of the eco-museum, to define its contents, for its management, and also represents its most loyal visitors. In major cities, eco-museums, which represent the local area, provide not only a memory bank, but also act as a focal point for the various multicultural demands and facilitate the acceptance of urban regeneration programmes.

## A different point of view: heritage tourism

A debate that lasted years has now clarified that cultural tourism and heritage tourism are not the same thing, even if they share the same assets (historical, artistic and cultural). Heritage tourism does not in fact define new types of artistic and cultural assets, but rather a different approach to the asset to be exploited in terms of tourism (Palmer 1999; Poria *et al.* 2001, 2003).

It encourages mechanisms of adhesion to or participation in communities of various types – belonging to such communities is seen as a value, and tourists consider themselves as 'heirs' (Gilli 2009a). A heritage experience, therefore, is not a cognitive, information-enhancing experience, but rather bonding and emotional, something that enhances our personal self. In this sense it can include not only the use of the aforementioned assets, but also the use of the natural environment (mountains, hills, parks, waterfalls) (Palmer 1999). Visiting a heritage site means consolidating links with a part of history that is not just generic but is part of our personal space and roots. In cultural tourism, too, the idea is to involve the tourist in an experience, and this happens thanks to the widespread use of multimedia communication. However, in heritage tourism the experience is not aimed at spurring simple participation, but rather a deep sense of belonging.

The growth of heritage tourism since the 1980s is due to many factors: local administrations are favourable to this kind of tourism since it strengthens the social cohesion of the local community, and it stimulates in the tourist a sense of respect towards the area. The perspective of heritage tourism is very much in line with that of searching out and building one's own identity, which is considered one of the levers of post-modern tourism (Dann 1996). Interest in this type of tourism is also driven by its flexibility, since underlying a process of building an identity there are processes of selection that are much more developed than in the past, which leave the person with more freedom to choose which past to belong to, and they no longer are bound only to pay homage to their own family background (Giddens 1991).

Since heritage tourism means a sense of belonging in relation to a community, there can be different types of community, at a local, national and supranational level. A typical example of supranational heritage tourism is American domestic tourism. Visits to the residences of American presidents aim to enhance the sense of belonging. The same can be said for visiting national parks which, through their grandeur, tell us of a mythical golden age. In a multiethnic America, with just a few centuries on which to found its roots, parks, which have no cultural or linguistic characterisation, are the ideal place for supranational heritage and can evoke the power and majesty of America (Battilani 2001). In France, an example of celebrating national heritage is the Festival of the Republic (14 July), and there are works of art (such as *The Raft of the Medusa* by Gericault or *Liberty Leading the People* by Delacroix) which help strengthen the nation's values. In Italy, the most common level of heritage tourism is local, in which the local community is of limited size (a town, an alpine valley, a district), perhaps reflecting the role that the local community still plays in Italy. Many rural museums and eco-museums house both cultural tourism and heritage tourism, two segments that are compatible in terms of marketing.

## Box 12.1 Case study: celebrations for the 150th anniversary of the unification of Italy

While many European nations have developed both local and national heritage tourism, in Italy national heritage tourism is at the very beginning (Richards 1996). This is tied to historical and political reasons. On the one hand, a united Italy has only 150 years of common history (1861) and the process of unification is in many ways ongoing, at a time when the validity of the very idea of the nation-state is being questioned, and given other options such as supranational (Europe) or even global groupings. 'Feeling Italian' is then made difficult by the party political disputes that accompanied the birth of the Republic (1946): historically it was the right which continued a tradition celebrating 'nationalism', which to the left smacked too much of Mussolini's nationalist-imperialist propaganda and so was unacceptable. To this we may add in Italy, too, the creation of parties such as the Northern League, which glorify sub-national identities, often with xenophobic undertones, disappointed by politics that remains centred on Rome, but also distrusting of political globalisation. The result of this process is that until a few years ago the Italian flag was considered a right-wing symbol and not an expression of national pride. If we consider all the literature on the extent to which a sense of belonging can develop social cohesion, a sense of the state and sensitivity to shared assets, the damage caused by these political disputes has been much greater than the simple failure to develop national heritage tourism. Things have changed in recent years. A crucial role was played by former President Ciampi (1999–2006). He was determined to transmit to Italians that national patriotic sentiment which derives from the feats of the Risorgimento and the Resistance, and which is clear in the national anthem by Mameli, in the flag and in the sites that have an important place in the country's history. The impact continued in following years, while the celebrations for the 150th anniversary of the unity of Italy (2011) were being prepared. These preparations were undertaken with a minimum of fanfare and without a precise programme, at least until 2010, and left individual regions with the task of organising their own tourism events. Besides the above political problems, another problem is that the locations that symbolise the construction of Italy's unity vary in terms of their contribution, as well as the fact that there have been three capitals of Italy and not just one (Turin, Florence and, finally, Rome). To give one example, this meant for Turin, which is seeking to maximise its tourism potential, the need to combine regional heritage initiatives regarding Turin as the capital of the State of Savoy and not of Italy. The media, too, have had a role in gradually grasping the importance of the event: from the national TV networks to the newspapers over the course of the year there were numerous interventions by historians, intellectuals and, finally, politicians who have gradually 'converted' to the idea of nation, above all on the crest of popular consensus which was perhaps a surprise to many, but which gained pace over the weeks. The newspaper *La Stampa* (which is based in Turin) sold a flag with the paper for only €1 and it sold out in just a few days. The celebrations for the unity of Italy started on a rainy day on 17 March 2011 and in some cities were more muted, but in others saw huge crowds. In Turin, one of the most involved as it was the former capital of Italy the celebrations were not just an urban phenomenon but spread everywhere, as could be seen from the numerous flags hanging from balconies in the countryside and in mountain villages. Each of them celebrated, through exhibitions, guided itineraries, processions and parades, the values of the Risorgimento and the Resistance. Even if the impact of this event still has to be assessed, it cannot be denied that it has had a significance that has gone beyond a mere formality and is one of profound feeling. This 'feeling Italian' was also facilitated by the detachment that the Italians have in regard to their political leaders and to the Italian politics that is bringing the country to its knees. The progressively diminishing credibility of Italy's image on the international scene has helped to drive a reaction that is not party political but a question of identity, as if to say that Italy is different from the image presented in the international media, and to promote the 150th anniversary of the unification of Italy as an opportunity to show it.

## Conclusions

Italy has a long-standing tradition in cultural tourism going back to the time of the Grand Tour. This competitive advantage, however, has made it difficult to renew or transform its international tourism image. Cultural tourism in Italy today is very different from the past, open to contemporary art, multimedia, and tangible and intangible culture. In Italy, too, heritage tourism is spreading, above all locally, thanks to the creation of rural museums and eco-museums destined to strengthen the values of local identity and a sense of belonging. For important historical and political reasons, national heritage tourism in Italy is almost non-existent. The celebrations for the 150th anniversary are an important milestone for the construction of tourism routes to celebrate the values of the country. The advantages of developing this type of tourism are evident, and go beyond tourism itself: an increase in the sense of the state, greater awareness of the role of citizens, defence of the values of the Constitution, greater social cohesion – something that is particularly important at a time when Italy is increasingly becoming a destination for migrants and must develop a more structured response to the problem of welcoming and integrating them. We believe that the development of national heritage tourism could make a significant contribution in this sense.

## Acknowledgement

Monica Gilli gratefully acknowledges the financial support from the Regione Lombardia, with the European Social Fund (ESF), for her research activity.

## References

Battilani, P. (2001) *Vacanze di pochi, vacanze di tutti. L'evoluzione del turismo europeo*, Bologna: Il Mulino.
Brilli, A. (1995) *Quando viaggiare era un'arte. Il romanzo del Grand Tour*, Bologna: Il Mulino.
——(2006) *Il viaggio in Italia. Storia di una grande tradizione culturale*, Bologna: Il Mulino.
Cavalcanti, O. (1984) 'I musei etno-demo-antropologici nei dibattiti e nei convegni degli ultimi due decenni', *Musei e Gallerie d'Italia* XXVIII(77): 18–28.
Dann, G.M.S. (1996) *The Language of Tourism: A Sociolinguistic Perspective*, Wallingford, UK: CABI.
Giddens, A. (1991) *Modernity and Self-identity: Self and Society in the Late Modern Age*, Cambridge: Polity Press.
Gilli, M. (2009a) *Autenticità e interpretazione nell'esperienza turistica*, Milano: FrancoAngeli.
——(2009b) 'La città come destinazione turistica *multipurpose*', in Nuvolati, G. and Piselli, F. (eds) *La città: bisogni, desideri, diritti*, I, Milano: FrancoAngeli, 133–48.
Ginsburgh, V. and Mairesse, F. (1997) 'Defining a Museum: Suggestions for an Alternative Approach', *Museum Management and Curatorship* 16(1): 15–33.
Maggi, M. and Falletti, V. (2000) *Gli ecomusei. Che cosa sono, che cosa possono diventare*, Torino: Allemandi.
Palmer, C. (1999) 'Tourism and the Symbols of Identity', *Tourism Management* 20: 313–21.
Poria, Y., Butler, R. and Airey, D. (2001) 'Clarifying Heritage Tourism', *Annals of Tourism Research* 28(4): 1047–49.
——(2003) 'The Core of Heritage Tourism', *Annals of Tourism Research* 30(1): 238–54.
Prentice, R. (2001) 'Experiential Cultural Tourism: Museums & the Marketing of the New Romanticism of Evoked Authenticity', *Museum Management and Curatorship* 19(1): 5–26.
Richards, G. (1996) 'Production and Consumption of European Cultural Tourism', *Annals of Tourism Research* 23(2): 261–83.
Savelli, A. (1998) *Sociologia del turismo*, Milano: FrancoAngeli.

## Further reading

Bennet, M. (1995) 'Heritage Marketing: The Role of Information Technology', *Journal of Vacation Marketing* 3: 272–80. (Relationship between marketing and heritage.)

Crang, M. (1999) 'Nation, Region and Homeland: History and Tradition in Dalarna, Sweden', *Ecumene* 6: 447–70. (Management of a heritage site.)

Lowenthal, D. (1989) 'Nostalgia Tells it Like it Wasn't', in Shaw, C. and Chase, M. (eds) *The Imagined Past: History and Nostalgia*, Manchester: Manchester University Press, 18–32. (Idealization of the past in heritage tourism.)

Moscardo, G. (1996) 'Mindful Visitors: Heritage and Tourism', *Annals of Tourism Research* 23(2): 376–97. (Role of interpretation in heritage tourism.)

Robb, J.G. (1998) 'Tourism and Legends: Archaeology of Heritage', *Annals of Tourism Research* 25(3): 579–96. (Relation between heritage tourism and authenticity.)

# 13

# Potential methods for measuring the economic impacts of cultural tourism

*Tereza Raabová, Petr Merta and Alena Tichá*

## Introduction

Cultural tourism is one of the most rapidly growing forms of tourism. Tourism is considered to be an important factor in regional and local economic development, whereas culture is often considered to be a sector that requires subsidies. This view has been countered by various analyses of the economic impact of culture, which have shown that culture is an important factor for supporting domestic and international tourism and a generator of economic growth of tourist destinations.

One of the most effective links between culture – either tangible (historical monuments, either movable or immovable), or intangible (art, festivals, concerts, exhibitions, theatre plays, etc.) – and economic benefit is the money that tourists spend on entrance fees, accommodation, boarding, transport, etc. As cultural facilities are usually subsidised by the state or municipalities, it is important to measure the rate of return of such financial support.

Tourism influences the whole community and its costs and benefits affect everyone in the destination. Studies focused on economic impacts provide quantified estimates of these relationships and they help us to understand the influence of tourism on regions. Quantification of tourism economic impacts plays an important role in planning and developing local, regional or national economies.

Although a study of economic impacts can be made for any destination, institution or activity, it is particularly popular among cultural organisations. Above all, impact studies help to enhance the importance of the particular organisation or field of culture in the eyes of politicians, potential sponsors and the general public. Municipalities or regions also often want to know the economic importance of cultural activities in their area. Economic impact studies therefore are often used to support political decisions in the fields of tourism and culture development.

Economic impacts are often quantified by means of the following economic indicators:

- turnover;
- gross value added, or gross domestic product (GDP);
- tax incomes; and
- improvement of balance of payments (in the case of international tourism).

The social or socioeconomic indicators that are influenced by cultural tourism and that are measurable are the following:

- employment rate (job creation); and
- employees' incomes.

## Why should we measure economic impacts and benefits?

The study of economic impacts can be beneficial not only for cultural organisations themselves, but also for their sponsors, grant-giving bodies or subsidy providers.

The managers of cultural organisations can use impact studies for an evaluation of their organisations' economic importance and they can also use it as an argument for requesting financial support. Donors nowadays are more likely to support organisations that can persuade them of their efficiency and ability to bring new capital to the region.

Funding organisations can use these studies in decision making. If all major organisations or at least organisations that are asking for subsidies had their studies of economic impacts elaborated it would have simplified the subsidy requests evaluation and therefore it would be one of the criteria in subsidy policies. Of course, though, economic success or efficiency cannot be the only criteria in subsidy policies for cultural projects. The most important are immanent and social values of culture, which are impossible or hard to quantify.

Another advantage of such studies is their use by state and local authorities in developing strategies for tourism and culture. For example, visitor surveys can yield important information about visitor spending, length of stay, etc. This information can be used for economic predictions in connection with decision making but also for planning of regional tourism development (Raabová 2010).

## Methods of measuring economic impacts and benefits

Various methods of economic analysis can be used to measure the economic impacts and benefits of projects and economic activities. Some of them are already widely used (these are mostly based on commonly used economic analysis), while others are being developed for potential application in both private and public sectors, considering not only pure economic results, but also non-economic values of culture for society.

In this chapter, we introduce a few commonly used methods of project evaluation that we consider to be appropriate for the field of cultural tourism. Each of the methods is designed for a particular purpose; each has a different form and structure of input and output data. Some of the methods are more suitable for use before the realisation of a project (ex-ante) and the others can be used after the project has been finished (ex-post).

(A) *Ex-ante methods*: used mostly for investment decision making, usually before the event or culture activity starts (music festival, theatre festival, reconstruction of historical sites, etc.).
- Cost-utility methods:
  - cost–benefit analysis (CBA)
  - cost-minimisation analysis (CMA)
  - cost-effectiveness analysis (CEA)
  - cost-utility analysis (CUA)
- multicriteria analysis (MCA)
- value analysis (VA)

(B) *Ex-post methods*: evaluation tools used during and after the realisation of the project. They are appropriate for the evaluation of the project's success and its economic return on investment.
- input-output analysis (including input-output multipliers)
- common comparative method
- economic benefits framework

Of the methods listed, cost–benefit analysis and input-output analysis are the most common methods, so we will place special emphasis on those methods in the following sections.

## Cost–benefit analysis (CBA)

CBA is often used for public-sector project evaluation and has been popular as a tool to assist public decision making, not in terms of producing the ideal project but simply by proposing the optimum solution for the community out of the spectrum of possibilities (Dupuis 1985).

To analyse a specific project, we examine the expenditure of resources (costs) now and consequent benefits secured both now and in the future. CBA usually applies the following terminology:

- *Costs* are a volume of resources we have to invest to produce demanded goods or services. They can be regarded as the capital costs of the project (Throsby 2001).
- *Utility* is total satisfaction due to the consumption of goods and services.
- *Benefit* is defined as a monetary appraisal of utility. It comprises collective (both consumers' and producers') surpluses.

The major part of the cost–benefit analysis relates to the assessment of benefits. The benefits are not usually just financial and are not always easy to quantify. Therefore, beside the standard (narrowed) CBA, an 'extended CBA' was developed. The narrowed CBA analyses just the direct costs and benefits of an investment. The extended CBA is usually called 'the analysis of social costs and social benefits' and it contains not only financial, but also non-monetary considerations and items that are not easily measurable in monetary terms.

The project benefits may be divided into use values and non-use values, some authors (e.g. Throsby 2001) also cite externalities. The *use values* include direct benefits, which can be quantified, for example as entrance fee revenues. The *non-use values* can be of three types:

- Existence value: people may regard the existence of a cultural project or asset to be of value to themselves or to the community, even if they do not benefit from it themselves.
- Option value: people may wish to maintain the option that some day they or their children may have the possibility of benefiting from the cultural asset or project.
- Bequest value: people may gain benefit from the project through the knowledge that the cultural asset will be passed on to future generations.

The externalities arising from the project are positive or negative spillovers that affect other economic agents. They are not easily quantifiable and must be treated with some caution (see Throsby 2001: 79).

The most difficult and least objective part of cost–benefit evaluation is the process of quantification of the non-monetary costs and benefits. There are three methods for the direct valuation of a cost or benefit:

- the value may be based on that of an alternative good or service available on the market;
- it may be deduced from the value of the complementary private good or service, which enables the intensity of demand for the public good to be measured in terms of the amount of the cash costs relating to its consumption; or
- it may be inferred from that of an associated product that exists on the market (Dupuis 1985).

All the mentioned benefits should be considered for a longer period, usually several years. The magnitude of these benefits can be seen as rate of return on the initial investment (costs). To be able to compare the costs and all benefits arising over several years, we need to discount the future benefits (and costs) to a present valuation, so that it can be aggregated in terms of present monetary values. The difference between the present value of benefits and present value of costs is defined as net present value (NPV):

$$NPV = B - C$$

where $B$ is present value of benefits (in monetary units), and $C$ is present value of costs (in monetary units).

In addition to the calculation of the NPV, we can also use the aspect of efficiency from invested monetary unit. This is expressed by a following formula:

$$B/C \geq 1$$

The main advantage of a cost–benefit analysis is that the use of this method is actually very clear; it enables us to estimate some of the benefits in advance (e.g. benefits of a festival taking place in a particular region), including various benefits in a form of visitor arrivals, improvement of cultural life, indirect advertising of the particular region or creation of new job positions. When compared with the expected costs of the investment, this analysis provides to organisers and investors a picture of the possible return rate of their investment.

The main disadvantage is that the quantification of the non-monetary costs and benefits is always subject to individual approaches of evaluators and can be manipulated. The discount rate is also a subject of discussion, as this can have significant influence on the results.

## Input-output analysis

Input-output analysis is considered as the most accurate and the most sophisticated among the methods for calculation of economic impacts of an institution, activity or a project (Stynes 1997). This analysis is based on tables of use and supply that are published by the statistical office of the particular country. The input-output model represents the interdependences between different branches of national economy and can serve as a tool to calculate input-output multipliers (see Figure 13.1). With these multipliers, we can quantify direct, indirect and even induced impacts of a new investment and its influence on regional economic indexes (turnover, gross added value, employment rate, employees' incomes or firms' profits). This method can quantify economic impacts of a project including all the multiplied effects coming from the whole supply chain.

Although there are various definitions of the direct and indirect impacts, the majority of the authors (e.g. Stynes et al. 2000; Australian Government 2001) use the following terminology:

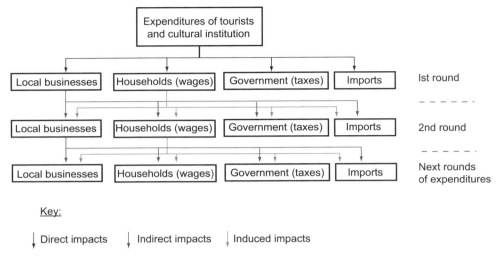

*Figure 13.1* Direct, indirect and induced impacts
Source: (Raabová 2011)

- Direct effects: the changes in the economy that are caused by direct expenses of a cultural organisation or their visitors (e.g. production growth of the direct suppliers of products and services demanded by visitors or the organisation itself).
- Indirect effects: the changes in the economy that are caused by subsequent suppliers' production in the consequence of further related economic activity in an analysed region (direct suppliers demand goods and services from their sub-suppliers and these sub-suppliers demand other goods and services from their own sub-suppliers), so this can be understood as the changes that involve all other production activities brought up by relations between direct suppliers and their subcontractors in the local economy.
- Induced effects: the changes in economic activity that are caused by employees of all involved organisations and their spending of wages earned due to a particular cultural event.

Many studies and models of economic impacts do not involve induced effects in the calculation of the total effect on the local economy, in order to maintain conservative results and to avoid overestimation of the total impacts.

## The calculation process

The required input data for input–output analysis can be divided into two streams (only one can be considered if needed):

1 Data on the volume and structure of expenses that visitors incur during their visits (the best source is a visitor survey running during the project).
2 Data on the volume and structure of expenses of the organisation itself, the amount of employees and total attendance (usually taken from internal data of the institution).

For all input data we need to know how much money flowed to which industries in the economy (hotels, restaurants, transport, etc.). After that, we need to adjust the input data and prepare it for the multiplier process. This means we deduct value-added tax (VAT), payments for imported goods (money going out of the economy) and retail margins (they must be linked with retail industry). Then the adjusted data are linked to multipliers of production, GDP, employment rate or employee compensation for individual industries. Once all the data are multiplied, we can sum the results of all industries for each indicator (see Figure 13.2).

The most difficult part of the process is the calculation of multipliers for each industry. For this phase it is necessary to have an up-to-date symmetrical input-output table capturing monetary flows between all industries in an economy. Such a table is regularly published by the statistical office of each country. Then we need to calculate a Leontief inverse matrix:

$$L = (I - A)^{-1}$$

where $I$ = identity matrix, and $A$ = input-output table matrix.

Then we form the column totals of the $L$ and to get output multipliers for each column, i.e. each industry. To calculate multipliers for other indicators (gross value added, compensation of employees, operating surplus of companies, etc.), we need to multiply a proper row of the normalised input-output table and the Leontief inverse.

Because of this difficulty, many economic impact studies are not based on proper input-output multipliers calculated for each industry, but on a unique guessed or estimated multiplier, usually used as a production multiplier. However, such calculated impact has no special significance for the interpretation (and often is left without any explanation of what the number means). In fact, the number obtained by simple multiplication of expenditures could be interpreted as total impact on production, which includes duplications of inputs (in case an input material goes through more supply chain rounds, the production multiplier counts it for each round again). Consequently, it is better to calculate impact on gross value added, business profits, etc., upon structured input-output multipliers. Also, every country has a different economy structure and different multipliers, so it is not appropriate to 'borrow' multipliers from another study.

The difficulty of multiplier calculations can be reduced by construction of a model, which works with built-up multipliers and is very easy to use for cultural users. The users only need to prepare input data (visitor expenditures, origin, motivation of visit, project expenditures, etc.) and the model uses all its pre-calculated multipliers to calculate economic impacts of the project and its visitors. We can find examples of such models in Canada, some of which are available online: EIMAH – Economic Impact Model for Arts and Heritage (by Canadian Heritage); TREIM – Tourism Regional Economic Impact Model (by the Ontario Ministry of Tourism, Culture and Sport).

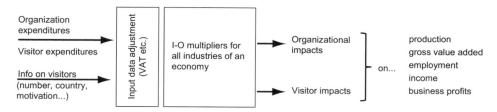

*Figure 13.2* Process of calculation of economic impact via input-output analysis

## Total impacts and net benefits

Obviously, every dollar or euro spent has some economic impact, and so each organisation has some economic impact on its suppliers, employees, etc. However, the majority of this money would be spent within the region anyway. In order for economic impacts to be 'net benefits' for the region (its economy) where the analysed cultural organisation or project is situated, they must represent a new or additional injection of funds into a defined economy. Consequently, the net benefits are generated usually from two sources:

1 Economic impacts associated with attributable spending by arts/culture patrons who reside outside the defined economy; and
2 Economic impacts associated with attributable spending by arts/culture organisations from funds originating outside the defined economy.

The advantage of this method is mainly the possibility of quantifying direct, as well as multiplied effects of the first investment. If we use multipliers calculated from official statistical input-output data of an economy, the results are based only on strict numbers and cannot be influenced by subjective estimates.

The main disadvantages of using net benefits are the volume of financial data required and the time required for calculation, which mean that these studies are usually conducted by specialised economics companies. Other disadvantages of this method are the fact that it does not compare initial costs and successive impacts, and that it does not capture non-monetary (social) costs and benefits of the project.

---

### Box 13.1 Case study: Prague Quadrennial

A number of economic impact studies for big international festivals and cultural events are based on input-output multipliers (e.g. Bregenz Festspiele 2004; Edinburgh Festivals – BOP Consulting 2011; Prague Quadrennial of performance design and space 2011).

For example, the study of IHS (Institut für Höhere Studien) on the Bregenz Festspiele in Austria in 2004 estimates that the festival budget was €20 million. It was co-financed by subsidies from the public sector. The subsidy volume was 28.5 per cent of the whole budget (€5.7 million). The tax income collected due to the festival was about €21 million, which means that each euro given by the state was paid back four times. Then the study quantifies total direct impact of the event on volume of business-sector production as approximately €167 million. The festival also creates approximately 1,150 full-time jobs.

Similarly, a new study for the Prague Quadrennial of performance design and space 2011 shows that visitors spent around CZK 164.2 million (€6.6 million) for subsidiary expenditures, such as accommodation, boarding, shopping, etc. The total expenditure of visitors at this event had an impact on production in the Czech economy of CZK 245.7 million (€9.8 million) and employees of all hotels, restaurants, shops and their suppliers earned gross wages amounting to CZK 36.6 million (€1.5 million) (see Table 13.1).

In addition, the expenditures of the event organiser reached about CZK 68 million (€2.7 million), a significant part of which was covered by foreign grants and contributions. The total economic impact of the event and its visitors together amounted to CZK 310.9 million (€12.44 million) in increased gross added value and around CZK 83.5 million (€3.34 million) in GDP. Expenditures by the organiser and visitors generated 166.7 whole-year full-time job positions. The Czech state profited from around CZK 53.6 million (€2.14 million) paid in taxes and social and health insurance (Raabová 2011).

*Table 13.1* Example of calculations of economic impacts of Prague Quadrennial 2011

| | A | B | C = A – B | D | E = C × D | F | G = C × F |
|---|---|---|---|---|---|---|---|
| Visitor expenditures to industries | Attributed expenditures | VAT, other taxes, etc. | Adjusted expenditures | Output multiplier | Total output impact | Income multiplier | Total income impact |
| restaurants | €1,387,855 | €225,362 | €1,162,493 | 2.005 | €2,330,799 | 0.324 | €376,648 |
| accommodation | €5,375 | €480 | €4,895 | 1.891 | €9,256 | 0.291 | €1,424 |
| local transport | €40,091 | €6,682 | €33,409 | 2.029 | €67,787 | 0.271 | €9,054 |
| other industries | – | – | – | – | – | – | – |
| Total visitor impact | €6,576,671 | €761,419 | €5,746,724 | | €9,826,331 | | €1,465,724 |

## Comparison of cost–benefit analysis and input-output analysis

Both cost–benefit analysis and input–output analysis can be used for economic evaluation of a cultural project. However, each method is suitable in different cases. Economic impact based on input–output analysis refers to the tracking and measurement of money as it changes hands within a given geographic area. Net benefit in cost–benefit analysis refers to a comparison of benefits and costs (or the social benefits and social costs) to see if the former more than offset the latter. Impact is a concept related to the absolute size of monetary spending, while net benefit is concerned with the relative size of components of that spending, as well as other non-monetary considerations (King 2003).

*Table 13.2* Cost–benefit analysis versus input-output analysis

| Cost–benefit analysis | Input-output analysis |
|---|---|
| better for long-term evaluation | better for annual evaluation ex-post |
| usually used before starting a project (ex-ante) | usually used for existing projects (ex-post) |
| suitable for decision making of investment | suitable for advocacy of grants and contributions |
| compares costs and benefits over several years | expresses only benefits (flow of money spent) |
| may include non-monetary (social) aspects | stays just on statistical numbers |
| easier, but more suggestible | more demanding calculation of multipliers |
| risk of misuse when quantifying social aspects | risk of misuse if wrong (borrowed or guessed) multipliers applied |

## Socioeconomic benefits framework

The economic benefits framework was developed in Canada (Whiting 1999), with the aim of involving not only the strict economic values but also other values in the evaluation of cultural organisations. So the framework tries to broaden the results of brief input-output analysis, to encompass also some features of cost–benefit analysis and other methods.

The Canadian generalised framework of socioeconomic benefits provides a logical method of describing the benefits derived from the culture sector in a 'supportive fashion'. The framework applies current approaches to economic valuation, including the total economic value approach. This concept attempts to illustrate and quantify the economic values derived from a particular activity, area or institution. It comprises the use value, as well as the non-use value of the institution/activity, including all the indirect benefits such as the option value, bequest value and existence value (Whiting 2001).

The framework is based on two fundamental principles: first, there are three categories of beneficiaries of the various programmes and products of culture/heritage institutions; and second, the value of the benefits within these benefit categories differs from different perspectives of valuation (or different account registers).

*Table 13.3* Total economic benefits framework

*Generalized framework of total benefits of cultural tourism*

| *Type of benefit:* | | |
| --- | --- | --- |
| Personal | Commercial | Social |
| *Definition:* | | |
| Benefits accruing to stakeholders (tourists, residents) | Benefits from the net redistribution of commercial activity from one area to another | Indivisible social benefits |
| *Benefit components:* | | |
| Use values:<br>• Direct use<br>• Indirect use<br>• Future use<br><br>Non-use values:<br>• Option value<br>• Existence value<br>• Bequest value | Impacts from stakeholder and producer spending on management and development e.g. increased place attractiveness, increased organisational capacity, 'eventfulness', etc. | Health effects<br>Education benefits<br>International responsibilities and agreements (e.g. UNESCO)<br>External contributions<br>Business location decisions<br>Scientific benefits (e.g. conservation research)<br>Identity – place image and attachment<br>Community cohesion<br>Quality of life |

Source: (After Whiting 2001)

## Conclusion

The methods mentioned above can help to express economic impacts of cultural activities or heritage sites in particular countries or regions. The two most common methods are cost–benefit analysis and input-output analysis. The third focused method is the Canadian economic benefit framework, which tries to cover most benefits of both cost–benefit and input-output analysis.

## Acknowledgement

This chapter was written under the Czech Mapping of Cultural and Creative Industries (DF11P01OVV031) project.

## References

Australian Government (2001) *Multipliers for Culture-Related Industries*, Canberra: Australian Government – Department of Communication, IT and the Arts.

BOP Consulting (2011) *Edinburgh Festivals Impact Study*, London: BOP Consulting.

Bregenz Festspiele (2004) *Kunstschöpfungist Wertschöpfung*, Vienna: Institut für Höhere Studien (IHS).

Dupuis, X. (1985) *Applications and Limitations of Cost-benefit Analysis as Applied to Cultural Development*, Paris: UNESCO, CC-88/WS/33.

Government of Canada, Department of Canadian Heritage (2008) *Economic Impact Model for Arts and Heritage*, www.pro.rcip-chin.gc.ca/sommaire-summary/mieap-eimah-eng.jsp (accessed 27 March 2012).

Heilbrun, J. and Gray, C.M. (2001) *The Economics of Art and Culture*, second edn, New York: Cambridge University Press.

Hollands, R. (2007) *Prague Fringe Festival Audience Survey Report*, Newcastle: University of Newcastle.

King, E.M. (2003) *Accounting for Culture: A Social Cost-Benefit Analysis of the Stan Rogers Folk Festival*, Halifax, Nova Scotia: Dalhousie University.

Leontief, W. (1951) 'Input-Output Economics', *Scientific American* 4: 15–21.

Merta, P. and Tichá, A. (2011) *Quantification of Value of Historic Buildings*, 10th International Conference Organization, Technology and Management in Construction, University of Zagreb, Faculty of Civil Engineering.

Mikš, L., Tichá, A., Košulič, J. and Mikš, R. (2008) *Optimalizace technickoekonomických charakteristik životního cyklu stavebního díla*, Brno: CERM.

Ochrana, F. (2005) *Nákladově užitkové metody ve veřejném sektoru*, Prague: Ekopress.

Raabová, T. (2010) *Multiplikační efekty kulturních odvětví v české ekonomice*, Prague: Arts and Theatre Institute.

——(2011) *Analýza ekonomického dopadu: Pražské Quadriennale 2011*, Prague: Economicimpact.

Richards, G. (2007) *Cultural Tourism: Global and Local Perspectives*, New York: Haworth Press.

Stynes, D.J. (1997) *Economic Impacts of Tourism*, Illinois Bureau of Tourism, Department of Commerce and Community Affairs.

Stynes, D.J., Propst, D.B. Chang, W.H. and Sun, Y. (2000) *Estimating Regional Economic Impacts of Park Visitor Spending: Money Generation Model Version 2 (MGM2)*, East Lansing, Michigan: Department of Park, Recreation, and Tourism Resources, Ann Arbor: Michigan State University.

Throsby, D. (2001) *Economics and Culture*, Cambridge: Cambridge University Press.

Whiting, P. (1999) *Heritage Institutions in Canada: Impacts and Benefits*, Stella, ON: The Outspan Group Inc.

——(2001) *Socio-Economic Benefits Framework, Cultural Sector*, Stella, ON: The Outspan Group Inc.

## Further reading

Australian Government (2001) *Multipliers for Culture-Related Industries*, Canberra: Australian Government – Department of Communication, IT and the Arts. (Explanation of multiplier calculations.)

Layard, R. and Glaister, S. (1994) *Cost–Benefit Analysis*, Cambridge: Cambridge University Press. (Basic literature on cost-benefit analysis.)

McLennan, W. (1995) *Information Paper: Australian National Accounts: Introduction to Input-Output Multipliers*, Australian Bureau of Statistics, Catalogue No. 5246.0. (Explanation of multiplier calculations.)

Throsby, D. (2001) *Economics and Culture*, Cambridge: Cambridge University Press.

Whiting, P. (2001) *Socio-Economic Benefits Framework, Cultural Sector*, Stella, ON: The Outspan Group Inc.

# 14

# The economic impacts of cultural tourism

*Juan Gabriel Brida, Marta Meleddu and Manuela Pulina*

## Introduction

There is a core of studies that emphasise the contribution of cultural tourism from an economic and methodological perspective. In recent years there has been a convergence between culture and everyday life, driven by the ongoing process of culture democratisation enhanced by a generalised higher level of education. This new cultural trend leads to an increase in the number of people visiting cultural attractions. Cultural tourism can be viewed as an important lever for economic development since it is characterised by push and pull forces similar to those of general tourism activity (Brida and Pulina 2010). As the United Nations Educational, Scientific and Cultural Organization (UNESCO 2005) reported, cultural and natural heritage tourism is the most rapidly growing international sector of the tourism industry. Although it is difficult to estimate the actual size of this phenomenon, the Organisation for Economic Co-operation and Development (OECD) and the UN World Tourism Organization (UNWTO) estimated that in 2007 cultural tourism accounted for 40 per cent of all international tourism, up from 37 per cent in 1995 (OECD 2009).

The cultural tourism industry includes many attractions such as museums, galleries, festivals, architecture, heritage sites, artistic performances, as well as attractions related to food, fashion, language and religion. Museums have a predominant role within the industry and are very often the main tourist attraction for a city. Starting from the 1990s, their role has changed as cultural institutions able to achieve a range of economic functions, often as part of complex urban redevelopment strategies (Tufts and Milne 1999). Museums indeed have been defined as an efficient marketing tool for urban tourism (Jansen-Verbeke and van Rekom 1996) and as a flagship of urban development (Hamnett and Shoval 2003). Besides, there is a significant body of literature that explores the relationship between museums and their economic impact (Dunlop *et al.* 2004; Stynes *et al.* 2004; Frey and Meier 2006; Plaza 2006, 2008; Kinghorn and Willis 2008; Çela *et al.* 2009; Choi *et al.* 2010). The main findings from this strand of economic literature reveal that museums have significant multiplier effects on the local economy, in terms of higher income and employment. Hence, a focus is placed on the applied methodologies to value economic impacts of such a cultural attraction. These approaches provide useful empirical tools that can be generalised and extended to a broad range of case studies. Empirical evidence is provided on the effects that museums and galleries have on the economy, mainly via stated preferences techniques, revealed preferences techniques and impact analysis. Accordingly, the existing literature can be divided into two main strands of research: microeconomics and macroeconomics.

## The microeconomic level

In microeconomics terms, the economic value of cultural tourism can be defined as the set of benefits that it is able to exert within society. Other than a financial or commercial value, welfare is generated by the use values or non-use values associated with the bundle of public goods composing the cultural supply. The use value is determined by the maximum amount of money individuals are willing to pay (WTP) to visit a cultural attraction. In addition, individuals may attribute a value even just knowing that the site exists (non-use value). Semantically, a site is defined as an option value if individuals visit it in the future; with respect to future generations, it will be a bequest value; finally, if the value is merely attributed to the preservation of a site, then it is defined as an existence value.

Use and non-use values may be elicited applying revealed preferences (RP) or stated preferences (SP) methods. RP includes those studies where the monetary value is revealed through a complementary though real market: hedonic price and travel cost methods.

In SP a sample of respondents are asked to state what they would hypothetically be willing to pay, or willing to accept, for a given good or bundle of commodity characteristics. SP variants include contingent valuation (CV) and choice modelling (CM). CV surveys involve more direct questions about respondents' willingness to pay.

On the one hand, only a few studies have adopted the revealed preference analysis to provide an economic valuation of museums. For example, Bedate *et al.* (2004) provide an application of travel cost to four heritage sites in Spain, amongst which is the museum of Burgos, characterised by a collection of archaeological items and fine arts. Boter *et al.* (2005) apply travel time for comparing the relative value of competing museums in the Netherlands. To this end, they explicitly take into account the different museums' distance to the population and the differences in willingness to travel. Fonseca and Rebelo (2010) employ a travel cost to estimate the demand curve in the Museum of Lamego (Portugal). They apply a standard Poisson model which reveals that the probability of visiting the museum is positively influenced by education level and being a female, and negatively by the travel cost.

On the other hand, there are more examples of stated preference applications. Mazzanti (2003) applies a multi-attribute choice experiment to measure the economic value and assess user preferences at the Galleria Borghese Museum in Rome. Amongst other methods, Sanz *et al.* (2003) propose a parametric, contingent valuation, estimation to evaluate the WTP of both visitors and residents for the national museum of sculpture in Valladolid (Spain). Bedate *et al.* (2009), via a contingent valuation, estimate the WTP of a representative sample of residents and visitors to the art museum of Valladolid, Spain. They find that visitors expressed a higher WTP than residents, though the latter were enthusiastic at the prospect of new cultural facilities. Colombino and Nene (2009) consider the case of Paestum (Italy) and present an analysis of tourists' preferences in relation to different museum services. Overall, respondents are more interested in extended opening hours, enhanced guided tours within the archaeological site and interactive teaching labs. However, they show less interest in transforming the site into a place of leisure and entertainment. Lampi and Orth (2009), via a contingent valuation method, measure visitors' WTP for a visit to the free-entrance Museum of World Culture in Sweden. The results show that four out of the six target groups are less likely to visit the museum after the implementation of a low fee; however, those who are regular culture consumers state that they are willing to visit the museum regardless of the fee level. Choi *et al.* (2010) employ a choice modelling analysis to evaluate the economic value of the Old Parliament House in Australia, currently operating as a museum of social and political history. They find that respondents positively value some of the attributes: extending the period of temporary exhibitions, hosting various events as well as restoration facilities. Moreover, they calculate that temporary exhibitions and events contribute AU$17.0 million and AU$21.8 million, respectively, to nationwide welfare annually.

A drawback of this kind of analysis is the tendency of the responses to be highly similar across surveys and individuals tend to accept even amounts above their true maximum WTP. Furthermore, a strategic bias occurs when respondents provide answers that are not their true preferences in an attempt to influence the provision of cultural goods. Given these limitations, it is quite difficult to extend specific empirical results to other case studies in order to enable one to provide a comprehensive picture of the phenomenon under investigation.

As a further strand of research, probabilistic approaches such as count models can also be used to explore the interrelationship between cultural tourists and museum visitors, with respect to a representative sample of survey respondents. The case study sketched here analyses empirical data obtained from a survey undertaken in one of the best-known futurism museums, the Museum for Modern and Contemporary Art, in Rovereto, Italy, in 2009. Considering revealed preferences data, the analysis focuses on the different factors influencing the intention to revisit this cultural site. The theoretical model was based on the hypothesis that an individual maximises his/her utility given the number of times s/he visits the heritage site and further socioeconomic variables, subject to time and income constraints. From an empirical perspective, the study employed a zero-truncated Poisson model, as the number of visits to the museum (the dependent variable) cannot be zero. The findings reveal that socio-demographic characteristics positively influence the probability to return. Also, as reported in other studies, the temporary exhibitions offered by the museum had a significant impact, with an incidence rate ratio of almost two times. Additionally, no matter how much the visitors spend on accommodation, they are less likely to revisit if they travel in groups, by train or on foot, are further from their place of origin and spent longer visiting the museum.

## The macroeconomic level

Cultural tourism, just as tourism activity in general, stimulates other economic industries through direct, indirect and induced effects. An increase in tourism expenditure will lead to an additional activity in related industries, and the change will be greater than the initial injection in spending, via multiplier effects. Cultural tourism has, in fact, a heterogeneous and *sui generis* nature that involves multiple aspects that interact with geographical, environmental, political, sociological and economic elements. Indirect impacts are generated by the production changes associated with the presence of cultural tourists which leads to an increase in demand for a wide bundle of services such as restaurants, hotels and other facilities. Since these businesses re-invest profits derived from the direct activity, the final outcome is an increase in jobs and disposable income. Households employ this additional income in the economy to satisfy their needs (i.e. housing, transport, food and so on), generating an induced impact. Therefore, economic impacts deriving from cultural tourism activities can affect the overall economy.

Empirically, input-output (I-O) models are widely applied to assess overall impacts of cultural tourism and museums on the economy (Dwyer *et al.* 2004). They consist of a mathematic technique connecting money flows between sectors of the economy that assesses inter-dependencies between these sectors (Fletcher 1989; Crompton *et al.* 2001). Inputs employed within the production process across various industries are transformed into outputs accounting for the contribution to the economy. These models enable one to calculate the proportion of wages and taxes deriving from sales. Based on the concept of recirculation of income, multipliers are computed from I-O models embodying the total effects (direct, indirect and/or induced) then divided into the direct effect produced by cultural tourism.

In analysing the multiplier effects, Dunlop *et al.* (2004) apply an input-output analysis to provide evidence on effects of museums and galleries on the Scottish economy. Overall, arts museums and galleries scored an income multiplier equal to 1.65, meaning that every £1 of income paid by museums and galleries supports a further £0.65 worth of income in other sectors. The employment multiplier is 1.64 meaning that every one job within the museums and galleries sector supports a further 0.64 jobs in other sectors. Çela *et al.* (2009) investigate the economic impact of heritage sites at the Silos and Smokestacks National Heritage Area in Iowa via an I-O model. The empirical findings show that non-residents made a total contribution of US$103 million and created 1,981 jobs that encourage institutions and managers to preserve and enhance their heritage, in 37 counties of north-east Iowa. The results led to an output or gross sales multiplier of 1.66 (sales total impact/sales direct impact) generated by an additional tourist spending of $1.

Plaza (2006) analyses the impact of the Guggenheim Museum of Bilbao (GMB), in the Spanish Basque region, on tourism demand, employing an autoregressive moving average (ARIMA) econometric analysis. The results suggest that the GMB contributed to a rise of 740,904 tourism overnight stays per year and generated 907 new full-time jobs as a result of its opening. However, the author advises caution in reading this outcome. The GMB case cannot in fact be generalised, as many factors tend to influence the success of a museum that requires continuous innovation and new activities to keep public interest alive. Expanding on previous studies, Plaza (2010) analyses the economic role of the GMB in creating new jobs. Through regional tourism Satellite Accounts the author estimates a creation of 1.25 jobs for every 1,000 visitors.

From the literature review, it also emerges that only a few studies have investigated the impact of museums on the growth of urban tourism especially by employing causal econometric specifications. Carey *et al.* (2011) investigate the long-term relationships between cultural tourism and tourism flows in the capital city Wellington (New Zealand) over the 1998–2009 period. The findings assess the positive impact of this museum as a cultural attraction of tourists to urban centres.

## Conclusions

In this section, the contribution of cultural tourism has been analysed from an economic and methodological perspective. A particular emphasis has been given to museums as major cultural attractions being able to stimulate positive externalities in local economies.

On the whole, the reviewed literature has shown that stated preference applications, logistic and causal econometric models are still very rarely used in the literature. Besides, computable general equilibrium (CGE) models, as extension of I-O models, may also be implemented to investigate the interrelationships between cultural tourism and other sectors. Such models provide policy makers with useful guidance concerning a variety of policy scenarios and international shocks, although they are hardly ever used to evaluate cultural tourism.

## References

Bedate, A., Herrero, L.C. and Sanz, L. (2004) 'Economic Valuation of the Cultural Heritage: Application to Four Case Studies in Spain', *Journal of Cultural Heritage* 5: 101–11.

——(2009) 'Economic Valuation of a Contemporary Art Museum: Correction of Hypothetical Bias Using a Certainty Question', *Journal of Cultural Economics* 33: 185–99.

Boter, J., Rouwendal, J. and Wedel, M. (2005) 'Employing Travel Time to Compare the Value of Competing Cultural Organizations', *Journal of Cultural Economics* 29: 19–33.

Brida, J.G. and Pulina, M. (2010) *A Literature Review on Tourism and Economic Growth*, Working Paper 10–17, CRENoS, Cagliari and Sassari University.

Carey, S., Davidson, L. and Sahli, M. (2011) *Capital City Museums and Tourism Flows: an Empirical Study of the Museum of New Zealand Te Papa Tongarewa*, IATE conference, 4–7 July, Bournemouth, UK.

Çela, A.C., Lankford, S. and Knowles-Lankford, J. (2009) 'Visitor Spending and Economic Impacts of Heritage Tourism: A Case Study of the Silos and Smokestacks National Heritage Area', *Journal of Heritage Tourism* 4(3): 245–56.

Choi, A.S., Ritchie, B.W., Papandrea, F. and Bennett, J. (2010) 'Economic Valuation of Cultural Heritage Sites: A Choice Modeling Approach', *Tourism Management* 31(2): 213–20.

Colombino, U. and Nene, A. (2009) 'Preference Heterogeneity in Relation to Museum', *Tourism Economics* 15(2): 381–95.

Crompton, J.L., Lee, S. and Shuster, T.J. (2001) 'A Guide for Undertaking Economic Studies: The Spring Fest Example', *Journal of Travel Research* 40(1): 79–87.

Dunlop, S., Galloway, S., Hamilton, C. and Scullion, A. (2004) *The Economic Impact of the Cultural Sector in Scotland*, www.christinehamiltonconsulting.com/wp-content/uploads/2011/10/Economic-Impact-Report.pdf (accessed 24 October 2011).

Dwyer, L., Forsyth, P. and Spurr, R. (2004) 'Evaluating Tourism's Economic Effects: New and Old Approaches', *Annals of Tourism Research* 25: 307–17.

Fletcher, J. (1989) 'Input-output Models', in Baum, T. and Mudambi, R. (eds) *Economic and Management Methods for Tourism and Hospitality Research*, Chichester: John Wiley & Sons, 14–29.

Fonseca, S. and Rebelo, J. (2010) 'Economic Valuation of Cultural Heritage: Application to a Museum Located in the Alto Douro Wine Region – World Heritage Site', *Pasos* 8(2): 339–50.

Frey, B.S. and Meier, S. (2006) 'The Economics of Museums', in Ginsburgh, V.A. and Throsby, D. (eds) *Handbook of the Economics of Art and Culture*, Vol. 1, Amsterdam: Elsevier, 1017–47.

Hamnett, C. and Shoval, N. (2003) *Museums as Flagships of Urban Development*, Oxford: Blackwell.

Jansen-Verbeke, M. and van Rekom, J. (1996) 'Scanning Museum Visitors: Urban Tourism Marketing', *Annals of Tourism Research* 23: 364–75.

Kinghorn, N. and Willis, K. (2008) 'Measuring Museum Visitor Preferences Towards Opportunities for Developing Social Capital: An Application of a Choice Experiment to the Discovery Museum', *International Journal of Heritage Studies* 146: 555–72.

Lampi, E. and Orth, M. (2009) 'Who Visits the Museums? A Comparison Between Stated Preferences and Observed Effects of Entrance Fees', *Kyklos* 621: 85–102.

Mazzanti, M. (2003) 'Discrete Choice Models and Valuation Experiment', *Journal of Economics Studies* 30 (6): 584–604.

OECD (2009) *The Impact of Culture on Tourism*, Paris: OECD, www.em.gov.lv/images/modules/items/OECD_Tourism_Culture.pdf (accessed 26 December 2011).

Plaza, B. (2006) 'The Return on Investment of the Guggenheim Museum Bilbao', *International Journal of Urban and Regional Research* 30: 452–67.

——(2008) 'On Some Challenges and Conditions for the Guggenheim Museum Bilbao to be an Effective Economic Re-activator', *International Journal of Urban and Regional Research* 322: 506–17.

——(2010) 'Valuing Museums as Economic Engines: Willingness to Pay or Discounting of Cash-flows?' *Journal of Cultural Heritage* 11: 155–62.

Sanz, J.A., Herrero, L.C. and Bedate, A.M. (2003) 'Contingent Valuation and Semi Parametric Methods: A Case Study of the National Museum of Sculpture in Valladolid, Spain', *Journal of Cultural Economics* 27: 241–57.

Stynes, D.J., Vander Stoep, G.A. and Sun, Y.-Y. (2004) *Estimating Economic Impacts of Michigan Museums*, Department of Park, Recreation and Tourism Resources – Michigan State University.

Tufts, S. and Milne, S. (1999) 'Museums: A Supply-Side Perspective', *Annals of Tourism Research* 26(3): 613–31.

UNESCO (2005) *Innovative Policies for Heritage Safeguarding and Cultural Tourism Development*, Proceedings of the International Conference Moscow, 25–27 November 2005, Moscow: UNESCO.

## Further reading

Bedate, A., Herrero, L.C. and Sanz, J.A. (2009) 'Economic Valuation of a Contemporary Art Museum: Correction of Hypothetical Bias Using a Certainty Question', *Journal of Cultural Economics* 33: 185–99. (The impact of applying different bias corrections for double-bounded dichotomous economic valuation exercises.)

Choi, A.S., Ritchie, B.W., Papandrea, F. and Bennett, J. (2010) 'Economic Valuation of Cultural Heritage Sites: A Choice Modeling Approach', *Tourism Management* 31(2): 213–20. (Choice modelling application in cultural economics.)

Dunlop, S., Galloway, S., Hamilton, C. and Scullion, A. (2004) *The Economic Impact of the Cultural Sector in Scotland*, www.christinehamiltonconsulting.com//up-content/uploads/2011/10/Economic-Impact-Report.pdf. (Measuring the volume of economic activity that is supported, both directly and indirectly, by the cultural sector.)

Fonseca, S. and Rebelo, J. (2010) 'Economic Valuation of Cultural Heritage: Application to a Museum Located in the Alto Douro Wine Region – World Heritage Site', *Pasos* 8(2): 339–50. (Travel cost to estimate the curve of culture demand.)

Lampi, E. and Orth, M. (2009) 'Who Visits the Museums? A Comparison Between Stated Preferences and Observed Effects of Entrance Fees', *Kyklos* 621: 85–102. (A contingent valuation method to investigate changes in visitors' compositions as a consequence of the introduction of entrance fees.)

Mazzanti, M. (2003) 'Discrete Choice Models and Valuation Experiment', *Journal of Economics Studies* 30 (6): 584–604. (A choice experiment technique as a tool aimed at measuring multi-attribute economic values, assessing visitors' preferences.)

# 15

# The economic value of cultural tourism

## Determinants of cultural tourists' expenditures

*Celeste Eusébio, Maria João Carneiro
and Elisabeth Kastenholz*

## Introduction

The cultural tourism market is often referred to as one of the most rapidly growing segments, accounting nowadays for about 40 per cent of international tourist movements, with evidence pointing to a continuous increase of the market since the 1990s (Richards 2007) and to important economic impacts of this tourist segment at the destination level (Eusébio 2006). The importance of this market justifies increasing efforts in researching its features, behaviours and motivations.

It is in this context that the Association for Tourism and Leisure Education (ATLAS) Cultural Tourism Research Programme (www.tram-research.com/atlas/) was launched in 1991, with the support of DGXXIII (now part of the Enterprise Directorate) of the European Commission. Over the past 15 years, the project has engaged in monitoring the market, its profile, behaviours and trends through visitor surveys and studies of cultural tourism policies and suppliers.

Empirical evidence suggests that the market of cultural tourists tends to include travellers with relatively high tourism expenditures, but little is still known about what factors most influence these expenditure patterns.

In this chapter the ATLAS data collected in 2004, and based on a survey of cultural tourists in 19 countries from diverse continents (Europe, Asia, Australasia and North America), are used for analysing the determinants of visitor spending. Results concerning daily individual visitor spending as well as the factors that influence these amounts are presented. More specifically, a log-linear regression model is used to estimate the cultural tourists' daily expenses per capita, with independent variables being those reflecting their socio-demographic profile, motivations, travel behaviour and perception of the destination.

The results permit a more profound understanding of the cultural tourism market and its potential as a tool of economic development in its destination areas. Destination management and marketing implications are also briefly discussed.

## Cultural tourism

In the tourism literature there is no consensus about the meaning of 'cultural tourism'. Although widely used, the concept is also widely misunderstood, partly due to the difficulty of defining culture in the first place (Reisinger and Turner 2004); it is a concept with a very broad scope and the object of analysis in several scientific fields, such as sociology, psychology, anthropology and inter-cultural communication. Some researchers use a narrow definition of culture, while others choose a broader one. However, one may broadly distinguish *material* and *non-material* culture, with a trend observable 'away from product-based to process-based or "way of life" definitions of culture' (OECD 2009: 25).

Some define cultural tourism as 'special interest holidays (vacations) essentially motivated by cultural interests', while, in a broader sense, all 'activities with a cultural content as parts of trips and visits with a combination of pursuits' may be considered (Medlik 2003: 48). McKercher and du Cros (2002: 6) suggest that 'cultural tourism is a form of tourism that relies on a destination's cultural heritage assets and transforms them into products that can be consumed by tourists', while Stylianou-Lambert (2011: 419) emphasise the 'diversity of tourist experiences' associated with culture in the tourism context.

In this chapter the technical definition suggested by Richards (1996: 24) is adopted: 'all movements of persons to specific cultural attractions, such as heritage sites, artistic and cultural manifestations, arts and drama outside their normal place of residence'.

According to Europa Nostra (in OECD 2009: 21), 'more than 50 per cent of tourist activity in Europe is driven by cultural heritage and cultural tourism is expected to grow the most in the tourism sector'. According to Richards (1996, 2007), the market of cultural tourism tends to be composed of travellers with high education, high socioeconomic status, often having occupations related to the cultural industries and education. In fact, one may predict an increase in world cultural tourism, because of an observable expansion of educational opportunities worldwide (Richards 2007). Studies further suggest that this segment is one of the most important markets in terms of economic benefits to the destination (Taylor *et al.* 1993). Also the heterogeneity of this market must be acknowledged (Medlik 2003; Kim *et al.* 2007; Richards 2007).

That is why cultural tourism is increasingly studied by planners and managers of destination areas, since a better understanding of the market permits an improved design and promotion of cultural tourism experiences. Some features of the market have already been identified, but factors influencing cultural visitors' expenditures are rarely studied, except for the study undertaken by Taylor *et al.* (1993).

## Factors determining cultural visitors' expenditures

Few researchers have investigated the factors influencing expenditure patterns of cultural visitors. However, those studies published about the topic reveal that the determinants of an individual's expenditures may include socio-demographic profile, motivations, travel behaviour and features of destination image (Perez and Sampol 2000; Eusébio 2006; Cho 2010; Kim *et al.* 2010; Goh and Law 2011).

As far as a visitor profile is concerned, empirical evidence shows that expenditure tends to be positively correlated with educational level (Woodside *et al.* 1987; Goh and Law 2011) and available income (Woodside *et al.* 1987; Agarwal and Yochum 1999; Cannon and Ford 2002; Seiler *et al.* 2002; Jang *et al.* 2004; Oh and Schuett 2010). Kastenholz (2005) and Perez and Sampol (2000) demonstrated that spending patterns were also related to visitors' place of residence or nationality (expenditure increasing for international travellers). The role of age was not conclusive, with some (e.g. Jang *et al.* 2004) revealing a positive correlation between age and total expenditure, others revealing the inverse relationship (e.g. Mudambi and Baum 1997), and still others not revealing any statistically significant relationship (Agarwal and Yochum 1999; Seiler *et al.* 2002; Goh and Law 2011).

Trip motivations or benefits sought have been considered in some studies. Kastenholz (2005) showed that culturally interested rural tourists tended to spend more while those interested in socialising and fun tended to spend less. Wang *et al.* (2006) showed that those seeking excitement spent more than those seeking stability. Mehmetoglu's (2007) study revealed that people who travelled for status enhancement tended to spend more than people travelling for other motives.

The knowledge that a visitor possesses of a tourism destination could also be a determinant of a visitor's expenditure level. Godbey and Graefe (1991) and Jang *et al.* (2004) showed that first-time visitors spent more than repeat visitors, although in this context the overall benefit of repeat visits should not be neglected. Oh and Schuett (2010) argue that findings regarding spending patterns of repeat visitors are somewhat inconsistent.

As far as travel context is concerned, group size was shown to be positively correlated to overall expenditure levels and negatively correlated to daily per capita spending (Agarwal and Yochum 1999; Seiler *et al.* 2002). Similar results were obtained for length of stay (Taylor *et al.* 1993; Perez and Sampol 2000; Jang *et al.* 2004; Kastenholz 2005; Mehmetoglu 2007). According to Agarwal and Yochum (1999) and Laesser and Crouch (2006), visitors on prepaid package or organised group tours tend to spend less per person, per day than those travelling independently.

The kind of accommodation used at the destination was also shown to be a significant determinant in some models of tourist expenditure. Mudambi and Baum (1997) observed that those visitors to Turkey using registered hotels spent more than other visitors. Agarwal and Yochum (1999) and Laesser and Crouch (2006) corroborated this conclusion, observing that the visitors staying in hotels or motels spent the most, while those staying with friends or family spent the least.

Last but not least, perception of destination features may influence the tourist expenditure level. However, at the micro level, few studies analyse this relationship. Perez and Sampol's (2000) model is one of the few incorporating the visitors' opinions on price as a determinant of expenditures, showing that tourists who considered the Balearic Islands expensive or very expensive tended to spend more at the destination than others.

## Determinants of the cultural visitors' expenditures: a worldwide survey

### *Methodology of the study*

For analysing the determinants of cultural visitors' expenditure levels, data from the 2004 survey wave of the ATLAS Cultural Tourism Project were used (Richards and Munsters 2010). Questionnaires were administered to visitors to cultural attractions, with respondents requested to provide information about their socio-demographic characteristics, travel motivations, travel behaviour, the image they held about the destination, satisfaction and expenditures undertaken at the destination. Motivations were assessed through ratings of Likert-type scales (ranging from 1 'disagree', to 5 'agree') for four motivational items. To report on their destination image, respondents rated 12 items reflecting destination image features, using an association scale from 1 'very little', to 5 'very much'. Finally, satisfaction with the visit was rated on a scale from 1 'very dissatisfied', to 10 'very satisfied'. For this study, 3,363 questionnaires were used. The next two sections provide an analysis of the sample profile and a discussion of results concerning determinants of visitors' expenditures.

## Profile of the sample

The questionnaires were administered in 19 countries around the world. Although the majority were administered in Europe, e.g. in Portugal (39 per cent of total) and Spain (8 per cent), a lot were also collected in countries located on other continents, such as Australia (6 per cent), China (4 per cent) and Brazil (3 per cent).

The sample is quite balanced in terms of gender and has some diversity regarding age (St.Dev. = 13.029), with the average age being 38 years (see Table 15.1). There is a predominance of people with a higher education degree (63 per cent), corroborating the findings of other studies which associate cultural tourism with high educational levels. However, a wide variety in gross annual household income (St.Dev. = 20,510) is observed, which is on average €28,859. The majority of the visitors were international tourists (57 per cent).

Visitors seem to be primarily motivated to expand their cultural knowledge, showing a strong desire to know the destination's culture (3.94), and learn new things (3.72), but they also want some entertainment (3.62). The sample also reveals a wide diversity regarding travel behaviour, for example considering the size of the travel group (St.Dev. = 3.100) and the length of stay at the destination (St.Dev. = 4.88). However, visitors travel mostly in groups of two to three persons and tend to spend close to five nights at the destination (see Table 15.1). Despite an average of 1.76 previous visits to the destination, the majority of respondents (59 per cent) had never visited the destination before. Respondents primarily use hotel accommodation (44 per cent) and only a few travel by plane (24 per cent) and on a package arrangement (18 per cent). A high preference for visiting museums (56 per cent), monuments (56 per cent), historic sites (54 per cent) and religious sites (42 per cent) is also visible.

For identifying a reduced number of destination image dimensions, a principal component analysis of the 10 items of this construct was undertaken. Three dimensions emerged using a varimax rotation and the eigenvalue criterion for dimension extraction:

- Cultural diversity and uniqueness: associated with 'festivals and events', 'linguistic diversity', 'multicultural region', 'a fashionable place to be', 'culturally distinct region' and 'lively atmosphere'.
- Built heritage: including 'historic architecture', 'authentic sights' and 'museums and cultural attractions'.
- Traditions and hospitality: encompassing 'regional gastronomy', 'customs and traditions' and 'hospitable local people'.

The three dimensions explain about 56.5 per cent of variance and have reasonable values of internal consistency (all Cronbach alpha values above 0.65) (Tabachnick and Fidell 1996). The analysis also presents appropriate KMO (0.812) and the Bartlett's test values (Chi-squared = 31 388.62, sig. = 0.000). Visitors seem to associate mostly the visited destinations with built heritage (3.68) and traditions and hospitality (3.47) and are highly satisfied with the destination (7.99) (see Table 15.1).

Regarding the expenditures undertaken at the destination, no homogeneous expenditure pattern is observable. The total average expenditure at the destination for all persons in the travel group is about €940 (Table 15.1). The majority of the total expenditure refers to accommodation (about €337 on average), and transportation (€254), a considerable amount is also spent on food and drink and shopping (€191 and €178, respectively), with expenditures on attraction admissions being much lower. The average expenditure per person, per day is about €62.50. An analysis of the potential determinants of the individual daily spending is presented in the next section.

*Table 15.1* Profile of the visitors

| Variables | N | (%) | Mean | St.Dev. |
|---|---|---|---|---|
| *Socio-demographic profile* | | | | |
| Gender | | | | |
| Male | 1,787 | 53 | | |
| Female | 1,568 | 47 | | |
| Age | 3,363 | | 37.98 | 13.029 |
| Highest level of education | | | | |
| Primary school | 74 | 2 | | |
| Secondary school | 596 | 18 | | |
| Vocational educational | 551 | 17 | | |
| Bachelor degree | 1,388 | 41 | | |
| Master's or Doctoral degree | 740 | 22 | | |
| *Annual household gross income* | 3,363 | | 28,859 | 20,510 |
| *Place of residence* | | | | |
| Domestic visitor | 1,445 | 43 | | |
| Foreign visitor | 1,918 | 57 | | |
| *Motivations*[a] | | | | |
| Learn new things | 3,363 | | 3.72 | 1.217 |
| Entertainment | 3,363 | | 3.62 | 1.223 |
| Culture | 3,363 | | 3.94 | 1.087 |
| Sightseeing | 3,363 | | 3.57 | 1.236 |
| *Expenditure* | | | | |
| Total expenditure | | | | |
| Transportation | 2,786 | | 254.03 | 811.725 |
| Accommodation | 1,565 | | 336.73 | 758.732 |
| Food & drink | 2,188 | | 190.78 | 329.291 |
| Shopping | 1,731 | | 178.33 | 460.044 |
| Attraction admissions | 1,633 | | 75.76 | 346.096 |
| Total | 3,363 | | 940.99 | 2151.953 |
| *Individual daily spending* | 3,160 | | 62.50 | 61.430 |
| *Travel behaviour* | | | | |
| *Size of travel group* | 3,363 | | 2,68 | 3,100 |
| *Length of stay at the destination (in nights)* | 3,363 | | 4,88 | 6,429 |
| *Number of previous visits* | 3,363 | | 1.76 | 3.785 |
| *Type of accommodation used* | | | | |
| Hotel | 1,466 | 44 | | |
| Other | 1,897 | 56 | | |
| *Type of transportation used* | | | | |
| Plane | 796 | 24 | | |
| Other | 2,567 | 76 | | |
| *Organization of the trip* | | | | |
| Use of a package tour | 598 | 18 | | |
| Other | 2,765 | 82 | | |

*Table 15.1 (continued)*

| Variables | N | (%) | Mean | St.Dev. |
|---|---|---|---|---|
| *Attractions visited* | | | | |
| Museums | 1,892 | 56 | | |
| Monuments | 1,865 | 56 | | |
| Art galleries | 619 | 18 | | |
| Religious sites | 1,418 | 42 | | |
| Historic sites | 1,798 | 54 | | |
| Theatres | 330 | 10 | | |
| Heritage/crafts centre | 754 | 22 | | |
| Cinema | 362 | 11 | | |
| Pop concerts | 168 | 5 | | |
| World music events | 132 | 4 | | |
| Classical music events | 89 | 3 | | |
| Dance events | 174 | 5 | | |
| Traditional festivals | 514 | 15 | | |
| | | | | |
| *Image of the destination[b]* | | | | |
| Traditions and hospitality | 3,363 | | 3.47 | 0.871 |
| Cultural diversity and uniqueness | 3,363 | | 3.14 | 0.767 |
| Built heritage | 3,363 | | 3.68 | 0.909 |
| | | | | |
| *Satisfaction[c]* | 3,339 | | 7.99 | 1.375 |

Notes:
[a] Measured using a Likert type scale from 1 (disagree) to 5 (agree).
[b] Measured using a Likert type scale from 1 (very little) to 5 (very much).
[c] Measured using a Likert type scale from 1 (very unsatisfied) to 10 (very satisfied).

## Determinants of cultural visitor expenditures per person and per day

For identifying the determinants of cultural tourists' expenditure levels a multiple regression model was carried out. According to the review of 27 expenditure studies that used micro-data conducted by Wang and Davidson (2010), this is the model specification most frequently used in modelling individuals' expenditure.

The dependent variable for this study is the expenditure per person and per day of cultural visitors. The independent variables included socio-demographic characteristics, travel motivations, travel behaviour and destination image (see Table 15.2).

First, a power model is adopted.

$$CVE_i = \alpha A_i^{b_1} Y_i^{b_2} LNT_i^{b_3} E_i^{b_4} C_i^{b_5} S_i^{b_6} TT_i^{b_7} TA_i^{b_8} TP_i^{b_9} TO_i^{b_{10}} LS_i^{b_{11}} SG_i^{b_{12}} NPV_i^{b_{13}} CD_i^{b_{14}} BH_i^{b_{15}} TH_i^{b_{16}} \quad (1)$$

This power model was transformed to carry out a log-linear regression by using the logarithm of both the dependent variable and of the continuous independent variables.

$$\begin{aligned} \ln CVE_i = {} & \alpha + b_1 \ln A_i + b_2 \ln Y_i + b_3 \ln LNT_i + b_4 \ln E_i + b_5 \ln C_i + b_6 \ln S_i \\ & + b_7 TT_i + b_8 TA_i + b_9 TP_i + b_{10} TO_i + b_{11} \ln LS_i + b_{12} \ln SG_i \\ & + b_{13} \ln NPV_i + b_{14} \ln CD_i + b_{15} \ln BH_i + b_{16} \ln TH_i \end{aligned} \quad (2)$$

*Table 15.2* Regression model explaining travel expenditure per person and per day

| Variables | Measurement | Expected sign |
|---|---|---|
| **Dependent variables** | | |
| Travel expenditure per person and per day | lnCVE = natural logarithm of travel expenditure per person and per day | |
| **Independent variables** | | |
| Socio-demograpic profile | | |
| Age | lnA = natural logarithm of age | + |
| Annual household gross income | lnY = natural logarithm of annual household gross income | + |
| Travel motivations | | |
| Learn new things | lnLNT = natural logarithm of travel motivation learning new things | + |
| Entertainment | lnE = natural logarithm of travel motivation entertainment | + |
| Culture | lnC = natural logarithm of travel motivation finding more about culture | + |
| Sightseeing | lnS = natural logarithm of travel motivation sightseeing | + |
| Travel behaviour | | |
| Type of travel | TT = 1 if international travel; 0 domestic travel | + |
| Type of accommodation used | TA = 1 if hotel was used; 0 otherwise | + |
| Type of transportation used | TP = 1 if plane used to travel to destination; 0 otherwise | + |
| Organisation of the trip | TO = 1 if a package tour was used; 0 otherwise | − |
| Length of stay at the destination | lnLS = natural logarithm of number of days at the destination | − |
| Size of travel group | lnSG = natural logarithm of size of travel group | − |
| Number of previous visits | lnNPV = natural logarithm of number of previous visits | − |
| Cognitive image of the destination | | |
| Cultural diversity and uniqueness | lnCD = natural logarithm of the mean of the factor "cultural diversity and uniqueness" | + |
| Built heritage | lnBH = natural logarithm of the mean of the factor "built heritage" | + |
| Traditions and hospitality | lnTH = natural logarithm of the mean of the factor "traditions and hospitality" | + |

In the case of length of stay and number of previous visits it was necessary to add 1 to the original variable before calculating its logarithm. This procedure of using the logarithm of dependent and independent variables is already widely adopted in the tourism field, as shown in Wang and Davidson's (2010) review study.

The ordinary least square (OLS) and the enter regression procedure were used to obtain the regression model. Further, the multivariate regression assumptions were analysed. As shown in Table 15.3 the multiple regression model does not present problems at this level.

Table 15.3 Variables and research hypotheses

| | Unstandardized coefficients | | Standardized coefficients | | | Colinearity statistics | |
|---|---|---|---|---|---|---|---|
| | β | Std. Error | β | t | Sig. | Tolerance | VIF |
| Age (lnA) | 0.193 | 0.054 | 0.056 | 3.583 | 0.000 | 0.813 | 1.230 |
| Annual household gross income (lnY) | 0.217 | 0.021 | 0.170 | 10.448 | 0.000 | 0.754 | 1.327 |
| Type of travel (TT) International Domestic | 0.174 | 0.017 | 0.166 | 9.983 | 0.000 | 0.718 | 1.393 |
| Type of accommodation used (TA) Hotel Other | 0.224 | 0.016 | 0.215 | 13.606 | 0.000 | 0.801 | 1.248 |
| Type of transportation used (TP) Plane Other | 0.219 | 0.020 | 0.180 | 11.198 | 0.000 | 0.774 | 1.292 |
| Organization of the trip (TO) Use of a package tour Other | 0.107 | 0.021 | 0.079 | 5.072 | 0.000 | 0.817 | 1.224 |
| Length of stay at the destination (lnLS) | −0.417 | 0.024 | −0.268 | −17.640 | 0.000 | 0.865 | 1.157 |
| Size of travel group (lnSG) | −0.392 | 0.029 | −0.194 | −13.442 | 0.000 | 0.955 | 1.048 |
| Number of previous visits (inNPV) | 0.014 | 0.023 | 0.009 | 0.587 | 0.557 | 0.780 | 1.282 |
| Motivations | | | | | | | |
| Learning new things (lnLNT) | −0.088 | 0.045 | −0.032 | −1.950 | 0.051 | 0.737 | 1.357 |
| Entertainment | 0.034 | 0.039 | 0.013 | 0.879 | 0.379 | 0.929 | 1.076 |
| Culture (lnC) | 0.074 | 0.054 | 0.022 | 1.358 | 0.174 | 0.730 | 1.370 |
| Sightseeing | 0.095 | 0.040 | 0.036 | 2.392 | 0.017 | 0.899 | 1.112 |
| Cognitive destination image | | | | | | | |
| Cultural diversity and uniqueness (lnCD) | −0.161 | 0.072 | −0.036 | -2.218 | 0.027 | 0.753 | 1.327 |
| Built heritage (lnBH) | −0.089 | 0.063 | −0.022 | −1.421 | 0.155 | 0.813 | 1.231 |
| Traditions and hospitality (inTH) | 0.243 | 0.067 | 0.059 | 3.633 | 0.000 | 0.765 | 1.308 |
| Constant | | | | | | | |

| Model diagnostics | |
|---|---|
| R | 0.578 |
| $R^2$ | 0.334 |
| Adjusted $R^2$ | 0.33 |
| Standard error | 0.42435 |
| F-statistic | 104,688 (0.000) |
| Normality: Kalmogorov-Smirnov Test (α) | 0,043 (0.000) |

The log-linear regression model is significant (F = 104.688; sig. = 0.000) and explains 33 per cent of the variance ($R^2$ = 0.33). All independent variables, with the exception of 'number of previous visits', some travel motivations – 'entertainment' and 'find out more about the culture of the destination' – and the cognitive destination image 'built heritage', have a statistically significant influence on the dependent variable.

Concerning the socio-demographic profile of visitors, the results obtained show a positive influence of age and household income on travel expenditure per person/day, corroborating other studies in this field (e.g. Cannon and Ford 2002; Jang *et al.* 2004; Thrane and Farstad 2011).

As far as travel behaviour is concerned, those staying in hotels present a higher individual daily spending than other visitors. Additionally, individual daily spending tends to decrease with increasing travel group size. Similarly, the individual daily spending is likely to decrease as length of stay increases. A potential reason for this is that as the number of persons in the travel group rises, the travel budget has to be divided among a larger number of individuals, resulting in a lower available amount per person. These results are consistent with prior research (e.g. Taylor *et al.* 1993; Jang *et al.* 2004; Wang and Davidson 2010). Additionally, people travelling by plane present a relatively higher spending pattern, corroborating results obtained by Thrane and Farstad (2011). The type of travel undertaken by cultural visitors also influences travel expenditure, with international trips showing higher expenditure levels when compared to domestic trips, as also found by Kastenholz (2005). The option of buying a package tour also reveals a significant but lower influence on individual daily spending, with those travelling on a package tour spending more money per day than others. This result contradicts our hypothesis. However, literature in this domain is scarce, revealing the need to continue studying this relationship. The number of previous visits is insignificant in the estimated model, consistent with some prior studies (e.g. Wang *et al.* 2006), revealing no significant difference in expenditure between first-time and repeat visitors.

Regarding travel motivations, the results presented in Table 15.3 show a positive influence of the travel motivation 'sightseeing' on travel expenditure per person/per day. Two of the four cognitive destination image dimensions show a statistically significant impact on daily individual expenditures: a positive influence of the factor 'traditions and hospitality' and a negative influence of the factor 'cultural diversity and uniqueness'. Although some micro-model studies integrated destination image variables for explaining expenditure level (e.g. Perez and Sampol 2000), the results are inconclusive and do not permit a valid comparison.

## Conclusions

The findings of this study are important due to the low number of cross-section micro-level studies undertaken in the tourism field to identify the determinants of cultural visitor spending.

This chapter highlights the important role that socio-demographics, motivations, travel behaviour and destination image may have as determinants of the individual daily spending of cultural visitors. As expected, income positively influences this kind of expenditure. International tourists, those travelling in smaller groups, staying in hotels and using a package arrangement are segments of high economic value in the cultural tourism market. Developing marketing strategies specifically designed to appeal to these groups should be a priority, not only through specific promotional strategies, but also through adaptations in product development. International travellers, for example, stand out as an interesting market segment, presenting a higher spending pattern, suggesting the importance of promoting the destinations' cultural heritage abroad and providing information in several languages when presenting and interpreting this type of heritage.

An interesting finding is that although visitors are more likely to associate the destination with built heritage, it is when visitors associate the destination with traditions and hospitality that they are likely to have higher expenditures. Preserving and recreating traditions may also permit visitors to live a more interesting, appealing and involving experience than they would have through built heritage alone. Traditions and hospitality – that is, the immaterial culture – are important elements in generating revenues.

Visitors travelling primarily for sightseeing also present higher expenditure levels compared to other visitors, which points to the importance of heritage conservation, of exploring the aesthetic appeal of buildings as well as their scenic environment.

The range of potential determinants of individual daily spending analysed in the present study was limited to some variables. However, the impact of other variables on daily spending would also be interesting to analyse, such as the range of cultural attractions visited at the destination. Future research could also identify segments of visitors with different patterns of expenditures regarding the kind of expenditures undertaken (e.g. those who spend most on accommodation; those who prefer staying in cheaper accommodation and spending more on cultural activities). Recognising the differences that exist among segments helps direct the promotion to the right target markets and create offerings best adapted to each. Studying the determinants of the daily expenditures of the cultural visitors in specific components of the tourism product – e.g. accommodation and shopping – would also help determine the most valuable cultural visitors regarding these components.

## References

Agarwal, V.B. and Yochum, G.R. (1999) 'Tourist Spending and Race of Visitors', *Journal of Travel Research* 38(4): 173–76.

Cannon, T.F. and Ford, J. (2002) 'Relationship of Demographic and Trip Characteristics to Visitor Spending: An Analysis of Sports Travel Visitor Across Time', *Tourism Economics* 8(3): 263–71.

Cho, V. (2010) 'A Study of the Non-economic Determinants in Tourism Research', *International Journal of Tourism Research* 12: 307–20.

Eusébio, C. (2006) *Assessment of Regional Economic Impacts of Tourism: The Case of Regional Centro of Portugal*, PhD dissertation, Aveiro University.

Godbey, G. and Graefe, A. (1991) 'Repeat Tourism, Play, and Monetary Spending', *Journal of Travel Research* 18: 213–25.

Goh, C. and Law, R. (2011) 'The Methodological Progress of Tourism Demand Forecasting: A Review of Related Literature', *Journal of Travel & Tourism Marketing* 28(3): 296–317.

Jang, S., Bai, B., Hong, G. and O'Leary, J.T. (2004) 'Understanding Travel Expenditure Patterns: A Study of Japanese Pleasure Travellers to the United States by Income Level', *Tourism Management* 25(3): 331–41.

Kastenholz, E. (2005) 'Analysing Determinants of Visitor Spending for the Rural Tourist Market in North Portugal', *Tourism Economics* 11(4): 555–69.

Kim, H., Cheng, C.-K. and O'Leary, J.T. (2007) 'Understanding Participation Patterns and Trends in Tourism Cultural Attractions', *Tourism Management* 28(5): 1366–71.

Kim, S.S., Prideaux, B. and Chon, K. (2010) 'A Comparison of Results of Three Statistical Methods to Understand the Determinants of Festival Participants' Expenditures', *International Journal of Hospitality Management* 29: 297–307.

Laesser, C. and Crouch, G.I. (2006) 'Segmenting Markets by Travel Expenditure Patterns: The Case of International Visitors to Australia', *Journal of Travel Research* 44(4): 397–406.

McKercher, B. and du Cros, H. (2002) *Cultural Tourism: The Partnership Between Tourism and Cultural Heritage Management*, New York: Haworth Hospitality Press.

——(2006) 'Culture, Heritage and Visiting Attractions', in Buhalis, D. and Costa, C. (eds) *Tourism Business Frontiers: Consumers, Products and Industry*, Amsterdam: Elsevier/Butterworth Heinemann.

Medlik, S. (2003) *Dictionary of Travel, Tourism and Hospitality*, third edn, Oxford: Butterworth/Heinemann.

Mehmetoglu, M. (2007) 'Nature-based Tourists: The Relationship Between Their Trip Expenditures and Activities', *Journal of Sustainable Tourism* 15(2): 200–15.

Mudambi, R. and Baum, T. (1997) 'Strategic Segmentation: An Empirical Analysis of Tourist Expenditures in Turkey', *Journal of Travel Research* 36(1): 29–34.

OECD (2009) *The Impact of Culture on Tourism*, Paris: OECD.

Oh, J. and Schuett, M.A. (2010) 'Exploring Expenditure-based Segmentation for Rural Tourism: Overnight Stay Visitors Versus Excursionists to Fee-fishing Sites', *Journal of Travel and Tourism Marketing* 27(1): 31–50.

Perez, E.A. and Sampol, C.J. (2000) 'Tourist Expenditures for Mass Tourism Markets', *Annals of Tourism Research* 27(3): 624–37.

Reisinger, Y. and Turner L.W. (2004) *Cross-cultural Behaviour in Tourism: Concepts and Analysis*, Amsterdam: Elsevier/Butterworth/Heinemann.

Richards, G. (ed.) (1996) *Cultural Tourism in Europe*, Wallingford: CABI.

——(ed.) (2007) *Cultural Tourism: Global and Local Perspectives*, New York: Haworth Press.

Richards, G. and Munsters, W. (2010) *Cultural Tourism Research Methods*, Wallingford: CABI.

Seiler, V.L., Hsieh, S., Seiler, M.J. and Hsieh, C. (2002) 'Modelling Travel Expenditures for Taiwanese Tourism', *Journal of Travel & Tourism Marketing* 13(4): 47–59.

Stylianou-Lambert, T. (2011) 'Gazing from Home: Cultural Tourism and Art Museums', *Annals of Tourism Research* 38(2): 403–21.

Tabachnick, B.G. and Fidell, L.S. (1996) *Using Multivariate Statistics*, New York: Harper Collins.

Taylor, D., Fletcher, R. and Clabaugh, T. (1993) 'A Comparison of Characteristics, Regional Expenditures, and Economic Impact of Visitors to Historical Sites with Other Recreational Visitors', *Journal of Travel Research* 32(1): 30–35.

Thrane, C. and Farstad, E. (2011) 'Domestic Tourism Expenditures: The Non-linear Effects of Length of Stay and Travel Party Size', *Tourism Management* 32: 46–52.

Wang, Y. and Davidson, M.C.G. (2010) 'A Review of Micro-analyses of Tourist Expenditure', *Current Issues in Tourism* 13(6): 507–24.

Wang, Y., Rompf, P., Severt, D. and Peerapatdit, N. (2006) 'Examining and Identifying the Determinants of Travel Expenditure Patterns', *International Journal of Tourism Research* 8: 333–46.

Woodside, A.G., Cook, V.J. and Mindak, W. (1987) 'Profiling the Heavy Traveller Segment', *Journal of Travel Research* 25(3): 9–14.

## Further reading

Barry, K. and O'Hagan, J. (1972) 'An Econometric Study of British Tourist Expenditure in Ireland', *Economic and Social Review* 3(2): 143–61. (Determinants of travel expenditures.)

Crouch, G.I. (1994) 'The Study of International Tourism Demand: A Survey of Practice', *Journal of Travel Research* 32(4): 41–54. (Determinants of travel expenditures.)

Davies, B. and Mangan, J. (1992) 'Family Expenditure on Hotels and Holidays', *Annals of Tourism Research* 19: 691–99. (Determinants of travel expenditures.)

Lim C. (1997) 'An Econometric Classification and Review of International Tourism Demand Models', *Tourism Economics* 3(1): 69–81. (Determinants of travel expenditures.)

Pizam, A. and Reichel, A. (1979) 'Big Spenders and Little Spenders in US Tourism', *Journal of Travel Research* 18(2): 42–43. (Determinants of travel expenditures.)

Qiu, H. and Zhang, J. (1995) 'Determinants of Tourist Arrivals and Expenditures in Canada', *Journal of Travel Research* 34(2): 43–49. (Determinants of travel expenditures.)

Spotts, D.M. and Mahoney, E. (1991) 'Segmenting Visitors to a Destination Region Based on the Volume of their Expenditures', *Journal of Travel Research* 2: 24–31. (Determinants of travel expenditures.)

# 16

# Can the value chain of a cultural tourism destination be measured?

*Juan Ignacio Pulido Fernández and Marcelino Sánchez Rivero*

## Introduction

The concept of the value chain was made popular by Porter (1985) as a basic instrument to describe the progress of the activities within a business organisation, generating value to the final customer. In this way, according to Porter, it is possible to analyse the origin of the competitive advantage of a certain organisation, by the systematic examination of all the activities that are carried out and the way in which they interact.

This term has begun to be used in the context of tourist destinations management, even though, so far, the contributions to this issue are still limited and not always successful, given that most of those who apply it in this field (especially in the area of development co-operation) have not yet realised that tourism is not exactly a sector (and even less a product), lacking then its application of the necessary holistic vision that tourism requires, along with the integration of the group of actors involved in its development and management.

The complexity of the value chain of a tourist destination goes even beyond this, since the product itself is not what consumers actually value, but the experience that is generated by its consumption, and this experience has a space-time double dimension that complicates the conceptualisation and subsequent management of the value chain of tourist destinations.

Notwithstanding this, the references to the need of managing the value chain of the tourist destination as a key factor for competitiveness are constantly increasing.

## The use of the value chain in tourist destination management

Nooteboom (2007) proposed the use of the term value chain for the analysis of the service sector, concluding that not only is it perfectly applicable, but it is also a very useful tool for the detection of inefficiencies in the allocation of resources by this kind of business, even for its suppliers, as it allows the identification of opportunities and obstacles for the commercialisation of its products.

In the field of tourism, most of the few attempts to apply the value chain have taken place, mainly, in the hotel, transport and travel agency sectors, and they have been oriented not as much towards the analysis of the value chain as to that of the supply chain (among the latest,

Fantazy *et al.* 2010; Hong and Yan 2011; Li and Tang 2009; Tang *et al.* 2009; Zhang *et al.* 2009). It is worth setting these two concepts apart. The supply chain refers to the input and output logistics of a business, but used as a technique for the optimisation of raw materials, intermediate and final goods flow (Beamon 1998). However, the value chain is the set of relations among value aggregation processes that primary, intermediate and final goods share.

To date, there are few published research papers about the tourism value chain, more specifically about tourist destinations (Poon 1993; Evans *et al.* 2003; Yilmaz and Bititci 2006; Zhao *et al.* 2009; Yunpeng *et al.* 2011, among others).

As stated by Zhao *et al.* (2009: 522–23), the tourism value chain can be defined as the process of transference of tourist products from suppliers to consumers, which generally consists of tourist products, tourism intermediaries – from traditional or e-commerce – and tourists.

In spite of the early adaptation of the concept of a value chain for the tourism industry made by Poon (1993), the scientific literature about tourism management has not paid much attention to the management of its value chain until recent times, and thus systems or models for the analysis of the value chain in this field have not yet been consolidated (Yilmaz and Bititci 2006).

From Poon's adaptation, Fabricius (2001: 76) proposed a value chain based on two types of activities: primary and support. Primary activities would be those taking place in the 'production process of the tourist product' (creation, marketing, distribution, after-sales service), while support activities would make the development of the former possible.

For their part, Evans *et al.* (2003) adapted the value chain for the analysis of the tourist product, highlighting as basic activities all those business activities with which the tourist product is provided: transport, destination services, commercialisation activities with wholesalers, retailers and travel agencies, marketing actions and customer service; and as support activities, all those organisms and policies that manage, support or work against the tourist product itself, together with the employment of new technologies and information systems, the human resources and the suppliers.

Yilmaz and Bititci (2006) consider that the tourism industry involves diverse actors, being the tourism demand satisfied by their common efforts. They propose a model to measure the performance of the tourism value chain, although their approach starts from a biased conception of the chain, as only the private agents implicated in the tourist destination development are included.

Mitchel and Phuc (2007) studied the value chain of a tourist product in Vietnam, but considering only the agents directly linked to the tourist activity, such as travel agents, transport companies or accommodation enterprises.

On the other hand, Zhao *et al.* (2009) suggest a demand-based reconfiguration of the concept of value chain based on e-commerce. In contrast to the previously mentioned authors, they consider that the actors that enable the tourist consumption are not only those who provide tourist services or who act as intermediaries, but also those agents who supply basic services.

Yunpeng *et al.* (2011) lay emphasis on the incorporation of ICT and the way in which it transforms the value chain of tourism and contributes to an improved information exchange, promoting efficiency between the different links and the actors involved in the decision-making process. As indicated by these authors, 'a tourist destination serves as a "resources collection" to achieve the value of the complete industry in a particular region' (Yunpeng *et al.* 2011: 193), and so research must be focused on the possibilities of optimisation of the tourist destinations' value chain.

The value chain of a cultural destination should have the configuration shown in Figure 16.1. The proposed model comprises nine links, organised, at the same time, in three stages that follow the logical time sequence in the process of generation of value of a destination to its potential clients.

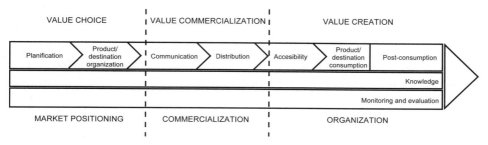

*Figure 16.1* Value chain of the cultural destination

Yilmaz and Bititci (2006: 342) try to justify the little interest of researchers (policy makers and tourism managers) in the management of the value chain of a destination by reason of the complexity in measuring its results. For them, the systematic character of the tourist activity impedes a more holistic view of it. The 'interdependent' nature of tourism amplifies the demanding requirements over all the agents involved in the provision of the services that shape a high-quality tourist product. It is hence argued that for the construction of a system which satisfies the client in every step of the value chain and guarantees the efficiency of the procedures in each stage, a solid system to measure the performance of every implicated agent is required.

Until now, as Kaplinsky (2000: 122) already acknowledged, the concept of the value chain 'is merely a descriptive construct, at most, providing a heuristic framework for the generation of data'. The aim of researchers should be, therefore, to generate an analytic structure that allows measuring the performance of every agent of the chain involved in the generation of value oriented to the final client. That would further an active management of the value chain of the destination.

## Methodological approaches to measure the value chain of a cultural destination

From a practical point of view, the measurement of the value chain of a tourist destination is not easy, for two fundamental reasons: the multidimensional character of the destination and the interdependence between these dimensions. There are several difficulties, therefore, that can be encountered in the measurement of the value chain. More concretely, the following questions can be asked:

- How can we reconcile the diverse interests of the agents involved in the value chain so that the global utility of the tourist destination can be maximised?
- How can the efficiency of a tourist destination be maximised by transforming an assembly of inputs in outputs?
- How does the external environment affect the value chain of a tourist destination and, more concretely, how does this environment influence the connections among the different links of the value chain?
- How can we quantify the different links in the value chain and how can the influence of these links on each other be determined?

To try and answer each one of these questions, a solution will be offered using different methodologies.

## Multi-criteria decision techniques

In the value chain of a cultural tourist destination a multitude of agents intervene (planning authorities, landlords, travel agents, suppliers, distributors, etc.). These often have conflicting interests and they often apply different criteria in their management of tourist activities. Given this complexity it is impossible to opt for a single criterion or choose only one alternative from among all those available, since in this case the interests of only one actor will be satisfied, generating dissatisfaction among the other actors in the value chain. It is necessary, therefore, to combine different criteria and available alternatives to maximise the utility for all the agents involved in the value chain of the destination.

The so-called multi-criteria decision techniques (Romero 1996; Zopounidis and Pardalos 2010; Shi *et al.* 2011) are used to solve this problem, which has the advantage that all parties concerned participate in the decision-making process, provide information, and seek a consensus that maximises the value generated by the value chain of the cultural destination.

The problem of multi-criteria analysis is defined on the basis of a group of alternatives $\mathbf{A} = \{A_1, A_2, \ldots, A_m\}$, of a group of states of nature $\mathbf{S} = \{S_1, S_2, \ldots, S_p\}$, of a group of criteria $\mathbf{C} = \{C_1, C_2, \ldots, C_n\}$. Now then, for every alternative $A_i$ and for every state of nature $S_k$, we assume that $C_j = C_j(A_i; S_k)$, so that $C_j : A \times S \rightarrow C \subset \mathbf{P}^n$ is characterised by its group of attributes $C_j = \{C_1, C_2, \ldots, C_n\}$. Once identified the group of criteria $C_j(A_i) = (C_1(A_i), C_2(A_i), \ldots, C_n(A_i))$ that will operate as the base to support the decision-making process, the mathematical problem to be solved is:

$$\max C_j(A_i) = \max(C_1(A_i), C_2(A_i), \ldots, C_n(A_i))$$

Multi-criteria decision techniques are generally classified according to the use of a value function to find the optimal decision or not. Those based on the value function are grouped under the generic denomination of multi-criteria utility theory, including, among others, the additive aggregate method, the UTA method or the VISA programme. On the other hand, those that are not based on the value function are known as multi-criteria classification methods (Electre and Promethee are the most commonly used).

## Data envelopment analysis

The value chain of a tourist destination is no more than a productive process that generates added value upon converting inputs into outputs. The economic objective of each actor that operates in the value chain is to maximise the value added, which involves maximising outputs and minimising inputs. One must consider, also, that the outputs of each actor in a link of the value chain are inputs for the actors in the following links of the chain. Therefore, the efficiency of each tourist actor (understood as the difference between outputs and inputs) is interrelated with that of the other actors. The final objective of the cultural tourist destination is to maximise the efficiency of all the actors that intervene in the value-creation process.

On the basis of the concept of efficiency, understood as the quotient between the output and input of a tourist business, data envelopment analysis (Charnes *et al.* 1978; Ramanathan 2003; Cooper *et al.* 2011) is a technique focused on frontiers rather than central tendencies. In opposition to the traditional regression, in which a line around core data is tried to be adjusted, data envelopment analysis attempts to identify the analysis units (tourist agents, in this case) that move further away from middle values and, subsequently, are more efficient or more inefficient.

Considering $n$ agents involved in the value chain of a cultural destination, and denoting $x_{ij}$, the quantity of input $i$ used by the agent $j$ and $y_{rj}$, the quantity of output $r$ employed by that same agent, the data envelopment analysis aims at maximising the relative efficiency of every agent of the value chain. Consequently, considering a total of $n$ inputs and $m$ outputs in the value chain of a cultural destination, this problem of optimisation of the efficiency for the agent $t$ would be formulated as follows:

$$\text{Max}\,Z_i(u,v) = \frac{\sum_{r=1}^{m} u_r y_{rt}}{\sum_{i=1}^{n} v_i x_{it}}$$

subject to:

$$\frac{\sum_{r=1}^{m} u_r y_{rj}}{\sum_{i=1}^{n} v_i x_{ij}} \quad for\ j = 1, 2, \ldots, p$$

$$\frac{u_r}{\sum_{i=1}^{n} v_i x_{i0}} \geq \varepsilon > 0 \quad for\ r = 1, 2, \ldots, m$$

$$\frac{v_i}{\sum_{i=1}^{n} v_i x_{i0}} \geq \varepsilon > 0\ for\ i = 1, 2, \ldots, n$$

The problem of optimisation posed calculates the optimal weights $u_r^*$ and $v_i^*$ of the outputs and inputs, respectively, which allow the achievement of the efficient frontier (that is, the maximum relative efficiency). The comparison between the real relative efficiency of every agent of the value change and this efficient frontier permits the identification of the agents that are more efficient (those placed on the efficient frontier or close to it) and those with the highest levels of productive inefficiency (which deviates from its efficiency frontier). The correction of the inefficiency problems of certain actors that intervene in the chain will lead to an increase in the value that it generates.

## Artificial neural networks

The management of the value chain of a cultural tourism destination is highly influenced by the external environment, both social and economic, in which the destination is located. This influences in great measure the capacity to generate added value for each destination specifically. For example, the generation of value of a tourist attraction declared a World Heritage site by the United Nations Educational, Scientific and Cultural Organization (UNESCO) will be very different if this attraction is found, for example, in Peru or in Nigeria, than if it is located in Spain or Italy, as the economic and social conditions of these countries are very different.

Therefore, the environmental conditions determine the form of the value chain of a cultural tourism destination and, above all, the relationships among the phases of the value chain. It is very important, consequently, to incorporate information about the environment. To measure the direct effect of the environmental conditions on some phases of the value chain and their indirect effect on others, one can use techniques associated with artificial neural network analysis.

Due to the existing interrelation between the different elements of the value chain, artificial neural networks can be applied to determine the value of each connection that comes to a specific part of the value chain to produce the expected output. They can also be used as a complement to the multi-criteria decision techniques to model the utility functions of the destination agents, in order to predict the tourist demand of the destination and introduce uncertainty in the decision–making process.

Artificial neural networks (Hu 2002; Isasi and Galván 2004; Olmeda 2007) reproduce the operation of a biological neural network. Thus, the neural network is constituted by a set of neurons (in this particular case, neurons would be different links of the value chain), where each neuron receives, coming from a previous neuron $o$ from outside, information through a set of variables (inputs). That information is processed inside the neuron applying a transference function. The result obtained from that transference function is transmitted to the following neurons (links) of the neural network (value chain) throughout weighted connections (synapses) that are established between each other.

To be more precise, an artificial neural network is a directed graph, in which the nodes are neurons and the connections are synapses. Every node $i$ (neuron or link of the value chain) is associated to a state variable $x_i$; every connection between the node $i$ and the node $j$ is related to a weight $w_{ij} \in \Re$. Besides, every node $i$ involves a threshold $\theta_i$. Finally, a transference function $f_i(x_i; w_{ij}; \theta_i)$ that provides the new state of the node is defined for every node.

In so doing, it can be affirmed that an artificial neural network is an application $f : \Re^n \times W \rightarrow \Omega \subset \Re^p$, where the set $W$ is identified as weight space.

As can be observed, the output that the neural network offers depends on both the input from outside and the weight of the connections between neurons. Therefore, the aim of neural networks is to determine the weight of these connections so that the network produces the expected output, given a certain input. This process of estimation of the coefficients of synaptic connections is called *learning*.

## Structural equation models

Most of the links in the value chain of a tourist destination that are presented in Figure 16.1 present two essential characteristics: they are not directly observable (which obliges us to seek indicators that permit their quantification); and they cannot be measured through a single indicator. Elements such as communication, distribution, accessibility, the post-consumption phase and, above all, the two elements present in all the phases of the value chain (knowledge and evaluation) require the use of indicators that permit us to appraise their contribution to the global process of value generation in a tourist destination. In addition, the 'latent' links (which cannot be observed directly) are often interrelated, so that some are the causes of others. Thus, for example, it seems logical to assume that the organisation of the destination product will influence the communication about the destination, and that this in turn will influence the distribution of the destination product. However, some relationships among phases of the value chain may be not consecutive. For example, how does the organisation of the destination product affect accessibility or how does communication affect the post-consumption experience? Does knowledge affect all the links in the value chain to the same extent? As we can see, the analysis of the relationships among the phases of the value chain of a tourist destination generate a multitude of questions, which can be addressed through structural equation modelling techniques.

Given the interrelationships existing between the different links of the value chain, structural equations models (Schumacker and Lomax 2004; Kline 2005) allow the simultaneous measurement of the relationships between a set of independent variables and a set of dependent variables. Thus, presuming that the links of the cultural destination value chain and the three stages in which the links are organised are 'latent' variables, this technique permits the identification of casual relations between them.

That set of techniques is based on the analysis of the covariance between the variables that measures the different links of the value chain, with a twofold objective: understanding the correlation structures existing between a set of observed variables; and explaining most of the variances of the related variables using an a priori model that incorporates latent variables. The formulation of an a priori model implies the introduction by the researcher of the variables that are supposed to affect other variables of the value chain as well as the direction of these effects. Then the specification a priori of the model reflects the researcher hypotheses, which can be contrasted by means of the available data.

The structural equations model is composed of two sub-models: a structural model and a measurement model. The matrix expression of the *structural model*, which involves the effect of a latent variable over any other latent variable of the model, is the following:

$$\eta = \mathbf{B}\eta + \Gamma\xi + \zeta$$

being $\eta$ the vector of latent endogenous variables; $\xi$ the vector of exogenous latent variables; $\mathbf{B}$ the matrix of co-efficients of endogenous latent variables that quantifies the existing relations in those endogenous variables; $\Gamma$ the matrix of co-efficients of the exogenous latent variables that holds the existing statistical relations among them; and $\zeta$ the vector of random perturbation.

On the other hand, the *measurement model*, which specifies the existing relations between latent and observed variables, consists of two matrix expressions, one for the indicators of endogenous latent variables and the other for the indicators of exogenous latent variables, i.e.:

$$\mathbf{y} = \Lambda_y\eta + \varepsilon$$

$$\mathbf{x} = \Lambda_x\xi + \delta$$

being the vector of indicators of endogenous latent variables; $\Lambda_y$ the measurement co-efficient matrix $\lambda_{ij}$ between the observed indicator $Y_i$ and the endogenous latent variable $\eta_j$; $\varepsilon$ the vector of measurement errors for the endogenous latent variables; $\mathbf{x}$ the vector of indicators for the exogenous latent variables; $\Lambda_x$ the matrix of measurement co-efficients $\lambda_{ij}$ between the observed indicator $X_i$ and the exogenous latent variable $\xi_j$; and $\delta$ the vector of measurement errors for the indicators of exogenous latent variables.

Once all the parameters of the model are estimated, different goodness–of–fit tests can be applied. In that sense, it is possible to distinguish between adjustment measures of the global, measurement and structural models.

## Conclusion

Recent literature reveals an increasing interest in analysing the value chain of tourist destinations. As Cooper *et al.* (2008) admit, until recently, each agent avidly competed in its 'own' segment of the value chain, taking no notice of the importance of collaborating with other members of the chain. However, in the future, integrated management will prevail, overcoming the current separate management of individual sectors such as accommodation, transport, intermediary services, etc.

This research study presents four techniques that can be used to solve three questions that determine the generation of value in the value chain of the cultural destination, stakeholders' decision-making processes and the productive efficiency of businesses, and the relationships between the links in the chain.

So far, there are few published studies on this matter, and most of them refer not to the value chain of a destination, but rather to the supply chain of some tourist businesses. There is a need, then, to generate a debate about the possibilities of measuring the variety of activities required to, as Kaplinsky (2000) states, conduct a product or service from its conception, through the diverse intermediate production stages, to its delivery to the consumer, disposition and final disposal.

# References

Beamon, B.M. (1998) 'Supply Chain Design and Analysis: Models and Methods', *International Journal of Production Economics* 55: 281–94.

Charnes, A., Cooper, W.W. and Rhodes, E. (1978) 'Measuring the Efficiency of Decision-making Units', *European Journal of Operational Research* 3: 429–44.

Cooper, C., Fletcher, J., Fyall, A., Gilbert, D. and Wanhill, S. (2008) *Tourism: Principles and Practice*, fourth edn, Essex: Pearson Education.

Cooper, W.W., Seiford, L.M. and Zhu, J. (2011) *Handbook on Data Envelopment Analysis*, International Series in Operations Research & Management Science, volume 164, New York: Springer.

Evans, N., Campbell, D. and Stonehouse, G. (2003) *Strategic Management for Travel and Tourism*, Oxford: Butterworth-Heinemann.

Fabricius, M.P. (2001) *Competitive Strategies for Tourism Destinations*, unpublished MBL Research Report, Pretoria: University of South Africa.

Fantazy, K.A., Kumar, V. and Kumar, U. (2010) 'Supply Management Practices and Performance in the Canadian Hospitality Industry', *International Journal of Hospitality Management* 29: 685–93.

Hong, L. and Yan, J. (2011) 'Construction the Tourism Supply Chain Focusing on the Tourism Destination as the Core', 2011 International Conference on E-Business and E-Government, ieeexplore.ieee.org/stamp/stamp.jsp?tp=&arnumber=5881759 (accessed 15 November 2012).

Hu, C. (2002) *Advanced Tourism Demand Forecasting: Artificial Neural Network and Box-Jenkins Modelling*, ProQuest Information and Learning Company's UMI Dissertation Services, Michigan.

Isasi, P. and Galván, I. (2004) *Redes de neuronas artificiales: un enfoque práctico*, Madrid: Pearson-Prentice Hall.

Kaplinsky, R. (2000) 'Spreading the Gains from Globalisation: What Can be Learned from Value Chain Analysis?' *Journal of Development Studies* 37(2): 117–46.

Kline, R.B. (2005) *Principles and Practice of Structural Equation Modelling*, New York: Guilford Press.

Li, Q. and Tang, F. (2009) 'An Integrated Model and Coordination Mechanism of Tourism Supply Chain Management', 2009 International Conference on Test and Measurement, 51–54, ieeexplore.ieee.org/stamp/stamp.jsp?tp=&arnumber=5413006 (accessed 15 November 2012).

Mitchel, J. and Phuc, L.C. (2007) *Final Report on Participatory Tourism Value Chain Analysis in Da Nang, Central Vietnam*, Vietnam: Vietnam Private Sector Support Programme.

Nooteboom (2007) 'Service Value Chains and Effects of Scale', *Service Business* 1(2): 119–39.

Olmeda, I. (2007) 'Redes neuronales en turismo', in López, D. and Pulido, J.I. (eds) *La actividad turística española en 2006*, Jaén: Asociación Española de Expertos Científicos en Turismo and Editorial Universitaria Ramón Areces, S.A., 51–58.

Poon, A. (1993) *Tourism, Technology and Competitive Strategies*, Wallingford: CABI.

Porter, M.E. (1985) *The Competitive Advantage: Creating and Sustaining Superior Performance*, New York: Free Press.

Ramanathan, R. (2003) *An Introduction to Data Envelopment Analysis: A Tool for Performance Measurement*, New Delhi: Sage Publications.

Romero, C. (1996) *Análisis de las decisiones multicriterio*, Madrid: Ingeniería de Sistemas.

Schumacker, R.E. and Lomax, R.G. (2004) *A Beginner's Guide to Structural Equation Modelling*, London: Lawrence Erlbaum.

Shi, Y., Wang, S., Kou, G. and Wallenius, J. (2011) *New State of Multiple Criteria Decision Making in the 21st Century*, Berlin: Springer.

Tang, F., Qiu, C. and Jiang, S. (2009) 'Supplier Selection of Tourism Supply Chain Based on Information Entropy and Matter-element Model', International Conference on Management and Service Science, ieeexplore.ieee.org/stamp/stamp.jsp?tp=& arnumber=5305439 (accessed 15 November 2012).

Yilmaz, Y. and Bititci, U.S. (2006) 'Performance Measurement in Tourism: A Value Chain Model', *International Journal of Contemporary Hospitality Management* 18(4): 341–49.

Yunpeng, L., Yongqiu, X., Min, N., Yu, H. and Lina, Q. (2011) 'Research on Dynamic Optimized Approach of Value Chain in Tourist Destinations', in R. Lee (ed.) *Computer and Information Science*, Berlin: Springer-Verlag, 191–99.

Zhang, X., Song, H. and Huang, G.Q. (2009) 'Tourism Supply Chain Management: A New Research Agenda', *Tourism Management* 30(3): 345–58.

Zhao, L., Cao, G. and Liu, M. (2009) 'The Reconfiguration of Tourism Value Chain Based on E-Commerce', in *Proceedings of 2009 International Conference on Management of e-Commerce and e-Government*, IEE Computer Society: 522–25.

Zopounidis, C. and Pardalos, P. (2010) *Handbook of Multicriteria Analysis*, Berlin: Springer.

# PART III

# Social patterns and trends

This section partly draws on some of the theories and issues that are pertinent to sociological enquiry, as well as geography and political economy. Earlier studies of the sociology of tourism focused on the idea that tourism was merely a form of escapism from the monotony or anomie of everyday life (Boorstin 1964). However, the sociology of tourism in a globalised world has produced a multiplicity of tourist gazes and there are now countless mobilities (Urry 2002), causing rapid and radical changes in tourist typologies and categorisations, which are becoming more fluid. Consumer psychology, mass media, communications and new technologies have had a major influence on the sociology of tourism. Issues relating to tourism as a form of citizenship, a human right, problems of social exclusion and how to increase the accessibility of tourism are all critical issues in cultural tourism studies too.

Mobility has become a highly significant topic in tourism research in recent years. It transcends disciplinary boundaries in its coverage of political, technological, social and cultural developments. Mobility is clearly at the heart of our understanding of tourism with its global transport networks, international business connections and policy frameworks, flows of images and representations, exchange of cultures and social interactions. It is important also to consider the concept of immobility in the context of tourism, as it has a significant bearing on the nature of host-guest interactions (i.e. where hosts never travel beyond the destination). There are also political issues relating to border control, political and social conflicts and safety issues which can hinder the development of tourism. Kevin Hannam and Sujama Roy in this section analyse the relationship between cultural tourism and the new mobilities paradigm. They argue that tourism is now an integral rather than marginal part of everyday social and cultural life; however, it is becoming harder to distinguish between tourism and other mobilities. Karolina Buczkowska gives an interesting example of a specific kind of social mobility, which is the ERASMUS phenomenon. Students travel and study or work in a foreign environment and, she argues, become 'ambassadors of cultural tourism' in the process.

The themes of embodiment and performance are alluded to by Hannam and Roy, and are then discussed in more depth by Kevin Meethan in this section. Corporeal and social performances in tourism mean that the self is being contingently produced. Tourists are rarely conscious of their performances, although they are likely to be somewhat predictable in the sense that their experiences are usually foregrounded by historical, social and cultural education or even indoctrination, as well as media representations and images. There may be elements of improvisation in tourism, especially when it involves interactions with host communities; however, the theme of 'staging' has also been well-documented in tourism studies. Meethan suggests that cultural tourism studies would benefit from a more reflexive analysis of the individual's experience, including elements of multi-sensory engagement and performance.

The age-old social phenomenon of hospitality is revisited in this section by both Tom Selwyn and David Picard to illustrate its traditional origins as a social and cultural phenomenon. David Picard's chapter considers cosmopolitanism rather than globalisation as a meta-narrative for understanding global tourism and encouraging more ethical approaches. He argues that this is a political and philosophical movement with the guiding principles of world citizenship and the defence of equality. He questions the power-based decisions that traditionally have dominated international organisations, often hampering the development of a more ethical tourism industry. He suggests that a return to the traditional and historical meaning of hospitality, as outlined by several philosophers, may be the key to redressing imbalances in tourism and increasing its positive role in world citizenship. Tom Selwyn discusses the important role of hospitality in forging human relationships with strangers, foreigners or even perceived enemies which can take us beyond hostility. Traditionally, guests were even seen as being touched with a divine or sacred quality, whereas today these are often overlooked in favour of commercial efficiency.

The natural human orientation towards the darker side of life is explored by Karel Werdler in this section, but one chapter does not really do justice to the growing interest in dark tourism. The new millennium has so far proved to be fairly turbulent, with its global terrorism, environmental catastrophes, economic and political crises, therefore the interest in disaster tourism is unlikely to wane anytime soon. Whole books have been devoted to the theme of dark tourism (e.g. Lennon and Foley 2000), as tourists are increasingly drawn to both historical and contemporary sites which commemorate past tragedies. Smith *et al.* (2010) summarise the categorisation of dark tourism which seems to have emerged in recent years. This ranges from Rojek's (1993, 1997) concepts of 'black spots' and 'sensation sites' – the former referring to places marking death, the latter to sites where a disastrous event took place – to Seaton's (1996) 'thanotourism' where visitors are motivated by an interest in death, to Tunbridge and Ashworth's (1996) 'heritage of atrocity' or 'dissonant heritage'. Werdler provides an interesting in-depth analysis of 'Dark Exhibitions', including artists' different representations of death and dying, the activities used to engage visitors, and their motivations and responses. This chapter makes us question the most effective and sensitive ways to depict difficult and emotional subjects at cultural attractions and sites.

Non-religious or secular spirituality is a subject that is not explored by the authors in this section, but is alluded to by Erik Cohen in his work on tattoo tourism and the religious signs and symbols that are misused or misunderstood by tourists. It is important to note that in many tourist-generating countries, especially in the West, a slow but steady spiritual revolution is taking place in which secular spirituality is taking over from traditional religion (Heelas and Woodhead 2005). This means that tourists are increasingly inclined to copy those aspects of religious or spiritual practices that they find most appealing without much concern for their origins. Cohen's (1996) earlier work on tourism described how the quest for a 'spiritual centre' is an integral part of tourism, especially when people feel socially alienated. This often involved a process of sampling 'alternative' rituals. Tattoos can provide a permanent reminder or marker of this spiritual journey.

## Summary of the chapters in this section

**Kevin Hannam** and **Sujama Roy** argue that tourism is now an integral part of everyday social and cultural life alongside other mobilities with which it has a 'fluid interdependence'. Mobilities and immobilities tend to take place in tourism 'cultural contact zones', which are the sites of complex interactions and identities. Although cultural tourists may be more inclined towards immobility for some of their stay so that they can fully engage with the location and its people, they may also experience cultural encounters while on the move (i.e. during travel to a destination). Urry's (2007) five independent 'mobilities' are used to analyse cultural tourism, including corporeal travel as an embodied experience, physical movement of objects (such as cultural souvenirs), imaginative travel including images of places and peoples, virtual travel (e.g. fantasies, myths and simulations), and communicative travel via media, internet and mobile phones. However, the authors suggest that there is a need for better maps of the sensuous and emotional geographies of cultural tourism, especially the notion of performativity.

**Karolina Buczkowska** discusses a particular form of mobility in cultural tourism that has become a widespread social phenomenon, and that is the travel of ERASMUS students. This includes those studying and undertaking internships abroad, usually for a period of three to twelve months. They therefore spend considerably longer in a destination than many other tourists, and usually have access to increased information about the place, its history, its people and their social and cultural traditions. They can therefore become far more immersed in the atmosphere and absorb the place more leisurely and profoundly. She argues that ERASMUS students have increasingly become 'ambassadors' of cultural tourism because of their special status in representing their country for extended periods abroad, their development of close relationships with local people, and their enhanced understanding of social, intellectual and linguistic aspects of culture.

**Kevin Meethan** analyses in more depth the notion of embodiment and performance, especially insofar as it relates to human agency and individuation in society. In tourism, performance can relate to the staging of rituals or spectacles by communities, or the gathering of certain 'props' in order to enact the role of an individual tourist. He suggests that performance is an integral or embodied part of everyday life, sometimes involving improvisations, including in our interactions with others. However, he also suggests that individuals sometimes have little agency or freedom to improvise and are forced to conform. This is not only because of enforced political or social regimes, but also because many of our experiences (including tourism) are already foregrounded by history, society, culture, media, etc. Embodied practices also take place in constantly shifting and interactive spaces, not on an empty, static stage. Wider narratives of society, including collective memory, are as influential as personal narratives, although the reflexive, engaged, sensory performance of the individual is still highly significant.

**David Picard** analyses the relationship between cosmopolitanism and hospitality, which he links closely to philosophical and political debates. Cosmopolitanism has become an international meta-narrative which advocates world citizenship and hospitality in its traditional sense (i.e. the welcoming of strangers or foreigners into one's home or land). Cosmopolitan ethics are now being seen as a guiding moral for many international organisations and nations wishing to address issues of unequal treatment of people, unequal flows of tourists, and inhospitable treatment of certain groups of people. Alternative tourism discourses are invented to address these issues, but they rarely succeed as they are not deeply embedded enough in the whole of the tourism and hospitality industries. However, education, inter-cultural dialogue, and the promotion of hospitality in its traditional sense can play a key role in this development.

**Tom Selwyn** analyses the phenomenon of hospitality using a highly original approach, exploring the main themes as depicted in works of art. He argues that traditional understandings of hospitality have been lost as the industry increasingly focuses on commercial efficiency. He suggests that hospitality was traditionally based on a number of fundamental premises, such as symbolic manifestations of social status and political power, an exchange of honour, but also a recognition of the sacredness or 'divinity' of guests. This relates partly to the offering of 'sanctuary' to visitors. Hospitality can also be a direct expression of pleasure, excesses and hedonism, but still be bound by rules of social etiquette. He also discusses the relationship between hospitality and hostility, at first glance polar opposites, but on closer examination, inextricably linked both etymologically and conceptually. The word originally refers to strangers or foreigners, but also to enemies. Refugees from political conflict may be accommodated in tourist spaces or seek asylum amongst foreigners in other countries. Overall, the concept refers to the establishment of relationships, not all of which can be harmonious but can still be hospitable rather than hostile.

**Karel Werdler** analyses the phenomenon of dark tourism and its role in the field of cultural tourism. Using a case study of the Netherlands, he explores different categories of dark tourism. This includes military or war heritage, prisons, cemeteries, funerary art and exhibitions. This is followed by an in-depth study of dark exhibitions over the past 20 years. He examines the content of the exhibitions, such as the main themes, and the number of visitors. He focuses on those exhibitions that have dealt with death and dying, including the representation used by different artists to depict the phenomenon or process. He especially notes those exhibitions that provided some kind of interactive visitor experience deemed unique or innovative. He examines the reactions of visitors to the exhibitions, as well as their original motivation to visit. Interestingly, many of them were positive, indicating that the treatment of dark and dissonant subjects is not something to be shied away from in the development of cultural tourism, but to be carried out with as much sensitivity as possible. This need not exclude innovative and creative approaches.

Finally, **Erik Cohen** examines the rather unusual subject of tattoo tourism, which he rightly identifies as being under-researched in cultural tourism studies. Tattooing has become a much more mainstream activity in Western, middle-class society in recent years, and this interest has extended to tourism. This includes tattoo-related events, such as international tattoo conventions and exhibitions. In particular, tourists tend to visit Thailand, where the art of tattooing also has cultural and spiritual significance and is considered to be a 'living tradition'. Although it is not a Buddhist custom, some tattoos are actually performed by Monks in temples. However, there are concerns that the meaning and significance of many designs and symbols may not be fully understood by foreigners and could be misused. This is especially true of religious symbols, which have been deemed inappropriate by the Thai Ministry of Culture, a controversial intervention which was thought by some to compromise artistic freedom and business development.

# References

Boorstin, D. (1964) *The Image: A Guide to Pseudo-Events in America*, New York: Harper & Row.

Cohen, E. (1996) 'A Phenomenology of Tourist Experiences', in Apostopoulos, Y., Leivadi, S. and Yiannakis, A. (eds) *The Sociology of Tourism: Theoretical and Empirical Investigations*, London: Routledge, 90–111.

Heelas, P. and Woodhead, L. (2005) *The Spiritual Revolution*, Oxford: Blackwell.

Lennon, J. and Foley, M. (2000) *Dark Tourism: The Attraction of Death and Disaster*, London: Thomson.

Rojek, C. (1993) *Ways of Escape: Modern Transformations in Leisure and Travel*, London: Macmillan.

——(1997) 'Indexing, Dragging and the Social Construction of Tourist Sights', in Rojek, C. and Urry, J. (eds) *Touring Cultures: Transformations of Travel and Theory*, London: Routledge, 52–74.

Seaton, A.V. (1996) 'Guided by the Dark: From Thanatopsis to Thanatourism', *International Journal of Heritage Studies* 2(4): 234–44.

Smith, M.K., Hart, M. and MacLeod, N. (2010) *Key Concepts in Tourist Studies*, London: Sage.

Tunbridge, J.E. and Ashworth, G.J. (1996) *Dissonant Heritage: The Management of the Past as a Resource in Conflict*, London: John Wiley & Sons.

Urry, J. (2002 [1990]) *The Tourist Gaze: Leisure and Travel in Contemporary Societies*, London: Sage.

——(2007) *Mobilities*, Cambridge: Polity.

# 17

# Cultural tourism and the mobilities paradigm

*Kevin Hannam and Sujama Roy*

## Introduction

This chapter reviews work from what has been termed the 'new mobilities paradigm' (Sheller and Urry 2004). The mobilities paradigm arguably allows us to place travel and tourism at the centre of social and cultural life rather than at the margins. Such tourism mobilities are often viewed as being bound up with both everyday, mundane journeys as well as the exotic encounters that have been the mainstay of much analysis in cultural tourism. The study of cultural tourism landscapes, meanwhile, has frequently privileged the visual in terms of the tourist gaze. Thus tourism landscapes have been 'read' as relatively 'flat' representations in much previous research. On the other hand, more recent research has engaged with new theories to argue that cultural tourism is experienced through tourists' own bodies through diverse mobility practices involving new technologies.

For instance, Larsen (2005: 81) has suggested that road and rail travel allows the traveller to experience landscapes and 'virtual otherness' while simultaneously being 'on the move'. Jacobsen (2001: 100) refers to this phenomenon as the 'passing gaze' – the process of viewing or 'consuming' places while in motion, while Sachs (1992: 155) adds that motor tourism 'embodies an individual way of experiencing landscapes'. Hence, this chapter argues that the mobilities paradigm allows us to analyse cultural tourism as 'more than representational' as simultaneously both visual and embodied through the concept of performativity. To begin with the chapter outlines the concept of tourism mobilities before discussing how this might be applied in the development of a research agenda for cultural tourism studies. Finally, the chapter reviews the recent theoretical academic literature that has developed the notion of the 'more-than representational' and the performative.

## Tourism mobilities

Tourism is increasingly viewed not as an ephemeral aspect of social life that is practised outside normal, everyday life. Rather it is seen as integral to wider processes of economic and political development and even constitutive of everyday life (Franklin 2003; Edensor 2007; Hannam and Knox 2010). Indeed, Franklin and Crang (2001: 3) point out that, 'tourism has broken away from its beginnings as a relatively minor and ephemeral ritual of modern national life to become a significant modality through which transnational modern life is organised'. Thus, Sheller and Urry (2004: 1) write in their book *Tourism Mobilities*:

> We refer to 'tourism mobilities', then, not simply to state the obvious (that tourism is a form of mobility), but to highlight that many different mobilities inform tourism, shape the places where tourism is performed, and drive the making and unmaking of tourist destinations. Mobilities of people and objects, airplanes and suitcases, plants and animals, images and brands, data systems and satellites, all go into 'doing' tourism ... Tourism mobilities involve complex combinations of movement and stillness, realities and fantasies, play and work.

Furthermore, Sheller and Urry (2006: 1) go as far as to argue that: 'It seems that a new paradigm is being formed within the social sciences, the "new mobilities" paradigm.' Broadly, they argue that the concept of mobilities is concerned with mapping both the large-scale movements of people, objects, capital, and information across the world, as well as the more local processes of daily transportation, movement through public space, and the travel of material things within everyday life (Hannam *et al.* 2006).

Again, tourism is increasingly seen as a process that has become integral to social and cultural life. It is not just about the purchase of second homes and the interconnections between tourism and migration. Rather, everything seems to be in perpetual movement throughout the world. *Most* people *travel* – academics, terrorists, tourists, military people, business people, homeless people, celebrities, migrants, refugees, backpackers, commuters, students, friends – filling the world's planes, trains, ships, buses, cars and streets. In the contemporary world all sorts of political, technological, financial and transportational changes have been critical in significantly lowering the mobility barriers for many. Tourism, leisure, transport, business, travel, migration and communication are thus all blurred and need to be analysed together in their fluid inter-dependence rather than discretely (Hannam *et al.* 2006; Sheller and Urry 2006).

On the one hand, moving between places physically or virtually can be a source of status and power for some tourists such as backpackers (see Richards and Wilson 2004; Hannam and Ateljevic 2007; Hannam and Diekmann 2010). On the other hand, where mobilities are coerced it can generate economic and cultural dislocation as with many migrants and refugees around the world (see Gill *et al.* 2011). Such mobilities and immobilities become particularly apparent in the so-called tourism 'cultural contact zones' at the interstices of different countries, where notions of citizenship can become highly contested and where multiple identities become increasingly fluid (see Bianchi 2000; King and Christou 2011). Analysing contemporary mobilities thus involves examining many consequences for different peoples and different places located in the fast and slow lanes of societies (Hannam *et al.* 2006; Sheller and Urry 2006).

## A mobilities agenda for cultural tourism

This section sketches out a rough agenda for cultural tourism research from a mobilities perspective. For example, we need to ask questions of how and *when* cultural tourists may become migrants, for instance (O'Reilly 2003). The relations between migration, return migration, transnationalism, and tourism need to be further researched. Of course, the ways in which physical movement pertains to upward and downward social mobility are also central here. In such a context we need to examine how cultural tourism becomes part of this social mobility and how it relates to new cultural identities and notions of cultural citizenship, particularly in the cultural contact zones mentioned above. Moreover, it is perhaps too obvious to perceive tourists as being continually on the move, as being hyper-mobile when in fact being a cultural tourist sometimes has more to do with being in places, of being relatively immobile and in the relative slow lane, through choice or finance. Places, technologies and 'gates' enhance the mobilities of some while reinforcing the immobilities (or demobilisation) of others. Such (im)mobilities are also, of course, heavily gendered, and age-specific (Hannam *et al.* 2006; Hannam 2009).

At an ontological level, studies of cultural tourism within the broader context of global human mobilities also need to be brought together with more 'local' concerns about everyday transportation, material cultures, and spatial relations, as well as with more 'technological' concerns about mobile information and communication technologies and emerging infrastructures of security and surveillance (Hannam 2009). Social and cultural life seems full of multiple and extended connections often across long distances, but these are organised through certain nodes. Mobilities thus entail distinct social spaces or 'moorings' that orchestrate new forms of social and cultural life – for example, stations, hotels, motorways, resorts, airports, leisure complexes, cosmopolitan cities, beaches, galleries, roadside parks and so on. Or connections might be enacted through less privileged spaces, on the street corners, buses, in subway stations, public plazas and back alleys. Also *contra* much transport research the time spent travelling is not dead time that people always seek to minimise. While the transport literature tends to distinguish travel from activities, the emerging mobilities paradigm posits that social and cultural activities occur while on the move – that being on the move can involve sets of 'occasioned' activities (Lyons and Urry 2005).

Cultural tourism research from the perspective of the mobilities paradigm would thus examine the embodied nature and experience of the different modes of travel that cultural tourists undertake, seeing these modes in part as forms of material and sociable dwelling-in-motion, places of and for various activities (see Jokinen and Veijola 1994; Crouch 2000; Johnston 2001; Featherstone *et al.* 2004). These 'activities' can include specific forms of talk, work, or information-gathering, but may involve simply being connected, maintaining a moving presence with others that holds the potential for many different convergences or divergences of physical presence (Hannam *et al.* 2006).

Moreover, according to Urry (2007: 47), there are five interdependent 'mobilities' that produce social and cultural life organised across distance. These can all be related to forms of contemporary cultural tourism:

- 'Corporeal' travel. This involves the travel of people for work, leisure, family life, pleasure, migration and escape, organised in terms of contrasting time-space modalities (ranging from daily commuting to lifetime exile). A great deal of conventional research in cultural tourism has examined aspects of such corporeal travel conceptualised as embodied experiences (Rodaway 1994; Veijola and Jokinen 1994; Crouch 2000) or hybrid ethnic experiences (Meethan 2003; Coles and Timothy 2004; Diekmann, this volume), or both (Ali and Holden 2006; Stephenson 2006; King and Christou 2011). Conversely, using an explicit mobilities perspective, recent work has considered how the technologies of travel have effected new cultural forms, including new cultural identities (D'Andrea 2006) and subjectivities (Conradson and Latham 2007).
- The 'physical' movement of 'objects' to producers, consumers and retailers, as well as the sending and receiving of presents and souvenirs. Again, a great deal of tourism research has examined the significance of souvenirs (Hannam and Knox 2010). However, from a mobilities perspective it is the movement of these souvenirs, gifts and more everyday

things that is of particular interest in terms of material cultures of mobility. There is now a growing interest in the ways in which material 'stuff' helps to constitute tourism, and such stuff is always in motion, being assembled and reassembled in changing configurations (Sheller and Urry 2006). We can see this clearly in studies of the cultures of food and tourism, for example (see Hall and Sharples 2003).

- The 'imaginative' travel effected through the images of places and peoples appearing on and moving across multiple print and visual media. Again, studies of imaginative travel have been a mainstay of recent cultural tourism research, particularly as destinations have sought to explicitly brand themselves as cultural places (Richards 2001; Cronin 2008) or as mobile cities as in the case of Singapore (Oswin and Yeoh 2010), using ever more complex destination management systems. Moreover, the connections between films and tourism have been explicitly researched in this context (Beeton 2005; Law *et al.* 2007). Furthermore, Germann Molz (2006), for example, has used 'cyberethnography' to explore the interplay between round-the-world travel and round-the-world travellers' websites through a method combining web-surfing, in-person and e-mail interviewing, and interaction in websites and in discussion groups.

- 'Virtual' travel often in real time thus transcending geographical and social distance. Drawing on the above imaginative travel, virtual travel has also led to new forms of cultural tourism. In their classic paper on 'Techno-Orientalism', Morley and Robins (1992) demonstrated the ways in which Japanese acquisition of former Western cultural assets such as media companies has led to the recognition of the power of the latter in the contemporary world. Moreover, we can see a latent orientalism at work in many computer games produced by Nintendo and Sony. As Schwartz (2006) notes, the fantasy worlds of game spaces involve mythological constructs and processes of Othering, and as Gale (2008) has demonstrated, such virtual worlds are, nowadays, an important element in the contemporary cultural tourist pre-experience (Hannam and Knox 2010).

- The 'communicative' travel through person-to-person messages via the Internet and mobile phone use. Communicative travel has become central to twenty-first-century life and a great deal of recent research has begun to examine the connections between mobile phone use and forms of cultural tourism. In this context, Melanie Smith (2009: 220) tells us that:

  many tourists are actively engaging in the kinds of activity that they could quite feasibly do at home (e.g. shopping for global brands, eating international fast food, watching sport on satellite TV). Media pervade some people's lives to the point that they watch their favourite soap opera or football team play while they are in beach bars abroad. Work and leisure are scarcely differentiated as tourists increasingly check e-mails, carry around laptops, and are glued to the ubiquitous mobile phone whilst on holiday!

## Box 17.1 Case study: cultural tourism and mobilities at the Darjeeling Himalayan Railway (DHR)

As we have noted, critical to the recognition of the materialities of mobilities is the re-centring of the corporeal body as an affective vehicle through which we sense place and movement, and construct emotional geographies (Crouch 2000; Bondi *et al.* 2005). Imaginative travel, for example, involves experiencing or anticipating in one's imagination the 'atmosphere of place'. Atmosphere is neither reducible to the material infrastructures nor to the discourses of representation. There is a complex, sensuous relationality between the technologies of travel and the cultural tourist (Rodaway 1994). Hence, we arguably need better maps of the sensuous, emotional geographies of cultural tourism in a mobile context (Hannam *et al.* 2006). In particular, the notion of performativity has been put forward as a way of understanding these inter-dependent relations.

The notion of performativity is thus concerned with the ways in which people know the world without knowing it, the multi-sensual practices and experiences of everyday life which include both the representational and the non-representational. As Adey (2010: 149) notes, 'This is an approach which is not limited to representational thinking and feeling, but a different sort of thinking-feeling altogether'. It is recognition that diverse mobilities such as walking, driving, dancing or jumping on and off a train involve various combinations of thought, action and feel-ing. Forms of mobility in cultural tourism, then, can be simultaneously representational and non-representational – a point which the cultural theorist Walter Benjamin made back in the early part of the twentieth century and which Anne Friedberg (1994) has termed the 'mobilized virtual gaze'. This can be illustrated below in the case of the embodied performance of the Darjeeling Himalayan Railway (DHR), a 'toy train' in India (Roy 2011).

One of the most significant performances of people that the DHR induces because of its track and its slow speed is that one can get on and off the train while it is on the move and it is in this process that it is argued that the DHR negotiates between place and people, not by being a stage for performance but by being itself an actor and taking initiative into this process. This becomes most evident from the stories of the people who belong to the locale as this is one of the everyday, but nevertheless is still an exciting performance for them:

> Whenever I travel, I make journey by the toy train, I quickly get off from the running train to a loop just to enjoy a cup of tea, until the train has made a full circle to come up. I keep chatting with the local people and as the train comes up I get on it. I still do enjoy this nostalgia.
>
> *(Local male resident and tour operator, aged 44)*

This performance is juxtaposed with cultural tourists' performances in experiencing the journey. In terms of the differences between locals and tourists in their experience of the DHR, a resident jokingly replied: 'Tourists do not hang out of the train neither can they jump on and off the train which we do.' For tourists to observe the performance from inside the train adds another dimension to their experience, as we found from a comment like this one from a domestic tourist:

> It serves useful human purposes and, at the same time delights a traveller's heart. We see anyone can get into it and anyone can also get off from it. It is a safe journey by all means. Unlike other trains it has an appearance and a route which do not arouse any fear of risk in people's mind …
>
> *(Domestic male tourist, aged 65)*

Hence the performance of getting on and off the train relates to the notion of performativity where the self is contingently produced, and thus it becomes one of the corporeal and social performances that makes the journey of the DHR 'touristic' for outsiders.

## Conclusion

In conclusion, this chapter has reviewed work from what has been termed the 'new mobilities paradigm' (Sheller and Urry 2004). The mobilities paradigm arguably allows us to place travel and tourism at the centre of social and cultural life rather than at the margins. Such tourism mobilities are often viewed as being bound up with both everyday and mundane journeys as well as the exotic encounters that have been the mainstay of much analysis in cultural tourism. The chapter has outlined the concept of tourism mobilities before discussing how this might be applied in the development of a research agenda for cultural tourism studies. Finally, the chapter has reviewed the recent theoretical academic literature that has developed the notion of the 'more than representational' and the 'performative', and how it might take the analysis of cultural tourism further, illustrated by the case of the Darjeeling Himalayan Railway.

## References

Adey, P. (2010) *Mobility*, London: Routledge.

Ali, N. and Holden, A. (2006) 'Post-colonial Pakistani Mobilities: The Embodiment of the "Myth of Return" in Tourism', *Mobilities* 1(2): 217–42.

Beeton, S. (2005) *Film-induced Tourism*, Clevedon: Channel View.

Bianchi, R. (2000) 'Migrant Tourist Workers: Exploring the Contact Zones of Post-industrial Tourism', *Current Issues in Tourism* 3(2): 107–37.

Bondi, L., Smith, M. and Davidson, J. (eds) (2005) *Emotional Geographies*, London: Ashgate.

Coles, T. and Timothy, D. (eds) (2004) *Tourism, Diasporas and Space: Travels to Promised Lands*, London: Routledge.

Conradson, D. and Latham, A. (2007) 'The Affective Possibilities of London: Antipodean Transnationals and the Overseas Experience', *Mobilities* 2(2): 231–54.

Cronin, A. (2008) 'Mobility and Market Research: Outdoor Advertising and the Commercial Ontology of the City', *Mobilities* 3(1): 95–116.

Crouch, D. (2000) 'Places Around Us: Embodied Lay Geographies in Leisure and Tourism', *Leisure Studies* 19: 63–76.

D'Andrea, A. (2006) 'Neo-Nomadism: A Theory of Post-identitarian Mobility in the Global Age', *Mobilities* 1(1): 95–120.

Edensor, T. (2007) 'Mundane Mobilities, Performances and Spaces of Tourism', *Social & Cultural Geography* 8(2): 199–215.

Featherstone, M., Thrift, N. and Urry, J. (eds) (2004) 'Cultures of Automobility (Special Issue)', *Theory, Culture and Society* 21: 1–284.

Franklin, A. (2003) *Tourism: An Introduction*, London: Sage.

Franklin, A. and Crang, M. (2001) 'The Trouble with Tourism and Travel Theory?' *Tourist Studies* 1(1): 5–22.

Friedberg, A. (1994) *Window Shopping: Cinema and the Postmodern*, Berkeley: University of California Press.

Gale, T. (2008) 'The End of Tourism, or Endings in Tourism?' in Burns, P. and Novelli, M. (eds) *Tourism and Mobilities: Local-Global Connections*, Wallingford: CABI, 1–14.

Germann Molz, J. (2006) 'Cosmopolitan Bodies: Fit to Travel and Travelling to Fit', *Body and Society* 12 (3): 1–21.

Gill, N., Caletrío, J. and Mason, V. (2011) 'Introduction: Mobilities and Forced Migration', *Mobilities* 6(3): 301–16.

Hall, C.M. and Sharples, L. (2003) 'The Consumption of Experiences or the Experience of Consumption? An Introduction to the Tourism of Taste', in Hall, C.M., Sharples, L., Mitchell, R., Macionis, N. and Cambourne, B. (eds) *Food Tourism Around the World: Development, Management and Markets*, Oxford: Butterworth-Heinemann, 1–24.

Hannam, K. (2009) 'The End of Tourism? Nomadology and the Mobilities Paradigm', in Tribe, J. (ed.) *Philosophical Issues in Tourism*, Clevedon: Channel View, 101–16.

Hannam, K. and Ateljevic. I. (eds) (2007) *Backpacker Tourism: Concepts and Profiles*, Clevedon: Channel View.

Hannam, K. and Diekmann, A. (eds) (2010) *Beyond Backpacker Tourism: Experiences and Mobilities*, Clevedon: Channel View.

Hannam, K. and Knox, D. (2010) *Understanding Tourism: A Critical Introduction*, London: SAGE.

Hannam, K., Sheller, M. and Urry, J. (2006) 'Editorial: Mobilities, Immobilities and Moorings', *Mobilities* 1(1): 1–22.

Jacobsen, J. (2001) 'Nomadic Tourism and Fleeting Place Encounters: Exploring Different Aspects of Sightseeing', *Scandinavian Journal of Hospitality and Tourism* 1(2): 99–112.

Johnston, L. (2001) '(Other) Bodies and Tourism Studies', *Annals of Tourism Research* 28(1): 180–201.

Jokinen, E. and Veijola, S. (1994) 'The Body in Tourism', *Theory, Culture & Society* 11(3): 125–51.

King, R. and Christou, A. (2011) 'Of Counter-Diaspora and Reverse Transnationalism: Return Mobilities to and from the Ancestral Homeland', *Mobilities* 6(4): 451–66.

Larsen, J. (2005) 'Families Seen Sightseeing: Performativity of Tourist Photography', *Space and Culture* 8(4): 416–34.

Law, L., Bunnell, T. and Ong, C. (2007) 'The Beach, the Gaze and Film Tourism', *Tourist Studies* 7(2): 141–64.

Lyons, G. and Urry, J. (2005) 'Travel Time Use in the Information Age', *Transport Research Part A: Policy and Practice* 39(2–3): 257–76.

Meethan, K. (2003) 'Mobile Cultures? Hybridity, Tourism and Cultural Change', *Journal of Tourism and Cultural Change* 1(1): 11–28.

Morley, D. and Robins, K. (1992) 'Techno-Orientalism: Futures, Foreigners and Phobias', *New Formations* 16: 136–56.

O'Reilly, K. (2003) 'When is a Tourist?' *Tourist Studies* 3(3): 301–17.

Oswin, N. and Yeoh, B. (2010) 'Introduction: Mobile City Singapore', *Mobilities* 5(2): 167–75.

Richards, G. (ed.) (2001) *Cultural Attractions and European Tourism*, Wallingford: CABI.

Richards, G. and Wilson, J. (eds) (2004) *The Global Nomad*, Clevedon: Channel View.

Rodaway, P. (1994) *Sensuous Geographies: Body, Sense and Place*, London: Routledge.

Roy, S. (2011) *A Cultural Politics of Mobilities and Post-Colonial Heritage: A Critical Analysis of the Darjeeling Himalayan Railway (DHR)*, unpublished PhD thesis, University of Sunderland, UK.

Sachs, W. (1992) *For the Love of the Automobile: Looking Back into the History of Our Desires*, Berkeley: University of California Press.

Schwartz, L. (2006) 'Fantasy, Realism, and the Other in Recent Video Games', *Space and Culture* 9(3): 313–25.

Sheller, M. and Urry, J. (eds) (2004) *Tourism Mobilities: Places to Play, Places in Play*, London: Routledge.

——(2006) 'The New Mobilities Paradigm', *Environment and Planning A* 38(2): 207–26.

Smith, M. (2009) *Issues in Cultural Tourism Studies*, London: Routledge.

Stephenson, M. (2006) 'Travel and the "Freedom of Movement": Racialised Encounters and Experiences Amongst Ethnic Minority Tourists in the EU', *Mobilities* 1(2): 285–306.

Urry, J. (2007) *Mobilities*, Cambridge: Polity.

Veijola, S. and Jokinen, E. (1994) 'The Body in Tourism', *Theory, Culture and Society* 11: 125–51.

# 18

# Erasmus students

## The 'ambassadors' of cultural tourism

*Karolina Buczkowska*

## Introduction

'Cultural tourism seems to be omnipresent, and in the eyes of many it also seems to have become omnipotent' – the words of Greg Richards (2007: 1) reflect the continuous intensification of tourist interest in culture in all its aspects. Openness to learning and tourist experience characterises mainly young people and results from their ability to establish contacts easily, from their knowledge of foreign languages, and from their lack of anxiety or fear of the unknown. Jensen (2006) believes that travelling and mobility in themselves have become a part of the lifestyle of young people. Richards (2007: 15) points out that among cultural visitors, 'The single largest age group is between 20 and 29, and almost 40 percent of visitors are under 30'. Students are a dominant group among young travellers as they have a lot of free time during their studies: 'Young travellers, and particularly students, are important for cultural tourism because of the strong link between cultural consumption and education. Highly educated people tend to consume more culture …' (Richards 2007: 15). It has been believed lately that 'the European student environment is undergoing radical change. More and more students go to study abroad and these experiences – as they declare it – change their lives' (Boomans *et al.* 2007: 55).

One of the most popular forms of foreign studies is the Erasmus Programme of international student exchange, which includes student mobility for study and work placements. About 200,000 students participate in the programme annually, spending from 3 to 12 months in the partner country. For many European students, the Erasmus Programme is their first experience of living and studying abroad. It might be argued that the Erasmus Programme is a cultural phenomenon of our times.

## The Erasmus Programme

The Erasmus Programme of the European Union (EU) supports student and staff mobility, including studying or doing an internship abroad, exchanges of teaching staff and training for university administrative staff (European Parliament 2006). The Erasmus Programme forms a major part of the EU Lifelong Learning Programme (LLP), implemented between 1987 and 2013. The programme is named after the Dutch philosopher Desiderius Erasmus of Rotterdam, who lived and worked in the fifteenth and sixteenth centuries in many places in Europe to expand his knowledge and gain new insights. Erasmus is also an acronym meaning *EuRopean community Action Scheme for the Mobility of University Students.*

Students who want to participate in the Erasmus Programme must be studying for a degree or diploma at a tertiary-level institution and must have already completed their first year. The internship lasts between three months and a whole academic year in another European country. The Erasmus Programme guarantees that the period spent abroad is recognised by the student's home university when they return. The principle is that students do not pay extra tuition fees to the university that they visit and they can apply for a special Erasmus grant to help them cover the additional expense of living abroad.

Currently there are more than 4,000 higher institutions participating in Erasmus across the 33 countries involved in the LLP/Erasmus Programme, and over 2.2 million students have already taken part. The number of Erasmus students has grown dramatically, from 3,200 in the academic year 1987/88 to reach 213,000 students in the academic year 2009/10 (Table 18.1). The figures underline how much students' mobility and fondness for travel have developed in the last 20 years.

*Table 18.1* Growing number of Erasmus students 1987/88–2009/10

| Academic year | Number of students |
| --- | --- |
| Erasmus | |
| 1987/88 | 3,244 |
| 1988/89 | 9,914 |
| 1989/90 | 19,456 |
| Erasmus | |
| 1990/91 | 27,906 |
| 1991/92 | 36,314 |
| 1992/93 | 51,694 |
| 1993/94 | 62,362 |
| 1994/95 | 73,407 |
| Socrates I – Erasmus | |
| 1995/96 | 84,642 |
| 1996/97 | 79,874 |
| 1997/98 | 85,999 |
| 1998/99 | 97,601 |
| 99/2000 | 107,666 |
| Socrates II – Erasmus | |
| 2000/01 | 111,092 |
| 2001/02 | 115,432 |
| 2002/03 | 123,957 |
| 2003/04 | 135,586 |
| 2004/05 | 144,037 |
| 2005/06 | 154,421 |
| 2006/07 | 159,324 |
| Lifelong Learning Programme – Erasmus | |
| Study plus placement 2007/08 | 182,697 |
| Study plus placement 2008/09 | 198,523 |
| Study plus placement 2009/10 | 213,266 |
| Total | 2,278,414 |

Source: (European Commission 2011b).

## The general benefits of the LLP/Erasmus Programme for students

Participation in the Erasmus Programme offers various benefits to students. It favours not only learning and understanding of the host country but it also creates a sense of community among students from different countries. As the Erasmus website and other sources report:

> Studies show that a period spent abroad not only enriches a student's life in the academic field but also facilitates the acquisition of inter-cultural skills, language skills and self-reliance. A crossborder mobility period is a key asset on every CV that enhances the employability and job prospects of graduates (Erasmus: I am one of the two million who did it!)
>
> *(European Commission 2011a)*

> These who went abroad are equipped with new ideas, tools, and visions: inter-cultural knowledge and competences, new technologies, new communication tools, ease to travel, but also the urge of adventure.
>
> *(Boomans* et al. *2007: 55)*

> Erasmus teaches, brings people closer together, helps them overcome prejudice and stereotypes.
>
> *(Fundacja Rozwoju Systemu Edukacji 2007)*

The quality of student exchange experiences has been monitored over the years, with all Erasmus students completing questionnaires on return from their period abroad. These data indicate that Erasmus offers students many benefits. The programme enables them 'to acquire European experience' and is valued because it offers them:

- cultural benefits, such as learning about new countries and languages;
- academic benefits in experiencing other models of education and learning;
- professional benefits, as foreign studies become an asset in the eyes of employers; and
- personal benefits, such as increased tolerance, openness to other cultures and people, self-reliance, and getting rid of complexes.

(European Commission 2009)

---

### Box 18.1 Case study: cultural preferences of Polish Erasmus students

Poland has been participating in the Erasmus Programme for over 10 years and the programme is currently very popular among Polish students. To check what kind of motivations students follow when they decide to go and how significant the culture of the visited places is for them, I carried out research in the academic community in Poznań, Poland. With the help of a questionnaire survey, I interviewed 2,510 students from 24 higher education institutions in Poznań in 2010 (140,000 people studied in Poznań at that time; the calculation of the appropriate sample size was done by the Data Processing Centre at Eugeniusz Piasecki University School of Physical Education in Poznań, Poland).

The results of the research show that 22 per cent of students had either participated in or intended to participate in the programme. Almost half of the students indicated no interest in the programme at all (Table 18.2).

Table 18.2 Completed or planned studies abroad as part of the Erasmus Programme

|  | Number | Percentage |
|---|---|---|
| Already completed studies abroad | 89 | 4 |
| Planned to study abroad | 456 | 18 |
| No possibility to study abroad | 839 | 33 |
| No interest in studying abroad | 1,124 | 45 |
| Total | 2,508 | 100 |

Those students who have already completed or are planning to study abroad as a part of the Erasmus Programme or a similar academic exchange, were often motivated by the possibility of improving their foreign language skills and getting to know the culture of other countries. For almost half of those surveyed the essential incentive was the desire to study (understood as 'being at the university') abroad or making friends from other countries. The least important motivating factor was the host university's curriculum. Each student surveyed named three different motivations on average (see Table 18.3).

Table 18.3 Motivations for LLP/Erasmus Programme stay

|  | Number (n=545) | Percentage |
|---|---|---|
| I want/ed to improve my language skills | 388 | 71 |
| I want/ed to get to know the culture of a different country | 327 | 60 |
| I want/ed to study in a different country | 323 | 59 |
| I want/ed to make friends from other countries | 254 | 47 |
| The university where I was/am going offered/offers an interesting curriculum | 71 | 13 |
| Other | 38 | 7 |

The research reveals that many Polish students are cultural tourists. As many as 39 per cent are interested in culture to a large extent and every second student indicated a medium level of interest. From a cultural tourism point of view, those students who have already been on an Erasmus exchange have an even greater interest in culture. For almost 66 per cent of these students, the culture of the places visited is of significant interest, and for 31 per cent of them it is of medium interest. None of the Erasmus students was indifferent to the cultural aspects of the host country (see Table 18.4).

Table 18.4 Interest in the culture of the places visited among all students and among former Erasmus students

|  | All students (no.) | All students (%) | Erasmus students (no.) | Erasmus students (%) |
|---|---|---|---|---|
| Significant interest | 970 | 39 | 56 | 63 |
| Medium interest | 1,257 | 50 | 28 | 31 |
| Minimum interest | 219 | 9 | 5 | 6 |
| No interest | 61 | 2 | 0 | 0 |
| Total | 2,507 | 100 | 89 | 100 |

The question about the interest in the culture of the visited countries was accompanied by another: do you consider yourself a cultural tourist? Every fifth student answered: 'Yes, always' and more than half of them answered 'Yes, sometimes'. Around 50 per cent of former Erasmus students felt that they were sometimes cultural tourists, a similar level to the percentage for all students. However, many more former Erasmus students (37 per cent) considered themselves permanent cultural tourists (see Table 18.5).

*Table 18.5* The cultural tourist identity of students

|  | All students (no.) | All students (%) | Erasmus students (no.) | Erasmus students (%) |
|---|---|---|---|---|
| 'I am always a cultural tourist' | 464 | 19% | 32 | 37% |
| 'I am sometimes a cultural tourist' | 1,393 | 55% | 44 | 50% |
| 'I am never a cultural tourist' | 298 | 12% | 4 | 5% |
| 'I don't know what a cultural tourist is' | 346 | 14% | 7 | 8% |
| Total | 2,501 | 100% | 87 | 100% |

## Why are Erasmus students the ambassadors of cultural tourism?

Ambassadors are the highest ranking diplomats representing a particular nation, usually accredited to a foreign sovereign, government, or an international organisation. Their duties include representing their country, performing activities that promote it – especially those of cultural, scientific and economic character, as well as creating friendly relations between their own country and the host country (Polish Government 2001). Similar duties must be performed by Erasmus students even though they have not been given any formal position.

Universities realise that Erasmus students represent both their universities and their countries, so they try to select only the best students for the programme – those who know foreign languages, who stand out, who have comprehensive interests, and those who are interested in the chosen countries.

Research conducted on the youth tourism market by the Association for Tourism and Leisure Education (ATLAS) and the World Youth Student Educational Travel Confederation (WYSE), indicated that for young travellers the single most important motivation was 'discovering other cultures' (Richards 2007: 15), which is one of the main motivations of cultural tourism. It helps to assume that this information refers mainly to Erasmus and other exchange students. My own research also indicates that these students are cultural tourists and that, through their approach and behaviour, they deserve to be recognised as the ambassadors of cultural tourism. In the following analysis, observations on cultural tourism have been adopted from a publication by Buczkowska (2011: 24–27), while the behaviour of Erasmus students has been analysed on the basis of (participant) observations and interviews with about 200 outgoing and incoming Erasmus students, through contacts gained as Programme Co-ordinator at Eugeniusz Piasecki University School of Physical Education in Poznań, Poland, as well as through the analysis of the Erasmus Programme documentation.

One of the fundamental features of cultural tourism is the preparation necessary for travel. The European Quality Charter for Mobility, obligatory reading for Erasmus students, emphasises the necessity of good preparation: 'before departure, participants should receive general preparation tailored to their specific needs and covering linguistic, pedagogical, legal, cultural or financial aspects'. Moreover, we read about the importance of linguistic aspects:

> language skills make for more effective learning, inter-cultural communication and a better understanding of the host country's culture. Arrangements should therefore include a pre-departure assessment of language skills, the possibility of attending courses in the language of the host country and/or language learning and linguistic support and advice in the host country.
>
> *(European Parliament 2006)*

Without a doubt, Erasmus students are aware of the culture of their destination and are assumed to have prepared themselves for the trip properly.

Cultural tourism aims at presenting and explaining the chosen culture or cultural idea and it is based on the '3 x E' formula – education, entertainment, and emotions/excitement – which offers experiences with three basic elements: diversity, interactivity and context. Erasmus students often choose to study abroad because they personally want to experience things they have previously only heard or read about, so they choose the places that are particularly interesting to them and which they want to get to know. During the exchange stay, they usually travel a lot and experience the culture of the visited places in various ways: sightseeing, studying, meeting the local community, partying, shopping, cooking, etc. The effect of this in-depth experience is not only broadened knowledge, albums full of photos and beautiful memories, but also (in the case of Erasmus students from Poland) BA and MA theses written at the end of the studies and thematically referring to the places visited during the Erasmus exchange.

Cultural tourism not only provides experiences but also requires from tourists active participation in different cultural activities, as well as being in good psycho-physical shape (constant movement plus constant concentration). Students studying in foreign countries and in non-native languages are prepared, if necessary, for intensive intellectual work and they are interested in learning about different cultural aspects of the places visited.

Cultural tourism trips are often organised for individuals or small groups – as an alternative to mass sightseeing tourism – so that their participants are guaranteed a unique, distinctive experience of a particular place. Erasmus groups studying at various universities are rarely numerous or monocultural, and these students usually travel around in groups, which often facilitates their contact with different cultures.

Cultural tourism also has all the features of alternative and/or sustainable tourism: it is supposed to be gentle and responsible towards cultural and natural environments; it is characterised by avoiding negative and boosting positive social, cultural and ecological influences on people and the environment surrounding them; by emphasising the contact with native culture of the areas visited, it preserves traditional values and communities. Thus it is more authentic and it cares more about existing cultural heritage. Moreover, cultural trips take place in an atmosphere of tolerance, respect for otherness and the attempt to engage in dialogue. Erasmus students must possess these qualities, otherwise they would not decide to go and study abroad, to stay in multicultural groups for several months, to have frequent contact with local communities, or to travel during their exchange period.

Time is also a particularly important issue when talking about cultural tourism. Tourists get a lot of it because cultural tourism refrains from hasty visits to many sites in favour of the in-depth study of a chosen few (their appearance, characteristic features, history, people connected with them, their true nature, etc.). Cultural tourism cannot stand 'the rush' because it is only the possibility of 'savouring' the visited place that brings the measurable effects – cognitive effects. Erasmus students have several months to get to know the city and region of their studies, thus they do it at a leisurely pace, returning to previously visited sites, and they live and breathe them. Apart from sightseeing and studying those places, they can peacefully 'absorb' them.

## Conclusion

The features of cultural tourism presented in this chapter should leave no doubt that Erasmus students are cultural tourists and the characteristics of their travel behaviour mark them out as ambassadors of this kind of tourism. We can only hope that future Erasmus students will possess a high level of knowledge and interest in the culture of the countries and regions visited so that their cultural tourism experiences are beneficial for them and their hosts. Cultural experiences gained during educational exchanges generate advantages now and will bring further advantages in the future, as they influence the current tourism styles and the future lives of former Erasmus students.

I would agree with the words of the political scientist Stefan Wolff, who said 'Give it 15, 20 or 25 years, and Europe will be run by leaders with a completely different socialization from those of today, referring to the so-called Erasmus generation' (ERASMUS Forum 2012).

## References

Bennhold, Katrin (2005) 'Quietly Sprouting: A European Identity', *International Herald Tribune*, www.iht.com/articles/2005/04/26/news/enlarge2.php (accessed 21 November 2009).

Boomans, V., Krupnik, S., Krzaklewska, E., Lanzilotta, S. (2007) *Generation Mobility*, Brussels: Erasmus Student Network AISBL.

Buczkowska, K. (2010) 'Wyjazdy polskich studentow w ramach programmeu LLP/Erasmus w kontekscie turystyki kulturowej' [LLP/Erasmus programme trips of Polish students in the context of cultural tourism], in E. Puchnarewicz (ed.) *Wielokulturowosc w turystyce*, Warsaw: Wyzsza Szkola Turystyki i Jezykow Obcych, 87–104.

——(2011) *Cultural Tourism – Heritage, Arts and Creativity*, Poznan: AWF.

ERASMUS Forum (2012) Cultural Phenomenon, www.erasmus-exchange.info/viewtopic.php?f=11&t=12 (accessed 25 April 2012).

European Commission (2007) *20-lecie Erasmusa* [Erasmus's 20th anniversary], www.erasmus.org.pl/index.php/ida/24/ (accessed 16 December 2011).

——(2009) Erasmus w Polsce od roku 1998 [Erasmus in Poland since 1998], www.erasmus.org.pl/index.php/ida/174/ (accessed 12 November 2009).

——(2011a) Erasmus: I Am One of the Two Million Who Did It! ec.europa.eu/education/pub/pdf/higher/2million_en.pdf, 7 (accessed 16 December 2011).

——(2011b) ec.europa.eu/education/Programmemes/llp/erasmus/statisti/table1.pdf (accessed 16 December 2011).

European Parliament (2006) *Recommendation (EC) No. 2006/961 of the European Parliament and of the Council of 18 December 2006 on Transnational Mobility within the Community for Education and Training Purposes*, European Quality Charter for Mobility, Official Journal L 394 of 30.12.2006, europa.eu/legislation_summaries/education_training_youth/lifelong_learning/c11085_en.htm (accessed 20 December 2011).

Fundacja Rozwoju Systemu Edukacji (2007) *20 lat Erasmusa 1987–2007* [20 years of Erasmus 1987–2007], Warsaw: Fundacja Rozwoju Systemu Edukacji.

Jensen, M. (2006) 'Mobility Among Young Urban Dwellers', *Young: Nordic Journal of Youth Research* 14(4): 343–61.

Polish Government (2001) *The Foreign Service Act*, 27 July [Ustawa o służbie zagranicznej z, 27 lipca 2001 r.].

Richards G. (2007) 'Introduction: Global Trends in Cultural Tourism', in Richards, G. (ed.) *Cultural Tourism: Global and Local Perspectives*, London: Routledge, 1–19.

## Further reading

Boomans, V., Krupnik, S., Krzaklewska, E., Lanzilotta, S. (2007) Generation Mobility, Erasmus Student Network AISBL. (An extended research study on 12,000 Erasmus students' mobility.)

Buczkowska, K. (2011) *Cultural Tourism – Heritage, Arts and Creativity*, Poznan: AWF. (Review of different definitions and typologies of cultural tourists.)

Richards G. (2007) 'Introduction: Global Trends in Cultural Tourism', in Richards, G. (ed.) *Cultural Tourism: Global and Local Perspectives*, London: Routledge, 1–19. (Contribution about important aspects of cultural tourism.)

# 19

# Performing and recording culture

## Reflexivity in tourism research

*Kevin Meethan*

## Introduction

I would like to begin by briefly outlining two broad contextual factors that underpin my position in writing this contribution. The first is a broad shift in society towards a greater sense of individuation. I have written about this in more detail elsewhere (Meethan 2012a), but the main points are worth mentioning here. In short, within our society, dominated as it is by consumption, individual identity is more negotiable than it has been in the past. As a consequence, we have seen the individual and the idea of embodiment become central concerns within mainstream social theorising in a number of cognate disciplines. The second factor is the question of human agency, of how much choice we as individuals actually have, and the extent to which our actions are constrained by contextual factors beyond our individual control. We need then to examine the relationship between embodiment and action, and in order to do this I would like to focus on action as performance, and reflect on how such a concern poses some interesting questions that relate to both theory and method, and the relationship between the individual, culture and space.

## Performing places and performing in places

There are two general senses in which we use the term performance (at least in the English language). The most obvious one is where we imply some form of conscious presentation and some audience, a form of deliberate and purposive action. For example Mock (2000: 5), writing about performance art, notes that it involves a cyclical process that encompasses conception, development, presentation, reception and reflection. There is then some notion here of conscious intent, a deliberate act of staging, a suspension of disbelief perhaps on the part of the audience.

We recognise a performance as a conscious and deliberate staging of actions that requires an audience, and we can look at the ways in which ritual is a form of performance, which has long been recognised in anthropology (Hughes Freeland 1998) and how ethnicity can be performed as a tourist spectacle (Crain 1996; Abram *et al.* 1997; Nicks 1999; Edensor 2000; Salazar 2005; Meethan 2010), while at a more individual level Hyde and Oleson (2011) note that packing for holidays is akin to assembling a wardrobe of costumes and props for the performance of being a tourist. Performance in this sense, I would argue, is a form of social interaction, a way of negotiating both self and other as we enact our daily lives. Certain actions are more or less consciously performed as purposive action, directed towards the achievement of certain goals. The point I wish to make here is that we need to regard performance not as something that is set apart from our daily lives but rather as a form of embodied practice – or sets of practices – that engage all the senses, and are as much visual as they are tactile, aural and olfactory, and while such engagement may involve the self-consciousness of staging at some point, it has also a more mundane side to it as well.

Social life as we know is on the one hand defined by rules and conventions but on the other is open to interpretation and indeed improvisation. In a recent attempt to place creativity (and hence agency) at the centre of anthropological enquiry, Ingold states that: 'There is no script for social and cultural life. People have to work at it as they go along. In a word, they have to *improvise*' (Ingold 2007: 1, emphasis in original). This is a rather stark assertion, even if he later concedes that there are at least 'scripts within it' (ibid.: 12; see also Hastrup 2007).

Clearly Ingold is writing in the tradition of phenomenological approaches, and while I have a great deal of sympathy for this, I also feel that there is a need here for some careful qualification. While social life does involve many instances of improvisation, we can also point to as many situations where improvisation is simply ruled out, or is not sanctioned. The important point to make is that there is danger here of overestimating the role of agency and the freedom that individuals actually have. In an ideal sense Ingold is right, and while it is true that life (again to quote Ingold) '… cannot be fully codified as the output of any system of rules and representations' (Ingold 2007: 12), there are certainly situations where experiences are ordered, where there are official scripts (or narratives) to which one has to conform; to simply focus on individual actions neglects the context, the scripts are not incidental, but are of crucial importance.

One example that I have in mind are the people from the UK (and indeed elsewhere) who travelled to the Soviet Union in the 1920s and 1930s in order to see for themselves what was occurring. What they actually saw was, perhaps unsurprisingly, carefully managed and deliberately staged, and served only to confirm pre-existing ideas that the visitors bought with them – either of the positive or the negative kind. As Wright puts it, '… visiting investigators had little on which to base their assessment of Soviet Russia except the fleeting occasions when the script in their heads seemed suddenly to correlate with the appearances passing before their eyes' (Wright 2007: 229).

Less extreme examples abound in tourism. We only need think of the ways in which tour guides and guidebooks, novels, TV shows and films, other media and forms of visual culture as much as history provide us with a ready-made script or template that we can apply to the situation and the place in which we find ourselves. Even before we enter tourist space we are primed for it (see Crouch and Lübbren 2003; Adolfsson *et al.* 2009; Reijnders 2011). All our tourist encounters are to some extent foregrounded in both our individual memories and knowledge of place as much as the cultural milieu in which we, as social beings, interact with each other (Bærenholdt *et al.* 2004). The exercise of agency then is always, to a greater or lesser extent, constrained by our material circumstances as much as our hopes and expectations. To regard embodiment and performance in this way is to see them as a process by which the self is constantly being created and recreated, is enacted into being (Wearing *et al.* 2010); it is, as Crouch (2002: 209) would say, a way of doing tourism, the 'practice of space'.

## Space, memory and culture

A further point to consider is that this enactment into being takes place within and across space. This cannot be simply regarded as an empty stage onto which we project ourselves; instead, we have to consider how space is affected by, and the effects it has on, embodied practices. Space is not inert, but is a combination of both the metaphorical and the material. For example, Bærenholdt *et al.* (2004: 32) point out that tourist places are '… simultaneously places of the *physical environment, embodiment, sociality, memory* and *image*' (emphasis in the original).

To talk of memory in this context requires us to consider the relationship between public and private memory (Climo and Cattell 2002). The former refers to what we can loosely describe as a kind of general history, the narratives of which are more or less shared, a stock of taken-for-granted knowledge, often rooted in discourses of the nation or the people, if not both. In terms of space and culture, certain sites and monuments act as the physical embodiment of national values and virtues and these can include sites of historical importance, sites of remembrance such as shrines, sites of religious worship, and also museums, art collections, parks and landscapes − even sites of imagined, fictive events (Reijnders 2011).

Private memory, on the other hand, is our own sense of self, our biography, the scripts and narratives of our individual lives. This may well contain elements of public memory that are shared between and across generations, for example public rituals of remembrance. Different generations will also have different shared memories (a point I will return to below) and individual memory then combines the grand narratives of history and nation with the personal narrative of the individual. In this sense the performance of embodied place, '… cannot be separated from the place as environment [which is] … the sediments of embodied practices over generations' (Bærenholdt *et al.* 2004: 46). This stress on process is an important one as the environment is not simply inert matter (see also Crouch 2004), but has been fashioned by practices as well as fashioning those practices. Similarly, Strathern and Stewart (2007: 96) write in relation to landscapes that 'Embodied knowledge is crucial to the understanding of landscape, because such knowledge is gained by traversing the landscape itself', and this, I would argue, holds true for all forms of space which, as Kuehling (2007: 177) puts it, '… incorporates sensations of all senses'.

To summarise so far, I have argued that we need to have a greater recognition of the individual within tourism, and also that this in turn means we have to acknowledge that the individual interacts with space and is situated in space, and that in turn this interaction, and situatedness is mediated by the wider narratives of society as much as one's own personal narrative. As we traverse space we also traverse memory and culture, we encounter it as embodied experiences as we perform and negotiate our sense of self. In turn, this raises some interesting methodological issues: if we accept that embodiment and experience − the sensory realm in short − is the subject matter of enquiry, the question is how we actually access that realm.

## Walking and recording: embodiment and method

The development of approaches and theoretical models that focus on notions of individuality, embodiment and reflexivity also means that the role of the researcher comes under scrutiny (Meethan 2011). It has long been recognised, within anthropology at least, that the researcher, in particular those adopting immersive methods such as participant observation, cannot be regarded as neutral data gatherers whose accounts are a direct and unproblematic record of what truly occurred (Denzin 1997). What we need to account for is that the researcher (in any field of enquiry) will necessarily bring with them a set of assumptions and predispositions as much as any tourist does, and as Denzin comments, 'Through our writing and our talk we enact the worlds we study' (Denzin 1997: 422). We also need to consider that within our current cultural context we privilege the written word over other forms of recording and presenting what we regard as valid data, whereas as Pink points out, researchers '… often describe how they came to moments of realization about the other people's meanings and values serendipitously through their own seemingly "same" sensory embodied experiences' (Pink 2007: 244).

Of course there is nothing new about the researcher immersing themselves in the culture they are studying; after all, that is the purpose of participant observation. The question here is to what extent do the experiences of the researcher actually inform and feed into the overall analysis, in effect becoming a form of auto-ethnography (Meethan 2011)? For the purposes of this chapter I would like to consider the ways in which an informed engagement with the practice and performance of being a tourist – the 'doing of it' to use Crouch's (2002) term – can be a way of gaining a different form of understanding to that we more habitually associate with tourism research and analysis. This approach draws on the ethnographic tradition (as mentioned above), which has more recently been developed into a concern with the practice of walking and recording as a method (Pink 2007; Ingold and Vergunst 2008; Edensor 2010; Pink *et al.* 2010).

In the summer of 2011 I visited Berlin, and while there I made a number of visits to sites where what remains of the Berlin Wall still stand. The purpose was partly to see for myself what it had actually looked like; partly to see how these sites had become monuments, places of memory and tourism (Häussermann and Colomb 2003); and partly to see how an approach based on ideas of embodiment and the reflexive performance of the researcher could actually be applied in the field.

## Gedenkstätte Berliner Mauer: the Berlin Wall Memorial

I have no personal memory of life before the wall. I remember watching it come down on television in 1989, and my recent knowledge of it has been a post hoc construction from public memory and other historical sources, overshadowed by the fact that to people of my generation the Berlin Wall (or the Anti-Fascist Protection Barrier as the DDR (Deutsche Demokratische Republik) euphemistically called it) stood as the overarching symbol of a Europe divided into two opposing ideological camps. As such its existence was, and still is, part of a wider historical narrative, familiar to many through numerous espionage novels and films (Mews 1996), as well as generating its own historiography (for example see Waldenburg 1990; Schürer *et al.* 1996; Funder 2003; Burgan 2007; Manghani 2008; Taylor 2008; Ahonen 2011; Hertle 2011).

The memorial itself, completed in 2011 and located along Bernauer Strasse, is a linear park 1.4 kilometres in length, comprising a documentation centre, a visitor centre/bookshop, an outdoor exhibition, a chapel of reconciliation (built on the site of a church demolished to make way for the wall), and the last complete section of the actual wall itself. As well as being a site of significance in its own right, the memorial also provides a narrative interpretation of its construction and effect on the population presented on information boards in both German and English (see Ward 1996). The wall itself was developed over a period of time (Hertle 2011) and in its final stage was in fact two walls, inner and outer, containing a narrow strip of sand some 20 or so metres wide. Known as the death strip, this was floodlit at night and patrolled by armed guards, and sand of course would show any footprints.

Like any other tourist, as I walked along the memorial I took photographs, using a camera not only to provide my own memories of the visit, but also more consciously as a convenient way of recording spaces and places (see Meethan 2012b for a fuller account of ethnographic walking/photographing as method). During the time I spent there, people were wandering around in small groups, and despite it being a sunny day, the atmosphere was rather subdued. Pictures of those who died attempting to cross are framed by bare rusting iron which mirrors the brutal concrete and iron construction of the wall itself, a shrine for their memory as well as a reminder of a divided city, country and Europe, and a warning for the future.

*Figure 19.1* The Berlin Wall as a shrine: portraits of those who died attempting to escape to West Berlin

The first thing that struck me about the wall was its outer surface, the one that had faced West Berlin. In many of the photos I had seen, the wall had been a bright polychromatic dazzle of graffiti and paintings, but here it was pock marked, eroded grey concrete with the rusting reinforced steel rods showing through. This I later found out was not the result of natural weathering or cheap construction, but had been caused by eager souvenir hunters, out to claim a small piece of the wall. Even today, over 20 years after the event, postcards containing a fragment of the true wall, encased in a plastic bubble can be found in many of Berlin's souvenir shops. The irony of a wall built to keep capitalism out succumbing to the processes of tourism commodification was very much in my mind.

The remaining complete section of the wall is opposite the Document Centre, and from here a rooftop terrace enables you to see the whole complex. From there, the path that the wall took is clearly visible for some distance in both directions. It was at that point that the sheer scale of it became apparent. Here the outer wall shows no sign of souvenir hunters; the remaining segment has been sandwiched between two massive metal walls, which, when viewed from street level, loom menacingly overhead. Behind the inner wall, in what was once East Berlin, a small opening has been cut to allow a brief glimpse across the death strip. Again, the experience was claustrophobic and is a reminder of just how final and definite this barrier was.

Along the gable ends of houses, which have been painted white, iconic black and white images stare down from what was the eastern side, as if black and white not only symbolises the stark reality of the wall, but also implies a monochrome and bleak existence for those in the east (see also Funder 2003). Colour photographs do, of course, exist and can be found on many tourist postcards and other wall memorabilia, but none are reproduced on the gable ends; here colour has been reduced to muted greys and the patina of rusty iron. At places bare metal posts emerge from the ground marking both inner and outer walls, and I wondered what would

*Figure 19.2* The wall as seen from the roof of the Document Centre, looking towards what was once East Berlin

happen in the future – would it be restored to what it looked like on its completion, or would it be allowed to decay and fall into eventual ruin? As Edensor (2008) notes, ruins disrupt, but in this case we have a deliberate and self-conscious attempt to create the effect of disruption, of disunity and discord: the wall is a ruin and a rebuke.

There was no doubt that the memorial is a stage, an arena deliberately designed to encourage both engagement and identification. Visitors – tourists – walk along the route of the wall, and on either side of it paths follow the line of the death strip. There is no triumphalism here; this is not a victor's monument, but neither is it a simple open-air museum. Rather it is a place where we can clearly see the intersection of private and public histories (see Ward 1996). For those who want to read up on the history of the wall, the bookshop offers many titles in many languages in addition to postcards and other images. While in many respects the memorial resembles any other generic tourist attraction, it is also a sombre and rather chilling reminder of a divided world.

## Conclusion: reflections on theory and method

The purpose of this chapter has been to raise a number of issues that touch on both theory and method in relation to the position of the individual in contemporary (Western, developed) society, and ways in which we both experience and remember places. As I mentioned above, I approached the memorial with both personal memories of the wall as having existed (albeit from a distance and via the media) along with some academic knowledge of European history, and also my knowledge of tourism and tourist commodification. My knowledge of the wall then was foregrounded by a number of factors, and I was also very conscious that the majority

*Figure 19.3* The end of Ackerstrasse, formerly in East Berlin, showing the development of the wall at that site

of students to whom I will show my pictures also have lived in a world in which the wall has always been a thing of the past, a trace of a different world.

The experience of being there – of actually walking the route and touching the wall – added another dimension, the sensory element which has, to some extent, been underplayed and under-recognised in tourism research. Another point to make is that my walking along and into that space was also a performance in a number of ways. I was a cultural tourist, but also a data gatherer, and a tourist analyst. As such, I was embodying and performing three distinct but inter-related roles, as well as responding to the cues and surroundings that the memorial itself embodied. My final point is that what this visit, recording and subsequent reflection has brought out is a personal knowledge and experience of culture that is as much sensual as intellectual, and is composed from a variety of sources that are personal as much as public. As we walk through space we are engaging and performing with it; we are reflecting and interacting with it; and it is this engagement and interaction on which we need to focus and take as our subject matter.

# References

Abram, S., Waldren, J. and MacLeod, D.V. (eds) (1997) *Tourists and Tourism: Identifying with People and Places*, Berg: Oxford.

Adolfsson, P., Dobers, P. and Jonasson, M. (eds) (2009) *Guiding and Guided Tours*, Göteburg: BAS.

Ahonen, P. (2011) *Death at the Berlin Wall*, Oxford: Oxford University Press.

Bærenholdt, J., Haldrup, M., Larsen, J. and Urry, J. (2004) *Performing Tourist Places*, Aldershot: Ashgate.

Burgan, M. (2007) *The Berlin Wall: Barrier to Freedom*, Minneapolis: Compass Point.

Climo, J. and Cattell, M.G. (2002) *Social Memory and History: Anthropological Perspectives*, Washington, DC: AltaMira Press.

Crain, M.M. (1996) 'Negotiating Identities in Quito's Cultural Borderlands: Native Women's Performances for the Ecuadorean Tourist Market', in Howes, D. (ed.) *Cross Cultural Consumption: Global Markets, Local Realities*, London: Routledge, 125–37.

Crouch, D. (2002) 'Surrounded by Place: Embodied Encounters', in Coleman, S. and Crang, M. (eds) *Tourism: Between Place and Performance*, New York: Berghahn Books, 207–18.

——(2004) 'Tourist Practices and Performances', in Lew, A.A., Hall, C.M. and Williams, A.M. (eds) *A Companion to Tourism*, Oxford: Blackwell, 85–96.

Crouch, D. and Lübbren, N. (2003) *Visual Culture and Tourism*, London: Berg.

Denzin, N. (1997) *Interpretive Ethnographic Practices for the Twenty-First Century*, Thousand Oaks, CA: Sage.

Edensor, T. (2000) 'Staging Tourism: Tourists as Performers', *Annals of Tourism Research* 27(2): 322–344.

——(2008) 'Walking Through Ruins', in Ingold, T. and Vergunst, J.L. (eds) *Ways of Walking: Ethnography and Practice on Foot*, Farnham: Ashgate, 123–41.

——(2010) 'Walking in Rhythms: Place, Regulation Style and the Flow of Experience', *Visual Studies* 25 (1): 69–79.

Funder, A. (2003) *Stasiland: Stories from Behind the Berlin Wall*, London: Granta.

Hastrup, K. (2007) 'Performing the World: Agency, Anticipation and Creativity', in Hallam, E. and Ingold, T. (eds) *Creativity and Cultural Improvisation*, Oxford: Berg, 193–206.

Häussermann, H. and Colomb, C. (2003) 'The New Berlin: Marketing the City of Dreams', in Hoffman, M., Fainstein, S.S. and Judd, D.R. (eds) *Cities and Visitors: Regulating People, Markets, and City Space*, Oxford: Blackwell, 200–18.

Hertle, H.H. (2011) *The Berlin Wall Story: Biography of a Monument*, Berlin: Ch. Links.

Hughes Freeland, F. (ed.) (1998) *Ritual, Performance, Media*, London: Routledge.

Hyde, K. and Oleson, K. (2011) 'Packing for Touristic Performances', *Annals of Tourism Research* 38(3): 900–19.

Ingold, T. (2007) 'Introduction', in Hallam, E. and Ingold, T. (eds) *Creativity and Cultural Improvisation*, Oxford: Berg, 1–24.

Ingold, T. and Vergunst, J.L. (eds) (2008) *Ways of Walking: Ethnography and Practice on Foot*, Farnham: Ashgate.

Kuehling, S. (2007) 'The "Anthropology of Landscape" as a Research Method', in Wassman, J. and Stockhaus, K. (eds) *Experiencing New Worlds*, New York: Berghahn Books, 176–86.

Manghani, S. (2008) *Image Critique and the Fall of the Berlin Wall*, Bristol: Intellect Books.

Meethan, K. (2010) 'Touring the Other: Buffalo Bill in Europe', *Journal of Tourism History* 2(2): 117–32.

——(2011) 'Narrating and Performing Tourist Space: Notes Towards Some Conceptual and Methodological Issues', in Mansfield, C. and Seligman, S. (eds) Narrative and the Built Heritage – Papers in Tourism Research, Saarbrücken: VDM, 129–40.

——(2012a) 'Tourism, Individuation and Space', in Wilson, J. (ed.) *New Perspectives in Tourism Geographies*, London: Routledge, 61–66.

——(2012b) 'Walking the Edges: Towards a Visual Ethnography of Beachscapes', in Andrews, H. and Roberts, L. (eds) *Liminal Landscapes: Travel, Experience and Spaces In-between*, London: Routledge.

Mews, S. (1996) 'The Spies are Coming in from the Cold War: The Berlin Wall in Espionage Novels', in Schürer, E., Keune, M.E. and Jenkins, P. (eds) *The Berlin Wall: Representations and Perspectives*, New York: Lang, 50–60.

Mock, R. (2000) *Performing Processes: Creating Live Performance*, Bristol: Intellect.

Nicks, S. (1999) 'Indian Villages and Entertainments: Setting the Stage for Tourist Souvenir Sales', in Phillips, R.B. and Steiner, C.B. (eds) *Unpacking Culture: Art and Commodity in Colonial and Postcolonial Worlds*, Berkeley: University of California Press, 301–15.

Pink, S. (2007) 'Walking with Video', *Visual Studies* 22(3): 240–52.

Pink, S., Hubbard, P., O'Neill, N. and Radley, A. (2010) 'Walking Across Disciplines: From Ethnography to Arts Practice', *Visual Studies* 25(1): 1–7.

Reijnders, S. (2011) *Places of the Imagination: Media, Tourism and Culture*, Farnham: Ashgate.

Salazar, N. (2005) 'Tourism and Glocalization: "Local" Tour Guiding', *Annals of Tourism Research* 32(3): 628–46.

Schürer, E., Keune, M.E. and Jenkins, P. (eds) (1996) *The Berlin Wall: Representations and Perspectives*, New York: Lang.

Strathern, A. and Stewart, P.J. (2007) 'Actors and Actions in "Exotic" Places', in Wassman, J. and Stockhaus, K. (eds) *Experiencing New Worlds*, New York: Berghahn Books, 95–108.

Taylor, F. (2008) *The Berlin Wall: A World Divided*, London: Harper Collins.

Waldenburg, H. (1990) *The Berlin Wall*, New York: Abbeville Press.

Ward, J.J. (1996) 'Remember When It Was the Antifacist Defense Wall? The Uses of History in the Battle for Public Memory and Public Space', in Schürer, E., Keune, M.E. and Jenkins, P. (eds) *The Berlin Wall: Representations and Perspectives*, New York: Lang, 11–24.

Wearing, S., Stevenson, D. and Young, T. (2010) *Tourist Cultures: Identity, Place and the Traveller*, London: Sage.

Wright, P. (2007) *Iron Curtain: From Stage to Cold War*, Oxford: Oxford University Press.

## Further sources

History of the Berlin Wall www.chronik-der-mauer.de/index.php/de/Start/Index/id/652147 (accessed 15 November 2012)

Berlin Wall Memorial www.berlin.de/mauer/gedenkstaetten/berliner_mauer/index.en.php (accessed 15 November 2012)

# 20

# Cosmopolitanism and hospitality

*David Picard*

Cosmopolitanism is a philosophical and political movement defending equality among humans and the idea of world citizenship as guiding principles. Cosmopolites claim that overcoming ethnic communalism and nationalism as institutions to define social identity, and promoting instead world citizenship and the principle of universal hospitality, will create conditions for lasting peace among people. Cosmopolitanism is a core element of the political rhetoric and policy agendas of major international organisations such as the United Nations Educational, Scientific and Cultural Organization (UNESCO). It also has flowed into the realms of modern tourism discourse and practice where it constitutes a new meta–narrative. This chapter briefly introduces the history of the cosmopolite movement and then explores different connections with tourism discourse, policy and practice. In this exploration, the anthropological and philosophical concept of hospitality is a constant element of reflection, demonstrating the potentials and limits of the cosmopolite movements to contribute to inter-cultural dialogues and more peaceful relations between people and nations.

## Cosmopolitanism and the claim to universal hospitality

Cosmopolitanism sources its leading metaphors from accounts of the life of Greek philosopher Diogenes, who was born in Sinope and died in Corinth in the fourth century BCE. In one of these accounts, Diogenes meets Alexander the Great, who is on his passage through Corinth. Alexander asks the philosopher if he has ever been surprised by anything. Diogenes replies that yes, indeed he has, and explains that when he was looking for the bones of Alexander's royal father he was surprised to find that there was no way to distinguish between these noble bones and those of commoners and slaves (Arumugam 2006: 15). In a different account, Alexander asks him if he could do him a favour, as he personally liked the philosopher. Diogenes, who has been sleeping under a tree responds that yes, indeed he could do him a favour by moving out of the sun, so that he could continue to sleep. In maybe the most famous account, which gives the cosmopolite movement its name, Diogenes is asked where he comes from, as a means to identify himself. He replies that he is a 'citizen of the world' (*kosmopolitês*) (Laërtius 1925: 63), implying that he does not belong to any specific state or reign. Important in these accounts is not the question of their historic authenticity, but how they are mobilised by various political and philosophical movements to articulate values and make political claims about what society should look like. By mocking the king with regard to the sameness of royal, commoner and slave bones, or by claiming world citizenship, Diogenes opposes the idea of social hierarchy based on geographical or social origin. Various political militants in later epochs mobilise these and other accounts of Diogenes' mockeries and claims as metaphors to criticise social inequalities and express claims to a more equal society. In 1795, German philosopher Immanuel Kant asserted that a world of perpetual peace would only be achieved by means of a 'law of world citizenship' based upon conditions of 'universal hospitality'. He explains that the 'right of a stranger not to be treated as an enemy when he arrives in the land of another' would allow 'the human race [to] gradually be brought closer and closer to a constitution establishing world citizenship'. Kant's ideological framework emerges from his idea that knowledge evolves in the interplay between experience and a priori concepts, and not in either pure reason or sensitivity, as stressed by the dominant philosophical traditions of his time. Kant explains that as a result of the limits of the human mind and sensitivity, we cannot understand a thing in itself or even whether it exists as a real thing at all – he uses God, the soul and freedom as examples – but we can still act on the supposition of its being real (Kant 2005). In this sense, God, soul and freedom are no longer necessarily absolute concepts of pure reason, but socially constructed ideas of practical reason. The moral imperative of doing good, which Kant considers the highest moral virtue, is subjected to free will, and not to the obedience to God or nature. Accordingly, for Kant, the only unconditioned principle of human life lies in the innate right of freedom. Kant vigorously criticises the injustices – exploitation of resources, enslavement of people, indebtedness of foreign economies – committed by the European colonial states, pointing in particular towards the British Empire (he refers to the English as the 'commercial people') who mobilise humanity to their ends rather than treating humanity as an end in itself. Kant's philosophy would have a lasting influence on subsequent philosophers, state philosophies, and also flow into the constitutional texts of many newly formed republican states and the *Charter of the United Nations*. The connection Kant makes between cosmopolitanism, hospitality and peace would remain a constant issue in future debates about how to treat foreigners and organise interpersonal relations in a transnational society. A prominent thinker influenced by Kant's thought is French philosopher and political activist Jacques Derrida, whose claim to absolute hospitality often comes up in contemporary debates on how to 'deal' with illicit immigrants in Western countries. The concept of absolute hospitality pushes the stakes set by Kant even higher, making hospitality an unconditioned moral ideal, an idealised pure reason of interpersonal relations (Derrida and Dufourmantelle 2000). While in Kant's concept of hospitality strangers shall not be harmed and will be offered protection until they move on (because they are thought to move on), in Derrida's hyperbolic vision strangers shall actively be welcomed without consideration of who they are, where they come from, how much money they have or how much prestige they can provide. Hospitality, in this sense, is an actively performed act of gratitude and goodness, a morally elevated pure reason in itself, which for Derrida defines the overarching virtue of being human. In a global societal context that for many observers is defined by an increasing polarisation between a rich North and a poor South, Derrida's notion of absolute or pure hospitality enjoys widespread success among many political activists and civil society organisations which seek out alternative models to organise the working of world society.

## Cosmopolitanism in tourism discourse and practice

Tourism evolves within a globally integrated social space creating contact and lasting economic and social relations between people and institutions that are a priori strangers to each other and who escape most traditional forms of local, national or global governance (Lanfant 1995). To ensure the physical and moral integrity of tourists and the people and sites they visit, different bilateral agreements and international conventions between state parties set out rules for the management of tourist flows and infrastructures and the economic and political resources mobilised by the tourism sector. Notable examples are bi- and multilateral visa agreements between state parties, regulations for global industry standards set out by the UN World Tourism Organization (UNWTO), and normative frameworks regulating global culture and cultural property rights set out by different international conventions by the World Trade Organization (WTO) and other UN agencies. Despite their often-universalising claims, most of these international frameworks are not based on an equal-to-equal base. Visa regulations in particular do not apply universally, but favour citizens of specific countries, usually with the explicit aim of supporting national policy agendas, the promotion of foreign direct investment or the development of international tourism. Citizens who hold the nationality of countries with an above-average gross domestic product (GDP), in particular those from the industrially developed countries of Europe, America and South-East Asia, usually find themselves here in a privileged position. They can relatively easily travel to almost any country in the world, while citizens from most other countries confront relatively important constraints when applying for tourist visas to visit other countries (Bookman 2006). The observance of the unequal governance of international flows of people against the backdrop of an accelerated global political and economic integration observed over the past 30 years has brought about renewed claims for a cosmopolitan ethics as a guiding model to govern world society and citizenship. These renewed claims surface among others in the field of tourism and travel where they have led to the formation of new discourses and meta-narratives, new types of tourist products and also experiments with new forms of economic production processes and resource governance models. Lanfant and Graburn (1992) show how the countercultural claims by the 'Alternative Movements' arising in Germany and the USA in the 1960s, rejecting consumer culture and by extension mass tourism, set the base for new discourses and concepts regarding 'alternative' forms of tourism during the 1980s. Alternative Tourism is then presented as expressing a New Order of the World, based on the cosmopolite principles of equality of exchanges, respect of the cultural integrity and authenticity of the visited, and the sustainable use of resources by the tourism sector (Lanfant and Graburn 1992). From the 1990s onwards, the concept of alternative tourism shifts into various other guises, re-appearing most notably as 'ecotourism', 'sustainable tourism' and also 'responsible tourism'. The success of these new concepts may be related to their polysemous nature, which allows them simultaneously to respond to mainstream society claims for more equal forms of international development, fair, and socially integrated tourist products in destination countries and a more sustainable model of tourism production at the global scale. Picking up on the increasingly mainstreamed alternative tourism rhetoric, new tourist products emerge throughout the 1990s and 2000s ranging from up-market eco-chic boutique hotels inside nature parks and reserves, guided adventure ecotourism trips in four-wheel-drive cars and buses, to community-run eco-lodges and guesthouses developed within sustainable-tourism development frameworks. At the same time, many traditional mass-tourism operators reinvent themselves as socially responsible enterprises working within local development agendas. Corporate social responsibility programmes, carbon footprint offset systems and self-imposed environmental standards become a norm for most of the large international hotel, travel and transport corporations. While rhetorically performing an alternative tourism discourse responding to the cosmopolite concerns by their mainly Western tourist audiences, these new products remain mass-produced and integrated into the global systems of capitalist production that frames the international tourism economy. Few community-run projects manage to become economically viable, often as a direct result of the imposition of idealistic models of community utopia by international development agents, ignoring the inner hierarchies and social relationships that govern community life at a local scale (Picard 2008). What changes from earlier forms of tourism production is that anti-tourism, pro-community discourse (Wheeler 1994) becomes part of the product, while the production processes of the industry remain dominated by the economically and politically powerful centres of world society. In practice the cosmopolite principle of (more) equality claimed by these new forms of tourism is rarely, if ever realised. In practical terms the achievement of this aim highly depends on criteria not directly linked to tourist consumption or experience, e.g. local access to tourism job markets and hotel value chains, the presence of professional training facilities, the socially fair public redistribution of tax income generated by the tourism sector. At a different level, the claim to forms of tourism that respect the cultural integrity and authenticity of destinations visited often leads to the creation of what Dean MacCannell (1992) calls 'post-savages'; in a post-modern economic setting, local people stage forms of imagined authenticity defined by outsiders as a means to access and participate in the realms of a wider global modernity. As a result, tourism reveals itself as a global theatre stage (following Erwin Goffman's (1959) notion of everyday life as a theatrical stage) in which various fractions of world society perform roles for each other. The role of destinations seems to be here to enact those mythical figures and metaphors – divine natures, primitive cultures, human genius, the progressing history of humanity, contact between cultures, time and death – which allow their touristic audiences to make sense of their own lives (Picard 2011). As suggested by earlier anthropologists such as Nelson Graburn (1977) or Dean MacCannell (1976), tourism constitutes a ritual ground through which modernity maintains and reproduces itself. In this sense, tourism certainly allows the invocation and celebration of cosmopolite values, but rarely, if ever the realisation of such values as principles guiding the inner working of the industry itself.

## UNESCO, tourism and the promotion of cultures of peace

UNESCO has recently recognised 'that tourism, which brings individuals and human communities into contact, and through them cultures and civilizations, has an important role to play in facilitating dialogue among cultures … and thereby contributes to the construction of peace in the minds of men and women' (Bouchenaki 2006: 4). UNESCO was created in 1946, in the aftermath of the Second World War, with the explicit aim to generate conditions that would allow humanity to live in lasting peace. The constitution of the organisation states that 'ignorance of each other's ways and lives has been a common cause, throughout the history of mankind, of that suspicion and mistrust between the peoples of the world through which their differences have all too often broken into war' (UNESCO 1946). The agency opposes the doctrine of inequality of people and races and, picking up on the ethics of Immanuel Kant's cosmopolite philosophy, instead propagates education as a means to achieve intellectual and moral solidarity among humanity. It makes learning from and about others the guiding principle of its endeavours. One of UNESCO's globally most visible and also most successful normative actions is its World Heritage programme, created by the 1972 World Heritage Convention. The convention allows UNESCO, in collaboration with state parties, to create a list of localised properties that represent an 'outstanding universal value' in terms of their historic, aesthetic, artistic or cultural importance for humanity as a whole. The programme today includes almost 1,000 sites distributed throughout the world. Most of these sites are successful tourism attractions, in many cases only as a result of the attribution of World Heritage status. Visited, studied and contemplated by tourists, these sites generate a new type of global topography through which a specific configuration and interpretation of world history as a unifying narrative framework to tell the story of common humanity, of world citizenship, is put on display. During the 1990s critics stressed the bias of the World Heritage programme towards sites that express or embody a specific European philosophical perspective on world history. The leading maxim of this perspective is that learning from others, including past generations, will allow us to progress in life, as if history were underpinned by a logic leading to a higher moral end eventually found in God, as most theological movements would suggest, or in humanity, as the European humanist philosophers of the eighteenth and nineteenth centuries propose. In this sense, the cosmopolitanism UNESCO talks about is a specific one based upon a certain doctrine of time and history, with education being a means to reach a form of cosmopolite humanity as an end. Other cosmopolitanisms based upon different values to define world citizenship are observed in other social contexts and other times, both in the past and in the contemporary world (Rosello 2001; Appiah 2006; Beck 2006). There is a good deal of proof that inter-cultural dialogue and the promotion of peaceful relations among humans effectively lead to more peaceful relations and more cosmopolite feelings of belonging. Tourism has here the potential to play a role as it effectively brings people into contact. At the same time, as demonstrated above, tourism always runs the risk that forms of inter-cultural dialogue or exchange are packaged by a quickly adapting tourism industry, making the philosophy of UNESCO's specific form of cosmopolitanism an economically certainly successful, yet politically widely meaningless merchandise.

## Anthropologies of hospitality: encompassing the magic of the guest

To make sense of the diverse forms of cosmopolitanism that emerge in the global world and in tourism in particular, it seems useful to return to the notion of hospitality and approach it from an anthropological (and no longer from a philosophical) perspective. The anthropological approach is based less in the pursuit of a political project or goal (such as creating world citizenship or conditions for peace), than in the observation of social practices as they occur on a quotidian base in everyday life. In the social field of tourism and other forms of intersubjective contact, a priori strangers enter into the social spaces of others. People meet and new social spheres emerge, generating new relations and new forms of governance. Hospitality practice represents here one form of governing contact, creating procedures and spaces to contain others and their potentially harmful qualities or intentions, in many cases, but not always, also to encompass and appropriate such qualities to increase the power or prestige of the host. In the early twentieth century, Georg Simmel (1950) produced one of the first sociological analyses of hospitality. He discusses how the ambivalent unity of nearness and remoteness involved in every human relation is organised in the specific phenomenon of the stranger. The latter, he explains, is able to challenge notions of strangeness and possibilities of commonness among hosts and guests, and thus both to accentuate or to dissipate conceptions of Self and Other. Hospitality is understood here in terms of a dialectic cycle through which Self and Other are separated and brought back into contact, only to be once again separated. The prerequisite condition of hospitality is the delineation of Other as a distinguished moral entity, estranged of Self, yet possibly part of Self in a hidden or uncanny way (Kristeva 1991). The ambivalent relationship between host and guest would remain the centre of attention for most ensuing anthropological studies of hospitality. In 1952 Hocart stresses the a priori uncertain nature of strangers and guests, who, he asserts, are seen in various historical contexts – in ancient Greece, India and Fiji – as potentially divine messengers or returning ancestors. Within a system of anticipated reciprocity, they are treated with due respect and are offered hospitality; in return (because there is an expected return), the host expects favours either in later life or directly from God. Similarly, for Julian Pitt-Rivers strangers belong to the 'extra-ordinary' world, which makes them, in the belief of hosts, a 'suitable vehicle for the apparition of the Gods' (Pitt-Rivers 1977: 101). He defines the social logic of hospitality in terms of a double strategy aimed at both socializing and containing strangers, by transforming them into guests, and to anticipate a form of future reciprocity based on the idea that God will repay what was given for free. In other approaches, the extraordinary, often supernatural qualities associated with strangers and other potential guests generate a more immediate kind of reciprocity. Hospitality practice can be seen here as a form of symbolic and material assimilation or encompassment of guests and their potentially powerful qualities. For Claude Lévi-Strauss (1974), the symbolic and sometimes material consumption of enemies and dead family relatives is a method to nullify ontological Otherness and pertain the power of the Other in the Self. The principle of this ceremonially performed symbolic cannibalism resurfaces in the context of tourism. The seduction of strangers and their presentation as familiar guests, allies or quasi-kin, both techniques inscribed in hospitality practices and observed in a variety of contexts (Sahlins 1995), directly aims to increase the political and symbolic power of the host within their specific social context. The magic associated with foreign guests helps to empower the host – or simply satisfy their desires to attract and encounter foreign goods and people (LiPuma 2000). In view of this wider logic, the anthropological study of hospitality can be further enlarged to include any form of practice by means of which a priori strangers and strange worlds (which may be also people, spirits, material cultures, or abstract models, techniques and knowledge) are accommodated and encompassed. With some rare exceptions (Lashley and Morrison 2007), the recent literature on hospitality focuses almost exclusively on commercial host-guest relationships, usually without connecting to the earlier literature on the social logic of hospitality. This divide between commercial and non-commercial hospitality often seems ideologically driven, sourcing its rationale from the anti-modernist sentimentalism of much philosophical discourse of the twentieth century. Here a religiously elevated modernist conception of the authentic as true and morally superior is usually opposed to anything commercial, marketed or mass-produced, which, in turn, is considered 'inauthentic' (Benjamin 1968). Beyond the ideological straitjacket of such convictions, it may make sense to rethink commercial hospitality and its relation to cosmopolitanism, and explore tourism in terms of a highly theatrical field of societal and individual encounters and participations. Hotels that offer commercial hospitality are one of the players, usually enterprises with the objective to participate in the global hotel business game, that provide their owners and employees with social identity, and make them earn money as an indicator of how successfully they play the game. States and international organisations such as UNESCO mentioned above represent another type of player, the objectives of which are to achieve strategic policy objectives, e.g. the maintenance and increase of national wealth, the creation of jobs and infrastructures, social cohesion and well-being. States and international organisations use tourism to achieve such objectives – to generate income, to formulate and show off narratives about social belonging and authenticity, to create and ceremonialise social inclusion and exclusion. Minorities use tourism and hospitality as a stage to express claims of particularity. Tourists experience fantasy worlds, meet foreign people, learn from them and learn, above all, about themselves. In the contemporary world, a large share of tourism flows escape the prism of state-orchestrated attractions and tourism master plans. Websites such as CouchSurfing.org, based on computer-mediated hospitality, allow direct engagement between hosts and guest in private settings (Buchberger and Picard n.d.). The social actors involved in these and all other tourism and hospitality practices always will continue to have expectations, fantasies and also fears with regard to the respective Other. Yet, it is these practices that effectively generate new forms of social sphere, with the potential to approach forms of cosmopolitanism as a common ethical framework.

# References

Appiah, K.A. (2006) *Cosmopolitanism: Ethics in a World of Strangers*, London: Penguin.

Arumugam, R. (2006) *Alexander: Son of Olympias*, TTS World.

Beck, U. (2006) *The Cosmopolitan Vision*, Cambridge: Polity Press.

Benjamin, W. (1968) *Illuminations*, New York: Harcourt, Brace & World.

Bookman, M.Z. (2006) *Tourists, Migrants and Refugees: Population Movements in Third World Development*, Boulder, CO: Lynne Rienner Publishers.

Bouchenaki, M. (2006) 'Preface', in Robinson, M. and Picard, D. (eds) *Tourism, Culture and Sustainable Development*, Paris: UNESCO, 4–5.

Buchberger, S. and Picard, D. (n.d.) *Cosmopolitanism 2.0: Tourism and Computer Mediated Hospitality in the Early 21st Century*, Farnham: Ashgate, forthcoming.

Derrida, J. and Dufourmantelle, A. (2000) *Hospitality: Anne Dufourmantelle Invites Jacques Derrida to Respond*, translated by R. Bowlby, Palo Alto, CA: Stanford University Press.

Goffman, E. (1959) *The Presentation of Self in Everyday Life*, Garden City, NY: Doubleday.

Graburn, N.H.H. (1977) 'Tourism: The Sacred Journey', in Smith V.L. (ed.) *Hosts and Guests: The Anthropology of Tourism*, Philadelphia: University of Pennsylvania Press, 17–32.

Hocart, A.M. (1952) 'The Divinity of the Guest', in Hocart, A.M. (ed.) *The Life-Giving Myth*, London: Methuen and Co, 78–86.

Kant, I. (2005 [1790]) *The Science of Right*, translated by W. Hastie, Adelaide: University of Adelaide Library, ebooks.adelaide.edu.au/k/kant/immanuel/k16sr/ (accessed 15 November 2012).

——(n.d. [1795]) *Perpetual Peace: A Philosophical Sketch*, trans. V. Ferraro, www.mtholyoke.edu/acad/intrel/kant/kant1.htm (accessed 15 November 2012).

Kristeva, J. (1991) *Strangers to Ourselves*, New York: Columbia University Press.

Laërtius, D. (1925) 'Diogenes', in *Lives of the Eminent Philosophers, Book VI*, translated by Robert D. Hicks, en.wikisource.org/wiki/Lives_of_the_Eminent_Philosophers/Book_VI#Diogenes (accessed 15 November 2012).

Lanfant, M.-F. (1995) 'International Tourism, Internationalization and the Challenge to Identity', in Lanfant, M.-F. Allcock, J.B. and Bruner E.M. (eds) *International Tourism: Identity and Change*, London: Sage Publications, 24–43.

Lanfant, M.F. and Graburn, N.H.H. (1992) 'International Tourism Reconsidered: The Principle of the Alternative', in Smith, V.L. and Eadington, W.R. (eds) *Tourism Alternatives*, Chichester: John Wiley & Son, 88–112.

Lashley, C. and Morrison, A. (eds) (2007) *In Search of Hospitality: Theoretical Perspectives and Debates*, Oxford: Butterworth-Heinemann.

Lévi-Strauss, C. (1974) *Tristes Tropiques*, New York: Atheneum.

LiPuma, E. (2000) *Encompassing Others: The Magic of Modernity in Melanesia*, Ann Arbor: University of Michigan Press.

MacCannell, D. (1976) *The Tourist: A New Theory of the Leisure Class*, New York: Schocken Books.

——(1992) *Empty Meeting Grounds: The Tourist Papers*, London: Routledge.

Picard, D. (2008) *Regional Strategic Action Plan for Coastal Ecotourism Development in the South Western Indian Ocean*, Quatre-Bornes: Indian Ocean Commission/RECOMAP Programme.

——(2011) *Tourism, Magic and Modernity: Cultivating the Human Garden*, New York: Berghahn.

Pitt-Rivers, J. (1977) 'The Law of Hospitality', in Pitt-Rivers, J. (ed.) *The Fate of Shechem, or the Politics of Sex*, Cambridge: Cambridge University Press, 94–112.

Rosello, M. (2001) *Postcolonial Hospitality: The Immigrant as Guest*, Stanford, CA: Stanford University Press.

Sahlins, M.D. (1995) *How 'Natives' Think: About Captain Cook, For Example*, Chicago, IL: University of Chicago Press.

Simmel, G. (1950) 'The Stranger', in Wolff, K. (ed.) *The Sociology of Georg Simmel*, New York: Free Press, 402–8.

UNESCO (1946) *Constitution*, Paris: UNESCO.

Wheeller, B. (1994) 'Egotourism, Sustainable Tourism and the Environment: A Symbiotic or Shambolic Relationship?' in Seaton, A.V. (ed.) *Tourism: The State of the Art*, Chichester: John Wiley & Son, 647–54.

# 21

# Hospitality

*Tom Selwyn*

The ideas and practices that we know as hospitality lie at the core of cultural tourism and the aim here is to suggest how we might define the term. Additionally, given the nature of this book, the chapter also follows the theme of hospitality by accompanying a cultural tourist into several art galleries to discover what he or she might learn about hospitality from some familiar paintings.

Amongst the many forms hospitality takes we may count the meal at home with invited family members and friends, the banquet to honour a distinguished visitor, corporate events put on by companies for their clients, the offering of a temporary resting place to a traveller by friend or acquaintance, the hospitality advertised and offered by hotels and tourist destinations, and the giving or withholding of hospitality by a state to refugees and asylum seekers.

As to the contemporary 'hospitality industry', it is both multivalent and enormous. Some would argue that modern, market-based, commercial hospitality has 'democratised' the practice of hospitality, making it more 'egalitarian' in the sense that we are all 'free' to enter the market and buy whatever hospitality we want, wherever, and whenever we want it. Others would argue that corporate hospitality, or that of hotels, theme parks, and the myriad Disney worlds and McDonald's of Western and Eastern cities, mark the triumph of individual and corporation over every other social form. Whichever of these two positions we choose to hold we may come to agree, following the line of argument traced below, that the modern world has turned hospitality on its head.

We may make a final preliminary point (to which we will return). One of the few rivals in size to the 'hospitality industry' is the arms industry. This fact reminds us that hospitality is etymologically and conceptually intertwined with hostility and that any definition of the former would be the poorer without a word about the latter and the relation between the two.

So what exactly *is* hospitality? When is it offered? Who is it for? What is it for?

Hosts offer guests hospitality by giving them a combination of space, food, warmth, respect, and an opportunity to initiate or consolidate relationships. In traditional societies, heads of families and kin groups offered hospitality to others by giving feasts that signalled alliances between groups in the interests of celebrating partnerships in marriage, trade, or other co-operative activity. In most societies, but particularly those with members spread over geographically large spaces, the significance of being hospitable to strangers is particularly pronounced, for it is clearly necessary in such landscapes to have systems of converting strangers into friends and potential enemies into allies. An early anthropological study of hospitality (Hocart 1952) suggested that the honour traditionally offered by host to guest is based on the idea that guests are tinged with the sacred. Furthermore, according to first sociological and anthropological principles, the relationship between host and guest is grounded in the nature of social life itself: it would be difficult to imagine how society would be possible without hospitality.

Thus it is wholly to be expected that, just as in ancient Greece and Rome, ideas in Jewish, Christian, and Islamic traditions stress the fact that the giving of hospitality is a virtuous, noble and moral obligation rooted in the natural order of things. One of the responsibilities of the medieval European guilds, for example, was to make provision for the poor, sick, and old. A hospital was originally a house designed to give hospitality to pilgrims, and the duty of hospitallers, such as the Knights of Malta, was to provide pilgrims with *hospitium*, lodging and entertainment. Furthermore, one may read seventeenth-century sermons by priests who referred to biblical sources (such as the book of Genesis in which the hospitality of Abraham to the three 'angels' is described) to explain to their congregations that hospitality is a virtue that consists of giving kindness to strangers and looking after the poor.

However, hospitality was and is seldom all virtue and good works. Hospitality is routinely linked not only to symbolic manifestations of social hierarchy and political power but also to pleasures marked by excess. For example, we read of descriptions of banquets in courts and baronial homes in England from the Norman period onwards that include references to the consumption not only of huge quantities of different types of food and drink – both of which are, of course, ingredients of central significance to most hospitality events – but also congenial post-prandial activities, sometimes of a sexual nature.

Traditional hospitality, rather like the relationships embedded within the practices associated with Maussian Gift exchange (Mauss 2002), are in fundamental ways distinct from the relationships formed in the market place. This takes us back to hospitality in our own market-driven societies. Not surprisingly most recent books and articles on the subject look at hospitality from the point of view of the commercial 'hospitality industry'. Much of this literature is concerned with the way hospitality is managed in hotels, tourist resorts, cruise ships, casinos, sporting venues, and sites of what one prominent American sociological critic, George Ritzer (1993) neatly terms 'eatertainment'. The fast-food restaurant, for example, runs on principles not of virtue and altruistic sociability but of commercial efficiency, predictability, calculability, and control by 'managers' who are not concerned with the identity of guests as persons or their relations with hosts, but with paying clients as sources of financial profit. Modern hotels are in many obvious senses temples dedicated to the individual and individual desire. In these spaces we are no longer in the company of families, households, tribes, villages, or cities – institutions that have traditionally articulated relationships with more distant kin, or members of other households, distant tribes, and cities through acts of hospitality – but with corporations selling hospitality to clients in market places of commercial services. In these senses, today's 'hospitality industry' has cut loose from its own foundations.

Furthermore, bearing in mind that the word hospitality is derived, amongst other terms, from the Latin *hostis* (enemy) and Greek *xenos* (stranger, guest, host), what of hospitality's etymological cousins, hostility and xenophobia?

Many anthropologists (particularly those working in regions such as New Guinea or the Amazon basin) have recorded the role of feasts in dispute settlement: describing how fights routinely transform into feasts. By contrast, it is not hard to explain why, in environments of limited resources and/or fragile political alliances, hospitality can change quite rapidly into hostility: how feasts may turn into fights. However, hospitality and hostility have one thing in common. Both express the existence of a relationship. The 'opposite' of hospitality is not hostility but the denial that a relationship exists at all.

The thought brings us directly to hostility in the modern world.

The recent wars in Afghanistan, Iraq, and Libya have led to a large number of refugees/ asylum seekers travelling to northern Europe, Australia and elsewhere. Despite the fact that from the earliest, including biblical, times the refugee has always been thought to be the most needy of hospitality, it is becoming harder for refugees, including and even particularly from these countries, to find hospitality in the global North. Sometimes the same hotels and institutions that welcome tourists serve as detention centres for refugees (Lenz 2010). Thus we may suggest that hostility in the contemporary world is associated, inter alia, with figures such as the permanent refugee, landscapes with rigidly defended borders, internment camps for those without papers and, above all, of the lonely stranger unmediated by hospitality.

We are now ready to go with a discerning cultural tourist into several of the world's leading art galleries in order to pick out some familiar paintings that help us identify some elementary features of hospitality and hostility.

Starting his or her journey in the Hermitage, St Petersburg, our cultural tourist may stand in front of Rembrandt's *Abraham Offering Hospitality to the Three Angels* (circa 1630) and recall Hocart's observation about 'the divinity of the guest'. Rembrandt places Abraham by his tent in the desert looking out for passing travellers. Three men come by and Abraham says that he would like their permission to give them hospitality. He cooks them a calf, washes their feet, and shows them a tree for shade. The Hebrew text is purposefully ambiguous about whether the discussion between Abraham and the men/angels is between them in the plural or in the singular. If the latter, the implication would be that the 'angels' are, in fact, a single god. Furthermore the men (or God) predicted that Abraham's wife would have a child – which greatly surprised Abraham and Sarah since both were elderly.

Airlifted to the National Gallery of Art in Washington our tourist will encounter Bellini's *The Feast of the Gods* (1512–14), a picture that may be read as a joyous celebration of the fact that companionship and collective consumption of food and drink lie at the core of hospitality. Bellini introduces us to gods, drowsy with drink, in a forest clearing. Bacchus appears and amorous feelings are in the air. One of the serving girls carries a Ming vase in her arms and there is another bowl on the ground overflowing with fruits. The painting serves as a reminder that the Greek word *Symposion* means drinking and/or being together and that Plato's (1951) *Symposium* is written as a record of discussions about erotic love between friends at a banquet given by an Athenian citizen for his friends. In this sense both Plato and Bellini trace the links between hospitality, food, drink, love, and collective life and order.

The next stop, the Musée d'Orsay in Paris, houses a powerful portrait of King Louis XIV at the Versailles court offering courtly hospitality to *Le Grand Condé* (1878), serving to remind our tourist that hospitality events, of whatever kind, are embedded within and surrounded by rules of etiquette. In this particular case the orientalist painter Jean-Léon Gérôme places King Louis at the top of the expansive stairs of the palace with General Louis de Bourbon, Le Grand Condé, bent double in a bow of honour at the bottom of the stairs. Representatives of the army, clergy, and court look on in ceremonial clothes. The entire scene is symbolically suffused by complex inter-weavings of power, potential threat and actual alliance.

Bearing the memory of this noble host and guest in mind whilst crossing the English Channel to London's Wallace Collection, our art-loving tourist will readily discover another image that reminds her that hospitality is always underscored by reciprocal exchanges of honour. Holbein's *King Solomon and the Queen of Sheba* (1535) illustrates the fact well. Although this tells yet another story about a royal meeting set within a rich display of power and status, few observers would demur from the suggestion that honour routinely finds a place in hospitality activities irrespective of the wealth of hosts or guests.

Hospitality events are symbolically accompanied by references to home, home making, and the sense that home is a primary symbolic marker of social inclusion and exclusion. Our tourist will, no doubt, have seen Murillo's *Return of the Prodigal Son* (1667–70) in the National Gallery of Art in Washington and will be interested to link this to the artist's *The Expulsion of the Prodigal Son* (1660s) in the National Gallery of Ireland in Dublin. Murillo's paintings invite observers to conclude that to offer a guest – in the case of these paintings a family member who had previously been expelled from the family – hospitality at home is to affirm that host and guest share commonalities of beliefs, values and ideas about what is acceptable and what unacceptable in both the making of home and the nature of the hospitality used symbolically to affirm it.

Doubling back to the USA before crossing the Pacific to Australia, our cultural tourist may choose to visit Yale University Art Gallery to see one of the all-time iconic American paintings, namely Edward Hopper's *Western Motel* (1957). This is a powerful reminder not only that a principal function of hospitality is the transformation of a stranger into a friend but also that one of the preconditions of hostility is the presence of the unmediated and alienated other. Hopper presents us with a portrait of a woman sitting on her own in a motel beside a road. We don't know who she is, where she comes from, where she is going, who she is meeting. Being alone and cut off from any biographical or social context she appears, quite precisely, as a symbol of the absence, or even the opposite, of hospitality.

Following the lonely and unknown woman in Hopper's *Motel* our tourist may cross the Pacific for a final duo of pictures (a photograph and a painting) to a country the political rhetoric and symbolism of which seems, in the first decade or so of the twenty-first century, to be traumatised by the fear of strangers, refugees and asylum seekers. Rosemary Laing's *Welcome to Australia* (2004), exhibited in various galleries during the period, including the Museum of Contemporary Art in Sydney in 2006, is a frightening image of an internment camp for refugees and those without papers, whilst Jan Nelson's *International Behaviour* (2000), permanently exhibited in the National Gallery of Victoria, Melbourne, consists of a boat in the high seas, listing, possibly about to sink, crowded with figures. Both Jan Nelson and Rosemary Laing have won numerous prizes in Australia and elsewhere for their work. Both artists demonstrate the extent to which some painters, photographers, like other artists and intellectuals, find themselves, at certain times at the cutting edge of efforts to promote open borders and the regimes of state hospitality that these imply. Their works are not only powerful symbols of the shape and character of contemporary hostility in a world stained by war, but of the fact that one of the rivals to the hospitality industry in terms of size is the global arms industry.

In her book, *Mezzaterra: Fragments from a Common Ground* (2004), Adhaf Souef argues that the history and culture of the Mediterranean region, if interpreted in a particular way, inspires us to think optimistically about how a more convivial future for a war-weary world might be imagined. We might add that the region is one in which hospitality has flourished, sometimes punctuated by periods of hostility. Additionally, we might expect our art-loving tourist, by now exhausted by the buffeting of emotions that portrayals of the juxtaposition of hospitality and hostility has induced, to seek rest and refuge – sanctuary (the ultimate space, arguably above all, of hospitality) even – in that part of the world from which derived much of the inspiration behind many of the paintings he or she has seen (ironically perhaps) in the galleries of the global North. We might suggest that a good place to end his or her artistic tour might be the municipal library, opened in 2004, of one of the great Mediterranean port cities, Marseille.

What is striking about the *Alcazar* library is that this huge building – a former music hall in Belsunce, known colloquially as the 'Arab Quarter', a part of the city in which a large part of the population has links with North Africa, sub-Saharan Africa, the Far East, and many other parts of the world is a haven of cosmopolitanism – is a congenial space for young and old, Muslim, Jew and Christian, men and women.

From a light and airy desk in the library, our tourist might reflect upon the nature of a region in which war, conflict and antagonism were routinely reported by the media to start with hostility between Muslims, Christians and Jews in a part of the world destined to be torn apart by ethnic, cultural and religious differences. He or she might further reflect how remarkable (but in many ways how remarkably easy) it has been for the municipality of Marseille city, with the help of regional and national authorities, to have managed to provide, very precisely in the terms of the approach to hospitality taken here, a space of hospitality in which people from all round the Mediterranean, as well as way beyond its shores, can feel themselves at home in the world.

We set out by asking what hospitality is, when it is offered, and who and what it is for. We have thought about the different forms hospitality takes and about the different spaces and contexts in which we find it. We have also learnt from an art-loving cultural tourist.

In the end, we might agree that hospitality brings together hosts and guests for occasions in which social relationships are symbolised by the reciprocal giving of goods, services, well-being, honour and status. It is routinely offered on occasions when strangers are welcomed to mark the making of alliances between new friends – in places as diverse as the public spaces of the city and/or the more private spaces of family celebrations. Whether the act of hospitality is large or small, richly or poorly endowed, grand or modest, hospitality is in a fundamental sense *for* society itself, symbolising, as it often does, moments of coming together and transition. The children and grandchildren come to lunch, a baby is born or given a name, a parent dies, a stranger is incorporated into the group, an enemy is converted into a friend, the farm workers or office staff are treated to an annual party, a peace agreement is signed, hostility is transformed into hospitality, migrants of all kinds find new geographical spaces to live and work: all these and many more are examples of moments when relationships are solidified, established, maintained and celebrated.

## References

Hocart, A.M. (1952 [1927]) 'The Divinity of the Guest', in *The Life Giving Myth*, London: Methuen.
Lenz, R. (2010) '"Hotel Royal" and Other Spaces of Hospitality', in Scott, J. and Selwyn, T. (eds) *Thinking Through Tourism*, New York: Berg.
Mauss, M. (2002 [1923]) *The Gift*, London: Routledge.
Plato (1951) *The Symposium*, trans. Walter Hamilton, Harmondsworth: Penguin.
Ritzer, G. (1993) *The McDonaldization of Society*, Thousand Oaks, CA: Pine Forge.
Selwyn, T. (2000) 'An Anthropology of Hospitality', in Lashley, C. and Morrison, A. (eds) *In Search of Hospitality*, Oxford: Butterworth Heinemann.
Souef, A. (2004) *Mezzaterra: Fragments from the Common Ground*, London: Bloomsbury.

## *Paintings*

Bellini, 1512–14 *The Feast of the Gods*, National Gallery of Art, Washington.
Gérôme, Jean-Léon, 1878, *Le Grand Condé*, Musée d'Orsay, Paris.
Holbein, 1535, *King Solomon and the Queen of Sheba*, Wallace Collection, London.
Hopper, Edward, 1957, *Western Motel*, Yale University Art Gallery, New Haven.
Murillo, 1660s, *The Expulsion of the Prodigal Son*, National Gallery of Ireland, Dublin.
Murillo 1667–70, *Return of the Prodigal Son*, National Gallery of Art in Washington.
Nelson, Jan, 2000, *International Behaviour*, National Gallery of Victoria, Melbourne.
Rembrandt, *circa* 1630, *Abraham Offering Hospitality to the Three Angels*, Hermitage, St Petersburg.

## *Photograph*

Rosemary Laing, 2004, *Welcome to Australia*, exhibited in various galleries including the Museum of Contemporary Art, Sydney in 2006.

# 22

# A darker type of cultural tourism

*Karel Werdler*

## Introduction

Within the extensive range of cultural tourism phenomena, regarded as one of the oldest and most important generators of tourism (Richards 1996; McKercher and du Cros 2002), one can easily recognise certain subcategories, as were described by various academics (Bonink 1992; Munsters 2007). Within his typology of cultural historical resources Munsters identifies attractions that belong to the category of cultural tourism in a wider sense, such as monuments, churches and museums, but also includes certain theme parks and folkloristic festivals and events. A more precise category is reserved for attractions such as archaeological digs, castles and their period gardens, thematic museums and art festivals. With this typology he emphasises the representatives of the so-called 'high culture' and not those of the so-called 'low culture' (Munsters 2007). However, there are also some types of cultural tourism that seem less easy to categorise and that show distinguishing marks of both 'high-brow culture' and 'low-brow culture'. Dark Tourism, defined by Stone as 'the act of travel and visitation to sites, attractions and exhibitions which have real or recreated death, suffering or the seemingly macabre as the main theme', might be regarded as one of those (Stone 2006: 146). Stone also suggested that there are different types of this dark tourism, ranging from a lighter version to the darkest appearance. The so-called dark fun factories like the dungeons that are found in some Western European cities belong to the first category, and the extermination camps of the Second World War, or a more recent location such as the 'Killing Fields' of Cambodia, belong to the other, darkest side of the spectrum (Stone 2006). Between these two extremes one can further discern other venues such as educational exhibitions, but also former prisons, cemeteries and battlefields that are often described as specific niches of tourism (Bristow and Newman 2005; Holguin 2005; Tarlow, in Novelli 2005; Hitchcott 2009; Turnell-Read 2009).

## Dark exhibitions and collections in the Netherlands

What about dark tourism as an expression of cultural tourism in the Netherlands? Is there a demand for this type of product, is there any supply, and are there any organisations involved in a professional and/or commercial manner? It will not be possible to answer all these questions in this chapter, but our research has shown that the latter two questions can be answered in a positive manner. The Netherlands offers quite a few attractions that can be characterised as objects for dark tourism and that act as national or local tourism resources. Some of the better-known examples are the historical Gevangenpoort (Prison gate) Museum in The Hague and the Amsterdam Dungeon as a representative of the lighter category. When we focus on the other end of the spectrum we see that there are many sites and locations that belong to the heritage of the Second World War, with the Anne Frank House in Amsterdam probably being the best-known example of this category. Apart from these resources there are quite a number of cemeteries in the Netherlands that attract visitors who do not have a direct relationship with the deceased. Their interest seems mainly focused on funerary art and customs of a certain period, or on the graves and monument of the famous (Bergen and Clement 2010; Werdler 2011). There are also some commercial organisations offering excursions in the Netherlands and abroad to cemeteries and battlefields. There are also some associations that express a specific interest for funerary culture and/or military history that also offer excursions to their members and other interested parties. Within this chapter the focus will now be directed towards a commercially exploited phenomenon and one that concurs with the conceptual definition of cultural tourism that emphasises motivational drivers (Richards 1996). This specific phenomenon was discerned by Seaton as, '… material evidence or symbolic representations of death in locations unconnected with their occurrence …' (Seaton 1996: 237), and by Stone as 'Dark Exhibitions' (Stone 2006: 153) – in short, exhibitions offering a proposition related to death and dying. Over the last 20 years there have been quite a few exhibitions that could be described as dark exhibitions and which made the theme of death the main proposition of their exhibits. These were identified by introducing specific search terms into internet search machines and by additional desk and field research. When not enough information could be found using these methods, representatives of the museum were approached for more detailed information and some even offered copies of their annual reports. Existing museums that focus on providing information on and insight into such phenomena as the Second World War, imprisonment and justice were not taken into account. Browsing through the web, three permanent collections and 20 different temporary exhibitions were found that complied with the description of dark exhibitions. One of the permanent exhibitions is the recently opened Funerary Museum in Amsterdam, which seems to concur with the opinion that there is a remarkable growth in specialised museums for specific audiences (MacDonald 1992). The earliest temporary exhibition dates back to 1980; the most recent opened in November 2011. After the inventory the exhibitions themselves were subdivided into those that highlighted the relationship between the phenomenon of death and (modern) art, those that focused on funerary traditions and rituals often from a cultural-anthropological point of view, and those that explicitly exhibited human remains. The complete overview of findings of both temporary exhibitions and museums with a permanent collection is presented in Tables 22.1 and 22.2.

## Exhibition characteristics

From this inventory several preliminary conclusions may be drawn. First of all it is difficult to obtain precise visitor numbers from the exhibitions that were held during this period. Some museums did not collect such data or have them available for before 2000. Others did not bother to list the visitor numbers since the exhibition was part of a visit within a permanent collection. This was the case with the FOAM photography museum in Amsterdam and also with the exhibition in Artis Zoo. However, in this last case the curator responsible optimistically assumed that roughly one-third of the zoo visitors also included the temporary exhibition

*Table 22.1* Dark exhibitions in the Netherlands, 1980–2011

| Exhibition/year | Location | Type/exhibits | Visitors |
|---|---|---|---|
| Dood en begraven, 1980 *(dead & buried)* | Centraal Museum Utrecht | Funerary culture Holland | unknown |
| Rouw sterft nooit, 1998 *(grief never dies)* | Museum Boerderij, Staphorst | Funerary culture of the region | 10,000 |
| Botje bij Botje, 1998 *(bone by bone)* | Kunsthal, Rotterdam | Human and other remains | No data available |
| Rituelen rond dood in Middeleeuwen, 1999 *(medieval death rituals)* | Catharijne Convent, Utrecht | Death rituals in the Middle Ages | 25,000 |
| Vrolik's preparaten, 2000 *(preparations of Dr.Vrolik)* | Zoological Museum – Artis, Amsterdam | Human preparations | 50,000–65,000 (approx. one-third of all zoo visitors) |
| Doods rituelen bij Dogon, 2000 *(Dogon death rituals)* | Grote Kerk, Goes | Funerary rituals of the Dogon/Africa | unknown |
| Rituelen rond leven en dood, 2000 *(rituals of life and death)* | Stratemakerstoren, Nijmegen | Funerary rituals | No data available |
| De Dood leeft, 2005 *(death is alive)* | Zuiderzee Museum, Enkhuizen | Theme month dedicated to death | 22,000 |
| Bodies, 2006 | Beurs van Berlage, Amsterdam | Body Worlds 'copy', human preparations | 340,000 |
| Plaats delict, 2008 *(crime scene)* | FOAM, Amsterdam | Police photographs of crime scenes | unknown |
| Uitva(art) 2009 *(Funerary-art)* | Stichting Rondzegster, Elburg | Art and funerary objects | unknown |
| Rouw + Toekomst van de Dood, 2009 *(grief + future of death)* | Krabbedans and Design Academy Eindhoven | Artists on grief and future of death | 1,327 |
| Herinner me, 2010 *(Remember me)* | Krabbedans and Design Academy Eindhoven | Artists on remembrance | 2,322 |
| Ik-RIP, 2010 *(I – RIP)* | Mediamatic, Amsterdam | Artists on Death | 2,022 |
| Bodyworlds, 2010 | Las Palmas, Rotterdam | Human preparations, von Hagen Expo | 200,000 |
| Rituelen, 'In Paradisum', 2010 *(rituals I.P.)* | Museum van de Vrouw, Echt | Funerary culture and women | 1,826 |
| me-EATing, 2010 | Perron, Tilburg | Artists on Death | 675 |
| De Dood, 2010 *(Death)* | Arti et Amicitiae, Amsterdam | Artists on Death | 300 |
| Doodgewoon, 2010 *(death – ordinary)* | Hilversum Museum, Hilversum | Funerary culture | 3,000 |
| De Dood leeft, 2011 *(death matters)* | Tropen Museum, Amsterdam | Global funerary and grief cultures | Open 3/11/2011 |

*Table 22.2* Permanent collections related to dark themes

| Museum | Location | Type/exhibits | Visitors |
|---|---|---|---|
| Vrolik Museum, since 1984 | Amsterdam Medical Centre | Human and animal preparations | Unknown |
| Tot Zover, since 2008 | Amsterdam | Funerary culture and temp. exhibitions | approx. 5,000/year |
| Centrum funeraire cultuur, since 2008 | Driebergen | Funerary culture of the region | 200–250/year |

in their visit. It comes as no surprise that in the case of the Vrolik Museum there are no data available. The museum is hidden away in one of Amsterdam's largest hospitals, and there are no signs indicating its exact location or even its existence, and once a visitor has arrived, he or she can walk in freely without any admission restrictions. Another conclusion that might be drawn regards the specific topics of the exhibitions. Most of them (seven) presented exhibits on local and/or national funerary rituals and traditions, creating a link between the visitor and local culture (Dodd and van Hemel 1999), and two more offered a more global and cultural anthropological approach, as with the exhibition highlighting the Dogon from Mali and the one in the Tropen Museum (Museum of the Tropics). In the case of the exhibition in Hilversum the curators combined traditional cultural historical objects such as mementos made from the hair of the deceased with the work of modern artists on the theme of death. The artists' views on death and grief were further exhibited in six temporary exhibitions and will be examined in more detail later. Although human remains were the object of just four exhibitions, the number of visitors surpassed the total of all other exhibitions combined (540,000 versus 108,000 visitors), indicating a greater interest in this specific type of object and especially in collections like that of Body Worlds and related 'blockbusters'. In fact, one might even argue that the collection of photographs showing dead or mutilated bodies at crime scenes exhibited at FOAM comes close to this category and furthermore this suggests that visitors are drawn to museums because they contain objects outside their normal experience (Falk and Dierking 1992). The exhibitions that made a connection between death and dying on one side and art or artistic impressions on the other were rather diverse in their approach and it was found that even some of the more 'traditional' exhibitions artfully experimented in their communication with visitors. For example, in Enkhuizen visitors could write their condolences in an online register and even design their own tombstones, and in Hilversum a funerary fashion show was organised. The other exhibitions used a wide variety of activities to inform and entertain their visitors. Apart from traditional exhibitions of objects, there were lectures, performances, movies, music, symposia and even the opportunity to enjoy a meal. The curators of *me-EATing* drew a link between food and death, and stated that the two concepts are closely connected, dead meat being a symbol for love, suffering, beauty and decay. Other exhibitions were more practical in their approach, asking questions about what might happen to one's online profile after dying and if it would be possible to make arrangements for an online memento. During *Uitva-art* artists showed how they could contribute to a funeral by means of sculpture, flower arrangements, urns and other memorial objects, and even poems and music. More innovating and surprising were some of the suggestions and activities offered in Eindhoven and Amsterdam. At the first, one artist offered personified glass rings that could hold tears of grief, and in the latter visitors were invited to design a sarcophagus for a loved one.

## The visitors

How did the public react to the exhibitions and what was their motivation to visit ? These are important questions, but not easy to answer since no research was undertaken at the time. One way of shedding some light on the public's reactions is looking for newspaper articles on the exhibitions describing the attraction and the personal view of the journalists. Apart from press releases from the venues themselves only a few publications were discovered and these mostly focused on the exhibitions where human remains were exposed. Two of them deserve a closer look. The *Bodies* exhibition in Amsterdam led to a heated discussion in the (local) press between supporters and opponents, and referred to the possible use of the bodies of executed Chinese criminals (*Trouw*, 14 Nov. 2006). The other exhibition that created some commotion, even internationally, was *Bone by Bone* in 1998. I argued that most visitors are attracted because they might be shocked and being shocked is fascinating. It was mostly the exhibition of an Inuit mummy that led to protest from the Arctic Peoples Alert and an outcry in the Danish press (*Ravage* 273/274, 18 Dec. 1998), making it clear that the ownership of human remains might involve multiple stakeholders and that tourists are not the only group to be considered (McKercher and du Cros 2002). This question is even harder to answer, but here again other resources might give some idea of the visitor's frame of mind. Both *Body Worlds* and the exhibition *Doodgewoon* in Hilversum gave visitors the opportunity to write down their reactions in a visitor's book and the author had the opportunity to read some of these comments. It was remarkable to find that most reactions at the Body World exhibition were positive, using expressions such as interesting and impressive, and that many of the visitors somehow referred to a professional (medical) background. The visitor book in Hilversum provided no additional background on the visitors but here again the word 'interesting' dominated the listings. It was also clear that visitors to *Body Worlds* came from all parts of the country and even from abroad, and those visiting Hilversum were mostly from the local area. Another remarkable finding was the fact that many of the visitors in their comments referred to 'we', indicating that the visit was done within a group, confirming the suggestion made by Falk and Dierking that museum visiting is often undertaken within a social context (Falk and Dierking 1992).

## Conclusions and suggestions

A brief chapter such as this cannot be expected to offer grand schemes on cultural tourism or on dark exhibitions as part of the dark tourism phenomenon. It does, however, demonstrate that there is a lively interest in the Netherlands in exhibitions and permanent collections that offer their visitors a chance to encounter objects and remains that are connected with death and dying, and that this specific type of cultural tourism includes both producers and consumers. It also demonstrated that these exhibitions are not focusing on just one aspect of death and dying but that different interpretations are possible. Apart from the traditional and historical approach there were exhibitions that had a cultural anthropological departure point or that made a connection with (modern) art. Especially this last group, one might add, illustrated the '... blurring of boundaries between high art and low art' (Richards 1996: 314). Furthermore, it was made obvious that those exhibitions that showed human remains such as *Body Worlds* and *Botje bij Botje* not only attracted the largest numbers of visitors, but also provided enough material for discussion between opponents and supporters and justified questions about the (cultural) sensitivity and/or appropriateness of these exhibitions or specific objects. With these conclusions the author hopes to make a small contribution to the larger field of cultural tourism research and maybe indicate new directions for further research. Since many of the exhibitions had taken place in the past and the author was only able to visit a fraction of them, no research could be undertaken in such categories such as interpretation and visitor management, which both play an important role in cultural tourism. Just as with further research into the motivational aspects of the visitors to dark tourism exhibitions, sites and attractions, this omission should offer future researchers new and interesting challenges.

## References

Bergen, M. and Clement, I. (2010) *Wandelen over Zorgvlied* [Zorgvlied itineraries], Amsterdam: Klapwijk & Keijzers.

Body Worlds (2009) *The Original Exhibition of Real Human Bodies*, official catalogue, Heidelberg: Arts & Sciences.

Bonink, C. (1992) 'Cultural Tourism Development and Government Policy', MA dissertation, Rijkuniversiteit Utrecht.

Bristow, R. and Newman, M. (2005) *Myth vs Fact, an Exploration of Fright Tourism*, proceedings of the Northeastern Recreation Research symposium, GT-NE-326, 215–21, www.fs.fed.us/ne/newtown_square/publications/technical_reports/pdfs/2005/326papers/bristow326.pdf (accessed 15 November 2012).

Catharijneconvent (2001) *Jaarverslag 2000*, Utrecht: Catharijneconvent.

Centraal Museum Utrecht (1980) *Dood en begraven* [Death and Burial], exhibition catalogue, Utrecht.

Dodd, D. and van Hemel, A. (1999) *Planning Cultural Tourism in Europe*, Amsterdam: Boekmanstichting.

Falk, J.H. and Dierking, L. (1992) *The Museum Experience*, Washington, DC: Washington Books.

Hitchcott, N. (2009) 'Travels in Inhumanity', *French Cultural Studies* 20: 149–64.

Holguin, S. (2005) 'National Spain Invites You, Battlefield Tourism During the Spanish Civil War', *The American Historical Review* 110(5), www.historycooperative.org/journals/ahr/110.5/holguin.html (accessed 15 November 2012).

MacDonald, G.F. (1992) 'Change and Challenge: Museums in the Information Society', in Karp, I., Kreamer, C.M. and Lavine, S.D. (eds) *Museums and Communities*, Washington, DC: Smithsonian Institution Press, 158–81.

McKercher, B. and du Cros, H. (2002) *Cultural Tourism: The Partnership Between Tourism and Cultural Heritage Management*, New York: Haworth.

Moscardo, G. (1996) 'Mindful Visitors, Heritage and Tourism', *Annals of Tourism Research* 23: 376–97.

Munk, E. (1998) 'Botje bij botje: een beetje tentoonstelling', *Ravage* 273/274, 18 December 1998.

Munsters, W. (2007) *Cultuurtoerisme*, fourth edn, Antwerpen/Apeldoorn: Garant.

Museum Vrolik (1990) *Guide*, Amsterdam: University of Amsterdam.

Novelli, M. (ed.) (2005) *Niche Tourism – Contemporary Issues, Trends and Cases*, Oxford: Butterworth-Heinemann.

Richards, G. (1996) *Cultural Tourism in Europe*, Wallingford: CABI.

Seaton, A.V. (1996) 'Guided by the Dark, from Thanatopsis to Thanatourism', *Journal of Heritage Studies* 2(4): 234–44.

Stone, P. (2006) 'A Dark Tourism Spectrum, Towards a Typology of Death and Macabre Related Tourist Sites, Attractions and Exhibitions', *Tourism, An Interdisciplinary International Journal* 52(2): 145–60.

Tarlow, P.E. (2005) 'Dark Tourism: The Appealing "Dark" Side of Tourism and More', in Novelli, M. (ed.) *Niche Tourism – Contemporary Issues, Trends and Cases*, Oxford: Butterworth-Heinemann, 47–58.

*Trouw* (2006) 'Omstreden expositie toont Chinese lijken' [Disputed expo shows Chinese corpses], 14 November 2006.

Turnell-Read, T.P. (2009) 'Engaging Auschwitz, An Analysis of Young Travellers' Experiences of Holocaust Tourism', *Journal of Tourism Consumption and Practice* 1: 26–52.

Werdler, K. (2011) *Dark Tourism and the Dutch Popular Press*, in Conference proceedings, Educational Travel Foundation Conference, ETF London.

# 23

# Tattoo tourism in the contemporary West and in Thailand

*Erik Cohen*

## Introduction

Tattooing and travel are closely related: tattooing is by itself a 'travelling culture' (Clifford 1997) par excellence; as de Mello (2000: 14) points out, it is 'an especially mobile aspect of culture … carried on the bodies of native people who migrate or on the body of travelers coming home from exotic places'; and 'tattoo tourism', as travel motivated by the desire to observe or participate in tattoo-related events, or to acquire a tattoo of a particular design or from a noted tattooist, is an emergent variety of 'special interest' tourism.

Tattooing underwent a renaissance in the Western world in recent decades (Velliquette *et al.* 1998) as one variety of a broader spectrum of body-modification practices, and put forward a claim for recognition as an 'art' (Jeffreys 2000; Atkinson 2003; Nagle 2009). Michael Atkinson (2003: 4) reports that an estimated '15 to 20 per cent of North Americans are now tattooed'. Tattooing is increasingly penetrating mainstream, middle-class, white Western society (de Mello 2000: 2), though it continues to signify a '(symbolic) rejection' of that society (ibid.: 14; parentheses in original). In the process, tattooing symbols were de-coupled from their traditional meanings and associations with particular low-class and semi-deviant social groups (ibid.: 4), and became expressions of aesthetic predilections and tokens of personal identity.

Tattoos have been transformed from 'standardized, formulaic designs executed by craftsmen to custom-designed, fine art images executed by professionally trained artists' (de Mello 2000: 4). Older, conventional designs are unpopular among contemporary tattooists; they tend to search for novel designs, and to assign tattoos with 'new meanings derived from non-Western culture, giving them an exotic, primitive flavor' (de Mello 2000: 4; see also Turner 1999).

Looking for distinction, tattooists tend to 'search the planet for cultures whose designs have not yet been discovered' (de Mello 2000: 14). Among the non-Western countries, one of the principal destinations of that search is Thailand.

The revival of tattooing was accompanied by a proliferation of tattoo-related events, particularly in the USA. National and international tattoo conventions, started in the 1970s, have recently proliferated. In the first eight months of 2011 there were close to 270 tattoo conventions and exhibitions around the globe, most of them in the USA, but also in many European and Latin

American, and some Asian countries. Tattoo conventions are a highly commercialised business, with glitzy advertisements on the Internet, and a variety of activities, attracting large audiences. The larger ones, such as the 'Biggest Tattoo Show on Earth' in Las Vegas, and the National Tattoo Convention, feature tattoo shows, exhibitions and contests in a wide range of categories, such as the best black-and-grey tattoo, the best portrait, the most patriotic and the most unusual tattoo. Tattoo artists put up their booths during such events, offering their original designs to visitors. Such conventions bring together people from widely different social backgrounds. One of the leading researchers of the tattoo scene reports that 'White Americans, middle-class and working-class, from the cities, suburbs and small towns – all wearing tattoos borrowed many times over from many different cultures – gather once a year to show off their tattoos and to honor the best' at the National Tattoo Convention (de Mello 2000: 2).

However, despite its growing significance, 'tattoo tourism' has elicited little, if any interest on part of tourism researchers. Ted Pothemus makes an important theoretical opening by pointing out that 'in tattoo conventions it is now commonplace for different tattooists to put up stalls where anyone … can witness the act of someone being tattooed … Thus have some purely intimate rituals become more openly public and therefore performative – the experience [of the tattooee] transformed by the presence of the audience' (Pothemus 1998: 85). The performative character of tattooing, and of events associated with it, however, has not been further explored by tourism researchers, notwithstanding the current interest in performativity in tourism (e.g. Knudsen and Waade 2010).

Asian countries, in some of which tattooing has been a common practice in the past, became popular goals for Western tattooists in search of distinctive designs. In response, countries such as South Korea, the Philippines and Thailand staged their own international tattoo conventions. I shall here present a case study of Thailand, as the leading destination of Asian tattoo tourism.

## Tattoo tourism in Thailand

In contemporary Thailand, 'the marking of the body for magical reasons, for protection, strength, influence and invulnerability is still a living tradition'. Such tattooing 'is accompanied by the uttering of magical formulae; the tattooer may rib the client's skin and blow sharply upon the markings in order to impart power, and … there is a … ceremony intended to raise the full forces which slumber in the design' (Terwiel 1977: 6). Tattooing is a magic ritual, and the tattooists often claim to be in a trance or possessed by a spirit during their work (Hoskin 1993: 18–19).

The figurative motifs on magical tattoos 'are most commonly animals … [or] figures from classical Thai mythology, such as the monkey warrior Hanuman [or the mythical ascetic thaumaturg reushi] …' (Hoskin 1993: 19–20). The most popular animals are monkeys, eagles, dragons, tigers, lions, Nagas (mythical serpents) and a double-tailed, luck-bringing lizard. The tattoos are accompanied by magic spells (katha) and symbols, written in khom (Khmer) letters and often arranged in complex, 'cabalistic' diagrams (yan [yantra]). It should be noted that tattooing is not a Buddhist custom, though it is in some temples performed by monks. However, traditional designs do not usually include Buddha images, or images of Hindu deities, popular in Thailand, such as Brahma, Indra or Ganesha.

As elsewhere in Asia, tattoos in contemporary Thailand are 'especially popular among people whose work puts them close to danger, for example, soldiers, policemen and taxi-drivers' (Otaganonta 1988: 46), and, one should add, members of the underworld.

Traditional Thai tattooists used 'magical homemade dyes' and 'simple equipment: rattan thorns; several sewing needles … embedded in a wooden handle; a pointed brass engraver; or needles crafted from nails', and applied these implements manually. In contrast, 'tattooists who cater to the international community … use imported electric equipment … and hygienic, colorful dyes' (*Manager* 1991).

Traditional tattoos are dispensed primarily by old-time tattooing masters, and specialist Buddhist monks. The Buddhist temple presently best known for its designs is Wat Bang Phra, in Nakhom Phathom province in central Thailand; its late, highly venerated abbot introduced the temple's specific tattooing style. This consists mostly of images of various animals and of the thaumaturg *rueshi*, densely surrounded by mantras, tattooed primarily on the back (see Figure 23.1). Several monks continue to impart the abbot's designs, with electric tattooing guns, to devotees from around the country. Visitors are permitted to observe the process, turning the tattooee's painful experience into a performance, as Pothemus (1998) pointed out. Wat Bang Phra also offers arm tattoos to foreigners, but is less prepared to let them have the complex designs executed in the temple on Thai devotees' backs.

*Figure 23.1* Complex tattoo in the distinct Wat Bang Phra style, 2011
Source: (Photo by the author [F/7946]).

The temple celebrates a unique annual 'Tattoo Festival' (actually a ritual of homage (*wai khru*) to the late temple abbot). The festival attracts thousands of adherents who have been tattooed there, and a large number of devotees and domestic and foreign tourists, among the latter some tattoo enthusiasts (Yongrit 2003; Cohen 2009); one or two of the latter actually take part in the proceedings (see Figure 23.2).

In the course of the festival, many assembled devotees are possessed by the spirit of one of the animals tattooed on their back and, imitating the animal's movements, run in a frenzy towards the big statue of the late abbot, only to be stopped by 'catchers' spread out in front of it (Cohen 2009). This spectacle is the principal attraction of the event for tourists, who walk around the rows of sitting worshippers, hunting for shots of rising runners, irrespective of the disturbance they cause to the proceedings. However, despite the presence of an audience, I came to the conclusion that 'the Tattoo Festival is an inner-directed "ritual" and not a performance. The frenzied possessed adherents are oblivious to the observers … as they run blindly towards the stage' (Cohen 2009: 53). This raises some important wider questions regarding the circumstances under which a public event becomes a 'performance' in Pothemus's (or Goffman's) sense.

The distinct style of the temple's tattoos in 2009 apparently inspired a foreign photographer to line up systematically tens of devotees to take photos of the tattoos on the bodies, with the intention to offer them for publication in the British journal *Tattoo*; the temple's tattooing style might thereby be brought to the attention of the international tattoo community.

Some other temples besides Wat Bang Phra also proffer tattoos to foreigners, but most of the latter get their tattoos in some of over 500 tattoo studios in the country (Wechsler 2009). Many of these are tourist-oriented, and located in popular tourist destinations, such as in the back-packer enclave of Khao San or the Chatuchak Weekend Market in Bangkok, in Chiang Mai, the capital of the north, in Thailand's principal seaside resort, Pattaya, or on Phuket island in the south. Jack Wong, the son of Jimmy Wong, Thailand's 'greatest tattoo guru who established the country's first tattoo studio', points out that 'Currently, customers are spoiled for choice

*Figure 23.2* Tattooed foreign visitor participating in the prayer at the 'Tattoo Festival', 2009
Source: (Photo by the author [F/6928]).

with countless tattoo styles, such as letters, graphics, tribal motifs, animals, and zodiac signs' (Laiyok 2010: 13) – and, one should add, images of Buddha, Ganesha and other deities. The studios are 'usually decorated inside and out with colorful pictures of designs or photos of clients covered in tattoos' (Wechsler 2009: 8).

Thailand is presently the most popular destination for tattoo tourists in Asia; growing numbers of foreigners come to Thailand to acquire a tattoo (Karnjanatawe 2008). The tourist clientele can be roughly divided into two groups: occasional tattoo-purchasers and aficionados. The former often decide spontaneously to acquire a tattoo in one of the studios in a popular tourist destinations. They can choose between permanent tattoos and temporary tattoos, executed with henna or ink, or even tattoo designs from adhesive stickers. Substitute tattoos are also available: shops offer fabrics with multicolour 'tattoo-sleeves' (Chanarat 2008), and T-shirts, imprinted with complex *yan* diagrams. Tattoos thus become commodified souvenirs for the mass tourist market.

Foreign tattoo aficionados seek out particular tattoo masters, with a wide reputation, who offer expensive, customised tattoos (Laiyok 2010: 13). A complex tattoo may cost up to 30,000–40,000 baht (approx. US$1,000–1,330) (Chaisatien 2007; Karnjanatawe 2008). The reputation of Thai tattooing gained a significant boost when in 2004 the renowned actress Angelina Jolie, a tattoo aficionado, acquired a tiger tattoo from one of the country's most prestigious Thai tattoo masters (Pornpitagpan and Puttarugsa 2005: 1). Two years later, in 2006, its reputation was further expanded when the tattoo master Jimmy Wong organised the First Annual World Tattoo Festival in Bangkok, which attracted 70 tattoo artists from around the world (Fry 2006). This was followed in the last few years by similar festivals in Bangkok, in Pattaya (Karnjanatawe 2008), and in Hua Hin, a popular up-scale resort.

Until recently, the Thai authorities did not interfere with the flourishing tourist-oriented tattoo business. However, in June 2011 the Thai Culture Minister noted 'that a number of foreigners coming to Thailand are interested in having their skin tattooed with Buddhist images or Hindu god Ganesh in several parts of their bodies such as arms, legs, ankles or chest. The Minister indicated that using religious objects as tattoo patterns is inappropriate according to Thai tradition and culture'. He observed that 'Some of the tourists deem religious tattoo patterns a fashion without any religious respect'. His Ministry 'hence asked provincial governors nation wide … to inspect tattoo studios and seek their cooperation not to use sacred objects of all religions on tattoo patterns. The Minister then announced that he will ask the Office of the National Culture Commission to issue a law banning people from using sacred objects or holy beings in Buddhism or any other religion as tattoo patterns' (National News Bureau of Thailand 2011, quoted in Saiyasombut 2011).

This is remarkable because 'sacred objects or holy beings', such as thewada (heavenly beings, or lesser deities) and high Chinese gods are common on protective tattoos worn by Thai and, respectively, Sino-Thai men. Even Buddha images appeared occasionally in traditional tattoos (e.g. Hoskin 1993: 37, upper-left illustration). The Minister's instruction would thus prohibit tattooists from inscribing on their clients' skin some fairly common motifs. The statement is also ironic, since in Thai popular culture a disassociation has taken place between the sign and symbol of other religions. Young Thai girls thus frequently wear a cross as a decoration, but are astounded when asked whether they are Christian.

> The Minister's pronouncement got a mixed reception. Some tattooists agreed with its intention. A female tattooist in a tourist area in Bangkok complained that 'Many foreigners don't understand the symbols, and they want a Ganesh below the waist, like on the hip or ankle … It's the same as putting a Buddha statue in a nightclub or a toilet'.
>
> *(Erkel 2011: 1)*

However, the pronouncement also provoked resistance; people questioned the right and propriety of the Ministry's intervention (*Bangkok Post* 2011); some tattooists complained that it obstructs free expression in their art (Erkel 2011), and implicitly, by restricting the range of permissible motifs, affects their flourishing business.

Widely perceived as intended to target foreigners, the Ministry's instructions also met with some derision, as picking on a minor issue while disregarding the widespread commercialisation of Buddhism in Thailand (Biggs 2011; Vanijaka 2011). It was thus perceived as an additional instance of the authorities over-reacting to any alleged threat to the Thai 'regime of images' (Jackson 2004; Cohen n.d.), while ignoring serious social issues.

## Conclusions

In the contemporary West, tattooing is a counter-cultural practice, gradually penetrating mainstream society; this is accompanied by an expansion of the 'tattoo community' (de Mello 2000), and an accompanying growth of tattoo tourism. Contrariwise, in Thailand, tattooing used to be a widely accepted magico-religious practice, which in modern times persevered mainly among lower strata and marginal social groups. Thai tattooing recently acquired a worldwide reputation and attracted a growing number of foreign tourists, but the designs lost much of their symbolic significance. The tattooing business flourished, but got into trouble when it deployed designs that allegedly offended Buddhist culture. The two instances of tattooing tourism thus manifest contrasting dynamics: in the West, tattooing tourism constitutes one expression of the movement of practices of body-modification from the margins into mainstream culture. In Thailand, the growth of tattoo tourism, and the associated introduction of designs, some of which are allegedly offensive to Buddhism, provoked an official reaction intended to defend mainstream culture from practices seen to be prompted by tourist demand, and to protect the unsullied image of Thailand the authorities seek to project to the world.

## References

Atkinson, M. (2003) *Tattooed: The Sociogenesis of a Body Art*, Toronto: University of Toronto Press.
*Bangkok Post* (2011) 'Buddha Curbs "Stifle Expression"', 3 June: 4.
Biggs, A. (2011) 'An Unholy Stink over Drilled Ink', *Bangkok Post, Brunch* 4(23): 6.
Chaisatien, A. (2007) 'Vision in Ink', *The Nation* (Bangkok) 12 July: 5B.
Chanarat, S. (2008) 'Fashion Statement or Suicide?' *Bangkok Post, Guru* 4 July: 6–8.
Clifford, J. (1997) 'Traveling Cultures', in Clifford, J., *Routes*, Cambridge, MA: Harvard University Press, 17–46.
Cohen, E. (2009) 'Spirit Possession and Tourism at Thai Festivals: A Comparative Study', *Tourism Recreation Research* 34(1): 45–54.
——(n.d.) *Fetuses in a Thai Buddhist Temple as Chaotic Irruption and Public Denouement*, forthcoming.
de Mello, M. (2000) *Bodies of Inscription: A Cultural History of the Modern Tattoo Community*, Durham, NC: Duke University Press.
Erkel, E.K. (2011) 'Ink Wars', *Bangkok Post*, 5 June: 1, 4.
Fry, E. (2006) 'Tattoo is in the Family', *Bangkok Post*, 11 June: P2.
Hoskin, J. (1993) *The Supernatural in Thai Life*, Bangkok: Tamarind Press.
Jackson, P.A. (2004) 'The Thai Regime of Images', *Sojourn* 19(2): 181–218.
Jeffreys, Sh. (2000) '"Body Art" and Social Status: Cutting, Tattooing and Piercing from Feminist Perspective', *Feminism & Psychology* 10(4): 409–29.
Karnjanatawe, K. (2008) 'Indelible Memories', *Bangkok Post*, 5 June: H4.
Knudsen, B.T. and Waade, A.M. (2010) *Re-investing Authenticity: Tourism, Place and Emotions*, Clevedon: Channel View Publications.
Laiyok, S. (2010) 'Body Art', *Bangkok Post, My Life*, 25 February: 2.

*Manager* (1991) 'Tattooed for Success', No. 31: 68–70.

Nagle, J.M. (2009) *Tattoo Artist*, New York: Rosen.

National News Bureau of Thailand (2011) 'Culture Ministry Alerted by Religious Tattoo Patterns', 31 May.

Otaganonta, W. (1988) 'The Beauty of Tattoos: It's More than Skin-deep', *Bangkok Post*, 8 June: 31, 46.

Pornpitagpan, N. and Puttarugsa, A. (2005) 'Pain to Talismanic Gain', *Bangkok Post, Outlook*, 21 March: 1, 8.

Pothemus, T. (1998) 'The Performance of Pain', *Performance Research* 3(3): 83–87.

Saiyasombut, S. (2011) 'Thai Culture Ministry to Crack Down on Religious Tattoos on Foreign Skin', asiancorrespondent.com/56307/ (accessed 26 October 2012).

Terwiel, B.J. (1977) 'Tattooing in Thai History', *Bangkok Post,* 9 October: 6–7.

Turner, B.S. (1999) 'The Possibility of Primitiveness: Towards a Sociology of Body Marks in Cool Societies', *Body & Society* 5(2–3): 39–50.

Vanijaka, V. (2011) 'A Portrait of a Dysfunctional Family', *Bangkok Post*, 5 June: 11.

Velliquette, A.M., Murray, J.B. and Creyer, E.H. (1998) 'The Tattoo Renaissance: An Ethnographic Account of Symbolic Consumer Behavior', *Advances in Consumer Research* 25: 461–67.

Wechsler, M. (2009) 'Tattooists Turn Flesh into Fantasy', *Bangkok Post, Spectrum* 2(1): 8–11.

Yongrit, R. (2003) 'Spirited Tattoos', *The Nation*, 2 May: 8A.

# PART IV
# Community and development

This section focuses on the development of cultural tourism and the implications for local communities. Increasing globalisation and mobility is rapidly changing our notions of what community means and is often leading to the fragmentation and erosion of communities, whether they be rural tribal communities in a developing country or ethnic urban communities in a developed one. The growth of new technology means that virtual communities are starting to become almost as important as actual ones; however, there is no doubt that tourists are still fascinated to visit real communities in other countries. Often this can be the result of a certain nostalgia for a true notion of community which seems to have been lost within modern living, as well as a quest for exotic, elusive, authentic cultures.

The interaction between tourists and local people originally provided a new source of anthropological enquiry in the second half of the twentieth century (Holden 2005), but has since become a major focus of cultural tourism studies. Within anthropological studies, there has always been considerable emphasis on the impacts of tourism on the cultures, traditions and lifestyles of local residents and the complex interactions between hosts and guests, going back to Smith's seminal work of 1977. In recent years there has been a noticeable shift from largely negative ethnographic critiques of the cultural impacts of tourism to a more balanced discussion of travel and tourism as a social and cultural phenomenon. Anthropologists have been studying acculturation for decades; however, it is now recognised that tourism is only one of many factors that can lead to permanent cultural change. For example, several accounts in Macleod and Carrier's (2010) book focus on the positive benefits of tourism and the growing empowerment of local communities, and also in Donald Macleod's chapter in this section. Globalisation is not always a negative process for local people. As stated by Friedman (1999), 'healthy glocalization' (the intersection between the global and the local) is ideally a process by which local communities incorporate aspects of foreign cultures that enrich them, but reject others that would negatively affect their traditions or identity.

Some of the issues that have become central to studies of community-based tourism include image creation, representation and the construction of social identities, which all directly or indirectly address the concept of power and are embedded within discourses of political economy. Michael Ireland in this section focuses on the role of visual anthropology in depicting the lives of communities, and Jarkko Saarinen discusses some of the problems of community representation in marketing. Other important themes include the commodification of culture, whether it is a handicraft, festival, a piece of art, a ritual or a celebration. Whereas in some cases the culture can lose its original meaning for local people, a process of 'cultural involution' can also take place where local people rediscover and regain pride in their heritage because of the growing interest of tourists (McKean 1989). Much emphasis also traditionally has been placed on the concept of authenticity (MacCannell 1976; Graburn 1977), debates about which have become increasingly complex. MacCannell (1976) suggested that remote communities have no concept of authenticity and consequently did not develop a system of 'frontstage and backstage' to protect their privacy. Once visitors began to arrive, communities engaged in 'staged authenticity', setting up contrived events to satisfy their guests. However, the increasing education and empowerment of local communities may enable them to make conscious and informed decisions about which elements of their culture they choose to present to tourists and how they do this (i.e. the degree of staging versus authenticity). In this section, Michael Hitchcock gives an interesting example of this phenomenon in the case of souvenirs.

In recent years there have been stronger connections between the theories and practice of cultural tourism and sustainable, responsible, ethical and ecotourism. Philip Sloan and his co-authors in this section refer to the phenomenon of 'social entrepreneurship' and how this can be applied to local communities. This demonstrates a degree of economic empowerment through business development which can change the whole lives of local communities for the better. Although ecotourism is a form of tourism that was originally more concerned with environmental than cultural issues, its development encourages the use of indigenous guides, local products and local resources (Zeppel 2006). The study of tribal and indigenous groups has become an important sub-area in cultural tourism studies to the extent that whole books are devoted to this phenomenon (e.g. Butler and Hinch 1996, 2007; Johnston 2005; Ryan and Aicken 2005; Zeppel 2006). Cultural tourism is one way in which displaced or politically marginalised indigenous peoples can start to rebuild their communities and to renew their sense of pride in their culture and identity. The view is now fairly widespread that the cultures of indigenous people should not be fossilised, but instead treated as living cultures. There is also more recognition of intangible heritage. There has been a positive shift in the literature from looking mainly at the impacts of tourism on indigenous lifestyles and cultures to documenting and advocating political self-determination and more active participation of indigenous peoples in tourism development. This is reflected in the chapters in this section by Xerado Pereiro, Jarkko Saarinen and Anna Thompson-Carr.

## Summary of the chapters in this section

**Donald Mcleod** provides an analysis of commodification in cultural tourism including reference to authenticity. He emphasises the positive nature of tourism interactions where a stronger sense of cultural identity can sometimes emerge amongst local communities, despite the pressure of globalisation. He cites examples where communities have empowered themselves to control tourism development. The central focus of his chapter is, however, on the concept of 'cultural configuration', which involves the intentional manipulation of culture to present only certain dimensions. Although this can be for contentious political reasons, it can also result in benefits for a destination which wants to project a positive image. This phenomenon is aptly illustrated using a case study of La Gomera in the Canary Islands. He also writes of the discrepancies between what local people want to show and what tourists want to see, and issues of identity, especially amongst non-tribal communities who have rarely been the subject of anthropological enquiry.

**Michael Hitchcock** presents a study of souvenirs, a much wider subject than commonly thought, which has links to most major disciplines in humanities and the social sciences (including anthropology, sociology and museum ethnography). He analyses the difficulties of establishing authenticity, especially where hosts exaggerate their culture to make it seem more 'primitive', in line with tourists' wishes. The connections to the sense of national or local identity with which souvenirs are imbued is also discussed, as well as the feeling of political solidarity or empathy which may sometimes be engendered in the purchaser. The theme of commodification is explored, highlighting the difficulties of knowing which souvenirs are traditional and which are touristic. However, the latter can sometimes still be admired or valued for their craftsmanship. Designs and approaches to production will inevitably change as a result of tourism and other global factors iterating the fact that culture is never static and cannot be fossilised. Tourists often need to understand the intentions of the producer, adding an interesting dimension to host-guest relations.

**Michael Ireland** considers the field of visual anthropology and documentary films in particular. He specifically looks at the process of indigenous cultural change and how this is captured by film-makers for different audiences of anthropologists and tourists. Its ethnographic value is debated and the extent to which it can depict communities as they really are, given that it is abridged (although not fictionalised). He suggests that such films do not have to be made by ethnographers, as long as depiction of everyday life and culture is accurate, representative and not idealised. He uses a case study of *The Last Place in England* about West Cornwall. The role of the indigenous community in shaping their own portrayal is fascinating, especially as it verges on the hostile! This illustrates the film-maker's refusal to shy away from the authentic but less positive aspects of culture, something which is relatively rare in cultural tourism, but from which tourists may ultimately benefit.

**Xerado Pereiro** discusses the phenomenon of indigenous tourism in Latin America. He especially highlights the positive impacts of tourism development, including the revitalisation of culture, poverty alleviation and raising the global profile of indigenous groups. He also acknowledges the negative effects, such as acculturation, exploitation, de-characterisation and displacement. However, his own case study presents an example of the 'adaptive' view of indigenous tourism, which accepts that both negative and positive impacts of tourism can take place, but encourages the community to adapt creatively to the changes. This is only possible in cases where the indigenous group is empowered to take political control of development and still retains the right to say no. His case study of the Kuna people in Panama demonstrates a positive example of an empowered indigenous people who have clearly asserted their needs and objectives.

**Jarkko Saarinen** similarly emphasises the need for active involvement of indigenous people in the development, management and operation of tourism. He highlights the political nature of the terminology relating to indigenous, native and tribal people, which tends to be criticised by academics and especially anthropologists. The westernisation of the construct has, he argues, often led to ethnographic visions which are misrepresentative. However, in lieu of more appropriate and representative terminology, the term indigenous continues to be used. More importantly, indigenous development should be based on involvement that includes ownership, control, direct economic benefits, social sustainability, questions of representation (e.g. marketing) and respect for culture, identities and traditions. His case study of the Ovahimba people in Namibia illustrates the problems that arise when cultures are selectively depicted and somehow fossilised as 'primitive' and 'exotic'.

**Anna Thompson-Carr** concludes the focus on indigenous tourism by analysing the development of Māori tourism in New Zealand. Unlike many forms of indigenous tourism,

Māori tourism has a long history dating back over 100 years and has become a 'must see' experience of New Zealand. She discusses the problems of categorising Māori tourism as there are so many diverse businesses and attractions, and Māori are much more deeply integrated into New Zealand society than many other groups. As a result, the cultural elements used to attract tourists tend to go beyond stereotypes and there has been a conscious effort on the part of national agencies to increase the number of Māori participants in ventures. The relationship between ecotourism and cultural tourism has been increasingly recognised as being important in Māori tourism, as the cultural and the natural heritage are inextricably linked. Preserving the authenticity of landscape is one of the main issues that emerges from the case study of the Te Ana Māori Rock Art Centre.

Finally, **Philip Sloan**, **Willy Legrand** and **Claudia Simons-Kaufmann** discuss the role of the tourism industry and businesses in the context of cultural tourism, providing best-practice case studies of three destinations that have successfully implemented responsible tourism and hospitality based on social entrepreneurship. This includes contributions to social improvement, such as benefiting local communities economically, enhancing environmental conservation, improving education, and preserving local culture. This chapter partly dispels the myth that it is impossible to be a responsible business and still make a profit, as well as demonstrating ways in which tourism and hospitality businesses can not only involve local people, but also preserve cultures. Examples are given of small lodges and hotels in India, Tanzania and Peru, all of which show how local communities have become involved in business developments.

## References

Boorstin, D. (1964) *The Image: A Guide to Pseudo Events in America*, New York: Harper and Row.
Butler, R. and Hinch, T. (eds) (1996) *Tourism and Indigenous Peoples*, London: International Thomson Business Press.
——(eds) (2007) *Tourism and Indigenous Peoples: Issues and Implications*, Oxford: Butterworth-Heinemann.
Friedman, T. (1999) *The Lexus and the Olive Tree: Understanding Globalization*, New York: Anchor Books.
Graburn, N.H.H. (1977) 'Tourism: The Sacred Journey', in Smith, V.L. (ed.) *Hosts and Guests: The Anthropology of Tourism*, Philadelphia: University of Pennsylvania Press, 33–47.
Holden, A. (2005) *Tourism Studies and the Social Sciences*, London: Routledge.
Johnston, A. (2005) *Is the Sacred for Sale?: Tourism and Indigenous Peoples*, London: Earthscan.
MacCannell, D. (1976) *The Tourist: A New Theory of the Leisure Class*, New York: Schocken.
McKean, P.F. (1989) 'Towards a Theoretical Analysis of Tourism: Economic Dualism and Cultural Involution in Bali', in Smith, V.L. (ed.) *Hosts and Guests: The Anthropology of Tourism*, second edn, Philadelphia: University of Pennsylvania Press, 119–38.
Macleod, D.V.L. and Carrier, J.G. (eds) (2010) *Tourism, Power and Culture: Anthropological Insights*, Bristol: Channel View.
Nash, D. (1977) 'Tourism as a Form of Imperialism', in Smith, V.L. (ed.) *Hosts and Guests: The Anthropology of Tourism*, Oxford: Blackwell, 33–47.
Ryan, C. and Aicken, M. (eds) (2005) *Indigenous Tourism: The Commodification and Management of Culture*, Oxford: Butterworth-Heinemann.
Smith, M.K., Hart, M. and MacLeod, N. (2010) *Key Concepts in Tourism Studies*. London: Sage.
Smith, V.L. (1977) *Hosts and Guests: The Anthropology of Tourism*, Oxford: Blackwell.
Zeppel, H. (2006) *Indigenous Ecotourism: Sustainable Development and Management*, Wallingford: CABI.

# 24

# Tourism, anthropology and cultural configuration

*Donald Macleod*

## Tourism and its impacts on culture

Anthropologists have particular approaches to culture, illustrated by the following definitions:

> That complex whole which includes knowledge, belief, art, morals, laws, customs, and any other capabilities and habits acquired by man as a member of society.
>
> *(Tylor 1871)*

> The way of life of a people.
>
> *(Kuper and Kuper 1985)*

Definitions of culture have changed over time, varied between people and places; however, there is a general approach that sees culture in a broad and holistic way, which has serious implications for the way anthropologists engage with tourism and tourists, as this chapter illustrates.

Numerous aspects of culture may be commodified, that is turned into a commercial product, including festivals, rituals, dances, handicrafts, art, folklore and buildings. With the increase of tourism worldwide and the growth of interest in the culture of other communities there has come a pressure and a drive to commercialise culture. This can have positive and negative impacts on the indigenous population and anthropologists have been particularly aware of this as their professional research enables them to gain a rich understanding of culture from the local perspective. Greenwood (1989) was strongly critical of the commercialisation of a festival in Spain, which led to a fundamental change in its meaning for local citizens, whereas in the same volume McKean (1989) saw the benefits for the people of Bali of the commercialisation of ceremonial dances and handicrafts, a process he called 'cultural involution' after Geertz (1963). Crucial to this debate has been the concept of 'authenticity', in the sense of whether a cultural trait loses its authenticity, or original meaning and purpose. Many scholars in anthropology have examined this concept and some regard it as central to the analysis and understanding of tourism (MacCannell 1976; Selwyn 1996: 21).

Anthropologists have been particularly interested in the impacts of tourism on the host community (e.g. Smith 1989a; Nash 1996; Macleod 2004; Cole 2007). Impacted aspects of the culture, in its broadest sense, include a change in the modes of livelihood (e.g. displacement from farming to service industry), a challenge to local morals and codes of conduct regarding gender roles, sexual behaviour, religion, as well as family organisation and identities. Both Smith (1989b) and Graburn (1989) were of the opinion that mass tourism has the largest impact through the demands of tourists for services similar to their home environment, leading to major infrastructural changes and economic transformations. In contrast, Macleod (1999, 2004) argued that change is more encompassing when 'alternative' tourists, such as backpackers, visit a community, because they tend to communicate more directly and on a more equal level with local inhabitants, using local accommodation not exclusive hotels, purchasing products in local shops, and are more likely to establish relationships with the indigenous population, therefore impacting on the family, moral attitudes, ideas and local economy. All this leads to a change in the host culture, which furthermore can increase their awareness of their own distinct attributes in relation to foreign visitors. A stronger sense of local identity might develop, despite the pressures of globalisation. Culture is something that undergoes change at different rates, but is never static. With the advent of tourism we have one of the most powerful forces impacting on host community cultures ever experienced. This is one of the reasons for the increased interest in the 'other' and cultural heritage.

## Cultural heritage and power

The heritage of a particular culture may, in part, become commodified, or used for marketing purposes, as an attraction. As the definition of culture is wide, so is the variety of cultural heritage, both tangible and intangible. Examples from World Heritage sites to the smallest carving, from national dances to a nursery rhyme, may be included. One of the most interesting areas of analysis and research is investigating what aspects of a culture are promoted to tourists as its cultural heritage, and how the entire process is organised: it is here that power becomes the underlying foundation and a phenomenon worthy of serious examination. Who decides whether something should be deemed as representing a culture, nation or community, and why? What is the cultural icon, the World Heritage site, the statue, telling us about the society that promoted it?

In an edited volume (Macleod and Carrier 2010), anthropologists explored some of these questions and the answers are varied and stimulating, as follows. Joy (2010) writes about the conflict over the materials and style used in the repair of buildings at the World Heritage site in Djenné, Mali, where locals seek to use inauthentic materials to maintain their property. A struggle has developed which exemplifies different goals of the indigenous African population compared to the authorities based at the United Nations Educational, Scientific and Cultural Organization (UNESCO). The demands of tourists inevitably play a part, influencing the shape of indigenous tourism, as noted by Theodosopoulos (2010) when examining the Embera people of Panama. Their ethnic identity and relatively exotic qualities make them attractive to tourists and become displayed in brochures and websites. This, however, raises concerns about their authentic cultural forms, some believing that tourism has debased their local culture. Nevertheless, Theodosopoulos argues that the Embera are able to benefit and strengthen their livelihood through control of tourism (see also Pereiro, this volume).

Ethnic identity is something upon which cultural tourism can have a profound impact: for example, in Belize a drive towards an overarching national identity has given way to promoting multiculturalism, with four regional 'Houses of Culture' replacing a planned National Museum (Holmes 2010). In Brazil, a similar drive for cultural tourism has led to an emphasis on identifying distinguishing cultural traits for distinct regions. This has led to an emphasis on 'blackness' in one area, with a renewed stress on African roots. One problematic consequence of this is a more racial understanding of groups, leading to changes in public health strategies and associations of blackness with particular religions (Calvo-Gonzalez and Duccini 2010).

The way that the tourism industry portrays the destination cultures in order to entice tourists is something that Selwyn (1996) has addressed. Sommer and Carrier (2010) continue this theme by considering how the tourism industry in Jamaica assigns meanings to different sets of people and the activities associated with them, such as fishers and traders. This research exposes the power of the industry to shape, portray and influence the destination, a process which I shall describe by a new term, 'cultural configuration', which embraces cultural representation, stereotyping, commodification and branding.

Cultural tourism exemplifies some elements of cultural configuration, in that specific aspects of a culture can be turned into commodities to be consumed by tourists, and an entire national culture can be framed so as to be attractive to tourists, such as Bali (Picard 1995); aspects of a culture may be edited out, muted or ignored. Cultural configuration is the deliberate manipulation of a culture, or part of it, to achieve a pre-conceived objective. Of course, it is not always detrimental to the culture, and may prove a positive boost – look at how Glasgow has gained from being rebranded as a European City of Culture (di Domenico 2001). In fact, cultural tourism is much more influential than it at first appears and the repercussions need to be appreciated in their totality.

## Box 24.1 Case study: commemorating cultural heritage on La Gomera

La Gomera is one of the Canary Islands, an autonomous region of Spain located near the west coast of Morocco. It was colonised by Spain in the fifteenth century and has a port capital, San Sebastian, which retains a central core of Spanish colonial architecture, including the first church built in the Spanish colonies, the original Count of La Gomera Tower and numerous buildings associated with Christopher Columbus, who docked his ship at the port before venturing across the Atlantic. This historic heritage is promoted strongly by the tourism authorities, which occasionally call the island 'La Isla Columbina' and celebrate Columbus Day annually, events that are oriented towards an external overseas market as well as generating local pride. Nevertheless, many local people prefer to emphasise their pre-Hispanic 'Guanche' roots associated with the indigenous population that the Spanish colonisers suppressed. This leads to a tension, a contestation of cultural heritage.

A recent and controversial event was the erection of a large statue in 2007: some four metres high, it is dedicated to Huatacuperche, the Guanche leader of a revolt against the representative of Spain on the island, the Count of La Gomera. Huatacuperche managed to kill the Count and was killed himself in the skirmish. The statue was sponsored by a Canary Island coalition of political parties, and might be seen as symbolising the independent identity of the islands in relation to Spain. Additionally, it is placed by a beach in front of the island's flagship hotel and is becoming an iconic representation of the island's individuality, always useful for promotional purposes; indeed, the figure is appearing on the front pages of tourism literature.

Another monument was established in 2005 to commemorate the departure of a *barco fantasmal* (ghost boat), the 'Telemaco', which left in the 1950s for Venezuela, in a risky and illegal voyage enabling Gomeros to escape the grinding poverty – *la miseria* – of the island. The monument is composed of a large stone with metal plaque, together with an ex-fishing boat named 'Telemaco'. This celebrates an event dear to the hearts of the local people (a popular film *Guarapo* also features the event). Moreover, it indicates the political economy of cultural heritage memorials, in that it is exceptional, being oriented to the local people, not overtly seeking to promote a political point or increase visitation to the island. The above examples illustrate a type of cultural configuration through representation in monuments, and exemplify how economic power often decides whether cultural heritage becomes celebrated. Now, at the beginning of the twenty-first century, a vital dimension of the island's cultural heritage and identity, its fishing community, is diminishing, leading to a potential loss of associated materials, knowledge and skills; this is a way of life that deserves a form of commemoration and recording as much as any other.

## Cultural tourism in a global context

Identity is a subject that has been of keen interest to many anthropologists, especially as related to ethnicity (see Banks 1996: 142–44). Identity is highly relevant to cultural tourism attractions, and forms part of the reason why tourists visit a unique place, people, cultural performances and buildings. Anthropologists gain a deep insight into places and people through fieldwork and often detail the emic perspectives of the local population on their own perceived identity as well as their critical view of the identity promoted by the tourism industry. The discrepancy between what the tourists want from the people they view, especially with so-called 'indigenous' tourism, and how the community of local people want to be seen, or how they perceive themselves, has been noted by anthropologists including Smith (1989c) and Swain (1989). It has been argued that the tourism industry exploits some communities, although it may as well be said that some local people are able to exploit tourists. The issue of control over tourism is crucial, as exemplified in the account of the Kuna people (Swain 1989) as well as Theodosopoulos (2010).

In the early days of the discipline, the majority of anthropologists were investigating pre-literate, pre-industrialised societies; however, over time there has developed a vast body of research on complex, industrialised societies, and some anthropologists have researched the issue of identity in cities and its relationship with tourism. Dahles (1996) showed how a particular group of citizens in Amsterdam developed a city tour to reflect their own interests, and thereby create a new commodified aspect of the identity of Amsterdam in contrast to the stereotypical vision delivered by standard tours. Cohen (1997) examines the fraught relationship that people have in Liverpool with the iconic pop group 'The Beatles', and how it continues to shape the tourist product and the identity of the city. Atkinson (1997) gives a rich insight into the importance of jazz music to the people of New Orleans, its various meanings and relevance to economic survival, and its socio-political status in relation to the rest of the USA which is tied to the ethnic composition of the city.

These examples display the ability of anthropology to portray the intricate details of a society, a culture, illuminating its variety and complexity. Anthropology also places its subject matter into the wide embrace of the global context, which may include a colonial history, the Modern World System, as well as comparison with other cultures. This approach is apparent with some recent work which places cultural tourism into a broad context. Boissevain (2010) describes how the maritime heritage of Malta, a major attraction, is being threatened by commercial and other property interests, in which the island's tourism success has stimulated a commodification of landscape. In another examination of Malta based on built heritage, Rountree (2010) draws attention to the multiple meanings and interpretations of the island's ancient archaeological heritage, in particular the views and practices of pagans. In this work Rountree reveals a different perspective which would have relevance to a wider international community of pagans. Similarly, Rabo (2010) draws on the perspective of a specific group, in this case local traders operating in a World Heritage site bazaar in Syria; he is able to examine their views about contemporary politics, economics and their own country, illustrating their involvement with global media and their attitude to the market, which contrasts with the saccharine portrayal of the site by tourism interests. Anthropologists continue to enrich our knowledge of cultures and place cultural tourism into a wider context – one which is fine grained, complex and always challenging.

# References

Atkinson, C.Z. (1997) 'Whose New Orleans? Music's Place in the Packaging of New Orleans for Tourism', in Abram, S., Waldren, J. and Macleod, D.V.L. (eds) *Tourists and Tourism: Identifying with People and Places*, Oxford: Berg, 91–106.

Banks, M. (1996) *Ethnicity: Anthropological Constructions*, London: Routledge.

Boissevain, J. (2010) 'Tourists, Developers and Civil Society: On the Commodification of Malta's Landscapes', in Scott, J. and Selwyn, T. (eds) *Thinking Through Tourism*, Oxford: Berg, 93–116.

Burns, P. (1999) *An Introduction to Tourism and Anthropology*, London: Routledge.

Calvo-Gonzalez, E. and Duccini, L. (2010) 'On "Black Culture" and "Black Bodies": State Discourses, Tourism and Public Policies in Salvador da Bahia, Brazil', in Macleod, D.V.L. and Carrier, J.G. (eds) *Tourism, Power and Culture: Anthropological Insights*, Clevedon: Channel View Publications, 134–52.

Cohen, S. (1997) 'More than the Beatles: Popular Music, Tourism and Urban Regeneration', in Abram, S., Waldren, J. and Macleod, D.V.L. (eds) *Tourists and Tourism: Identifying with People and Places*, Oxford: Berg, 71–90.

Cole, S. (2007) *Tourism, Culture and Development: Hopes, Dreams and Realities in East Indonesia*, Clevedon: Channel View Publications.

Dahles, H. (1996) 'The Social Construction of Mokum: Tourism and the Quest for Local Identity in Amsterdam', in Boissevain, J. (ed.) *Coping with Tourists: European Reactions to Mass Tourism*, Oxford: Berghahn Books, 227–46.

di Domenico, M. (2001) 'Re-imaging the City: Heritage Tourism Strategies for Regeneration in Dundee', in di Domenico, C., Law, A., Skinner, J. and Smith, M. (eds) *Boundaries and Identities: Nation, Politics and Culture in Scotland*, Dundee: University of Abertay Press, 191–214.

Geertz, C. (1963) *Agricultural Involution*, Berkeley: University of California Press.

Graburn, N.H.H. (1989) 'Tourism: The Sacred Journey', in Smith, V.L. (ed.) *Hosts and Guests: The Anthropology of Tourism*, second edn, Philadelphia: University of Pennsylvania Press, 21–36.

Greenwood, D. (1989) 'Culture by the Pound: An Anthropological Perspective on Tourism as Cultural Commoditization', in Smith, V.L. (ed.) *Hosts and Guests: The Anthropology of Tourism*, second edn, Philadelphia: University of Pennsylvania Press, 171–86.

Holmes, J.T. (2010) 'Tourism and the Making of Ethnic Citizenship in Belize', in Macleod, D.V.L. and Carrier, J.G. (eds) *Tourism, Power and Culture: Anthropological Insights*, Clevedon: Channel View Publications, 153–73.

Joy, C. (2010) 'Heritage and Tourism: Contested Discourses in Djenné, A World Heritage Site in Mali', in Macleod, D.V.L. and Carrier, J.G. (eds) *Tourism, Power and Culture: Anthropological Insights*, Clevedon: Channel View Publications, 47–63.

Kuper, A. and Kuper, J. (eds) (1985) *The Social Science Encyclopaedia*, London: Routledge and Kegan Paul.

MacCannell, D. (1976) *The Tourist: A New Theory of the Leisure Class*, New York: Schocken Books.

Macleod, D.V.L. (1999) 'Tourism and the Globalization of a Canary Island', *Journal of the Royal Anthropological Institute* 5(3): 443–56.

——(2004) *Tourism, Globalisation and Cultural Change: An Island Community Perspective*, Clevedon: Channel View Publications.

McKean, P.F. (1989) 'Towards as Theoretical Analysis of Tourism: Economic Dualism and Cultural Involution in Bali', in Smith, V.L. (ed.) *Hosts and Guests: The Anthropology of Tourism*, second edn, Philadelphia: University of Pennsylvania Press, 119–38.

Macleod, D.V.L. and Carrier, J.G. (eds) (2010) *Tourism, Power and Culture: Anthropological Insights*, Clevedon: Channel View Publications.

Nash, D. (1996) *Anthropology of Tourism*, Oxford: Pergamon.

Picard, M. (1995) 'Cultural Heritage and Tourist Capital: Cultural Tourism in Bali', in Lanfant, M., Allcock, J.B. and Bruner, E.M. (eds) *International Tourism, Identity and Change*, London: Sage Publications, 45–65.

Rabo, A. (2010) 'Enchanted Sites, Prosaic Interests: Traders of the Bazaar in Aleppo', in Scott, J. and Selwyn, T. (eds) *Thinking Through Tourism*, Oxford: Berg, 117–38.

Rountree, K. (2010) 'Tourist Attractions, Cultural Icons, Sites of Sacred Encounter: Engagements with Malta's Neolithic Temples', in Scott, J. and Selwyn T. (eds) *Thinking Through Tourism*, Oxford: Berg, 183–208.

Selwyn, T. (ed.) (1996) *The Tourist Image: Myths and Myth Making in Tourism*, Chichester: John Wiley & Sons.

Smith, V.L. (ed.) (1989a) *Hosts and Guests: The Anthropology of Tourism*, second edn, Philadelphia: University of Pennsylvania Press.

——(1989b) 'Introduction', in Smith, V.L. (ed.) *Hosts and Guests: The Anthropology of Tourism*, second edn, Philadelphia: University of Pennsylvania Press, 1–20.

——(1989c) 'Eskimo Tourism: Micro-Models and Marginal Men', in Smith, V.L. (ed.) *Hosts and Guests: The Anthropology of Tourism*, second edn, Philadelphia: University of Pennsylvania Press, 55–82.

Sommer, G. and Carrier, J.G. (2010) 'Tourism and Its Others: Tourists, Traders and Fishers in Jamaica', in Macleod, D.V.L. and Carrier, J.G. (eds) *Tourism, Power and Culture: Anthropological Insights*, Bristol: Channel View Publications, 174–98.

Swain, M.B. (1989) 'Gender Roles in Indigenous Tourism: Kuna Mola, Kuna Yala, and Cultural Survival', in Smith, V.L. (ed.) *Hosts and Guests: The Anthropology of Tourism*, second edn, Philadelphia: University of Pennsylvania Press, 83–104.

Theodosopoulos, D. (2010) 'Tourists and Indigenous Culture as Resources: Lessons from Embera Cultural Tourism in Panama', in Macleod, D.V.L. and Carrier, J.G. (eds) *Tourism, Power and Culture: Anthropological Insights*, Clevedon: Channel View Publications, 115–33.

Tylor, E.B. (1871) *Primitive Society: Researches into the Development of Mythology, Philosophy, Religion, Language, Art and Culture*, London: John Murray.

# 25

# Souvenirs and cultural tourism

*Michael Hitchcock*

## Introduction

Souvenirs are mementos of places and occasions and, though often regarded as ephemeral, may be counted among the most valued items purchased during a vacation (Littrel 1990: 229). Items purchased on holiday are meaningful and are often more than simple mementos of time and place. Souvenirs acquired during a holiday are associated with the travel experience, but are also linked to a generalised image of a culture, or even a specific town or village. Many tourists read around the subject to find out more about their purchases, and some become specialist collectors and experts. Specialist tours involving handicrafts form a small but increasingly important niche market. Other tourists are oriented towards clothing and ready-to-wear jewellery as expressions of taste and identity.

If souvenirs are defined as objects kept to recall occasions, places or people, then it becomes clear that the worlds of souvenir and museum collecting are inter-related. Museums often serve as material and cultural memory banks, and it is not far-fetched to argue that there is common ground between the content of museum collections and the mementos purchased by tourists. This raises some contradictions for both museum staff and their visitors, since both often express an interest in what is perceived to be genuine (Teague 2000: 194–95). In contrast, souvenirs and assorted turistica and replicas are often regarded as inauthentic and thus not worthy of the attention of serious scholars, collectors and museum visitors. This is not to say that the collections of museums are based entirely on items made specifically for sale to tourists, but simply to recognise that there is some overlap between the two concerns and to argue that souvenirs merit serious scrutiny. The situation is further complicated by the fact that many museums are major retailers and derive a considerable source of revenue from the sale of souvenirs and reproductions.

The body of literature concerning souvenirs is diverse and it would be reasonable to suggest that all the major disciplines in the humanities and social science have at some point considered this topic. An overarching cross-disciplinary analysis, though undoubtedly worthwhile, lies beyond the confines of this volume and it is the intention of this chapter to concentrate on the related subject fields of sociology, anthropology and museum ethnography. Even within these cognate disciplines discussions concerning souvenirs are highly eclectic, but what is significant is that many of the authors take as their starting point the edited volume entitled *Ethnic and Tourist Arts* (Graburn

1976). Before the appearance of this volume many commentators tended to disparage the study of tourist arts as a legitimate field of anthropological and sociological investigation (Cohen 1993a: 1). The publication of Graburn's book marks the start of more objective and substantive research, as is confirmed by the growing number of books and articles devoted to this field of enquiry.

The purpose of this chapter is to build on Graburn's own work and the papers that engage with him, and it is helpful to refer to one of his more recent considerations of the subject. In a paper published in 2000, Graburn provides some observations that can serve as an opening for this discussion. Drawing on his work among the Inuit, he describes how the indigenous people of the Canadian and American Arctic were drawn into the world system as trappers; only later did tourism become important. They produce souvenirs to satisfy the following quite different demands. First, they provide buyers with attractive arts and crafts. Second, they strive to control the outside world's image of themselves. Third, they aim to be commercially viable in an increasingly competitive world. Running through these observations are a number of related questions which, for the sake of convenience, can be divided into themes that help to orientate this chapter: authenticity, identity, consumption and commodification.

## Authenticity

Souvenirs are signs of the tourist's travels and are thus often taken as tangible proof of where he or she has been. In these contexts it is perhaps not surprising that many of the questions that have been asked about souvenirs should concern authenticity. Questions concerning authenticity have been the subject of a number of celebrated essays in the social sciences (e.g. MacCannell, Graburn, Baudrillard). It is not the intention here to document the cut and thrust of this debate, but to draw attention to what light these perspectives may shed upon the study of souvenirs. The tourism industry does provide consumables such as souvenirs, but whether or not gullible tourists assume that they are authentic remains a moot point. Souvenirs are mementos of the out of the ordinary experience of the holiday and as such may be likened to holiday photographs, but they are also a great deal more besides.

Littrel *et al.* (1993: 205–5), for example, argue that authenticity is usually defined by the tourists, who often place emphasis on the hand-made, particularly with regard to quality and the time invested in its manufacture. These purchases not only evoke memories of the special people encountered on a holiday, but may also be considered to be objects that stand as generalised symbols of the developing world. For one of Littrel's respondents study the souvenir was not so much valued for its authenticity, but because of its strong empathetic response to the artisan as a representative of the poorer people of the world (Littrel 1990: 238). A similar theme is addressed by Graburn who argues that many tourist arts depend for their appeal on a definable ethnicity, an expression of the perceived cultural difference between the tourist and the person living in the tourist destination, the touree (Graburn 1987: 396).

Tourists seem to ignore evidence of encounters with modernity, but tourees know this and thus make their objects more authentically primitive, according to the codes of this interaction, in order to convey these messages. The resuscitation of ancient crafts, particularly around important archaeological sites, is also a feature of souvenir production. The artisans may have little historical connection with the ancient culture that produced the prototypes that they copy. The goods that they learn to produce are often sold as antiques and, indeed, antiquing has become a style of manufacture (Cohen 1993a: 3).

The authenticity of the artefact is linked by purchasers to the perceived authenticity of the experience. The purchase of the souvenir, as is noted by Evans, often represents the only interaction between the tourist and the touree beyond the confines of the hospitality industry.

The person with whom the tourist interacts in the marketplace is often assumed to have a close cultural link to the items being sold, but this is not necessarily the case. Souvenirs move along the hub and spoke distribution systems of market economies and may involve quite different producers and retailers. Goods drawn from the length and breadth of the vast Indonesian archipelago may, for example, be purchased in Kuta Beach, Bali, often without any information whence they came. Production may also be delegated to a client group such as the Zapotec/ Mixtec who work in the style of the Dineh (Navaho). Sometimes ethnic groups become so closely associated with particular kinds of goods and services that others cash in on their reputation. Much of the trade in Sumba textiles has little to do with the island of that name and originates in factories in Java where cheap copies are mass produced.

Deirdre Evans-Pritchard (1989) adds moreover that the items bought by tourists are often judged by the yardstick of what is in museums or private collections. This is a problematic issue as far as this volume is concerned, since many items of great aesthetic and ethnographic value in Western museums were originally collected as souvenirs. It is not only the tourists who orientate themselves by museum collections, but also many producers. As Wilkinson (2000) notes, museum objects are used by many Ainu as points of reference and other indigenous peoples elsewhere doubtless to the same. As the contributors to *Souvenirs: The Material Culture of Tourism* (Hitchcock and Teague 2000) acknowledge, the existence of such objects in museums is problematic. Within many museums no sharp line is drawn between archaeology and anthropology, and many place material from contemporary cultures in what is now referred to as the developing world alongside ancient cultures. Many of these artefacts were collected by travellers and tourists and have at least a partial history as souvenirs. Some are nothing but souvenirs.

Fascination with ancient artefacts and curios of the kind seen in museums and historic sites is stimulated by emotional responses to the past and the attendant social attitudes (Evans Pritchard 1993: 14). The relationship between tourism and the collection of antiquities is not a twentieth-century phenomenon. Marketing the past has long been well established in tourism, especially with regard to the Grand Tour. The authenticity of religious relics came under attack in the seventeenth and eighteenth centuries in Europe, and the void was filled by a demand for antiquities (ibid.: 15). The collection of arts and curiosities is not simply a Western phenomenon, but the pervasive attitudes towards the past that influence modern tourism have European and American origins. The commodification of the past through the antiquities market for tourists and collectors has helped to shape the growing heritage industry (Cohen 1993a: 6).

## Identity

MacCannell's (1992) views about the intersection of different exchange values and the appearance of reconstructed markers of identity are helpful when considering the material culture of tourism. The World of Goods draws attention to the metaphorical use of goods as indicators of cultural categories (Douglas and Isherwood 1979). As part of the information system material culture helps to make and maintain social relationships. Those who understand the codes of the information system share agreed values concerning goods as category markers. Goods are particularly sought after if there is ambiguity in the social hierarchy (Miller 1987: 136). Through the acquisition and display of goods associated with higher status, low-ranking people strive to emulate those above them. Fashion is part of a rapidly changing information system and may include and exclude on the basis of knowledge and understanding. More recent studies discuss the triumph of consumerism (Selwyn 1996) and the transcendent and identity-related experiences of shopping (Miller 1998).

These themes emerged at various points in *Souvenirs: The Material Culture of Tourism* (Hitchcock and Teague 2000), and it is the intention here to highlight a few examples. Crozier, for example, discusses individualised souvenirs, especially those made directly for purchasers, whereas Tythacott explored the aesthetic preferences and personalities behind the creation of cabinets of curiosities. Implicit in West's account of Philla Davis's travels and collections is the idea that identity may be in some ways created and mediated with the aid of souvenirs. Philla Davis's motorbike, festooned with the tools of her trade, conjures up an image of an adventurous and self-reliant woman, whose social capital was enhanced through travel. Mars and Mars focused on the symbolic qualities of gifts bought for people in different kinds of relationships with the purchasers. Their rich ethnography of the material culture of the Wake's Week holiday maker reveals much about the inter-connectedness of identities in working-class Lancashire. Souvenirs reveal as much about who one is as with whom one wishes to be identified, as is particularly the case with political memorabilia. Historians, like tourists, may seek out objects because of their associations, often eschewing the material culture associated with unpopular causes. Thus, as Bradley noted, successful movements such as the Suffragettes are over-represented in the material record.

The Suffragette souvenirs may be regarded as a forerunner of what has become known in the international crafts trade as the solidarity market. These goods are sold cheaply for charity as symbols of association to promote various causes. The purchaser does not necessarily have high expectations and may not even like the product: quality is secondary, it is the message that counts. Solidarity souvenirs arrive on the international market from time to time, some of the most striking being from Mexico. Dolls in Indian dress wearing sinister masks and bandoliers appeared during the Chiapas insurgency of the mid-1990s, though it remained unclear whether the profits from their sale went to Zapatista causes. Assertions of indigenous identity, though often denigrated by elites, may paradoxically stimulate the interest of tourists.

The Kente cloths described by Grieco may also be partly understood in terms of solidarity. Adopted by black Americans as generalised symbols of African pride and affinity, textiles from Ghana are traded in both the tourist and international craft markets. In *Building on Batik* Graburn (2000) likens Kente to other kinds of what he refers to as pride cloths such as batik cloth from Indonesia, Māori cloaks, Fijian tapa and Navaho blankets. Similar observations may be made of the storyboards of Papua New Guinea discussed by Dougoud (2000). Likewise, Butler (2000) has drawn attention to the re-interpretation of Scotland's identity with regard to tartan, tourism and national consciousness.

Souvenirs and national emblems have similar properties, but as is indicated by a chapter in *The Invention of Tradition* (Morgan 1983), they may become entangled almost accidentally. In that chapter the author argues that visitors to Wales, who often recorded their impressions of the Welsh peasantry, were struck by the cloaks and high crowned hats worn. It would appear that what had been fashionable in lowland England in the 1620s had survived among the poor in Wales. The Welsh woman's attire, though not in any sense a national costume, had by the 1830s been turned into a caricature of Wales, becoming part of the illusion of Welshness reproduced on Victorian postcards and in dolls (Morgan 1983: 79–85). The processes by which a local folk art may become a national iconic souvenir are documented by Hanefors and Selwyn (2000) with regard to the Dalecarlian horse of Sweden. Adding an unusual twist, however, the authors show how the globally overexposed Swedish tourist has come to eschew souvenirs of other cultures in favour of more home-grown fare like the horse.

## Consumption and commodification

The production and consumption of souvenirs involves a pattern of exchange that intersects diverse groups of producers and consumers. These transactions often involve middlemen as interpreters, ranging from street hawkers to sophisticated gallery owners. The discourse between the purchaser and vendor provides opportunities to negotiate the meanings associated with the souvenir. As Shenhav-Keller (1995: 152) argues, Jewish tourists visiting Israel often come with a set of expectations reflecting individual concerns about identity. The way tourists respond to souvenirs is partly dependent on their reaction to specific symbolic codes. The Jewish tourist does not simply buy souvenirs as evidence of travel, but as a component of the construction of identity.

Shops selling souvenirs are a vital ingredient in the social creation of reality and may be organised in particular ways that enhance the authenticity of the goods being sold (Shenhav-Keller 1995: 146). The sale of souvenirs also takes place in special zones and following Berger, it is useful to consider Goffman's celebrated distinction between backstage and frontstage. Tourists may be permitted to pass beyond the front region and visit the society that allegedly lies behind, though a firm distinction cannot always be readily drawn between these areas since there are what Cohen (1988: 372) has called, 'false backs'. When the staging becomes too obvious, the attraction becomes less authentic (Brown 1996: 37).

Another frequently cited perspective is Graburn's (1976: introduction) contention that goods destined for tourists may be regarded as those that are outwardly directed, in contrast to those used that are inwardly directed and are retained for traditional purposes. In some contexts, especially where there is a long experience of international trade, it may be difficult to distinguish between a touristic and traditional artefact. Goods are often made for a domestic artefact in which tourists may share a similar background to the makers. Attitudes to goods may change over time and, as Hill (in Hitchcock *et al.* 1993: 11), has shown, goods made for tourists in one period may be appreciated by the culture that made them in another. There are, for instance, examples of Balinese kris from the early days of tourism being valued on account of the quality of workmanship invested in their production. It may be useful to regard Graburn's distinction as a kind of continuum which is more sharply marked in the developing world where the backgrounds of producers and consumers differ markedly.

Debates about tradition versus modernity have been around a long time and what many authors in Graburn's (1976) famous volume suggest is that it is not particularly helpful in the case of souvenirs to argue that one necessarily negates the other. Traditional artefacts are continuing to be turned into commodities and new designs go on being created to satisfy new markets. Not only are the designs affected by these changes, but so are the social relations of production. Occupational roles associated with a particular gender, for example, may be disrupted during the process of commodification. Purchasers of souvenirs are often able to identify standardised styles and genres, such as idyllic landscapes and picturesque representations of indigenous peoples. By working within these widely accepted genres, the makers of souvenirs modify their work, often adopting a set of symbols that are assumed to be meaningful to tourists. Souvenirs are, therefore, not characterised by the holistic system of signs that is often a feature of inwardly directed goods.

Commodification transforms the original meaning of an object and its attendant symbolic codes. In order to identify specific genres and interpret what are perceived to be artistic codes, the purchaser must understand some of the intentions of the producer. The exchange is often characterised by ambiguity since the maker's original intentions and the buyer's response often diverge. These rules are perceived by those involved in the artistic exchange, though the rules operate at many levels and are often modified and broken. Souvenirs do not comprise a unified set of objects and cultural meanings, though they often hint at the experience sought by tourists.

# References

Brown, D. (1996) 'Genuine Fakes', in Selwyn, T. (ed.) *The Tourist Image: Myths and Myth Making in Tourism*, Chichester: John Wiley & Sons, 33–48.

Butler, R. (2000) 'The Role of Tartan in the Development of the Image of Scotland', in Hitchcock, M. and Nuryanti, W. (eds) *Building on Batik: The Globalization of a Craft Community*, Aldershot: Ashgate, 323–37.

Cohen, E. (1988) 'Authenticity and Commoditization in Tourism', *Annals of Tourism Research* 15: 371–86.

——(1993a) 'Introduction: Investigating Tourist Arts', *Annals of Tourism Research* 20: 1–8.

——(1993b) 'The Study of Touristic Images of Native People: Mitigating the Stereotype of a Stereotype', in Butler, R. and Pearce, D. (eds) *Tourism Research: Critiques and Challenges*, London: Routledge, 36–69.

Douglas, M. and Isherwood, B. (1979) *The World of Goods*, New York: Norton.

Dougoud, R.C. (2000) 'Souvenirs from Kambot (Papua New Guinea): The Sacred Search for Authenticity', in Hitchcock, M. and Teague, K. (eds) *Souvenirs: The Material Culture of Tourism*, Aldershot: Ashgate, 223–37.

Evans Pritchard, D. (1989) 'How They See Us: Native American Images of Tourism', *Annals of Tourism Research* 16(1): 89–105.

——(1993) 'Ancient Art in Modern Context', *Annals of Tourism Research* 20: 91–98.

Graburn, N.H.H. (ed.) (1976) *Ethnic and Tourist Arts: Cultural Expressions from the Fourth World*, Berkeley: University of California Press.

——(1987) 'The Evolution of Tourist Arts', *Annals of Tourism Research* 11(3): 393–420.

——(2000) 'Traditions, Tourism and Textiles: Creativity at the Cutting Edge', in Hitchcock, M. and Nuryanti, W. (eds) *Building on Batik: The Globalization of a Craft Community*, Aldershot: Ashgate, 338–54.

Hanefors, M. and Selwyn, T. (2000) 'Dalecarlian Masques: One Souvenir's Many Voices', in Hitchcock, M. and Teague, K. (eds) *Souvenirs: The Material Culture of Tourism*, Aldershot: Ashgate, 253–83.

Hitchcock, M., King, V.T. and Parnwell, M.J.G. (eds) (1993) 'Introduction', in *Tourism in South-East Asia*, London: Routledge.

Hitchcock, M. and Nuryanti, W. (eds) (n.d.) *Building on Batik: The Globalization of a Craft Community*, Aldershot: Ashgate.

Hitchcock, M. and Teague, K. (eds) (2000) *Souvenirs: The Material Culture of Tourism*, Aldershot: Ashgate.

Littrel, M.A. (1990) 'Symbolic Significance of Textile Crafts for Tourists', *Annals of Tourism Research* 12: 228–45.

Littrell, M.A., Anderson, L.F. and Brown, P.J. (1993) 'What Makes a Craft Souvenir Authentic?' *Annals of Tourism Research* 20: 197–215.

MacCannell, D. (1989 [1976]) *The Tourist: A New Theory of the Leisure Class*, New York: Schoken.

——(1992) *Empty Meeting Grounds: The Tourist Papers*, London: Routledge.

Miller D. (1987) *Material Culture and Mass Consumption*, Oxford: Blackwell.

——(1998) *A Theory of Shopping*, Cambridge: Polity.

Morgan, P. (1983) 'From Death to a View: The Hunt for the Welsh Past in the Romantic Period', in Hobsbawm, E. J. and Ranger, T. O. (eds) *The Invention of Tradition*, Cambridge: Cambridge University Press, 43–100.

Selwyn, T. (1996) 'Introduction', in Selwyn, T. (ed.) *The Tourist Image: Myths and Myth Making in Tourism*, Chichester: Wiley, 1–32.

Shenhav-Keller, S. (1995) 'The Jewish Pilgrim and the Purchase of a Souvenir in Israel', in Lanfont, M.F. (ed.) *International Tourism: Identity and Change,* London: Sage, 143–57.

Teague, K. (2000) 'Tourist Markets and Himalayan Craftsmen', in Hitchcock, M. and Teague, K. (eds) *Souvenirs: The Material Culture of Tourism*, Aldershot: Ashgate, 194–208.

Wilkinson, J. (2000) 'Tourism and Ainu Identity, Hokkaido, Northern Japan', in Hitchcock, M. and Teague, K. (eds) *Souvenirs: The Material Culture of Tourism*, Aldershot: Ashgate, 157–65.

——(2001) 'The Return of Ainu Material to Hokkaido for Temporary Exhibitions to Increase the Awareness of Ainu Culture', *Journal of Museum Ethnography* 13: 55–61.

# 26

# Documenting culture through film in touristic settings

*Michael Ireland*

## Introduction

This chapter looks at five factors underlying cultural tourism: change, culture, ethnography, the destination, and 'beyond'. Change refers primarily to the socioeconomic transformations brought about by tourism as a process at work within the host culture and the culture of the visitor. Just how this change is documented is central to the issues raised in this chapter. Change within the culture of a tourist destination is recorded both in formal and informal ethnographies of place. These ethnographies, once written, are set free of their touristic setting and the indigenous cultures from which they originate, through the process of publication in the academic press and popular media.

Just how these accounts of ethnography move beyond place and the extent of their ethnographic value in describing host and tourist cultures has attracted interdisciplinary interest from anthropologists studying tourism, students of tourism management, film and media studies, and specialist fields, namely visual anthropology. It is this latter field that provides inspiration for this chapter, because visual anthropology, like tourism studies, is a relatively new area for serious academic interest. Both fields of study have an interest in what ethnographies of tourist settings tell their audiences about a place and people they may be yet to visit. The focus of this chapter is the medium that brings academic and touristic audiences together: the documentary film.

## The issues raised

The documentary film is important to cultural tourism because it explores the social life of people who become the objects of the tourist gaze (Urry 1990). In doing so the documentary becomes a special kind of ethnographic film, not necessarily directed or shot by anthropologists, but having content with a wider cultural interest. For example, a drama documentary shot to entertain and educate is likely to have an 'ethnographicity' (Oliver de Sardan 1999) that tells the audience something of the indigenous culture.

This ethnographic knowledge derived from such sources will be fragmented, yet it paints a picture of the tourist setting where it was shot. In the process the cinematic technique constructs a special kind of cultural document, sharing aspects of social reality that the tourist and student of anthropology both hope to find. These realities will of course be viewed differently: by the tourist in the quest for authenticity; and by the anthropologist attempting to construct academic knowledge from what they observe. What unites them is the claim to a world beyond the screen, at once acting as a locale for fieldwork and holiday destination.

Films differ in how academic and lay audiences view them. Students of tourism will want to know what the footage can tell them about the social and economic impacts of tourism phenomena on primarily remote communities, whereas the potential tourist viewing the film will look for something more elusive, fragments of lost cultures and ways of life, for example the Celtic periphery of Britain, or 'Cornishness' (Ireland 1998). Notwithstanding these very different perspectives, the film becomes a special kind of cultural document and a stimulus for both research and tourist endeavours. There is by no means agreement on the role of the documentary film as a source of ethnographic knowledge. The next section of the chapter examines in more detail some of the issues raised in the literature in the last decade.

## Literature review

In trying to convey knowledge about a culture through film there is a process of construction for the audience which involves fictionalisation (Samuel 1994, cited in Piccini 1996). Piccini (1996) addresses this point in *Filming Through the Mists of Time* by making reference to characterisations of Celtic cultures. Piccini cites the work of Whetter (1973) and Deacon (1992) on Cornishness, drawing together Cornwall's past industries and cultural landscapes with contemporary tourism. To set the ethnographic record straight, Piccini (1996: S97) argues that 'filmmakers have an excellent opportunity to discuss current issues involving the construction of knowledge and of past and present identities'.

In reply to Piccini, Banks (1996: 98–99) expresses reservations about the ability of film to show communities as they are, saying that 'it is unlikely the Celts would have recognised themselves from accounts of their practices'. This is a rather pessimistic view of what is possible. Documentary film makers working in the Celtic periphery do in fact show their audience divisions in social structures that are recognisable to the community.

This point is taken up by Nolley (1997) in the paper, 'Finding Alternatives to Gossip: Reflexivity and the Paradigm of the Traditional Documentary'. Nolley explores the relationship between the 'documentary image and the real world', asserting that 'the documentary film promises the possibility of reference beyond itself, reference to the world beyond the screen' (Nolley 1997: 267). It is this second idea of a world beyond that is of interest to tourists and the tourism industry. A version of a culture yet to be visited 'speaks directly [to the tourist] from the documentary [being] screened. What is seen is of course an abridged view of everyday life, but it is not fictionalisation. Instead the reconstruction of events in a community is "carefully planned" but "actual enough in one sense"' (Nolley 1997: 267). Film-makers would do better not to ignore cultural change which they might find personally uncomfortable, but incorporate the subjects into their documentaries, for example external forces such as tourism.

Tomaselli (1999: 185) addresses the central concern of 'the relationship between knowledge and the visual'. Referring to field work in Africa, he is critical of the expropriation of culture from its setting, to be conserved and exhibited in museums to be the focus of cultural tourists. Tomaselli laments the blending together of the 'ethnospiritual and ecoscience' to form a base for ecotourism and cultural tourism. This leads to indigenous people being placed within a paradigm that is more acceptable to proper scientific study. He points to conservation and development paradigms being used to veil what is cultural tourism. An example of this is the 'Bushmen being returned to their cultural enclaves ... to re-join the animals' (Tomaselli 1999: 187).

Tomaselli (1999: 187–88) refers to this process as the emergence of 'anthro-tourism' where 'people would have been required to wear skins and pretend to be wild'. This kind of staged authenticity has been well documented; the challenge for us is to distinguish what it is we see! This relationship between knowledge and the visual, on the one hand, and knowledge about peoples on the other, is a prime concern in visual anthropology (Tomaselli 1999: 185). What is needed is a way of seeing behind the scenes, so to speak, to establish what social reality is and what fiction is. One way this can be achieved is to look for the 'ethnographicity of a film' (Oliver de Sardan 1999: 15).

Oliver de Sardan's work is significant in that it changes in the way we see film genres, pushing beyond debates about what is and what is not ethnographic and worthy of academic study. The argument is that the distinction between ethnographic cinema and documentary film is false (Oliver de Sardan 1999: 13). Both genres are based on the same premise, an agreement to provide an accurate representation without idealisation; this is referred to as a 'realist pact'. Oliver de Sardan's work is important principally because he disagrees with the view that ethnographic films must be made by ethnographers (Oliver de Sardan 1999: 14). Instead we should be concerned with the content of the film. For example, the emicness of the film, so that the images we see 'open a window on the point of view' of the subjects (Oliver de Sardan 1999: 16). If this can be achieved then it is 'close to the primary objective of anthropology', so when watching a documentary film what we see is not actors but people who act 'their own roles instead of playing roles of people in a script' (Oliver de Sardan 1999: 15).

Jenssen (2005) has further explored the synergy between the anthropological method and the documentary, with reference to early definitions. He offers a modern definition of the anthropological film 'as an attempt to understand human beings by showing their environment, their acts and their activities of daily life' (Jenssen 2005: 292–93). What is important for Jenssen is not arguments over definitions or terminology but the knowledge created through the film. In creating knowledge about a people, their culture and environment, the film maker is providing an archive for others to use. In so doing the film can be a source for secondary analysis by social scientists and tourists alike. Palmer (2009) has extended this usage to research in tourism where 'the visual has been employed as both data and evidence'. There are also good examples of where the documentary has been used for teaching, such as the Channel 4 series *Strangers Abroad* (1986), which charted the history and field methods of anthropologists.

We have now moved to a position put forward by Picton (2011), where we are less concerned about what is and is not an ethnographic film, and instead consider the genre as cultural documents arranged along a continuum of 'ethnographicness'. Picton points to popular 'soaps' about British life (e.g. *EastEnders*) as valuable for what they say about 'culturally specific rules of their production and about the culture of the maker and subject without being anthropological per se' (Picton 2011: 424). It is this approach to the documentary film that I take in discussing the case study, *The Last Place in England* (Yorkshire Television 1982). This case study is a cultural document, important for what it says about the subjects and the film maker.

## Box 26.1 Case study: *The Last Place in England*

This case study introduces the reader to Sennen Cove, in West Cornwall, Britain, through the eyes of a special category of visitor: the documentary film maker. His experiences as visitor and film maker are used to present, through the medium of film, a picture of life in *The Last Place in England*. The case study also demonstrates how data gathered from the making of the documentary can support observations made in the field. The case shows the film maker treading a fine line between an accurate portrait of a people's way of life and something which might be considered too real. The point is that the documentary film can never document facts alone, for even if it provides no moral context for what we see, the audience will. Therefore exact definitions of the film are not so important; what is important is what the documentary can tell us about culture. The methodology used here is a combination of participant observation on location and a life history approach with the producer, Barry Cockcroft.

### The producer and his method

Cockcroft described his method of work for the Yorkshire Television magazine programme 'Country Calendar'. He said: 'They [the stories] were easy to find, I felt more comfortable there [in the Yorkshire Dales] the ideas came better and quicker and seem to settle better.' His work in the Dales began to associate him with outdoor life in the public's mind. As Barry put it, 'I began to become associated with small people in large landscapes'.

A northern evening daily newspaper summarised his work as specialising in searching out people whose way of life is disappearing, capturing a culture that is 'isolated physically and on a different time scale' (*Evening Post* 1974: 11).

### Filming in West Cornwall

The documentaries made in Cornwall were inextricably linked to Cockcroft's experiences as a tourist. He came to St Ives as a tourist almost a decade before he made the films.

He said, 'I didn't go there with the intention of making films, I went down there because I liked the place. They [the people of St Ives] lived differently in that they had different points of reference. I realized they had many similarities to the hill farmers that I had been filming for years'.

This quotation captures much of the man versus nature theme that has been the hallmark of the early documentary film-makers of this tradition. From 1977 to 1982 Cockcroft made four documentaries in West Cornwall. *The Last Place in England* deals with life in Sennen Cove and Land's End, and provides a portrait of Cornish culture sought after by cultural tourists.

### The Last Place in England

The documentary uses interviews with locals to illustrate the community relationship with the outside world, the collective memory of historical events and emic view of tourist–local relations. The nature of the relationship is made clear in a scene where Cockcroft interviews the local secretary of the lifeboat. He defines his own position in the village and other incomers. He says, 'Strangers are not welcome [at the catch of mullet shoal]. I mean I would still regard myself as a stranger, obviously'. Just how outsiders come to accept this definition is clear from one of the scenes in the sequence. Cecil, a retired fisherman and former member of the lifeboat crew, expressed the view of people other than locals watching the mullet caught. He said, 'Local people don't mind local people, but when bloody strangers come around 'e and want to know the in and outs. I don't know the "ins and outs" about they and what they do. But they always want to know ours' (see Figure 26.1).

*Figure 26.1* Barry Cockcroft (Yorkshire TV Producer) with the Sennen Cove Lifeboat and Crew
Source: (© M. Ireland).

Having observed the making of the documentary and watched the screened version, my conclusion must be that the indigenous people, like the film-maker, effectively blended myth with reality. This is presented to the audience as 'a picture of a society which was almost hostile to the outside world' (Cockcoft 1982).

## Discussion and conclusion

This chapter has addressed the need for a change to the way we see films about settings that are tourism locations. We need to be less concerned about definitions and filmic technique and more aware of the ethnographic content. In other words what can the film tell the audience about place and culture?

In documenting culture the film becomes a source of knowledge for both academics and tourists. The value of the film as cultural document is reflected in modern definitions of the anthropological film which are also very close to the interests of cultural tourists. Academic and tourist audiences are not naive; both are aware that what is seen on the screen is an abridged version of everyday life.

The case study in this chapter provides us with an emic view of Cornish culture. The film maker has not been afraid to address issues that are uncomfortable for the audience. This is achieved through sequences containing dialogue with significant ethnographic content. In the quest for authenticity, the documentary attempts to validate its subject's words with historical evidence.

Fieldwork in Sennen Cove has shown that far from presenting the viewer with a fictional account, the film-maker has in fact captured the way in which cultural knowledge is shared with the outside world. If viewed with a critical eye, the documentary film can provide an invaluable source of knowledge about touristic settings.

## References

Banks, I. (1996) 'Comments', in Piccini, A., 'Filming Through the Mists of Time: Celtic Constructions and the Documentary', *Current Anthropology* 37(1), Supplement: Special Issue: Anthropology in Public (Feb. 1996): S98–99, University of Chicago Press.

Cockcroft, B. (1982) Interview transcript (interview conducted in Leeds).

Deacon, B. (1992) *Vive la difference? The Cornish Identity*, unpublished manuscript.

*Evening Post* (1974) 'The TV Stories That Won't Let Barry Go', *Evening Post*, 4 November, Leeds, England.

Ireland, M. (1998) 'What is Cornishness? The Implications for Tourism', *Tourism Culture and Communication* 1(1): 17–26.

Jenssen, T.S. (2005) 'Cool and Crazy: Anthropological Film and the Point of Convergence Between Humanities and Social Science', *Visual Anthropology* 18(4): 291–308.

Nolley, K. (1997) 'Finding Alternatives to Gossip: Reflexivity and the Paradigm of Traditional Documentary', *Visual Anthropology* 9(3–4): 267–84.

Oliver de Sardan, J.P. (1999) 'The Ethnographic Pact and Documentary Film', *Visual Anthropology* 2(1): 13–25.

Palmer, C. (2009) 'Moving with the Times: Visual Representations of the Tourism Phenomenon', *Journal of Tourism Consumption and Practice* 1(1): 74–85.

Piccini, A. (1996) 'Filming Through the Mist of Time: Celtic Constructions and the Documentary', *Current Anthropology* 37(1), Supplement: Special Issue: Anthropology in Public: S87–S111.

Picton, O. (2011) 'Anthropologists Working "at Home": On the Range of Subjects and Forms of Representation in Film, and What Makes These Ethnographic', *Visual Anthropology* 24(5): 421–36.

Tomaselli, K.G. (1999) 'Psychospiritual Ecoscience: The Ju/'hoansi and Cultural Tourism', *Visual Anthropology* 12(2–3): 185–95.

Urry, J. (1990) *The Tourist Gaze*, London: Sage.

Whetter, J. (1973) *A Celtic Tomorrow*, St Austell: Mebyon Kernow.

## Further reading

Caplan, P. (2006) 'Tribes and Tribulations', *Anthropology Today* 22(2): 22–23.

——(2005) 'In Search of the Exotic: A Discussion of the BBC2 Series Tribe', *Anthropology Today* 21(2): 3–7.

(These articles both provide a critical review of Bruce Parry's series *Tribe*, first televised in 2004.)

## Filmography

Channel Four Television, n.d., *Strangers Abroad*, London: England.
Yorkshire Television, 1982, *The Last Place in England*, Leeds, England.

# 27

# Understanding indigenous tourism

*Xerado Pereiro*

Indigenous tourism has many synonyms, including ethnic tourism, ethnotourism, ethno-ecotourism and aboriginal tourism. In spite of this ambiguity, indigenous tourism emerged as an important research field in the 1990s (Mercer 1995; Butler and Hinch 1996; Picard and Wood 1997; Moscardo and Pearce 1999; Zeppel 2007: 310). Many bibliographical references were compiled by the Canadian Tourism Commission (1997) for Canada. More recently, Kutzner *et al.* (2007) collected 323 references on indigenous tourism. In 2011, 41 papers related to indigenous tourism were published in the *Bulletin of Latin American Research*. The term 'ethnic group' is cited 57 times in the key words of CABI index of 2002, making it one of the most popular terms in the index since 1990, along with the concepts of history, sustainability and cultural heritage (Hall *et al.* 2007: 37).

In the 1990s indigenous tourism was defined as the ensemble of first-hand experiences with indigenous cultures (Harron and Weiler 1992), a form of cultural collection (Volkman 1990), as well as a field of co-ethnic relations (van den Berghe 1994a) characterised by the attraction of the others and their culture, the different and 'ethnic exoticism', i.e. the native as a 'touristised' object of curiosity. At the same time, anthropologist Valene Smith defined indigenous tourism as:

> ... that segment of the visitor industry which directly involves native peoples whose ethnicity is a tourist attraction ... Indigenous tourism involves four interrelated elements: the geographic setting (habitat), the ethnographic traditions (heritage), the effects of acculturation (history), and the marketable handicrafts.
>
> *(Smith 1996: 283, 287)*

Edward Bruner (1995: 224) writes about the tourist necessity for primitiveness that masks the life of indigenous people. In indigenous tourism, indigenous ethnicity (Vermeulen and Govers 2003) is reconstructed for tourists (MacCanell 1984, 1992; Grünewald 2003), to enable them to consume the indigenous culture, transferring identities and ethnic places into the global tourism market. This type or mode of tourism is related to the Western tourists' belief that indigenous peoples are the preservers of the true human values and that they are closer to nature than people in the tourists' places of origin.

While indigenous tourism is linked to processes of commodification of culture and cultural and natural heritage, at the same time it is also related to the processes of indigenous politicisation and empowerment, indigenous social movements and social movements for alternative and anti-globalisation tourism (see, for example, the debates of World Forum of Portalegre 2002 at www.ivt-rj.net/destaques/forum/index.htm). This process must be seen as a process for social construction of identities and not just as a mercantile product.

## The effects of tourism on indigenous Latin American communities

If we analyse the scientific literature on indigenous tourism in Latin America, there are three types of interpretative analysis: those that respond to the positive or optimistic view of tourism; those that respond to a negative or critical view of tourism; and those that construct a vision of creative adaptation to the changes brought by tourism. Let's look at these views in some detail.

### The positive or optimistic view of indigenous tourism

In the 1990s, authors such as Pitchford (1995) presented an optimistic picture of indigenous tourism, by stating that it can revitalise arts, promote cultural creativity and produce a positive platform for the presentation of such human groups. It is a perspective followed by authors such as Ryan and Aicken (2005) and Barreto (2007). The latter defends the idea that tourism is not only the engine of change among host communities, but sometimes the changes produced are not as negative as it is asserted. When talking about the positive effects of indigenous tourism, the scientific literature highlights among other things the meeting of different peoples, cultural exchange and the stimulus for craft production (Getino 1991: 123). According to many authors, tourism in indigenous communities can create more respect for them by helping to maintain or revitalise languages and traditions (Mastny 2003: 28), bringing economic benefits and fighting extreme poverty.

Examples of this positive view include studies by Ingles (2002) on the Peruvian Amazon, Maldonado (2006) on the REDTURS network (www.redturs.org), Espinosa (2010) on the Saraguro Rikuy network of community tourism in Ecuador (see www.turismosaraguro.com), and Chernela (2011) for Kuna ecotourism. Another example is the Mundo Maya project (Morales and Marías 2007: 131), an initiative of regional tourism co-operation in which Mexico, Guatemala, Belize, El Salvador and Honduras are taking part. In this project women make blouses and other products with indigenous motifs for visitors, as well as corn and chilli. According to these and many other reports, tourism revitalises indigenous communities, gives them economic profits and allows them to show their cultural identity to the world.

### The negative view of indigenous tourism

A second approach is more critical of the effects of tourism on indigenous populations (Gascón Gutiérrez 2005; Gascón and Cañada 2005; Johnston 2006; Vigna 2006; Cañada 2010), and is the central focus of many scientific reports on indigenous tourism in Latin America. There are many examples that follow this line, but I would like to highlight some exemplary cases, very significant and with a major impact on academia.

Some issues of the *Cultural Survival Quarterly* (see www.culturalsurvival.org) from 1982 to 1990 served as a warning of the negative effects of tourism on indigenous groups. Another example is the work of anthropologist Pierre van den Berghe (1994b), who analysed the case of San Cristobal (Chiapas, Mexico) and the changes produced by and through tourism. If in the 1960s the community received a few backpackers, in the 1980s it began to receive hundreds of tourists who sought an ethnically exotic, untouched, 'primitive' and 'authentic' community, generating a radical alteration in the indigenous lifestyles.

Thus Pierre L. van den Berghe (1994b: 10) defined indigenous tourism, which he saw as ethnic, as follows: 'The ethnic tourism is the latest wave of expansion of exploitative capitalism to the remotest periphery of the world system.' For this author, tourism would be a new kind of Western conquest and tourists would be neo-conquerors. One of the most critical and most accurate analysts of tourism development in Latin America, Ernest Cañada (2010: 11), said that it is necessary to question the official discourse that attributed to tourism a major role in reducing poverty. He argues that the increased economic weight of tourism has been preceded by a crisis in agriculture and has resulted in what he calls 'tourism without development' and an 'unsustainable tourism model' (Cañada 2010: 12). Governments have barely considered the private sector and foreign capital as a key in tourism, concentrating their investment in the sun and sand model (large, international all-inclusive chain resorts, cruises and residential real estate tourism).

Another example to be considered is the case of Cancun, in the Quintana Roo region (Mexico), in which tourism development involved the de-characterisation of the Mayan population, the loss of their language, their dresses and their socio-cultural space. In addition, tourism eventually displaced 65 per cent of the Mayan population (Arnaizburne 1996), destroyed communal land ownership and consolidated private property and inequality exacerbated by consumer culture (Pi-Sunyer *et al.* 2001).

## The adaptive view of indigenous tourism

This third perspective can appreciate both sides of tourism and considers that while tourism can bring positive and negative impacts, it also forces communities to re-adapt creatively (Mowforth *et al.* 2008; Pérez Galán 2011). An example of this third analytical perspective is the work of Grünewald (2001). This Brazilian author has worked with the Pataxó indigenous people in north-eastern Brazil, who have developed a tourism industry that has given them a different status and a new instrumental cultural production. They have shown their creative and inventive culture from the selection of various origins, as illustrated by Peter Anton Zoettl's documentary (2010) on the Coroa Vermelha Pataxó community.

My own work on Kuna indigenous tourism (Pereiro and de León 2007; Pereiro *et al.* 2011) in Panama illustrates how tourism is a double-edged sword which has different kinds of effects, but if it is controlled politically by the indigenous group, it could generate a better distribution of its benefits, a reduction or mitigation of its negative impacts, a creative adaptation to the local-global relationships and a positive ethnic assertion in the perception of the Kunas. Thus, the Kunas' almost monopolistic tourism development is part of their strategy for survival and cultural adjustment. Far from being passive and indifferent, the Kunas use tourism as a tool for achieving economic objectives (reducing poverty), political objectives (reclaiming their lands, seas and territories), environmental objectives (conserving their environment) and socio-cultural objectives (increasing their cultural rights and collective self-esteem).

From this perspective, it can be said that indigenous tourism, rather than a simple product derived from cultural tourism to diversify the tourism system, could be thought of as an alternative way to make tourism more reflective, ethical and educational. However, this would only be possible if it were done in a planned way (Butler and Hinch 1996), controlling its speed, shape, resources and empowerment for indigenous peoples. This is what some authors call socially responsible tourism, community-based tourism and awareness travelling (Rodríguez Miranda 2011: 10).

## Conclusions

The international literature on indigenous tourism is enriched in its diversity by paying more attention to the Latin American context and its prospects in Spanish and Portuguese. In that sense I have discussed the three perspectives on indigenous tourism in Latin America: optimistic, negative and adaptive. These perspectives basically align with the platforms for scientific knowledge of tourism mentioned by Jafari (2001, 2005) and currently employ different models of analysis and intervention.

The first perspective sees indigenous groups being able to benefit from tourism, focusing only on one side of tourism development. This view supports and legitimises the commodification of indigenous tourism. The second perspective warns about the negative impacts of tourism on indigenous communities in Latin America and questions the lack of benefits for the indigenous people, as most of the profits go to the tourism-generating countries and the intermediary companies. This perspective gives a wake-up call for the critical observation of tourism, advocating alternative models of tourism (e.g. community tourism, fair tourism, responsible tourism, ethical tourism …) that are not simply cosmetic or marketing strategies.

Finally, the adaptive perspective is thoughtfully positioned to overcome the previous dichotomous duality, viewing the positive and negative effects of tourism as contextually dependent. This perspective supports the need for more indigenous political participation and control of the tourism development according to principles that benefit the indigenous people as much as possible, but without forgetting the indigenous peoples' right to say no to tourism and to manage their own natural and cultural resources.

If we look at the wide variety of case studies, we see that there is little consensus when interpreting indigenous tourism development. Researchers are more critical in cases that analyse models of mass tourism aggressive to culture and to the environment, and they are more optimistic when the models of tourism development are participatory, community-based, environmental and responsible.

## References

Arnaizburne, S.M. (1996) 'Desarrollo turístico y medioambiente en el Caribe Continental', *Estudios y Perspectivas en Turismo* 5(2): 259–86.

Barreto, M. (2007) *Turismo y Cultura. Relaciones, contradicciones y expectativas*, La Laguna (Tenerife): Pasos (ebook at www.pasosonline.org).

Bruner, E.M. (1995) 'The Ethnographer/Tourist in Indonesia', in Lanfant, M.F., Allcock, J.B. and Bruner, E.M. (eds) *International Tourism: Identity and Change*, London: Sage, 224–41.

Butler, R. and Hinch, T. (eds) (1996) *Tourism and Indigenous Peoples*, London: Thompson.

Cañada, E. (2010) *Impactos del turismo en los países del sur y turismo rural comunitario. Material de apoyo*, Madrid: Foro Turismo Responsable.

Canadian Tourism Commission (1997) *Aboriginal Tourism: A Bibliography*, Vancouver: Tourism Reference and Documentation Centre, www.canadatourism.com (accessed 7 April 2010).

Chernela, J.M. (2011) 'Barrier Natural and Unnatural: Islamiento as a Central Metaphor in Kuna Ecotourism', *Bulletin of Latin American Research* 30(1): 35–49.

Espinosa, M. (2010) 'Turismo Comunitario en Saraguro – Ecuador', in SODEPAZ (co-ord.) *Turismo y Desarrollo: Experiencias desde la Cooperación Internacional*, Madrid: SODEPAZ, 65–117.

Gascón, J. and Cañada, E. (2005) *Viajar a todo tren*, Barcelona: Icaria.

Gascón Gutiérrez, J. (2005) *Gringos como en sueños. Diferenciación y conflicto campesino en el sur andino peruano ante el desarrollo del turismo*, Lima: Instituto de Estudios Peruanos.

Getino, O. (1991) *Turismo y Desarrollo en América Latina*, México: Editorial Limusa.

Grünewald, R.A. (2001) *Os Indios do Descobrimento Tradicao e Turismo*, Rio de Janeiro: Contra Capo.

——(2003) 'Turismo e etnicidade', *Horizontes antropológicos* 20: 141–59.

Hall, C.M., Williams, A.M. and Lew, A.A. (2007) 'Turismo: conceitos, instituições e temas', in Hall, C. M., Williams, A.M. and Lew, A.A. (eds) *Compêndio de Turismo*, Lisboa: Instituto Piaget, 23–41.

Harron, S. and Weiler, B. (1992) 'Review: Ethnic Tourism', in Weiler, B. and Hall, C.M. (eds) *Special Interest Tourism*, New York: Wiley, 82–94.

Ingles, P. (2002) 'Welcome to My Village: Hosting Tourists in the Peruvian Amazon', *Tourism Recreation Research* 27(1): 53–60.

Jafari, J. (2001) 'Toward an Ethics Platform for Tourism', *Annals of Tourism Research* 32(4): 962–84.

——(2005) 'El turismo como disciplina científica', *Política y Sociedad* 42(1): 39–56.

Johnston, A.M. (2006) *Is the Sacred for Sale? Tourism and Indigenous Peoples*, London: Earthscan.

Kutzner, D., Maher, P.T. and Wright, P. (2007) *Aboriginal Tourism: A Research Bibliography*, Prince George: University of Northern British Columbia: Outdoor and Tourism Management Programme – Publication Series 2007–02, www.unbc.ca/assets/ortm/research/report_2007_02_aboriginal_tourism_bibliography.pdf (accessed 7 April 2010).

MacCanell, D. (1984) 'Reconstructed Ethnicity Tourism and Cultural Identity in Third World Communities', *Annals of Tourism Research* 11(3): 375–91.

——(1992) *Empty Meeting Grounds*, New York: Routledge and Kegan Paul.

Maldonado, C. (2006) *Turismo y comunidades indígenas: Impactos, pautas para autoevaluación y códigos de conducta. Documento de trabajo número 79*, Ginebra: Oficina Internacional del Trabajo (OIT).

Mastny, L. (2003) *Ecoturismo. Nuevos caminos para el turismo internacional*, Bilbao: Bakeaz.

Mercer, D. (1995) 'Native People and Tourism: Conflict and Compromise', in Theobald, W.F. (ed.) *Global Tourism – The Next Decade*, Oxford: Butterworth-Heinnemann, 124–45.

Morales, G. and Marías, D. (2007) 'Turismo en comunidades indígenas', *Revista Ábaco* 54: 123–33.

Moscardo, G. and Pearce, P.L. (1999) 'Interpretación del turismo étnico', *Annals of Tourism Research en Español* 1: 147–66.

Mowforth, M., Clive, C. and Munt, I. (2008) *Tourism and Responsibility: Perspectives from Latin American and the Caribbean*, London: Routledge.

Pereiro, X. and de León, C. (2007) *Los impactos del turismo en Kuna Yala. Turismo y cultura entre los kuna de Panamá*, Madrid: Editorial Ramón Areces.

Pereiro, X., Martínez, M., Ventocilla, J., del Valle, Y. and de León, C. (2011) *Estudio estratégico del turismo en Kuna Yala (Panamá)*, Panamá: SENACYT (unpublished research report).

Pérez Galán, B. (2011) 'Nuevas y viejas narrativas turísticas sobre la cultura indígena en los Andes', in Prats, L.L. and Santana, A. (eds) *Turismo y patrimonio. Entramados narrativos*, La Laguna (Tenerife): Pasos (ebook at www.pasosonline.org), 27–48.

Picard, M. and Wood, R.E. (eds) (1997) *Tourism, Ethnicity and the State in Asian and Pacific Societies*, Hawaii: University of Hawaii Press.

Pi-Sunyer, O., Thomas, R.B. and Daltabuit, M. (2001) 'Tourism on the Maya Periphery', in Smith, V.L. and Brent, M. (eds) *Hosts and Guests Revisited: Tourism Issues of the 21st Century*, New York: Cognizant, 122–40.

Pitchford, S.R. (1995) 'Ethnic Tourism and Nationalism in Wales', *Annals of Tourism Research* 22: 35–52.

Rodríguez Miranda, R. (ed.) (2011) *Construyendo resistencias. Experiencias de turismo local*, Madrid: Foro Turismo Responsable.

Ryan, C. and Aicken, M. (eds) (2005) *Indigenous Tourism: The Commodification and Management of Culture*, Oxford: Elsevier.

Smith, V.L. (1996) 'Indigenous Tourism: The Four Hs', in Butler, R. and Hinch, T. (eds) *Tourism and Indigenous Peoples*, London: Thomson, 283–307.

van den Berghe, P. (1994a) *The Quest for the Other: Ethnic Tourism in San Cristobal México*, Seattle, WA: University of Washington Press.

——(1994b) 'Marketing Mayas: Ethnic Tourism Promotion in Mexico', *Annals of Tourism Research* 22(3): 568–88.

Vermeulen, H. and Govers, C. (eds) (2003) *Antropologia da Etnicidade. Para Além de Ethnic Groups and Boundaries*, Lisboa: Fim de Século.

Vigna, A. (2006) 'Los "falsarios" del ecoturismo: Grandes proyectos privados en América Central', *Le Monde Diplomatique* (July), www.lemondediplomatique.cl/Los-falsarios-del-ecoturismo.html (accessed 25 April 2012).

Volkman, T.A. (1990) 'Visions and Revisions: Toraja Culture and the Tourist Gaze', *American Ethnologist* 17(1): 91–110.

Zeppel, H. (2007) 'Indigenous Ecotourism: Conservation and Resources Rights', in Higham, J. (ed.) *Critical Issues in Ecotourism. Understanding a Complex Tourism Phenomenon*, Oxford: Elsevier, 308–48.

Zoettl, P.A. (2010) *Capa de Índio, documental antropológico*, Lisboa: author edition.

## Further reading

Barreto, M. (2007) *Turismo y Cultura. Relaciones, contradicciones y expectativas*, Tenerife: Pasos (ebook at www.pasosonline.org). (Cultural and indigenous tourism from a Latin American perspective.)

Gascón Gutiérrez, J. (2005) *Gringos como en sueños. Diferenciación y conflicto campesino en el sur andino peruano ante el desarrollo del turismo*, Lima: Instituto de Estudios Peruanos. (A good ethnography about the effects of tourism on indigenous areas of Peru.)

Gmelch, G. (2003) *Behind the Smile. The Working Lives of Caribbean Tourism*, Bloomington: Indiana University Press. (A treatment of work cultures in tourism areas of the Caribbean.)

Pereiro, X. (2009) *Turismo cultural. Uma visão antropológica*, La Laguna (Tenerife): Pasos (ebook at www. pasosonline.org). (A university handbook written in Portuguese about the relationship between culture and tourism from an anthropological point of view.)

Pereiro, X. and de León, C. (2007) Los impactos del turismo en Kuna Yala. Turismo y cultura entre los kuna de Panamá, Madrid: Editorial Ramón Areces. (A working paper about the effects of tourism in Kuna Yala, Panama, which won an award at FITUR – Madrid in 2007.)

Ryan, C. and Aicken, M. (eds) (2005) *Indigenous Tourism: The Commodification and Management of Culture*, Oxford: Elsevier. (Case studies on indigenous tourism from Australia, Canada and New Zealand.)

Salazar, N.B. (2006) 'Antropología del turismo en países en desarrollo: análisis crítico de las culturas, poderes e identidades generados por el turismo', *Tabula Rasa* 5: 99–128. (A very good paper about the role of anthropology in studying tourism.)

Smith, V.L. and Eadington, W.R. (eds) (1992) *Tourism Alternatives: Potentials and Problems in the Development of Tourism*, Philadelphia: University of Pennsylvania Press. (A classic scientific book about alternative ways of developing tourism with many cases on indigenous tourism.)

# 28

# Indigenous tourism and the challenge of sustainability

*Jarkko Saarinen*

## Introduction

During the past two decades, there has been a growing interest in indigenous tourism. By utilising Ryan's (2005) considerations on the issues in increasing the focus on indigenous tourism research, the main reasons for the touristic interests are related to the changes in the tourism industry and indigenous societies themselves. Although cultural elements and differences have attracted tourists for a relatively long time, the recent changes in the modes of tourism production and consumption have created growing markets for new and varying forms of cultural tourism activities, such as indigenous tourism. These changes in tourism are largely based on wider movements in Western production systems and related consumption modes from Fordism towards post-Fordism (Urry 1990), or from a mass scale to more individualised patterns of production and consumption. This has created growing and new kinds of demands for tourism, involving possibilities for a wide range of activities, attractions and cultural learning opportunities (Poon 1993; McIntosh 2004), for example, including the emergence of indigenous tourism.

While tourism has grown and transformed, the indigenous communities and their socio-economic environments have also changed – or they are dramatically changing. In many places, traditional livelihoods have lost their ability to provide economic survival and well-being for the people, or their future viability is seen as being challenged by the people. In addition, the general modernisation of the surrounding societies of indigenous people has created both external and internal pressures for communities to be involved with ongoing socioeconomic development processes and their outcomes. At the same time, the indigenous people have become more aware and also critically concerned about their role and position in societies and development, including tourism. In addition, international and national agreements on indigenous rights have supported their position (see Sinclair 2003; Greene 2004). Thus, on the one hand, the increasing tourism demand has provided possibilities for the development of tourism based on the attractiveness of indigenous communities and cultures. On the other hand, the agreements and evolved indigenous people's need to be actively involved in, benefit from and also control the ways in which tourism is operating and managed in their everyday environment has supported the development of indigenous tourism, i.e. a tourism activity in which 'indigenous people are directly involved, either through control and/or by having their culture serve as the essence of the attraction' (Hinch and Butler 1996: 9).

Although there are many ongoing processes, elements and aims that support the symbiotic relationship between tourism and indigenous communities, the co-existence is not always harmonic, but is characterised by conflicts, costs and uneven power relations. Indeed, for indigenous people, the tourism industry may represent a competing resource user, outside interests and a non-local development that does not 'derive from processes internal to those societies' (Urry 1990: 64). Therefore, many scholars have emphasised the need for sustainable and community-based tourism development in the context of indigenous people (see Hinch and Butler 2007). This chapter aims to discuss the nature of indigenous tourism and the relationship between tourism development and indigenous people. First, the idea of indigenous people is critically discussed, followed by the discussion of indigenous tourism, its definitions and limits to growth in tourism development.

## Indigenous people: native, primitive, what!?

The concept and idea of indigenous people is a contested one and, thus, a much debated issue in literature (see Barnard 2006). The term is also highly political (Kuper 2003) and it is often used synonymously with 'aboriginal' or 'native' people. In general, the concept refers to a culturally distinct group of people that was living and occupying a region before the present group(s) dominating the region and prior to the creation of nation-states (see Saugestad 2001). This kind of definition relates to international agreements and policy documents by the United Nations (UN 2004, 2007) and the International Labour Organization (ILO), for example. The widely used Article 1 of the ILO's Indigenous and Tribal Peoples Convention defines indigenous people as:

> peoples in independent countries, who are regarded as indigenous on account of their descent from the populations which inhabited the country, or a geographical region to which the country belongs, at the time of conquest or colonization or the establishment of present state boundaries and who, irrespective of their legal status, retain some or all of their own social, economic, cultural and political institutions.
>
> *(ILO 1989: 1)*

The ILO Convention also makes a distinction between indigenous people and tribal people, as there are tribal groups that are not indigenous – a native – in the sense of the previous definition in the countries in which they presently live. These kinds of groups are the Maasai in East Africa or the San (Basarwa) and OvaHimbas in southern Africa, for example, who have not lived in the region that they inhabit longer than some other cultural groups (see Barnard 2006). However, in the UN definitions, the terms indigenous and tribal are used as synonyms 'when the peoples concerned, identify themselves under the indigenous agenda' (UN 2004: 3). Indeed, many tribal groups identify themselves as indigenous and native, both culturally and politically.

These policy-oriented or legal definitions of indigenous people are widely used, but academically, the idea of indigenous people or indigeneity turns out to be problematic and many anthropologists have recently strongly debated and criticised the term in research contexts. Kuper (2003: 395), for example, notes that the current idea of indigenous people represents an essentialist and anthropologically obsolete and nostalgic notion based on a 'false ethnographic vision'. Barnard (2006: 2) continues that indigenous 'is simply a new word for "primitive"', originating its content from the previous traditionalist Kalahari debate and the search for the 'most primitive', primal cultures (Urkultur) in nineteenth- and early twentieth-century anthropology. For the critics, the indigeneity represents a Western, i.e. originally externally formed and driven construct, involving historically contingent hierarchic cultural connotations.

Based on the academic critics of the idea of indigeneity, it would be fair to assume that the concept of indigenous tourism is also contaminated by the legacies of colonialism and cultural hierarchies and thus should be avoided or even rejected in academic tourism research. However, while the hardest critics would reject the concept in any academic uses as being too politicised (see Kuper 2003), some scholars would use the very same argument for keeping the concept in the academic arena (see Guenther 2006). Indeed, there are very few, if any concepts in social sciences that are not contested or politically used. By accepting the politically loaded and socially constructed nature of the concept, Saugestad (2001: 43) has indicated four criteria for indigenous people: first-come (i.e. descended from people who were there before the others); non-dominance (i.e. under the dominance of others); cultural difference (i.e. different from the majority); and self-ascription (i.e. a willing identification to indigenous peoples). These kinds of principles could provide support for local communities in protecting their culture, traditions, knowledge and resources in changing circumstances and development, and many indigenous groups are actually utilising the political nature of indigeneity and have turned it towards economic and recently into corporative uses (see Brown 1998; Greene 2004). In this respect, tourism also provides a fruitful and highly important context for utilising the idea of indigeneity in local development, but not without challenges and risks.

## Indigenous tourism and the challenge of sustainability

A basic notion of indigenous tourism refers to tourism which 'directly involves native peoples whose ethnicity is a tourist attraction' (Smith 1996: 283). The critical issue here is what the direct involvement means. Smith (1996) has further identified four influential elements in the development potential of indigenous tourism: habitat, history, handicrafts and heritage (4Hs). These elements refer mainly to the cultural difference and attractiveness of indigenous people, but they also indicate, at least indirectly, the needs of ownership or control in indigenous tourism management. In this respect, Hinch and Butler (1996, 2007) have further conceptualised the idea by including the need for indigenous people to be involved with tourism, either through control and/or by serving the indigeneity as the essence of the attraction.

Although these widely used definitions for indigenous tourism can still partially exclude the element of control, many tourism scholars prefer a more comprehensive definition in practice. Hinch and Butler (2007: 5), for example, have emphasised the importance of control as the key issue in indigenous tourism development (see also Li 2006). In this way, the concept also resonates better with Saugestad's (2001) four criteria of indigenous people including the cultural difference, but also involving, directly and indirectly, the elements of ownership, power and identity. By including the element of control as the condition for indigenous tourism development, the concept also becomes close to the idea of community-based tourism (CBT). The CBT represents a sustainable form of tourism (Telfer and Sharpley 2007: 124), which aims to respect the socio-cultural authenticity of local communities, conserving their cultural and natural heritage and traditional values by ensuring viable, long-term economic processes, providing socioeconomic benefits that are fairly distributed to all stakeholders. Both indigenous and community-based tourism aim to ensure that members of the local communities hold a sufficient degree of control over the tourism activities, its limits and the resources used (see Scheyvens 2002). The control can be based on participatory planning, land and other resource leasing systems or (joint) ownership in business (Ashley and Roe 2002). If such control can be achieved, it is more likely that indigenous people receive a significant share of the economic benefits of tourism in the forms of direct revenues and employment, upgraded infrastructures, the environment and housing standards, etc. (see Stronza 2007).

The issue of control is not only a matter of direct benefits, but also of how indigenous people are used in tourism and depicted as tourist attractions. In this respect, two major goals can be seen in indigenous tourism development (see Telfer and Sharpley 2007). First, it should be socially sustainable, which refers to the key role of indigenous local control and participation in tourism operations and the shared socioeconomic benefits. Second, indigenous tourism should imply respect for local cultures, identities and traditions. Therefore, especially when keeping in mind the problematic connotations of the primitivity of the academic idea of indigeneity, the indigenous people and communities that are involved with tourism should be depicted in ways that are ethically sustainable and acceptable. Therefore, the question of representation, i.e. how indigenous people are illustrated and used in tourism marketing and products, is crucial for the people and the sustainability of tourism development (Cohen 1993; Saarinen 1999; Hunter 2011).

---

## Box 28.1 Case study: the representations of OvaHimbas in Namibian tourism promotion

OvaHimbas (or Himbas) are an ethnic minority who mainly live in north-west Namibia and south-west Angola (Bollig and Heinemann 2002). They are traditional pastoralists, but recently some OvaHimba communities have turned in part towards tourism-related activities. In a strict sense, the OvaHimbas are not indigenous as they have not lived in the region as long as some other cultural groups. Based on their minority position, however, the OvaHimbas have many parallels with indigenous people in the sense of the UN definition system (see UN 2004: 3). They have distinct traditions and cultural features, especially the OvaHimba female hairstyle, clothing and their tradition of using a mixture of ochre, butter fat and herbs to cover their skin are highly recognisable, which also makes them widely used in the promotion of Namibian tourism. Although OvaHimbas live mainly outside the main tourism zones of the country (see Weaver and Elliot 1996; Henrichsen 2000) and represent around 1 per cent of the total population, they dominate the local cultural dimensions (images) of Namibia in tourism (Saarinen and Niskala 2009).

The representations of OvaHimbas in the Namibian tourism promotion were analysed based on the contemporary printed tourism marketing material consisting of 32 brochures with a total of 1,154 photo images. The material was collected from the Namibian Tourism Board office in Windhoek and it has been analysed in detail by Saarinen and Niskala (2009). The analysis was done by utilising a content analysis in which the coding of images was based on the theoretically driven and empirically formed categories (see Rose 2001). These categories referred to the common themes of indigenous people in tourism-related literature, such as primitiveness, exotic/otherness and erotic dimensions in depictions (see Hall 1992; Waitt 1999; Echtner and Prasad 2003), which were empirically traced from the tourism brochures.

Based on the tourism promotion material, the representations of OvaHimbas are dominated by female depictions (Saarinen and Niskala 2009) and a clear majority of the images depicted 'half-dressed' (as some of the advertising texts described the issue) women or women with children. In contrast to women, OvaHimba men were very rarely included in tourism promotion material and even the family oriented depictions in village settings didn't include men. This OvaHimba female-dominated dimension of place promotion has also been noted by Kanguma (2000) and the resulting gender imbalance in tourism marketing refers to the historically contingent modes of representing indigenous people as primitive, exotic and erotic objects (see Edwards 1996). The role of OvaHimbas in tourism promotion is to be a passive and posing object for tourists to gaze at: they 'symbolize the colonized subject' (van Eeden 2006: 345). In the tourism promotion materials this ethnic and gendered landscape of north-west Namibia for tourists to consume is supported by advertised tourist products such as 'Oryx and Himba Safaris' equating OvaHimbas with local fauna in the 'touristic gazing' practices. This creates and refers to the processes of 'primitivisation' and 'zooification' that have been typical elements in colonial Western travel literature when depicting indigenous cultures and peoples (see Saarinen 1999; Waitt 1999; Wels 2004). The created otherness and images of static and unchanged culture are supported by representations of 'timeless' desert landscapes.

However, the critical issues in tourism promotion are not only linked to cultural depictions or the possible questions of ethics in marketing. Western tourists visit the OvaHimba villages based on these images and related expectations (see Rothfuss 2000) and, thus, in order to satisfy non-locally created and maintained expectations and attract visitors to their villages, the OvaHimbas are trapped by playing their role as an unchanged, static culture (Saarinen 2011, 2012). These kinds of tourism representations and practices become problematic when thinking back to the basic premises of indigenous tourism as an activity that should manifest a respect for the local cultures and people.

In addition, the created images and related tourism practices may have an effect on how OvaHimbas, or indigenous people in general (Bruner 1991), perceive their role in tourism and the possibilities to participate in, have control, and benefit from, tourism (Saarinen 2012). It is likely that the reproduced primitive and exotic role that the OvaHimbas play in the tourism system may keep them as passive recipients of tourists and tourism operations which they cannot really control or participate actively in. While they receive much-needed benefits from international tourists, this kind of tourism system may support socioeconomic and power structures in tourism-community relations that keep the OvaHimbas mainly as objects and separated from the actual decision-making processes in regional and local tourism development (Saarinen and Niskala 2009).

## Conclusions

The concept of indigenous tourism is important, and although the idea of indigenous people may academically involve historical negative connotations to uncivilised cultures, the term is usable in policy–relevant and management–oriented studies that focus on the relations between indigenous people and change. For many indigenous communities, the modern tourism industry represents a major force of change and while tourism can create unwanted outcomes and images, it can also provide possibilities and new ways for local indigenous communities to maintain and value their culture (Grunewald 2002), create well-being and survive in changing socioeconomic and political environments. In order to benefit from tourism, there need to be frameworks that mitigate the negative impacts and optimise the positive ones, based on the principles of sustainable tourism and, especially, the community-based approaches in sustainability.

However, as Hinch and Butler (2007: 4) state, this 'nirvana has yet to be achieved and there are systemic causes for this failure'.

A major source of systemic failure may be the very nature of tourism itself and the ways in which it operates and constructs destination spaces. According to Getz (1999: 24), a touristic space is 'an area dominated by tourist activities or one that is organized for meeting the needs of visitors'. This means that the needs and values of the customers are the leading guidelines in market-driven economic tourism activities. From the perspective of indigenous people, one possible outcome of this process can be the marginalisation of local communities and lifestyles, which may be concretised not only in representations, but also in discursive practices such as land-use planning and economic investments that favour non-locally oriented tourism development rather than an indigenous one. Therefore, the emphasised elements of local control, with the respect of the difference, identity and integrity of indigenous culture as the core attractions and values in indigenous tourism development, are crucial both at conceptual and practical levels.

## References

Ashley, C. and Roe, D. (2002) 'Making Tourism Work for the Poor: Strategies and Challenges in Southern Africa', *Development Southern Africa* 19: 61–82.

Barnard, A. (2006) 'Kalahari Revisionism, Vienna and the "indigenous peoples" debate', *Social Anthropology* 14: 1–16.

Bollig, M. and Heinemann, H. (2002) 'Nomadic Savages, Ochre People and Heroic Herders: Visual Presentation of the Himba of Namibia's Kaokoland', *Visual Anthropology* 15: 267–312.

Brown, M. (1998) 'Can Culture be Copyrighted?' *Current Anthropology* 39: 193–222.

Bruner, E. (1991) 'Transformation of Self in Tourism', *Annals of Tourism Research* 18: 238–50.

Butler, R. and Hinch, T. (eds) (2007) *Tourism and Indigenous Peoples*, London: International Thomson Business Press.

Cohen, E. (1993) 'The Study of Touristic Images of Native People: Mitigating the Stereotype for a Stereotype', in Pearce, D.G. and Butler, R.W. (eds) *Tourism Research: Critiques and Challenges*, London: Routledge, 36–69.

Echtner, C.M. and Prasad, P. (2003) 'The Context of Third World Tourism Marketing', *Annals of Tourism Research* 30: 660–82.

Edwards, E. (1996) 'Postcards: Greetings from Another World', in T. Selwyn (ed.) *The Tourist Image. Myths and Myth Making in Tourism*, Chichester: John Wiley & Sons, 197–222.

Getz, D. (1999) 'Resort-centred Tours and Development of the Rural Hinterland: The Case of Cairns and the Atherton Tablelands', *Journal of Tourism Studies* 10: 23–34.

Greene, S. (2004) 'Indigenous People Incorporated?' *Current Anthropology* 45: 211–37.

Grunewald, R. (2002) 'Tourism and Cultural Revival', *Annals of Tourism Research* 29: 1004–21.

Guenther, M. (2006) 'The Concept of Indigeneity', *Social Anthropology* 14: 17–19.

Hall, S. (1992) 'The West and the Rest', in Hall, S. and Gieber, B. (eds) *Formations of Modernity*, London: Polity Press and Open University, 275–332.

Henrichsen, D. (2000) 'Pilgrimages into Kaoko: Herrensafaris, 4x4s and Settler Illusion', in Miescher, G. and Henrichsen, D. (eds) *New Notes on Kaoko*, Basel: Basler, 159–85.

Hinch, T. and Butler, R. (1996) 'Indigenous Tourism: A Common Ground for Discussion', in Butler, R. and Hinch, T. (eds) *Tourism and Indigenous Peoples*, London: International Thomson Business Press, 3–21.

——(2007) 'Indigenous Tourism: Revisiting Common Ground', in Butler, R. and Hinch, T. (eds) *Tourism and Indigenous Peoples*, London: International Thomson Business Press, 1–12.

Hunter, W.C. (2011) 'Rukai Indigenous Tourism: Representations, Cultural Identity and Q Method', *Tourism Management* 32: 335–48.

ILO (International Labour Organization) (1989) Indigenous and Tribal Peoples Convention No. 169, Geneva: General Conference of the International Labour Office.

Kanguma, B. (2000) 'Constructing Himba: The Tourist Gaze', in Miescher, G. and Henrichsen, D. (eds) *New Notes on Kaoko*, Basel: Basler, 129–32.

Kuper, A. (2003) 'The Return of the Native', *Current Anthropology* 44: 389–402.

Li, W.J. (2006) 'Community Decisionmaking: Participation in Development', *Annals of Tourism Research* 33: 132–43.

McIntosh, A.J. (2004) 'Tourists' Appreciation of Maori Culture in New Zealand', *Tourism Management* 25: 1–15.

Poon, A. (1993) *Tourism, Technology and Competitive Strategies*, Wallingford: CABI.

Rose, G. (2001) *Visual Methodologies: An Introduction to the Interpretation of Visual Materials*, London: Sage.

Rothfuss, E. (2000) 'Ethnic Tourism in Kaoko: Expectations, Frustrations and Trend in a Post-Colonial Business', in Miescher, G. and Henrichsen, D. (eds) *New Notes on Kaoko*, Basel: Basler, 133–58.

Ryan, C. (2005) 'Introduction: Tourist-host Nexus – Research Considerations', in Ryan, C. and Aicken, M. (eds) *Indigenous Tourism: The Commodification and Management of Culture*, Oxford: Elsevier, 1–11.

Saarinen, J. (1999) 'Representations of Indigeneity: Sami Culture in the Discourses of Tourism', in Sant, P.M. and Brown, J.N. (eds) *Indigeneity: Constructions and Re/presentations*, New York: Nova Science Publishers, 231–49

——(2011) 'Tourism, Indigenous People and the Challenge of Development: The Representations of Ovahimbas in Tourism Promotion and Community Perceptions Towards Tourism', *Tourism Analysis* 16: 31–42.

——(2012) 'Tourism Development and Local Communities: The Direct Benefits of Tourism to Ova-Himba Communities in the Kaokoland, North-West Namibia', *Tourism Review International* 15: 149–57.

Saarinen, J. and Niskala, M. (2009) 'Local Culture and Regional Development: The Role of OvaHimba in Namibian Tourism', in Hottola, P. (ed.) *Tourism Strategies and Local Responses in Southern Africa*, Wallingford: CABI, 61–72.

Saugestad, S. (2001) *The Inconvenient Indigenous*, Uppsala: Nordic Africa Institute.

Scheyvens, R. (2002) 'Backpacker Tourism and Third World Development', *Annals of Tourism Research* 29: 144–64.

Sinclair, D. (2003) 'Developing Indigenous Tourism: Challenges for the Guianas', *International Journal of Contemporary Hospitality Management* 15: 140–46.

Smith, V.L. (1996) 'Indigenous Tourism: The Four Hs', in Butler, R. and Hinch, T. (eds) *Tourism and Indigenous Peoples*, London: International Thomson Business Press, 283–307.

Stronza, A. (2007) 'The Economic Promise of Ecotourism for Conservation', *Journal of Ecotourism* 6: 210–30.

Telfer, D. and Sharpley, R. (2007) *Tourism and Development in the Developing World*, London: Routledge.

UN (2004) *The Concept of Indigenous Peoples*, New York: Department of Economic and Social Affairs, United Nations, www.un.org/esa/socdev/unpfii/documents/workshop_data_background.doc (accessed 15 November 2012).

——(2007) The United Nations Declaration on the Rights of Indigenous Peoples, New York: United Nations, www.un.org/esa/socdev/unpfii/documents/DRIPS_en.pdf (accessed 15 November 2012).

Urry, J. (1990) *The Tourist Gaze*, London: Sage Publications.

van Eeden, J. (2006) 'Land Rover and Colonial-Style Adventure', *International Feminist Journal of Politics* 8: 343–69.

Waitt, G. (1999) 'Naturalising the "primitive": A Critique of Marketing Australia's Indigenous Peoples as "Hunter-gatherers"', *Tourism Geographies* 1: 142–63.

Weaver, D. and Elliot, K. (1996) 'Spatial Patterns and Problems in Contemporary Namibian Tourism', *Geographical Journal* 162: 205–17.

Wels, H. (2004) 'About Romance and Reality: Popular European Imagery in Postcolonial Tourism in Southern Africa', in Hall, C.M. and Tucker, H. (eds) *Tourism and Postcolonialism: Contested Discourses, Identities and Representation*, London: Routledge, 76–94.

## Further reading

Barnard, A. (2006) 'Kalahari Revisionism, Vienna and the "Indigenous Peoples" Debate', *Social Anthropology* 14: 1–16. (Contextualizing review with commentaries on the idea of indigeneity.)

Butler, R. and Hinch, T. (eds) (2007) *Tourism and Indigenous Peoples*, London: International Thomson Business Press. (A collection of case studies on indigenous tourism.)

Ryan, C. and Aicken, M. (2005) (eds) *Indigenous Tourism: The Commodification and Management of Culture*, Amsterdam: Elsevier. (A collection of case studies on indigenous tourism.)

Smith, V.L. (ed.) (1989) *The Host and Guests: The Anthropology of Tourism*, Philadelphia: University of Pennsylvania Press. (A classic textbook on host-guest relations in indigenous and ethnic tourism.)

UN (2007) *The United Nations Declaration on the Rights of Indigenous Peoples*, New York: United Nations. (A key example of international agreements on indigenous peoples and their rights.)

# 29

# Māori tourism

## A case study of managing indigenous cultural values

*Anna Thompson-Carr*

## Introduction

This chapter reviews Māori cultural tourism developments during the past 25 years, with a focus on southern Māori tourism ventures. The involvement of Māori in the management of cultural values that are subjected to commodification for tourism purposes provides insights as to how an indigenous culture can be at the forefront of the management, ownership and delivery of tourism experiences. In comparison to many cultural groups, and despite the history of experiences of colonisation such as segregation or loss of lands, Māori are socially integrated within New Zealand society and consequently are the controllers of indigenous tourism experiences in the country. The Te Ana Māori Rock Art Centre will be discussed in-depth as a case study of how collective approaches can authentically and ethically provide an indigenous cultural tourism experience.

## The Māori people

Māori refer to themselves as the *tangata whenua* or 'people of the land' and are officially recognised as the indigenous people of New Zealand (Graham 1998; Statistics New Zealand 2012). Māori are of Polynesian origin and many identify themselves as individuals through *iwi* (tribal) affiliation (O'Regan 1990; Orbell and Moon 1996). Prior to the European settlement of New Zealand, Māori had developed a distinct system of values and knowledge that remains today as *kaupapa Māori* or a Māori way of doing things. In 1840 the Treaty of Waitangi was signed and it is the founding document by which the British Crown and New Zealand Māori agreed to the settlement of New Zealand by British subjects (Graham 1998; Solomon 1998). Under the Treaty the traditional rights of Māori were to be protected. However, throughout the mid-to-late nineteenth century a combination of colonisation, government legislation, land wars and land confiscations disenfranchised Māori society, with many individuals and *iwi* losing their lands (Sinclair 1992; Walker 1992). The consequence is that the majority of New Zealanders with Māori ancestry live outside their traditional *rohe* (boundaries of tribal homelands).

Despite this, many people of Māori descent retain strong links with the land of their ancestors through involvement in *marae*-based activities where they can learn or gain knowledge of legends or stories of their homelands or revisit these areas for traditional purposes such as the gathering of food and resources or events on the *marae*, such as *tangi* (Sinclair 1992; Walker 1992, 1996).

From the mid-1970s an intense revival of pride in Māori culture resulted in increased Māori pressure on government for recognition of Māori to exercise these traditional rights, and involvement in tourism has been seen as a means to gain employment and income from culture, if undertaken in a culturally appropriate manner. The past two-to-three decades have seen an increased awareness of Treaty obligations by the New Zealand government, with consequent legislation reflecting the spirit of the Treaty of Waitangi. Treaty Settlements have resulted in financial compensation, and the return of traditional lands or resources to *iwi* ownership with opportunities to develop tribal assets and financial independence through economic ventures such as tourism.

Each region has a *marae* managed by *hapu* (sub-tribe) representatives through a *runanga* or management committee. These representatives are vital for providing feedback to, or informing the cultural appropriateness of, various tourism or cultural ventures. Most museums and art galleries in Aotearoa New Zealand have *iwi* representatives on organisational boards, and museum exhibits or displays are developed with the direction of Māori staff employed in the institutions. Most cultural and natural heritage managers in New Zealand are assisted and informed on matters regarding cultural ownership, or authenticity issues, through consultation processes and communication with local *runanga*. Some organisations are also informed on matters concerning management and policy development through relationships with runanga where *iwi* employees, volunteers or staff (some renumerated for their services, others doing it out of a sense of obligation or pride in being Māori). In comparison to many other indigenous or First Nations peoples, Māori have infiltrated every level of New Zealand society and are actively involved in health, education, politics and business. The Treaty of Waitangi has resulted in government legislation ensuring the role of Māori in society, for example, on conservation lands managed by the Department of Conservation, while Māori are active as staff members within the Ministry and department organisational structure or through active consultation (Carr 2004).

Despite such empowerment, race relations are not always smooth as poverty, crime, imprisonment, poor health and low educational achievement exist amongst members of Māori society.

## Māori tourism

Māori tourism has been broadly defined as 'an opportunity provided within the composite tourism product for the tourist to have contact with Māori culture' (Barnett 1997: 473). Māori culture has been utilised within national tourism promotion for over a century as a 'unique' feature of the New Zealand product, and a 'must see' component of the New Zealand experience for international travellers (Tourism New Zealand 2003a). Ingram (1996: n.p.) identified two types of Māori tourism experiences as:

> Unique, indigenous, cultural experiences, such as: hangi and concert performances, Māori arts and crafts. Māori owned tourism activities that are not culturally Māori but are special because they give the visitor a unique Māori perspective and interpretation i.e. ecotourism products or Māori owned accommodation.

Yet a third category was identified by researchers: the category of Māori-owned activities with a non-Māori theme (McIntosh *et al.* 1999). However, the reality is that it is difficult to categorise Māori tourism. There are diverse business models for Māori tourism attractions, from owner-operator to *iwi* collectives, joint investments with non-Māori, perhaps even overseas owners, and all may have varying layers of cultural elements within the products, or none at all depending on the choices made by the Māori owners.

Rotorua is the destination most associated with Māori by international visitors (Ryan 1997, 1998; Ryan and Pike 2003; Carr 2004, 2006). The Māori people of Rotorua have been involved with tourism since the 1860s and many visitors anticipate encountering and experiencing Māori tourism attractions in the region (Walsh 1996; Barnett 1997; Wikitera 2006). The traditional Rotorua tourism experience of Māori culture has centred upon staged shows, featuring *hangi*, *poi* and *haka*, within Rotorua *marae* or commercial hotel settings. From the Māori perspective the *waiata*, legends, stories, art and information shared with visitors are *taonga*. Often elders or *kaumatua* have a say in what is conveyed and the highly trained performers are very selective in what is appropriate for tourism (Walsh 1996; Tahana and Opperman 1998). Such 'front stage' Māori tourism attractions were, until the late 1990s, the predominant type of visitor experience of Māori culture (Barnett 1997; Tahana and Opperman 1998; McIntosh *et al.* 1999; van Aalst and Daly 2002; Ryan and Pike 2003).

In 1993 the New Zealand Tourism Board (NZTB) acknowledged that alongside natural environments and wilderness areas, there was an increasing demand for cultural tourism. The NZTB identified that the 'strong culture of the Māori – unique to New Zealand – is a major aspect of our national heritage which enhances New Zealand's appeal to world travelers' (NZTB 1993: 4). The 1996 NZTB International Visitor Survey (IVS) findings indicated that Māori cultural activities were attended by 36 per cent of all international visitors to the country. Māori cultural elements that have extended beyond the traditional stereotypes of the Māori people as warriors, performers of *haka* and dusky maidens were included in promotional material, with the realisation that 'the unique culture of the Māori people is a strong and attractive element of our national heritage' (NZTB 1996: 1).

By the mid-1990s Māori tourism development had garnered support and resourcing at a national level with active strategies implemented by Te Puni Kokiri/Ministry of Māori Development (TPK/MMD 1998). In 2001 a report identified the tourism sector as providing a number of growth opportunities to Māori tourism ventures (The Stafford Group 2001). The report explored Māori tourism opportunities but was criticised for a dominance of non-Māori participants whose opinions directed the future of Māori involvement in tourism (Armstrong 2002). The Stafford Group Report omitted analysis of non-commercial attractions that conveyed cultural perspectives, in particular interpretive material at natural or historic sites. Despite being non-commercial, such interpretation provides opportunities for the *iwi* to convey the tribal identity to the visiting public. Instead, the report focused on the development of commercial attractions which yield economic, rather than socio-cultural, benefits.

The relationship between Māori and tourism, particularly the need to ensure cultural sustainability within commercial Māori tourism attractions, has been widely reported upon. Academic studies include Te Awekotuku (1981), Tahana and Opperman (1998), McIntosh *et al.* (1999), Ryan (2002), Pihema (2002), Ryan and Pike (2003), Wikitera (2006) and Amoamo (2008). Such studies invariably found negative impacts and benefits of tourism on the culture, with concerns reflecting issues of authenticity, control and ownership of cultural intellectual property. Generally, studies acknowledge a long association of Māori with tourism that dates back over 150 years, but also the future economic potential as demand for cultural tourism increases (Carr 2007). International visitors are generally more interested in Māori culture than domestic visitors (Te Puni Kokiri 1998; Ryan 2002; Carr 2006). It has been widely accepted amongst Māori tourism operators that domestic and international visitor markets will not always want traditional Māori experiences, yet there are opportunities to develop tourism activities that enable personal encounters, or some incorporation of cultural values, within contemporary settings, particularly with ecocultural tourism or the interpretation of cultural values within nature-based settings.

## Promoting Māori tourism

Since the mid-1980s there has been steady growth and diversification of Māori tourism products ranging from traditional cultural-based performances based in Rotorua to a wide range of cuisine, accommodation, transportation, nature and adventure products; Māori owners, employees and operators spanning all levels and sectors of the tourism industry, including at political and national levels. Te Puni Kokiri (TPK) and TNZ databases indicate a flourishing Māori tourism sector consisting of over 250 operations dispersed from Northland to Southland (TPK 1998; TNZ 2003a, 2003b).

TNZ's promotional activity since 1998 has utilised diverse, non-traditional images of Māori, including landscape features with cultural significance for Māori, for example Aoraki/Mount Cook or the Rotorua thermal areas. TNZ have a strategy to employ and train Māori staff within the organisation in a variety of roles including marketing and promotion. These Māori staff assist with the appropriate marketing of cultural tourism products, with an emphasis on international marketing activities. In addition to staff development TNZ's *Three Year Strategic Plan 2003–2006* had a strategic outcome to 'Naturally express through the campaign the values of New Zealand's Māori cultural identity' (TNZ 2003a: 3). The *New Zealand Tourism Strategy 2015* (Ministry of Tourism 2007) included sections about commitment to principles of the Treaty of Waitangi, with emphasis on integrating cultural values of *kaitiakitanga* and *manaakitanga* through partnership with *tangata whenua* for product development to enable protection of the integrity and authenticity of the culture and the environment (TNZ 2003a: 8).

The NZ Māori Tourism Council is an active force in Māori tourism marketing both nationally and internationally, with a website, brochures, offshore marketing clusters, social media activities and branding of cultural experiences – the Living Landscapes project. Over 110 Māori tourism operations or cultural tourism experience providers such as Te Papa (the national museum in Wellington) or Puke Ariki (a regional museum in Taranaki) are members of, and marketed by, the Council (NZ Māori Tourism Council 2012).

By 2011, and separate from (yet in collaboration with) Tourism NZ and the NZ Māori Tourism Council activities, nine Māori regional tourism organisations (RTOs) had been established throughout the country to advance regional initiatives and support owner-operators and business development. The Māori RTOs have a nationwide presence with particularly strong clusters in the Rotorua Lakes, Northland and major cities (Auckland and Wellington). Māori tourism entrepreneurs now provide a variety of tourism experiences, many with a cultural focus, but equally there may be Māori-owned and -operated tourism businesses with a non-cultural focus. For instance, the Otago Māori Business Network KUMA (Te Kupeka Umaka Māori Ki Araiteuru): KUMA has recently produced a website and brochure entitled Tiki Tour (Māori Guide to the Lower South Island) to showcase Māori-owned and -operated tourism attractions including wine trails, accommodation, cultural landscape attractions, boat trips and adventure tourism activities. Tiki Tour showcases several businesses under the management and ownership of Ngāi Tahu Tourism Holdings, some of which have no cultural elements whatsoever visible to the public, and the Te Ana Rock Art Centre.

## Ngāi Tahu and Te Ana Māori Rock Art Centre

Ngāi Tahu are the recognised *iwi* (Māori tribe) of Te Waipounamu, the South Island of New Zealand, their rights as *tangata whenua* being affirmed within the Ngāi Tahu Claim Settlement Act 1998, which recognised the traditional relationships between the *iwi* and the natural world (O'Regan 1989, 1990; Evison 1993; Russell 2000; TRONT 2002). Te Runanga o Ngāi Tahu (TRONT) is the formal structure that manages *iwi* issues, social, cultural and economic interests. Ngāi Tahu *rohe* (traditional lands) cover almost 50 per cent of the geographical area of New Zealand, including the majority of the South Island and Stewart Island (O'Regan 1989, 1990). During the 1990s, Ngāi Tahu invested in diverse tourism interests, including businesses within non-cultural sectors, notably two Queenstown-based operations, Shotover Jet and Pipeline Bungy. By 2011 Ngāi Tahu Tourism had developed a number of visitor attractions throughout the South Island (see Table 29.1). Financial feasibility was a strategic necessity to ensure the solid growth of the tribe's assets but cultural integrity underpinned the management of the ventures. As part of their cultural development policy Ngāi Tahu had a philosophy to present an *iwi* perspective of natural heritage throughout the South Island (O'Regan 1990; TRONT 1998, 2002, 2012). Cultural elements exist within the marketing and management of most commercial ventures but not all businesses interpret Ngāi Tahu culture or values to visitors. Separate to the tribal investments are independently owned and operated businesses managed by individual members of the *iwi*, or as partnerships between *whanau* (families) or *hapu* (sub-tribes).

The most renowned Ngāi Tahu tourism business is the ecotourism company, Whale Watch Kaikoura (WWK), which has achieved international acclaim and awards. WWK was owned by Kaikoura *whanau* and was not initially managed through TRONT. Marine mammal and wild-life viewing is the primary product; however, aspects of Māori cultural heritage are subtly incorporated into the ecocultural tourism experience. The company philosophy is one that promotes strong *iwi* identity, boats are named after tribal ancestors and Māori motifs are incorporated into logos and other design features. The legend of *Paikea*, the Whale Rider, is illustrated and reproduced in text on the wall of the Whale Watch Kaikoura Visitor Centre, offering visitors a traditional interpretation and history of the *iwi* relationship with the natural world.

*Table 29.1* Visitor attractions developed by Ngāi Tahu Tourism Ltd

| |
|---|
| Whale Watch Kaikoura |
| Shotover Jet, Queenstown |
| Dart River Safaris, Glenorchy |
| Huka Jet, Taupo |
| Aqua Taxi |
| Abel Tasman Freedom Kayaks |
| Franz Josef Glacier Guides |
| Hollyford Track |
| Rainbow Springs/Kiwi Encounter, Taupo |

Source: (Ngāi Tahu Holdings 2012)

## Box 29.1 Case study: Te Ana Māori Rock Art Centre

Pre-European rock art sites are located throughout Otago and Canterbury, in the South Island. As an immovable cultural heritage resource with historic values they are threatened by vandalism, climatic conditions and land-use pressures. The conservation, preservation and management of rock art is the domain of the Ngāi Tahu Māori Rock Art Charitable Trust. The Trust was partially funded by TRONT in partnership with Meridian Energy (a hydro-electricity company that negotiated use of water holding cultural values for Ngāi Tahu). From a cultural perspective the Trust, a non-profit organisation established in 2002, is also involved in research, documentation (through a collaboration of professional archaeologists and *iwi* members using GPS), and celebration of the 550+ rock art sites (Eddington and Symon 2008). The Trust is regarded as *kaitaiki* (guardian) of the rock art, with *runanga* members from Moeraki, Arowhenua and Waihao playing particularly active volunteer roles with the mindset that the *iwi* is culturally enriched by the rock art. A key consideration for *iwi* is the need to maintain cultural integrity and authenticity with any commodification of the art or landscape. Alongside the cultural need to protect the rock art, via methods such as stock fencing to protect sites, the art is nationally significant as artistic remnants of the cultural landscape of Aotearoa New Zealand. Tourism, education and public demand mean that there are opportunities for visitation to sites, the most accessible being road-side attractions called Maerewhenua and Takiroa in the Waitaki Valley of North Otago (see Figure 29.1). Visitation to such sites is usually managed by *iwi* members in consultation with private landowners, Department of Conservation (DOC) or the NZ Historic Places Trust (NZHPT).

*Figure 29.1* Takiroa Rock Art site

In October 2007 the trust formed Te Ana Whakairo (TAW) Ltd, a charitable entity to develop a visitor centre to showcase the various dimensions of the rock art. TAW and the Trust raised funds through grants, contestable funding applications and investment from the local *runanga*. The centre's interpretation was developed by an international design agency – Story Inc. (which is based in New Zealand but developed exhibits at museums and visitor centres throughout the world) – in consultation with the Trust, TAW, the three *runanga* (Moeraki, Waihao and Arowhenua) and other *iwi* members. Most critically the content of the displays, including video, holograms, imagery, recordings, art and written material including traditional legends and traditional ecological knowledge, was written and interpreted with the guidance of the Trust directors, *runanga* representatives and rock art centre staff, most significantly the rock art curator, Amanda Symon.

The Te Ana Māori Rock Art Centre (based in Timaru) was officially opened in 2010 and through interactive, static and audiovisual displays, alongside personally guided tours, showcases Ngāi Tahu cultural values and the rock art (see Figure 29.2). Story-telling about the landscape and people's relationships with the rock art enhance the visitor experience at the centre. The underlying values of the centre include the need for 'authenticity', with the presentation of information about the rock art sites to visitors to the centre. At all times the *mana* (integrity and cultural significance) of the rock art and cultural values must be considered and guide decisions that safeguard the rock art for present and future generations (thus the *mana* of the rock art is prioritised over any economic opportunities).

*Figure 29.2* Visitors at Te Ana Māori Rock Art Centre, Timaru

Numerous challenges exist for the centre as it becomes a financially viable ecocultural tourism attraction that serves the needs of the local Timaru and South Canterbury communities, Ngāi Tahu and visitors. The centre is becoming increasingly renowned as showcasing the rock art as an aspect of the cultural landscape of the South Island, despite facing challenges, since opening, as a result of visitor numbers into the region decreasing with the Christchurch earthquake and the global recession.

## Acknowledgements

The author would like to acknowledge the members of the runanga, Ngāi Tahu Māori Rock Art Charitable Trust and Te Ana Whakairo Ltd, particularly Gerard O'Regan and Amanda Symon, who were mentors and colleagues during her time on TAW.

## References

Amoamo, M. (2008) 'Decolonising Māori Tourism: Representation and Identity', unpublished thesis, University of Otago.

Armstrong, K.R. (2002) *Issues Regarding Museum Evaluation and the Visitor Experience: A Case Study of 'Signs of a Nation' in the Museum of New Zealand*, Te Papa Tongarewa, unpublished Master of Tourism Thesis, Victoria University of Wellington, Wellington.

Barnett, S.J. (1997) 'Māori Tourism', *Tourism Management* 18(7): 471–73.

Carr, A.M. (2004) *Visitor Experiences of Cultural Landscapes*, unpublished thesis, University of Otago.

——(2006) 'Lakes, Myths and Legends: The Relationship Between Tourism and Cultural Values for Water in Aotearoa/New Zealand', in Hall, C.M. and Harkonen, T. (eds) *Lake Tourism: An Integrated Approach to Lacustrine Tourism Systems*, Clevedon: Channel View Publications, 83–100.

——(2007) 'Strengthening of Identity Through Participation in Tourism Guiding', in Butler, R. and Hinch, T. (eds) *Tourism and Indigenous Peoples*, second edn, Oxford: Butterworth-Heinemann, 113–27.

Eddington, S. and Symon, A. (2008) *Ngāi Tahu Rock Art Charitable Trust AGM Report 2007–8*, Timaru: Ngāi Tahu Rock Art Charitable Trust.

Evison, H. (1993) *Te Wai Pounamu, the Greenstone Island: A History of the Southern Māori During the European Colonization of New Zealand*, Christchurch: Aoraki Press.

Graham, D. (1998) 'The New Zealand Government's Policy', in A. Quentin-Baxter (ed.) *Recognising the Rights of Indigenous Peoples*, Wellington: Institute of Policy Studies, 3–21.

Ingram, T. (1996) *Māori Tourism Development: A Strategic Plan and Policy for Ministry of Māori Development*, Wellington: Te Puni Kokiri.

McIntosh, A., Hinch, T. and Ingram, T. (1999) *Māori Attractions in Aotearoa, New Zealand: Setting a Context for Sustainable Tourism*, Centre for Tourism, University of Otago.

Ministry of Tourism (2007) *New Zealand Tourism Strategy 2015*, Wellington: Ministry of Tourism.

Ngāi Tahu Holdings (2012) www.ngaitahuholdings.co.nz/Subsidiaries/Tourism.php (accessed 29 January 2012).

NZ Māori Tourism Council (2012) Living Landscapes, www.livinglandscapes.co.nz/index.php?option=com_content&view=category&layout=blog&id=44&Itemid=72 (accessed 29 January 2012).

NZTB (1993) *New Zealand: Conservation Estate and International Visitors*, Wellington: New Zealand Tourism Board and Department of Conservation.

——(1996) *International Visitor Survey*, Wellington: New Zealand Tourism Board.

O'Regan, T. (1989) 'The Ngāi Tahu Claim', in I. Kawharu (ed.) *Waitangi: Māori and Pakeha Perspectives of the Treaty of Waitangi*, Auckland: Oxford University Press.

——(1990) 'Māori Control of the Māori Heritage', in Gathercole, P. and Lowenthal, D. (eds) *The Politics of the Past*, Cambridge: Cambridge University Press, 95–106.

Orbell, M.R. and Moon, G. (1996) *The Natural World of the Māori*, Auckland: David Bateman.

Pihema, W.T. (2002) 'Boundaries of Desire: How Hapu and Whanau Mitigate the Vectors of Power During the Establishment of a Māori Tourism Attraction', unpublished thesis, Wellington, Victoria University.

Russell, K.J. (2000) Landscape: Perceptions of Kai Tahu I Mua, Āianei, Ā Muri Ake, unpublished thesis, University of Otago.

Ryan, C. (1997) 'Māori and Tourism, a Relationship of History, Constitutions and Rites of Tourism', *Journal of Sustainable Tourism* 5(4): 257–78.

——(1998) 'Māori and New Zealand Tourism', in Robinson, M. and Boniface, P. (eds) *Tourism and Cultural Conflicts*, Oxon: CABI, 229–45.

——(2002) 'Tourism and Cultural Proximity: Examples from New Zealand', *Annals of Tourism Research* 29: 952–71.

Ryan, C. and Pike, S. (2003) 'Māori-based Tourism in Rotorua: Perceptions of Place by Domestic Visitors', *Journal of Sustainable Tourism* 11(4): 307–21.

Sinclair, D. (1992) 'Land Since the Treaty', in King, M. (ed.) *Te Ao Hurihuri: Aspects of Māoritanga*, Auckland: Reed Books, 85–105.

Solomon, M. (1998) 'The Context for Māori (II)', in Quentin-Baxter, A. (ed.) *Recognising the Rights of Indigenous Peoples*, Wellington: Institute of Policy Studies, 60–84.

The Stafford Group (2001) *He Matai Tapoi Māori: A Study of Barriers, Impediments and Opportunities for Māori in Tourism*, Wellington: Ministry of Māori Development and the Office of Tourism and Sport.

Statistics New Zealand (Te Tari Tatau) (2012) www.stats.govt.nz/browse_for_stats/people_and_communities/maori/census-snapshot-maori.aspx (accessed 28 January 2012).

Tahana, N. and Opperman, M. (1998) 'Māori Cultural Performances and Tourism', *Tourism Recreation Research* 23(1): 23–30.

Te Awekotuku, N. (1981) *The Sociocultural Impact of Tourism on the Te Arawa People of Rotorua*, New Zealand: University of Waikato.

Te Kupeka Umaka Māori Ki Araiteuru (KUMA) (2011) *Tiki Tour Māori Guide to the Lower South Island*, www.kuma.org.nz (accessed 29 October 2012).

Te Puni Kokiri (TPK) (1998) *Māori Tourism Directory*, Wellington: Ministry of Māori Development Te Puni Kokiri.

Tourism New Zealand (TNZ) (2003a) *Tourism New Zealand 3 Year Strategic Plan 2003–2006*, Wellington: Tourism New Zealand.

——(2003b) *New Zealand's Ideal Visitor: The Interactive Traveller*, Wellington: Tourism New Zealand.

TPK/MMD (1998) *Māori Tourism Directory*, Wellington: Ministry of Māori Development (Te Puni Kokiri).

TRONT (Te Rūnanga o Ngāi Tahu) (1998) *Te Karaka Special Edition, Crown Settlement Offer: Consultation Document From the Ngāi Tahu Negotiating Group*, Christchurch: Ngāi Tahu Publications.

——(2002) *Draft Ngāi Tahu 2025: te manaka o iwi*, Christchurch: Ngāi Tahu Publications.

——(2012) *About Te Runanga o Ngāi Tahu*, www.ngāitahu.iwi.nz (accessed 21 January 2012).

van Aalst, I. and Daly, C. (2002) *International Visitor Satisfaction with their New Zealand Experience: The Cultural Tourism Product Market – A Summary of Studies 1990–2001*, unpublished report, Wellington: Tourism New Zealand.

Walker, R. (1992) 'The Relevance of Māori Myth and Tradition', in King, M. (ed.) *Te Ao Hurihuri: Aspects of Māoritanga*, Auckland: Reed Books, 171–84.

——(1996) 'Contestation of Power and Knowledge', *The Politics of Culture He Pukenga Korero Ngahura*, Autumn, 1(2): 1–7.

Walsh, B. (1996) 'Authenticity and Cultural Representation: A Case Study of Māori Tourism Operators', in Hall, C.M. and McArthur, S. (eds) *Heritage Management in New Zealand and Australia*, Melbourne: Oxford University Press, 202–8.

Wikitera, K.-A. (2006) *Whakarewarewa Tourism Development: A Critical Analysis of Place and Space*, unpublished thesis, Auckland University of Technology.

# 30

# Social entrepreneurship and cultural tourism in developing economies

*Philip Sloan, Willy Legrand and Claudia Simons-Kaufmann*

## Introduction

Tourism has become a major activity in our society and an increasingly important sector in terms of economic and social development (Giaoutzi and Nijkamp 2006). Edgell (2006) supports this theory, suggesting that tourism 'has the potential to participate in, change, and improve the social, cultural, economic, political, and ecological dimensions of our future lifestyles'. Virtually all nations practise tourism as a development strategy using it as a means of 'earning foreign exchange, creating employment, promoting deprived regions and developing infrastructure' (Singh 2003: 41). It has become apparent that the tourism industry can play an economically sustainable role in combating poverty, conserving the environment, community development and poverty alleviation. This chapter looks at the various ways in which the phenomenon of social entrepreneurship is being used in the context of cultural tourism and hospitality in developing countries to bring about improvements to the lives of members of local communities. Developing countries typically have comparative advantages in tourism. They not only possess land, sun, sea and adventure possibilities but also assets like wildlife, landscape and cultural experiences, which are all demanded by consumers from richer and often more densely populated countries.

Recently, it has been recognised that entrepreneurship is an important factor driving the growth of social emancipation and the integration of disadvantaged minorities (Reis and Clohesy 1999). Paton (2003) made similar observations and drew attention to the emergence of these new forms of business governance by introducing the concept of hybrid services, such as organisations promoting social entrepreneurship. As emphasised by Fowler (2000), any socially minded enterprise such as tourism requires a specific type of capability to manage a not-for-profit organisation under one roof. As the term social entrepreneurship implies, it is multi-disciplinary and draws on what were previously two distinct research directions ('society' and 'entrepreneurship'). Due to its increasing prominence in communities and businesses and due to an increasing awareness of its potential contribution to the economy the topic recently has received considerable attention in different fields of research. In the words of Mair and Marti (2006) 'the variegated nature and multiple expressions of social entrepreneurship make it a fascinating playground for different perspectives and literatures, and at the same time, suggest that it should be studied through diverse theoretical lenses'.

However, the emerging field of literature is still largely phenomenon-driven, and appears to lack a comprehensive theoretical framework (e.g. Mair and Marti 2006). Social entrepreneurship research has so far drawn on insights and theoretical frameworks such as organisation theory, management literature, entrepreneurship literature, social movement theory, development studies, corporate social responsibility and social innovation literature (Sharir and Lerner 2006). Hence, there is at present no consensus around a specific definition or clearly defined academic understanding of social entrepreneurship. A common thread running through all academic literature is the element of social problem-solving as the primary mission for social entrepreneurial organisations. Social entrepreneurship is not a philanthropic or charity approach to poverty reduction; it offers an approach based on the strategic use of market forces to promote social improvements. It can be broadly characterised by a tendency towards combining efforts across private, public and civil society sectors in the search for solutions to present societal problems (Johnson 2000). Johnson states 'with its emphasis on problem-solving and social innovation, socially entrepreneurial activities blur the traditional boundaries between the public, private and non-profit sectors, and emphasize hybrid models of for-profit and non-profit making activities' (Johnson 2000: 1).

Similarly, private-public partnership organisations also achieve the same objectives employing market-based strategies to achieve a social purpose. It seems that there is a fine line between the degree to which an organisation employs so called 'enterprise-based' strategies as opposed to general non-profit-based strategies. This reveals unanswered questions to definitions within current academic research on social entrepreneurship. For the purposes of this research the authors prefer the definition created by Alford 'a process that creates innovative solutions to immediate social problems and mobilizes the ideas, capacities, resources, and social arrangements required for sustainable social transformation' (Alford et al. 2004: 262). Here, the social mission is explicit; it is about applying and mastering entrepreneurial skills in order to solve a social problem. In brief, social entrepreneurial activities can be seen as initiatives that mainly focus on creating social value and where the creation of economic value, if present, is seen as a necessary means to ensure financial viability (Mair and Marti 2006).

Although numerous studies have been carried out in the field of entrepreneurship as a driving force for social change following purely capitalist doctrine (e.g. Scott and Venkataraman 2000) in the field of tourism and hospitality research, little attention has been paid to social entrepreneurship. During the last 21 years only 2 per cent of the articles published in the top hospitality and tourism journals have addressed the topic (Lin 2008). A recurring theme in the literature on social sustainability in tourism is the significance of the community and local development (e.g. Edgell 2006), where the importance of a participatory planning and development process is stressed. Moreover, socially equitable tourism should not merely involve the community, but a substantial share of the profits should benefit the local population. Again, academics agree that this is beneficial for both tourism organisations and the host community: 'the full involvement of local communities in the tourism sector not only benefits them ..., but also improves the tourism experience' (Edgell 2006: 23). This principle is fundamental to cultural tourism that takes place in developing countries and focuses on or affects the traditions and lifestyles of local communities.

The participatory planning process should also include other stakeholders and the public. Edgell (2006: 23) emphasises that 'consultation between the tourism industry and local communities, organizations, and institutions is essential if they are to work together and resolve conflicts of interest'. Basu (2003) emphasises that the development of destinations should be fundamentally built around local participation, representation and empowerment, the promotion of local interests, the preservation of local landscapes, cultures and heritage, and the matching of the industry to local carrying capacity. Singh (2003: 33) supports this, as 'community involvement in policy framing, planning and development of local resources and monitoring success and failure of the project' lead to a more 'authentic, meaningful and satisfying experience for both the visitor and the visited'. Singh argues that there are a great number of examples where tourism development contributes towards economic growth, but where societal effects were ignored. Therefore, Singh (2003: 39) concludes that 'no tourism development however ingeniously conceived can foster sustainability if it fails to respect the needs and aspirations of the local people. It has to be a community industry to become viable, sustainable and self-perpetuating'. Consequently, sustainable tourism and hospitality development should not only involve the local population, but should actively preserve local culture.

## The case studies: introduction

Research was undertaken in small lodges and small hotels catering almost uniquely for tourists within three selected destinations: Kumily in India, Chumbe Island in Tanzania, and Inkaterra in Peru. As well as supplying a 10–15-page written report on their ventures, respondents also answered an open ended online questionnaire. These respondents were all instigators of the projects and had continued in the role of project leaders. They were asked to provide details of local culture, livelihoods, the environment and economic development. In addition, they were asked to describe the development of their projects pointing out not only successes but also the problems they encountered. The case studies are three very different socially and ecologically diverse destinations, yet provide examples of all the principles of social entrepreneurship within tourism and hospitality. While each has their own goals and challenges to meet, each destination strives to regenerate damaged biodiversity, educate local communities in rural cultures and maintain financially successful hotel lodges that reach a wide customer base of travellers and vacationers.

Kumily focuses on environmental conservation and community development as part of the India Ecodevelopment project. Luxury hospitality is not the primary goal; 'home stays' have been developed as the best option to minimise environmental impacts and encourage cultural diversity. Chumbe Coral Park focuses on regenerating the natural richness of the coral reef and to providing meaningful employment opportunities for local fishermen whose fish stocks had diminished in recent years. By educating the local population, the coral park gradually has been regenerated to its previous pristine condition. Fishermen, farmers, forestry workers and lodge operatives have learnt to understand the carrying capacity of their activities and to work with nature. Inkaterra strives to create luxury accommodation right in the heart of tribal homelands and rich biodiversity. With limited technological and financial resources the challenge for Inkaterra was to develop sustainable tourism and hospitality operations without harming the cultural traditions of the local community.

---

### Box 30.1 Chumbe Island Coral Park Ltd in Zanzibar, Tanzania

This case study on Chumbe Island Coral Park focuses on sustainability initiatives established by the hotel and a marine research centre. It strives to work with the local people on issues of education, sustainable fishing, preservation of coral-rag forests and, of course, the coral reefs in Zanzibar, Tanzania.

Chumbe Island is registered with the World Conservation Monitoring Center and has exceeded anticipated goals in community aid and in the protection of biodiversity. Chumbe Coral Park organises excursions for local schools offering educational programmes on the reef and forest

---

habitat as well as classes in children's snorkelling and swimming. Village fishermen, who previously practised fishing in all areas of the reserve, now respect the boundaries of the coral park and fish only outside the protected areas. Previously the coral reef was not valued by local people and the relationship between the resort developers and the fishermen was strained. The fishermen did not want to accept that this was not their fishing territory. They agreed to learn from former fishermen-turned-park rangers and slowly began to understand that the fish would slowly migrate outside the boundaries, which would be to the fishermen's benefit.

Through providing fishermen with the opportunity to become park rangers, a form of social entrepreneurial tourism has developed. The park rangers now manage the Coral Reef Sanctuary. To support the local economy, Chumbe purchases local food produce from spice and fish markets which provides around 90 per cent of the needs of the hotel lodge restaurant. Buying locally grown produce supports farmers in the region, while local women are employed to cook and serve meals based on local traditions. These women are also employed as operatives in the Chumbe lodge hotel. Job opportunities are also offered by international research institutions that have set up a highly reputable marine research centre. Profits from the hospitality operations are re-invested into conservation area management and free island excursions are provided for local school children through environmental educational programmes.

## Box 30.2 The Periyar Tiger Reserve, Kumily in Kerala, India

The social entrepreneurial mission of the Kumily project leaders reveals the importance of linking community development with biodiversity conservation within protected areas without harming the livelihood of local people or degrading the natural environment by means of tourism. The Periyar Tiger Reserve in Kumily is now on the brink of being a major tourism destination due to its immense natural beauty and rich flora and fauna. The challenge faced by the leaders of this community-based sustainable tourism and hospitality venture is to protect the site from environmental degradation and social upheaval.

This form of responsible tourism is now successfully being used not only to sustain but also regenerate the environment whilst providing a livelihood for local people and tribes. Originally funded by the India Ecodevelopment Organisation Project, the Periyar Tiger Reserve produces not only benefits for the environment and well-being for local people but also revenue for the local economy that funds improvements to local infrastructure such as roads and schools.

One of the key benefits is the integration of tourists into the life of the villages by introducing them to local activities based on traditional knowledge. Tourists lodge with local people in so called 'homestays', where the villagers open up their homes to the Westerners, who both gain valuable insights into local culture and provide financial support to a traditional way of life. Locals also work as guides, rickshaw drivers and plantation farmers, who in turn provide food products to their visitors. They also have the opportunity of working in the local hotels where they make no secret about learning the trade while harbouring the hope one day to have their own accommodation operation. Fortunately local tribes have a very tightly knit community spirit and strong culture that withstands the sometimes obvious Western, consumer behaviour.

## Box 30.3 Inkaterra – pioneering ecotourism in Peru

This case study focuses on Inkaterra Amazonica and how they have over the years pioneered a new form of social entrepreneurship and environmentally friendly tourism in Latin America. The project has given much-needed support to local cultures through staff trained to develop a sustainable retreat resort. All have expert knowledge of surrounding ecosystems and the immense regional biodiversity. Inkaterra has successfully created a market for high-quality, luxurious, sustainable hospitality and tourism.

Jose Koechlin, owner and founder, has created three sustainable hotel complexes in the jungles of the Peruvian rainforest. His priority was to form a team capable of offering new knowledge and skills to local indigenous communities who could combine the benefits of tourism dollars with environmental stewardship and care for local people. The first hotel project was in the Ese'eja-Sonene community, where travellers were introduced to local communal traditions exemplified by hunter-gatherer lifestyles. Another benefit to the communities is the training given to locally educated personnel to represent the interests of Inkaterra in local government. Benefits such as accommodation, food, airfare and insurance are provided to the local staff of Inkaterra. This, along with educational support, health campaigns, and agro-forestry workshops raising the awareness of biodiversity are just some of the activities of Inkaterra in their contact with local communities. However, difficulties have been experienced with national legislation that prevents local people who do not have at least five years' previous experience from being employed as guides. There are also concerns in hiring locals from the Amazonian communities in the hotels, since their culture is not easily adapted to Western accommodation expectations.

Inkaterra works to achieve 'authentic nature travel' and is behind several research projects on biodiversity, natural resource management and conservation of natural reserves. They are also presently supporting a rescue centre for spectacled bears. Due to the rich local biodiversity requiring specialised knowledge, some tours are led by members of indigenous communities who have intimate knowledge of the flora and fauna.

In addition to providing an example to all social entrepreneurs and environmental stewards, Inkaterra is now a profit-making organisation. Starting from humble beginnings in the Amazonian rainforest where services are practically non-existent, the organisation overcame enormous difficulties in obtaining equipment and in creating jobs for the indigenous population who, although they were more than happy to co-operate, required extensive training. This conversion to the principles of sustainable tourism and hospitality has been achieved in such a way as not to endanger cultural heritage

## Conclusions

The case studies in this survey demonstrate the effectiveness of social entrepreneurship within cultural tourism and hospitality ventures as a tool for sustainable development in several under-developed economies around the world. Poverty alleviation and environmental regeneration have now become goals not only of some governments and non-governmental organisations but also of forward-thinking individuals in their quest for a fairer society and harmonious natural environment. The case studies show that this has been achieved in the context of social entrepreneurial business management. All three respondents maintain that their ventures are now financially solvent, although no precise start-up investment information was given to allow for precise financial analysis. By using modern business management techniques these social entrepreneurs have achieved economic respectability for all stakeholders including their indigenous employees, environmental stewardship and social progress. Thus, this study provides evidence that the popular perception that companies cannot combine financial profitability, the promotion of social values and environmental responsibility is flawed. It can also be concluded that the social entrepreneurial model of cultural tourism and of hospitality operations are perfectly suitable for local populations with no previous understanding of the hospitality product or international visitor standards. In all the destinations the staff and in some cases the lower and middle management positions were occupied by local employees with little or no education.

Models of social entrepreneurship are wide and varied. The authors hypothesise that hospitality operations in Western economies could find synergies with groups of single parents, senior citizens, and the physically and mentally disabled in a similar way. More research is needed to obtain a deeper understanding of the mechanisms that hospitality operations could employ to support deprived sections of Western society. Social entrepreneurship is a new business model that can provide the inspiration currently sought by corporations of all sizes that wish to become more socially responsible.

## References

Alford, S.H., Brown, L.D. and Letts, C.W. (2004) 'Social Entrepreneurship and Societal Transformation: An Exploratory Study', *Journal of Applied Behavioral Science* 40(3): 260–82.

Basu, P.K. (2003) 'Is Sustainable Tourism Development Possible? Broad Issues Concerning Australia and Papua New Guinea', in Ghosh, R.N., Siddique, M.A.B. and Gabbay, R. (eds) *Tourism and Economic Development: Case Studies from the Indian Ocean Region*, Aldershot: Ashgate, 140–49.

Edgell, D.L. (2006) *Managing Sustainable Tourism: A Legacy for the Future*, New York: Haworth Hospitality Club.

Fowler, A. (2000) 'Breaking the Politics of the Aid Chain – The Case for a Systems Approach to Impact Measurement', *@lliance* 5(3): 31–32.

Giaoutzi, M. and Nijkamp, P. (eds) (2006) *Tourism and Regional Development: New Pathways*, Aldershot: Ashgate.

Johnson, C. (2002) 'Mintel Report on Sustainable Development in Hotels', *Travel and Tourism Analyst* 5 (3): 1–24.

Johnson, S. (2000) *Literature Review on Social Entrepreneurship*, Edmonton, Alberta: The Canadian Centre for Social Entrepreneurship, University of Alberta.

Lin, L. (2008) 'A Review of Entrepreneurship Research Published in the Hospitality and Tourism Management Journals', *Tourism Management* 29(5): 1013–22.

Mair, J. and Marti, I. (2006) 'Social Entrepreneurship Research: A Source of Explanation, Prediction, and Delight', *Journal of World Business* 41(1): 36–44.

Paton, R. (2003) *Managing and Measuring Social Enterprises*, London: Sage.

Reis, T. and Clohesy, S. (1999) *Unleashing New Resources and Entrepreneurship for the Common Good: A Scan, Synthesis and Scenario for Action*, Battle Creek, MI: W.K. Kellogg Foundation.

Scott, S. and Venkataraman, S. (2000) 'The Promise of Entrepreneurship as a Field of Research', *Academy of Management Review* 25(1): 217–26.

Sharir, M. and Lerner, M. (2006) 'Gauging the Success of Social Ventures Initiated by Individual Social Entrepreneurs', *Journal of World Business* 41: 6–20.

Singh, T.V. (2003) 'Tourism and Development: Not an Easy Alliance', in Ghosh, R.N., Siddique, M.A.B. and Gabbay, R. (eds) *Tourism and Economic Development: Case Studies from the Indian Ocean Region*, Aldershot: Ashgate, 30–41.

# PART V
# Landscapes and destinations

This section focuses on the role that landscapes and destinations play in cultural tourism. The concept of landscape has been the subject of several books over the past few years (e.g. Ringer 1998; Aitchison *et al.* 2001; and de Haan and van der Duim 2008). Historically, landscapes were often viewed by tourists with a mixture of awe and wonder, especially mountain landscapes which sometimes inspired fear too. Early Grand Tourists tended to follow the trail of the classics, for example, visiting landscapes described by Virgil, Horace and Cicero, or later the Romantic poets. Aesthetics has always been an important element of landscape-based tourism, with tourists travelling exclusively to visit the world's most beautiful landscapes and monuments – for example the Seven Wonders of the World or World Heritage sites. In recent years, however, there has been something of a 'democratization' of landscape, whereby sites have begun to be valued for their historical or cultural value, rather than their beauty. For example, many industrial landscapes have made their way onto the World Heritage site list.

The philosopher Alain de Botton (2003) described how travellers are drawn to 'sublime' landscapes because of the spiritual feelings they engender, making them feel part of an infinite and universal cycle. Some tourists actually do visit spiritual landscapes which may or may not be associated with religion (e.g. the Santiago de Compostela pilgrimage), which have cultural connections to ancient civilisations (e.g. Macchu Picchu), or may be the original homeland of First Nations (e.g. Native American Indian or Aboriginal landscapes).

Well-being can be enhanced through contact with natural landscapes. Although the appreciation may be based on nostalgia or sentimentalism about rural idylls of the past, visitors' appreciation can also go way beyond conventional notions of 'the picturesque' and romanticised simplifications of nature (Todd 2009). Kaur Kler (2009) uses theories of environmental psychology to explain tourists' preferences for natural and restorative landscapes. Viewing natural scenes has been proved to improve mental well-being, increase alertness, and reduce stress.

Many landscapes have become associated with literary or artistic works or figures (see Robinson and Andersen 2004), such as the poet Wordsworth's Lake District or the Yorkshire Moors of the Brontës. This has now been extended to include film tourism landscapes, such as 'Middle Earth' from *The Lord of the Rings* in New Zealand or *Harry Potter* country in the UK. However, many of these landscapes are merely imaginative or socially constructed, therefore the visitor may experience some degree of confusion or disappointment when confronted with the actual landscape which may not bear much resemblance to the perceived or fictionally represented one.

Discourses of social and cultural geography have frequently been used to analyse landscapes, often within the framework of theories of space and place. In this section, David Crouch revisits some of the theoretical debates about these concepts and applies them directly to land-scapes and destinations. Space is no longer thought to be static but full of energy and flows. Place derives its meaning from the human experiences which take place therein. Landscapes are partly shaped by the agencies which produce and represent them, but also by the visitors who consume them, whose activities and energies affect their character, nature and atmosphere.

Landscape can be highly politicised with regards to issues of ownership, usage, appropriation, displacement or exclusion. Landscape has been particularly contentious in the case of cultural landscapes which were home to indigenous peoples and 'First Nations'. Landscape can also be gendered or sexualised, with many spaces being unwelcoming or unsafe for women or gay communities. Post-colonial landscapes tend to be strewn with reminders of dominant and sometimes oppressive regimes and decisions need to be made about which elements of the landscapes should be preserved. Joan Henderson touches on this in her analysis of South-East Asian cities. She looks at the rapidly growing urban landscapes where decisions about conserving traditional heritage are sometimes at odds with the need or desire to provide modern developments.

Landscapes are rapidly evolving, especially in the case of rural landscapes where the forces of globalisation and urbanisation are leading to the transformation of whole regions and communities. Marjan Melkert and Wil Munsters in this section discuss issues relating to the authenticity of landscape, arguing that there are very few landscapes that have not been transformed somehow by human intervention. Myriam Jansen-Verbeke and her co-authors document the development of rural landscapes in detail especially in the context of rural China. They focus in particular on the challenges of managing tourism in areas that are somewhat remote and under-developed. Lóránt Dávid, Bulcsú Remenyik and Béla Zsolt Gergely analyse the potential for niche tourism development in the under-visited and relatively unknown rural landscapes of Transylvania.

The management of landscapes and tourism destinations more generally has been transformed in recent years via the phenomenon of 'destination management'. This approach has been adopted in many countries throughout the world with the establishment of DMOs (or destination management organisations), even though the meaning and nature of the approach varies con-siderably and the definition of a destination is sometimes unclear. It can be a whole town, a seaside resort, or even a landscape, but destinations vary in terms of scale and structure, therefore management approaches need to be adapted accordingly. Destination management tries to ensure that all interests are met including those of the host community, the tourism industry, the public sector and the tourists themselves. Impacts must be managed, quality standards should be maintained, and the destination needs to stay competitive. Simon Woodward makes interesting recommendations in this section for destinations which are university towns or which contain university campuses.

Overall, it is clear that almost all landscapes and destinations are politically, socially and culturally constructed and represented. Those that are visited are transformed from spaces into places by the energy and activities of their visitors; they are not merely static or passive receptacles. Landscapes are enlivened and transformed by the presence and experiences of visitors, which can radically change not only their atmosphere but their basic structure and form. As a result, tourism must be carefully managed in these locations, possibly through the relatively new approach that is destination management, which should provide an integrated and sustainable way of supporting cultural dynamism alongside environmental protection and social sensitivity.

## Summary of the chapters in this section

**David Crouch** revisits debates relating to space and place in the context of tourism. Using the works of spatial and cultural geographers, he traces the development of theories relating to these two concepts, concluding that they are essentially different. It is agreed that space is not fixed and static but fluid and dynamic, full of changing flows and energies. Place is based on people's experiences of and engagement with a space, however the process by which places are constructed in tourism is not always well understood. The term landscape also conveys a construct which occurs or 'erupts' in a way that is not always pre-scripted or mediated. Perceptions and experiences of both landscapes and destinations will include matters of culture brought from the visitor's own lives and backgrounds. The visiting of landscapes and destinations is no longer merely spectatorial. Visitors are instead active and creative in the making of cultural tourism for themselves and others.

**Marjan Melkert** and **Wil Munsters** discuss the concept of authenticity in the context of landscape with a focus on the material objects themselves rather than the visitors' experience. The notion of authenticity in this context is considered as being different from historical 'reality' or original artefacts, i.e. some authors have argued that it is impossible for replicas or reconstructions to be authentic. In the context of landscape, the original may be the prehistoric landscape before human interference; however, most landscapes now have been transformed agriculturally or culturally. Such processes may be considered to be authentic, thus most landscapes combine what is original and authentic. However, the latter process reflects the period in which the transformation took place, including any interpretation. It is sometimes difficult to identify the 'authors' and to understand the multi-layered dynamic of landscape development over time. Ethically, reconstructions should be identifiable in order to be distinguished from conservation and restoration, and to adhere to a sense of authenticity and coherence, even if originality in its true sense is an impossibility.

**Joan Henderson** considers landscapes and destinations in South-East Asian cities, especially the tension between conservation and urban development. Heritage tends to be politically contentious and it can be difficult to reconcile the need for conservation with the desire for modernisation, especially when land is scarce. Old structures may sometimes be used for contemporary developments, but they are not always financially or practically viable, they may be unsympathetic or exclude or displace local residents. South-East Asian cities have the added complication of colonial legacies, which may now seem dissonant to local people. Slums may also be a common feature of cities which project a very different image to the outside world. The complexity of managing the global and the local, the past and the present, and retaining or creating a sense of place is a constant challenge for urban planners. The value of heritage in this context is a hotly debated issue, especially as international tourists may find it decidedly more appealing than intra-regional tourists who tend to prefer contemporary developments (e.g. shopping malls, events).

**Simon Woodward** analyses the role of universities and campuses in the development of destinations. This includes not only the built heritage but also the intangible heritage associated with university life and the experiences of the students and staff. The author suggests that many university destinations might benefit from being considered within the framework of DMOs in order to enhance their product development, image and identity, and tourist experience. There are also certain conflicts which may need to be resolved between tourists' and students' needs, such as access to campuses during term time, the freeing up of accommodation during holidays, even the content and presentation of museum collections or programming of art centres. The impacts on the built heritage, host communities and atmosphere of place also need to be considered when developing academic landscapes as tourist destinations.

**Myriam Jansen-Verbeke**, **Yehong Sun** and **Qingwen Min** consider the heritage value of agricultural landscapes, territories and communities that are gradually disappearing due to globalisation and urban development. Models of 'dynamic conservation' have therefore been developed by the United Nations World Tourism Organization (UNWTO) and UN Educational, Scientific and Cultural Organization (UNESCO) (amongst others) in order to balance conservation and economic revitalisation. The chapter focuses in particular on the urbanisation and industrialisation of the countryside, which is typical of development in many Asian regions, and China in particular. This includes creating sustainable and competitive forms of cultural tourism by promoting traditional and authentic ways of life, including creative use of intangible heritage. However, this can be challenging due to insufficient infrastructure or lack of local expertise. Tourism needs to be developed in such a way as to maximise social, economic and cultural resources for poor local communities. This may happen through an understanding of the tourism value chain, intelligent visitor management, adequate monitoring systems, and a clear awareness of the impacts of tourism on rural heritage.

**Lóránt Dávid**, **Bulcsú Remenyik** and **Béla Zsolt Gergely** analyse the way in which special interest tourism products can be used to develop rural landscapes. The focus is on a case study of Gyimes in Transylvania which is typical of many rural areas that are struggling to establish mainstream tourism products and are concentrating instead on niche markets. Due to its special status as a former part of the Hungarian Kingdom (until the First World War), this region attracts ethnic tourists from Hungary who may be nostalgic or interested in genealogy or roots. There are also pilgrimage routes, some of which are Catholic, but others which are connected to the 'thanatourism' of Second World War sites. Finally, gastro-tourism is explored as a potentially attractive product because of the uniqueness of local cuisine which combines both Hungarian and Romanian traditions. Such a landscape clearly has potential like many rural areas that have a distinctive character and history, but the challenge will be to develop the area to the extent that it can become an internationally known tourism destination rather than just a regional one.

## References

Aitchison, C., MacLeod, N.E. and Shaw, S. (2001) *Leisure and Tourism Landscapes: Social and Cultural Geographies*, London: Routledge.

de Botton, A. (2003) *The Art of Travel*, London: Hamish Hamilton.

de Haan, H. and van der Duim, R. (2008) *Landscape, Leisure and Tourism*, Eburon Academic Publishers.

Kaur Kler, B. (2009) 'Tourism and Restoration', in Tribe, J. (ed.) *Philosophical Issues in Tourism*, Bristol: Channel View, 117–34.

Ringer, G. (1998) *Destinations: Cultural Landscapes of Tourism*, London: Routledge.

Robinson, M. and Andersen, H. (eds) (2004) *Literature and Tourism: Essays in the Reading and Writing of Tourism*, London: Thomson International.

Todd, C.S. (2009) 'Nature, Beauty and Tourism', in Tribe, J. (ed.) *Philosophical Issues in Tourism*, Bristol: Channel View, 154–70.

# 31
# Space and place-making
## Space, culture and tourism

*David Crouch*

## Introduction

Space and place are habitually used in tourism literature, yet frequently merge as one, general 'thing'. In this chapter I bring to the fore rich themes of debate concerning space and place, and culture. In the first section, rather than 'fix' space and/or place, I invite engagement with these ideas, avoid narrow definition and recommend consideration of meaning. Second, I include landscape, another familiar term that tends to presume its reference point in tourism work, to bear on the discussion of space. Third, these unravelled 'certainties' are brought directly into our thinking concerning cultural tourism in a way that seeks to engage in the complexity and fluidity, the multiple sites of 'doing tourism'.

## The matter of 'making'

The 'making' of space and place, akin to the making of 'destinations' is familiar in tourism literature, not least in terms of cultural tourism. In this piece I attend to the notions of place and space that have more recently come to be significant in geography, particularly through the work of social and cultural geography. I consider these explanations in relation to the use of these and related terms in tourism, particularly from a perspective of what we understand the label 'cultural tourism' to mean; its significance and use. As with most rich debates, this discussion reflects the complexity of the terms and the dynamic of their occurrence in the material, social and cultural world.

Space and place have been themes habitually debated in geography for a very long time. Tim Cresswell's (2004a) valuable introductory text arrives at a reasoning that 'space' is the fabric of somewhere, the materiality, buildings and streets, hills and trees that we may encounter, and the mediated constructions relating to the space; 'place' is embedded with our own experience of that space. Such consideration contrasts greatly with two books familiar to tourism studies: sociologist Urry's *Consuming Places* (1995) and *The Tourist Gaze* (1990). In the former, the emphasis is on places as being constructed through literature, advertising and so on; in the latter, that our experience of tourist sites is led by a detached looking. Doreen Massey (1994), another geographer with a particularly critical attention to explain, argues somewhat differently. She points to the power of spatial co-ordinates – economic, physical, social and political – that position any particular site or location, perhaps destination; these are turned by our human work, or engagement with that space, into place.

More recently Massey has gone further into the complexity of what space is, how it occurs, what influences space. The idea of how space occurs is perplexing and fascinating. We usually assume it is there, simply 'there'. From her engagement with much developing literature, she reasons that space is a participatory and dynamic energy: '(a) coming together of the previously unrelated, a constellation of processes rather than a thing. This is place as open and internally multiple ... not intrinsically coherent' (Massey 2005: 141). Space is more that the contextual co-ordinates of the social, economic and political; more than the materials and their physical and metaphorical assemblage, of building material, vegetation, rock and so on. *Space* is increasingly recognised to be always contingently related in flows, energies and the liveliness of things; therefore always 'in construction', rather than fixed and certain, let alone static (Massey 2005). What space 'is' and how it occurs is crucially rendered unstable and shifting; matter and relations in process. It may be *felt* to be constant, consistent and uninterrupted, but that feeling is subjective and contingent.

British geography's recent interest in the French theorists Deleuze and Guattari (2004) has focused upon their notions of territory, space and spacing. In geographically pertinent terms this space is highly contingent, emergent in the cracks of everyday life, affected by a maelstrom of energies well beyond human limits. What interests them is the potential of space to be constantly open to change and becoming, rather than only or mainly as the more settled. Interpreted in terms of individuals' participation in space, in making space through 'spacing', space and life cohabit in holding on to the familiar and going further into what is unknown.

Adjustments are produced through which life can be negotiated, always in tension in an unlimited array, or immanence of possibility. Moreover, life does not work to a given script or prefigured world, not even linearly with our own memory and its spaces. As anthropologist Tim Ingold (2007) has argued, creativity in what we do and how we feel does not work to a given script either, a point to which I will return in a moment. To a degree this process happens in an embodied way; it could not do otherwise, as Deleuze insists upon the possibility of everything being involved in this process, not merely mental reflexivity, and potentially including memory of other times and spaces engaged relationally. Thus, Deleuze introduces a notion of *spacing*, where the individual is constantly active in projecting and feeling meaning of the material world she or he engages. Spacing happens in highly intense and in less urgent moments.

The American geographer Yi-FuTuan positions 'place' as:

> the centre of meaning constructed by experience, not only through the eyes and mind but also through the more passive and direct modes of experience, which resist objectification ... At one end of the spectrum, places are points in a spatial system, at the other end of the spectrum places form a nexus of strong visceral feelings ... which presuppose rootedness in the locality and emotional commitment to it that are increasingly rare.
>
> *(Tuan 1975: 152)*

Yet de Certeau inverts these terms and their constituent processes: '... space is a practised place ... the street geometrically defined by urban planning is transformed into a space by walkers ... i.e. place constituted by a system of signs' (de Certeau 1984: 118). Such an approach turns on its head what we understand by space and by place. Place becomes more than understood in tourism, as its sites and destinations constituted by its (marketing) signs. Either way, there is an assertion of place and space being essentially different.

Whilst 'place' may continue in popular exchange, it seems superfluous in the face of the interpretive power of 'spacing'. The term *place* may have significant fluid connotations, but it is also archetypal in, for example, popular tourism literature: the synagogue or temple to be visited, the 'vibrant city'. These 'places' offer new fixity. It is difficult to relate place to process conceptually.

## Landscape

There is a similar debate concerning what 'landscape' is. Cresswell (2004b), again, has elsewhere argued that such a term is redundant if we have the terms of space and place; landscape merely a notion that works from, and conjures up kinds of visual representation rather than anything that is lived. Hence he considers that the problem with 'landscape' is its habitual use that implies the obliteration of life.

In a way similar to Massey's reflections on space, landscape is also *not* the mere bits and pieces; the arrangements of physical or material components of a site that can be apprehended in our experience, as being outside of me, outside of us ourselves (Crouch 2010b). Acknowledging the lively, awkward, uneven and pregnant vitality of Deleuze and Guattari's thinking about space enables us to move beyond landscape as being fixed.

Being aware of 'a landscape' is not really the point, as it is neither our awareness of 'place'. The landscape is not 'out there'; it is not prepared for us. It emerges in our relationship, in feeling, in what we do, in how we approach it, physically, mentally, that landscape *occurs*. It is in the moment of the event, the act we engage, in looking, but also engaged, encountered in other sensuous manners: in hearing, touch and so on. Memory can be engaged, and frequently is, in how we participate in making the landscape occur, yet memory is itself fluid, with each current moment being a recreation of a moment of memory, and that memory is not the same. It can inform, inflect, but may also be erased in the new moment. Similarly with mediated images of landscape in or from film, advertising and so on. These may well be created presentations of landscape, but they are not the landscape, or space, that we actually encounter: they may merely influence, inflect something into our own experience. Individuals, as Ingold (2007) has argued, are creative too, in their doing, feeling, memory and relations with things, other humans and other than human life.

Spacing relates to a degree to the earlier place and landscape work of humanistic geographers who were drawing on the work of the philosopher Merleau-Ponty (1962). Spacing goes much further than this work, and emphasises capacity and energies for change that is abrupt, non-linear and non-accumulative, and which includes influences that are other than human. 'Landscape' erupts in a commingling or clash of many impulses in our journeys, definitely not felt as pre-scripted.

Landscape as signified through spacing can have a gentle yet cumulative politics, profound in its feeling and ideas. Landscape as practice is forwarded into process, as dynamic rather than either 'outside' experience or only focused through particular physical character of encounters. Landscape emerges from its mediated fixity as 'this' or 'that' into something articulate; the dynamic and complex character of landscape in process, working away from the particularly fixed character familiarly associated with landscape in and as representation. Landscape's purported fixed and steady character which we find to be instead shuffling, unstable and lively.

## Space, landscape and the enlivening of our interest in and understanding of cultural tourism

Cultural tourism is habitually used to designate particular character in tourism 'places', destinations, as that which draws tourists to them, as well as the character of the tourist experience at those sites, even that shapes it and, perhaps, in the memory of experience there. Taking up the above discussion, in this section I reflect upon the familiar uses and meanings of space and other terms in relation to destinations and for cultural tourism and cultural tourists. Understanding journeys and creativity crucial to understanding the non-prefigured, not-stable character of space, and cultural tourism provides a valuable example of journeys.

Life happens in multiple journeys, of different measurable distances, spaces, registers or intensities. Meanings relating to space and landscape cut across and commingle in this lively complexity. Our journeys are at least somewhat fluid. Tourism, for example cultural tourism, fits into these journeys.

As this contribution has gathered, it is evident that space is not out there; we participate in its making, its occurrence. Similarly with the culture of our *doing tourism* (Crouch 1999). The very notion of doing tourism (being a tourist) is itself active, participatory, lively, not merely 'in receipt of'. Thus, spaces, places to include a popular usage, and landscapes may have some material, ancient buildings, mosques or churches, wildlife, funfairs, stretches of beach, steep rocky surface; famous shopping malls, gambling sites, visiting a World Heritage site; engaging in 'music holidays' and beer; joining a charter holiday trip to rediscover a fantasy of Englishness or whatever our own nation seems to be (recently excellently captured by Hazel Andrews 2011). Each has matters of culture – what we bring to it from our own lives. These are all cultural tourism – just as we acknowledge that each of these spaces, the feeling of doing tourism, is affected at least in part by us; by our doing. Moreover, varied and repetitive spaces of our own experience, at different times and spaces, become components of the context through which our experience (of culture) in this moment comes to have feeling and meaning.

We affect what *is* – what the culture is – in our experience of whatever it is. We are participants, as in the way considered above for constituting space, landscape, in making tourism cultural. We are components of, participants in, making culture. Culture concerns meanings, values, attitudes, and how we live, our practices. As cultural studies has explained, mediated, iconic or inherited culture is a significant shaping of the meaning we may hold, feel or acknowledge. Yet those influences and matters such as gender, class, ethnicity, are not determining. The term 'cultural tourism' can emerge, then, as an oxymoron: it asserts the fixed character of culture, where we become merely spectators, not active in its making or in the creativity of our own lives. Creativity is an important part of culture, always in the making, and all we bring to any site we may visit. Participating with our own culture can also affect the character and style of the visit in which we engage, or anyone else for that matter. Culture in tourism is all-embracing.

With regard to particular interests in available, pre-figured cultures situated in particular sites of cultural heritage, or, rather, particular projections or presentations of cultures, visited as tourists, these understandings become particularly pertinent (not 'more cultural'). We participate in making heritage. Heritage is, like space, place and landscape, not 'out there' – made available for visiting – but in our own participation (Crouch 1999). Like landscape, heritage, or any kind of tourism site or activity explicitly associated or recognised by its prefigured association with a particular cultural moment (e.g. music sites, 11 September, and so on), becomes also informed through combinations of different times and life durations and rhythms, different registers and intensities of experience in our own lives. Landscape emerges as a continual process, emergent in the expressive and poetic character of spacing: creative, contingent, awkward and not blocked in representations.

The human, practical participation by a tourist in such culture becomes understood as creative rather than spectatorial. Individuals are expressive and poetic. As is increasingly becoming acknowledged, doing tourism does not happen in a wholly separate world; we live in our culture, its meanings, values, feelings. We cannot help have that culture with us as we engage in the fluid, continuing but contingent process of encountering and participating in the world, in life and its material stuff, wherever we are. Our individual and group culture may shift, unsettle, or be affirmed in our experiences; influenced by the site, but also our experience of the site influenced by our selves. Similarly of the tourist destination, its character is inflected by our own individual and shared culture, our everyday, lived experience of being in the world, of activity, which is also creative.

## References

Andrews, H. (2011) *The British on Holiday*, Clevedon: Channel View.

Cresswell, T. (2004a) *Place: A Short Introduction*, Oxford: Blackwell.

——(2004b) 'Landscape and the Obliteration of Practice', in Anderson, K., Domosh, M., Pile, S. and Thrift, N. (eds) *Handbook of Cultural Geography*, 269–81.

Crouch, D. (ed.) (1999) *Leisure/tourism Geographies: Practices and Geographical Knowledges*, London: Routledge.

——(2009) 'The Perpetual Performance and Emergence of Heritage', in Waterton, E. and Watson, S. (eds) *Culture, Heritage and Representation: Perspectives on Visuality and the Past*, Aldershot: Ashgate, 57–74.

——(2010a) *Flirting with Space: Journeys and Creativity*, Farnham: Ashgate.

——(2010b) 'Flirting with Space: Thinking Landscape Relationally', *Cultural Geographies* 17(1): 5–18.

de Certeau, M. (1984) *The Practice of Everyday Life*, trans. S. Rendell, Berkeley: University of California Press.

Deleuze, G. and Guattari, F. (2004) *A Thousand Plateaus*, London: Continuum.

Ingold, T. (2007) *Lines: A Brief History*, London: Routledge.

Massey, D. (1994) 'Power-geometry and a Progressive Sense of Place', in Bird, J., Curtis, B., Putnam, T., Robertson, G. and Tickner, L. (eds) *Mapping the Futures: Local Cultures, Local Changes*, London: Routledge.

——(2005) *For Space*, London: Sage.

Merleau-Ponty, M. (1962) *The Phenomenology of Perception*, trans. C. Smith, London: Routledge.

Tuan, Yi-Fu (1975) 'Place: An Experiential Perspective', *Geographical Review* 65(2): 151–65.

Urry, J. (1990) *The Tourist Gaze*, London: Sage.

——(1994) *Consuming Places*, London: Routledge.

## Further reading

Andrews, H. (2011) *The British on Holiday*, Clevedon: Channel View. (A ground-breaking tourism text, by an anthropologist, on the culture of tourists.)

Cresswell, T. (2004a) *Place: A Short Introduction*, Oxford: Blackwell. (An enjoyable introduction to matters of place (and space.)

——(2004b) 'Landscape and the Obliteration of Practice', in Anderson, K., Domosh, M., Pile, S. and Thrift, N. (eds) *Handbook of Cultural Geography*, 269–81. (A critical consideration of the plight of landscape.)

Crouch, D. (ed.) (1999) *Leisure/tourism Geographies: Practices and Geographical Knowledges*, London: Routledge. (Focuses upon recent innovative work on tourism and leisure practices, culture and tourism.)

——(2009) 'The Perpetual Performance and Emergence of Heritage', in Waterton, E. and Watson, S. (eds) *Culture, Heritage and Representation: Perspectives on Visuality and the Past*, Aldershot: Ashgate, 57–74. (An empirically engaged discussion of heritage as constantly being (re)figured.)

——(2010a) *Flirting with Space: Journeys and Creativity*, Farnham: Ashgate. (A wide ranging and informed discussion that engages matters of space and human activity, practice, feeling and attitudes relating with space; inter-disciplinary, empirical and conceptual.)

——(2010b) 'Flirting with Space: Thinking Landscape Relationally', *Cultural Geographies* 17(1): 5–18. (A critical contribution to understanding how landscape 'occurs', in complexity of moments, memory fragments, and mediated influences, using many examples.)

Massey, D. (2005) *For Space*, London, Sage. (A passionately argued case by a world renowned geographer for considering space in an original, relevant way.)

Urry, J. (1995) *Consuming Places*, London: Routledge.

# 32

# The development of the historic landscape as a cultural tourism product

*Marjan Melkert and Wil Munsters*

An important issue within the field of cultural tourism research is the question of how the quality of the supply can be kept in line with visitors' expectations and how it can be improved and even be renewed. Whoever wants to know more about this issue may turn to the writings of Pine and Gilmore (1999; Gilmore and Pine 2007) as these are by many considered as important sources for tourism and heritage studies. However, cultural tourism involves more than just the (visitor's) experience and it is perfectly possible to speak of the material objects themselves in terms of value and authenticity (Melkert and Munsters 2010). For those who specialise in the study of aspects of the material world such as excavations, historic buildings and museums, or whole places and landscapes, this observation is not new. To these researchers the question of what is authentic and why it is labelled as such has always been a subject matter of their investigations. An application of their ideas, methodologies and ethics to the field of cultural tourism research opens new possibilities for the development of the cultural tourism supply while starting from the material world. It puts tools in the hands of those who want to improve the quality of the cultural offer composed by objects and ensembles. The focus of this article is on how this approach works out for the largest possible ensemble: the cultural-historic landscape.

## Measurement criteria for the value of the historic landscape

A model to measure in an objective way the value of the historic landscape does not have to be developed as a completely new research tool. Such a model has already been the subject of research in relation to a smaller sort of material ensemble: the historic interior. For de Mensch (2001) interiors have the special capacity to make the past almost tangible. The world of the interior convinces by its coherence which is linked to the measure in which it is detailed and authentic. For landscapes it is also possible to use three criteria: coherence, detail and authenticity, and their inter-relationship. These criteria help us to study the appearance of a landscape.

- Coherence: what kind of elements are present and what is their inter-relationship (e.g. waterways and watermills or sets of elements that are to be linked to one period in time)?

- Detail: how much and what kind of detail is to be found and what is their inter-relationship (e.g. standard orchards *with* their surrounding hedges *and* wrought iron gates)?
- Authenticity: how much and what kind of authentic material is there to be found (e.g. historic buildings)? How is it inter-related or related to detail?

As authenticity is a buzz word today, it deserves to be dealt with first. In order to evaluate the authenticity of landscapes an operational definition is required. Denslagen (2004) proposes an interesting definition of authenticity in his book *Romantic Modernism*. First he states that authenticity is something else than the original. The original is the state in which the object was presented for the first time. 'Authentic' applies only to the (historic) material substance and nothing else. Even if the historic object has been either changed or even damaged, it remains authentic. In this light, a replica, or reconstruction, can never be labelled as authentic in relation to the real historic objects they replace or make complete. This straightforward definition is completely in line with the Charter of Venice (ICOMOS 1964).

By using this definition for landscapes it is possible to determine what is original, and what is authentic. Original is the pre-historic landscape before human interference. There is hardly any of it left in Europe. At the time of the arrival of hominidae (*ca.* 100,000–30,000 BC), the original landscape had undergone some minor changes. Later, with the arrival of the first farmers (*ca.* 5,000 BC) agricultural practices created the first cultural landscape. The first appearance of this agrarian landscape, in that time, may be seen as the original for that period. Likewise, the first traces of the different forms of agrarian use of fertile landscapes (edible landscapes) that have replaced one another through the ages may all be labelled as original for their period. On the other hand, the state in which they arrive in the present is to be called authentic, even when it is altered or damaged. This approach forces researchers to focus carefully and precisely on the remains of the time frames that they investigate. Each and every situation is different and researchers have to be aware of this in order to avoid misinterpretations.

A landscape that comes from a certain period and that shows elements that are original and authentic as a coherent whole may be expected to foster the visitor's experience of historic reality. Here Denslagen's (2004) and de Mensch's (2001) approaches converge. The observation of the quality of the detailed traces from different periods in a landscape and the way they interfere with each other becomes important in this light. It may be worthwhile to examine if different sorts of relationships may be measurable in visitors' experiences and if they can even contribute to create the so-called 'historical sensation', defined by the Dutch historian Huizinga as a (sublime) historic experience (Ankersmit 2007). For example, can the loss of authentic detail account for a landscape being less attractive for the cultural tourist? If so, this may help to find arguments that underpin the different choices that can be made in order to strengthen the coherence of the cultural-historic landscape as a whole.

## The authorship of the historic landscape

De Mensch (2001) also states that what we can learn from the historic interiors and especially those in historical museums, is that they are regarded as an historic reality by the visitor. The reason is that these cultural attractions themselves are recognised by the visitors as institutions that are specialised in putting authentic objects on display. Nowadays, however, in the field of heritage, the difference between historically real and fake has become blurred by the tendency to focus on the visitor's experience. This sometimes happens at the cost of the truth of the stories that are being told and of the authenticity of the objects that are being shown. According to de Mensch (2001), visitors are generally unaware of this 'forged authenticity' as they are confronted with a credible interpretation where different levels of reality are being integrated with each other. So, presentations of interiors where objects from different backgrounds are being put on display in a 'natural' coherence (habitat) go close to and even beyond the limits of authenticity. It is an old approach that emerged in the nineteenth century as the so-called 'naturalistic' staging. The focus lies on storytelling, a technique that comes from the field of folklore. Historic scenery is swift to appear. The source of inspiration is to be found in the historic genre of paintings, where the general type is considered to be more important than the individual case. For example, in the research of historic farms, types were introduced. Naturally, the historic farms were never constructed to conform to a type and they existed long before the classification. At the same time the 'period room' appears that encompasses both rooms that are original and sometimes even 'in situ', and later constructed interiors as well. Nowadays, actors are added, in the tradition of the 'living history' or 're-enactment' in order to add narrative or even biographic elements. These presentations aim to produce a vivid visitor experience. This practice is not limited to historical houses and open-air museums, but is also to be found outside in landscapes as well.

*Figure 32.1* At festive occasions we meet flint experts at Neanderthaler sites
Source: (Photo Lennard Grensschap 2005)

De Mensch (2001) postulates that this 'heritage' approach requires a new ethics with regard to authenticity as a label and in the presentation of historic interiors in museums in general. There is a difference between the original historic interior and the added narrative or biographical aspects. In practice, the difference may be difficult to spot but in the process of conservation and restoration both approaches demand completely different ethics. The added narrative or biographic elements materialised in assembled objects reflect the vision of the time in which they were made or the historic period that they 'portray'. The authorship of this interpretation lies with the responsible conservator, whereas the original inhabitants are the 'authors' of original rooms that have been handed down through history, and document their own time.

For landscapes it is very possible to observe this difference as well by asking the question: who is the author? Is it the original farmer or is it someone else? We can discern quite a range of possibilities and Denslagen's (2004) definitions of the original and the authentic will be of help here as well:

- The pre-historic landscape where there has been no human activity. This type of landscape is very rare.
- The cultural-historic landscape handed down with all the changes that have been brought about in land use and agricultural practices. Some 7,000 years of agricultural activity have shaped this kind of landscape. The farmers are the 'authors'.
- Reconstructions of pre-historic natural landscape. The conservators are the 'authors'.
- Reconstructions of cultural-historic landscape. Here we could speak of 'classic' and 'light' versions. An example of the 'classic' version is the reconstructed pre-historic landscape to be found in open-air museums like the Butser experiment in the UK. The 'light' version is characterised by the camouflage of present-day agricultural land use with small natural historic landscape elements like hedges and orchards. The conservators are the 'authors'.

## The dynamics of the historic landscape

For the conservation and presentation of historic interiors there are different points of view to be observed. De Mensch (2001) states that in every interior there are three aspects that are linked to each other: space, the mix of the objects within it, and the order in which they have been placed. The sum of these three aspects constitutes the appearance of the whole, which can undergo two forms of dynamics: gradual ones and abrupt ones. Gradual dynamics result from renewal, modernisation and adaptation. Abrupt dynamics are related to periodic or ad hoc changes, such as the introduction of a Christmas tree or the setting of a table in the room. In landscapes, too, gradual changes occur such as the removal of the cow from the Dutch meadow into the mega-stables built by the agro-industry. Periodic changes in landscapes may be linked to the different stages of growth and the pruning of fruit trees and hedges. Objects can be subject to different dynamics as well. In historic interiors, paintings tend to be rather static and cups of tea come and go rather dynamically. In landscapes we see the same. Crops in the fields change every season. Dust roads slowly change course because of different circumstances. Buildings seem to be the most static kind of object in a landscape because as long as people have a use for them they will continue to be. Here it is easy to discern between the actions that have a quick or a slow effect on the outlook of the landscape. A change of crops is fairly quick, but a newly planted standard orchard takes years of good maintenance to mature and grow beautiful. When studying the landscape, the moment and stage in the development of the appearance at a given week, month or year should be taken into account. Consequently, the less that is known of space, mix and order, the more care has to be taken with the subject matter. For de Mensch

(2001) the original (if present) and the authenticity of space, mix and order should be tampered with as little as possible. The advice that may be distilled from these ideas for working with landscapes while improving them as a cultural tourism offer, is the following:

- Recognise and preserve whatever is original.
- Recognise and preserve whatever is authentic.
- Foster coherence.
- Take care that reconstructions are recognisable as such. The substance matter and aesthetic form should be of the highest quality possible and preferably sustainable!

This is, again, quite in line with the Venice Charter as well: conservation goes before restoration; restoration is to be preferred to reconstruction; and reconstructions have to be recognisable as such. The last principle offers space for present-day interventions, creating the new originals of our age in the ever ongoing history of the place.

## The biography of the historic landscape

In order to document all the aspects of landscapes that have been mentioned above, many different sources that are linked to a specific landscape may be scrutinised for information. The synthesis of these may be an illustrated description that comes close to a biography of the landscape in question. The methodology of the Historic Critical method (Melkert and Vos 2010) should be applied to the sources. This approach helps to select scientifically sound examples and put the right questions to them. The following examples of written and audiovisual sources may well be included, to mention just a few of them:

- Geological studies.
- Archaeological research results.
- Historic maps and geographical studies.
- Old drawings, prints, paintings, photographs and films.
- Nature surveys and studies.
- Studies into the local history and the history of buildings and settlements.
- Categorical monument surveys.

Another crucial source of information is the information that experts, inhabitants and visitors can point out about the landscape. Interviews and dialogues with experts and locals during excursions on the spot may provide more insight into how the landscape is being/may be 'read' and interpreted (Buizer 2008). Classical surveys with questionnaires may be carried out amongst visitors, but also visitor-employed diaries, photographs and videos (see Richards and Munsters 2010). The result of these studies: a biography of the landscape to be used to argue the right policy choices in the process of developing it for cultural tourism purposes.

## Box 32.1  Case study: the Historic Landscape Park Voerendaal, Province of Limburg, the Netherlands

A quick scan shows that the area where the community of Voerendaal wants to develop the Historic Landscape Park Voerendaal has undergone many major changes during the past 50 years. This is also the first impression one receives when visiting. It is almost impossible to walk or cycle properly around the area without being forced to use quite busy provincial roads (80 kilometres per hour). The land consolidations from the second half of the twentieth century are to blame, as in the process roads have disappeared and huge fields for large-scale farming have been created. New (historic) walks and cycling routes have to be constructed as part of the cultural tourism product. The pattern of ancient roads and paths could be studied in order to seek possibilities for reconstructions. The creation of a golf course is another land-consuming intervention made quite recently. Luckily, it is well dressed with hedges and trees, so it does not cause a lot of visual damage. From the archaeological record we know that in Roman times this area was the heart of the major grain-producing region for the troops stationed on the river Rhine. The remains of one of the largest Roman villas in this part of Europe lie here, but if you have no idea where the site is located, it is very hard to find. Nevertheless, its presence lends weight to the 'branding' of the area in a Roman fashion. Today, there are still quite a number of farmers active in the area, including some biological farmers. This provides opportunities for developing the concept of the 'edible landscape'. In the South-Limburg region, spelt, a crop known from Roman times, is being reintroduced. The edible landscape may therefore very well be integrated into the historic landscape. When considering what the Historic Landscape Park Voerendaal already has to offer, it is easy to find the historic 'hooks' on which to hang the modern cultural tourism product.

*Figure 32.2* 'Roman' soldiers marching on Roman tracks help visitors to experience the history of the region. This is evidence-based storytelling

Source: (Photo Lennard Grensschap 2005)

# References

Ankersmit, F. (2007) *De Sublieme Historische Ervaring*, Groningen: Historische uitgeverij.

Buizer, M. (2008) *Worlds Apart*, Wageningen: Alterra.

Denslagen, W. (2004) *Romantisch Modernisme*, Amsterdam: Uitgeverij SUN.

Gilmore, J. and Pine, J. (2007) *Authenticity: What Consumers Really Want*, Boston, MA: Harvard Business School Press.

de Graaf, B. (1993) 'Limburg 1802–7 Landschap en vegetatie in beeld gebracht', *Natuurhistorisch Maandblad*, 82–83.

ICOMOS (1964) *The Venice Charter*, Paris: ICOMOS.

Melkert, M. and Munsters, W. (2010) 'Objective Authenticity in Cultural Tourism: Thinking the Unthinkable', *Journal of Hospitality & Tourism* 8(2): 14–29.

Melkert, M. and Vos, K. (2010) 'A Comparison of Quantitative and Qualitative Approaches: Complementarities and Trade-offs', in Richards, G. and Munsters, W. (eds) *Cultural Tourism Research Methods*, Wallingford: CABI, 33–51.

de Mensch, W. (2001) 'Tussen narratieve detaillering en authenticiteit', in Kleijn, H.C.M. (ed.) *Interieurs belicht*, Zwolle: Waanders Uitgevers.

Pine, J. and Gilmore, J. (1999) *The Experience Economy*, Boston, MA: Harvard Business School Press.

Richards, G. and Munsters, W. (2010) *Cultural Tourism Research Methods*, Wallingford: CABI.

# Further reading

Renes, H. (2010) *Op zoek naar de geschiedenis van het landschap*, Hilversum: Uitgeverij Verloren. (Handbook for research of historical landscapes.)

# 33

# Finding a place for heritage in South-East Asian cities

*Joan Henderson*

## Introduction

There are inherent tensions between the conservation of built heritage and urban development, with both competing for space and financial resources. Tourism is an additional complication in cities popular with visitors and has an uneasy and contested relationship with heritage. Tourists can damage the physical fabric of built heritage together with more intangible aspects because of overuse and excessive commercialisation, but they are also a potentially positive force in support of conservation. The interconnectedness of heritage, urban development and tourism, and the difficulties and dynamics of the relationship are evident in many larger South-East Asian metropolitan centres, which are the focus of this chapter. The region's urban environments are developing rapidly there in ways that have destroyed much built heritage and threaten the survival of any that remains. Tourist interest is frequently cited in arguments for protecting heritage, but other policy goals appear to take priority and the future is one of some uncertainty.

## Built heritage and its meanings

Heritage is multi-faceted and encompasses buildings, structures and spaces from the past which have historic significance. Built heritage performs numerous roles, not least that of tourist attraction, and has an economic and commercial value that is partly fixed by the market. Its socio-cultural worth is harder to quantify and embraces aesthetic, historic, social, spiritual and symbolic qualities (de la Torre 2002). Perceptions and evaluations of heritage depend on the individual and group and are shaped by wider circumstances. Cultures may attribute different degrees of importance to heritage and its preservation and level of economic development has consequences for funds available for conservation and restoration as well as technical expertise. Politics also can be a critical influence over official interpretations and presentations of heritage and its safeguarding. Governments regularly seek to exploit history and its legacies in pursuit of a political agenda, sometimes inspired by hegemonic motives (Henderson 2009). In addition, geographical location and whether the setting is urban or rural may affect the meanings and merit allotted to heritage and the nature of conservation policies.

There are likely to be intense pressures in many cities to develop scarce land in the urban core and maximise its revenue-generating potential, possibilities that must be reconciled with the demands of heritage conservation. Some argue that conservation is compatible with urban development and can be complementary. Heritage is capable of earning income directly and indirectly by making cities more liveable and endowing them with uniqueness, which is employed in branding and promotion to entice visitors and businesses (Ebbe 2009). In certain cases, proximity to heritage sites can enhance the value of property and land and restored buildings may command a premium price, as demonstrated in Malaysia (Nor *et al.* 2007). Proponents contend that money thus raised by urban heritage contributes to both overall economic development and conservation efforts, from which everyone benefits. Adaptive reuse is commonly proposed as a means of resolving any frictions between conservation and development and permitting buildings to survive, sometimes by performing a leisure or tourism function. In theory, it allows the adaptation of old structures for contemporary usage in a fashion that respects their architectural integrity and the importance of the site (Langston *et al.* 2008). Critics, however, complain about inappropriate and unsympathetic conversions and occupants. There are also financial and practical restrictions on what can be done (Cohen 2001; Feilden 2003) and a danger that the purchase and rental costs of converted properties are beyond the means of residents. Locals are thereby excluded and alienated from their own heritage in a manner illustrated by so-called lifestyle businesses, such as the expensive fine dining restaurants and luxury boutique hotels that have opened in historic properties once serving a public purpose in Singapore.

Socio-cultural rewards must also be considered and a city's heritage can assist in cultivating feelings of civic pride and belonging. Tangible reminders of earlier eras offer connectivity and continuity with the past (Girard 2006), affording comfort and reassurance in a world of change and upheaval. Colonisation introduces another dimension to any discussion of heritage (Yeoh 1996) and many of the countries in South-East Asia have a history of rule by European powers and also by Japan during the Second World War. These experiences are reflected in the extant British colonial architecture in Singapore and Kuala Lumpur and French designs in Vietnam's capital of Ho Chi Minh City. Jakarta also has a Dutch colonial district, but the buildings are in very poor repair. How to deal with evidence of occupation and oppression is a question for all post-colonial societies, one option being neglect. Other responses include obliteration for ideological or pragmatic reasons, yet manifestations of foreign interference may be retained because of their capacity to be harnessed to nation building. Capital and other cities often were the scenes of pivotal events on the journey to independence and are home to potent symbols of a common struggle towards freedom from the imperial yoke, which are deemed to foster feelings of national identity and unity. Such sentiments may also be a channel for consolidating the position of entrenched political elites.

## Losing and conserving heritage in South-East Asian cities

As suggested in the above account, the debate about the place of heritage in the modern world is not confined to the West and resonates in cities across much of Asia, which have expanded at a fast pace in recent decades. Expansion has been fuelled by economic advances and inward migration, with mainland China providing some striking illustrations. The trend is also apparent in South-East Asia (Page 2001; Rimmer and Dick 2009) and the physical alterations to parts of many of the region's capitals, which include Bangkok (Thailand), Jakarta (Indonesia), Kuala Lumpur (Malaysia) and Manila (the Philippines). The city state of Singapore is another example, albeit one distinguished by its wealth and the control exercised over the urban planning process.

Transformations of this sort are regularly hailed by officials as a sign of progress and prosperity, although problems facing administrators cannot be overlooked. For instance, transport systems struggle to cope and traffic congestion is severe, despite some investment in projects such as light railways. Great disparities in income amongst urban dwellers and a rise in migrants from rural areas in search of a better life are a potential cause of unrest. Persistent poverty leads to slums still being found in the cities of poorer countries, at odds with projected images. These are formidable difficulties and failure to find solutions to these has adverse outcomes for city sustainability and the experiences of those living and working there, and for visitors. National and municipal governments therefore confront numerous challenges in managing twenty-first-century South-East Asian cities besides that of what to do with built heritage, given more pressing matters that have a higher priority (Srinivas 1999).

Every city has its own story and personality, but some general patterns of modernisation can be discerned. Urban landscapes commonly comprise towering skyscrapers in central business districts, large multi-storey shopping malls and busy highways. The architecture is modern with few references to the location, failing to convey a sense of place and imposing a global character on the centres of the region's capitals. Much built heritage has been lost to urban development at a speed that indicates that the residue of the historic cores and districts is vulnerable (Martokusumo 2002; Ghafar Ahmad 2006; Jones and Shaw 2006). Doubts about their future are intensified by expectations that the very strong impetus towards growth will persist and economic objectives continue to take precedence in inner-city policy making (Steinberg 2008). Many buildings from the past are low rise and perceived by some as an unproductive use of land, the preference being to clear the site and build high-rise commercial and residential blocks, which earn more money. As a consequence, vernacular architecture such as shop-houses (terraced properties in which lower floors were traditionally devoted to business and upper storeys to accommodation) is being replaced by an international, homogenised style.

Long-standing settings for daily life and traditional trades are thus also disappearing and the case study examines one such instance of a locale under threat. While inspiring the affection of locals and curiosity of tourists, these areas are frequently an embarrassment to governments and do not match their visions of a city of sleek modernity. Observers note a similar official attitude to cooked food hawkers (te Lintelo 2009) and the prospects of these remnants of earlier eras are precarious. Even when there are conservation initiatives, these may be directed to political ends by seeking to reinforce the authority of incumbent regimes, some of which have been in office since independence (Henderson 2002; Peleggi 2005). Commerce may also be at the forefront of decisions and undermine the effectiveness of conservation work. Heritage management as a whole is made more difficult by deficiencies in urban planning, inadequate controls and poor general governance linked to bureaucratic inefficiencies and the corruption and cronyism that are endemic in much of the region (Westcott 2003).

Nevertheless, awareness of the need for some conservation is expressed in official statements of commitment and intent as well as urban plans and tourism strategies. Heritage is seen to contribute to the well-being of society and help in binding a people together. Solidarity is especially sought after in multi-ethnic states such as Indonesia, Malaysia and Singapore, where cultural heritages can be competing and there are suspicions about the privileging of the majority race. Conserving heritage can therefore be a politically charged issue and vote winner or loser. There is an additional appreciation that cultural heritage in its assorted forms has tourist appeal, especially for long-haul visitors. Saving heritage aids in maintaining the popularity of city destinations and their competitive advantage, highlighting that which renders them unique (Chang et al. 1996). Tourist interest is informing official decision making and is having an effect on the formal valuation of heritage, attractiveness to tourists bolstering the rationale for conservation which can be partly funded by their spending. Heritage is, however, deemed to be less of a draw for the intra-regional leisure travellers who dominate international movements in South-East Asia and for whom shopping, purpose-built facilities and various events are key reasons for city visits.

---

## Box 33.1 Case study: the case of Kampung Baru

Kampung is the Malay word for village and Kampung Baru in the Malaysian capital of Kuala Lumpur dates from the late nineteenth century when much of the country was under British colonial rule. The administration was concerned about the rising number of outsiders moving into Kuala Lumpur and displacing indigenous Malays. An area of around 223 acres was therefore reserved for Malay farmers and incorporated several small settlements already on the riverside site, which were eventually amalgamated. Ownership of land was restricted to Malays and originally carried certain obligations pertaining to cultivation. Prior to 1900, there were 12 recognised land holdings and the number exceeded 4,000 by 2011 in a proliferation attributed to the nature of Islamic inheritance laws (Ar 2009).

The settlement has seen some changes over the years and there are a few multi-storey accommodation blocks, but it remains primarily a low-rise area of traditional wooden houses on stilts and family restaurants. Its architecture and ambience make it one of the last neighbourhoods in the city where a distinctive Malay way of life is followed. It is also seen as a bastion of Malay patriotism and representative of the resilience of traditional culture. These special qualities are emphasised by the contrast with the encroaching urban landscape of skyscrapers, including the Petronas twin towers, which was the tallest such construction in the world when it opened in 1998. The towers are a component of Kuala Lumpur City Centre (KLCC), a precinct of multi-million-dollar projects that is separated from Kampung Baru by the river. KLCC is a deliberate attempt to create a new city centre unconnected to the original, and is symbolic of Malaysia's aspirations to full development status in the near future.

Such ambitions make Kampung Baru an anomaly for many city officials and there have been various attempts at development and integration with the surrounding metropolis. The latest plan was announced in 2010 and describes the setting up of a Kampung Baru Development Corporation (KBDC). Kampung Baru is envisaged as a world-class tourist and cultural hub, main commercial area and residential district. Its unique Malay identity will be retained, but given modern appeal. Residents are assured that they will not be relocated and will have the right to determine the form of development most suited to their requirements. Despite these promises, the proposals met with an unenthusiastic response and the relevant legislation was delayed. Opponents were worried about the loss of the essential character of the place and introduction of un-Islamic activities and businesses such as pubs and clubs if ownership were opened up to non-Malays as proposed.

---

## Conclusion

Contentious issues of heritage and its management within an urban context extend beyond South-East Asia and apply worldwide. The fast pace of growth in the region's cities and notably in capitals does, however, heighten the urgency of the dilemma of securing an appropriate balance between the demands of heritage conservation and economic dictates. The necessity for

South-East Asian countries to advance economically and raise standards of living for citizens is keenly appreciated, and sacrificing some built heritage to forward these objectives might be considered a price worth paying, comprehensive and costly conservation being a luxury available only to wealthier countries. Shortages of expertise, an absence of planning and insufficient funds may also undermine conservation activity. At the same time, there are arguments in favour of conservation and tourism has a part to play in defining the importance attached to heritage and endeavours to conserve it. Nevertheless, other, more powerful forces are at work, and cultural tourism in the twenty-first century must be prepared to accommodate the realities of life in different destinations.

# References

Ar, A.N.A. (2009) 'Legacies of an Urban Village: Kampung Baru History, Architectural Features and Heritage', Paper presented at the PAM CPD Seminar 2009, Kuala Lumpur, 8 August.

Chang, T.C., Milne, J., Fallon, D. and Pohlmann, C. (1996) 'Urban Heritage Tourism: The Global-Local Nexus', *Annals of Tourism Research* 23(2): 284–305.

Cohen, N. (2001) *Urban Planning, Conservation and Preservation*, New York: McGraw-Hill Professional.

de la Torre, M. (2002) *Assessing the Values of Cultural Heritage: Research Report*, Los Angeles, CA: The Getty Conservation Institute.

Ebbe, K. (2009) 'Infrastructure and Heritage Conservation: Opportunities for Urban Revitalisation and Economic Development', Directions in Urban Development Note, World Bank Urban Development Unit, February.

Feilden, B.M. (2003) *Conservation of Historic Buildings*, Oxford: Elsevier.

Ghafar Ahmad, A. (2006) 'Cultural Heritage of Southeast Asia: Preservation for World Recognition', *Malaysian Town Plan* 3(1): 52–62.

Girard, L.F. (2006) 'Celebrating our Urban Heritage', *Global Urban Development Magazine* 2(1): 1–10.

Henderson, J.C. (2002) 'Built Heritage and Colonial Cities', *Annals of Tourism Research* 29(1): 254–57.

——(2009) 'The Meaning, Marketing and Management of Heritage Tourism in Southeast Asia', in Timothy, D.J. and Nyaupane, G.P. (eds) *Cultural Heritage and Tourism in the Developing World: A Regional Perspective*, London and New York: Routledge, 73–92.

Ho, K.C., Teo, P. and Chang, T.C. (eds) (2001) *Interconnected Worlds: Tourism in Southeast Asia*, Oxford and New York: Pergamon.

Jones, R. and Shaw, B.J. (2006) 'Palimpsests of Progress: Erasing the Past and Rewriting the Future in Developing Societies: Case Studies of Singapore and Jakarta', *International Journal of Heritage Studies* 12(2): 122–38.

Langston, C., Wong, F., Hui, E. and Shen, L.Y. (2008) 'Strategic Assessment of Building Adaptive Reuse Opportunities in Hong Kong', *Building and Environment* 43: 1709–18.

Martokusumo, I.W. (2002) 'Urban Heritage Conservation in Indonesia: Experiences from the Inner-city of Bandung and Jakarta Kota', in P. Nas (ed.) *The Indonesian Town Revisited*, Munster/Singapore: LIT Verlag-Institut of Asian Studies, 374–89.

Nor, A.Y., Lim, Y.M., Lee, L.M. and Tan, S.F. (2007) 'Urban Conservation as a Development Strategy to Revitalize Real Estate Market: An Analysis of Property Transactions in Georgetown Penang', *Journal of Construction in Developing Countries* 12(2): 43–61.

Page, S. (2001) 'Gateways, Hubs and Transport Interconnections in Southeast Asia: Implications for Tourism Development in the Twenty First Century', in Ho, K.C., Teo, P. and Chang, T.C. (eds) *Interconnected Worlds: Tourism in Southeast Asia*, Oxford and New York: Pergamon.

Peleggi, M. (2005) 'Consuming Colonial Heritage: The Monumentalism of Historic Hotels in Urban South-East Asia', *Asia Pacific Viewpoint* 46(3): 255–65.

Rimmer, P.J. and Dick, H.W. (eds) (2009) *The City in Southeast Asia: Patterns, Processes and Policy*, Honolulu: University of Hawaii Press.

Srinivas, H. (1999) 'Prioritizing Cultural Heritage in the Asia-Pacific Region: Role of City Governments', *Asia Urbs*, November, www.gdrc.org/heritage/heritage-priority.html (accessed 27 June 2011).

Steinberg, F. (2008) 'Revitalization of Historic Inner-City Areas in Asia', Manila: Asia Development Bank, www.adb.org/Documents/Reports/revitalization-inner-city/Revitalization-Inner-City.pdf (accessed 28 December 2011).

te Lintelo, D.J. (2009) 'The Spatial Politics of Food Hygiene: Regulating Small-scale Retail in Delhi', *European Journal of Development Research* 21: 63–80.

Westcott, C. (2003) 'Combating Corruption in Southeast Asia', in Kidd, J.B. and Richter, F.J. (eds) *Fighting Corruption in Asia: Causes, Effects and Remedies*, Singapore: World Scientific Press, 237–69.

Yeoh, B. (1996) *Contesting Space: Power Relations and the Urban Built Environment in Colonial Singapore*, Kuala Lumpur: Oxford University Press.

## Further reading

Goh, R. and Yeoh, B. (eds) (2003) *Theorizing the Southeast Asian City as Text: Urban Landscapes, Cultural Documents and Interpretative Experiences*, New Jersey: World Scientific Books. (A commentary on urban experiences of modernization and underlying discourses.)

Shaw, B.J. and Jones, R. (1997) *Contested Urban Heritage: Voices from the Periphery*, Aldershot: Ashgate Publishing. (A wide range of cases about heritage conflicts and commercialisation.)

Timothy, D.J. and Nyaupane, G.P. (eds) (2009) *Cultural Heritage and Tourism in the Developing World: A Regional Perspective*, London and New York: Routledge. (Discussion of cultural heritage and tourism issues within the context of less developed countries.)

Winter, T. (2009) *Conserving Heritage in South East Asian Cities: Planning for Continuity and Change*, The Getty Conservative Institute, www.getty.edu/conservation (accessed 27 June 2011). (A summary of the critical issues.)

# 34

# Campus tourism, universities and destination development

*Simon Woodward*

## Introduction

This chapter explores a rarely examined aspect of cultural tourism, namely the contribution of universities to the development and experience of tourist destinations. Drawing on a wide range of examples, it demonstrates how universities, which often are amongst the oldest cultural organisations in a destination, can contribute to the development of tourism in their host communities through the provision of products and services. Also examined is the contribution of the intangible heritage associated with aspects of university life to the development of a place brand, a concept currently at the forefront of destination marketing.

Other than in China, where it has been identified as a phenomenon worthy of investigation partly because of the rapid scale in which it developed in the last decade or so (Ming 2007), campus tourism has generally been the subject of little academic interest. Yet throughout the world, many university quarters function as popular tourist destinations. In the UK, towns such as Oxford and Cambridge owe much of their appeal as a destination to their university heritage, whilst in the USA the town of Cambridge, Massachusetts, markets itself principally on the basis of the presence of Harvard University. In these and many other cases, such as Salamanca and Alcalá de Henares in Spain, Heidelberg in Germany or the area around the Al-Azhar University and Mosque in Cairo, the historic buildings associated with centuries of learning provide an iconic and attractive physical presence that helps the destination build its sense of place.

However, universities are not only able to provide a tangible, built heritage component within a destination. They also offer an intangible heritage product that manifests itself in the institutionally unique cultures and ceremonies, activities and events (formal and informal) associated with university life. So the May Balls in Cambridge, commencement ceremonies at universities across the USA and the *vappu* celebrations on 1 May in Finland all bring aspects of university culture into the public domain. One must also consider how the facilities provided by universities for their students are increasingly being used to support tourism more generally, as universities provide seasonal accommodation for leisure tourists, host conferences and seminars, mount major sporting events, and open up their museums, galleries and cultural venues to the public.

## Developing and branding university towns as destinations – a framework for analysis

All destinations inevitably experience fluctuations in demand at some time (Butler 2006) and try to anticipate and respond to this through product innovation, marketing and other activities designed to secure competitive advantage. In most instances this is delivered through partnerships of public sector, private sector and civil society, with destination management organisations (DMOs) seeking to identify a 'place brand' that differentiates their destination in the marketplace (Anholt 2005, 2007; Govers and Go 2009). This chapter seeks to demonstrate why DMOs should make sure that university authorities are invited to contribute to all efforts seeking to develop tourism in the destination.

The framework for presenting and analysing the contribution of universities to tourism is provided by the recent work of Govers and Go (2009) on place branding and their development of a '3-gap place branding model' (see Figure 34.1). This allows us to place within a broader context product-related topics such as university residential accommodation, museums, galleries and sports facilities on the one hand, and place-image aspects such as the heritage of learning establishments and the contribution of students to create a particular culture in the destination (i.e. the intangible heritage associated with universities) on the other. It will also highlight from a practical perspective where universities may need to become more involved with DMOs in the future in order to ensure that they are able to make a positive contribution to destination development and branding.

Looking at the model presented in Figure 34.1, some key issues to consider are as follows:

- How universities are able to provide aspects of the product offering that attracts tourists to a destination and that supports their visit.
- How some universities are able to make a significant contribution to place identity through events associated with university life.

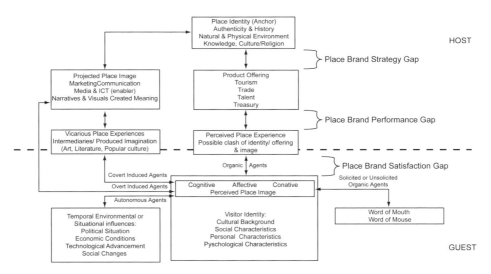

*Figure 34.1* The 3-gap place branding model

*Figure 34.2* Brasenose College, Oxford, which attracts around 6,000 paying visitors a year
Source: (Photograph © Gail Simmons).

- How the presence of university students contributes to place making by developing and supporting products and by projecting a place image.
- How universities and university towns are sometimes represented in popular culture, and the impact this has on the final place experience for tourists.

## University facilities as tourism products

### Residential accommodation

Most universities provide accommodation for some, if not all of their students. In general, these halls of residence or dormitories provide the basic residential and leisure facilities required by students living away from home. With undergraduate terms or semesters generally lasting around 30 to 32 weeks per year, much of the accommodation is thus available for alternative use during vacations.

Research investigating the use of student accommodation during vacations identified two main types of campus-based tourism – special-interest tourism that includes an element of learning (e.g. conferences, language schools, study tours), and general tourism, where visitors use the accommodation but otherwise do not engage with the university's resources (Connell 1996). Because of the nature of university residential accommodation, there are also opportunities to locate social tourism on campus, highlighting the potential contribution that universities can make to developing destinations and broadening market access (Connell 2000).

Within the UK, the scale of this activity is now at such a level that commercial operators are actively co-ordinating the marketing of university accommodation to the group tourism market in particular. One such company based in Sheffield, Venuemasters (www.venuemasters.co.uk), represents more than 100 UK universities and colleges, helping them to market their residential, meeting and associated facilities to domestic and international buyers. No information is currently available on the scale of this market overall, though some universities are reported to earn considerable sums from this business. For instance, Warwick University in the English Midlands generates more than £20 million per annum through renting out its accommodation to business, conference and leisure tourists.

There are, however, institutional challenges associated with using residential accommodation for other paying guests during vacations. Connell (1996) reported some unease amongst international postgraduate students asked to move out of their accommodation outside of term time, as well as perceptions that other guests were better catered for than students. Whether this is a widespread issue or confined to the one institution where her fieldwork was carried out is unknown. However, it does reflect a concern expressed in some quarters at the conflict between public (tourist) access to university spaces and the use of those spaces for learning by students and faculty, demonstrating the risk of universities contributing to the 'place brand satisfaction gap' when the quality of the anticipated experience is compromised through conflict with the host community.

## Museums, galleries and other cultural spaces

University museums across the world, generally based on original teaching collections, seek to bridge the gap between education, research and broader access to heritage and culture. Research carried out on university museums in the UK (Kozak 2007), Australia (Mack and Llewellyn 2000), Japan (Kinoshita and Yasui 2000), Mexico (Herreman 2000), and the Philippines (Labrador 2000) confirms both the potential of university museums to broaden access to a wide range of heritage assets, but also some of the challenges associated with this.

The need to accommodate both 'regular' tourists, teaching programmes and academic researchers can place pressures on curators because of the need to satisfy the primary audience whose study and teaching needs may be very different from those of visiting cultural tourists, not all of whom will be seeking the same level of engagement with the collection. Such issues can be exacerbated when the resources available to university museums are limited (Stanbury 2000). Yet at the same time, there is an opportunity for university museums to use their collections both to celebrate their institutional heritage and at the same time develop a particular institutional identity that appeals to a wide range of audiences (Kozak 2007).

Interestingly, this is also an area where there is a potential divergence between the aims and objectives of university museum and gallery curators on the one hand, and destination managers on the other. There is a belief in some quarters (see, for example, Hammond *et al.* 2006) that university museums and galleries are well placed to be particularly provocative in their display and interpretation of collections because of the tradition within universities of promoting critical thinking. Yet this may not fit easily with some tourists' perceptions of universities being repositories of 'tradition' and 'heritage'. An historic city destination the brand of which celebrates these attributes may find it hard at the same time to find a place for contemporary and challenging art, design and museum displays that seem opposed to how the core brand values of the destination are being presented and perceived in the cultural tourism marketplace.

There is a long tradition in the USA, in particular, of university arts centres being opened up for public use and this is becoming increasingly formalised in college policies. For instance, one of the oldest institutions of higher education in the USA, the College of William and Mary, recently published a strategy identifying how it could use its resources to support the development of tourism in and around its home town of Williamsburg and the wider Tidewater area of Virginia (College of William and Mary 2011). Key amongst the proposals is a conscious effort to increase public engagement with its theatrical and musical events, art exhibitions and its lecture programmes. This emphasis on the performing and fine arts as well as the more traditional university culture provides an exemplar of what could be developed at other universities in popular destinations. However, unless this access is managed to avoid potential conflict between the primary user, the academic, and the secondary market – the tourist – once again there is a risk that the 'place brand satisfaction gap' expand still further.

## Architecture and the built heritage

One final point to consider in terms of tangible heritage is the role of architecture and the built environment. Again, there is plenty of precedent here. In terms of historic properties, the view of iconic university buildings such as King's College Chapel from The Backs in Cambridge, or the roofline of Oxford's 'Dreaming Spires', are often used as key images to promote those destinations to tourists. However, the profile of a university, and therefore of the destination as well, can be enhanced when some of its buildings are designed by world-renowned architects. Signature buildings such as Frank Gehry's University of Toledo Center for Visual Arts in Ohio, the university library in Cottbus, Germany, designed by Herzog and De Meuron, and the AET Faculty Building at Broadcasting Place, Leeds, UK, designed by Feilden Clegg Bradley and named best tall building in the world for 2010 by the Chicago-based Council on Tall Buildings and Urban Habitat, are all examples of university architecture as destination. Whilst such buildings are certain to strengthen a location's appeal to a certain niche market, the level and nature of tourist activity associated specifically with the presence of such iconic signature structures is unknown and offers an interesting avenue for future research.

## The contribution of events and activities to place identity

There are two types of events and activities to consider here: tourism associated with ceremonies related to academic life, and events associated with the university that attract a broader audience. The scale and impact of the first theme, tourism associated with ceremony, has, as far as can be established, not been researched in any systematic way. However, anecdotal evidence from any university will confirm that these ceremonies inevitably create a short-term demand for accommodation, hospitality and related services in a destination.

In Boston, Massachusetts, the presence of some 50 universities and colleges is sufficiently important for a whole website to have been developed to attract potential students to the destination. The site, www.studyboston.com, presents a particular perspective on the destination designed to attract students but at the same time is also supporting a niche market, that of familiarisation visits when families attend open days. This often requires the purchase of over-night accommodation by families living some distance away, and at least one hotel, the Royal Sonesta in Cambridge, Massachusetts, actively targets the families of prospective students visiting universities and colleges in and around Boston. The obverse situation is also beginning to appear, with institutions like the College of William and Mary in Virginia actively seeking to develop formal relationships with hotels that will become the 'preferred hotels' for William and Mary tourists and visitors (College of William and Mary 2011). It is likely that this kind of relationship will become increasingly common as destinations build on the presence of universities in their midst, and is a subject worthy of further research from a destination management perspective.

In terms of university-hosted events that attract broader audiences, one area that has received some attention in recent years is the impact of college sports on local economies. This is relevant to the current discussion for two reasons: first, because of the direct tourism impacts associated with such events as they attract visitors to the destination; and second, because of the strong place image associated with many US college teams. College football in particular plays a key role in US sports culture, with some 48 million spectators attending college games each year, more than twice the number that attend professional NFL games (Baade *et al.* 2008).

Yet despite the large number of spectators involved, with some games attracting more than 100,000 spectators, including many overnight visitors, the net economic gain of college football is in reality relatively modest. Research undertaken in two Florida towns, Gainesville and Tallahassee, home to the University of Florida and Florida State University, respectively, reports a relatively modest net economic gain of around US$2 million per game (Baade *et al.* 2011). Nonetheless, the high profile associated with winning teams is reported to assist in building awareness and appreciation of the university and the town within which it is located (Baade *et al.* 2008), and thus would appear to be of particular relevance to the broader issue under discussion here – namely, how universities contribute to the development of competitive identity in a destination. In this instance, universities are contributing both to the product offering but also to the place image and hence its overall identity.

This contention that US college football plays a powerful role in helping develop tourism in university towns is strengthened by the work of Gibson *et al.* (2003), who looked at motivations of tourists attending University of Florida (the Gators) games in Gainesville. They use the term 'pilgrimage' to describe the behaviour of many spectators, including those who are not University of Florida alumni yet who still follow the team. Interestingly, that research also found an additional level of allegiance to the university itself amongst alumni who followed the team, suggesting that there is a hierarchy of identification with the institution. Again, this raises another dimension of the role of (some) universities in contributing significantly to the place brand and competitive identity of a destination.

## The role of university students in place making

The one thing that university towns have in common, no matter where they are located, is the presence of a large number of students. As anyone who has lived or worked in a university town will know, students often contribute considerably to the sense of place in the destination. Yet to date this topic has received little attention in the academic literature, although a recent study of university students in Melbourne found some evidence of the importance of cultural production associated with students in creating a sense of place in and around a university quarter (Shaw and Fincher 2010).

Whilst the dispersal of student activity away from the immediate environs of the campus or university precinct can create benefit in terms of developing a sense of place for a destination, at the same time it can also increase potential conflict between the students and the host population. This is particularly the case with international students who are demonstrably, by their visual appearance, culturally different from the host community (Krahe *et al.* 2005).

More research is required on the ways in which university quarters and the surrounding student areas are perceived by tourists, particularly those who are not otherwise associated with the university. This is particularly important given experience in China, for example, where increasing public access to university campuses by tourists, including families of prospective tourists, are creating such levels of disturbance that the sense of place and atmosphere desired by students and faculty is being lost. For instance, the level of disturbance associated with tourist activity on campus at Peking University has led to a total ban on tours as well as a restriction on other public access (*China Daily* 2006).

The findings of such work would greatly assist in identifying strategies for avoiding possible clashes between campus user groups, but also would help to confirm how access to university quarters could help bridge any 'place brand satisfaction gap' in university towns.

## Representation of universities in popular culture

At times it is not the heritage of the university itself that directly attracts tourists, but the association that a particular building or campus may have with popular movies or TV shows. For instance, Princeton University reported a significant increase in demand for its guided tours by people attracted to the campus because the movie *A Beautiful Mind* was filmed there (Cooper 2002). Similar benefits have been seen around some of the Oxford colleges where the long-running TV detective series *Inspector Morse* was shot, and where, more recently, the Hollywood movie *The Golden Compass* was filmed. The potential impact of that single movie alone was estimated by the city's tourism bureau as being in the region of 1 million additional visitors and £15 million in visitor spend (Hamilton 2007), with part of the city's appeal as a destination being the university and college buildings featured in the movie.

Again, turning to the model prepared by Govers and Go (2009), this immediately demonstrates how some parts of the university estate in a destination feed into the creation of what they term the 'vicarious place experience' through its commodification by popular culture. However, there is a potential risk of trespass and even conflict if tourists are not able to access some of the locations or views made famous in the movie that attracted them to the destination in the first place. This problem can be exacerbated when the location presented in the movie or TV show is in fact somewhere else. For instance, despite being set at Harvard University in Boston, Massachusetts, most of the scenes in the Reese Witherspoon movie *Legally Blonde* were shot at the University of Southern California (USC 2009), and the famous Great Court Run depicted in the 1981 movie *Chariots of Fire*, supposed to take place at Trinity College, Cambridge, was in fact shot at Eton College. Thus the mis-representation of university places and spaces in popular culture could in fact create conflict with DMOs seeking to build a coherent place identity based around product, image and place experience, again contributing to the 'place brand performance gap'.

## Concluding comments

The development of place identity is crucial to successful destination marketing and, as has been shown above, universities around the world are well placed to contribute to this by offering products and by projecting images of the destination to a wide range of audiences and markets. Yet there remains, in many areas, the potential for conflict between the day-to-day life of the university and the broader aspirations to develop tourism in the destination. As far as can be established, to date only the College of William and Mary in Virginia, USA, has prepared its own tourism strategy (College of William and Mary 2011). It is hoped that the opportunities and the challenges identified in this paper will encourage many more to follow suit and, in doing so, work alongside DMOs in trying to reduce the gaps between the place brand, the product offer and the visitor experience.

## References

Anholt, S. (2005) *Brand New Practice: How Branding Places and Products Can Help the Developing World*, Oxford: Butterworth-Heinemann.
——(2007) *Competitive Identity: The New Brand Management for Nations, Cities and Regions*, Basingstoke: Palgrave Macmillan.
Baade, R.A., Baumann, R.W. and Matheson, V.A. (2008) 'Assessing the Economic Impact of College Football Games on Local Economies', *Journal of Sports Economics* 9(6): 628–43.
——(2011) 'Big Men on Campus: Estimating the Economic Impact of College Sports on Local Economies', *Regional Studies* 45(3): 371–80.

Butler, R.W. (2006) 'The Concept of a Tourist Area Cycle of Evolution: Implications for Management of Resources', in Butler, R.W. (ed.) *The Tourism Area Life Cycle Vol.1: Applications and Modifications*, Clevedon: Channel View Publications, 3–12.

*China Daily* (2006) Peking University Bans Campus Tourism, www.chinadaily.com.cn/china/2006–7/25/content_648334.htm (accessed 14 February 2012).

College of William and Mary (2011) *Tourism Task Force Final Report*, Williamsburg, VA: College of William and Mary.

Connell, J. (1996) 'A Report of Tourism on University Campus Sites', *Tourism Management* 17(7): 541–50.

——(2000) 'The Role of Tourism in the Socially Responsible University', *Current Issues in Tourism* 3(1): 1–19.

Cooper, S. (2002) 'Campus Tourism Increases as Spectators Flock to Film Sites', *Daily Princetonian*, 2 April 2002, www.dailyprincetonian.com/2002/04/02/4764/ (accessed 14 February 2012).

Gibson, H., Willming, C. and Holdnak, A. (2003) 'Small-scale Event Sport Tourism: Fans as Tourists', *Tourism Management* 24(2): 181–90.

Govers, G. and Go, F. (2009) *Place Branding: Glocal, Virtual and Physical Identities, Constructed, Imagined and Experienced*, Basingstoke: Palgrave Macmillan.

Hamilton, G. (2007) 'Tourists to Flock to Lyra's Oxford', www.oxfordmail.co.uk/news/1870455.tourists_to_flock_to_lyras_oxford/ (accessed 14 February 2012).

Hammond, A., Berry, I., Conkelton, S., Corwin, S., Franks, P., Hart, K., Lynch-McWhite, W., Reeve, C. and Stomberg, J. (2006) 'The Role of the University Art Museum and Gallery', *Art Journal* 65(3): 20–39.

Herreman, Y. (2000) 'University and Museum in Mexico: A Historical Partnership', *Museum International* 52(2): 33–38.

Kinoshita, T. and Yasui, R. (2000) 'University Museums in Japan: A Time of Transition', *Museum International* 52(3): 27–31.

Kozak, Z.R. (2007) *Promoting the Past, Preserving the Future: British University Heritage Collections and Identity Marketing*, PhD thesis, St Andrews: University of St Andrews.

Krahe, B., Abraham, C., Felber, J. and Helbig, M.K. (2005) 'Perceived Discrimination of International Visitors to Universities in Germany and the UK', *British Journal of Psychology* 96: 263–81.

Labrador, A.P. (2000) 'Educating the Muses: University Collections and Museums in the Philippines', *Museum International* 52(3): 4–9.

Mack, V. and Llewellyn, R. (2000) 'Australian University Museums and the Internet', *Museum International* 52(2): 19–24.

Ming, L. (2007) Research in Campus Tourism: Actuality, Problems and Advice – A Literature Review of 10 Years Research in Campus Tourism in China, DOI: CNKI:SUN:ZTKB.0.2007-06-030 (accessed 8 April 2012).

Shaw, K. and Fincher, R. (2010) 'University Students and the "Creative City"', *Journal of Policy Research in Tourism, Leisure and Events* 2(3): 199–220.

Stanbury, P. (2000) 'University Museums and Collections', *Museum International* 52(2): 4–9.

USC (2009) Campus Filming Office, www.usc.edu/pr/filming/usc_in_film/films.html (accessed 14 February 2012).

# 35

# Cultural heritage resources of traditional agricultural landscapes, inspired by Chinese experiences

*Myriam Jansen-Verbeke, Yehong Sun and Qingwen Min*

## Can traditional agricultural landscapes and habitats survive the twenty-first century?

An increasing concern about 'keeping traditions alive' and a growing interest in 'using the past to built a better future' is more than a nostalgic movement or a search to redefine cultural identities in a globalising world (Friedman 2008). Creating more awareness about the irreversible process of disappearing 'values' has recently become an important objective of academic research, conservation policies and spatial planning. However, values are mental constructs, changing over time and historically rooted in variable geographical and ethnic contexts. 'Universal values' and 'collective values' tend to be widely questioned, whereas more consensus is possible in identifying and mapping local and individual values. There even is a possible controversy between global values and their projection on the local level (George *et al.* 2009).

This might explain why top-down approaches to heritage preservation in regional tourism development are neither applicable nor effective in specific local conditions. When assessing the 'heritage' value of agricultural landscapes, territories and communities, the emphasis is on the generic cohesion between natural and environmental resources, geomorphology, biodiversity, production systems and the rural habitat of local farmers. Historic, unique agricultural systems are the result of a continued inter–generational transfer of knowledge, but seem to be doomed to disappear in many parts of the world. The cumulative and interconnected pressure of urbanisation, industrialisation, globalisation of living standards, intensified mobility and, last but not least, the power of agribusiness induce important mutations in traditional agricultural landscapes (Guibert and Jean 2011).

The high risk of irreversible destruction of unique and vulnerable landscapes and their territorial, physical, cultural and social capital has motivated the United Nations Food and Agricultural Organization (FAO), the UN Educational, Scientific and Cultural Organization (UNESCO) and the UN World Tourism Organization (UNWTO) to launch awareness campaigns and to develop models for 'dynamic conservation' (Min 2009). What appears to be a contradiction in terms has initiated an academic 'exploration fever' to find liveable and sustainable compromises between preventive conservation modes for 'valuable landscapes' with global forces of economic revitalisation.

## Dynamic preservation of agricultural heritage sites: why?

Powerful globalisation waves are indeed eroding the diversity of rural habitats. The most tangible and visible impact can be observed in the built environment, the villages and their infrastructure. The speed of the morphological metamorphosis seems to be related to the physical distance of the heritage landscapes and sites to the densely and highly urbanised metropolitan regions. The time-distance factor between urban and peripheral rural areas is considered to be crucial also in the persistence of a significant cultural and economic gap. The call to protect or restore traditional landscapes raises obvious questions about which historic landscapes and which heritage assets need to be preserved.

The current debate on physical and functional preservation of traditional agricultural land-scapes and communities is often approached in a fragmented way. Obviously, the implementation of preservation policies for the built heritage in rural areas cannot be dissociated from the wider context of social and economic processes, global technical innovations and above all the spatial impact of demographic trends in an increasingly mobile society. Mobility flows of people and thoughts have led to a greater uniformity in visions and expectations regarding quality of life, even about environmental aesthetics and the valorisation of traditional architecture.

Trans-disciplinary studies are required to analyse the impact of ongoing mutations in the physical environment and human habitat, to identify the vectors of change and the power of different agents (Jansen-Verbeke 2008). Arguments to sustain traditional production systems emphasise the cohesion between landscape, people and their livelihood, the importance of safeguarding biodiversity in rural territories, and the intergenerational transfer of knowledge.

The aim of this chapter is to reflect critically on the meaning of newly introduced concepts and policies, such as 'dynamic conservation', valorisation of traditional habitats and built heritage, preservation of rural ways of life and agricultural production systems and eventually the con-stitutive role of tourism (Hollingshead *et al.* 2009). How can this growing interest in rural heritage be explained? Why has the development of cultural tourism to rural areas become a priority policy and a key issue in regional planning in many countries? The driving forces behind this global trend include:

- The urbanisation and industrialisation of the countryside, typical of development in many Asian regions, and China in particular (Sun *et al.* 2008).
- Pressure on traditional agricultural production from global market forces and changing food demands, increasing the dichotomy between urban and rural areas.
- Increasing mobility and resulting orientation to urban employment poles.
- Revalorisation of the 'peaceful' countryside, as a pleasant residential setting, temporarily or permanently.

However, the question is whether this predominantly European-American trend will also affect – on a large scale – rural areas in China in the near future. Taking into account the very strong and rapid process of urbanisation in China on the one hand, long distances and mobility constraints on the other, the model of an urbanised rural countryside might not be for tomorrow. Yet, in combination with the impact of demographic and social changes, various forms of gentrification in rural villages are already appearing (Timothy 2011). The aesthetic upgrading is very visible and an ambition to create or recreate 'a sense of place' and to position landmarks is part of the 'staged authenticity model' in many places. The so-called 'conservative architecture' is the subject of an ongoing debate about authenticity, conservation versus innovation, and aesthetics versus functionality.

Changes in architectural style, size, materials and also location preferences for residences, are gradually transforming the morphology and the outlook of many a rural village. In most cases this is a market-driven development. Public buildings and public spaces, streets and squares are 'modernised' in order to meet the expectations of a qualitative living environment, reaching for a 'better life'. The visual metamorphosis of rural villages is often reinforced by important modifications in the agricultural production system and as a consequence its once prominent role in the community livestock. In rare cases it is part of a cultural government plan to protect traditional villages and eventually develop these sites as 'cultural villages' with a clear economic mission; places for a visitor centre, a small museum, souvenir shops, handicraft atelier and, of course, nostalgic places for visitors to stay, eat and drink.

The selection of iconic heritage buildings to be renovated as a landmark and to function as a visitor centre, a museum or other public function, is an important decision and the outcome of a power test between different stakeholders. In many ways this could be an incentive for more restoration policies and upgrading of the physical environment.

## Heritage assets and territorial capital

The present challenge is to identify the heritage assets that potentially support or reinforce the territorial capital and open new economic perspectives. A wide range of environmental characteristics resulting from an historical trajectory is marked by the impact of human interactions; the man-made capital refers to the built environment, the architecture of houses and complexes of public buildings. Monuments and landmarks are part of the cultural capital, as are cultural activities and events. This is actually the most vital aspect of cultural capital, grounded in traditions, folklore, handicrafts, all represented now in a contemporary version.

In fact, a lively awareness of cultural heritage in rural regions and communities in China has always been part of the local culture and traditions (see Box 35.1). More recently, external incentives for revalorisation of cultural capital became a driving force in recreating cultural identity, and hence a valuable resource for new or renewed cultural activities.

This process reinforces the development of territorial cultural capital and provides favourable incubation conditions for creating sustainable and competitive forms of cultural tourism. Preservation of built heritage, with the purpose to create an appropriate and attractive setting for a contemporary presentation and interpretation of intangible heritage, both for residents and visitors, seems to be an important drive.

Attractive images and stories about 'typical' rural villages, 'authentic' local people and their traditional way of life, are potential resources for an innovative cultural economy. A creative use of intangible heritage (folklore, music, costumes, dances, games and festivities, local arts and rural crafts …) offers real opportunities, not only in the perspective of preservation, but also in terms of finding new areas of employment.

A prime condition to safeguard the territorial heritage assets is the consensus about the values of the past for a common and better future, to be shared by local stakeholders and external agents. However, the restoration or preservation of traditional buildings and built heritage in general is but one aspect of the current process of 'heritagisation'.

The attractiveness of traditional villages as places to live and to visit is based on variable perceptions and criteria (Sun *et al.* 2011). When it comes to developing attractive places for various forms of rural cultural heritage tourism, the role of exogenous forces and decision makers needs to be assessed, in particular.

Growing competition means that the capacity to anticipate the volatile preferences of domestic and international tourism markets is a key advantage. Often expectations regarding tourism potential of a village or region are high, even when knowledge about trends in the market and tourist preferences is lacking. Local communities need guidance on how actually to benefit from the dynamics of a very competitive global tourism market. The images of attractive landscapes and 'typical' villages can be strong assets in the destination planning and marketing, but they have to be used effectively.

## Agents and stakeholders

A consensus between stakeholders about heritage preservation implies a research-based selection process. The focus tends to be on 'typical' buildings in vernacular style and traditional infrastructure with a history. A progressive re-valorisation of traditional agricultural systems and the perception of urgency regarding preservation policies are complex challenges, highly dependent on the level of knowledge and involvement of different stakeholders. Strategic visions about new uses and users of the built environment need to mature in a network of decision makers. Divergent appreciations of stakeholders accentuate the paradox between preservation policies and local development plans (Sun *et al.* 2011).

Who are the owners and guardians of the traditional houses? Who invests in their renovation? Above all, what are the selection criteria for deciding on preservation or renovation? Aesthetics, comfort, location and accessibility, iconic value and alternative uses are all important in generating additional income and effectively re-enforcing the economic capital of the community. Clearly, the dynamics of rural areas also depend on the role and the stakes of 'outsiders' in the transformation of the traditional landscape and habitat; expats, visitors, tourists, regional authorities and business companies (Guibert and Jean 2011). What are the shared visions of 'external' decision makers on the rural heritage to be 'used' for various forms of cultural activities and rural tourism?

Although there is confusion in the literature and in tourism promotion material about concepts such as rural tourism, farm tourism, ecotourism, green tourism, heritage and cultural tourism, etc., there are clear opportunities for 'traditional village tourism' in rural heritage landscapes (Timothy 2011). The ambition to generate additional income from tourism is a hidden agenda behind most investments in restoration or renovation of rural heritage. Cultural tourism attractions are being developed in different settings and in various ways. As in many rural places, basic tourism infrastructure is still lacking, as well as human, institutional and physical resources; new tourism businesses are usually bottom-up and 'spontaneous' initiatives. The priority is to increase access to natural or cultural resources for individual visitors, rather than developing specific, sustainable products or services embedded in the tourism value chain.

This initial stage of exploration and above all of 'trial and error' in the tourism market can be referred to as an 'artisanal stage of tourism'. As tourism demand increases, more emphasis is put on the production and consumption of tourism goods and services, with an eye for the quality of tourist experiences. In this stage of local tourism development, the priority is often to create adequate accommodation to meet the demand of guests; bed and breakfast accommodation, home stays or special, small-scale complexes in villages, using schools, for instance, or other public buildings. The message of the UNWTO is to keep the capacity low as long as there is no regular tourist demand, which means accepting a slow growth model. The most crucial stage is when important and often irreversible decisions for the future are taken regarding preservation and restoration of heritage buildings, vernacular architecture, location of museums, visitor centres, hotels and not least the design of public spaces and tourist facilities.

## Preservation policies in partnership with tourism strategies

The hypothesis is that preservation policies for heritage assets in traditional rural villages and unique agri-cultural landscapes can benefit from a strong partnership with the emerging cultural economy, where cultural programmes and tourism ambitions meet (Timothy 2011). This requires an integrated planning process – research based, and with participation of experts from different disciplines and local and external stakeholders. Finding the right balance in the decision-making process is probably the most difficult mission, in particular when it concerns issues that transcend the local context.

In remote, rural areas such as the south-west of China (e.g. Yunnan) where tourism opportunities have only recently entered the mind of local leaders and the mental map of tourists visiting China, strategies are still poorly developed. How can local stakeholders become shareholders in this – largely unknown – 'import business'? A major challenge is the capacity to anticipate the short- and long-term impacts of these 'new activities'.

Governments, whether at local, regional or state level, still lack the understanding and management skills to deal with important tourism issues in regions that are branded as heritage landscapes with iconic rural villages. The sectoral approach to tourism development rapidly becomes inadequate. Tourism, even at low development levels, becomes a powerful sector, infiltrating many, if not all, aspects of the local community and habitat. At this point, local and regional governments realise that policies need to proceed to more strategic considerations such as, 'how can we develop tourism as an effective instrument in building local economic social and cultural resources?'

A positive impact of tourism in rural villages implies finding ways to improve the livelihood of the local community. A top priority is creating job opportunities for younger people in the region, in tourism-related organisations, in hospitality, in commercial activities, in the creative sector of events and souvenirs, arts and crafts.

In order to realise actual improvements in human, social and economic capital, an almost technical understanding of the tourism value chain is required. So far, most analyses of 'tourism as a vector of change' are based on fragmented field surveys, more qualitative than quantitative methods, often with small and questionable samples of respondents. Structural knowledge accumulation through dispersed, explorative projects, rarely comparable and temporary snapshots, fails to simulate future scenarios in which the sovereignty of tourism is well understood (Hollingshead *et al.* 2009).

In view of dynamic preservation policies for traditional agricultural landscapes, the introduction of tourism holds real risks of unbalancing the historical cohesion in the system and irreversibly affecting the territorial capital. The physical impact of tourism on rural habitats – even with small-scale infrastructure and limited numbers of visitors – can hardly be quantified. The main reason is that identifying and measuring tourist footprints in the vulnerable eco-system in a scientific way is a complex mission. Physical changes in the built environment are the best 'measurable' indicator; space claims for tourism infrastructure, the use of public space for traffic, parking lots, signboards, waste bins, etc. New 'place-images' are created. The metamorphosis is not only visible in the landscape but also in the mindset of the local population. Rather briskly they become aware of an alternative to their hard labour in the fields. An open window on the 'outside' world is undeniably colouring the life expectations of the younger generation in a pertinent way.

Many negative impacts of tourism can be anticipated, avoided or reduced through an intelligent visitor-management policy, translated into practical guidelines in the field. Keeping within limits of acceptable change is the task of authorities, local and regional, who have the tools to monitor carrying capacity and to develop adapted policies for a small-scale tourism development in the rural villages. The introduction of a monitoring system and the appointment of 'local stewards' can be effective, and also means job creation for younger people. This example confirms again the strong interdependency of territorial heritage resources and the economic capital of the region.

## Two examples in Chinese rural areas

Rural China is changing and the policy of 'Building the New Socialist Countryside (BNSC)', launched in 2005 (the 11th 'five-year plan') speeded up the process of change. The good intentions of the BNSC policy are obvious; the objective is to improve the countryside environment and the livelihood of the farmers. However, negative side effects include the destruction of the special traditions of rural areas, especially the traditional buildings. Even though the heritage preservation policy in China is pretty strict, not every valuable element could be included yet, especially in rural areas. Many heritage sites are damaged in the rapid process of modernisation and urbanisation. Some traditional buildings have survived because they are closely connected to the daily life of people. The value of some traditional buildings is not fully realised, however, and the owners have no qualms about destroying them.

Two typical examples were selected to explain the preservation of built heritage in rural areas – one in Zhejiang Province, south-east China, and another in Guizhou Province, southwest China. Architectural heritage is one of the most important assets in traditional agricultural landscapes and sites, but is in fact increasingly threatened by modern society progress. Research indicates that architectural heritage that is well integrated in the life of local people is more easily preserved, whereas architectural heritage that is less connected with community life is threatened by many outside factors.

The two examples cannot cover the wide spectrum of rural landscapes in China, but only illustrate specific issues of the ongoing deals or compromises between preservation policies and tourism development models.

---

### Box 35.1 Case study: traditional houses in Longxian village

Longxian village is a traditional village located in Qingtian County, Zhejiang Province (south-east China). With the long history, extraordinary rice-fish farming systems and landscapes, it was selected as a pilot site in the Globally Important Agricultural Heritage Systems (GIAHS) project in 2005. The rice-fish farming system in Longxian village demonstrates an ingenious approach to generating ecological, economic and social benefits through encouraging essential ecological functions, and also provides rich resources to be valorised for tourism development, e.g. traditional landscapes, traditional knowledge, music, architecture, performances, folklore, etc. (Sun *et al.* 2010, 2011). This case study was carried out in the context of a PhD project (Sun *et al.* 2010).

The village has become an icon in the current debate on GIAHS about balancing preservation and renovation. Global forces such as urbanisation of the countryside, changing living standards and demographic processes are rapidly changing rural landscapes in China and the role of tourism as an agent of local preservation can be questioned. Since 2005, over 80 per cent of the traditional houses in Longxian village have been replaced by new buildings, and most of them are totally rebuilt.

This transformation in a small mountainous village in south-east China, with 188 farm households registered in local government statistics, is rather surprising but can be explained by the overseas Chinese history. Even though the rice-fish culture in this village was listed as the first GIAHS site in 2005, the conservation plan did not stop the drive of the villagers to build new houses. In fact, as the programme of GIAHS pays more attention to the preservation of biodiversity and agricultural landscape, new buildings were actually allowed. Moreover, villagers are very proud of their newly built, multi-storey houses.

Most of the traditional buildings in Longxian village are very old and vulnerable; the wooden-structured houses can very easily catch fire, and indoor equipment is inadequate for today's way of life. Since renovation is difficult and expensive, most villagers chose to rebuild.

This dilemma also applies to most of the wooden houses in Xiaohuang village. Several years ago a big fire destroyed most of the houses there, and now villagers rebuild their houses with stone and cement, while preserving the outside look of wooden structures. This also is the case with the houses of ethnic groups in Yunnan Province, for example the mushroom house of Hani ethnic groups in Honghe Prefecture. In fact, this applies to most wooden-structured houses in China.

*Figure 35.1* Iconic old house in Longxian village

There is a remarkable, iconic house in Longxian village, not fully wooden structured, and with a long history. Yang Minkang, a farmer born in the village, and his wife are running the place as a restaurant and farm stay for tourists. Today, it is very popular with tourists, who love to have their meals there. The owner is not just making a good living, but has considerably improved his economic situation by developing a business selling dried gold fish, a successful tourist product. The question is whether this one success story is representative of the new perspective of rural village areas in China.

## Box 35.2 Case study: drum tower in Xiaohuang village

These cultural landmarks to be found in Congjiang County villages, can be considered a good example of an endemic conservation policy, which means closely linked with people's daily life.

In Xiaohuang village (Congjiang County, Guizhou Province), also a GIAHS site because of the rice-fish-duck agricultural system, the traditional wooden drum tower is a symbol of the Dong people living here (see Figure 35.2). Every Dong village has its own drum tower, even today. Originally the drum tower was used for important events and worship ceremonies in the village. Today the function has not changed very much, but has become more spiritual. The layout of the village is based on the location of the drum tower. According to legend, the drum towers have been present for as long as the Dong people have been there. Documents prove the over 300-year history of the drum towers. People cannot live without their drum towers, as the towers are connected to their lives. Hence they decorate the drum towers with paintings of their food, their lives, and their big festivals and performances inside the towers.

*Figure 35.2* Drum tower in Xiaohuang village

There are currently more than 100 drum towers in the whole of Congjiang County, and three in Xiaohuang village alone. People love their drum towers and they conserve them as if their lives depended on it, although some young people are starting to forget the original meaning of the towers. From this example, we could conclude that the strong symbolic value for the local community guarantees a preservation concern, although the 'heritage site' might be used in changing ways.

## Paradoxes and challenges

In many places in the world, the ambition to 'recreate' landscapes of the past as carriers of heritage tourism today needs to be questioned seriously. A better understanding of key concepts such as 'dynamic conservation', 'preservation of heritage landscapes and villages', and the importance of 'territorial capital' is essential.

Most plans for local development in rural areas refer – in a rather naive way – to tourism as 'the goose that lays the golden eggs'. There are three major traps: first of all, the false expectations about the impact of investment in local tourism on the actual cultural and economic capital of the rural community; second, the lack of expertise to connect strategically with key actors in the tourism value chain. Knowing about the comparative advantages of the site, the richness and the vulnerability of the territorial heritage assets is a primary condition to enter the competitive tourism market.

Last but not least, the capacity of stakeholders and decision makers to anticipate the impact of 'heritagisation' and 'tourismification' in their region or place. Is the local community aware of the impact of the gentrification process in their rural traditional habitat? What are the views of residents on tourism improving the quality of their daily life?

At this stage, when rural heritage sites (local and regional authorities) in China develop ambitions to enter the tourism market, there are yet so many unknown variables to make realistic prognoses. Sharing some crucial questions with a wider forum can help to sharpen the perspectives and draw a research agenda to support policy making.

For instance, are local farmers and their families qualified and motivated stewards for safeguarding the territorial heritage? An important step is a public debate on environmental preservation methods in view of making the village more attractive for tourists: a place to visit, a place to stay, a place to spend money.

The most important challenge remains to find the best-fit methodological framework to understand local development conditions and tourism systems and act upon them. Preservation of cultural heritage is but one of the projects closely linked to tourism planning and creating 'images for the future'.

## Acknowledgements

This study was supported by the project Visiting Professorships for Senior International Scientists of the Chinese Academy of Sciences (CAS)-2010TZ21, and project FAO-GEF/GIAHS(GCP/ GLO/212/GEF).

We kindly acknowledge the support from the Institute of Geographic Sciences and Natural Resources Research (IGSNRR), CAS and the hard work of the GIAHS project group.

## References

Friedman, T. (2008) *Hot, Flat, and Crowded; Why the World Needs a Green Revolution – and How we Can Renew Our Global Future*, New York: Penguin.

George, E.W., Mair, H., Reid, D.G. (2009) *Rural Tourism Development: Localism and Cultural Change*, Clevedon: Channel View Publications.

Guibert, M. and Jean, Y. (eds) (2011) *Dynamiques des espaces ruraux dans le monde*, Paris: Armand Collin.

Hollingshead, K., Ateljevic, I. and Ali, N. (2009) 'World Making Agency, World Making Authority: The Sovereign Constitutive Role of Tourism', *Tourism Geographies* 11(4): 427–43.

Jansen-Verbeke, M. (2008) 'Cultural Landscapes and Tourism Dynamics: Explorative Case Studies', in Jansen-Verbeke, M., Priestley, G.K. and Russo, A.P. (eds) *Cultural Resources for Tourism*, New York: Nova Science, 125–44.

——(2009) 'The Territoriality Paradigm in Cultural Tourism', *Turyzm/Tourism* 19(1/2): 27–33.

Min, Q. (ed.) (2009) *Dynamic Conservation and Adaptive Management of China's GIAHS Theories and Practices*, Beijing: China Environmental Press.

Sun, Y., Chen, T. and Zhang, M. (2008) 'Sustainable Tourism Development Management of Local Cultural Landscapes', *Chinese Journal of Population, Resources and Environment* 6(2): 74–79.

Sun, Y., Jansen-Verbeke, M., Min, Q.W. and Cheng, S.K. (2011) 'Tourism Potential of Agricultural Heritage Systems', *Tourism Geographies* 13(1): 112–28.

Sun, Y., Min, Q.W., Cheng, S.K., Zhong, L.S. and Qi, X. (2010) 'Study on the Tourism Resource Characteristics of Agricultural Heritage Systems', *Tourism Tribune* 25(10): 57–62.

Timothy, D.J. (2011) *Cultural Heritage and Tourism: An Introduction*, Clevedon: Channel View Publications.

# 36

# Special interest cultural tourism products

## The case of Gyimes in Transylvania

*Lóránt Dávid, Bulcsú Remenyik and Béla Zsolt Gergely*

## Introduction

Gyimes is one of the few micro-regions of the Carpathian Basin that has a truly unique character. Here, traditional homestead farming and rural lifestyle support a distinctively rich folklore that has been passed down from generation to generation in its most intact form due to the isolation of this peripherally located and inherently secluded region. Given its abundance of natural and cultural resources, this territory could be a rightful contender for the United Nations Educational, Scientific and Cultural Organization's (UNESCO) much-acclaimed World Heritage list. Zoltán Ilyés dubbed it the Folklore Museum of Szeklerland. A fairly large volume of inbound tourist traffic to Romania is made up by visitors from Hungary – 39.4 per cent in 2008 (Dávid and Bujdosó 2009). In 2000 the number of tourists from Hungary was 1.2 million. By 2004 this had increased to 2.6 million, only to see a sharp decline in following years – 1.5 million in 2005 and 1.3 million in 2006 (Institutul National de Statistica 2007). These numbers clearly indicate that besides ethnic tourism, other products need to be developed in order to stop the downward trend in guest traffic.

New products have emerged, such as heritage tourism, religious tourism, thanatourism and gastro-tourism. By 2007 tourist flows started to grow, with the inbound tourist volume rising to 1.7 million, and tourism continued to grow to 1.9 million in 2008 and reached 2.1 million in 2009 (Institutul National de Statistica 2010).

## Competitiveness and product development

The Gyimes area is a little-known destination, but full of potential; development of competitive tourism products could result in an increased number of guests. As tourism of Gyimes is in its developmental stage, it does not offer a diversified tourism experience compared to its competitors in the area. At this point, Gyimes would like to get on the map of international tourism destinations; however, this cannot be done with commercial, mainstream tourism products. It should target a specialist, niche market with attractive and innovative products that stand out from the crowd of tourism products.

Locally conducted in-depth interviews revealed that difficulties in accessibility and weather conditions pose problems. The mountainous depressions of the region have a cool, wet climate (further affected by wind), therefore the high season is restricted to the summer months. Development of a full-blown tourism sector is further hindered by rudimentary research and development and a lack of effective visitor and destination management, as well as marketing.

## Development of competitive tourism products

### Ethnic tourism

Numerous definitions of ethnic tourism have been proposed by various authors, but one of the first definitions is attributed to Smith (1978), who used the term as tourism 'marketed to the public in terms of "quaint" customs of indigenous and often exotic peoples'. Essentially, people engaging in ethnic tourism are travelling for the purpose of observing the cultural expressions and lifestyles of truly exotic people and shopping for primitive wares and crafts. Dearden and Harron (1992: 84) defined ethnic tourism as travel 'motivated primarily by the search for first hand, authentic and sometimes intimate contact with people whose ethnic and/or cultural background is different from the tourist's'.

In a Central and Eastern European context, ethnic tourism applies to travel motivated by ethnic reunion – members of an ethnic group exploring their ethnicity in other locations. In the case of Gyimes, ethnic tourism would be exemplified by travellers with a Hungarian or Szekler background tracing their ancestry in Transylvania. The difference between the international and

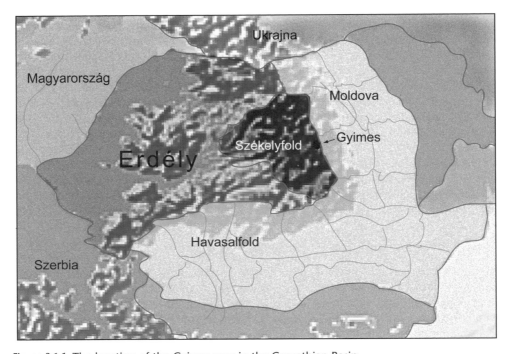

*Figure 36.1* The location of the Gyimes area in the Carpathian Basin

Central and Eastern European definitions derive from the different interpretations of the terms 'ethnic group' and 'nation', as the development of this tourism product has been induced by different historic processes. For the most part, ethnic tourism to the Gyimes area means the flow of tourists between two areas inhabited by populations that share a common ethnic background and identity (Horváth 2010).

Ethnic tourism is a fast-growing sector of the tourism industry worldwide, present on all continents (albeit in different forms). Its appearance started with the neocolonial era in the nineteenth century, when millions of Europeans chose emigration in the hope of a better life.

The development of ethnic tourism is most significant in America, Australia and Europe. Certain differences in ethnic tourism development on these continents should be pointed out. In the case of America and Australia the proportion of ethnic tourists and nostalgia tourists is relatively the same, whereas in the case of Europe ethnic tourism is characterised by a large number of nostalgia tourists. Nostalgia tourists visiting Western Europe come mainly from South-East Europe, countries of the Islamic world (Turkey, Arab countries) and Africa. Their mass immigration to Western Europe started in as early as the 1960s, but to this day their trips back home for vacationing or religious holidays are clearly traceable through border crossing statistics. Various diaspora communities maintain strong ties with their homeland and try to preserve their socio-cultural and religious identity; children in such communities are brought up with values that are rooted in their distinct history, culture, language, religion and way of life. Nevertheless, younger generations tend to loosen the ties with their ancestral homelands and become 'proper' tourists rather than nostalgia tourists (Ilyés 2007).

In the case of Szeklerland the premises that led to the emergence and development of ethnic tourism are rather particular. This territory was part of the Hungarian kingdom for 1,000 years, with somewhat autonomous governance (székely székek). A homogenous ethno-cultural area was established here, severed from Hungary and adjoined to Romania through the peace treaties of Trianon (1920) and Paris (1947). The Szekler community's efforts to preserve its ethnic identity through aspirations to autonomy and self-governance were at first welcomed by the Romanian government, but later during the dictatorial leadership of Nicolae Ceauşescu (1965–89) their civil liberties and basic human rights were curtailed and a hard-line assimilation policy was instituted against them. Endangerment of ethno-cultural identity of Transylvanian Hungarians in general, and that of the Szekler community in particular played an especially important role in the emergence of ethnic tourism in the region. As a reaction to discrimination and assimilation policies enforced against the Hungarian minority in Romania, the ties between Hungary and the minority community strengthened. As this unity between the two communities grew ever-stronger, it also accounted for the rapid growth of ethnic tourism in the region. The discriminative policies of the 1990s increased the number of Hungarians travelling to Romania. Autonomous aspirations were renewed with the aim of achieving ethno-cultural autonomy. The mid-2000s saw a decrease in the number of ethnic tourists, possibly tied to the outcome of the referendum on dual citizenship for ethnic Hungarians living in the adjacent states held on 5 December 2004, which was invalid due to low turnout (Horváth 2010). In 2010 the passage of the Act on Hungarian Nationality, which stipulates that naturalisation can be offered to a non-Hungarian citizen whose ascendant was a Hungarian citizen or whose origin from Hungary is probable, and whose Hungarian language knowledge is proved, will, it is hoped, have a positive impact on the growth of ethnic tourism.

An important question still remains: how did the Csík Depression (Ciuc Depression) and the Gyimes area become the beacon for this kind of tourism product? National history and geography education in Hungary places a marked emphasis on the kingdom of Hungary and the important role played by Hungarians in the Carpathian Basin. The geographical area of this study, Gyimes, lies deep within Romanian territory, far from the borders of today's Hungary, yet it is considered an important ethno-cultural area where memories of the 'Great Hungarian Past' are still vivid, and the population shares a common Hungarian ancestry, a common heritage of language and traditions, including food preferences, and a common religious faith. The area gives us a genuine picture of what life used to be in pre-industrialised 'rural Hungary' and cannot be studied in this form anywhere else.

Ethnic tourists in the region can be divided into the following groups:

- The patriotic, nationalistic, sentimental, heavy historic tradition and cultural memory-seeking tourist, whose interests include purchasing memorabilia related to 'Great Hungary'.
- There is a large number of families or their descendants returning to their Transylvanian homeland after emigrating to Hungary (nostalgia tourism), in a quest for their relatives and friends (genealogy/roots tourism).
- There is an important number of tourists travelling to the area via travel agency packages 'Transylvania tours'. They come for the rich history, folklore and gastronomy of this unique ethno-cultural region.
- The rising number of religious tourists is also another important movement as far as national unity is concerned; the vast majority of Szeklers are of Roman Catholic faith and their holy places are destinations that attract lots of visitors.
- There is an increasing amount of educational co-operation with Hungary, which results in a significant number of exchange students visiting as youth tourists.
- The growing economic ties with Hungary lead to an increasing number of people engaging in business tourism.

The decrease in tourist numbers in 2005 made it clear to all actors that tourism-based economic development cannot be solely based on ethnic tourism. In the 1990s the shortage of accommodation presented a real problem – tourists found board at private residences. From the mid-2000s Romania was eligible for Instrument for Pre-Accession (IPA) funds from the European Union (EU), which contributed to development of accommodation in Szeklerland. In order to increase the number of tourists there was a need to develop ancillary tourism products that could be linked to ethnic tourism – religious tourism, thanatourism, gastro-tourism. With Romania slated to become a member state of the Schengen Area and with the right to vote granted to Hungarian minority members holding dual citizenship, the whole dynamics of ethnic tourism is poised to change.

When developing special tourism products, it is very important to keep in mind that the main goal is to increase the number of tourists. In light of this it would be advisable to involve actors from the Romanian speaking community in the development process as well.

## Nostalgia tourism

According to international studies nostalgia tourists can be differentiated along the lines of their motivation to use their vacation to revisit a specific country or city with a sentimental association to their lives. Some international nostalgia tourism developed on account of migrant populations, which undertook their migration for different reasons: economics, politics or education (Fendl 1998). A poll of 500 people conducted by Expedia (expedia.co.uk) and Adrian Furnham, a senior professor of psychology at University College London revealed that more than one-quarter (27.7 per cent) went back to a destination where they had a memorable childhood vacation, while more than one-fifth (21.5 per cent) went to where they lived or studied in their younger years. This indicates that most nostalgia tourists are driven by a desire to relive their youth.

As the research shows, despite the potential for disappointment, two-thirds (66 per cent) had a positive experience revisiting a sentimental destination. Almost 9 out of 10 (88 per cent) had such a good time that they intended to go back for a third time.

In Hungary, nostalgia tourism developed under specific circumstances and therefore we are observing a specific type of nostalgia tourism in connection to Gyimes – it is a cultural exercise, a memory-fortification work, a series of activities undertaken to come to terms with the loss of the homeland, a mourning of sorts (Ilyés 2007). People engaging in 'homesick tourism' to Gyimes are primarily Csángós and Szeklers, who have been separated from their homeland. One of the reasons for their visit is to collect relics devoted to their bygone past (religious symbols mostly) and to use them as sanctified objects on their return. These 'icons' to their deceased world, although seldom of great material value, become priceless for their sentimental value and facilitate integration in the new world. Clinging to memories of the homeland and a heightened Hungarian nationalism are characteristic features of this type of homesick tourism.

Symbols of memory can be easily infused with religious significance. As Elisabeth Fendl (1998) observes, there is a close relationship between 'homesick tourism' and pilgrimages: returning to the lost homeland is a pilgrimage undertaken to visit religious shrines of the old country or other formerly unimportant sites (intimate corners, streets, houses of relatives, acquaintances), which become vested with 'religious' meaning. These pilgrimages, along with their religious purpose, offer a chance to meet relatives and acquaintances again, to feel good in the midst of like-minded people, to document this belonging together and to find a sense of rootedness.

Most of the visits are generated by journeys to the old country's cultural and natural attractions. Group city sightseeing can render new experiences for most tourists as they – partly due to their age or rural lifestyle – could not see the attractions of the homeland; in this capacity they are considered tourists in the classic meaning of the term (Ilyés 2007). Roman Catholic Church groups from Hungary return frequently to visit their homeland's famous pilgrimage sites. As part of the journey members of the group individually visit their ancestral villages and parental houses.

The Gyimes historic cultural landscape includes the anthropogenic morphological elements, characteristic land-use patterns and built environments and settlement structure. This region lags behind as far as social mobility and economic innovation are concerned, but sports tremendous value from the point of view of cultural landscape diversity – it is unique in the whole Hungarian language area.

Protection of the Gyimes historic cultural landscape is guaranteed, but an inscription in UNESCO's list of World Heritage sites would greatly contribute not only to the protection, but also to the development of these values. The establishment of an ethnic theme park with nature trails or 'explorable backroads' with the active collaboration of the locals is imperative. Within the framework of such a park, visitors could sample the rural lifestyle through tours of traditional farmsteads (barn, shepherd's hut), to watch farmers at work (animal farming, dairy production, horse-drawn ploughing, haymaking and logging), or tours that explore small villages and everyday Csángó life, remnants of the old border control system, sacred religious sites and rituals, with insights into how Csángó families practise their religion.

## Genealogy tourism

Genealogy tourism, also known as 'ancestry' and 'roots' tourism, is one such product that falls under the umbrella of culture and heritage tourism, and is travel aimed at visiting birthplaces of one's ancestors and getting acquainted with distant relatives. It is generally considered as a viable option for tourism product diversification (Csapó and Matesz 2007).

As far back as the nineteenth century a significant number of people left the Gyimes area and emigrated to North America. In the twentieth century (especially during the dictatorship of Ceauşescu), due to a decline of the living conditions and oppressive policy directed against ethnic Hungarians, a significant wave of migration fled to Hungary and other Central or Western European countries.

Roots tourism aims to organise the 'homecoming' of the uprooted Csángós and their descendants and to facilitate the rekindling of ties with long-lost family, relatives, friends or church. If there is a need for it, room and board can be provided in circumstances that bear the closest possible resemblance to the natural, human and spiritual environment of old times (Dávid and Bujdosó 2009). The main feature of the programme would be to recreate a nostalgic experience that would compensate for the lack of infrastructural amenities. Developing new genealogy/roots tourism products is not without challenges. A number of issues must be addressed before the full potential of roots tourism can be exploited. Local actors in the private tourism sector must recognise the potential of the roots tourism market. A suite of micro-products will need to be developed, including a fully computerised genealogical service and a network of supporting institutions to develop and sustain the product. This network should include a library and digitised archives with civil records of births, marriages and deaths to support genealogy tourism initiatives and, as far-fetched as it may seem, cutting-edge investigative resources such as laboratories that are able to perform DNA testing.

In the Gyimes area, roots tourism is extremely important to the local Csángós. The Csángó community of Gyimes as an ethnic group entered the limelight following the publication of a three-act play entitled *Wildflower of Gyimes* by playwright Istvan Geczy in 1897. The play became a favourite with small-town drama groups and was turned into a major feature film in 1939 under the guidance of Ákos Ráthonyi. The research of folksongs and folkdances, legends and archaic prayers made Gyimes the favourite micro-region of the Hungarian intelligentsia (Szilágyi 2007).

When travelling to Gyimes, Szeklers and Csángós are not only partaking in roots tourism, but they are engaging in cultural tourism as well – they visit the attractions that once symbolised their culture. Gyimes underwent a spate of cultural tangible and intangible heritage development once Romania became a member state of the EU. The main attraction for people wanting to explore this unique culture is the traditions and lifestyle of the Csángós living in the Tatros valley. The multi-cultural milieu that emerged here (Szekler, Hungarian, Csángó and Romanian), the outstandingly rich ancient folk poetry and the wide range of folk-dancing traditions all add to the colourful palette of attractive elements. According to the accounts of the Csángós of Gyimes, their ancestors fled to this wooded area to avoid conscription, and this tale dovetails into the etymology of their name as well: a *csángó* (wanderer) is someone who wandered away from their original community (Posch 2010). The Csángós explain their traditional folk garments with the fact that they were on the run – they dressed like the Moldavian Csángós so that nobody could see the deserter Szekler soldiers in them (Tankó 2008).

The Roman Catholic Church – protector and facilitator of the Hungarian culture in the region – plays a significant role in the establishment of genealogy tourism. Genealogy tourists seek their religious roots as well. Religious tourism here has taken off since the mid-1990s, but its development as a tourism product has only seen a breakthrough in the last few years. Development of the Saint Mary's Trail (Via Mariae) pilgrimage route and the increasingly important role played by Csíksomlyó (Şumuleu Ciuc) led to a growing number of religious visitors to Gyimes. There are quite a few religious tourism attractions in the region including the Holy Spirit Chapel, a favourite of pilgrims, the grand churches of Gyimesközéplok, Gyimesbükk and the church of Kontumác. In an effort to boost religious tourism it would make sense for local actors to revive the Feast of Saint Mary Magdalene Pilgrimage, which formerly rivalled the Pilgrimage of Csíksomlyó, attended by people from all over the Csík Depression.

Covering approximately 1,400 kilometres (about 1,000 miles) the Via Mariae runs along centuries-old pilgrimage trails and trading routes through Central Europe. The Via Mariae is a spiritual- and cultural-themed pilgrims' trail that for most of its length winds its way through scenic natural landscape. The route links close to 60 pilgrimage sites, some smaller, some larger, some important churches, and other religious establishments. The east–west axis of the route runs from Mariazell (Austria) to Csíksomlyó (Transylvania, Romania), via Budapest and Mariapócs in Hungary. Plans to include a north–south route that runs from Częstochowa (Poland) to Mdjugorje (Bosnia Herzegovina), via Esztergom, Budapest and Máriagyűd (Hungary) have been drawn up. These envisage a number of adjacent trails branching off the main route; the major setback is that the attractions are located far from each other. The Association of Via Mariae strives to provide pilgrims with a spiritual experience by including these treasures in the trail. Most of the trail has been marked; accommodation choices have been included in the pilgrim's guide. The association has created an online presence through the website http//mariaut.hu, which provides information and social-networking opportunities. They created an image, a sign system, and they involved local groups to carry out the logistics. Site visits, dry runs, placement of signs and their inclusion on tourist maps are ongoing. The association is in the process of building partnerships with all the stakeholders located along the route: dioceses, forestry authorities, local government and national park directorates. In Austria and Transylvania stakeholder organisations are working on networking and the preparation of cross-border co-operation grant proposals. Funding is raised mostly through private donations and membership fees, as well as through sales of religious books and memorabilia.

## Thanatourism

Thanatourism is an umbrella term for what is often identified as dark tourism, including trauma and disaster tourism, as well as other acts of travel to sites with a history of suffering and violent death. Seaton (2004) describes the phenomenon of thanatourism as 'travel to a location wholly or partially motivated by the desire for actual or symbolic encounters with death, particularly, but not exclusively, violent death'. In their search for the macabre, thanatourists are drawn to 'traumascapes' or attractions that range from sites of assassinations to those where natural disasters occurred (disaster tourism), from war memorials to concentration camp sites; travel to events that create an environment for catharsis, reflection and redemption, such as commemorations or even battle re-enactments also account for thanatourism (Pusztai 2006, see also Werdler, this volume).

Traumascapes of the Gyimes area include a Second World War battle site, the so-called Árpád defence line and several monuments erected in the memory of the fallen heroes (for example, the Soviet soldier war memorial in the woods of Gyimesbükk). Accommodated within the field of heritage tourism, battlefield tourism and guided tours of battle theatres with narratives intended to evoke the spirit of the epoch are becoming increasingly popular. Therefore, various organisations in Gyimes and concerned individuals who have a vested interest in promoting awareness, education and history should undertake the development of these sites (Dávid et al. 2007). Initiatives to commercialise similar trauma and battlefield tourism sites in an effort to attract tourists are being undergone all over Europe, from Italy to Poland, and Gyimes should not be left out. Renovation and proper development of the network of bunkers and fortifications of the Árpád line could add some actual Second World War history value to these structures and facilitate the creation of themed tours. The Árpád line was part of a defence system of reinforced concrete fortifications, bunkers, pillboxes, machine-gun posts, armour-piercing artillery casemates, anti-tank obstacles (concrete cones and pyramids), and wicker-lined trenches built between 1941 and 1944 to serve as a valley-blockade fortification system (Ilyés 2007).

Thanatourist-pilgrims add meaning to the object; they sanctify it and end up treating it as a quasi-religious relic (Seaton 2004). Until recently, the topic of Hungary's role in the Second World War has been taboo in public discourse, especially in Romania. Consequently, no efforts have been made to develop attraction elements related to the war. Showcasing Second World War-era weapons and innovative military technology, grave sites and other elements that add to the authenticity of the Árpád line, could be of interest to thanatourists visiting Gyimes. Worldwide, bunker trails are shrines of patriotism symbolising both national pride and memories of military glory of old.

## Gastro-tourism

A plethora of influences, both Western and Eastern have left their mark on Gyimes cuisine, the most marked of which are Hungarian and Romanian. Others are drawn from quite a colourful palette: Roman, Byzantine, Armenian, Turkish and Austrian. The whole region is farmland – they grow plants in the valley and raise livestock on the pasture-covered slopes of the surrounding mountains. This markedly sets the tone for the local cuisine – incorporating elements borrowed from eating habits of the Romanian mountain folk. Due to the shepherding lifestyle, corn-meal – a staple ingredient of the Romanian shepherd's diet – has made its way into Csángó cooking. It is used to prepare an ordinary weekday fare or a more festive Sunday family meal. Carrying a bag of cornmeal all the way uphill to the sheep farm made more sense to the Csángó than having to trot all the way downhill to the valley just to bake a couple of loaves of bread. Cornmeal mush was combined with feta cheese (juhtúrós puliszka) (Horváth 2010).

Csángó gastronomy still uses a wealth of medicinal herbs and spices that were once ingredients in old Hungarian cookbook recipes, but are hardly used today in Hungary, such as summer savoury, dill, caraway seeds, coriander, pine nuts and various mushrooms. Csángó soup is flavoured by adding tarragon to it, a herb that is almost gone from Hungarian cooking. Effective use of medicinal plants and herbs by Csángós to brew tea in order to obtain an enjoyable remedy for various ailments and conditions was described at length by several authors (Antalné Tankó 2008).

Nowadays, local eating habits are marred by high calorie intake – not a worry in the days of intensive manual labour carried out daily in the fields or woods. To compensate for this (mainly due to Romanian influences), they eat quite a high volume of green salads and vegetables such as tomatoes, onions and aubergines (eggplants). An even greater issue is a high volume of alcohol consumption embodied especially by large amounts of hard liquor (high alcohol content fruit brandy, the so-called *pálinka*). Cheap, mass-produced caraway seed pálinka seems to be the drink of choice of the local folk. This does not even qualify as pálinka and neither locals nor tourists should indulge in tasting it at all, let alone drinking it in large quantities.

Gyimes has not been sheltered from the effects of globalisation. Impacts of international cooking can be observed here as well. At the same time, wood-burning ovens and grilling are the most popular choices for preparing meat (e.g. grilled pork shoulder chops). When building his open fire grill, the Csángó will sprinkle freshly cut juniper twigs on top of the hot embers to add a unique, smoky flavour to the meat. This and other unique foods could make the Gyimes valley area an attraction for gastro-tourism enthusiasts.

## References

Antalné Tankó, M. (2008) *Gyimes-völgyi népi gyógyászat*, Budapest: Harmattan Kiadó.

Csapó, J. and Matesz, K. (2007) 'A kulturális turizmus jelentősége és szerepe napjaink idegenforgalmába', *Földrajzi Értesítő* LVI. évf. 3–4. füzet: 291–301.

Dávid, L. and Bujdosó, Z. (2009) 'Connection Between Tourism, Regional Development and Environmental Protection Along Borders', *DSM Business Review: An International Journal of Divine International* 1(1): 21–27.

Dávid, L., Jancsik, A. and Rátz, T. (2007) *Turisztikai erőforrások: A természeti és kulturális erőforrások turisztikai hasznosítása*, Budapest: Perfekt Kiadó.

Dearden, P. and Harron, S. (1992) 'Case Study: Tourism and the Hilltribes of Thailand', in Weiler, B. and Hall, C.M. (eds) *Special Interest Tourism*, London: Belhaven, 95–104.

Fendl, E. (1998) 'Reisen in die verlorene Vergangenheit – Überlegungen zum "Heimwehtourismus"', *Jahrbuch der Ostdeutschen Volkskunde* 41: 85–100.

Horváth, A. (2010) 'A területi turizmusfejlesztés lehetőségei a Székelyföldön', unpublished PhD thesis, University of Pécs.

Ilyés, Z. (2007) *A tájhasználat változásai és történeti kultúrtáj 18–20. századi fejlődése Gyimesben*, Eger: Eszterházy Károly College, Department of Geography.

Institutul National de Statistica (2007) *Territorial Statistics Romania*, www.insse.ro/cms/rw/pages/index.ro.do (accessed 15 November 2012).

——(2010) *Territorial Statistics Romania*, www.insse.ro/cms/rw/pages/index.ro.do (accessed 15 November 2012).

Posch, D. (2010) *Csángómagyarok Moldvában*, Székesfehérvár.

Pusztai, B. (2006) 'A thanaturizmustól a nyaralásig – gondolatok a turizmus történetéhez', *Turizmus Bulletin* X. évf. 3. szám.: 70–71.

Seaton, A.V. (2004) 'Háború és thanaturizmus: Waterloo, 1815–1914', *Aetas* 19. évf. 3–4. szám: 220–45.

Smith, V.L. (ed.) (1978) *Hosts and Guests: The Anthropology of Tourism*, Oxford: Blackwell.

Szilágyi, E. (2007) 'Gyimes kevésbé devalvált vidék', paper presented at Scientific Students' Associations Conference, Miskolc, 39.

Tankó, G. (2008) *Öregek faggatása, történelem, életmód, sors Gyimesben*, Csíkszereda: Státus Kiadó, 330.

# Part VI
# Regeneration and planning

The effects of globalisation and the widespread restructuring of urban and rural economies have created a need to regenerate many cities and regions. From the late 1970s onwards these processes were particularly noticeable in the inner city areas of major conurbations, as manufacturing industry moved to new locations leaving substantial gaps in the urban fabric. One of the most widespread strategies for plugging these gaps and kick-starting the local economy was to employ culture-led regeneration (Evans 2003; Miles and Paddison 2005; Vickery 2007).

Culture is increasingly being included in urban regeneration strategies as a means of stimulating physical redevelopment, adding animation to areas of the city and generating economic and cultural benefits. Miles and Paddison (2005) identify culture-led regeneration as part of the 'new orthodoxy' for cities in a competitive global environment. Part of this orthodoxy is that culture provides an ideal basis for regeneration, since it has the ability to generate a wide range of benefits for the local community as well as being able to generate (cultural) tourism. As Michael Hall points out in his contribution to this section, the convergence of culture and urban regeneration has been stimulated by the rise of postmodernism and the subsequent de-differentiation of culture and economy, and the growing use of culture as an economic development tool.

Vickery's (2007) review of culture-led regeneration shows that the concept emerged in the literature in the late 1980s and was made visible in the 1990s through practices of urban design and public art. He identifies four major categories of 'culture-led' urban regeneration:

- 'Flagship' cultural facilities, such as signature style architecture or a new cultural institution.
- Landmark sculptures or public art schemes.
- Innovative structural engineering, such as bridges or archways.
- Unique performances, events or festivals.

He traces the widespread implementation of such projects in the UK and elsewhere to a number of presuppositions, including the leading role of metropolitan areas, the importance of design in supporting quality of life, and the importance of culture in involving citizens, increasing social benefits and supporting the democratic process. More recently, culture-led regeneration has also been linked to the development of 'distinctive cities' (Turok 2009), which use culture as a convenient medium for making themselves distinctive in the growing field of inter-urban competition. As Richards and Wilson (2007) have pointed out in the case of cultural tourism, however, strategies aiming to produce cultural distinctiveness often end up having the reverse effect and generate 'serial reproduction' instead, as cities tend to adopt similar development models.

Zukin (1995: 268) also identified the rise of culture-led regeneration as part of the general development of the symbolic economy, the growth of which has arguably allowed cultural institutions to claim more space within cities. Museums, galleries, opera houses and theatres are now seen as an integral part of regeneration processes, and often form the centrepiece of planned regeneration projects (Hamnett and Shoval 2008), as in Bilbao (Guggenheim Museum), Manchester (The Lowry), Kanazawa, Japan (Twenty-First Century Art Museum), or Los Angeles (Getty Museum).

As Hall notes in this section, however, the benefits of these urban regeneration projects often produce little social benefit for residents and may in fact lead to the original residents being displaced by physical redevelopment and gentrification. In many cases (cultural) tourism may be seen as part of the problem, because tourist expenditure helps to change the local economy, pushing out the previous forms of economic activity and raising prices.

In many cities cultural attractions or whole districts or 'quarters' have become nodes in the 'liquid geography of global cultural consumerism', as Russo and Quaglieri-Domínguez describe it in this volume. The cities that are successful in this field not only tend to have lots of 'culture' and 'creativity', but also offer 'plug and play'-style facilities for the modern 'global nomad' (Richards 2010). These cultural sites are not just destinations, but relational spaces, in which the 'being there', 'being seen' and 'being cool' are more important than the cultural content itself.

The use of culture for regeneration is therefore often also linked to specific areas or 'cultural clusters' (Mommaas 2004), which are often underpinned by the development of intangible culture, including cultural events (Richards and Palmer 2010). A wide range of cultural and creative districts, quarters and clusters has therefore sprung up across the world. These are often developed as top-down responses to problems of urban or rural regeneration, but there are also a number of cases in which clusters have emerged from ad hoc groupings of artists and creative workers in run-down areas where work space is cheap. Such bottom-up clustering often becomes incorporated into more formal regeneration schemes as in the case of formerly squatted areas of Amsterdam or the development of artistic clusters in Brooklyn, New York (Zukin 2010).

The development of cultural clusters has also been linked to the emergence of 'ethnic quarters' in major cities where there are large concentrations of migrants. The trend towards culture-led regeneration has initiated a widespread use of such areas as tourist attractions, playing on the exotic difference between these visibly different populations and the surrounding city. Here, regeneration strategies are often linked to ideas about ethnic entrepreneurship. The contributions of Steve Shaw and Anya Diekmann to the current volume provide examples of how these processes work in cities such as London and Brussels.

The literature shows a strong tendency to link regeneration processes to urban areas where the problems of physical regeneration are often most acute, but restructuring has also created a need for regeneration in rural areas as well. A range of different strategies have therefore developed to link culture and tourism in the countryside. 'Artistic havens' (Wojan *et al.* 2007) act as magnets for rural tourists in the USA, festivals in areas such as the English Lake District become 'creative hubs' for the local community as well as tourists, and creative tourism programmes are often found in rural areas (Richards and Wilson 2007).

## Summary of the chapters in this section

This section begins with a contribution from **Greg Richards**, who examines the way in which culture has become an increasingly central part of the tourism experience and how culture in turn is increasingly linked to creativity. The development of 'creative tourism' stems from the idea that consumers increasingly want more active involvement with the culture of the places they visit. By developing creative experiences, usually in a process of 'co-creation' with tourists themselves, destinations can arguably avoid the problems of 'serial reproduction' so often seen in culture-led regeneration schemes and in the rise of 'mass cultural tourism'.

**Philip Long** and **Nigel Morpeth** develop a critique of the growing use of 'creative' approaches to development and cultural tourism in the following chapter. They point out that the development of the 'creative industries' is the subject of much debate, particularly as this seems to signal a turn from cultural to economic conceptions of creativity. Using the example of Sheffield, UK, as a postindustrial city that has turned to creative industry development, they underline the importance of creativity being allowed to develop for its own sake, not just as an engine for regeneration projects.

Also in the context of cities in the UK, **Clare Carruthers** examines the way in which cultural tourism has been used as a tool for economic regeneration, focusing on how strategies designed to differentiate cities often have the effect of creating homogenous, standardised environments. Evidence for the success of culture-led or tourism-based regeneration is often lacking, and where studies have been conducted the results are often disappointing. She uses the example of Liverpool (European Capital of Culture in 2008) to illustrate how success in attracting tourists and generating economic impacts may not always be linked to improvements in quality of life for local people.

**James Kennell** also points to processes by which culture is valorised and then commercialised through cultural tourism, which provides the marketplace of consumption necessary for the economic model that underpins cultural regeneration. He presents a model of cultural regeneration, and describes how the different elements of the model have changed as a result of the global economic crisis. This is creating debate about the value of public spending in areas of culture, tourism and regeneration, at the same time as private investment in tourism and regeneration is dropping and the lucrative cultural tourism market is shrinking. He points to alternative models of cultural regeneration, using the example of the Stokes Croft district of Bristol, UK, where artist-led initiatives have emerged. Such grassroots projects often contrast with official top-down development strategies.

In the case of Barcelona, **Antonio Paolo Russo** and **Alan Quaglieri-Domínguez** point to the way in which tourists themselves are transforming the cultural tourism geographies of cities. They point out that there is increasingly little distinction between tourist culture and local culture, and the tourists themselves become a force for shaping culture in the city. A framework for analysing the emerging cultural geographies of cities is presented, which relates the degree of embeddedness of visitors and residents in the destination and their degree of transience. This shows that visitors and residents represent end members of a mobility continuum, rather than being distinct groups. The destination becomes a relational space in which cultural exchange shapes a new geography of 'hotspots' in which tourism is performed and translated.

The concentration of cultural tourism in specific locations is an implicit part of many tourism and cultural development strategies, as **Michael Hall** describes in his analysis of regeneration and cultural quarters. He also identifies increasing debate around issues of commodification, identity, homogenisation, gentrification and regeneration in the context of cultural quarters or cultural districts. These also suffer from problems of serial reproduction as common models are copied around the world. This is clear in the case study of the SOL (South of Litchfield) cluster in Christchurch, New Zealand modelled on the SoHo district of New York.

**Stephen Shaw** reflects on how specific cultural quarters have been developed on the basis of visible ethnic minorities in many cities. Although many cities have a Chinatown or 'Little Italy', opinion is divided on their success as areas that can stimulate innovation, with many arguing that the exoticism of local populations is being marketed as a commodity. Drawing on a case study of Brick Lane, a Bangladeshi enclave in East London, he shows how ethnic difference has been packaged and marketed, with the area being transformed into 'Banglatown'. In particular he highlights struggles between stakeholder groups over the direction of development of such ethnic quarters, with local entrepreneurs and residents often resisting externally imposed labelling and stereotypical representations of their culture.

**Anya Diekmann** also examines the issue of exotic representations of ethnicity in an African cultural quarter in Brussels, Belgium. The city has made a top-down effort to develop migrant areas for tourism, which has often excluded local stakeholders from decision making around the development of tourism. Surveys of visitors show that very few consider themselves to be 'tourists', which could also explain the failure of tourism marketing efforts. The projected exotic image of the quarter is also at odds with the run-down inner city environment, and there is a lack of facilities for tourists.

## References

Evans, G. (2003) *Cultural Planning: An Urban Renaissance?* London: Routledge.

Hamnett, C. and Shoval, N. (2008) 'Museums as Flagships of Urban Development', in Hoffman, L.M., Fainstein, S.S. and Judd, D.R. (eds) *Cities and Visitors: Regulating People, Markets, and City Space*, Oxford: Blackwell.

Miles, S. and Paddison, R. (2005) 'Introduction: The Rise and Rise of Culture-led Urban Regeneration', *Urban Studies* 42: 833–39.

Mommaas, H. (2004) 'Cultural Clusters and the Postindustrial City: Towards the Remapping of Urban Cultural Policy', *Urban Studies* 41: 507–32.

Richards, G. (2010) Leisure in the Network Society: From Pseudo Events to Hyperfestivity? Tilburg: Tilburg University, www.docstoc.com/docs/68264365/Leisure-in-the-network-society (accessed 15 November 2012).

Richards, G. and Palmer, R. (2010) *Eventful Cities: Cultural Management and Urban Revitalisation*, London: Routledge.

Richards, G. and Wilson, J. (2007) *Tourism, Creativity and Development*, London: Routledge.

Turok, I. (2009) 'The Distinctive City: Pitfalls in the Pursuit of Differential Advantage', *Environment and Planning A* 41: 13–30.

Vickery, J. (2007) *The Emergence of Culture-led Regeneration: A Policy Concept and its Discontents*, Centre for Cultural Policy Studies, University of Warwick, Research Paper No. 9.

Wojan, T.R., Lambert, D.M. and McGranahan, D.A. (2007) 'The Emergence of Rural Artistic Havens: A First Look', *Agricultural and Resource Economics Review* 36: 53–70.

Zukin, S. (1995) *The Cultures of Cities*, Malden, MA: Blackwell.

——(2010) *Naked City: The Death and Life of Authentic Urban Places*, Oxford: Oxford University Press.

# 37

# Tourism development trajectories

## From culture to creativity?

*Greg Richards*

---

Culture and tourism were two of the major growth industries of the twentieth century, and in recent decades the combination of these two sectors into 'cultural tourism' has become one of the most desirable development options for countries and regions around the world. As the Organisation for Economic Co-operation and Development (OECD) report on *The Impact of Culture on Tourism* (2009) noted, cultural tourism accounted for almost 360 million international tourism trips in 2007, or 40 per cent of global tourism. In value terms, the contribution of cultural tourism is even greater, since cultural tourists are estimated to spend as much as one-third more on average than other tourists (Richards 2007).

However, the rapid growth of cultural tourism from the preserve of the elite Grand Tourists to a major industry in the last century has also caused problems. Growing numbers of tourists at major sites and in small communities has raised questions about the sustainability of this new form of mass tourism. In particular it has become harder for destinations to profile their culture among the welter of products on offer, each desperate to claim their uniqueness. There is a growing number of places in search of new forms of articulation between culture and tourism which can help to strengthen rather than water down local culture, which can raise the value accruing to local communities and improve the links between local creativity and tourism.

Many places are therefore turning to creative development strategies, or different forms of creative tourism in the process (Richards 2011). This chapter examines why and how cultural tourism is being transformed into creative tourism.

## The growth of cultural tourism

In order to understand the origins of creative tourism, we first have to look at the rise of culture as a form of tourism consumption. In the past, culture was not something strongly associated with tourism, which was viewed mainly as a leisure activity. In Europe, only a small number of relatively wealthy people used to undertake cultural tours with specific educational goals – the vast majority saw holidays as a time for rest and relaxation. This situation gradually changed during the twentieth century, as tourists became more experienced and started seeking new experiences on holiday, and more places began to recognise the value of culture as a potential means of generating tourism.

A number of vectors of cultural, social and economic change underlay the growth of cultural tourism. These included a fundamental shift in the nature of consumption, changing factors of production and changes in the nature of tourism itself.

## The trajectory of consumption – from basic needs to creative needs

As society has developed, so the basis of human needs and wants has also changed. As we became increasingly able to satisfy our basic needs for food and shelter, we turned our attention to the satisfaction of 'higher-order' needs, such as status and self-fulfilment. Scitovsky (1976) has described this development in terms of the shift from unskilled to skilled consumption, or from outer-directed to inner-directed consumption. People are no longer just concerned with accumulating goods, but they also want to develop themselves and their own consumption skills. People want to paint, draw, design, photograph, sing, do yoga – a whole range of activities that will build their own skills and develop their potential.

Ironically this growing desire for creativity coincides with a diminishing amount of available time in which to be creative. One route is to be creative in interstitial time at home, or via the Internet; another is through travel, as holidays often provide the only significant block of free time that a pressured creative class has. They are also demanding more 'real' experiences of everyday life.

## The trajectory of production – from goods to experiences

At the same time, the nature of production has shifted dramatically. Pine and Gilmore (1999) have shown that the previous stages of the economy based on the production of goods or services have been replaced by an economy specialised in the production of experiences. Increasing competition forces producers to differentiate their products by adding value, such as additional features or services. However, over time, competitors can reproduce these features and the value of the product, and therefore productivity declines. In the experience economy, the product is a unique experience for the consumer, which cannot be replicated so easily.

## The trajectory of tourism – from mass tourism to cultural tourism to creative tourism?

Tourism as an industry has also undergone major transformations in line with the rise of skilled consumption and the experience economy. Tourism is of course one of the phenomena closely identified with the rise of the service industries, and in many countries it is the most important single service industry. Tourism grew rapidly in the latter half of the twentieth century because the basic inputs were cheap and easy to mass produce. The rise of mass tourism also brought about several negative impacts, such as overcrowding, environmental problems, degradation of local culture, etc. Cultural tourism, in contrast, was often viewed as a 'good' form of tourism, which was small scale, high spend and low impact. Perhaps most importantly, cultural tourists themselves were perceived as desirable visitors, because they were usually wealthy, well heeled and well behaved.

In the past, cultural tourism was also largely based on cultural heritage – particularly those elements of heritage, such as museums and monuments, that can be consumed by a large number of people. In Europe, for example, Europa Nostra has estimated that 50 per cent of European tourism is related to such resources, and the Association for Tourism and Leisure Education (ATLAS 2009) research programme has shown that over 50 per cent of cultural tourists visit museums and monuments.

The convergence of these different trajectories of change in consumption, production and tourism style served to create a cultural tourism boom from the 1980s onwards. The ATLAS research has underlined how cultural visits have tended to grow as a proportion of tourism consumption, reaching 36 per cent of those surveyed in 2008. This growth, coupled with the perception of cultural tourism as high-value tourism, encouraged many countries and regions to develop specific cultural tourism programmes, and to design marketing efforts targeted at cultural tourists.

## Cultural tourism: a victim of its own success?

There is no doubt that tourism and culture are now inextricably linked, and that cultural tourism is a major segment of global tourism. However, there are also signs that cultural tourism is now becoming a victim of its own success. The work of Paolo Russo (2002) in Venice has underlined how historic city centres can suffer from a 'vicious cycle' of cultural tourism development, in which famous sites attract a large number of tourists, degrading the quality of experience and driving 'serious' cultural tourists away. The falling appeal of the destination forces suppliers to concentrate on new, lower-value markets, chiefly consisting of excursionists.

Other problems are also evident. There is a certain irony in destinations seeking to develop their uniqueness through cultural tourism. In fact, many places follow similar strategies in order to achieve their uniqueness, which ends up making those places feel and look the same. This is the problem of 'serial reproduction' described by Richards and Wilson (2006). Strategies based on iconic structures or mega-events are recognisable in cities across the globe, and the means of consuming these products are also becoming increasingly familiar: the tourist bus, the city card, the guided tour.

The major problem with this process of 'McCulturisation', to paraphrase Ritzer (1993), is that the very people targeted by these products are repelled by them. Just as cultural tourists are becoming more experienced, more sophisticated and better able to structure their own tourism experiences, so the cultural tourism product being offered is becoming more standardised, more rigid and less engaging. One cultural creative describes their dissatisfaction with (post)modern existence thus: 'I was accumulating experiences without changing very much'.

The ATLAS research has indicated that the experiences enjoyed most by cultural tourists tend to be those small-scale, less-visited places that offer a taste of 'local' or 'authentic' culture. Tourists increasingly say that they want to experience local culture, to live like locals and to find out about the real identity of the places they visit. Clearly, new types of cultural tourism products are needed.

The emergence of this new breed of cultural tourist coincides with the growth in 'prosumption' – the process by which the consumer becomes a producer of the products and experiences they consume. We are already used to doing a large element of the work in producing services, as Ritzer demonstrated in the case of fast food and Disney-style entertainment, but as people demand more individualised and engaging experiences, so the level of consumer involvement is increasing.

The skilled consumer often knows more about the experiences they are consuming than the people who are supposed to supply them. Not surprisingly, therefore, skilled consumers have begun to take the lead in experience production. Lifestyle entrepreneurs start lifestyle businesses, travellers construct their own itineraries on the Internet, compiling flights and hostel beds and combining these with couches borrowed from friends on social networking sites. These travellers no longer buy the packaged excursion, but creatively shape their own experiences, based on what they want to do, when they want to do it, where they want to do it, and with whom they want. These experiences usually emphasise active involvement in local culture, rather than the highlights of global culture.

## From cultural to creative tourism

Faced with these changes in the nature of experience production and consumption, destinations could continue offering the same mass cultural tourism products they always have, but they do this at the risk of losing a very important part of the market. Admittedly, these new forms of tourism are difficult for the traditional tourism sector to deal with, but there are major opportunities in working with rather than ignoring creative tourism.

Richards and Raymond (2000: 18) have defined creative tourism as:

> Tourism which offers visitors the opportunity to develop their creative potential through active participation in courses and learning experiences which are characteristic of the holiday destination where they are undertaken.

This definition has a number of important implications:

- Creative potential: the tourist is provided with the tools to develop their own creative potential, and to take something more than souvenirs home with them.
- Active involvement: the consumer is actively involved in the creative process, and this involvement creates the potential for genuine exchange and engagement with local people and local culture.
- Characteristic experiences: creativity can happen anywhere, but the important thing is to link the creative process to the destination and to anchor it in local culture, creativity and identity. This requires not just creativity on the part of the tourist, but also the destination.
- Co-creation: the concept of creative tourism implies a level of co-creation, or co-makership between visitors and locals. Co-creation covers an emerging body of knowledge about the way in which products, services and experiences are made jointly by producers and consumers. At its most crude, this concept involves using the consumer's knowledge of the product in order to improve it and to provide a closer fits with consumer needs. However, in the context of creative tourism there is usually a much more important dimension of co-creation at work, which involves a reversal of the normal power relationships attached to tourism. This is most evident in projects such as the Opuwo workshop in Namibia, where the Finnish designer Satu Miettinen (2008) has run craft workshops for tourists. These workshops are led by local women, who rather than serving tourists in bars or restaurants, or selling them trinkets in the market, now become their teachers and co-workers, guiding them in the skills required to make traditional objects and initiating them into their cultural significance.

## Examples of creative tourism experiences

Our research on the relationship between tourism and creativity suggest that there are a number of ways in which they can be linked in order to enhance the tourism product and the visitor experience. The forms of creative experience can range from more active involvement in formal courses, as primarily envisaged in the original formulation of creative tourism, to a more passive experience of creative environments as a background to other forms of tourism (Richards 2011). Creativity can either be the central motivation for tourism, as with the more formalised provision, or else a more peripheral experience in which the creativity of people and places adds 'atmosphere' and animation to the general tourist experience of places.

Creative experiences can also be delivered in a variety of ways, including the creation of networks, itineraries, courses and events. The summary below provides some examples. Many more examples can be found in Richards and Wilson (2006, 2007).

## Creative tourism networks

The original creative tourism network was founded in the city of Nelson, New Zealand, where Creative Tourism New Zealand was established as a network of creative businesses offering products to tourists (www.creativetourism.co.nz). The network provides a wide range of creative experiences, including bone carving, Māori language classes, weaving, felting and woodwork, and New Zealand gastronomy. The focus is very much on learning experiences, with a range of hands-on workshops being run by local tutors (Raymond 2007). Such initiatives make widespread use of local and indigenous culture as a stimulus for creativity (see also Thompson-Carr, this volume).

Creative Tourism Barcelona (www.barcelonacreativa.info) takes a slightly different approach, acting as an intermediary to link creative producers in the city with people from other parts of the world who want to engage in creative activities there. This more artistic approach to the development of creative tourism provides a platform through which potential creative tourists can indicate the types of creative activities in which they are interested, and they are then put in touch with local creative sector actors who can provide the facilities or resources to make it happen. Creative Tourism Barcelona has been instrumental in setting up the Creative Tourism Network, together with parts of France, Italy and Austria, and is currently working with travel companies such as Kuoni to distribute creative tourism products to a wider market.

Creative Tourism Austria (www.kreativreisen.at/en) provides a wider range of cultural and creative experiences, with an emphasis on adding creative elements to existing cultural tourism products, such as painting and cooking classes in a monastery, or walking tours themed around sheep herding. In contrast to the Barcelona initiative, the Austrian project relies heavily on involvement of the commercial sector, particularly local hotels. Paris has also begun to profile itself as a creative destination, offering a range of creative experiences in visual, performing and culinary arts, media, fashion and design, science and technology, and literature (creativeparis. info/en/).

More grassroots-based networks are also beginning to emerge, such as the 'Put a Face to Tourism' initiative in Galicia, Spain (www.ponlecaraalturismo.com). Here, members of the local creative community have developed guided tours around local neighbourhoods in the region, led by local creatives.

## Creative spaces

Particular spaces also have been developed to offer creative learning experiences to visitors in different parts of the world. For example, the Italian coffee producer Illy's Università del caffè provides courses on all aspects of coffee and coffee making at 11 different locations (http://unicaffe. illy.com/en/universita/around-the-world). Since 1999, approximately 22,000 students have graduated from this institution. The Valrhona chocolate company provides similar courses for gourmets and professionals in their L'Ecole du Grand Chocolat in southern France.

In Barcelona different forms of accommodation have tapped into the creative sector to develop new experiences. The Chic and Basic hotel has staged fashion shows, using its individually designed bedrooms to showcase the products of young, local designers. The Equity Point hostels group (www.equity-point.com/en/hostelart) runs a 'hostelArt' programme, giving young artists an opportunity to exhibit their work in hostel rooms and introducing young travellers to the creative sector in Barcelona. The Camping House Barcelona (www.barcelona-house.com/barcelona-house-philosophy) is a new concept in tourist accommodation, providing guests with the sensation of camping in the middle of the city, and adding design value to their stay.

### Events

Cities around the globe are busy developing their 'eventfulness' (Richards and Palmer 2010) in order to utilise the creative power of events to help the city achieve its wider cultural, social and economic goals. Many of the new types of events being developed are not just about passive audience attendance, but the active involvement of creative producers and others in the 'co-creation' of events.

In the Swedish city of Umea, for example, the European Capital of Culture for 2014 is being run on an open-source principle. Instead of the programme being designed by 'experts' in the cultural sector, the event is being planned and programmed with direct involvement of local people. For example, local school children created a blog which was used as the basic script for an opera performance to which they were later invited. By extending this open-source or co-creation concept to the national and international arena, this also becomes a strategy to develop creative tourism. The audience is not there simply to consume, but also to take an active part in producing the experience.

The Festes de Gràcia is a local festival in a district of Barcelona which has developed into a major celebration for the whole city. The key element of this event is the decoration of local streets by residents, using recycled materials. Each street is themed, and there is a high level of creativity involved in creating a totally new space from discarded items such as water bottles and milk cartons.

### Creative backdrops

Many cities have a reputation for being 'creative' in one way or another. In many cases this creativity is experienced by the visitor not so much in the direct consumption of creative activities, but rather through the general atmosphere or buzz of the place as a whole, which is generated by the creative sector. This strategy is also being employed in Shanghai and Beijing, as newly developing creative clusters are opened up and marketed to tourists.

## Criticism of creativity in tourism

As Long and Morpeth (this volume) point out, the relationship between tourism and creativity is not unproblematic. The range of examples of creative tourism presented in the current chapter indicates that creativity can be incorporated into tourism products in different ways, ranging from bottom-up initiatives stimulated by local creative producers to top-down imaging strategies designed to attract the creative class. The use of creativity to develop tourism also runs the risk of strengthening the tendency towards colonisation of the lifeworld by the forces of commerce. As Russo and Quaglieri-Domínguez (this volume) also point out, the increasing contact with 'local' culture facilitated by creative tourism initiatives may also be problematic. Whether one takes a critical or optimistic view of creative tourism initiatives therefore depends to a large extent on the intentions of the individual projects, and whether these succeed in delivering real benefits for local residents and indigenous creativity, the creative life of the destination or the creative experience of the tourist.

## Conclusion

The search for solutions to the growing problems of commodification and serial reproduction in cultural tourism are among the most important explanations for the growing utilisation of creative tourism development strategies. Creativity is seen as adding distinctiveness and can provide a link to local culture and creative producers. At the same time many tourists are seeking more involvement with local cultures through creative activities, and this trend is being stimulated by a range of creative tourism projects and networks in different parts of the world.

## Acknowledgement

A version of this chapter was previously published as Richards, G. (2010) 'Tourism Development Trajectories: From Culture to Creativity?' *Tourism and Management Studies* 6: 9–15.

## References

ATLAS (2009) *ATLAS Cultural Tourism Research Project*, www.tram-research.com/atlas (accessed 24 April 2012).

Miettinen, S. (2008) 'Creative Tourism as Tool for Local Empowerment', in Richards, G. and Wilson, J. (eds) *Changing Experiences: The Development of Creative Tourism*, ATLAS: Arnhem, 60–69.

OECD (2009) *The Impact of Culture on Tourism*, Paris: OECD.

Pine, B.J. and Gilmore, J.H. (1999) *The Experience Economy*, Boston: Harvard University Press.

Raymond, C. (2007) 'Creative Tourism New Zealand: The Practical Challenges of Developing Creative Tourism', in Richards, G. and Wilson, J. (eds) *Tourism, Creativity and Development*, London: Routledge, 145–57.

Richards, G. (ed.) (2007) *Cultural Tourism: Global and Local Perspectives*, New York: Haworth Press.

——(2011) 'Creativity and Tourism: The State of the Art', *Annals of Tourism Research* 38(4): 1225–53.

Richards, G. and Palmer, R. (2010) *Eventful Cities: Cultural Management and Urban Revitalisation*, London: Routledge.

Richards, G. and Raymond, C. (2000) 'Creative Tourism', *ATLAS News* 23: 16–20.

Richards, G. and Wilson, J. (2006) 'Developing Creativity in Tourist Experiences: A Solution to the Serial Reproduction of Culture?' *Tourism Management* 27: 1209–23.

——(2007) *Tourism, Creativity and Development*, London: Routledge.

Ritzer, G. (1993) *The McDonaldization of Society*, Los Angeles: Pine Forge Press.

Russo, A.P. (2002) 'The "Vicious Circle" of Tourism Development in Heritage Cities', *Annals of Tourism Research* 29: 165–82.

Scitovsky, T. (1976) *The Joyless Economy*, Oxford: Oxford University Press.

# 38

# Critiquing creativity in tourism

*Philip Long and Nigel D. Morpeth*

## Introduction

This chapter defines and critiques the concept of 'creativity', positioning it in its changing meanings and applications within society generally and in relation to tourism in particular. These observations are made acknowledging the shifting cultural landscapes within society from the Renaissance, to modern, post-modern and post-industrial societies and the emergence of the cultural economy. In discussing the melding of creativity and industry, now firmly established within the parlance of policy communities notably in Western, 'developed' economies, there are issues with the amalgamation of two concepts which are potentially dissonant and mutually exclusive in their respective meanings. This is consistent with the emergence, particularly in North American and European cities, of clusters of artistic and creative communities and *milieux* where their *raison d'être* is broader than (and perhaps antagonistic to) the pursuit of commercial gain and being appropriated and assimilated into creative industry and cultural tourism strategies.

In considering creativity and tourism it is important to note Packard's *The Wastemakers* (1960) and his timeless themes of 'ever mounting consumption' and 'creative obsolescence', which arguably underpin creative consumption as a *leitmotif* of contemporary societies. There is a controversial conflation of the terms creative and cultural and the assimilation of the 'creative industry' sectors as a central part of the so-called experience economies (Pine and Gilmore 1999). This underpins public-sector promotion and the corralling of the creative industries (and also tourism) as the panacea for de-industrialisation, a defining policy initiative of the previous UK New Labour government, for example (DCMS 2001, 2004). The current UK government, in reducing the funding for the cultural and creative sectors, is at the same time promoting the creative industries as important economic drivers during a period of economic crisis. In focusing on a case study of the UK city of Sheffield, we interrogate a so-called exemplar of good practice in the development and promotion of the creative industries in relation to tourism and emphasise that there are creative counter-narratives to 'official' versions of the creative sector and places.

## Conceptualising creativity in relation to tourism

'Creativity' needs to be conceived within particular social, historical and political circumstances as the term may not readily be translated and recognised in different cultural settings, cautioning against any grand generalisations and singular definitions. We acknowledge that the discussion and examples of creativity in this chapter draw on literature published in the English language and situated in 'developed' economies. Future research might encompass a broader global perspective.

This is particularly apposite in universal understandings of creativity from a spiritual dimension, and within creation and mystical narratives. From a Western perspective, the Renaissance and the epoch of the Enlightenment emphasised humanistic, romantic notions of '... conjuring something forth, giving form to what is inchoate, and bringing an inner voice or vision into being' (Negus and Pickering 2004: 4). Nevertheless, the ability to be creative, or the capacity to appreciate aesthetic qualities is not solely the preserve of those who are somehow divinely inspired and/or endowed with unique, inherent talents and capabilities (Robinson 2001). There is a risk of assigning the capacity to be creative as belonging to an elite, educated and privileged class (which parallels conceptions of the 'cultural tourist' and the supposed 'tourist/traveller' dichotomy). All people have the capacity to be creative in everyday life, as tourists and/or as workers in tourism occupations, for example. However, when the term is appropriated and conjoined with 'industry' and the everyday, creativity may seem to become routine and banal, and risk losing any particular meaning (Schlesinger 2007). We acknowledge that people practise creativity in daily life through consumption practices and expressions of taste and distinction as part of identity formation (relating to conceptions of 'cultural capital', and the creative consumer – Bourdieu 1984). Such tastes for 'creative consumption' may be shaped in part through our experiences as tourists and may also feed into our subsequent destination choices and behaviour as tourists.

The conflation of the 'cultural' and 'creative' with 'industry' is a source of considerable controversy and academic debate. Some critics argue that the 'creative industries' definition values culture primarily or even solely for its economic role, rather than for its much wider contribution to ideas, aesthetics and society. 'Culture industry' has negative connotations for some theorists drawing on the work of the Frankfurt School in its critique of the media in particular (Habermas 1987; Adorno 1991). For such critics, new and emerging media and technology organisations possess too much power in shaping socio-cultural change, with particular concerns about their impact on the young, poor and vulnerable and in the alienation of society at large (Schlesinger 2007; Raunig et al. 2011). For Raunig et al. 'creativity is astir: reborn, re-conjured, re-branded, resurgent ... the creative industries sound the clarion call to the Cultural Entrepreneurs. In the hype of the creative class and the high flights of the digital bohemians, the renaissance of "the creatives" is visibly enacted' (Raunig et al. 2011: 1). They also suggest that, 'culture making is a crucial industry in today's global battle for tourist cash, as such like any other industry, it is subject to government policy' (ibid.: 185). For critics, therefore, a defining feature of a creative market system-based economy is the search for constant innovation, production and consumption of consumer goods and images. Negus and Pickering (2004: 11) characterised this as an 'ever-rolling mobility of pleasure, frustrated desire, obsolescence and new desire rationally incorporated into a commodity system maintained by the techniques of advertising, publicity and marketing'. For Raunig et al. (2011: 185) 'culture is instrumentalized for its "value-generating" spin-offs ... [with the] value that is more valuable than all others [being] monetary, and where "art is conceived as an abstract quantity, another product, like baked beans"'. The economic valuation of creative outputs may also result in, '[an] idealised opposition between "authentic" and "artificial" forms of creativity that assumes the marketization of culture generates only a spurious creativity which consists of manufacturing devices for keeping people continually in the process of coming back for more new things' (Negus and Pickering 2004: 11).

In their 2006 paper, Richards and Wilson argue that there has been a proliferation and 'serial reproduction' of generic cultural attractions and destinations often linked with regeneration programmes and that these have resulted in some bland developments (such as retail and waterfront projects). Alongside this, they suggest a turn towards more sophisticated and complex markets as people (at least those with the resources to do so) engage in 'skilled consumption'. They argue that tourist practices can provide opportunities for the building of personal identities involving the acquisition of 'cultural capital' through creative pursuits and experiences, and that the tourism sector is increasingly developing and promoting packages, trails and products aimed at satisfying such demand. The implication of these arguments is that there is substantial scope for the tourism sector to work more closely with creative practitioners (although mutual misunderstanding may be observed at times as a consequence of different educational and perhaps occupational and ideological backgrounds – Fitzgibbon and Kelly 1997; Beck 2003), with some artists and neighbourhoods resisting being packaged and presented as tourist attractions.

It is necessary, therefore, not to lose sight that the 'critical evaluation of experience, both inner and drawn from social encounters and relationships, is based on far more than market efficiency and personal satisfaction' (Negus and Pickering 2004: 11). Therefore, the 'doing' of tourism as practitioner and tourist affords a means of creating difference and promoting self-discovery and 'self-making', and moments of creativity that 'flow' and are beyond purely economic value (Csíkszentmihályi 1997, 1999).

## The creative industries and tourism

While any industry sector (and not least tourism) may apply creativity and innovation to their processes and products, a cluster of sectors has been identified and demarcated by government departments, such as the UK's Department for Culture, Media and Sport (DCMS) which identifies 13 sectors comprising the creative industries to be 'those industries which have their origin in individual creativity, skill and talent which have a potential for job and wealth creation through the generation and exploitation of intellectual property' (DCMS 2001). These 13 sectors include: advertising; architecture; art and antiques; computer games; crafts; design; designer fashion; film and video; music; performing arts; publishing; software; and TV and radio.

The DCMS approach to the definition and mapping of the creative industries has been influential on policy elsewhere, with Higgs and Cunningham (2008) providing examples from South-East Asia and Australasia. However, there are issues and controversies in the definition of the creative industries (see, for example Hesmondhalgh 2002; Hartley 2005), with these including the complex and fragmented nature of these sectors and their close economic relationships with firms in the wider economy, which means that it is difficult to distinguish them from other industries (including tourism). A further definitional issue is that the creative industries are characterised by high levels of micro-businesses, firms employing fewer than 10 people, and businesses below the £64,000 value added tax threshold in the UK (DCMS 2004). Self-employment means that official data may not capture the creative industries accurately. This observation may also, of course, be applied to operators of such a scale in the tourism sector.

It is notable that in the UK, tourism is not identified formally as being a creative industry sector (nor food and drink, which could also make a claim for inclusion). This is perverse given that much of the work of destination managers and of private-sector tourism operators is characterised by creativity and innovation in, for example, product development, marketing and interpretation. There are some clear connections between tourism and creative industry practitioners through the development and application of new and emerging media in tourism, and through festivals and cultural events showcasing the creative identity of place. Nevertheless, this is patchy, uncoordinated and lacking in any clear strategic direction.

However, the sectors that are included in the creative industries all, more or less, have connections with tourism including through direct involvement (for example, advertising, publishers of travel literature and other tourism media), and also with particular destinations being featured in place promotion on the basis of their creative industries (for example in the 2011 Visit Britain marketing campaign which featured the endorsement of celebrity 'creative people' such as actors and fashion designers) and packages aimed at tourists that are centred on creative industry sectors (for example, theatre breaks).

There are long-standing connections between tourism, publishing and literature reflected in sites associated with authors and the settings of their work. Historically travellers' tales published as text and images (and increasingly distributed electronically) illustrated the tourist/traveller as creative actor and co-producer of the tourist experience. Screened adaptations of creative/ fictional literature, travel writing and their conveying of senses of character and place also draw the reader (or viewer) imaginatively (and perhaps physically as tourists) to their locations. Creativity may also be applied in the reinvention and inter-mediation of texts aimed at tourists, including guide books (e.g. Lonely Planet), site interpretation (using mixed media and mobile phone applications), and in the mapping of tourist space. New publishing technologies are changing the nature of 'reading', with opportunities emerging for the use of 'mobile literature' as guide and route planner. Writers and publishers are also 'playing' with and re-conceptualising tourism through drawing on ideas based in situationism and psycho-geographies. Examples include the writings of Ian Sinclair and Will Self, and the *Lonely Planet Guide to Experimental Travel* (2005). Some such work presents the act of being a tourist as akin to performance art.

The performing arts staged in theatres featuring creative re-interpretations of the classics (for example of Shakespeare at Stratford upon Avon and the Globe Theatre, London), along with plays, musicals, opera, dance, concerts, recitals and variety shows, have long been an important element in Britain's tourism product. In London's West End theatres, UK and overseas tourists together make up a substantial proportion of the audience, while a growing number of arts festivals and theatres elsewhere in the UK are also succeeding in attracting domestic and inter-national tourist audiences (Hughes 2000). 'Immersive' performance art (or 'street theatre') is also increasingly taking place on the streets and in the landscape, with some such work using ideas of travel and tourism as themes. At times there is a blurring between the performing and visual arts and tourism (see for example the French company *La Machine* and the work of the artist Christo as an example of a 'performance event', where large-scale works are unveiled and exhibited for a limited period, attracting large audiences and media coverage).

The visual arts have a longstanding regeneration presence within UK destinations, with artists such as Richard Long being noted for their work situated in the landscape and also its connections with travel (other examples include the use of artistic installations and creative design in public spaces in both rural and urban settings, such as the 'Sustrans' National Cycle Network routes in the UK). However, questions arise concerning how official tourism agencies reflect and promote controversial and politically infused work of artists such as Banksy. Does such work continue to be subversive, or is it now part of the tourist mainstream or both? Arguably Banksy can now be viewed as a 'mainstream' artist, with his 2010 exhibition in Bristol attracting huge attendances and his film *Exit Through the Gift Shop* (with a title referencing tourism) also being reasonably popular.

The relationship between fashion retailing and tourism is evident at famous shops such as Harrods, Selfridges and Harvey Nichols, and on the King's Road, Chelsea, in London. Prominent British designers who can convey some sense of national identity include Sir Paul Smith, who has ubiquitous global presence, and Dame Vivienne Westwood, who is internationally famous as a designer (and subcultural) icon and exhibitor.

However, arguably the greatest scope for links between creative practitioners and tourism is through the development and use of new and emerging digital technologies. Illustrative of this are the online 'communities' which share interests in digital arts (i.e. artworks created using computer technologies), and the festivals associated with this artistic genre. Theories of sub-cultures and 'neo-tribes' may be applied to analysing these people who both 'commune' online and also travel as tourists in attending such festivals (Muggleton and Weinzierl 2003; Novelli 2005; Marletta 2011). In her research, Marletta (2011) identifies high levels of interactivity online, sustained membership of the 'community', the presence of an expert 'fan culture', the development of relationships, ideas, information and critical debate and physical tourist movements and experiences linked with this 'community's' interests. Her work suggests implications and opportunities for the tourism sector in their seeking to engage with such communities.

These include the observation that 'viral' may be more influential than 'official' media, with the trusted nature of the source being critical with possible resistance to any sign of overt commercialisation. The issue of how to engage without alienating virtual communities is therefore a key consideration. The scope for applying mobile, online applications is apparent in tourism and the site of much innovation.

---

## Box 38.1 Case study: tourism and creativity – the case of Sheffield

The city of Sheffield in northern England is a good example of a 'post-industrial city' that has increasingly recognised the value and potential of its strong traditions of creative industry and their potential for attracting tourists. With a population of 500,000, Sheffield has an international reputation for metalworking including the manufacture of high-quality cutlery and jewellery, with the sector characterised in part by small workshops operated by 'Little Mester' craft workers. However, the large-scale steel manufacturing sector experienced plant closures and redundancies among its skilled workforce from the late 1980s, although the sector still survives with some companies thriving on the basis of their international competitiveness in specialised markets.

The city centre has been substantially re-shaped following an extensive property-led regeneration programme from the 1990s, funded in part through European Union (EU) 'Objective 1' designation (the 'Heart of the City' project). A notable component of this was the designation of a pioneering 'Cultural Industries Quarter' (CIQ) close to the city centre (Roodhouse 2006). The CIQ has been the subject of international interest and is home to artist studios such as Yorkshire Art-space, the Showroom Cinema, which hosts a number of high-profile film festivals, notably the International Documentary Film Festival, and galleries. However, the story has not always been one of success, with the most notable failure being the closure of the National Centre for Popular Music following very disappointing visitor admissions.

Sheffield has a strong musical scene and legacy, including the recent commercial and critical success of Arctic Monkeys, Richard Hawley and Jarvis Cocker and prominent contributors to 'synthpop' and electronic music from the 1980s, such as Human League, Cabaret Voltaire, the Thompson Twins and Heaven 17. Jarvis Cocker currently presents a critically acclaimed programme on BBC Radio 6 Music, as part of which he presented a personal and evocative 'Musical Map' of his home city. However, there is need for caution by tourism and cultural agencies in their desire to capitalise on such artistic interventions. The author of this case study recalls Richard Hawley during a public meeting dismissing the city's proposal to be the UK City of Culture (a designation awarded to Derry) as something that artists did not endorse.

The city also has a thriving theatre sector, with the Crucible celebrating its 40th anniversary during 2011. The city is also home to the critically acclaimed theatre company 'Forced Entertainment', the work of which interestingly has included reference to tourism. The author of this case recalls attending their *Nights in the City* performance, which involved both audience and performers on board a moving bus conducted by 'tour guides' who avoided facts in search of competing versions of urban space, from the official and the historical to the personal, the mythical and the imaginary. This work has also been adapted for performance in Rotterdam.

In recent years the city marketing agency 'Creative Sheffield' has demonstrated an increased awareness of the value of the city's cultural life and legacy, for example through its promotion of a festival programme that includes 'Galvanise', focused on the work of local metalworkers, the 'Off the Shelf' literature festival, and 'Tramlines' free music festival at venues across the city centre. Its marketing strap line for creativity is 'Independent and Authentic', redolent of the city's sense of self-sufficiency and craft-based heritage. The official recognition of the value of creativity in the city's tourism offer is welcome and had not been prominent in the work of the former 'Destination Sheffield' agency.

## Conclusions

Tourism destination management and arts and cultural agencies in the UK public sector have faced deep cuts in their funding under the coalition government since 2010 (e.g. Brown 2011). There are growing expectations that both sectors will work more closely with and be funded by the private sector, as well as contributing to the 'Big Society' agenda through closer involvement with local communities, with examples including 'social tourism' and 'access to the arts' initiatives. Both tourism and creative industry sectors thus share challenges and experiences of the 'changing landscape' regarding public funding of their work. However, there are opportunities for closer working. Both the tourism and creative sectors 'reside' within the DCMS (at least in England) as the arm's-length 'home' of national tourist boards Visit Britain and Visit England, and also of agencies with strong relationships with tourism including Arts Council England, English Heritage, Historic Royal Palaces, and Museums, Libraries and Archives.

Within a UK context the creative industries emerged as a dominant part of the so-called social milieu of 'Cool Britannia', redolent of previous governments' attempts to promote political paradigms previously articulated in the 'Swinging 60s' within the white heat of technological societal revolution. Currently, the UK government's intended epoch-defining mantra is 'Big Society'. We have argued within this chapter that creativity is a timeless and a vital element of civil society – an eternal thread in the lineage from the Renaissance to post-industrial and post-modern society. Ironically, within a period of economic recession and austerity measures, funding for the creative industries and tourism have diminished yet there is an expectation that the creative industries will continue to be a key driver of economic prosperity. In highlighting the case study of Sheffield we recognise the innovation of a city that originally invested in infrastructure of the creative industries in the mid-1980s and continues successfully to nurture local creative talent which has been showcased increasingly for a global audience. However, given the concerns about the corporatisation, commodification and commercialisation of creativity, Sheffield continues to demonstrate how local creative 'animateurs' and craft-makers are given the scope to be creative as an aesthetic pursuit for its own sake. Whilst we have noted that the tourism industry has recognised the connection with creativity and provides niche opportunities for creative consumption, there is a serendipity and disconnection between policy communities for tourism and creativity, even within the policy communities of the DCMS. We note the urban emphasis to this critique and that future research might consider the nature of creativity in rural settings to offset the concentration on the urban context.

## References

Adorno, T. (1991) *The Culture Industry: Selected Essays on Mass Culture*, London: Routledge.

Beck, A. (2003) *Cultural Work: Understanding the Cultural Industries*, Routledge: London.

Bourdieu, P. (1984 [1979]) *Distinction: A Social Critique of the Judgement of Taste*, trans. R. Nice, Cambridge, MA: Harvard University Press.

Brown, M. (2011) Arts Council England to Shake Up Museum Funding Programme, www.guardian.co.uk/culture/culture-cuts-blog/2011/aug/12/arts-funding-museums (accessed 15 November 2012).

Csíkszentmihályi, M. (1997) *Creativity: Flow and the Psychology of Discovery and Invention*, New York: Harper.

——(1999) 'Implications of a Systems Perspective for the Study of Creativity', in R.J. Sternberg (ed.) *Handbook of Creativity*, Cambridge: Cambridge University Press, 313–39.

DCMS (2001) *Culture and Creativity*, London: Department for Culture, Media and Sport.

——(2004) *Government and the Value of Culture*, London: Department for Culture, Media and Sport.

Fitzgibbon, M. and Kelly, A. (eds) (1997) *From Maestro to Manager: Critical Issues in Arts and Cultural Management*, Dublin: Oak Tree Press.

Habermas, J. (1987) *The Philosophical Discourse of Modernity: Twelve Lectures*, trans. F. Lawrence, Cambridge, MA: MIT Press.

Hartley, J. (ed.) (2005) *Creative Industries*, Oxford: Blackwell.

Hesmondhalgh, D. (2002) *The Cultural Industries*, London: Sage.

Higgs, P. and Cunningham, S. (2008) 'Creative Industries Mapping: Where Have We Come From and Where Are We Going?' *Creative Industries Journal* 1(1): 7–30.

Hughes, H. (2000) *Arts, Entertainment and Tourism*, Oxford: Butterworth-Heinneman.

Lonely Planet (2005) *Lonely Planet Guide to Experimental Travel*, Melbourne: Lonely Planet.

Marletta, D. (2011) *'Sharing Bits': Creating Sociability in the Age of the Digital Agora*, unpublished PhD thesis, Leeds Metropolitan University, UK.

Muggleton, D. and Weinzierl, R. (eds) (2003) *The Post-Subcultures Reader*, Oxford: Berg.

Negus, K. and Pickering, M. (2004) *Creativity, Communication and Cultural Value*, London: Sage.

Novelli, M. (ed.) (2005) *Niche Tourism: Contemporary Issues, Trends and Cases*, Oxford: Elsevier.

Packard, V. (1960) *The Wastemakers*, London: Verso.

Pine, B.J. and Gilmore, J.H. (1999) *The Experience Economy*, Boston, MA: Harvard Business School Press.

Raunig, G., Ray, G. and Wuggenig, U. (eds) (2011) *Critique of Creativity: Precarity, Subjectivity and Resistance in the Creative Industries*, London: Mayfly Books.

Richards, G. and Wilson, J. (2006) 'Developing Creativity in Tourist Experiences: A Solution to the Serial Reproduction of Culture?' *Tourism Management* 27: 1209–23.

Robinson, K. (2001) *Out of Our Minds: Learning to be Creative*, Chichester: Capstone.

Roodhouse, S. (2006) *Cultural Quarters: Principles and Practices*, Bristol: Intellect Books.

Schlesinger, P. (2007) 'Creativity: From Discourse to Doctrine?' *Screen* 48(3): 377–87.

# 39

# Cultural tourism development in the post-industrial city

## Development strategies and critical reflection

*Clare Carruthers*

## Introduction

The role of culture and tourism in urban development and regeneration strategies in the UK, Europe and North America is increasingly recognised at both a policy and planning level in economic urban regeneration, as more and more cities incorporate these elements into their overall process of economic urban renewal. In the last two to three decades the policy makers of many de-industrialised cities across North America and Europe have seen the development of their tourism industries as one possible means of economic regeneration as it had the potential to 'breathe new life into old cities' (Law 1996: 11). The Organisation for Economic Co-operation and Development (OECD 2009) identifies a number of both demand and supply factors leading to the convergence between tourism and culture, including post-modern consumption styles, increased interest in culture, the desire for more direct forms of experience, the use of cultural tourism as an economic development vehicle and the desire to improve the image of regions. This chapter examines that process as it has applied to UK cities, focusing on homogeneity versus unique identity, drawing critical reflections and presenting some considerations for future direction and sustainability.

## Homogenisation versus unique identities

Common features of these processes of development have included physical building and infrastructure improvements and projects and less tangible cultural elements, which have developed alongside renewed marketing campaigns and improved media coverage. Specific elements common in most cases include cultural flagship projects, such as The Burrell Collection, Glasgow, or the Angel of the North, Newcastle-Gateshead. The development of an ever-more expansive festival/event portfolio is also a key feature, in particular spurred on by the relative successes of Glasgow European City of Culture, 1990 and more recently Liverpool Capital of Culture 2008. In addition, these very large-scale events make a contribution to the role of improved images and marketing. The re-use of disused industrial space is another common response, with numerous examples including the Baltic Centre for Contemporary Arts, Newcastle-Gateshead, and Tramway, Glasgow.

Alongside these specific projects has been the role of waterfront regeneration schemes such as that of the regeneration of the Clydeside, Glasgow, the Albert Dock, Liverpool and the regeneration of Birmingham's canal network. Further supporting infrastructure developments include improved access and transport development and further development of the overall tourist offering in terms of accommodation, food and drink, entertainment and retail activities.

Richards and Wilson (2007b) note that ideas are often borrowed in attempting to distinguish one place from another on the grounds of culture, so that there is little cultural distinction. This is a theme echoed by Sigala and Leslie (2005: 238), in particular in relation to cultural tourism where they note that novelties 'begin to wear thin as tourists become blasé, tired of the same old thing, and search for the new and that which is different'.

Robinson and Smith (2006) discuss the culture of the everyday and the ordinary as including the experiences tourists have just because they are in a new or unfamiliar place, such as food, shopping and menus, and note that these important resources are not always recognised by host authorities, but in fact are far more likely to shape the overall experience for the cultural tourist since that is how most of their time is spent rather than formal visits to cultural manifestations housed in galleries and museums. Smith (2007) goes on to suggest that homogenised developments need to be complemented by development that reflects something of the local place and identity.

Richards (2001, 2002, 2009) and Richards and Wilson (2007a, 2007b) also discuss the development of creative tourism as a new market opportunity in light of increased competition in the cultural tourism market, and that destinations should consider developing creative capital as an extension to their cultural resources. In developing tourism that is not homogeneous Richards and Wilson (2006: 1210) suggest that cultural tourism be reoriented towards 'new models of creativity-led tourism', noting that the development of creativity and the creative industries has been emphasised more in the strategies of many cities throughout the late 1990s and early twenty-first century (Richards and Wilson 2007a).

## Critical reflections

These types of economic renewal and regeneration strategies in cities have attracted considerable critical attention. Much criticism focuses on the high degree of homogeneity that tends to exist in common responses, resulting in the 'high street effect', where every place possesses similar advantages in terms of the overall tourism product offering, notably in retail, accommodation, food and drink establishments and so on.

Bianchini and Schwengel (1991 in Chang et al. 1996: 286) refer to the 'Americanisation' and 'Europeanisation' of cities, where homogeneity occurs with 'the duplication of features such as waterfront zones, festival marketplaces, downtown malls and tourism-historic districts in a diverse array of cities'. This theme is also echoed by Swarbrooke (2000: 273), who warns against the danger of 'product standardization' that could in effect 'reduce the long term appeal of these destinations in the future'. Chang et al. (1996) also note that historically cities differ and it is these differences that should be the basis for competition, a theme which is also echoed by Law (1993).

Further criticisms focus on the social issues inherent in such strategies in that they have been, in the main, property-led booster strategies accompanied by place marketing initiatives that did not bear any resemblance to the realities of the local place (Judd 1995; Robinson 1999). They have been criticised for not delivering the promised results in terms of improved quality of life and employment multipliers for local communities and have resulted in gentrification, creating further economic and social divisions, divisions in spatial distribution between the centre and the periphery, and marginalisation of already fairly excluded communities (Parkinson and Judd 1988; Harvey 1989; Bianchini 1991; Zukin 1995; Eisinger 2000; Garcia 2004; Miles 2005).

The lack of a sufficient evidence base demonstrating the benefits of culture-led regeneration is also criticised (Judd 1995; Eisinger 2000; Garcia 2004; Evans 2005; Miles and Paddison 2005). In addition, the long-term, sustainable benefits and impacts of these strategies are also questioned (Parkinson and Judd 1988; Bianchini 1991; Zukin 1995; Miles 2005), and in particular these criticisms question the large public-sector investments in such strategies and the disregard of social and community needs in favour of attracting tourists and boosting the city image with high-profile cultural infrastructure projects (Garcia 2004).

Garcia argues that investment in cultural production is a more effective approach in guaranteeing 'a degree of control over the local economy and its sustainability in the long term' (Garcia 2004: 323). Bianchini (1991: 242) goes on to suggest that arts initiatives in more peripheral areas in a city could be strengthened or indeed created 'from scratch', but that these would need to be fully accessible and fully integrated with the provision of other local amenities. Such initiatives would co-exist alongside strategies that would make the central areas 'accessible, safe and attractive for all citizens' (Bianchini 1991: 243), and a more democratic model of cultural planning with co-operation between numerous agencies, where there is no sharp distinction between those policies aimed at tourists and those aimed at the local population.

Evans (2005) notes a distinct lack of evidence to support culture-led regeneration, while Garcia argues that the investment in high-profile events and cultural infrastructure are not 'framed in an assessment of long term cultural legacies or coherent strategies that seeks to secure a balanced spatial and social distribution of benefits' (Garcia 2004: 313). She draws on the case study of Glasgow 1990 to illustrate that often culture is used as an 'instrument for economic regeneration without being supported by properly developed urban cultural policy' (ibid.: 319), where the economic perspective overrides the social/cultural/community dimension. She criticises approaches to the monitoring of large, high-profile cultural events, specifically the European Capital of Culture event, calling for more monitoring and evaluation of them over the long term in the form of longitudinal studies that assess their true sustainability, impacts and legacies, not just in economic terms but in social and cultural terms as well. This theme is also addressed by Miles and Paddison (2005), who question the long-term sustainability of cultural regeneration.

---

### Box 39.1 Case study: Liverpool – the world in one city

Liverpool in the UK has seen a continual period of investment and development from the late 1980s onwards in its tourism and cultural infrastructure. Early examples include the redevelopment of the Albert Dock, with its mixed use-style regeneration. The first such project of its kind in the UK, it incorporates the Tate Gallery, the Maritime Museum, a TV news centre, shops, restaurants, cafes, bars, exhibition areas, hotel accommodation, The Beatles Story Exhibition and the International Slavery Museum.

Alongside this was the upgrading of existing cultural capital such as that of St George's Hall, a £23 million project, largely funded by Lottery money, as a major cultural venue and community hub. In addition, the designation of United Nations Educational, Scientific and Cultural

Organization (UNESCO) World Heritage site status in July 2004 to much of Liverpool's Waterfront further strengthened the position of the city as an important heritage and cultural destination.

The most significant recent development for Liverpool came in 2003 when it was announced as the host for the European Capital of Culture 2008. Central in the bid campaign for Liverpool was the role and input of the local community. Indeed, this was specifically identified as a deciding factor in awarding the designation (Richards and Palmer 2010). The bid strap line, 'The World in One City', was intended to convey the city's multiculturalism, not just in its present-day population mix but in its industrial heritage and multicultural past.

Like elsewhere, the process of development in Liverpool has not been without its critics, who raise concerns in relation to employment structure, social divisions, gentrification and the question of 'whose culture?' (Jones and Wilks-Heeg 2004: 342). However, a research project conducted by the University of Liverpool and John Moores University involved a longitudinal impact analysis of the event for the period 2005–10, which focused on economic, social and cultural dimensions. The report indicates that actually the city benefited from £4 billion worth of investment in physical infrastructure, with around £1.5 billion of that being completed in 2008 itself. In terms of tourism the year-long event in 2008 attracted 9.7 million additional visits, with additional direct visitor spend estimated at £753.8 million. However, Garcia et al. (2011) caution that the sustainable benefits of this event cannot be measured at such an early stage and that ongoing measurement and analysis is required to fully understand the sustainable aspects and legacies of such an event.

## Future directions and sustainability

With such intensified inter-urban competition and criticism of the social issues that may result from these processes, what is the way forward for cities wishing to continue their development and regeneration in this vein? It is clear that while there are certainly commonalities in much of the development that has taken place thus far, there is not a 'one size fits all' model, and that strategies for this type of development need to be flexible to account for unique local contexts and relevant opportunities.

It would appear also that there is a lack of any in-depth market research in relation to tourists' opinions and perceptions of such strategies and this is something that may need to be addressed, in particular in light of reduced public subsidy for many arts, cultural and tourism projects and organisations. Development decisions can therefore be made based on more accurate data on the market and what tourists seek from their experiences, in turn leading to more effective and targeted marketing.

Consideration also needs to be given at the policy and planning stage to the opportunities and challenges that are unique to the local place. Not only will this allow key challenges to be considered and addressed but it may contribute towards differentiating cities with similar competitive advantages, thereby avoiding the 'serial reproduction' of culture referred to by Richards and Wilson (2006, 2008).

Consideration might also be given to the development of tourist services provision that provides a more bespoke offering, including small-scale independents and speciality retailers, for example, thereby avoiding homogeneity of the offer. Development of this type could contribute towards the unique sense of local place and identity in these cities.

Opportunities to develop creative tourism as an extension to cultural tourism may also be considered in these cities, as advocated by Richards (2001, 2002, 2007, 2009) and Richards and Wilson (2007a, 2007b). In particular, cities that have been investing heavily in their creative economies as an element of the broader process of regeneration are well placed to fully develop and exploit such an opportunity. Again, development of this type could contribute towards the unique sense of local place and identity in these cities, avoiding the homogeneity already referred to here (Richards and Wilson 2006, 2007c). It is clear that simply mirroring what has happened elsewhere is no longer a viable option in an increasingly intensified market.

## References

Bianchini, F. (1991) 'Urban Renaissance? The Arts and the Urban Regeneration Process', in McGregor, S. and Pimlott, B. (eds) *Tackling the Inner Cities: The 1980's Reviewed, Prospects for the 1990's*, Oxford: Clarendon Press, 215–50.

Chang, T.C., Milne, S., Fallon, D. and Pohlmann, C. (1996) 'Urban Heritage Tourism: The Global-Local Nexus', *Annals of Tourism Research* 23(2): 284–305.

Eisinger, P. (2000) 'The Politics of Bread and Circuses: Building the City for the Visitor Class', *Urban Affairs Review* 35(3): 316–33.

Evans, G. (2005) 'Measure for Measure: Evaluating the Evidence of Culture's Contribution to Regeneration', *Urban Studies* 42(5/6): 959–83.

Garcia, B. (2004) 'Cultural Policy and Urban Regeneration in Western European Cities: Lessons Learned from Experience, Prospects for the Future', *Local Economy* 19(4): 312–26.

Garcia, B., Melville, R. and Cox, T. (2011) *Impacts 08 European Capital of Culture Research Programme: Creating an Impact: Liverpool's Experience as European Capital of Culture*, Liverpool: University of Liverpool and Liverpool John Moores University.

Harvey, D. (1989) 'Down Towns', *Marxism Today*, January 1989: 21.

Jones, P. and Wilks-Heeg, S. (2004) 'Capitalising Culture: Liverpool 2008', *Local Economy* 19(4): 341–60.

Judd, D.R. (1995) 'Promoting Tourism in US Cities', *Tourism Management* 16(3): 175–87.

Law, C.M. (1993) *Urban Tourism: Attracting Visitors to Large Cities*, London: Mansell Publishing.

——(1996) 'Tourism in British Provincial Cities: A Tale of Four Cities', in Law, C.M. (ed.) *Tourism in Major Cities*, London: Thompson, 179–205.

Miles, S. (2005) '"Our Tyne": Iconic Regeneration and the Revitalization of Identity in Newcastle Gateshead', *Urban Studies* 42 (5/6): 913–26.

Miles, S. and Paddison, R. (2005) 'Introduction: The Rise and Rise of Culture-led Urban Regeneration', *Urban Studies* 42 (5/6): 833–39.

OECD (2009) *The Impact of Culture on Tourism*, Paris: OECD.

Parkinson, M. and Judd, D. (1988) 'Urban Revitalization in America and the UK – The Politics of Uneven Development', in Parkinson, M., Foley, B. and Judd, D. (eds) *Regenerating the Cities: The UK Crisis and the US Experience*, Manchester: Manchester University Press, 1–8.

Richards, G. (2001) 'Cultural Tourists or a Culture of Tourism? Developments in the European Cultural Tourism Market', in Butcher, J. (ed.) *Innovations in Cultural Tourism: Proceedings of the 5th ATLAS International Conference Innovatory Approaches to Culture and Tourism*, Tilburg: ATLAS, 1–9.

——(2002) 'From Cultural Tourism to Creative Tourism: European Perspectives', *Tourism* 50(3): 225–33.

——(2007) 'Introduction', in Richards, G. (ed.) *Cultural Tourism: Global and Local Perspectives*, New York: Haworth Press, 1–24.

——(2009) *Tourism Development Trajectories – From Culture to Creativity?* Paper presented to the Asia-Pacific Forum on Culture and Tourism, Jeju Island, Republic of Korea, 3–5 June 2009.

Richards, G. and Palmer, R. (2010) *Eventful Cities: Cultural Management and Urban Revitalisation*, Oxford: Elsevier.

Richards, G. and Wilson, J. (2006) 'Developing Creativity in Tourist Experiences: A Solution to the Serial Reproduction of Culture?' *Tourism Management* 27(6): 1209–23.

——(2007a) 'The Creative Turn in Regeneration: Creative Spaces, Spectacles and Tourism in Cities', in Smith, K. (ed.) *Tourism, Culture and Regeneration*, Wallingford: CABI, 12–24.

——(2007b) 'Tourism Development Trajectories: From Culture to Creativity?' in Richards, G. and Wilson, J. (eds) *Tourism, Creativity and Development*, London: Routledge, 1–33.

——(2007c) 'Creativities in Tourism Development?' in Richards, G. and Wilson, J. (eds) *Tourism, Creativity and Development*, London: Routledge, 255–88.

——(2008) 'From Cultural Tourism to Creative Tourism: Part 2 Changing Structures of Collaboration', *Proceedings of the ATLAS International Conference*, Barcelona, 2005: 7–9.

Robinson, M. (1999) 'Tourism Development in De-industrializing Centres of the UK: Change, Culture and Conflict', in Robinson, M. and Boniface, P. (eds) *Tourism and Cultural Conflicts*, Wallingford: CABI, 129–59.

Robinson, M. and Smith, M. (2006) 'Politics, Power and Play: The Shifting Contexts of Cultural Tourism', in Robinson, M. and Smith, M. (eds) *Cultural Tourism in a Changing World: Politics, Participation and (Re)presentation*, Clevedon: Channel View, 1–17.

Sigala, M. and Leslie, D. (2005) 'The Future of the Past: Visions and Trends for Cultural Tourism Sector', in Sigala, M. and Leslie, D. (eds) *International Cultural Tourism: Management, Implications and Cases*, Oxford: Elsevier Butterworth-Heinemann, 234–40.

Smith, M.K. (2007) 'Introduction', in Smith, M.K. (ed.) *Tourism, Culture and Regeneration*, Wallingford: CABI, xiii–xix.

Swarbrooke, J. (2000) 'Tourism, Economic Development and Urban Regeneration: A Critical Evaluation', in Robinson, M., Sharpley, R., Evans, N., Long, P. and Swarbrooke, J. (eds) *Developments in Urban and Rural Tourism*, Sunderland: Business Education Publishers, 269–85.

Zukin, S. (1995) *The Cultures of Cities*, Oxford: Blackwell.

## Further reading

Avery, P. (2007) 'Born Again: From Dock Cities to Cities of Culture', in Smith, M.K. (ed.) *Tourism, Culture and Regeneration*, Wallingford: CABI, 151–62. (An examination of the changing role of dockland cities and urban regeneration strategies with specific reference to Albert Dock, Liverpool and Cardiff Bay, Cardiff.)

Avery, P.M. (2000) 'City Cultures as the Object of Cultural Tourism 2000', in Robinson, M., Sharpley, R., Evans. N., Long, P. and Swarbrooke, J. (eds) *Developments in Urban and Rural Tourism*, Sunderland: Business Education Publishers, 21–51. (A conceptual approach to examining city cultures, particularly cultural quarters and a case study of Temple Bar, Dublin, Ireland.)

Bailey, C., Miles, S. and Stark, P. (2004) 'Culture-led Urban Regeneration and the Revitalisation of Identities in Newcastle, Gateshead and the North East of England', *International Journal of Cultural Policy* 10(1): 47–65. (An in-depth longitudinal examination of the long-term social impacts of culture-led regeneration in Newcastle-Gateshead, with particular relevance to the Quayside regeneration.)

Law, C.M. (2002) *Urban Tourism: The Visitor Economy and the Growth of Large Cities*, second edn, London: Continuum. (Scope, scale, demand and strategy of urban tourism.)

Maitland, R. (2007) 'Tourists, the Creative Class and Distinctive Areas in Major Cities: The Roles of Visitors and Residents in Developing New Tourism Areas', in Richards, G. and Wilson, J. (eds) *Tourism, Creativity and Development*, London: Routledge, 73–86. (The role that tourism and tourists play, alongside residents in shaping creative spaces in cities.)

O'Brien, D. (2010) Measuring the Value of Culture: A Report to the Department for Culture, Media and Sport, London: DCMS, www.culture.gov.uk. (A report examining ways in which culture should/could be valued in the UK.)

Smith, M. (2009) *Issues in Cultural Tourism Studies*, second edn, Abingdon: Routledge. (Examination of the phenomenon of cultural tourism and issues therein.)

Throsby, D. (2010) *The Economics of Cultural Policy*, Cambridge: Cambridge University Press. (Examination of policies emphasising the links between the economic and the cultural.)

# 40

# After the crisis

## Cultural tourism and urban regeneration in Europe

*James Kennell*

Over the last three decades urban regeneration and tourism in Europe have become most closely linked through the phenomenon of cultural regeneration, an approach to urban development that has become a significant part of the suite of approaches to regeneration used by governments and regeneration agencies (Evans 2005; Smith 2007a; Vickery 2007). Landry (2000) argues that the reason why some post-industrial cities have prospered since the economic crises of the 1970s and 1980s is precisely because they made this turn to cultural investment and creativity in the context of urban decline and renewal. Evans highlights the potential for cultural development as a mode of action within the policy arena as one of the few available strategies that can engage with globalisation and 'capture the twin goals of competitive advantage and quality of life' (Evans 2005: 960), perhaps helping to explain its current popularity. Grodach and Loukaitou-Sideris (2007) reinforce this perspective, highlighting how cities pursue cultural development strategies to catalyse inward business investment, increase consumption by residents and tourists, improve city image and enhance local quality of life.

In the context of urban regeneration, culture is defined broadly, but can involve elements or combinations of:

- Architecture
- Heritage buildings and attractions
- Visual and performing arts
- Festivals and events
- Tourism development
- Entertainment and leisure complexes
- 'Culture as a way of life'.

(Smith 2007b: 2)

These elements are valorised and then commercialised through cultural tourism, which provides the marketplace of consumption necessary for the economic model that underpins cultural regeneration to be sustainable. This model has four components, shown in Figure 40.1, each of

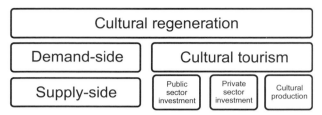

*Figure 40.1* Economic aspects of cultural regeneration

which has been significantly affected by the economic crisis that has been evolving in Europe since 2008. Each of these components will be analysed in turn below.

There are three key elements on the supply side for cultural regeneration projects which work to create the tourism products and services for the cultural tourism market. The first of these is public-sector investment. Many cultural regeneration schemes have relied on significant levels of state funding for key infrastructure and cultural facilities. For example, in the late 1990s, the councils of the cities of Newcastle and Gateshead in the north-east of England began to work together on a cultural regeneration strategy that was to bear fruit in 2002 with the opening of a major new contemporary art museum and an international-standard concert hall in a previously run-down industrial area on the Tyne river. This scheme has led to the growth of the cities' night-time economies (Miles 2010) and has helped to kick-start economic growth in the creative industries (Minton 2004). The value of tourism to the regional economy in Newcastle and Gateshead grew by 30 per cent year-on-year in the first five years after the new Baltic Gallery opened in 2002 (NEBG 2008). The investment required to develop this programme of cultural interventions in regeneration was led by the public sector, with over £200 million of state funding supplied by a consortia of public bodies from local government, regional development and the cultural sector (One North East 2011).

Attracting new private-sector investment is a key driver of contemporary regeneration. The metropolitan area of Lille, France, and its surrounding towns was suffering from the negative consequences of economic restructuring and deindustrialisation when the decision was taken to regenerate the city-region in the 1990s. This regeneration has had significant cultural components, and was driven by the successful bid of Lille to become European Capital of Culture in 2004, which had the newly refurbished Palais des Beaux Arts as its centrepiece venue. A town in the Lille metropolitan area, Roubaix, had previously been regarded as the 'worst town in France' (Cadell *et al.* 2008) and culture was central to its regeneration plans, including 'la piscine', a renovated Art Deco public baths, now a national museum of art and industry, and 'la conditione publique', a former industrial building from the region's once dominant textiles industry, now converted into a cultural hub with recording facilities, a concert hall, and theatre and exhibition spaces. The initial regeneration programme in Lille, which occurred at the time of the opening of the cross-channel Eurotunnel terminal in the city, was funded mainly from the private sector (FR3.5 billion from FR5 billion in total) and the city region has used public funding to leverage private-sector investment as the regeneration has continued. The private sector has led on the creation of new business and science parks, creating new industrial sectors populated by firms which have been attracted by the improved quality of life and renewed image of the area, including Haute-Bonne which is home to 60 scientific research laboratories. Inward investment and job creation in the Lille region has dramatically increased, with 15 per cent of new jobs coming from high-value knowledge industries (Bacon *et al.* 2008).

The third element of the supply side system for cultural regeneration is cultural production. This can involve the direct production of cultural goods and experiences by individuals, groups of producers and businesses, or indirect provision in the shape of exhibitions, touring performances, retail and other methods of supplying non-locally produced cultural output. Undervaerket in Randers, Denmark's sixth-largest city, is an example of a cultural regeneration project that has cultural production as its main driver. Randers has endured a long period of economic decline as traditional industries associated with shipping and clothing manufacture have shrunk. The city government also identified difficulties in the integration of newly arrived migrants into areas already suffering from socioeconomic problems. Part of the solution to this twin dilemma has been Undervaerket, a bazaar-style cluster of shops, market stalls, cultural and educational spaces (Undervaerket 2011). This new creative space brings craftspeople, including jewellers, glass blowers, graphic artists, ceramic artists, textile printers and weavers into close proximity to each other and to a concentration of ethnic businesses and facilities. Many of the projects in Undervaerket have involved using cultural production to break down barriers between immigrant and indigenous groups and new businesses have started up capitalising on the presence of imported craft traditions. The ERDF-funded UrbAct programme found that 'Its strength lies in the way it combines regeneration, job creation, training, small business support and tourism while at the same time harnessing cultural diversity to a cultural industries strategy' (Udix Alep 2005).

Uniting all three of these examples is the demand-side aspect of cultural regeneration: cultural tourism. It is through this form of tourism that cultural regeneration schemes derive a vital source of ongoing revenue, leading to business growth and increased local taxation. Cultural tourism also provides a shop window for promoting inward investment and relocation by businesses and individuals. Cultural tourism is seen as both a 'good' form of tourism in that it promotes sustainability and inter-cultural communication, and as a high-value industry because of the high-spending tourists who take part in it (Cengiz *et al.* 2006). This combination of sustainability and economic impact makes cultural tourism an attractive tool for policy makers seeking to regenerate an area through diversification and stimulation of its economy – a key aim of regeneration projects. In addition, the achievement of more wide-ranging outcomes is predicated on the knock-on benefits of income streams that have cultural tourism and private-sector growth at their base.

The global financial crisis that began in 2008 has had significant impacts on the global tourism industry. Tourism has experienced greater falls in spending than other industries, impacting negatively on the economic contribution that tourism makes to destinations (Sheldon and Dwyer 2010). By the first quarter of 2009, global tourism arrivals had dropped by 8 per cent and in Europe, international arrivals were down by 10 per cent (Smeral 2010). Although there has been some limited recovery since 2009, especially on inbound trips to the European Union (EU) and in low-cost markets (Eurostats 2011), internal demand is likely to remain suppressed by the effects of the crisis in the eurozone which is producing growing unemployment and significant drops in both public- and private-sector investment. Public-sector austerity and private-sector retrenchment are creating a crisis for cultural regeneration in Europe as a wide debate takes place about the value of public spending in areas of culture, tourism and regeneration, at the same time as private investment in tourism and regeneration is dropping and the lucrative cultural tourism market is shrinking. The one element of the supply side that does not bear a direct relationship to the economic crisis is cultural production, calling into question Kunzmann's assertion that 'Each story of regeneration begins with poetry and ends with real estate' (cited in Evans 2005: 959). After the crisis, poetry may be the only reliable component of cultural regeneration in Europe.

If it is cultural production that will be the driving force of cultural regeneration in the coming years, then the question must be asked what impact this might have on the urban environment and what relationship, if any, this will have to cultural tourism in Europe? The story of massive cultural investment in regeneration that had its beginnings in 1997 with the Guggenheim Museum in Bilbao may well have come to an end with the 2011 opening of Turner Contemporary in Margate, which benefited from £25 million of EU and UK government money, and which was intended to drive the regeneration of a prominent and now very deprived example of England's faded seaside towns. The gallery's 156,000 visitors in its first 12 weeks (Kent News 2011) have undoubtedly brought new money into the town, but, as with all models of cultural regeneration based on trickle-down economics, the future success of this intervention is precariously hitched to the economics of cultural tourism. In future, we should expect to see fewer large capital projects like these in cultural regeneration but instead, in those areas where the cultural route is valued and supported, higher levels of bottom-up activity, artist-led interventions in the urban fabric, and time-limited, event-driven approaches to cultural development, where cultural tourism is a more proportional aspect of the mix that sustains these projects. An example of how cultural regeneration can be driven from the bottom up, with minimal state or private investment, but maintaining the positive impacts of the cultural approach, is the People's Republic of Stokes Croft in Bristol, UK.

---

### Box 40.1 Case study: the People's Republic of Stokes Croft, Bristol, UK

Stokes Croft is the informal name for an area within Bristol, in the west of England, which has suffered from the historical decline of the city as an industrial and trading hub, but which has not benefited directly from the city's recent redevelopment as a financial and retail centre of regional importance. Stokes Croft is a diverse area that has seen high levels of immigration as well as playing host to transient populations of students, artists and squatters.

The People's Republic of Stokes Croft (PRSC) was formed in 2007 to bring together people from the local community to promote a positive sense of place for the area and to improve both its streetscape and its day-to-day life through the creation of a bottom-up cultural quarter. This is being achieved by groups of activists, individuals, residents and visitors, without dependence on public or private investment, building on the reputation of the area as creative and diverse, especially its international reputation for (often illegal) street art. Although the state, the third sector and private companies have been engaged in specific projects, the PRSC draws on local resources to achieve its aims and strongly resists attempts to direct the project from the outside. The aims of the PRSC align its objectives with the aims of cultural regeneration projects across Europe, which have attempted to link quality of life, creativity, tourism and sense of place:

> Our aim as a community will be to make the whole area a pleasure to visit, a place where people want to come and spend time … a place where people want to be. There is an enormous amount of traffic, vehicular and pedestrian, that passes through Stokes Croft every day, and our aim must be to make that experience as welcoming and as pleasant as possible. We will do this by attending to every aspect of the visual amenity of the area, by making the place feel loved, by positive energy. Stokes Croft as an area of outstanding creativity and individuality, as a gallery, as a sculpture, as a destination.
>
> (PRSC 2008: 1)

The PRSC has developed an artist-led regeneration plan (PRSC 2008), which contains details of specific short-, medium- and long-term projects, but recent projects in the area have included:

- Co-exist: a renovated 55,000-square foot former office building, taken over by a Community Interest Company and now home to a community kitchen, a restaurant, artist studios and a live music venue. This is a community-managed project that has attracted private investment from a property developer (Co-exist 2011).
- Stokes Croft StreetFest: organised in partnership with the Bristol Festival Community Group, this is a one-day festival celebrating local creativity, diversity and inclusiveness. It is preceded by a week of community action to improve the area and includes music, art, theatre, stalls, children's activities and workshops (Stokes Croft StreetFest 2011).
- Visit Stokes Croft: this is an independent tourist brand for the area with the tag line 'Bristol's Cultural Quarter'. The website promotes the attractions of the area, primarily the high volume and world-leading quality street art that adorns the many abandoned buildings, as well as giving useful tourist information such as directions, food and drink, and contact details (Visit Stokes Croft 2011).

*Figure 40.2* Visit Stokes Croft poster

As Europe struggles to return to economic stability and growth over the coming decade, the rhetoric of cultural regeneration will be sorely tested by the lack of public and private investment available to drive it from the top down. Clearly, not everywhere can follow this model of bottom-up activism in cultural regeneration, but the example of Stokes Croft shows how the aims of cultural regeneration strategies can be achieved without the involvement of celebrity architects, landmark galleries and huge levels of investment. Regeneration that is driven by cultural production and producers, such as is taking place in Stokes Croft, creates new resources for cultural tourism, but these resources may not always fit neatly into the strategies of destination marketing organisations and local authority planners. For cultural tourism to continue to impact on urban regeneration in times of austerity will require tourism and regeneration professionals to develop new ways of working in partnership with cultural producers at the street and community levels, because without these relationships a major driver of regeneration will be lost.

## References

Bacon, N., Faizullah, N., Mulgan, G. and Woodcraft, S. (2008) *Transformers: How Local Areas Innovate to Address Changing Social Needs*, London: NESTA.

Cadell, C., Falk, N. and King, F. (2008) *Regeneration in European Cities*, York: Joseph Rowntree Foundation.

Cengiz, H., Eryılmaz, S.S. and Eryılmaz, Y. (2006) 'The Importance of Cultural Tourism in the EU Integration Process', paper given at the 42nd I SoCaRP Congress, 14–16 September, Yildiz, Turkey.

Co-exist (2011) *Hamilton House*, coexistcic.squarespace.com (accessed 24 January 2011).

Eurostats (2011) *Winter Season Tourism Trends 2010–11*, Luxembourg: European Commission.

Evans, G. (2005) 'Measure for Measure: Evaluating the Evidence of Culture's Contribution to Regeneration', *Urban Studies* 42(5/6): 959–83.

Grodach, C. and Loukaitou-Sideris, A. (2007) 'Cultural Development Strategies and Urban Revitalisation: A Survey of US Cities', *International Journal of Cultural Policy* 13(4): 349–70.

Kent News (2011) 'Turner Contemporary Welcomes its 156000th Visitor', www.kentnews.co.uk/mobile/news/turner_contemporary_welcomes_its_156_000th_visitor_1_969560 (accessed 24 January 2012).

Landry, C. (2000) *The Creative City: A Toolkit for Urban Innovators*, London: Earthscan.

Miles, S. (2010) *Spaces for Consumption*, London: Sage

Minton, A. (2004) *Northern Soul: Culture, Creativity and Quality of Place in Newcastle and Gateshead*, London: DEMOS/RICS.

NEBG (2008) 'Tourism Growth Supports Jobs in the North East', www.nebusinessguide.co.uk/news/art/194/Tourism-growth-supports-jobs-in-North-East.htm (accessed 15 November 2012).

One North East (2011) Culture, www.onenortheastlegacy.co.uk (accessed 23 January 2011).

PRSC (2008) *Overall Game Plan for Stokes Croft*, Bristol: PRSC.

Sheldon, P. and Dwyer, L. (2010) 'The Global Financial Crisis and Tourism: Perspectives of the Academy', *Journal of Travel Research* 49(1): 3–4.

Smeral, E. (2010) 'Impacts of the World Recession and Economic Crisis on Tourism: Forecasts and Potential Risks', *Journal of Travel Research* 49(1): 31–38.

Smith, M. (2007a) 'Towards a Cultural Planning Approach to Regeneration', in Smith, M. (ed.) *Tourism Culture and Regeneration*, Wallingford: CABI, 1–11.

——(2007b) 'Conclusion', in Smith, M. (ed.) *Tourism Culture and Regeneration*, Wallingford: CABI, 175–78.

Stokes Croft StreetFest (2011) Stokes Croft StreetFest, stokescroftstreetfest.wordpress.com (accessed 23 January 2012).

Udix Alep (2005) *Quartiers en Crise*, www.qec-eran.org/urbact/underverkaet_ws7.htm (accessed 23 January 2012).

Undervaerket (2011) *Forside*, www.undervaerket.dk/Forside.html (accessed 23 January 2012).

Vickery, J. (2007) *The Emergence of Culture-led Regeneration: A Policy Concept and its Discontents*, Centre for Cultural Policy Studies Research Paper No.9, University of Warwick.

Visit Stokes Croft (2011) *Visit Stokes Croft*, visitstokescroft.wordpress.com (accessed 24 January 2011).

## Further reading

Florida, R. (2010) *The Great Reset: How New Ways of Living and Working Drive Post-crash Prosperity*, New York: Harper Collins. (Written by the researcher who coined the term 'the creative class', this book covers both the causes of the current economic crisis and explores a set of solutions that can be applied in cities to promote new growth.)

Miles, S. (2010) *Spaces for Consumption*, London: Sage. (This book looks at the phenomenon of the modern, globalised city and questions the place of culture and consumption within it. It has chapters on mega-events, theming and retail which analyse the importance of these aspects of tourism for understanding the development and regeneration of urban areas.)

Smith, M. (ed.) (2007) *Tourism Culture and Regeneration*, Wallingford: CABI. (This edited collection contains a range of contributions that vary from the strategic and conceptual to the very practical, and are based on a wide variety of international case studies.)

Throsby, D. (2010) *The Economics of Cultural Policy*, Cambridge: Cambridge University Press. (A very accessible cultural economics text for non-specialists that includes sections on the role of culture in urban and regional development and also on the links between tourism, cultural tourism and economic development.)

# 41

# From the dual tourist city to the creative melting pot

## The liquid geographies of global cultural consumerism

*Antonio Paolo Russo and Alan Quaglieri-Domínguez*

### Urban tourism as global cultural consumerism

Although the lack of incontrovertible statistical data catches the attention, commentators and professionals in the sector agree that urban tourism has been experiencing a stage of steady expansion for at least three decades now (Keller 2005). The example of Spain is illuminating. Although Spain arguably owes its status as one of the world's top tourism destinations to its archetypal 'sun, sea and sand' brand, overnight stays in the capital Madrid rose by 27 per cent between 2003 and 2006, to reach 13.5 million (INE 2011); stays in Barcelona in that same period surpassed 11.2 million, with a 28 per cent increase; stays in Valencia increased by 47.5 per cent, reaching 5.6 million. In all three cases, growth rates surpass the national average (around 20 per cent), while Spain's main beach destinations were virtually stagnating. Even when the global financial meltdown struck hard in Spain, in the 2006–09 period, urban destinations increased their market shares (Madrid +3 per cent, Barcelona +9 per cent, while the country as a whole slumped by –6 per cent). This trend is likewise confirmed in the most popular destination regions, and is changing the map of the 'visited world' at the fine scale (Richards 2007).

The growth of the importance of cities as destinations cannot be explained solely by their advantage as highly (and cheaply) accessible places. Rather, it seems to express a specificity of urban destinations, which hints at the increasing capacity of urban landscapes (and in general of the 'urban' as a cultural fact, as suggested by Delgado 1999) to connect with the expectations of a new generation of travellers, for whom the historical-architectural heritage, as well as the artificial 'leisurescapes' of the sun belt, are losing their traditional primacy as drivers of tourism.

As a reflection of a general trend in the knowledge society, expert travellers are less and less moved by the 'objects' that can be found in places, observed, photographed, and seldom anything deeper than that, and instead become increasingly interested in the experiences that they can have in places; their performances and the way they are shaped by – and in turn shape –

place become the very essence of such experiences, an end of travel in itself (Feifer 1985). From this point of view, many authors, notably Maitland (2008), cast doubts on the very definition of *cultural* tourism, advocating an ontological shift by which this should be about 'the culture of tourists', or more precisely about the cultural processes that are triggered by outsiders visiting a place, which may – and most often do – lead to transformations or 're-inscriptions' of the system of signs and values that make it meaningful, dissolving the duality between 'out there' and 'back home' in the practices of travel.

The shift, however, is also epistemological, because if it is true that cultural tourism is not about the object of the visit but rather about what a tourist does in a place, on one hand there are no more explicitly 'cultural' tourist destinations as separated from others that are 'non-cultural', and second, knowledge about cultural tourism implies a re-focus on the subjective nature of representations and performances of place (Ritzer and Liska 1997; Coleman and Crang 2002; Richards and Wilson 2006), which are notably very diverse – from mere 'gaze' to a deeper process of 'comprehension' of place – and mediated by agency to varying degrees, as underlined by Urry (1990).

As a result, (cultural) tourism cannot easily be 'bounded off' as a separated activity distinguishable from other mobilities (Maitland and Ritchie 2009), just as it is increasingly difficult to disentangle the cultural processes that are unequivocally 'local' – the destinations 'backstage', understood in objective terms as untouched by tourism – from the 'touristscapes', spaces constructed for and through tourism activity and the global mobilisation of their narratives (Edensor 2006). The 'everyday consumption landscape' (Maitland 2008) becomes the ideal environment in which such encounters and exchanges take place: hence, a strategic asset in the city's competitiveness.

From this point of view, which is becoming widely shared in the study of tourism, we claim that cities do attract more interest as destinations because this is where 'intermission' between visitors as not only spectators but transforming agents, is potentially more intense, diverse and problematic. As nodes in an a-geographic system that promotes global contents and meanings, open to global flows of users, or audiences, cities are attractive and at the same time more complex places to study – let alone to manage.

When questioned about their reason for choosing a destination, visitors to large cities tend to refer to specific experiences that can be had there, rather than to the objective features (sights, attractions) that they offer: food that can be eaten there, music that can be heard, smells, manifestations in which to take part (Richards 2007). Cities are diverse, powerful, 'noisy'. The manifold conflicts, dissonant voices and minority stances that populate contemporary cities multiply the dimensions and the depth of such 'intermission', offering narratives that are appropriated and re-elaborated by visitors according to their own cultural perspective.

## The social geography of tourist cities: an analytical framework

Along with the division between object (place) and subjects (tourists), a second 'barrier' is critiqued in this poststructuralist re-visioning of tourism: that between hosts and guests. Again Urry (2000) suggested that as the (urban) post-Fordist society becomes increasingly mobile as a condition of life, tourism loses much of its extraordinary character, not only in terms of 'persistence in place', but also in regard to the content of the tourist experience, and may just come to be considered one form of mobility, temporary and motivated (mostly) by leisure, which insists on cities as cruxes of different other mobilities. Indeed, new forms of leisure or non-work-driven mobility have emerged and are increasingly blurring with the mobility of residents: foreign students on an Erasmus stay (see Buczkowska, this volume) and visiting researchers, second-home owners, post-bohemians 'finding themselves' in some big cities for a few months and working on a part-time basis, health tourists on a treatment, etc. (Quaglieri-Domínguez and Russo 2010).

Martinotti (1993) questioned the capacity of places to be resilient in the face of the 'multiplication' of uses, populations and cultures, which sees tourism as a major agent. In his 'three populations' theory of urbanisation, he postulated that a sustainable city or urban region is one that negotiates between different populations characterised by varying degrees of stability and patterns of place consumption, achieving a dynamic balance. Though his classification of populations draws a line between residents, commuting workers, regional consumers and tourists, his intuition – supported by research into successful cities – could be further elaborated along the lines of Urry's mobilities paradigm: different populations flow constantly in and out of cities and regions, contributing to the socioeconomic development of places.

It is up to the cities and regions to accommodate such diversity and nurture the social and cultural connections or 'atmospheric' elements that determine their capacity to offer a distinct and stimulating atmosphere where, according to the logic of experience marketing, ordinary activities are transformed in memorable experiences. This can be seen to depend to a large extent on the nature of the encounters and inter-relations of visitors with other collectives with which they share such experiences, which are remarkably 'spatialised' according to specific (and largely idiosyncratic) patterns.

In order to manage and brand the tourist city, it is thus paramount to understand these processes, both from a cultural and from a spatial point of view: which urban collectives are meeting? What is the nature of their interaction, and of the landscape that is negotiated? Where do these encounters take place, and how can space be consequently 'adjusted' to facilitate or steer the process?

To address this issue, we introduced in an earlier work (Quaglieri-Domínguez and Russo 2010) an analytic framework to 'map' the social geography of distinct urban populations. We so do by charting a continuum of different audiences along two dimensions: levels of transience (how persistent, or 'volatile', a group is likely to be in relation with places), and the strength of their ties (cultural, affective, social and economic) that they develop with places (see Figure 41.1).

Groups located in the upper-right quadrant of Figure 41.1 could be formally described as 'residents', albeit temporary, while groups at the lower left would be counted as tourists in official statistics. The former, in fact, are likely to have a more persistent and stable relation with place, though there are important differences between, for instance, traditional residents with a work career in the 'Fordist' age and new collectives of mobile workers or immigrants. Mirroring their situation are visitors in the lower-left quadrant, ranging from the traditional 'mass tourist' – characterised by short transiences in place and volatile personal links with it – to more hybrid visiting populations who tend to have a more continuous relationship with place (by frequency of return or length of stay) and who do develop some links with it. Some of these populations can only be characterised in residual terms with respect to established classifications; they are positioned as 'interstitial groups' using the city and taking part in its cultural assets according to patterns that partially overlap with those of others – hence the 'liquidity' of this classification.

Such overlaps, however, do establish a relational space where place is collectively constructed in more or less desirable ways: each collective uses (and constructs through its practices) specific areas of the city, and where these spaces overlap – by chance or as result of pursued intermissions – meaningful, place-bending 'contacts' are produced. Visitors are less likely to live a deep, meaningful cultural experience of place when they only come in contact with members of the same group (which is a typical condition of mass tourism, using highly specialised touristscapes),

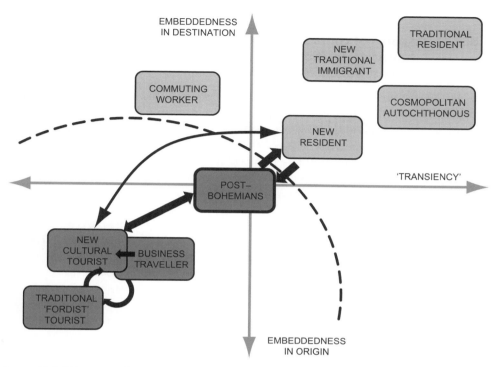

*Figure 41.1* Urban populations and evolutionary patterns
Source: (Adapted from Quaglieri-Domínguez and Russo 2010).

whereas contact with other tourist types or with resident populations may greatly influence the range of experiences and narratives to which they are exposed, which is – as we noted – a prerogative of global cultural consumerism, and this, as we will argue below, is not likely to take place in any type of artificial touristscape.

These relationships are also dynamic: a package tourist or a young traveller on a low budget could return as a high spender if he/she enjoys a positive experience of the place, just as tourists could become so engaged in local culture to be willing to move to the city as new residents – which may be the ultimate object of an attraction policy that considers mobility as a funda-mental force field in place development (Servillo *et al.* 2011). We charted the most significant evolutionary patterns with arrows in Figure 41.1.

To conclude, we have proposed that not only the urban space is continuously re-shaped by the encounters of different populations characterised by different cultures and patterns of mobility in relation to places, producing a social geography of the city, but also that such populations are dynamically related, further increasing the 'liquidity' of this geography.

We will try to illustrate this point through a short case study illustration of a city, Barcelona (Box 41.1), which has been utterly successful as a cultural tourist destination – a place that is not only visited because of its cultural landmarks, but also because of the 'cultural intermissions' that most visitors expect to experience there, and a place that has been gradually transformed and mobilised by tourism.

## Box 41.1 Spaces of contact in the development of a cultural tourist destination: illustrations from Barcelona and its post-bohemian population

At the centre of the scheme in Figure 41.1, Quaglieri-Domínguez and Russo (2010) positioned 'post-bohemians'. These are defined as a population group of mostly young adults, who live in a city for a short or medium period without being integrated into the formal labour market and mostly not making it onto official residence registers (they may include students on an international exchange and youngsters taking a 'sabbatical' in between studies or jobs); as such, they are formally counted as 'tourists' in official statistics. From a motivational point of view, however, their main defining characteristic is their temporary condition of economic inactivity that is dedicated to 'formative' cultural consumption.

Our research indicates that these young people seek to satisfy their need for change and mobility in places where they have a high chance of being exposed to a vibrant cultural milieu and enjoy a certain degree of freedom even when engaging in 'liminal' activities, and their practices are more similar to those of cosmopolitan urban residents than to that of tourists. They eagerly seek contact with public life, and in this sense do not look for the 'exclusivity' that characterises typical tourist experiences; instead, they value the heterogeneity of the city and the numberless opportunities for 'cultural zapping' (Minca 1996), by which they design their own urban experience without the support of the traditional touristic infrastructure (and in this sense they are not detectable through traditional statistical tools).

In international surveys and magazine articles, this group is seen to favour cities like Barcelona, Berlin, Paris, Venice, Amsterdam, Sydney, San Francisco or Buenos Aires. These are not necessarily the economic capitals of the world, but cities where, arguably, the rapid 'homing' of outsiders is facilitated: they offer plenty of opportunities for affordable cultural activities, easy access to low-paid, temporary jobs (also thanks to their status of tourism capitals) which suffice to 'fund' their stays – also serving as an opportunity to meet locals and learn their language and lifestyle – and relatively cheap housing (or squatted) space to be shared with other urban collectives.

Quaglieri-Domínguez and Russo (2010) made an exploratory 'ethnographic study' in the city of Barcelona, charting perceptions, motivations, relationships and spatial behaviour of this group through a number of in-depth interviews with a panel of people who fit the profile of post-bohemians, with the ultimate aim of understanding their importance for the development and transformation of a tourist city and propose a new approach to urban management that brings this potential into the open.

The Catalan capital offers an ideal context for this study, for it combines the heritage elements of a traditional tourist destination with a contemporary landscape that for global cultural consumers is not (only) something to be 'seen', but rather a scenario of cultural activity. The contact between post-bohemians and other urban collectives (traditional tourists, cosmopolitan residents, students) takes place in a number of 'new tourist spaces', the symbolic construction of which is remarkably different from the development and evolution of traditional touristscapes. These include places like Gràcia, the old anarchists' quarter, and a preferred residential area for exchange students, which, in spite of not having any tourist sites or traditional hotel establishments, recently has been discovered by tourists because of its hectic cultural activity bridging the 'militant vernacular' with the global ethnic-chic. Or the so-called 'gay example', the quadrilateral area in the nineteenth-century city 'chessboard' where gay communities (local and visiting) mingle in cafés, fashion shops, galleries and even themed hotel lounges. The regenerated water-front, the main legacy of the 1992 Olympic Games, in the public beaches of which locals, post-bohemians, immigrants and weekend tourists have their most intense contacts.

However, the most emblematic case is offered by the Raval neighbourhood in the Old City. The old *barrio chino*, for a long time considered a no-go area plagued by crime and marginality, has been gradually regenerated since the early 1980s through an important plan of urban reforms and the development of cultural infrastructure (theatres, university faculties, civic centres) (Russo and Capel-Tatjer 2007). One of the most cosmopolitan areas of Barcelona for its mix of immigrants of different origins, long-time residents, university students and creative workers, this neighbour-hood is also attractive to a large population of post-bohemians, due to cheap rents and centrality, but mostly due to its vibrant street life and artsy atmosphere (Degen 2003).

The contacts to which such an area owes its status as the new 'tourist hotspot' of Barcelona take place in specific spaces, like Plaça dels Àngels, where the MACBA – the iconic museum of contemporary arts designed by Richard Meyer – is located, together with the adjoining CCCB (Centre for Contemporary Culture of Barcelona) and FAD (Federation of Arts and Design), and two university faculties. Rather than for the rich cultural programmes of these institutions, this square is valued as a flagship scenario of 'café culture' and creative performances, such as those of a large international skaters' community that shares and animates this spot, while other audiences attend this urban spectacle or just pass through it. This square may also become a cricket play-ground for local Pakistanis, and it is the main stage of SONAR, the world-famous electronic music festival bringing into the city a dedicated audience of more than 80,000 young cultural consumers every June.

Another such space is the Rambla del Raval, 400 metres away from Plaça dels Àngels, a 50-metre wide promenade conceived as multi-functional and leisure space, opened in 2000 to increase the provision of public space in this densely built neighbourhood, reform the surrounding housing blocks, and extend regeneration to its more problematic southern end. Welcomed with scepticism by local residents during the initial stages of the renovation, after 10 years this 'new rambla' is a successful meeting-place for the varied resident community but also for many young tourists. It has given an opportunity to local immigrants to become integrated in the burgeoning tourism economy of the city, by developing a diverse offer of ethnic restaurants and 'hip' bars with a predominantly foreign audience, which represent an important addition to the supply of a city whose local culture is perceived as rather 'closed' to outsiders.

The multiple, overlapping uses of the two places mentioned above, among many others, are emblematic of the contact between different communities, which sees the post-bohemians as the driving agents, on account of their ability to *adapt* (to sometimes difficult living conditions), *perform* (due to their 'liminal' condition and cultural pursuits) and *transform* place (coming into contact with other groups and making it an attraction). The geography of this process is consequently fluid and mutable, especially as compared to the 'established' geography of cultural tourism produced by 'sights' and the dual consumption spaces developed around them. We tried to reproduce this distinction in Figure 41.2, based on the ethnographic study of the cited paper, which maps the traditional tourist spots of Barcelona and the blurrier areas where post-bohemians come into contact with other populations. These areas of contact were not necessarily developed as 'tourist areas' in the first place, and certainly the Raval spaces presented above were not; however, they have become, or are becoming, the spaces in the city with the most fertile opportunities for cultural experience. Urban policy in Barcelona is facing the huge challenge to maintain this 'field of opportunities' open and dynamic.

*Figure 41.2* Tourist points and spaces of 'contact' in Barcelona
Source: © Google 2009.

## Final remarks

We claim that a new approach to the study of cultural tourism (and to place management) is needed, which takes into account the liquid character of urban landscapes. This approach would recognise that tourists and other populations, 'acknowledged' and legitimised, or interstitial and almost invisible groups such as the post-bohemians of Barcelona in our example (but we could also quote foreign workers, business travellers, children, transgender, etc.), in fact 'co-create' space, through their social and cultural contacts, providing an opportunity to mitigate the typical problems associated to mass tourism: dualism, segregation and the loss of idiosyncrasy, or 'banalisation' of place.

We do not dispute that the quantitative relevance of global cultural consumers is small if compared with the persisting numbers of organised, intermediated 'mass tourists', and the associated supply structures that cater for this group of visitors. It is commonly pointed out in the tourist literature and in industry reports how the mass-tourist market has been revived by the rise of low-cost companies, by burgeoning participation rates from emerging economies, and in general by an ongoing 'democratisation' of travel.

Nevertheless, from the qualitative point of view, it is clear that attracting – and catering for – these global cultural consumers is of paramount strategic importance for cities. Their convergence with residents in terms of urban consumption and spatial behaviour overcomes the socio-economic and spatial unbalances associated with the 'Fordist' tourist model. Furthermore, their presence develops into critical mass that sustains a richer and more varied urban offer and, in turn, further attractiveness and retentiveness of cities (Russo *et al.* 2011).

Urban policy, hence, should not only recognise the existence of a city for residents and a city for (mass) tourists, to be appropriately regulated, but also of spaces of overlapping and inter-mission between these populations and their 'interstices', to be carefully managed in order to preserve the existing mix and accessibility.

## References

Coleman, S. and Crang, M. (2002) *Tourism: Between Place and Performance*, Oxford: Berghahn.

Degen, M. (2003) 'Fighting for the Global Catwalk: Formalising Public Life in Castlefield (Manchester) and Diluting Public Life in el Raval (Barcelona)', *International Journal of Urban and Regional Research* 27 (4): 867–80.

Delgado, M. (1999) *El animal public*, Barcelona: Anagrama.

Edensor, T. (2006) 'Sensing Tourist Space', in C. Minca and T. Oakes (eds) *Travels in Paradox: Remapping Tourism*, Lanham: Rowman and Littlefield, 23–45.

Feifer, M. (1985) *Going Places: The Ways of the Tourist from Imperial Rome to the Present Day*, London: Macmillan.

INE (2011) *Encuesta de ocupación hotelera*, www.ine.es/jaxiBD/menu.do?L=0&divi=EOT&his=1&type=db (accessed 15 November 2012).

Keller, P. (2005) 'A New Symbiotic Relationship Between Culture, Leisure and Tourism in the Urban Environment', *Proceedings of the UNWTO Seminar 'The Future of City Tourism in Europe'*, 19–20 May, Coimbra (Portugal).

Maitland, R. (2008) 'Conviviality and Everyday Life: The Appeal of New Areas of London for Visitors', *International Journal of Tourism Research* 10(1): 15–25.

Maitland, R. and Ritchie, B.W. (2009) 'City Tourism: National Capital Perspectives', in Maitland, R. and Ritchie, B. (eds) *City Tourism: National Capital Perspectives*, Wallingford: CABI, 14–26.

Martinotti, G. (1993) *Metropoli: La Nuova Morfologia Sociale della Città*, Bologna: Il Mulino.

Minca, C. (1996) 'Lo spazio turistico postmoderno', in E. Nocifora (ed.) *Il Viaggio. Dal 'Grand Tour' al turismo post-industriale*, Naples: Magma, 123–33.

Quaglieri-Domínguez, A. and Russo, A.P. (2010) 'Paisajes urbanos en la época post-turística. Propuesta de un marco analítico', *Scripta Nova. Revista Electrónica de Geografía y Ciencias Sociales* 14(323), www.ub.edu/geocrit/sn/sn-323.htm (accessed 15 November 2012).

Richards, G. (2007) *Cultural Tourism: Global and Local Perspectives*, London: Routledge.

Richards, G. and Wilson, J. (2006) 'Developing Creativity in Tourist Experiences: A Solution to the Serial Reproduction of Culture?' *Tourism Management* 27(6): 1209–23.

Ritzer, G. and Liska, A. (1997) '"McDisneyization" and "Post-Tourism": Complementary Perspectives on Contemporary Tourism', in C. Rojek and J. Urry (eds) *Touring Cultures: Transformations of Travel and Theory*, London: Routledge, 96–109.

Russo, A.P. and Capel-Tatjer, L. (2007) 'From Citadels of Education to Cartier Latins (and Back?): The Changing Landscapes of Student Populations in European Cities', *Geography Compass* 1(5): 1160–89.

Russo, A.P., Smith, I., Atkinson, R. and Servillo, L. (2011) Territorial Attractiveness and Mobility Flows Across Europe: A Regional Classification Proposal Based on Their Relationships, paper presented at the ERSA Congress 2011, 30 August– 1 September, Barcelona.

Servillo, L., Atkinson, R. and Russo, A.P. (2011) 'Territorial Attractiveness in EU Urban and Spatial Policy: A Critical Review and Future Research Agenda', *European Urban and Regional Studies*, doi: 10.1177/0969776411430289.

Urry, J. (1990) *The Tourist Gaze*, London: Sage.

——(2000) *Sociology Beyond Societies: Mobilities for the Twenty-first Century*, London: Routledge.

# 42

# Regeneration and cultural quarters

## Changing urban cultural space

*C. Michael Hall*

## Introduction

Although of major significance for urban branding and tourism, cultural quarters have become highly contested as a consequence of debates around issues of commodification, identity, homogenisation, gentrification and regeneration (McCarthy 2005). Cultural quarters should therefore be conceptualised within the framework of the development and promotion of distinct social and spatial areas (Bell and Jayne 2004; Evans 2004; McCarthy 2005; Hall 2008a). This chapter examines the significance of urban regeneration for tourism and highlights the relationship between regeneration and the cultural economy. This chapter notes the role of both material (hardware) and immaterial (software) aspects of cultural quarter development but concludes by noting that the distinction of different cultural quarters is increasingly being lost as a result of serial replication.

## Urban regeneration

The issue of regeneration has become a major theme for urban policy and planning in much of the industrialised world since the late 1970s. The impacts of ongoing economic restructuring, globalisation, and technological and policy change have meant that the basis for many urban economies has undergone fundamental shifts within which certain areas have been marked by both physical decline – e.g. vacant industrial property as a result of industry closures or new forms of production – as well as social changes such as social exclusion and deprivation as a result of changing labour markets and welfare systems. Undesirable changes in the urban economy have therefore led policy makers to rethink the means by which employment may be created and some of the impacts of restructuring can be overcome. Tourism and related services, such as culture, sport, leisure and retail, are usually regarded as key sectors in policy responses to perceived urban decline. Much of this is undertaken under the rubric of regeneration (Law 1992; Hall 2004; Evans 2005).

Importantly, the concept of regeneration includes both physical – i.e. concerned with material architecture and image, physical plant and infrastructure, urban design and form – and social/immaterial dimensions – i.e. concerned with improving the quality of life of those who already live in areas targeted for regeneration and/or attracting new permanent and temporary migrants (Page and Hall 2003). However, urban regeneration projects often result in the physical transformation of target areas with little social benefit for residents of such locations (Hall 2004). Indeed, the major social transformation of such areas may well be more in terms of the displacement of previous residents by new arrivals to such areas than any major improvements in the economic and social welfare of long-term residents. Nevertheless, even if social rejuvenation is a major goal of urban regeneration projects, the major mechanism to achieve this is usually via a physical transformation which can then be used to underlie new place branding strategies that in turn may serve to attract new capital investment, firm relocation and residents (Jayne 2006; Hall 2008b).

## Culture economy and urban regeneration

Culture, and cultural tourism in particular, is integral to many urban regeneration strategies (Jayne 2006). Culture in this context can be understood in both a narrow, commoditised sense with respect to specific cultural attractions, such as arts, heritage, museums and events, as well as in the wider notion of the ways of life of residents (which, of course, may also be commoditised via advertising, promotion and visitor consumption). Either way, the significant interactions between culture, urban political economy and regeneration have become enmeshed in the development of 'cultural economy' (Scott 2001). This is a concept that is broader in scope than an association with cultural industry, as significant as these might be for cultural tourism and the hosting of cultural events (Evans 2003; Gibson and Kong 2005; Quinn 2005; Kong 2007; Tucker 2008; Hall 2012). The contemporary importance of culture in urban political economy is therefore a result not only of the increasing explicit use of culture as an economic development strategy (e.g. European Capitals of Culture or the use of museums and art galleries as economic flagships), but also the growth of post-modernism and new conceptualisations of the culture-economy relationship (e.g. gender studies, ethnic networks, post-colonialism, sexual identities, performity, virtual space), which is sometimes referred to as the 'cultural turn' in the social sciences (Ribera-Fumaz 2009).

The attention given to the cultural economy has extended some of the more traditional foci of critical urban studies, and particularly the significance of urban entrepreneurialism: 'a public-private partnership focusing on investment and economic development with the speculative construction of place rather than amelioration of conditions within a particular territory as its immediate (though by no means exclusive) political and economic goal' (Harvey 1989: 8). Urban entrepreneurialism was particularly influential on some of the earlier studies of the political dimensions of urban cultural tourism (Boyle 1994; Hall 1994), especially as it reflected a recognition that 'urban politics can no longer be analysed in isolation from the larger political and economic forces that shape the development, restructuring, and redevelopment of urban spaces and places' (Jonas and Wilson 1999: 11).

One of the most significant implications of the extension of urban entrepreneurialism to the cultural economy is that it has provided a stronger dialectical articulation of the material (urban form, design and architecture) and the immaterial (place branding, marketing, identity, image) as co-created and co-produced urban economic practice (Jessop and Sum 2001). This approach has arguably been significant for at least three main lines of research that place regeneration projects within the context of cultural economic processes (Evans 2005; Hall 2012). First, the urban morphology of economic restructuring in which regeneration is tied to the cultural-material production of urban space (Evans 2003; Monclús 2009). Second, the development of the 'new' and 'symbolic' economy in which regeneration projects, including flagship museums and cultural events, in conjunction with the leisure and tourism sectors, are integral to post-modern economic and political urban competitiveness strategies (Malecki 2004; Turok and Bailey 2004; Connelly 2007; Hall 2007). Third, entrepreneurialism and ethnicity in which cultural discourses of race and ethnic difference become part of entrepreneurial place strategies (Hall and Rath 2007). However, place promotion and the accompanying transformation of urban space require distinct boundaries in order to be effectively commodified. This may be done via the (re)development and (re)branding of urban spaces for sport, such as stadia and event complexes; retail and shopping, including malls or the identification of specialist shopping streets and spaces; nightlife and entertainment districts, such casino development; and/or distinctive cultural precincts or quarters as is the focus here (Hall 1994).

## Cultural quarters

A cultural quarter is defined by Roadhouse (2010: 24) as 'a geographical area of a large town or city which acts as a focus for cultural and artistic activities through the presence of a group of buildings devoted to housing a range of such activities, and purpose designed or adapted spaces to create a sense of identity, providing an environment to facilitate and encourage the provision of cultural and artistic services and activities'. Roadhouse (2010) therefore distinguishes between a cultural quarter and a cultural industries quarter, the latter referring to an area focused on cultural business development that often has been initiated via 'top-down' government intervention, and the former being more of a geographically defined focal point for the location of cultural activity that is often regarded as more of a 'bottom-up' type of development. However, given that cultural quarters undoubtedly 'provide a context for the use of planning and development powers to preserve and encourage cultural production and consumption', and 'are often part of a larger strategy integrating cultural and economic development, usually linked to the regeneration of a selected urban area' (Roadhouse 2010: 24), attempts to distinguish a cultural quarter from a cultural industries quarter or cluster are likely to be quite arbitrary given the extent to which co-location and new cultural developments occur over time.

From a policy perspective, cultural quarters are regarded by governments as serving several significant roles as development catalysts within the broader field of 'culture-led' regenerations (Evans 2005; McCarthy 2006). Cultural industries are widely regarded as economically significant initiatives for the development of creative, innovative and more diversified economies (Smith 2003). Cultural quarters can specifically contribute to making attractive urban environments and can therefore serve to encourage the (re)location of mobile capital and people, as the attractiveness of locations not only provides for improved leisure and living spaces for residents but can also attract a significant number of tourists. The social and environmental aspects of quartering are also regarded as having social benefits such as providing a sense of collective belonging or enhanced local social identity (Miles 2005), which may enhance feelings of social inclusion (Bell and Jayne 2004), and may also lead to reductions in crime and provide a basis for more sustainable development (Darlow 1996). Although, as McCarthy (2005: 298) stresses, 'perhaps of greater urgency', cultural quarters are regarded as 'a means to enhance image via branding or re-branding in order to attract mobile capital and visitor income in the context of globalizing forces and city competition'.

The wide range of policy objectives for cultural quarters can nevertheless lead to significant implementation and assessment issues as some of the aims are potentially contradictory creating, as Mommaas (2004: 530) termed it, an 'ad hoc blending of arguments and opportunities', and confusion over even basic concepts (McCarthy 2005). Furthermore, the focus on cultural quarters for economic development and regeneration purposes also presents something of a paradox as, given the large numbers of cities that have adopted cultural quarters, such serial reproduction of regeneration strategies may potentially reduce the very heterogeneity that is meant to be their unique selling proposition (Bell and Jayne 2004; Malecki 2004; González 2011). As Dungey (2004: 411) observes, 'No major town or city's plans for regeneration [are] now complete without a designated cultural quarter, seeking to attract and develop knowledge economy industries in entertainment, arts, media and design'.

The benefits of quartering are also uneven. McCarthy (2005) argues that this is essentially because tourists along with other more permanent in-migrants are often from higher-income sectors of society, and leads to gentrification. He also suggests that city quartering may actually even increase urban social and economic fragmentation, since proximity does not imply sharing of values or even compatibility, while the quartering process may also lead to the homogenisation of a previously variable urban space. This in turn can lead to contestation on the part of those who may not wish to be, or their cities, residence, workplace and leisure spaces to be, culturally branded and quartered (Miles 2004; Jensen 2007). There is also mounting evidence to suggest that cultural quarters may not only be more distinctive but also more sustainable if they develop organically with only limited, or at least more appropriate public intervention. This is because some quarters are overly focused on design of the physical environment without there being adequate attention to the development of dense social and economic networks (Garcia 2004; Evans 2005; Hall 2008b). Kunzmann (2004: 399) even suggests that zoning the development of cultural and creative quarters and precincts 'would be counter-productive'.

## Box 42.1 Case study: cultural quarters and serial reproduction

The long-term success of 'designed' cultural quarters is often problematic given that consumption-oriented designscapes usually represent public–private interventions that aim to induce the development of distinct precincts rather than allowing for a slower, more 'bottom up' approach. Examples of where this has occurred include the South of Litchfield (SOL) development in Christchurch, New Zealand, and SoFo (South of Folkungagatan) in Stockholm, Sweden. Both sought to replicate the success of South of Houston, or SoHo, located in Manhattan, New York (Jansson and Power 2006; Hall 2008a). This case focuses on the former.

As with SoHo in New York, SOL occupies a former warehouse and lane district that dates from the 1880s. The lanes had been identified by the Christchurch City Council (CCC) as an integral component of the city's revitalisation strategy via public–private partnerships. One of the most significant aspects of the development was the extent to which the SOL designscape was influenced not only by public–private partnerships but also by architects, designers and design institutions (many of which were US based), which were referred to by the developers, Property Ventures, in their own materials (Hall 2008a).

As in Julier's (2005) analysis of Barcelona, it is noteworthy that in the case of SOL 'few of the mediatory forms and sites of consumption for such encounters had direct relationships with the institutions of governance and civil society', as well as also revealing 'that the most public of sites of encounter, urban design, and design exhibitions, provided interfaces between both designers and local government. These were key moments in the shaping and mediation of aesthetic content' (Julier 2005: 877). In the case of the Property Ventures website, for example, a 'knowledge center' listed the articles, websites and organisations that have influenced the company's philosophy, which is grounded in 'New Urbanism'. However, none of the links on the Property Ventures website with respect to new urbanism and their philosophy of development had any connection to any New Zealand sites or reports and were instead primarily US focused. Indeed, DPZ Pacific (Duany-Plater Zyberk, the Asia-Australasian arm of a design and urban development consultancy based in Florida) served as consultants to both Property Ventures for the SOL development and to the CCC for the Central City South redevelopment strategy in which SOL is located. The narrow range of design advice reflects McCarthy's (2005) concerns with respect to the replication of quarters, and corresponding problems of homogeneity between cities seeking to encourage inner-city regeneration.

The SOL case supports the argument that the process of serial reproduction of cultural quarters is linked to the involvement of a small number of cultural mediators (Evans 2005; McCarthy 2005). Although this may have allowed the dissemination of 'good practice', it also contributes to the propensity for the replication or emulation of solutions or suggestions incorporating an essentially similar mix of architectural, branding, design and planning elements in very different economic and socio-cultural contexts, 'with the associated risk of homogeneity and loss of local identity or distinctiveness' (McCarthy 2005: 300).

## Conclusion

This chapter has focused on the development of cultural quarters from both material and immaterial perspectives on regeneration and the cultural economy. It has stressed that an understanding of cultural quarters needs to incorporate both dimensions as a focus on the physical aspects of change alone means that the potential for social change and the role of quarters as a form of commodified space will be lost. Such an appreciation is also important in assessing the success of any regeneration project.

Despite their popularity as urban regeneration mechanisms, research also suggests that the effectiveness of cultural quarters is uneven at best. This is because there is often too much focus on the physical environment and insufficient attention on social and economic network creation. In addition, there is much concern about inappropriate public intervention in the creation of cultural quarters, and the need to stimulate more bottom-up initiatives though slower development. Unfortunately, many cultural quarters appear unsustainable as they are serial reproductions of other quarters and therefore make relatively little contribution to fulfilling regeneration aims of place distinctiveness and competitiveness.

## References

Bell, D. and Jayne, M. (2004) *City of Quarters: Urban Villages in the Contemporary City*, Aldershot: Ashgate.

Boyle, M. (1994) 'The Politics of Urban Entrepreneurialism in Glasgow', *Political Geography* 25: 453–70.

Connelly, G. (2007) 'Testing Governance – A Research Agenda for Exploring Urban Tourism Competitiveness Policy: The Case of Liverpool 1980–2000', *Tourism Geographies* 9: 84–114.

Darlow, A. (1996) 'Cultural Policy and Urban Sustainability: Making a Missing Link?' *Planning Practice and Research* 11: 291–301.

Dungey, J. (2004) 'Overview: Arts, Culture and the Local Economy', *Local Economy* 19(4): 411–13.

Evans, G. (2003) 'Hard-branding the Cultural City – From Prado to Prada', *International Journal of Urban and Regional Research* 27: 417–40.

——(2004) 'Cultural Industry Quarters: From Pre-industrial to Post-industrial Production', in Bell, D. and Jayne, M. (eds) *City of Quarters: Urban Villages in the Contemporary City*, Aldershot: Ashgate, 71–92.

——(2005) 'Measure for Measure: Evaluating the Evidence of Culture's Contribution to Regeneration', *Urban Studies* 42(5/6): 959–83.

Garcia, B. (2004) 'Deconstructing the City of Culture: The Long-term Cultural Legacies of Glasgow 1990', *Urban Studies* 42(5/6): 841–68.

Gibson, C. and Kong, L. (2005) 'Cultural Economy: A Critical Review', *Progress in Human Geography* 29: 541–61.

González, S. (2011) 'Bilbao and Barcelona "in motion". How Urban Regeneration "Models" Travel and Mutate in the Global Flows of Policy Tourism', *Urban Studies* 48(7): 1397–418.

Hall, C.M. (1994) *Tourism and Politics: Policy, Power and Place*, Chichester: John Wiley & Sons.

——(2004) 'Sports Tourism and Urban Regeneration', in Ritchie, B. and Adair, D. (eds) *Sports Tourism: Interrelationships, Impacts and Issues*, Clevedon: Channel View Publications, 192–206.

——(2007) 'Tourism and Regional Competitiveness', in Tribe, J. and Airey, D. (eds) *Advances in Tourism Research, Tourism Research, New Directions, Challenges and Applications*, Oxford: Elsevier, 217–30.

——(2008a) 'Servicescapes, Designscapes, Branding and the Creation of Place-identity: South of Litchfield, Christchurch', *Journal of Travel and Tourism Marketing* 25(3/4): 233–50.

——(2008b) *Tourism Planning: Policies, Processes and Relationships*, second edn, Harlow: Prentice Hall.

——(2012) 'The Political Analysis and Political Economy of Events', in Page, S. and Connell, J. (eds) *A Handbook of Events*, London: Routledge, 186–201.

Hall, C.M. and Rath, J. (2007) 'Tourism, Migration and Place Advantage in the Global Economy', in Rath, J. (ed.) *Tourism, Ethic Diversity and the City*, New York: Routledge, 1–24.

Harvey, D. (1989) 'From Managerialism to Entrepreneurialism: The Transformation of Urban Governance in Late Capitalism', *Geografiska Annaler B* 71: 3–17.

Jansson, J. and Power, D. (2006) *The Image of the City – Urban Branding as Constructed Capabilities in Nordic City Regions*, Oslo: Nordic Innovation Centre.

Jayne, M. (2006) *Cities and Consumption*, Abingdon: Routledge.

Jensen, O.B. (2007) 'Culture Stories: Understanding Cultural Urban Branding', *Planning Theory* 6(3): 211–36.

Jessop, B. and Sum, N.L. (2001) 'Pre-disciplinary and Post-disciplinary Perspectives', *New Political Economy* 6: 89–101.

Jonas, A.G. and Wilson, D. (1999) 'The City as a Growth Machine: Critical Reflections Two Decades Later', in Jonas, A.G. and Wilson, D. (eds) *The Urban Growth Machine: Critical Perspectives Two Decades Later*, Albany: State University of New York (SUNY), 3–18.

Julier, G. (2005) 'Urban Designscapes and the Production of Aesthetic Consent', *Urban Studies* 42(5–6): 869–87.

Kong, L. (2007) 'Cultural Icons and Urban Development in Asia: Economic Imperative, National Identity, and Global City Status', *Political Geography* 26: 383–404.

Kunzmann, K.R. (2004) 'Culture, Creativity and Spatial Planning', *Town Planning Review* 75(4): 383–404.

Law, C.M. (1992) 'Urban Tourism and Its Contribution to Economic Regeneration', *Urban Studies* 29(3/4): 599–618.

McCarthy, J. (2005) 'Cultural Quarters and Regeneration: The Case of Wolverhampton', *Planning, Practice & Research* 20(3): 297–311.

——(2006) 'The Application of Policy for Cultural Use Clustering', *European Planning Studies* 14(3): 397–408.

Malecki, E.J. (2004) 'Jockeying for Position: What it Means and Why it Matters to Regional Development Policy When Places Compete', *Regional Studies* 38(9): 1101–20.

Miles, M. (2004) 'Drawn and Quartered: El Raval and the Hausmannization of Barcelona', in Bell, D. and Jayne, M. (eds) *City of Quarters*, Aldershot: Ashgate, 37–55.

Miles, S. (2005) '"Our Tyne": Iconic Regeneration and the Revitalisation of Identity in Newcastle Gateshead', *Urban Studies* 42(5/6): 913–26.

Mommaas, H. (2004) 'Cultural Clusters and the Post-industrial City: Towards the Remapping of Urban Cultural Policy', *Urban Studies* 41(3): 507–32.

Monclús, F.J. (2009) *International Exhibitions and Urbanism: The Zaragoza Expo 2008 Project*, Farnham: Ashgate.

Page, S.J. and Hall, C.M. (2003) *Managing Urban Tourism*, Harlow: Prentice-Hall.

Quinn, B. (2005) 'Arts Festivals and the City', *Urban Studies* 42: 927–43.

Ribera-Fumaz, R. (2009) 'From Urban Political Economy to Cultural Political Economy: Rethinking Culture and Economy in and Beyond the Urban', *Progress in Human Geography* 33: 447–65.

Roadhouse, S. (ed.) (2010) *Cultural Quarters: Principles and Practice*, second edn, Bristol: Intellect.

Scott, A.J. (2001) *The Cultural Economy of Cities*, London: Sage.

Smith, M.K. (2003) *Issues in Cultural Tourism Studies*, London: Routledge.

Tucker, M. (2008) 'The Cultural Production of Cities: Rhetoric or Reality? Lessons from Glasgow', *Journal of Retail and Leisure Property* 7: 21–33.

Turok, I. and Bailey, N. (2004) 'Twin Track Cities? Competitiveness and Cohesion in Glasgow and Edinburgh', *Progress in Planning* 62: 135–204.

## Further reading

Bell, D. and Jayne, M. (2004) *City of Quarters: Urban Villages in the Contemporary City*, Aldershot: Ashgate. (Presents a number of different cases of urban quartering processes.)

Hall, C.M. (2008) 'Servicescapes, Designscapes, Branding and the Creation of Place-identity: South of Litchfield, Christchurch', *Journal of Travel and Tourism Marketing* 25(3/4): 233–50. (Case study of the role of the material and immaterial aspects of precinct creation in New Zealand.)

McCarthy, J. (2006) 'The Application of Policy for Cultural Use Clustering', *European Planning Studies* 14(3): 397–408. (Examines policy intervention for urban cultural cluster development.)

Roadhouse, S. (ed.) (2010) *Cultural Quarters: Principles and Practice*, second edn, Bristol: Intellect. (Presents a range of chapters and contributions on different dimensions of cultural quarters with considerable attention being given to Bolton in the UK.)

# 43

# 'Ethnic quarters'

## Exotic islands or trans-national hotbeds of innovation?

*Stephen Shaw*

## Introduction

Many commercial thoroughfares in areas known as Chinatown, Arab quarter, Punjabi market and so on, welcome cultural tourists. Marketed as 'ethnic quarters' (EQs), they often feature in the promotion of cities in North America, Europe and the Pacific Rim that are gateways to immigration. However, opinion is divided concerning the direction this is taking in the early twenty–first century.

*Figure 43.1* Montréal's historic Chinatown welcomes cultural tourists
Source: (Photo by author).

In the last two decades of the twentieth century, as post-industrial cities restructured their economies, critics characterised initiatives to regenerate EQs as top-down, formulaic and somewhat voyeuristic. Pessimists portrayed such areas as exotic islands surrounded by deprived neighbourhoods; enclaves re-presented as spaces of consumption to visitors from the white majority and international tourists. In time, the process would displace the very communities the identities of which it claimed to 'celebrate'. Nevertheless, recent commentators have detected a more benign globalisation-from-below, where nodes of trans-national networks intersect. *Inter*-cultural tourism should be nurtured in vibrant, well-connected places that are developing as hotbeds of innovation.

These polarised interpretations of EQs are examined critically here. The author argues for a more grounded analysis that gives greater weight to local context and agency. In particular, he foregrounds power relationships and alliances that develop over time between stakeholders (interest groups) within new frameworks of urban governance. In the UK, over the past 30 years, place-competition and downloading of responsibilities/resource allocation to regeneration partnerships between urban authorities and non-state agencies have enabled the narrow interests of particular ethnic minority businesses to prevail at specific places/times, sometimes to the detriment of other communities. However, the loosening of traditional hierarchies has sometimes provided opportunities to challenge them.

The author's published research is based on close analysis of documentation from the beginning to end of regeneration programmes (typically five years), photographic evidence of changing cityscapes and exit interviews with key informants, including programme directors, ethnic minority businesses, local politicians, officers and the consultants that they commissioned. He concludes that the processes of designing, planning and managing EQs are more complex, their outcomes far less predictable at 'street level', than urban policy theorists have assumed hitherto.

## Ethnic quarters as cosmopolitan spaces: cynical versus idealistic readings

In their study of ethnically diverse neighbourhoods in Montréal, Germain and Radice (2006: 113) distinguish two distinct 'camps' that have interpreted the re-presentation of EQs as cosmopolitan spaces:

> Crudely, there are the cynics who see it as an elitist ideology that strategically co-opts 'cultural' difference in order to sell experiences to urban consumers; and the idealists who still believe in its Enlightenment-inspired progressive potential to unite citizens and/or political movements and institutions across national and other boundaries.

The first camp builds upon a well-established thesis that markers of difference are extracted from other cultures for their exchange value: 'ethnic' food, drink and alternative medicines, clothing, furniture and furnishings, and souvenirs are progressively de-contextualised, transformed and homogenised. Szerszynski and Urry (2002: 461–62) note the influential critique by Marx and Engels (1952: 46–47) of the systematic appropriation of marketable features of other cultures: 'the bourgeoisie has through its exploitation of the world market given a cosmopolitan character to production and consumption.'

Contemporary observers may conclude that astute capitalists continue to select, adapt and trade on features of cultural difference that are valued by the privileged elite, and that the socio-cultural impact is demonstrated in the appropriation, not only of 'items', but also of entire cityscapes that the visitors experience. Global competition encourages cities to create cosmopolitan spaces in which to entertain affluent, footloose cosmopolites. Judd (1999: 36) draws attention to 'Disneyfied' Latin quarters, created through revitalisation programmes in the USA: islands in a 'sea of decay', e.g. Detroit's renovated Greektown. This exemplifies a trend towards tourist-oriented enclaves, 'more likely to contribute to racial, ethnic, and class tensions than an impulse toward local community' (ibid.: 53). Hackworth and Rekers (2005) discuss commercially oriented ethnic branding through business improvement area boards in Canada, e.g. Toronto's Little Italy.

In sharp contrast, commentators from the second camp see cosmopolitan spaces as catalysts that foster open-minded interaction: a 'willingness to engage with the Other' (Hannerz 1996: 103). The normative 'creative city' model (Landry and Bianchini 1995: 28) values opportunities for people with diverse cultures and lifestyles to interact productively, casually and without friction. Likewise, Sandercock (2003) advocates an evolving hybridity: a fusion of ideas or dynamic 'inter-cultural' exchange for a more tolerant and inclusive cosmopolis. This argument, developed further by Wood and Landry (2008), envisages urban environments within which merchants and creative intermediaries move with relative ease, negotiating paths between different 'worlds'. From this perspective, cultural and inter-cultural tourism is embedded within other aspects of the local economy and community life, complementing rather than over-whelming them.

## Showcasing ethnic quarters in UK cities

In the UK in the late twentieth century, cities that had been gateways for immigration and settlement began to consider the advantages of showcasing localities that could be re-presented in a positive light. By encouraging upscale leisure consumption and the development of cultural tourism, urban authorities across the political spectrum sought to draw a symbolic line under previous associations with poverty, bad housing, and in some cases ugly scenes of violence by racists among the white majority in the recent past.

The regeneration of inner-city areas in Birmingham was a notable example, but as Chan (2004) observes, the City Council's interventions in the 1980s and 1990s tended to confirm the 'exotic islands' argument, e.g. a proposed leisure complex with a Chinese flavour, comprising a casino, restaurant and nightclub oriented to business tourism. Nevertheless, greater civic appreciation of inter-culturalism from the beginning of the new millennium suggests a shift in the direction of the idealists. Henry *et al.* (2002) discuss an emerging globalisation from below, rooted in ethnically diverse areas of Birmingham but drawing strength from the trans-national networks of dispersed communities, including Pakistanis, black Caribbeans, Irish, Italians, Cypriots, Poles, Hungarians, Chinese and Yemenis. Inter-cultural exchange and fusion was encouraging innovation, e.g. *halal* Chinese food, the Birmingham *balti*, British *Bhangra* music, and a digital television channel broadcasting to Punjabi communities across Europe.

Competition between cities – and areas *within* cities – is deeply embedded in North American policy and practice, and since the 1980s UK governments have encouraged competitive 'urban entrepreneurialism' and 'place marketing', scaling down to small area revitalisation – EQs. Under 'City Challenge' and in 1994–2007 the 'Single Regeneration Budget' (SRB), they competed for central government grants. In making bids for SRBs and in managing successful schemes, they were required to collaborate with other public, commercial and community organisations, forming area-based partnerships. Typically, these were five-year programmes that crossed boundaries between authorities to target economically deprived areas. Under three successive New Labour governments (1997–2010), there was an increasing emphasis on meeting social objectives through SRB programmes: inclusion, capacity building and wider consultation (Shaw and Bagwell 2012).

Two examples of initiatives in emerging EQs supported through SRBs within London serve to illustrate how such partnerships stimulated and managed commercial hubs associated with Asian communities: Green Street, Newham, and Southall Broadway, Ealing, 6 miles east and 11 miles west of central London, respectively. In Green Street, a few traders diversified into fashion clothing and jewellery for wealthier Asian markets across the UK. Through inspired East–West fusions by young Asian designers, and SRB support, this attracted many non-Asian customers, and it became known as the 'New Asian Bond Street'. Thus, inter-cultural *haut couture* lured in ethnically diverse visitors; urban design and public art to enhance Green Street developed themes of 'togetherness', rather than overt ethnic branding. Likewise, a proposal to brand Southall Broadway as 'Punjabi Bazaar' was rejected. Today, its spice/food shops and restaurants attract customers from Asian and non-Asian cultures, and the area is promoted as an international gateway through London Heathrow airport, exploiting links with the rising 'tiger' economies (Shaw and Bagwell 2012).

More broadly, the devolution of responsibilities and resources to local partnerships at arm's length from urban authorities has assumed an increasingly important role in the regeneration of post-industrial cities, especially where traditional structures and processes have proved too 'slow and bureaucratic' to deal effectively with the complexities of delivery, and where agencies of state have 'lost the confidence' of local communities: a shift from government to urban *governance* (Newman *et al.* 2004; Taylor 2007). Managed by independent board members appointed to represent their public–commercial–community stakeholders, some SRB partnerships in the UK steered the physical form and functions of EQs towards the more contemporary model of a 'trans-national hotbed of innovation', as illustrated in Southall Broadway and Green Street. In the case study (Box 43.1), however, the initial vision to emulate the established, tourist-oriented Brick Lane in London's East End was closer to the traditional 'exotic island' model.

---

### Box 43.1 Case study: re-constructing Brick Lane as 'Banglatown'

Historic Spitalfields in the London Borough of Tower Hamlets (LBTH) accommodated successive waves of immigration from the 1600s, and Brick Lane became its main commercial thoroughfare. In the 1970s Asian entrepreneurs bought textile manufacturing and distribution premises from former Jewish owners, employing co-ethnic workers, mainly young men from Bangladesh. Unfortunately for the new immigrant community, poor living conditions were exacerbated by a steep decline in the textile industry, and attacks by neo-fascist youths. Despite the area's built heritage and proximity to central London (1 mile east), it seldom featured on the 'tourist map' of London at that time.

Somewhat against the odds, one or two enterprising café owners encouraged a rising trade from non-Asian customers, and from the early 1990s Brick Lane acquired a 'shabby chic', attracting artists and designers into Spitalfields. Bethnal Green City Challenge (1992–97) supported this nascent visitor economy, funding ornate street furniture and arches with Asian motifs to welcome visitors from the nearby City of London. City Fringe Partnership (1997–2002), identified and promoted the area as an 'emerging cultural quarter', in parallel with another SRB programme called Cityside (geographically overlapping and also during 1997–2002), which envisaged a 'quantum leap in the area's status as a visitor/cultural destination' (London Borough of Tower Hamlets 1996: 13).

Brick Lane was being reconstructed in both senses (Shaw and MacLeod 2000). Cityside allocated £1 million for 'raising the profile'. Its 'town management group' rebranded the locality as 'Banglatown' through media campaigns, and established two annual street festivals: Baishakhi Mela (in the spring) and Brick Lane (curry) Festival (in the autumn). Amending the recently approved development plan, part of Brick Lane was re-zoned in 1999 to permit change of use from shops to restaurants. Additionally, £300,000 in grants was made available for restaurant façades, plus £600,000 to upgrade pedestrian links with the City. Meanwhile, a former brewery was converted into design studios, nightclubs and exhibition space. In 2000 LBTH and Cityside drew up an 'environmental improvement scheme' to close Brick Lane permanently to vehicles, which would have opened new opportunities for al fresco dining in summertime (Shaw *et al.* 2004; Shaw 2008).

Previous claims that this proposal to create a pedestrian mall was favoured by the local community were brought into question when the scheme received an extremely hostile response from other businesses, as well as from residents who objected to the restaurant zone and proposed street closure. To the embarrassment of those who had championed the scheme, two years of consultation (2000–02) with local organisations, together with extensive surveys of nearby residents, revealed widespread concerns over displacement of local people and established firms from Brick Lane. Public engagement also highlighted sinister issues, especially drug-dealing and prostitution at the fringes of the night economy (Shaw 2008, 2011).

The dramatic increase in curry restaurants from eight in 1997, to 41 in 2002, created over 400 jobs for local, co-ethnic workers (Carey 2002: 12). Unlike their counterparts in Green Street and Southall Broadway, the customers were 'overwhelmingly white' with 70 per cent in the age group 25–34 years (ibid.: 4). However, the unprecedented public engagement in the early 2000s proved a watershed. Revised street design to accommodate multiple uses and users of the street, through traffic calming rather than full pedestrianisation (2002–06), projected Banglatown's image, with public art and decorations (e.g. murals and banners) that made reference to the locality's diverse communities and traditions (Shaw 2011).

## Micro-analysis and the bigger picture

As illustrated through the examples above, in most cases a small cluster of ethnic minority entrepreneurs emerge as the prime movers of regeneration. Their motivation is to diversify their customer base from the limitations of dependence on local and co-ethnic markets. They encourage higher-spending visitors to consume goods and services that they value as exotic. In doing so, they draw them into neighbourhoods that they may have avoided or even feared hitherto. Development of a nascent visitor economy can be stimulated further through symbolic re-presentation of the cityscape to create an agreeable Otherness, calculated to appeal to prospective customers. However, such action requires collaboration, not only between traders, but also with urban authorities whose interventions can enable or constrain development of EQs in accordance with the economic, social and environmental objectives of public policy. Thus, power relationships and alliances evolve to re-construct the imaginary as well as physical form of selected streets in disadvantaged neighbourhoods.

The example of Brick Lane in the 1990s illustrates the power of a small but ambitious group of entrepreneurs to reverse the zoning policy of a recently adopted development plan, and enable rapid expansion of curry restaurants. The proposed street closure would also have favoured their interests. During this phase, the pessimism of the 'cynical camp' would have been fully vindicated. However, in the early 2000s, opposition from other stakeholders was galvanised. Eventually, this informed a more inclusive approach, but the function and character of the street has changed irreversibly. At the time of writing (2012), serial reproduction of a successful formula has led to over-supply of an undifferentiated product. Around 60 restaurants offering similar menus compete aggressively with one another through on-street canvassing by waiters and discounted prices. It would be hard to argue that the balanced, sustainable vision of the 'idealistic camp' has been achieved over the last decade.

As with Green Street, Southall Broadway and other cases discussed above, interventions to nurture EQs have been legitimised by a mix of objectives that are not necessarily consistent with one another or 'joined up'. Many critics question urban policy rhetoric that espouses 'empowerment' of citizens (Swyngedouw 2005). In some cases, the shift from hierarchical, top-down government towards more pragmatic and 'participatory' governance has given sectional interests privileged access to decision making in ways that impact badly on other stakeholders. Nevertheless, some concede that there is potential for quieter voices within disadvantaged communities to become 'active subjects' and steer prevailing discourses to their own advantage (Taylor 2007). Thus, it has also created opportunities for others to articulate alternative views on future development in their localities. If circumstances are favourable, they may influence the formulation of more balanced strategies for the regeneration of EQs, with inclusive forms of *inter*-cultural tourism that bring longer-term social and environmental benefits to 'host' communities.

## References

Carey, S. (2002) *Brick Lane, Banglatown: A Study of the Catering Sector, final report*, Research Works Limited prepared for Ethnic Minority Enterprise Project and Cityside Regeneration, Hendon, London.
Chan, W. (2004) 'Finding Chinatown: Ethnocentrism and Urban Planning', in Bell, D. and Jayne, M. (eds) *City of Quarters: Urban Villages in the Contemporary City*, Aldershot: Ashgate, 173–91.
Germain, A. and Radice, M. (2006) 'Cosmopolitanism by Default: Public Sociability in Montreal', in Binnie, J., Holloway, J., Millington, S. and Young, C. (eds) *Cosmopolitan Urbanism*, London and New York: Routledge, 112–29.
Hackworth, J. and Rekers, J. (2005) 'Ethnic Packaging and Gentrification: The Case of Four Neighbourhoods in Toronto', *Urban Affairs Review* 41(2): 211–66.
Hannerz, U. (1996) *Transnational Connections: Culture, People, Places*, London: Routledge.
Henry, N., McEwan, C. and Pollard, J.S. (2002) 'Globalisation from Below: Birmingham – Postcolonial Workshop of the World?' *Area* 34(2): 117–27.
Judd, D. (1999) 'Constructing the Tourist Bubble', in Judd, D. and Fainstein, S. (eds) *The Tourist City*, New Haven and London: Yale University Press, 35–53.
Landry, C. and Bianchini, F. (1995) *The Creative City*, London: Demos in association with Comedia.
London Borough of Tower Hamlets (1996) *Eastside Challenge Fund Submission*; NB the name was changed to 'Cityside'.
Marx, K. and Engels, F. (1952 [1848]) *The Manifesto of the Communist Party*, Moscow: Foreign Languages.
Newman, J., Barnes, M., Sullivan, H. and Knops, A. (2004) 'Public Participation and Collaborative Governance', *Journal of Social Policy* 33: 203–23.
Sandercock, L. (2003) *Cosmopolis II: Mongrel Cities in the 21st Century*, London and New York: Continuum.
Shaw, S. (2008) 'Hosting a Sustainable Visitor Economy: Messages from London's Banglatown', *Journal of Urban Regeneration and Renewal* 1(3): 275–85.
——(2011) 'Marketing Ethnoscapes as Spaces of Consumption: Banglatown – London's Curry Capital', *Journal of Town and City Management* 1(4): 381–95.
Shaw, S. and Bagwell, S. (2012) 'Ethnic Minority Restaurateurs and the Regeneration of "Banglatown" in London's East End', in Aytar, V. and Rath, J. (eds) *Selling Ethnic Neighborhoods: The Rise of Neighborhoods as Places of Leisure and Consumption*, New York: Routledge, in press.

Shaw, S., Bagwell, S. and Karmowska, J. (2004) 'Ethnoscapes as Spectacle: Reimaging Multicultural Districts as New Destinations for Leisure and Tourism Consumption', *Urban Studies* 41(10): 1983–2000.

Shaw, S. and MacLeod N. (2000) 'Creativity and Conflict: Cultural Tourism in London's City Fringe', *Tourism, Culture and Communication* 2(3): 165–75.

Swyngedouw, E. (2005) 'Governance, Innovation and the Citizen: The Janus-face of Governance-beyond-the-state', *Urban Studies* 42(11): 1991–2006.

Szerszynski, B. and Urry, J. (2002) 'Cultures of Cosmopolitanism', *Sociological Review* 50(4): 461–81.

Taylor, M. (2007) 'Community Participation in the Real World: Opportunities and Pitfalls in New Governance Spaces', *Urban Studies* 44(2): 297–317.

Wood, P. and Landry, C. (2008) *The Intercultural City: Planning for Diversity Advantage*, London: Earthscan.

## Further reading

Aitchison, C., MacLeod, N. and Shaw, S. (2000) *Leisure and Tourism Landscapes: Social and Cultural Geographies*, London and New York: Routledge. (Conceptualises the wider relationships between landscape imagery and leisure and tourism consumption.)

Aytar, V. and Rath, J. (eds) (2012) *Selling Ethnic Neighborhoods: The Rise of Neighborhoods as Places of Leisure and Consumption*, New York: Routledge, in press. (Critically assesses the development of EQs in gateway cities with international comparison of extended case studies.)

Binnie, J., Holloway, J., Millington, S. and Young, C. (eds) (2006) *Cosmopolitan Urbanism*, London and New York: Routledge. (Provides insightful interdisciplinary perspectives on cosmopolitan space in contemporary societies.)

Lin, J. (2011) *The Power of Ethnic Places: Cultural Heritage and Community Life*, London and New York: Routledge. (Analyses social and political aspects of ethnic heritage sites in the USA.)

Sandercock, L. (2003) *Cosmopolis II: Mongrel Cities in the 21st Century*, London and New York: Continuum. (Offers examples of community-based projects that apply principles of inter-culturalism.)

Shaw, S. (2007a) 'Cosmopolitanism and Ethnic Cultural Quarters', in G. Richards and J. Wilson (eds) *Tourism, Creativity and Development*, London and New York: Routledge, 189–200. (Expands on the concept of innovation and creativity in EQs.)

——(2007b) 'Ethnoscapes as Cultural Attractions in Canadian World Cities', in Smith, M. (ed.) *Tourism, Culture and Regeneration*, Wallingford: CABI, 49–58. (Reviews developments in metropolitan Canada.)

——(2012) 'Faces, Spaces and Places: Social and Cultural Impacts of Street Festivals in Cosmopolitan Cities', in Page, S.J. and Connell, J. (eds) *The Routledge Handbook of Events*, London and New York: Routledge, 401–14. (Investigates the socio-cultural ramifications of events staged in EQs.)

Shaw, S. and Ferdinand, N. (2012) 'Events in Our Changing World', in Ferdinand, N. and Kitchin, P. (eds) *Events Management: An International Approach*, London: Sage, 5–22. (Reflects on the meaning of events, and projection of cosmopolitanism at different scales from 'world parties' down to local street festivals in EQs.)

Shaw, S. and Karmowska, J. (2004) 'Multicultural Heritage of European Cities and its Re-presentation Through Regeneration Programmes', *Journal of European Ethnology* 34(2): 41–56. (Compares the re-imaging of Spitalfields, London with Kazimierz, Cracow.)

# 44

# Ethnic tourism

## Who is exotic for whom?

*Anya Diekmann*

## Introduction

In the last two decades, urban tourism shifted from a heritage-focused supply to a broader offer (Maitland and Newman 2009). While 'traditional' urban tourism was concentrated mainly in and around historic city centres, the diversification of urban tourism has integrated new quarters and areas previously ignored by visitors. As Hoffman explains 'the differentiation of formerly standardized markets has valorized multiculturalism and diversity, giving rise to new forms of cultural capital and creating interest in formerly unattractive places' (Hoffman 2003b: 92).

The underlying idea of such policies was to develop disadvantaged areas and regenerate them through the creation of tourism activities (Zukin 1998), but also to demonstrate how inclusive and cosmopolitan a city can be (Shaw 2007). These developments concerned mainly former industrial areas and districts with a high rate of migrants shaping a city of quarters (Roodhouse 2006) allowing tourists to choose à la carte according to their interests. Myriad tourism assets could thus be created from art studios over fashion districts to ethnic markets and, in extreme cases, to slum tourism.

So-called 'ethnic quarters' became in many cities an interesting asset for tourism authorities (Rath 2007). Chinese quarters, Little Italys or Little Indias were promoted as a means of encountering the exotic. Indeed, ethnic quarters represent enclaves with an extensive variety of linguistic, religious, family and friendship entities. On the one hand they play the role of important storehouses of heritage that are often in the process of disappearing in developing 'home' countries abroad (Smith and Maryann 2001). On the other hand they embody a melting pot of many different cultures, composed of locals, immigrants, residents and users (Chang 1999). Many ethnic quarters grew indeed through the settlement of migrant workers in impoverished areas with little or no urban planning. However, as soon as the community members could afford to settle in a wealthier area they left the district. What remained were the shops and specialised service providers offering specific cultural goods and providing the opportunity of social exchange and contacts with other community members. Very important in that context is the food and beverages supply for being often emphasised by the tourism promotion as clusters of exotic restaurants (Conforti 1996; Trevor and Monder 2003; Selby 2004). These commercial ethnic belts (McLaughlin and Jesilow, 1998) attract community members, allowing them to distinguish themselves from the host country for a limited time and reaffirming their identities (Diekmann and Maulet 2009). However, the movement of people out of the district exacerbates the already problematic situation (dilapidated housing, high unemployment and high rates of crime) of the area. In fact, new migrants from other countries settle in the dilapidated area following the same path as their predecessors and generating a multicultural melting pot. Moreover, as highlighted by Hoffman, these areas are frequently characterised by a distinct 'ghetto' economy, social/spatial isolation and exclusion, negatively perceived culture, political patronage and social policies (Hoffman 2003b: 105). While Hoffman distinguishes this state as being a Fordist concept, it is indeed in many countries valid as long as regeneration has not been considered for the district under scrutiny. One regeneration process is tourism development. Yet, the type of development depends to a large extent on the geographical situation and connections to the main tourism clusters and urban spaces.

The chapter examines the concept of ethnic tourism by highlighting the ambivalence in promoting specific cultural communities as exotic to the 'tourist community', and in that 'excluding' a whole group of (potential) consumers, that often constitute the majority of visitors. Findings from a recent survey led in the sub-Saharan African precinct Matonge in Brussels will highlight the significance of community visitors. Moreover, the chapter will look into the promotional policies and how the tourism mediation shapes the communities and stakeholders in the development process, focusing on several examples.

## Ethnic tourism development

With the need for diversification and increasing competition between cities for attracting tourists, tourism authorities see in ethnic quarters a significant opportunity to distinguish their city. Indeed, multiculturalism and diversity have recently become a positive demographic characteristic for business and tourism and an aspect of flexible specialisation, which coincides with a saturation of traditional markets and heightened global competition (Hoffman 2003a; Fainstein and Powers 2005). Therefore, the provision of exotic experiences and sights representing 'otherness' are potential sources of economic revenue in a destination (Ooi 2002).

In the 1980s ethnic tourism referred to a 'first hand experience with the practice of another culture to provide tourists with more intimate and authentic experiences' (Greenwood 1982: 27) involving travel. However, since, the term has broadened in terms of definition and is nowadays widely understood as engaging 'in the cultural activities of a minority group within the tourist's own society' (Smith 2003: 30). McKercher defines ethnic tourism as 'emphasising the otherness of a place in terms of the tourist's frame of reference' (McKercher and du Cros 2002: 131). In a certain way, that means, for instance that an American tourist in a European country would consider a Chinese quarter to be exotic for he/she has a similar frame of reference as the host country. Another example is that South Americans consider the German districts there to be an ethnic destination independent of their home country. The 'exotic' and 'otherness' is thus to be understood in a very broad geographical and socio-cultural context. While in some places the community shapes the streetscapes through specific architectural features (e.g. Chinatown), in others they simply open shops and restaurants giving the district some recognisable ethnic features (e.g. the colours of the Italian flag used in most Little Italys) (Collins and Jordan 2009). Yet it is worthwhile repeating that in many ethnic precincts today the community has moved out and hardly any members of the community live in the quarters that become ethnic tourist attractions (e.g. Sydney's Little Italy – Mura and Lovelock 2009). In some cases, it goes so far that ethnic districts are entirely emptied of their community (e.g. Little Italy in Boston) and are transformed into purely tourist attractions providing food and other business (Conforti 1996). Through tourism development, sites like Brick Lane in London or Little India in Singapore have been alienated from their original community to become hip Asian dining areas (Chang 1999) and gentrified areas. Indeed, the ethnicity of the community may appear as an exotic backdrop but the original idea of meeting the 'other' turns into a purely commercial exchange. In the literature, ethnic tourism is often understood as engendering a positive impact such as improved tax revenues and increased personal income (Andereck *et al*. 2005). Conditions to achieve this are yet linked to the type of tourism planning and the degree of community and resident involvement.

However, not all cities can turn migrant quarters into tourist destinations. The presence of infrastructure and services such as public transport, restaurants and accommodation for tourists constitutes a key factor for tourism development. At the same time, the role and implication of the different actors, such as public authorities, users and residents – all those involved in or potentially concerned by the tourism planning process – are of primary importance.

## The stakeholders

The stakeholders in cultural tourism are numerous: the community that uses the district, the visitors (tourists and passers-by), the residents, the tourism authorities, the local authorities. There are two key developments: either the community decides to develop tourism (e.g. Harlem, NY), or the authorities decide to do so (e.g. Matonge in Brussels). The core issue, however, relates to the development model applied to the district. Murphy (1985) explains that in order to avoid top-down tourism planning, four components need to be considered: characteristics of the environment and accessibility; social and cultural issues; commercial and economic considerations; and the managerial framework.

As the ethnic community does not always live in the quarter, it may also constitute an incoming user-group as do the consumers or tourists. Integrative management approaches are therefore difficult for the 'to be visited' community as opposed to the residents, who might have very different interests when it comes to local development issues. Stakeholder theory (Sautter and Leisen 1999) or the collaborative planning model (Murphy and Murphy 2004) emphasise the importance of the integrated management of a destination if it is to benefit the community. A study in Matonge (Brussels) in 2008 highlighted the problematic of putting a precinct on the map as a tourist destination without informing the 'promoted community' (Diekmann and Maulet 2009). Indeed, in the case of Matonge, neither restaurants nor shopkeepers had been informed by the authorities that they were part of the new branding of the city and promoted as an 'exotic' destination within the city. Most of them learnt about it only through the current research.

The consequence of this poor involvement of the stakeholders and the lack of infrastructure and visual markers was that the tourism development related to the 'otherness' and the exotic did not achieve its goals of attracting visitors to the area. As service providers were not implicated and were even offended by the planning behind their backs, they expressed little interest in receiving tourists and providing, for instance, items that tourists are likely to purchase, such as postcards or souvenirs (Diekmann and Maulet 2009). The indifference towards tourism development is, however, also linked to the type of clients of the ethnic service and goods providers, composed mainly of members from the different central African communities, as shown in the next section.

## The tourists

While ethnic precincts attract more and more visitors who come for the 'exotic' experience, others come to purchase goods and gather with community fellows. In New York's Little Italy, probably half of the visitors on a Saturday afternoon are Italian-Americans; the same goes for Chinatown (Conforti 1996).

A survey was conducted in Brussels' African quarter Matonge in 2011 as part of a research project (Ouethy 2011). The rationale of the research was to identify the perception and behaviour of members of the ethnic community within the district and to analyse whether they consider themselves as tourists and how they were addressed by the tourism promotion of the area. Respondents of African origin were randomly chosen and 100 were interviewed in public spaces in March 2011. Although the results may vary slightly according to the time and place of the interview, the results showed that a broad majority of visitors from other countries are ethnic community members in a broad sense for they originate from a multitude of sub-Saharan countries in Africa. They come from neighbouring countries to purchase specific goods and meet friends and relatives, and/or visit places that represent their cultural environment. They come for nostalgic reasons, to share a bit of homeland with their children, to socialise with other community members, to exchange news with friends and family, and to consume the community's food and beverages. According to common definitions of tourism, this group of visitors are tourists because they stay for a couple of nights and come mainly for leisure purposes. Yet the visiting community members interviewed never considered themselves as tourists, but as visitors. While all respondents were of diverse African origin (Figure 44.1), many of them did not live in Brussels or even in Belgium (Figure 44.2).

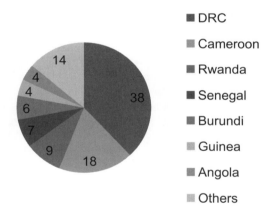

*Figure 44.1* Country of origin

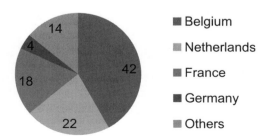

*Figure 44.2* Country of residence

The respondents of Congolese origin, representing 38 per cent, were the largest group. This is also due to the history of the Matonge, named after a famous district in Kinshasa. While the name indicates strong links with the Democratic Republic of Congo (DRC), other central African countries use the quarter as their social interface.

Indeed Congolese students settled in the area in the early 1960s and a broad cultural offer developed as a consequence, from specific shops, bars, restaurants and music clubs (outside DRC, Matonge has the most important Congolese music production). Due to the political developments in many countries in central Africa, the students were replaced by refugees and migrants, strengthening the position of Matonge as a location for social networking and exchange with ethnic community members and a place for buying specific goods from back home. While Matonge is considered generally to be one ethnic central African district, at present most of the nationalities mentioned in Figure 44.1 have their own community cafés and restaurants and thus distinct locations for their community activities.

Figure 44.2 shows the country of residence of the respondents. While 42 per cent of the visitors come from Belgium and are not necessarily 'tourists', many of them are excursionists coming from other cities in Belgium for the above-mentioned reasons. However, the graph shows the important number of people coming from neighbouring countries and, as shown in Figure 44.3, many of them considered their trip to be a leisure trip (Ouethy 2011).

Only 5 per cent of all respondents stayed in a hotel, while 59 per cent stayed with family and 20 per cent with friends (Figure 44.4). The major reasons for staying with friends and family are the existing opportunities and financial issues. It should be underlined, however, that no hotels are located in the ethnic precinct or in the immediate surroundings. Respondents wishing to stay in a hotel mainly choose the budget hotels near the railway station, three metro stops away (Ouethy 2011).

Another survey in public space with randomly chosen people in the same area in 2008 showed that only very few 'ethnic tourists' visit the quarter. Indeed, out of 100 people of various origins, only four (white) respondents declared themselves to be tourists. Other ethnic quarters have indeed more visitors from outsiders of the community for their tourism offer is more developed and involves the community. An example is Harlem, New York, where the

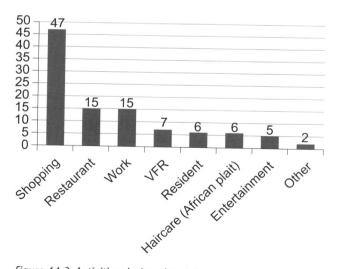

*Figure 44.3* Activities during the visit

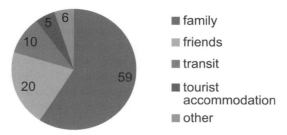

*Figure 44.4* Accommodation used

initiative to respond to the demand of foreign tourists to visit the district has been taken up by the Afro-American communities in the precinct. However, while the promotion targets foreign visitors, it does not advertise the community as 'exotic', but as part of the American heritage, and therefore also addresses community members.

## Promoting the ethnic precinct

The tourism authorities and the media, such as guidebooks, are responsible for the promotion of the destination. Since the need for diversification and competition between the cities came on the agenda in the late 1990s, ethnic precincts seem to be a promising promotion tool for tourism authorities. While tourism development is considered as an economic stimulus, the presence of different ethnic groups in a city emphasises its global status and its cosmopolitanism. In many cases, the presence of a specific ethnic community is based on a common and intertwined historical past such as, for instance, colonisation or labour migration. In that sense, the presence of the ethnic community shapes the image of the host country and contributes to the branding of the city.

In the current scheme of ethnic quarters as tourism destinations, the 'otherness' and the exotic are often promoted. The following examples come from official promotional materials of Matonge in Brussels.

Slogans like 'get a glimpse of Africa' (*Time Out Brussels* 2010), or 'your gaze will inevitably be attracted by the colourful stalls of Matonge'. 'This exotic blend …' (www.wallonie-tourisme.be), or 'Here, the whole of Africa is offered up to you: you'll find miles of multicoloured fabrics, and can fill up with exotic fruits, spices from distant lands and human warmth' (visitbrussels.be), or '… borders on the highly colourful Matongé quarter. Its inhabitants, who are mainly Africans, open up their doors and sunny terraces' (www.brusselsinternational.be). These accounts clearly distinguish amongst the focused visitor groups dwelling on the otherness of the place. Not-withstanding, the information given is not entirely correct, for there are hardly any stalls to be seen, and few inhabitants (2 per cent) are of central African origin. The visual markers are more those of urban decay and poorly maintained public space, very common to any impoverished urban district.

However, Matonge is not a unique case; most destinations promote their 'ethnic' quarter as an insight into 'otherness' and an 'exotic' environment. Identity and cultural distinction from a 'host' country where the community is not yet integrated highlights a certain paradox that is reinforced by the promotional slogans segregating the local community even more and merchandising it at the same time. An example is Singapore promoting its cosmopolitism with three different ethnic precincts: Chinatown, Little India and Kampong Glam (Arab quarter). The official description of the three quarters addresses visitors from other cultures than the community under scrutiny, though from a more heritage-oriented perspective than in Matonge: 'Today, it [Chinatown] carries an ethnic-heritage charm amidst modern influences. It has kept its roots by conserving pre-war shop houses and its century-old beliefs. This is truly a most beautiful part of Singapore, and a "must visit" for all new visitors!' (www.visiting-singapore.com/chinatown.html). The website explains further that 'Little India, Chinatown and Kampong Glam was restored, refurbished and now houses rows of conservation houses redeveloped as art galleries, curios shops and food eateries and restaurants' (www.visiting-singapore.com/kampong-glam.html). These places are thus highly commodified to meet alleged visitors' expectations of the post-modern lifestyle tourist, but not actually addressing community members. Henderson highlights the controversial situation and the role of tourism, which is seen to act as an instrument of both development and conservation (Henderson 2008). A comparable example is San Francisco, where Chinatown developed from a 'quaint and mysterious section of the city' (Page and Hall 2003: 154) into a tourist attraction. Indeed, dwelling on the otherness, San Francisco's tourism authorities promoted Chinatown as 'an exotic Chinese colony, and the dingy back alleyways were turned into picturesque little lanes' (Page and Hall 2003: 154).

## Conclusion

Promotion of ethnic quarters is used in many urban destinations as a substantial element of a multicultural and cosmopolitan branding of the city. While city branding aims to create emotional, mental and psychological connections or links between the different user groups – such as investors, residents and visitors – and the city, many promotions of ethnic quarters seem to exclude one significant user group – the community itself. However, in many ethnic quarters the ethnic community members constitute the core group of visitors. One explanation why they are hardly ever addressed by the official tourism promotion might be the fact that as community members, they shift from being tourists themselves to become part of the 'otherness' and underpin the ethnicity of the place.

The current policies of promoting ethnic quarters as exotic places seem, however, short-sighted. Indeed, with a significant number of visitors not being addressed, tourism development appears to be at risk in the long term, for it fails to provide services to all visitor groups. If tourism development in ethnic quarters is to contribute to regeneration and economic development, promotion should be aiming at more integration instead of segregating the communities and certainly not emphasising the exotic in comparison to local culture, but to evoke more common past and historical reasons for the presence of the communities to be visited. This integrative approach is indeed strengthened when the ethnic community and the local residents are involved in tourism planning and development, and contribute to the promotional message of the ethnic precinct.

## References

Andereck, K.L., Valentine, K.M., Knopf, R.C. and Vogt, C.A. (2005) 'Residents' Perceptions of Community Tourism Impacts', *Annals of Tourism Research* 32(4): 1056–76.

Chang, T.C. (1999) 'Local Uniqueness in the Global Village: Heritage Tourism in Singapore', *Professional Geographer* 51(1): 91–103.

Collins, J. and Jordan, K. (2009) 'Ethnic Precincts as Ethnic Tourism Destinations in Urban Australia', *Tourism, Culture and Communication* 9(1): 79–92.

Conforti, J.M. (1996) 'Ghettos as Tourism Attractions', *Annals of Tourism Research* 23(4): 830–42.

Diekmann, A. and Maulet, G. (2009) 'A Contested Ethnic Tourism Asset: The Case of Matonge in Brussels', *Tourism, Culture and Communication* 9(1): 93–106.

Fainstein, S.S. and Powers, J.C. (2005) Tourism and New York's Ethnic Diversity: An Underutilized Resource?, inside.gsd.harvard.edu/people/faculty/fainstein/docs/Diversity%20tourism%20edited%20version. pdf (accessed 16 November 2011).

Greenwood, D.G. (1982) 'Cultural Authenticity', *Cultural Survival Quarterly* 6(3): 27–28.

Henderson, J.C. (2008) 'Managing Urban Ethnic Heritage: Little India in Singapore', *International Journal of Heritage Studies* 14(4): 332–46.

Hoffman, L.M. (2003a) 'The Marketing of Diversity in the Inner City: Tourism and Regulation in Harlem', *International Journal of Urban and Regional Research* 27(2): 286–99.

——(2003b) 'Revalorizing the Inner City: Tourism and Regulation in Harlem', in Hoffman, L.M., Fainstein, S. and Judd, D. (eds) *Cities and Visitors*, Malden. MA: Blackwell, 91–112.

McKercher, B. and du Cros, H. (2002) *Cultural Tourism: The Partnership between Tourism and Cultural Heritage Management*, New York: Haworth Hospitality Press.

McLaughlin, C.M. and Jesilow, P. (1998) 'Conveying a Sense of Community Along Bolsa Avenue: Little Saigon as a Model of Ethnic Commercial Belts', *International Migration* 36(1): 49–65.

Maitland, R. and Newman, P. (2009) *World Tourism Cities: Developing Tourism off the Beaten Track*, London: Routledge.

Mura, P. and Lovelock, B. (2009) 'A Not So Little Italy? Tourist and Resident Perceptions of Authenticity in Leichhardt, Sydney', *Tourism, Culture and Communication* 9: 29–48.

Murphy, P. (1985) *Tourism: A Community Approach*, London: Methuen.

Murphy, P. and Murphy, A. (2004) *Strategic Management for Tourism Communities: Bridging the Gaps*, Clevedon: Channel View.

Ooi, C.S. (2002) *Cultural Tourism and Tourism Cultures*, Copenhagen: Copenhagen Business School Press.

Ouethy, T. (2011) *Le profil des touristes ethniques de Matongé*, Master's dissertation, ULB, Brussels.

Page, S. and Hall, M. (2003) *Managing Urban Tourism*, London: Prentice Hall.

Rath, J. (ed.) (2007) *Tourism, Ethnic Diversity and the City*, London: Routledge.

Roodhouse, S. (2006) *City Quarters: Principles and Practice*, Bristol: Intellect.

Sautter, E.T. and Leisen, B. (1999) 'Managing Stakeholders: A Tourism Planning Model', *Annals of Tourism Research* 26(2): 312–28.

Selby, M. (2004) *Understanding Urban Tourism: Image, Culture and Experience*, London: I.B. Tauris.

Shaw, S. (2007) 'Ethnic Quarters in the Cosmopolitan Creative City', in Richards, G. and Wilson, J. (eds) *Tourism, Creativity and Development*, London: Routledge, 189–200.

Smith, M.K. (2003) *Issues in Cultural Tourism Studies*, London and New York: Routledge.

Smith, V. and Maryann, B. (eds) (2001) *Host and Guests Revisited: Tourism Issues of the 21st century*, New York: Cognizant Communication Corporation.

Trevor, J. and Monder, R. (2003) 'South Asian Business in Retreat? The Case of the UK', *Journal of Ethnics and Migration Studies* 29(3): 485–500.

Zukin, S. (1998) 'Urban Lifestyles: Diversity and Standardisation', *Urban Studies* 35(5/6): 825–39.

# PART VII

# The tourist and visitor experience

There have been several significant developments in the field of visitor and attractions management in recent years, especially in many cultural cities. In the past, tourism had always tended to be somewhat scripted, with tourists being shepherded from one place to another with few opportunities for deviations from the prescribed route or schedule. Even in the earlier days of travel, the Grand Tour routes were largely pre-determined, which was then followed by the guidebooks of Baedeker and others and the tours of Thomas Cook or American Express. Whether tourism was aristocratic, bourgeois or mass, there were few spontaneous experiences to be had or it was thought that tourists may not cope adequately alone or may be subject to danger or inconvenience. Thus, the majority of tourists started to take on the characteristics of a sheep or a child, meekly following a trail, a travel guide or a tour without question.

However, in recent years, tourism literature increasingly refers to the desire to subvert such prescribed routes and activities. Performance theory (e.g. Edensor 2000) is referred to by Nikki MacLeod in this section, which analyses the increasingly active and interactive role of the tourist. There has been a rapid growth in the academic literature about the need for experiential developments (Pine and Gilmore 1999; Oh *et al.* 2007; Ek *et al.* 2008; Ritchie and Hudson 2009), and the role of the co-creation concept (Potts *et al.* 2008; Binkhorst and Dekker 2009), whereby the visitor is somehow actively involved in shaping his or her own experiences. In this section, both Sonia Ferrari and Zsuzsanna Horváth discuss the relationship between cultural tourism, the experience economy and co-creation. Here, the thoughts, feelings and personal backgrounds of the tourist all come into play as destination developers and service providers involve the tourist in the creation of their own experiences. This is especially evident in the field of creative tourism which involves tourists in local cultural processes, often alongside the hosts.

Gone are the days when it was enough for a museum or gallery to provide limited interpretation and visitors were expected to be passive receivers of extensive and not always very interesting information. For several decades already, interpretation theorists (e.g. Tilden 1977) had been advocating the need to provoke or shock visitors and to shake them out of their comfort zone. Interpretation should also be engaging, educational and informative (e.g. Uzzell 1989). This involves various interactive and playful modes of engaging with collections and exhibitions, including intangible heritage. Museums and galleries are increasingly using more complex and sophisticated interpretation methods and technology to create innovative visitor experiences. The 'new museology' trend of the late 1990s emphasised the need to focus on visitors rather than collections, including greater accessibility and wider public participation. The so-called 'post-museum' is involved in audience development strategies which encourage under-represented groups to participate in cultural activities. A clear understanding of visitor psychology is essential for this, as emphasised by László Puczkó in his chapter. It is important to develop the whole 'servicescape' to create a memorable experience from the moment a visitor enters a building, and a focus is also needed on different visitor segments.

Several writers have started to focus on the tourists' desire to experience the everyday life of a destination on the fringe or in alternative areas of cities (e.g. Maitland 2007). This means that there has been something of a shift away from tourists passively gazing at built heritage and landscapes to wanting to participate in and engage with real events and people. Gernot Wolfram and Claire Burnill discuss this phenomenon in this section with reference to the so-called 'tactical tourist'. The 'authenticity' of culture which can be found amongst local communities in a destination is becoming increasingly appealing. This is especially true in the case of ethnic communities, whose lives may seem colourful or exotic (Shaw 2007; Diekmann and Maulet 2009); however, it can also include the places frequented by ordinary, everyday people (e.g. bars, cafés, restaurants). Interestingly, even anthropologists are starting to focus more on the lives and behaviours of urban dwellers in developed economies, and not only tribal groups in developing countries (Macleod and Carrier 2010). Of course, it is still debatable as to how far visitors can truly gain access to the 'backstage' or people's lives (early tourism theorists like MacCannell 1976 suggested that they could not).

One of the other important aspects of the tourist or visitor experience is the spontaneous encounters that tourists enjoy when they are travelling (Richards 2001). Most of the authors in this section focus on experiences that are created or co-created by tourism or cultural attractions managers. However, much of tourism consists of unpredictable and surprising experiences which often involve local people and cross-cultural exchange. Not all of these may be entirely positive, but they can certainly be memorable. They can be mediated by the tourism industry to a certain degree, but less in the case of independent and backpacker travel. Tourists increasingly like to choose elements of their own experiences. In many hotels, there is a trend towards 'customization' of services so that the visitor has some degree of choice (even if it is just the type of pillow s/he sleeps on or the preferred menu for dinner). Many lifestyle and boutique hotels provide themed rooms so that visitors can state their preference for décor and atmosphere.

Overall, the tourist and visitor experience is becoming a somewhat sophisticated one including many elements of personalisation, customisation and choice. Integrated experiences are becoming common where it is harder to differentiate between leisure and tourism, fiction and reality, authenticity and inauthenticity, spontaneity and staging. It is often suggested that the 'post-tourist' does not care about such distinctions (e.g. Rojek and Urry 1997), but researchers need to look carefully at the psychology of different visitor groups and segments to be sure. This may include increasing cross-cultural understanding, as different nationality groups may respond in very different ways (for example, newly travelling groups of Chinese visitors will have very different expectations from independent and experienced European visitors). Age also plays a significant role and research often shows that there can be tensions between different age groups within the same facility as it is hard to cater for a range of ages simultaneously. In this section, one visitor segment is analysed in depth by Anna Leask and Paul Barron – Generation Y – but it would be useful to apply similar research to other segments across various nationalities. Only then can cultural tourism managers hope to afford tourists and visitors the optimum experience in their destinations and attractions.

## Summary of the chapters in this section

**Gernot Wolfram** and **Claire Burnhill-Maier** write about the so-called 'tactical tourist', a term that is based on de Certeau's (1988) concept of people who employ tactics to subvert dominant systems. Such tourists seek unique and individual experiences and wish to engage with the 'true destination', which can mean the everyday lives of people or a place's hidden treasures. They could be compared to the notion of 'creators', who represent a small but increasingly influential group of visitors. The term tourist has become somewhat pejorative, therefore such visitors may not even want to think of themselves or be defined as tourists. This has important implications for the development and promotion of visitor experiences, as tactical visitors will want a certain degree of independence, flexibility and spontaneity in what they see and do. A case study is given of Berlin, where this phenomenon has been handled rather well and visitors are encouraged to explore and immerse themselves in the everyday life of the city and its people by those who consider themselves to be 'experts in everyday life'.

**Nikki MacLeod** examines the way in which self-guided routes and trails are used within the context of visitor experience creation. Trails are frequently used as a visitor management tool and can be based on a wide range of themes such as history, industry, culture, gastronomy or famous people. Trails should ideally bring economic and social benefits for local communities, as well as directing and enhancing the visitor experience. However, it is noted that trail development relies on selective interpretation and is a highly structured mode of seeing. This means that a certain degree of freedom and spontaneity of the gaze is lost. Nevertheless, there is a growing trend towards subversion, as emphasised also in 'performance turn' theory, where visitors wish to be active rather than passive and sensually engaged in their experience of place. An analysis of 75 trails in England is used to demonstrate the fact that the optimal visitor experience is rarely created by trail developers, as they do not make enough use of some of the key tools of experience creation such as storytelling, interaction, personalisation and enrolment. This means that the tourist is often unable to become a fully embodied producer of his or her own experiences.

**Zsuzsanna Horváth** discusses the importance of memorable experience creation in the development of competitive and sustainable destinations. Tourism consumption experiences should reflect the opposite of everyday life and be unique, personal, but also surprising and unusual. The importance of the tourist in co-creation is emphasised here – especially the role of thoughts, feelings, imaginations and backgrounds. Creative tourism is used as one example of where the creative potential of the tourist is also considered in destination development and experience creation. This can even lead to the personal growth or development of the tourist, fulfilling aspirations, wishes and expectations. The importance of collective consumer creativity is highlighted, whereby new interpretations and discoveries are shared and discussed mainly using social media. Data were collected about the perceptions of 80 students with regards to the phenomenon of co-creation and memorable tourist experiences, and the findings corroborated the theory that visitors tend to value unexpected, sensual, interactive, colourful, personal, intellectual and spiritual experiences.

**Sonia Ferrari** provides a discussion of how museums and heritage sites are increasingly designing memorable visitor experiences or 'experiencescapes' in accordance with theories of 'edutainment', the Tourist Gaze, the experience economy, and co-creation. She emphasises the importance of engaging the five senses and the four spheres according to Pine and Gilmore (1999). Visitors need to be immersed in their experiences and continuously 're-enchanted'. Much of this can be achieved through interactive multi-media and multi-sensory techniques which are increasingly being employed at cultural attractions. Aspects of storytelling or theatre can be highly effective, especially where the visitor is also involved in the process through 'co-creation'. This means that the visitor can enjoy a personalised experience which is adapted to his or her own preferences and expectations. She uses a case study of the Palazzo Vecchio in Florence to illustrate elements of experiencescape development.

**László Puczkó** also focuses on visitor experiences at cultural attractions such as museums and galleries, but he emphasises the importance of interpretation and visitor psychology in the creation of experiences. He makes the significant point that cultural attractions are usually created by designers rather than psychologists, therefore visitor needs and expectations are not always well understood, especially as environmental stimuli can have vastly different impacts on different visitors. He emphasises the fact that most visitors need to be actively involved in cultural spaces in order to retain information and have a memorable experience; however, this can be relatively limited in many attractions. He concurs with theories about co-creation and 'prosumption', and suggests that this can be achieved through techniques such as 'chunking' or 'experience mapping'. This can include elements of interpretation, orientation, services and performance monitoring. An experience grid can be used to identify how beneficial, accessible, valuable and authentic a cultural space is. He concludes with a case study of Hungarian museums, which are slowly but successfully moving towards the creation of more engaging, interactive and memorable experiences.

**Anna Leask** and **Paul Barron** finally consider the needs of one segment of museum visitors, which is Generation Y. Generally born between 1979 and 1994, this group of visitors embody many of the characteristics of the visitors discussed so far in this section. They respond well to interactive, creative, experiential and technology-based attractions which offer them something fun and engaging. This group of consumers tend to share experiences using social media, with 'word-of-mouse' overtaking other forms of communication. Gen Y are thought to be the consummate experience seekers and appreciate the organisation of events that are child-free, include opportunities for socialisation, often take place at night or even through the night, are fun, and involve doing rather than listening. The authors use a case study of the National Museum of Scotland, which organises events after standard opening hours for the 18–30 age group, including a silent disco, socialising spaces, games and other online activities.

## References

Binkhorst, E. and Den Dekker, T. (2009) 'Agenda for Co-Creation Tourism Experience Research', *Journal of Hospitality Marketing and Management* 18(2): 311–27.

de Certeau, Michel (1988) *The Practice of Everyday Life*, Berkeley, CA: University of California Press.

Diekmann, A. and Maulet, G. (2009) 'A Contested Ethnic Tourism Asset: The Case of Matonge in Brussels', *Tourism, Culture and Communication* 9(1): 93–106.

Edensor, T. (2000) 'Staging Tourism: Tourists as Performers', *Annals of Tourism Research* 27: 322–44.

Ek, R., Larsen, J., Hornskov, S.B. and Mansfeldt, O.K. (2008) 'A Dynamic Framework of Tourist Experiences: Space-Time and Performances in the Experience Economy', *Scandinavian Journal of Hospitality and Tourism* 8(2): 122–40.

MacCannell, D. (1976) *The Tourist: A New Theory of the Leisure Class*, New York: Schocken.

Macleod, D.V.L. and Carrier, J.G. (eds) (2010) *Tourism, Power and Culture: Anthropological Insights*, Clevedon: Channel View Publications.

Maitland, R. (2007) 'Cultural Tourism and the Development of New Tourism Areas in London', in Richards, G. (ed.) *Cultural Tourism: Global and Local Perspectives*, New York: Haworth Press, 113–28.

Oh, H., Fiore, A.M. and Jeoung, M. (2007) 'Measuring Experience Economy Concepts: Tourism Applications', *Journal of Travel Research* 46: 119–32.

Pine, B.J. and Gilmore, J.H. (1999) *The Experience Economy: Work is Theatre and Everyday Business a Stage*, Boston, MA: Harvard Business School Press

Potts, J.D., Hartley, J., Banks, J.A., Burgess, J.E., Cobcroft, R.S., Cunningham, S.D. and Montgomery, L. (2008) 'Consumer Co-creation and Situated Creativity', *Industry and Innovation* 15(5): 459–74.

Richards, G. (2001) 'The Development of Cultural Tourism in Europe', in Richards, G. (ed.) *Cultural Attractions and European Tourism*, Wallingford: CABI, 3–29.

Ritchie, J.R.B. and Hudson, S. (2009) 'Understanding and Meeting the Challenges of Consumer/Tourist Experience Research', *International Journal of Tourism Research* 11: 111–26.

Rojek, C. and Urry, J. (eds) (1997) *Touring Cultures: Transformations of Travel and Theory*, London: Routledge.

Shaw, S. (2007) 'Ethnoscapes as Cultural Attractions in Canadian "World Cities"', in Smith, M.K. (ed.) *Tourism, Culture and Regeneration*, Wallingford: CABI, 49–58.

Tilden, F. (1977) *Interpreting Our Heritage*, Chapel Hill: University of North Carolina Press.

Uzzell, D.L. (ed.) (1989) *Heritage Interpretation: Vol 1: The Natural and Built Environment*, London: Belhaven Press.

# 45

# The tactical tourist

## Growing self-awareness and challenging the strategists – visitor groups in Berlin

*Gernot Wolfram and Claire Burnill-Maier*

## Introduction

In *The Practice of Everyday Life*, Michel de Certeau (1988) investigates the ways in which, throughout everyday situations, society seeks to challenge power relations. In a society that is arguably driven by markets and industry, economists and researchers seek to identify consumer habits and manipulate a seemingly docile populous with targeted marketing and carefully designed products and product placement. De Certeau describes these manoeuvres by dominant groups as 'strategies'. However, de Certeau argues that these strategies are responded to and challenged by 'tactics' deployed by a conscious public to subvert and undermine the 'strategists' and to claim small 'joyous victories'. He puts forward a case that popular culture is defined and shaped by a people who are not simply passive pawns trapped in an industrialised system, but that people are alert to and aware of their part in the system and will seek to find small ways in which to subvert it, and repeatedly deploy a 'wisdom' aimed at:

> ... playing and foiling the other's game ... People have to make do with what they have. In these combatants' stratagems, there is a certain art of placing one's blows, a pleasure in getting around the rules of a constraining space.
>
> *(de Certeau 1988: 18)*

De Certeau points out that consumers should not be underestimated by reductionist theorists and that through the deployment of tactical behavioural change, these tactics gain validity, and with this society is able to undermine and sometimes radically change the rules imposed upon them by dominant societal structures.

For the field of cultural tourism, this sociological concept is particularly important. It is essential to understand that there are groups of people who seek unique, individual tourist experiences 'far from the madding crowd' and 'off the beaten track'. Many visitors wish to find the 'true' destination and feel an affinity with local people. These groups seek escape from the well-known strategies of tourism marketing and popular tour programmes. They no longer

361

wish to define themselves as 'tourists' because the term has negative connotations for them. In Berlin, an interesting discourse has emerged from this growing phenomenon. Amongst the rising success of the city as a tourist destination with over 9 million visitors in 2010 (Amt für Statistik Berlin-Brandenburg 2011), more and more visitors look for individual and complex access to the city by shifting their self-awareness as tourists. In this chapter we make a clear distinction between traditional models of independent travellers (e.g. backpackers and alternative tourism), and 'tactical tourists' – the latter being defined as those able to reflect upon the problematic nature of the 'the tourist'.

In this text, we will focus on those visitors who may be described as 'tactical visitors', in accordance with de Certeau's theory. Those visitors who are seeking to evade the 'tourist traps' and find new insights to the city. By focusing on these groups, we shift the notion of 'tourist' from that which is a passive member of a 'target group' at which the city is marketed, to an active, independent figure who rejects the specifically targeted strategies of the tourist industry, and has the potential to, consciously or unconsciously, change the company and institutional strategies deployed by and within the tourist sector. We illustrate some of these changes and look at the ways in which tourist provision is adapting to these groups and how a new culture of tourism is emerging in the city. In viewing these tactical visitors, we are able to gain an insight into what attracts them to the city of Berlin, and by looking at their response to structural tourist offers and trends we can draw some implications for the future.

## The tactical tourist

All too often, conventional tourist industry approaches look upon the behaviour of tourists as passive consumers, not as considered visitors who react to corporate strategies. In seeking to promote and offer a 'true cultural insight' for its visitors, the tourist industry often succeeds merely in creating a mass market for the very things tourists would find 'at home':

> The mass tourist is less likely to adapt to the local cultures, and will seek amenities and standards found in the home country, while the independent traveller or backpacker will adapt more readily to an alien environment.
>
> *(Holloway 2006: 123)*

It can be argued, however, that the 'tactical tourists' become problematic in accordance with their successes. The result of the 'tactical out-manoeuvring' of mass tourism can be seen as both positive and negative for destinations, the industry, for culture, society, and can ultimately be seen to serve the very ends they sought to undermine.

The 'tactical tourist' can be likened to Horowitz's (2006) 'creators' as demonstrated in his 'creators, synthesisers and users' pyramid of influence. The 'creators' are a minority of those who ultimately make up the consumer market for the tourist industry; however, their sphere of influence, and their quality of contribution to it, is highly significant. Other independent travellers including backpackers can be seen as forming the 'synthesisers'; those who remain are largely tourists and follow the conventions of independent travel.

In Jennings's book *Net Blogs and Rock 'n' Roll* he uses a pyramid to illustrate value creation in the music industry. In his model he looks at how a tiny minority of music lovers have the most influence on the music industry. However, we have taken the idea of the pyramid to show how the 'tactical tourist', representing the smallest fraction of the tourist sector, could be argued as being those who are most likely to instigate tactical change in accordance with de Certeau's theory, with passive mass tourists, forming the largest number of the group, at the bottom. The

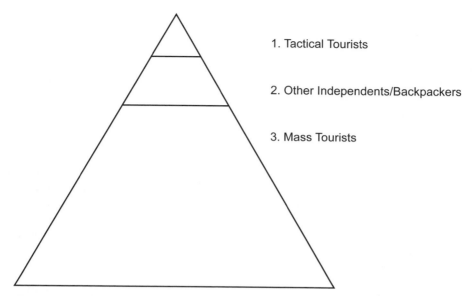

1. Tactical Tourists

2. Other Independents/Backpackers

3. Mass Tourists

*Figure 45.1* Tactical tourists form the smallest segment of the market, but are the most likely to seek original experiences

group at the top are original and seek new experiences, whilst the backpackers and mass tourists can be seen as representing mainstream tourism at the bottom (see Figure 45.1).

Here we see a very small number of 'tactical tourists', whose consumer behaviour has a large effect on the wider market, ultimately shaping and defining it. Through their 'tactical' choices, shifts in consumer behaviour can be observed, resulting in the 'flocking' of groups in the longer term – turning 'niche' markets into mainstream ones.

This dichotomous relationship between tactical tourists and mass tourism has been perhaps most lucidly illustrated in the growth of ethical tourism. Throughout the last two decades, demand for ethical tours and travel has increased significantly, and the travel industry has been forced to integrate ethics into conventional product offerings (Crane and Matten 2010). However, at this point, we would stress that de Certeau's 'tactics' should not be *merely* accounted for by so-called 'consumer sovereignty' whereby tourists simply shift allegiance according to what's on offer in the market place – though this is clearly an issue. Tactical tourism goes beyond 'voting with one's feet and taking business elsewhere'; it is about finding unique experiences that allow the tourist to be an independent individual – a 'counter-tourist' whilst gaining the experience of a new culture in new surroundings. Furthermore, as our case study illustrates, it goes beyond that of consumer behaviour and makes way for 'tactical' provision, whereby minority groups may manoeuvre themselves into the tourist market.

## Current trends and historical links

We will attempt to contribute to and highlight the significance of this discourse by examining a number of tourist opportunities that are offered in Berlin and can be understood as reactions to the changing behaviour of Berlin's visitors.

The city of Berlin may be divided up conveniently into a number of different cultural zones for tourist purposes. Following the fall of the Berlin Wall the areas of former East Berlin were frequented in particularly high numbers and (Hartmann and Kistner 2005), even today, visits to areas where the wall stood and places particularly pertinent to the Nazi period remain popular amongst tourists. Certain spaces have received a large degree of attention and were converted into public tourist attractions, such as the *Gedenkstätte Berliner Mauer* situated on Bernauerstrasse (see Meethan, this volume). A whole new tourist infrastructure was created in response to the increasing attention of international tourists.

In contrast to the purpose-built tourist areas, it is possible to turn one's attention to other areas of the city such as the quarters of Wedding, Neukölln and Marzahn. These areas have generally not been focal points for tourists and have not been subjected to the attentions of mass cultural programmes in the field of tourism. However, it is precisely here that new tourist interventions are emerging. These interventions are trying to attract tourists who wish to gain local knowledge and insights and who wish to behave in a counter-tourist context. Within these areas visitors will find the Stadtteilmuseen, which presents historical items from the households of working families in the nineteenth century as well as some largely unknown cultural memorials and sculptures. Perhaps most interestingly, though, artists and galleries are increasingly interested in staging events in empty apartments situated in one of the typical skyscrapers, a legacy from the former communist era, especially in Marzahn and Lichtenberg. A common goal of these interventions is that they present themselves as an opposite side of Berlin – a kind of 'hidden city'.

It is a noteworthy paradox, in many ways, that the very things that have, historically, attracted tourists to Berlin are to a great extent lost when tourists undertake a commercial tour of the city. Berlin is a city celebrated for its important role in the cultural and philosophical history of the German nation (and, indeed, the world). It is a city that has been defined by its reserved, hidden characteristics, secrecy and unrevealed mystery. In Franz Hessel's (1880–1941) book *Spazieren in Berlin* (Walking in Berlin, 1929), for example, he uses descriptions of hidden zones in public spaces to reflect hidden memories of the late 1920s. His close friend, the philosopher Walter Benjamin (1892–1940), in the memoires of his childhood, growing up in Berlin, *Berliner Kindheit um Neunzehnhundert* (Benjamin 2006), created a similarly intense topography of the city. Old and hidden courtyards, shabby streets and red-light districts fascinated him and in these dark and confusing zones of the megacity he saw convincing parallels with modern contemporary citizenship.

Berlin has puzzled and fascinated writers and artists alike, who have sought to capture the essence of the city. One could extend this row of writers, philosophers and artists who have formulated for themselves their own view and definition of the city, from Christopher Isherwood's *Good bye to Berlin* right up to Lou Reed and Metallica's album *Lulu* (Reed and Metallica 2011), the cover of which displays a flawed doll from the *Berliner Museum der Dinge* (www.museum derdinge.de).

The success of Hans Fallada's (1893–1947) last novel, *Jeder stirbt für sich allein* (Alone in Berlin), published in 1947 and republished in a new translation in the UK and in the USA in 2010, is a stark illustration of the appeal of Berlin. This later publication was an astonishing bestseller (Alberge 2010), and its success was obviously connected as much with the popularity of Berlin as a tourist destination for Americans as with the quality of Fallada's writing. Notably, most of the streets and places described in the novel still exist, but they do not form part of conventional sightseeing tours. They form a part of Berlin's so-called 'hidden places', which reveal a complex and contradictory history. As a consequence, these places in particular should be more interesting areas of the city from a tourist's perspective. Such places reveal fictional and real elements; they create an individual dialogue with the visitor because their quality is a specific mixture of knowledge the visitor has yet to gain and the experience of being in the actual spaces depicted (Webber 2011). Within the field of cultural tourism such places work as fields of distinction.

One can look at these places as so-called 'Heterotopias' – a term of the young Michel Foucault:

> There are also, probably in every culture, in every civilization, real places – places that do exist and that are formed in the very founding of society – which are something like counter-sites, a kind of effectively enacted utopia in which the real sites, all the other real sites that can be found within the culture, are simultaneously represented, contested, and inverted. Places of this kind are outside of all places, even though it may be possible to indicate their location in reality. Because these places are absolutely different from all the sites that they reflect and speak about, I shall call them, by way of contrast to utopias, heterotopias.
>
> *(Foucault 1967: 24)*

Tactical visitors, as we describe them, look for places where they decide by themselves what they see and experience because internal and external stimuli come in to play. That is, they engage with both the particular beauty or history of the physical place and their own sense of place that goes beyond what they see, relating to their broader knowledge of context which enables them to make a connection both with it and to it. The tactical tourist comes closest to experiencing Foucault's 'heterotopia'.

That these places are not currently placed at the fore of the city of Berlin's tourism strategy or indeed at the heart of the countless other mainstream tourist programmes, is their big advantage when considering the interests of tactical visitors. In order to serve the tactical tourists' interests, it is not of primary concern to consider gender, age, income, etc., as in conventional marketing, but to enquire: how and why do these visitors seek experiences that are not prescribed? (Kennedy 2009). Cultural destinations need to assist in the important process of challenging the sometimes problematic (lack of) self-awareness of tourists. Just as the level of consciousness concerning specific cultural destinations plays a significant role in the tactical tourist's choices, so too is the consideration of their role as 'tourist' and the way in which they are perceived. Particularly in Berlin, the very label 'tourist' has become a problematic term.

## The tourist as the enemy

For Berlin, one of the significant considerations for both the 'tactical tourist' and the providers of alternative tourist programmes is the heated debate surrounding tourism and tourists in Berlin. For example, in 2011 Berlin saw the beginning of a new campaign. Based on political and private initiatives, the campaign seeks to protect particular areas from the presence of tourists. What began as a local discussion has become so prominent that it was picked up by the foreign press. The UK's *Guardian* newspaper wrote of the campaign:

> … the anti-tourist movement really started getting column inches at the end of February, when the local Green party in the district of Kreuzberg-Friedrichshain put on an event under the banner, Help, The Tourists Are Coming! It was, said the organiser, Green MP Dirk Behrendt, an attempt to bring together residents, city planners and a representative from the Visit Berlin tourist office to discuss the effect foreign visitors were having on the area. It was held in the trendy Wrangelkiez, which in the past 10 years has become home to a string of budget hostels, noisy bars, restaurants and clubs such as Watergate and My Name Is Barbarella. More than 120 people attended the meeting. The bürgers of the Wrangelkiez aren't the only unhappy ones. Last year the residents of the very desirable

Gräfekiez, a pretty area around the canal further west in Kreuzberg, begged one travel guide to stop sending tourists in their direction.

*(Pidd 2011)*

Throughout the discourse, the term 'tourist' has turned out to have, both in the German and British media, very pejorative connotations. The year 2011 also saw a new website launched offering private accommodation for visitors to Berlin, and the website owners have chosen the title 'Stop being a tourist' – a carefully chosen name linguistically stressing the importance of 'not being a tourist'.

The consequence of this discourse leaves the state of tourism in Berlin in an interesting position. The city is now witnessing a shift whereby individual visitors try to find a new position within this controversial discourse – a position that makes clear that they see themselves as visitors but not as tourists. Can the two be distinguished? Put very simplistically, yes. On the one hand, visitors who seek to explore and immerse themselves in the everyday life of the city are welcomed by both the city and its people, whilst on the other hand, the occupants of the bars and hostels in Wrangelkiez seeking a superficial glance at the city can expect to be labelled as tourists. Moreover, our tactical visitors reflect very precisely on the ways in which they can escape from the context of the general tourism strategies. They position themselves in resistance to the expected mannerisms of tourists and go beyond the spaces that are pre-defined for them. This kind of exclusive non-compliance (denial) seems to be an important fact reflecting the changes of the wishes and needs of many individual visitors, especially in Berlin. One successful website bears the name 'Berlin Hidden Places' (www.berlin-hidden-places.de), and presents its idea as the following:

Berlin-hidden-places is presented in German and English. It is directed at potential lovers of Berlin, at people who want to get to know the city in depth, whether they come from abroad, from Germany or Berlin itself.

*(www.berlin-hidden-places.de/yuba_web3/wir_en.htm)*

The choice of the phrase 'in depth' indicates that at least two possible approaches to the city are conceivable: one superficial, the other 'in depth'. This is linked to a specific intellectual tradition (Walton 2005) and refers intertextually to the celebrated mysteries of this city.

## Box 45.1 Case study: Route 65 Wedding and Route 44 Neukölln

One of the most innovative projects to have emerged that illustrates the changing dynamic amongst visitors to Berlin is 'Route 65' (situated in Wedding) and its partner project 'Route 44' (Neukölln) (www.route65-wedding.de). Founded by the cultural association 'Kultur bewegt e.V.', the concept is that young migrants, living in these areas of the city, offer tours through their 'kiez' (the colloquial name for a particular residential area). The project caters for visitors who seek a different perspective of Berlin. It is for those who position themselves as sensitive to local demographics and who seek an understanding of the lives of everyday Berliners. It requires guests to leave the conventional mass tourist tracks and explore the city through the eyes of the young immigrant population of Berlin. Visitors are taken to places of interest unlikely to be on the usual tourist agendas, including hidden Pakistani mosques situated in quiet courtyards, hidden meeting places and special shops with products from the homeland of the immigrants. The project members define themselves as 'experts in daily life'.

Visitors to the project can expect to be taken to mosques, memorials, restaurants and bakeries, clubs, parks and immigrant social groups that form a central part of the daily lives of the 'guides'. As such, the routine behaviour of mass tourists becomes unacceptable. These visitors must necessarily:

- Adopt the position of 'partner' (as opposed to tourist).
- Be open to the culture and lifestyle of their guides.
- Be sensitive to the notion of 'otherness' and 'oneness' (shared cultures, and 'other' cultures).
- Behave appropriately within public spaces and sites such as mosques.
- Reflect the experience of discovering sites from an internal and external perspective.

## Practical consequences

Many museums, theatres and concert halls in Berlin have benefited from the huge success of the tourist industry within the city of Berlin over recent years. Germany's capital is seen as one of the most important cultural destinations in Europe, with 20 million overnight stays in hotels in 2010. An increasing number of hotels, bed and breakfasts, and private accommodation try to profit from and take part in this development by connecting accommodation offers with cultural activities. However, this huge success comes at a price. The influx of mass tourists has resulted in discontent amongst residents and indeed amongst the most aware of the tourists themselves.

Destinations are now attempting to avoid becoming 'typical tourist places'. Instead of providing a spectacle, they try to provide exclusive participation in the city. As with the pyramid in Figure 45.1, the tactical tourist's impact on those around them can be great – and instrumental in bringing about these cultural changes.

The paradox, of course, is that the tactical tourist's success will arguably result in the homogenisation of these new strategies to a set of predictable outcomes – forcing them to adopt new tactics in the future.

## References

Alberge, Dalya (2010) 'Hans Fallada's Anti-Nazi Classic Becomes Surprise UK Bestseller', *The Guardian*, 23 May, www.guardian.co.uk/books/2010/may/23/hans-fallada-thriller-surprise-hit (accessed 15 November 2012).

Amt für Statistik Berlin-Brandenburg (2011) www.statistik-berlin-brandenburg.de (accessed 15 November 2012).

Benjamin, W. (2006) *Berlin Childhood Around 1900: Hope in the Past*, trans. H. Eiland, Cambridge, MA: Harvard University Press.

Cooper, C., Fletcher, J., Fyall, A., Gilbert, D. and Wanhill, S. (2005) *Tourism: Principles and Practice*, third edn, London: Prentice Hall.

Crane, A. and Matten, D. (2010) *Business Ethics: Managing Corporate Citizenship and Sustainability in the Age of Globalization*, Oxford: Oxford University Press.

de Certeau, M. (1988) *The Practice of Everyday Life*, Berkeley: University of California Press.

Fallada, H. (2010 [1947]) *Alone in Berlin*, trans. M. Hofman, Harmondsworth: Penguin.

Foucault, M. (1967) *Of Other Spaces/Dits et écrits* (1984), Des espaces autres (conférence au Cercle d'études architecturales, 14 march 1967), *Architecture, Mouvement, Continuité*, 5, October 1984: 46–49.

Hartmann, R. and Kistner, F.P. (2005) *Berlin: A Tour Through the City Before and After the Wall Came Down*, Berlin: Edition Braus.

Hessel, F. (2011) *Spazieren in Berlin*, Berlin: Verlag für Berlin-Brandenburg.

Holloway, C.J. (2006) *The Business of Tourism*, seventh edn, London: Prentice Hall.

Horowitz, B. (2006) *Creators, Synthesizers, and Consumers*, blog.elatable.com/2006/02/creators-synthesizers-and-consumers.html (accessed 15 November 2012).

Jennings, D. (2007) *Net Blogs and Rock 'n' Roll*, London: Nicholas Brealey.

Kennedy, D. (2009) *The Spectator and the Spectacle: Audiences in Modernity and Postmodernity*, Cambridge: Cambridge University Press.

Page, S.J. (2007) *Tourism Management: Managing for Change*, second edn, Oxford: Butterworth-Heinemann.

Pidd, Helen (2011) 'Without Tourists, Berlin is Stuffed. But Try Telling That to the Angry Natives', *The Guardian*, 9 May, www.guardian.co.uk/commentisfree/2011/may/09/berliners-angry-over-tourists (accessed 15 November 2012).

Reed, L. and Metallica (2011) *Lulu*, music album (double disc with booklet), Mercury Records.

Walton, J.K. (2005) *Histories of Tourism: Representation, Identity and Conflict*, Clevedon: Channel View.

Webber, A.J. (2011) *Berlin in the Twentieth Century: A Cultural Topography*, Cambridge: Cambridge University Press.

# 46

# Cultural routes, trails and the experience of place

*Nicola MacLeod*

This chapter explores the growing field of self-guided routes and trails within the context of the visitor experience and considers the extent to which these popular cultural tourism products reflect contemporary thinking on visitors' engagement with tourism offerings. Self-guided routes and trails are found in both urban and rural contexts and provide an interpreted, themed journey which can be travelled on foot, by bicycle, horseback, car, or in some cases even followed underwater. Trails can vary in scale from the very local, for example a town trail, to the international, exemplified by the Council of Europe Cultural Routes project which has developed a number of long-distance, cross-border routes interpreting pan-European themes. Timothy and Boyd (2003: 51) have categorised trails as linear visitor attractions that can be mega (international), large (national and regional), or small (local), and note that the mega and large-scale trails are predominantly rural whilst smaller trails are almost always urban based.

The idea of travelling along a pre-determined route is not a new one. Indeed, trails may have been amongst the earliest artefacts produced by humans as a means of understanding their world as they found their way through it. Historically, the act of moving through the environment created cognitive connections and knowledge of place as well as producing a physical pathway (Turnbull 2007: 142), and these remain important aspects of trails today. Trails have a rich symbolism as many cultures have origin myths where the creator passes through empty space, according it meaning as they travel (Snead 2009). The path is often representative of the journey through life itself as exemplified in literature from John Bunyan's *The Pilgrim's Progress* (1678), to Jack Kerouac's *On the Road* (1957). In cultural terms, the trail is often characterised as liminal space, full of possibility and used as a setting for chance meetings or farewells in novels, poems and films (Snead 2009).

In the contemporary tourism destination, trails are developed to interpret a variety of stories ranging from local history (San Francisco's Gold Rush Trail, USA), industry (Ruhr Industrial Heritage Trail, Germany), food and wine (South African Wine Trail), to famous people (the Mozart Route) and historical events (the Pendle Witch Trail in Lancashire, UK). Trails are usually developed in partnerships, with local authorities taking the lead in trail development in the UK (Hayes and MacLeod 2008). The range of stakeholders involved typically includes tourism organisations, visitor attractions, civic societies, local history groups and businesses who will benefit from the additional visitor footfall. By their nature, trails form business clusters that should encourage interaction and community participation and this potential has recently been investigated by the Council of Europe in their report on the impact of European Cultural routes on small and medium-sized enterprises (SMEs) (Council of Europe 2011).

Trails have proved to be highly flexible in both the themes that they interpret and in the purposes to which they are put. In recent years, trails have been developed for conservation purposes, routing visitors away from sensitive sites, providing information on environmental issues and encouraging the use of public transport. Their potential as tools for economic development has been recognised (Strauss and Lord 2001; Bowker *et al.* 2007) and they can provide opportunities for the wider use of local facilities by visitors, enhancing their engagement with place. As al-Hagla (2010: 2) states, 'a heritage trail is one physical manifestation of the interactions between tourists, locals, and the host place'. Clearly visitor management and educational rationales are significant and the physical benefits of walking or cycling are promoted through trail use, with some trails having been specifically developed to address health issues (Geiger and Werner 2009). Trails are therefore seen to be a useful means of satisfying a range of objectives, often at very little cost as many trails consist simply of an interpretive leaflet showing a map with points of interest indicated. Other, more complex trails utilise interpretation panels, sign-posts and markers to guide the visitor. Increasingly, trails information is made available online with dedicated trail websites and interactive maps becoming more common (for example Scotland's Malt Whisky Trail on www.maltwhiskytrail.com).

Trail developers use trails as a tool for visitor management whilst providing an interesting route to follow. In developing trails, specific themes are chosen and sites selected in order to tell a particular story. The deliberate theming of place though constructs such as trails has come under scrutiny, from Relph (1976) and his 'museumisation' of space, to more contemporary authors who comment on the cultural significance of such themed spaces (e.g. Lukas 2007; Urry and Larsen 2011). Relph's critique of the museumisation of space centres around the imposition of the museum idioms of authority, selectivity and interpretation on public spaces and the trail's role of highlighting specific sites reflecting a chosen theme can certainly be seen as a contributing factor in this transformation of space, turning real places into trivial and inauthentic areas. Lukas (2007: 2) comments on the 'immutable and unifying nature that characterises a theme', suggesting that once a space has been themed, it is difficult to encourage visitors to see it in any other way. When considering the borrowed and reworked symbols and meanings that themed spaces utilise in their exploration of the *tourist gaze*, Urry and Larsen (2011) note that these themed 'countries' present appealing aspects of places which may not necessarily relate to actual historical or geographical reality and which may obscure dissonant or contested heritage. Indeed, trails can be seen as the ultimate expression of the tourist gaze as they are designed around visual signs and the route is literally a set of instructions to look at specific monuments, buildings or vistas. The points of interest on a trail are '… usually … those elements that can appeal to the visual sense and can help tell a story that is mostly structured around a clear chronological logic' (Markwell *et al.* 2004: 460). The trail directs the visitor's gaze away from that which is irrelevant or merely unsightly, thus promoting a highly structured mode of seeing that is said to be characteristic of the tourist's experience.

Of course visitors will always ignore instructions, sabotage arrangements and subvert the hegemonic message of a themed route, and indeed some trails have been designed to encourage visitors to dip in and out of the story and compare heritage themes with contemporary culture on the streets (Shaw and MacLeod 2000). This tendency of tourists towards creativity and subversion has been reflected in the recent 'performance turn' in critical studies of tourism which emphasises the active experience of tourism (Edensor 2000) and a multi-sensory 'embodied gaze' (Urry and Larsen 2011). This 'performance turn' suggests that tourists are no longer simply spectators of an organised scene but wish to be actively engaged, experiencing places sensually. This new way of thinking about tourist practices allows us to reconsider the role and potential of the trail as, 'in contrast to studies portraying tourism as an over-determined stage where tourists passively follow prescribed routes and scripts, the performance turn also uncovers creativity, detours and productive practices' (Urry and Larsen 2011: 192–93). To a certain extent, the trail has already been seen to have embraced aspects of the performance turn in encouraging a more embodied gaze through the increasing use of sound. Audio guides have long been used in museums and galleries but new digital technology has allowed the development of downloadable audio trails and mobile applications ('apps') to be used flexibly in the field. These audio trails can be followed en route using iPods, MP3 players and mobile phones, and are described as being 'more nuanced, embodied, complex, multi sensory methods of experiencing and representing our surroundings' (Butler 2007: 15). Typically they use music, recorded interviews and performance to create a soundscape to be listened to whilst following a map-based trail. An audio trail developed in Wapping in East London, for example, uses the tale of an elderly woman remembering a lost love as the basis for the walk through the area. Community groups were involved in the creation of the walk, which uses speech and sound effects to create a performance in which the user fully participates (Ball et al. 2005).

The performance turn in tourism studies can also be considered within the wider context of Pine and Gilmore's (1999, 2011) influential work on the experience economy, which suggests that contemporary consumers have moved beyond the mere consumption of products and services and are increasingly seeking unique and engaging experiences. The authors apply this new experience economy to all service providers but the concept is perhaps particularly apt in relation to the tourism and hospitality sectors where, for example, the Disney Corporation has been providing successful models of themed experiences since the 1950s (Bryman 1995). Several authors have specifically applied Pine and Gilmore's ideas to the tourism sector (Richards 2001; Oh et al. 2007; Ek et al. 2008), recognising that the tourism industry has had a pioneering role in the staging of experiences, and Visit Britain reported in 2010 that holidays will become more experiential in the future, concentrating on 'immersion' in experience rather than the destination itself (Visit Britain 2010).

Pine and Gilmore (1999) claim that experiences fall into four distinctive realms – the entertainment, education, aesthetic and escapist realms. Experiences are further characterised according to whether they require active or passive participation and whether they result in the absorption or immersion of the participant. Pine and Gilmore suggest that the most compelling experiences are those that encompass all four realms in the 'sweet spot' or 'optimal tourist experience', as Oh et al. (2007: 121) define it. In order to assist providers in designing experiences that hit this 'sweet spot', the authors propose four principles: provide a compelling theme; use positive cues to affirm the nature of the experience; provide memorabilia as a physical reminder of the encounter; and finally, utilise all four senses to fully enrol and engage participants (Pine and Gilmore 1999; Pine and Gilmore 2011). As tools for encouraging more engagement with place, trails may benefit from a more experiential approach to their design, as explored in the case study (Box 46.1).

Although the research presented in the case study did find examples of good practice in the production of engaging and creative trails, the findings suggest that trails are still being viewed as products rather than experiences by their developers. It would appear that more could be done to realise the potential of English town trails (and by extension, all routes and trails) to provide more interesting and interactive 'optimal tourist experiences' (Oh et al. 2007).

## Box 46.1 Case study: town trails and experiential design

This case study presents the results of research that was undertaken to explore how far experiential design principles have been adopted by trail developers. As the trails field is very diverse in terms of theme and scope, the authors selected town trails as the focus for their research. As Timothy and Boyd (2003: 52) suggest, town trails are usually more specifically theme-driven than longer trails, and the authors were keen to explore how far trail developers were exploiting the potential of their destinations in devising trails that contribute to the visitor experience.

### Methodology

Some 75 town trails in England were selected from an existing database of trails brochures. Content analysis of the trail brochures was undertaken to ascertain whether the experiential design principles proposed by Pine and Gilmore (1999) had been incorporated and, if so, to what extent. This analysis comprised both qualitative and quantitative dimensions, with both rhetorical analysis (focusing on the organisation and presentation of the message), and semiotic analysis (exploring the symbolic meanings of imagery and text) being undertaken. The main areas of investigation were storytelling, language, visual devices, positive cues, enrolment opportunities, engagement, and personalisation.

### Findings

Overall, the findings reveal that town trail developers are not fully realising the potential of their trails to create memorable visitor experiences and engage their users. Content analysis of the trail brochures produced the following results:

- *Storytelling*: only 16 per cent of the trails sample were found to deliver a highly coherent story.
- *Language*: the majority of trails (67 per cent) used fewer than 1,000 words to convey the story, and 73 per cent had fewer than 20 specific commentary points included in the trail. The majority of trails used rational rather than evocative appeals in the language, producing a rather spartan and didactic experience.
- *Visual devices*: the majority of trails presented photographic images of architectural features with illustrations and line drawings also used extensively. Very few images of people/communities or artefacts were found.
- *Positive cues*: over half the trails provided positive tangible elements to harmonise the user's experience. These included reference to interpretive panels (25 per cent), visitor centres (21 per cent) and signage (12 per cent).
- *Enrolment*: only 8 per cent of the trails analysed included some kind of enrolment activity that officially acknowledged the visitor's engagement with, or completion of, the trail. These usually related to the undertaking of a task en route.
- *Engagement*: 61 per cent of trails provided opportunities for active engagement with the trail, e.g. suggesting links to visitor attractions (29 per cent), relevant exhibitions (28 per cent), and events (20 per cent).
- *Personalisation*: only half the trails offered opportunities to personalise the experience, with 15 per cent suggesting alternative routes and varying length of trail, and 20 per cent suggesting links to other trails of potential interest.

Finally, the opportunity to include informal cultural products along with the more formal offerings was explored. Over 60 per cent of trails included informal cultural facilities (e.g. pubs, restaurants, shops and markets), but there is scope for the wider use of these more informal sites to enhance the visitor experience of the trail.

*(Adapted from Hayes and MacLeod 2007).*

As more recent critical approaches to tourism suggest, there is now more emphasis on the tourist as embodied producer of their own experiences, aided by carefully designed tourism offerings that allow them to explore and engage with place in a more sensory, interactive and ultimately more meaningful way. This chapter has suggested that trails may have a central role to play in this if better design is employed to encourage a more experiential and playful approach to learning about places. Thus trails may be one cultural tourism experience that transcends the absolute nature of the themed destination and moves it towards interaction and co-creation between developer, place and visitor.

# References

al-Hagla, K.S. (2010) 'Sustainable Urban Development in Historical Areas Using the Tourist Trail Approach: A Case Study of the Cultural Heritage and Urban Development (CHUD) Project in Saida, Lebanon', *Cities* 27: 234–48.

Ball, B., Day, K., Livergant, E. and Tivers, J. (2005) 'Wapping: The "Stage" for an Audio Trail', paper presented at Critical Tourism Research Conference on Tourism and Performance: Scripts, Stages and Stories, Sheffield, July 2005.

Bowker, J.M., Bergstrom, J.C. and Gill, J. (2007) 'Estimating the Economic Value and Impacts of Recreational Trails: A Case Study of the Virginia Creeper Rail Trail', *Tourism Economics* 13(2): 241–60.

Bryman, A. (1995) *Disney and his Worlds*, London: Routledge.

Butler, T. (2007) 'Memoryscape: How Audio Walks Can Deepen Our Sense of Place by Integrating Art, Oral History and Cultural Geography', *Geography Compass* 1(3): 360–72.

Council of Europe (2011) 'Impact of European Cultural Routes on SMEs', innovation and competitiveness, provisional edn, Strasbourg: Council of Europe.

Edensor, T. (2000) 'Staging Tourism: Tourists as Performers', *Annals of Tourism Research* 27: 322–44.

Ek, R., Larsen, J., Hornskov, S.B. and Mansfeldt, O.K. (2008) 'A Dynamic Framework of Tourist Experiences: Space-Time and Performances in the Experience Economy', *Scandinavian Journal of Hospitality and Tourism* 8(2): 122–40.

Geiger, B.F. and Werner, K.A. (2009) 'A Guided Walking Trail to Explore the Martin Luther King Jr. National Voting Rights Walk and Selma Antebellum Historic District', *International Journal of Heritage Studies* 15(5): 467–76.

Hayes, D. and MacLeod, N. (2007) 'Packaging Places: Designing Heritage Trails Using an Experience Economy Perspective to Maximise Visitor Engagement', *Journal of Vacation Marketing* 13(1): 45–58.

——(2008) 'Putting Down Routes: An Examination of Local Government Cultural Policy Shaping the Development of Heritage Trails', *Managing Leisure* 13: 57–73.

Lukas, S. (2007) *The Themed Space*, Lanham, MD: Lexington Books.

Markwell, M., Stevenson, D. and Rowe, D. (2004) 'Footsteps and Memories: Interpreting an Australian Urban Landscape Through Thematic Walking Tours', *International Journal of Heritage Studies* 10(5): 457–73.

Oh, H., Fiore, A.M. and Jeoung, M. (2007) 'Measuring Experience Economy Concepts: Tourism Applications', *Journal of Travel Research* 46: 119–32.

Pine, B.J. and Gilmore, J.H. (1999) *The Experience Economy*, Harvard: Harvard Business School Press.

——(2011) *The Experience Economy*, second edn, Harvard, MA: Harvard Business School Press.

Relph, E. (1976) *Place and Placelessness*, London: Pion.

Richards, G. (2001) 'The Experience Industry and the Creation of Attractions', in Richards, G. (ed.) *Cultural Attractions and European Tourism*, Wallingford: CABI, 55–69.

Shaw, S. and MacLeod, N. (2000) 'Creativity and Conflict: Cultural Tourism in London's City Fringe', *Tourism, Culture and Communication* 2(3): 165–75.

Snead, J.E. (2009) 'Trails of Tradition: Movement, Meaning and Space', in Snead, J.E., Erickson, C.L. and Darling, A. (eds) *Landscapes of Movement: Trails, Paths and Roads in Anthropological Perspective*, Philadelphia: University of Pennsylvania Press, 42–60.

Strauss, C.H. and Lord, B.E. (2001) 'Economic Impacts of a Heritage Tourism System', *Journal of Retailing and Consumer Services* 8: 199–204.

Timothy, D.J. and Boyd, S.W. (2003) *Heritage Tourism*, Harlow: Pearson.

Turnbull, D. (2007) 'Maps Narratives and Trails: Performativity, Hodology and Distributed Knowledges in Complex Adaptive Systems – An Approach to Emergent Mapping', *Geographical Research* 45(2): 140–49.

Urry, J. and Larsen, J. (2011) *The Tourist Gaze*, third edn, London: Sage.

Visit Britain (2010) 'Culture and Heritage Topic Profile', www.visitbritain.org/Images/Culture%20%26%20Heritage%20Topic%20Profile%20Full_tcm29-14711.pdf (accessed 31 October 2012).

## Further reading

Cheung, S.C.H. (1999) 'The Meanings of a Heritage Trail in Hong Kong', *Annals of Tourism Research* 26 (3): 570–88. (An interesting example of the socio-cultural significance of the trail within the context of dissonant heritage.)

Morgan, M., Elbe, J. and de Esteban Curiel, J. (2009) 'Has the Experience Economy Arrived? The Views of Destination Managers in Three Visitor-dependent Areas', *International Journal of Tourism Research* 11: 201–16. (Explores the extent to which experience economy concepts have been applied by destination managers.)

Puczko, L. and Ratz, T. (2007) 'Trailing Goethe, Humbert, and Ulysses: Cultural Routes in Tourism', in G. Richards (ed.) *Cultural Tourism: Global and Local Perspectives*, London: Haworth Press, 131–48. (A useful critical overview of the sector with guidelines on setting objectives, creating and operating cultural routes.)

# 47

# Cultural value perception in the memorable tourism experience

*Zsuzsanna Horváth*

## Introduction

Destinations around the globe are looking for creative solutions to common challenges in tourism development. It may be possible to identify broad and narrow types of creativity. In the broadest sense, everything that exposes one's identity to some kind of challenge or learning can be creative. In the modern risk society, creativity has become part of our everyday lives – a strategy for shaping multiple identities to cope with the fluidity of modern existence.

Tourism experience is embedded in the experience economy and many authors have argued that the central challenge facing tourism destination managers and planners is the design of effective tourism experiences (Ritchie and Hudson 2009). Creativity has been employed to transform traditional cultural tourism, shifting from tangible heritage towards more intangible culture and greater involvement with the everyday life of the destination. The emergence of 'creative tourism' reflects the growing integration between tourism and different place-making strategies, including promotion of the creative industries, creative cities and the 'creative class'. Creative tourism is also arguably an escape route from the serial reproduction of mass cultural tourism, offering more flexible and authentic experiences, which can be co-created between host and tourist (Richards 2011).

The growth of creative tourism was first defined as an extension or reaction to cultural tourism inasmuch as cultural tourists, creative consumers as they are, are searching for more engaging, interactive experiences that can contribute to their personal growth. In the area of individualisation, identity can be best developed in the process of collecting unique experiences. This can then be extended to tourism destinations (Morgan *et al.* 2009). Each tourist perceives the destination and the experience offered by the destination in their very special, individualised way which is the sum of their past life experience, education, attitudes – in other words, a whole series of personal characteristics. The focus of tourism experience creation is the individual, and the fulfilment of their aspirations, wishes and expectations relating to their personal growth.

The idea that the tourist as well as the destination can be creative in their use of the basic building blocks of tourism experience also opens up new perspectives on the nature of tourism itself. Allowing for multiple meanings in the tourism experience leaves room for the creativity of the tourist to interact with the placing and staging by producers in the role of performer.

Consumer experiences have a beginning and end point and typically are composed of a variety of environmental and internal components that trigger a multiplicity of emotional, physical and cognitive reactions to the consumption of goods and services. It is a blend of many individual elements that involve the consumer emotionally, physically, intellectually and spiritually (Shaw and Ivens 2002). A consumer is not seeking the fulfilment of their needs, but rather their aspirations, desires and dreams that can carry them further in personal improvement and growth. Shared experiences can create close bonds between tourists, a sense of community, contributing to the better identification of attributes that make each person individual, thus to gain recognition, status or kudos. This means, in practical terms, that the consumer will experience a state of flow when, immersed in the process of creation (or transformation), certain challenges will be offered, but (s)he is prepared to complete them. This transformation can be called the *creative process*, the *value creation* in tourism, and co-creation takes place when various stakeholders in the tourism experience are invited to participate in the process.

## Memorable tourism experience (MTE) research

Tourism management education, if its ultimate objective is to give an introduction to the modern trends in tourism management and marketing and to prepare future destination managers, must inevitably incorporate – together with all their theoretical and practical implications – the phenomena of experiential consumption and value co-creation.

A survey was undertaken to explore the perception of tourism management students of memorable tourism experience (MTE). The survey was of an exploratory nature as little previous research exists on the topic. A multi-method approach was used to research the nature of the MTE. Third-year tourism students were asked, by means of open-ended questionnaires and a subsequent focus-group interview, to reflect upon the nature and process of the formation of the MTE, without any prior elucidation on what exactly is meant by the term. It was also the objective of the survey to find out how they distinguish between 'ordinary' and 'extraordinary' (i.e. memorable) tourism experiences. Content analysis was then applied to the narratives of their most salient and memorable experiences.

The questionnaire and interview topics had not been discussed before in the framework of the tourism management courses, therefore it required some creativity and innovative thinking from the students to reflect on them. Value creation and co-creation were specifically terms that are not widely discussed in these courses so that students had to make a mental effort to work out what the terms mean and how to interpret these terms in the framework of tourism experience. By the same token, memorable tourism experience was a term on which they had to reflect without any prior introduction or elucidation on its meaning. The survey was in this respect exploratory and innovative: future tourism managers will have to use the intellectual capabilities of innovativeness and creativity to relate to the terms. It is exactly this relation to the 'solution' of this problem in which we were interested. The approaches the students selected in solving this problem will be reflected in their problem solving when facing the necessity for experience creation for their visitors at the destination.

## Theme 1: the MTE – definition of framework, description of the phenomenon and its components

This theme was directed at finding out the perception of the components, possible definitions, and description of the processes and outcomes of the experience. What makes a tourism experience extraordinary (memorable) in contrast to an 'ordinary' one?

## The tourist's mental processes

> The memorable experience starts from the phase when we get information about the destination, it continues throughout the visiting period, and the final phase comes slowly, after 1–2 months of the real visit, because all the impressions and memories reach a mature stage by that time.

> It's the interpretation of universal symbols at the destination.

> I think the stories that happen to us during the experience are the most important elements.

> MTE is basically a marketable story.

It is not so much the physical environment or the activities themselves, as the mental process of transforming the impressions that account for the experience. The tourist goes on a certain kind of mental, psychological journey that consists of transformation, absorption and thus, value creation. Tourists create stories during their experiences and they present these stories to others as memories of their trip. Storytelling acts to both consolidate and recover experiences from memory, and an appreciation of storytelling provides listeners with a deeper understanding (Tung and Ritchie 2011). Physical and intellectual activities during the experience are often at the same time exercises of the imagination, with the participants seeing themselves as acting out roles.

## The tourist's physical challenges and sensory experience

> Tourism is about experiential consumption where all the five senses take an active role in the absorption of new impulses.

This cluster, by its characteristics, is complementary to the previous one, inasmuch as it reflects on the physical aspects of the experience.

## Complexity

> Every single aspect of the journey contributes to the totality of the experience that we gain, I can't single out any.

The totality of internal and external impulses, influences and emotions as well as physical environment details have an impact on the formation of the experience. Individual elements cannot be identified as they act in conjunction with other elements and at the same time, the psychological and emotional state of the visitor is the foundation for the absorption of the experience. That is what makes a memorable experience so unique and unrepeatable (Gentile *et al.* 2007).

## Surprise

> It is the aspect of unforeseen, unexpected events and happenings that are in the core of the MTE.

> It is the component of surprise that is the best in a good trip.

Unexpected events make the experience extraordinary, in contrasted to, for example, an ordinary trip. Visitors' expectations of the memorable experience is the trait of uniqueness, something never seen or heard of which they can possess and thus distinguish themselves from the other tourists. Surprises make the trip not only unforgettable, but personalised inasmuch as this unexpected and unforeseen event happened to them only.

## Attitude and expectations

Immersion in MTE is largely influenced by the visitor's attitude and expectations, so it varies with the individual's emotional state, educational level and degree of preparedness.

The most important component of the MTE is the quality of the services at the destination that leaves us with a positive post-experience feeling.

Prior to the commencement of the trip, tourists, on the basis of information that they have gathered, formulate a set of 'minimum standards' which they expect to be delivered during the experience. Now, the actual delivery may be above or below this level of standard, and this will have an impact on the evaluation of the experience – to a better or to a worse degree.

## Theme 2: perceived value creation during the process of the MTE

In a way, the sub-theme intended to reiterate the first theme, but this time focusing more on the value creation aspect. This theme sought to deepen reflection on the experience and to find out the group's perception of value creation.

### Utilitarian

After the visit, we think back and evaluate and single out what aspect or experience was the most important – that will become the ultimate value.

Value co-creation is about receiving extraordinary service at the destination. Visitors, by their value expectations help destinations become better and better.

This cluster represents a quality-driven, utilitarian perception of the experience whereby the overall experience is dominated and therefore determined by the quality of the experience. In their perception, the core of the experience is the delivery of quality. The experience is a type of quality service that the visitors expect from the visit (Scott *et al.* 2009).

### Contribution to the building of social capital

It is the interaction with the locals at any particular destination that creates tremendous cultural value.

Visiting places of national history enhances patriotism; adds value to the social capital of that nation. The more citizens visit and the more visitors they attract by their narratives, the more developed the social capital becomes.

Interaction with co-visitors or personnel of the destination or practically any human being who has an active role in the delivery of the experience serves as an enabler of social development.

Shared experiences can create close bonds between people and a sense of community (Cova and Cova 2001) within which they can establish identity and gain recognition. Tourism experience can be a powerful building block in social capital.

### 'Serendipitous moment' – become one with the experience

Value is created when you feel that somehow you are part of the destination, and by way of adding part of your personality, experience or education, you add to the colourfulness of the destination.

During the experience, I let myself be carried away by a mixture of conscious and sub-conscious learning patterns, and all I have to do is to be exposed to it and absorb it.

Drawing on Hom Cary's (2004: 68) interpretation of the tourism experience, the term 'serendipitous moment' means a 'spontaneous instance of self-discovery and belonging', in which 'the moment simultaneously produces and erases the tourist as a subject and where one goes beyond 'being a tourist'. Other authors explain the process of 'immersion' in the experiences as a distinctive feature of the memorable tourism experience. Being one with the experience helps growth and this in itself is an extremely important element. It is the very essence of the experience economy to enable the shift of emphasis from the rational to the emotional aspects where the value of the experience can be measured by the positive self-development.

### Self-discovery: spiritual and intellectual growth

I consider spiritual growth during a visit a tremendous value.

I gain value from unique experiences that leave an imprint on my intellect and enhance my set of values.

This approach is most effective when it is based on shared values and allows the tourist to create their own experiences in a search for personal growth. Self-discovery and growth supposes a degree of consequentiality – that is, some personally perceived importance from the outcome of the trip, in the shape of permanent changes in the respondent's state of mind. It is in the moments of immersion in experience that the growth can start. Ultimately, experiences offer intellectual stimuli. Creative tourism involves not just 'being there', but reflexive interaction on the part of tourists. In creative tourism, the onus is on the tourists themselves to actively learn about their surroundings and apply that knowledge in order to develop their own skills (Richards and Wilson 2006).

## Theme 3: perception of value co-creation in social media

### Information, knowledge sharing as decision-making tools and networking

[T]he objective of the trip is not exclusively leisure, but also gaining new information, knowledge and networking, letting the circle of acquaintances know about the destination …

The role of social media is growing by the day. I can't see myself organising a programme without consulting one or more sites and discussing with my friends. On these occasions, we get information and share experience even without making a single step in the direction of the destination.

Planning for experiential consumption is an experience itself, and positive emotions such as anticipation and excitement are a part of this process. Some consumers enjoy vicarious vacationing and experience not only positive emotions in response to product stimuli, but also *positive* task-related affect: pleasure in the planning, an emotional dimension of the decision process.

## Trend setting and peer group evaluation

I only trust the opinion of my peer group when making an experiential decision as I am aware that I am continually being harassed by media, advertisements.

My age group [20–24] only trusts the narratives of peers. We do not accept any suggestions on leisure activities from older generations.

Social media is perceived as a trend-setting tool, the use of which is necessary if one wants to comply with the attitudes and behaviour patterns of the peer group. Interviewees often mention the fact of being harassed by offers on a multitude of marketing channels and they feel lost amidst this myriad information. The most practical means of evaluating offers is by the social media that the peer group favours, which provides a reliable set of information and evaluations on various consumption experiences, including memorable tourism experiences (Potts *et al.* 2008).

## Intellectual processes

Experience is shared by friends and family on the social media sites – the minute I see something exciting, I take a picture of it and load it on social media.

Social media is a tool for communicating the experience after it has been lived, absorbed and transformed in the traveller's mind.

Social media co-creation is perceived as an opportunity to instigate mental, intellectual work, the product of which is then offered to the peer group members. Social media as a modern platform for information exchange, often used as a marketing solution to create brand communities and awareness in the retail and services industries, has reached the domain of tourism. Tourism social media sites can have links to and from other sites, for example professional communities attaching the industry to the tourists/visitors, and strengthening the connection between the two. This win-win situation leads to more useful content, more business opportunities and invites more members to the communities.

## Challenges based on expectations

Marketeers could learn from the narratives on social media sites – positive experience is the best advertisement!

Social media is sometimes deceptive as narratives of memorable experiences are extremely subjective, what is ok for my friends, may not be an ok or satisfactory experience for me.

Responses suggest that social media value co-creation is about providing narratives of the memorable experience that can inspire and instigate community reader members to consider and go through the same experience. Thus, social media functions as a marketing tool that destination managers could use.

## Conclusion

This chapter has tried to provide new insights into the interpretation and understanding of the vast realm of memorable tourism experience by drawing on tourism management students' perceptions. It is essential to incorporate in the curriculum of future destination managers the concepts of tourism experience, value creation or co-creation and the role of social media sites in marketing the tourism experience.

What emerges from the research is that the interviewees had a very varied interpretation of the notion of the tourism experience, resulting from the fact that the experience is a very complex phenomenon and it is approached and lived according to the individual's emotional state, stimuli, education and a number of other factors. However, it was possible to set up clusters of characteristic features that represent the interviewees' perceptions. The managerial implication of the variety of approaches is that most probably these future managers will, when designing the memorable experiences, draw on their own aptitudes and stimuli, therefore contributing to more colourful and exciting experience creation. The success of destinations depends on how they market experiences in order to entice an increasingly sophisticated visitor.

Pertaining to value creation or co-creation, it is observed on the basis of the type of interpretations that the tourism management students had limitations in the usage of the term and that they had not been accustomed to the term. The clusters of value creation in the process of the memorable tourism experience and the social media value co-creation are almost identical, which suggests that in the perception of the interviewees, contemporary and memorable tourism experience is largely based on the use of social media and that the value creation processes are similar, if not identical.

As to the educational and managerial implications, it can be said that tourism management higher education institutions must pay more attention to the incorporation of modern tourism marketing subjects into the curricula in order to prepare future destination managers for successfully designing colourful, memorable tourism experiences.

## References

Cova, B. and Cova, V. (2001) 'Tribal Aspects of Postmodern Consumption Research: The Case of French In-line Roller Skaters', *Journal of Consumer Behaviour* 1: 67–76.

Gentile, C., Spiller, N. and Noci, G. (2007) 'How to Sustain the Customer Experience: An Overview of Experience Components that Co-create Value with the Customer', *European Management Journal* 25(5): 395–410.

Hom Cary, S. (2004) 'The Tourist Moment', *Annals of Tourism Research* 31(1): 61–77.

Morgan, M., Elbe, J. and Curiel, J. de E. (2009) 'Has the Experience Economy Arrived? The Views of Destination Managers in Three Visitor-dependent Areas', *International Journal of Tourism Research* 11: 201–16.

Potts, J.D., Hartley, J., Banks, J.A., Burgess, J.E., Cobcroft, R.S., Cunningham, S.D. and Montgomery, L. (2008) 'Consumer Co-creation and Situated Creativity', *Industry and Innovation* 15(5): 459–74.

Richards, G. (2011) 'Creativity and Tourism. The State of the Art', *Annals of Tourism Research* 38(4): 1225–53.

Richards, G. and Wilson, J. (2006) 'Developing Creativity in Tourist Experiences: A Solution to the Serial Reproduction of Culture?' *Tourism Management* 27: 1209–23.

Ritchie, J.R.B. and Hudson, S. (2009) 'Understanding and Meeting the Challenges of Consumer/Tourist Experience Research', *International Journal of Tourism Research* 11: 111–26.

Scott, N., Laws, E. and Boksberger, P. (2009) 'The Marketing of Hospitality and Leisure Experiences', *Journal of Hospitality Marketing and Management* 18: 99–110.

Shaw, C. and Ivens, J. (2002) *Building Great Customer Experiences*, New York: Palgrave Macmillan.

Tung, V.W.S. and Ritchie, J.R.B. (2011) 'Exploring the Essence of Memorable Tourism Experience', *Annals of Tourism Research* 38: 1367–86.

# 48

# An experiential approach to differentiating tourism offers in cultural heritage

*Sonia Ferrari*

## Introduction

Nowadays, many tourists are in search of active holidays and engaging, emotionally, physically, socially, psychologically and/or spiritually authentic experiences, rejecting mass tourism and standardised packages. In addition, tourists increasingly devise their holidays with the aim of learning, self-development and making contact with the local population. Due to the post-modern commodification of culture, visitors' experiences with cultural heritage require innovation and adaptation in order to offer them unique and meaningful personal events rather than the former passive activities. All around the world, numerous museums, heritage sites and cultural venues are now working in this direction, introducing new visitor models.

Memorable visiting experiences can be designed in museums and at heritage sites, not only for the segments of traditional demand but also for new ones which, in general, include younger guests. It is a way to transform cultural heritage into an 'experiencescape' (O'Dell and Billing 2005) – a place of enjoyment, socialisation, pleasure, emotions and amusement, offering visitors different kinds of valuable tourism, educational, cultural and entertainment experiences.

## Experience economy and cultural tourism today

In post-modern society, consumers, who are continuously in search of emotions and subjective and personalised consumption, do not demand goods and services, but memorable, unique, holistic and engaging experiences with a high symbolic content (Holbrook and Hirschman 1982; Addis and Holbrook 2001). The customer is not only buying a good, but also services and information, experiences and culture (Rifkin 2000), and wishes to have an active role during their consumption (Prentice 2001). This means that firms must be increasingly dedicated to trying to offer experience-based products, which can engage the customer emotionally, physically, mentally, socially and/or spiritually (O'Sullivan and Spangler 1998; Pine and Gilmore 1999; Fabris 2003: 203; Argano and Dalla Sega 2009).

Therefore, there is now much more emphasis than in the past on sounds and music, scents and fragrances, atmospheres, colours and images, tastes and interactivity to enrich goods and services. For example, it is common practice to use music in locations to make the visit more pleasant and more memorable (Krishna 2010: 149). Colours, fragrances and lights can have a similar impact. Sometimes the deprivation of one sense is used to exalt others. This is the case of *Dialogo al Buio*, an exhibition held using routes to be followed in complete darkness, accompanied by expert non-sighted guides, to experience new and unexpected emotions that amplify the perceptions of touch, smell and taste.

Pine and Gilmore (1999) have identified four different experience spheres on the basis of two parameters, the (active or passive) involvement of the guest and the type of relationship between the customer and the experience (which involves absorption, in other words physical or virtual involvement, and immersion, in other words mental involvement). These four spheres, which are called entertainment, education, escapism and the aesthetic experience, are not opposed to one another, but on the contrary are often mixed and lead to global, subjective, unique and tailored experiences. The best experiences are, in any case, those in which the visitor, by taking an active part, is completely immersed in the situation that they are experiencing. This requires the involvement of the five senses or the offer of something memorable (Smith 2009: 188). Generally, providers tend to offer a mixture of experiences that are judged more complete if enhanced by all four components. An example of this is *Emozioni da Museo*, an initiative at Palazzo Vecchio in Florence, which is described in the case study in this chapter (Box 48.1). Therefore, experiences that mix entertainment and education ('edutainment'), shopping ('shoppertainment'), or eating ('eatertainment') are increasingly common.

Tourism agencies, private and public bodies and destinations are also making an effort to offer events, packaging and atmosphere, involving physical settings, extravaganzas (Ritzer 1999), sensory designs and other differentiating elements, which allow tourists to enjoy meaningful experiences and create positive attitudes in them.

Continuous 're-enchantment' processes (Baudrillard 1993; Bauman 1993: 33) aim to make the 'cathedrals of consumption' even more magical, fascinating or fantastic. These are places where processes related to the purchase, supply, consumption and/or use of goods and services are undertaken, and are often important tourist attractions, destinations or infrastructure, such as retail centres, theme parks, museums and archaeological sites, etc. (Ritzer 2005: 68). Frequently they become multipurpose containers which simultaneously satisfy different needs (entertainment, socialising, shopping, education, eating, etc.). For example, museums often have an increasing range of support and auxiliary services that offer highly engaging experiences, which are sometimes unique and unforgettable, thanks to themed settings, events, atmospheres, tactile sensations, colours and images, sounds, fragrances, virtual realities, multi-sensory stimuli, theatre pieces, workshops and operators performing as actors in the setting. In some cases the 'cathedrals of consumption' are symbols of Western culture that have been exported and sold in other countries, as has been happening for some years with museums and art galleries, which are reproduced in multiple locations (such as the Guggenheim Museum which is now present, besides New York, in Bilbao, Berlin, Las Vegas, Venice and Abu Dhabi).

All this entails risks of mass reproduction of culture and art and the search for perfect imitation – in other words, the 'McDisneyisation' of culture, which is feared by experts in the sector, who are afraid that museums and cultural heritage are becoming the new theme parks (Swarbrooke 2000).

## Experiential cultural products and heritage

Nowadays, the field of museums and cultural heritage is greatly affected by shifts in demand and supply. In particular, there is increased competition to access ever-shrinking funds. Moreover, there has been an increase in consumers' attention towards the quality of their leisure enjoyment.

Furthermore, museums and heritage sites are frequently considered as institutions that can trigger virtuous processes of urban renewal. All this has fostered the development of cultural consumption, but, at the same time, has increased visitors' expectations and needs. In fact, consumers today are not only interested in satisfying their need for learning, but also wish to have more engaging types of experiences. In particular, there appears to be a strong demand for experiences providing inner growth and self-development in social, cultural, intellectual and emotional terms (Doering 1999).

Thus, the role of these institutions is changing, also due to the commodification of culture and to the merging of high and low culture in the post-modern era. They are trying to increase visitor attendance also by attracting new segments (especially families and young people).

It can be claimed that for all these reasons, heritage venues and cultural sites now ought to modify their image and their offer to become more market-oriented and to create more engaging visits. In fact, cultural heritage and 'museums are essentially experiential products' (Prentice 1996), and smells, colours, sounds, animations and interactions are potentially part of this product (Prentice 2001). Currently, significant efforts in this sense have been made above all by science museums, in which 'edutainment' and the need to make the visit engaging and fun, as well as instructive, for the youngest visitors and for school groups as well, has already seen a significant effort in this direction for a number of years. The role of cultural heritage today is broader, and safeguarding it requires growth in demand and adequate management to enable the public to perceive its value and the need to protect it.

There are numerous tools now available to management to achieve the above aims, by guaranteeing visitors not only learning experiences, but also entertainment, excitement and time for contemplation (Kotler and Kotler 1999: 187).

In this regard, it is interesting to note that in recent years a growing number of experts have been addressing the issue of multi-sensoriality in tourism, which in the past was overlooked in favour of the sole sense of sight. In particular, the latest edition of the book *The Tourist Gaze* (Urry 2002: 146), which previously concentrated on the use of sight, now also talks about other types of panoramas and perceptions beyond *visual landscapes*, such as 'soundscapes', 'smellscapes', 'tastescapes' and 'geographies of touch'. Examples are olfactory-based routes, touch and sound stimuli, and multimedia installations.

Thus the importance of 'sensescapes' (Quan and Wang 2004) is growing, being the settings that stimulate visitors' senses and manage to offer sensations other than the routine and everyday environment (Urry 2002: 155). Moreover, the supply system should be flexible and encourage some discretion in the use of the setting by various customers, in order to be able to allow them to undergo unique personal experiences, based on their own use of the 'servicescape' (Bitner 1992).

In addition, in order to enhance the experiences offered, often complementary or auxiliary components are added to the *core product*, such as restaurants, bars, shops, e-commerce, meeting areas, guided tours, conferences, concerts, programmes for teachers, workshops, etc.

The new technologies enable traditional services to be accompanied by innovative services, thanks to interactive multimedia resources, multi-sensory techniques and IT support; examples are audio guides with palm-tops, also for children, multimedia kiosks, digital archives of art works, virtual and audio-visual visits, and three-dimensional reconstructions of monuments (Falk and Dierking 1992; Bourgeon-Renault *et al.* 2006).

Given this background, locations use new means, other than information boards and traditional guided visits, to present the objects displayed in relation to other objects and to the visitor, for example through the reconstruction of an environment to mirror the original context of a work or historic moment or through particularly striking displays. One example is the Statue Room of the Egyptian Museum in Turin, in which the lighting and soundscape have been designed by

Dante Ferretti, a famous set designer, to recreate the atmosphere of the inside of the pyramids and make the works displayed even more powerful and striking, thus emotionally involving the visitor (Xanthoudaki 2003). In some locations it is possible to relive past eras thanks to historic re-enactments in period costume and reconstructions of environments and lifestyles of far-off places and times. An excellent example is the Butser Ancient Farm, in England, a real open-air workshop in which it is possible to experience aspects of everyday prehistoric life by tasting the meals of the age and taking part in celebrations, such as that for the start of the summer, building a hut using ancient techniques, etc.

Other innovations concern the introduction of new communication methods that guide and accompany the visit, such as animation or the use of actors who tell stories associated with the collection or the locations (Jackson *et al.* 2002), the offer of workshops where visitors can fashion objects using ancient techniques or can experience new sensations (for example, a short walk in a gravity-free environment), and the use of games to involve the youngest visitors who, while visiting an archaeological museum, as happens in Milan, can play the games that their ancestors used to play.

Finally, it is now common for cultural sites to use storytelling (Kotler 2003), thanks to new, professional roles (for example, actors, set designers, costume designers), or people normally responsible for back-office work (for example restorers), who increasingly work in the public gaze.

All the tools set out so far can increase the value of the experience, by enhancing its 'theatrical' aspect and ensuring that the place visited becomes a *setting* that offers a show (Falk and Dierking 1992; Bourgeon-Renault *et al.* 2006). They are transforming the enjoyment of culture by increasingly involving visitors, who are becoming the *co-creators* of their own experience. The aim is to shift the visitor's attention to playful elements, entertainment, emotional pull, thus stimulating their creativity, imagination, emotions and not only the traditional conflicting sentiments that are felt before an artwork: emotion or boredom, curiosity or lack of involvement (Zorzi 2004).

In designing the routes to enjoy the cultural resources of a location, it is therefore necessary always to take account of the fact that visitors are the co-designers and co-producers of their own experiences (Simonsen *et al.* 2010: 187). Therefore, they see and assess attractions, places and cultural events through their own personal way of interpreting them, linked to social, cultural and personal values that are highly varied. The expectations can also change markedly depending on whether the tourist is looking for the *authentic* or just an experience (Smith 2009: 189).

In conclusion, cultural heritage should be considered as *places of interpretation*, in which perceptions are sharply influenced for each consumer by imaginary and real representations of the past provided by the social, material and cultural environment of the place being visited and by the social, temporal and spatial dimensions (Sundbo and Darmer 2008: 181; Simonsen *et al.* 2010: 187). In designing an experience and in assessing it, it is necessary to take account of these dimensions, of space-time links, and of imaginary worlds and personal flights of fancy.

---

## Box 48.1 Case study: *Emozioni da Museo*

Palazzo Vecchio in Florence is a museum and also the seat of the Florentine Municipality. Inside Palazzo Vecchio the beauty is predominantly represented by the architecture and by the interior wall decorations, which have been realised over many centuries by important artists. The number of visitors to Palazzo Vecchio has increased over time, partly thanks to *Emozioni da Museo*, the initiative undertaken since 2001. The experience initially was dedicated mainly to children and teenagers, but from 2003 also to adults. In 2009 the museum attracted 361,462 visitors (Centro Studi TCI 2009).

*Emozioni da Museo* aims to make the use of Palazzo Vecchio even more engaging in terms of experience, through educational activities, study workshops, theatre for children and a lot more. It allows visits to parts of the historic building not previously open to the public and which are truly fascinating, such as secret passages accessible through openings hidden by frescoes. The study workshops facilitate the learning of ancient painting techniques, above all that of *affresco* painting. For the youngest visitors theatrical shows are put on. In addition, children can take part in constructing objects, playing games and dressing up. The activities take place accompanied by a facilitator, who impersonates a historic character from the court, such as Giorgio Vasari, the architect and painter of Duke Cosimo I de' Medici.

*Emozioni da Museo* transforms the museum into an 'experiencescape' (O'Dell and Billing 2005), which offers different kinds of valuable tourism, educational, cultural and entertainment experiences. These activities all seek to introduce the audience to new, integrated ways of using the museum, based on the use of multiple senses and by proposing animations, shows, interactive workshops and multimedia events every day of the year. Moreover, inside Palazzo Vecchio, two interactive laboratory rooms and two small museum theatres have been created.

Research was carried out to investigate users' behaviour in *Emozioni da Museo* activities, in order to acquire knowledge about attitudes, expectations, preferences and satisfaction levels for a more engaging use of arts in experiential terms (Ferrari and Veltri 2008). A survey was administered to a non-random sample of 400 visitors to Palazzo Vecchio who were interviewed before and after their visit. The research findings show the positive outcomes of the initiative, which is still unique in the Italian museum context. Palazzo Vecchio, through *Emozioni da Museo*, is addressing the key target group and is managing to satisfy visitors' expectations, although these are quite high.

The initiative could in the future improve in terms of its communication, thus creating more realistic expectations and attracting a greater number of visitors and new market segments. Anyway, the results of the survey confirm the validity of *Emozioni da Museo* as a means to enrich the offer of Palazzo Vecchio, repositioning it in experiential terms and improving its *functional image* (determined by the benefits that visitors are offered) (Vaughan 2001).

## Conclusions

Cultural tourism, in the sense of a travel experience that involves personal enrichment achieved thanks to direct contact with another culture, lifestyle, or population, can be considered as highly creative and adaptable, but difficult to control, since it is not standardised and is not completely foreseeable in all its components (Richards 2001, 2011). In order for the enjoyment of culture to be a unique and memorable experience, it is not sufficient for the physical environment to be highly engaging and stimulate all the senses. It is also necessary for the visitor to have an active role during the experience and, thanks to a certain degree of freedom in the interaction, be able to adapt it to their own preferences and expectations. Therefore, it is necessary not only to engage visitors, but also to make them become real partners in the processes used, thus allowing them to enjoy a highly personalised and flexible experience (Cova 2003: 122).

## References

Addis, M. and Holbrook, M.B. (2001) 'On the Conceptual Link Between Mass Customisation and Experiential Consumption: An Explosion of Subjectivity', *Journal of Consumer Behaviour* 1: 50–66.

Argano, L. and Dalla Sega, P. (2009) *Nuove organizzazioni culturali. Atlante di navigazione strategica*, Milano: Franco Angeli.

Baudrillard, J. (1993) *Symbolic Exchange and Death*, London: Sage.

Bauman, Z. (1993) *Postmodern Ethics*, Oxford: Backwell.

Bitner, M.J. (1992) 'Servicescapes: The Impact of Physical Surroundings on Customers and Employees', *Journal of Marketing* 56 (April): 57–71.

Bourgeon-Renault, D., Urbani, C., Petr, C., Le Gall-Ely, M. and Gombault, A. (2006) 'An Experiential Approach to the Consumption Value of Arts and Culture: The Case of Museums and Monuments', *International Journal of Arts Management* 9(1): 35–47.

Centro Studi TCI (2009) *Dossier Musei 2009*, Milano: TCI.

Cova, B. (2003) *Il marketing tribale*, Milano: Il Sole 24 Ore.

Doering, Z.D. (1999) 'Strangers, Guests or Clients? Visitor Experiences in Museums', paper presented at the conference: Managing the Arts, Performance, Financing, Service, Weimar, Germany, March.

Fabris, G. (2003) *Il nuovo consumatore: verso il post-moderno*, Milano: Franco Angeli.

Falk, J.H. and Dierking, L.D. (1992) *The Museum Experience*, Washington, DC: Whalesback Books.

Ferrari, S. and Veltri, A.R. (2008) 'L'approccio esperienziale nell'offerta dei beni culturali. Il caso di "Emozioni da Museo"', *Finanza, Marketing e Produzione* 4: 66–95.

Holbrook, M.B. and Hirschman, E.C. (1982) 'The Experiential Aspects of Consumption: Consumer Fantasies, Feelings, and Fun', *Journal of Consumer Research* 9 (Sept.): 132–40.

Jackson, A., Johnson, P., Rees Leahy, E. and Walzer, V. (2002) *Seeing it for Real: An Investigation into the Effectiveness of Theatre and Theatre Techniques in Museums*, Executive Summary and Abridged Report, Manchester: Centre for Applied Theatre Research.

Kotler, N. (2003) 'Creativity and Interactivity: New Way to Experience, Market and Manage Museums', working paper, Melbourne, Australia: Deakin University.

Kotler, N. and Kotler, P. (1999) *Marketing dei musei*, Torino: Edizioni di Comunità.

Krishna, A. (ed.) (2010) *Sensory Marketing: Research on the Sensuality of Products*, New York: Routledge.

O'Dell, T. and Billing, P. (2005) *Experiencescapes: Tourism, Culture, and Economy*, Copenhagen: Copenhagen Business School Press.

O'Sullivan, E.L. and Spangler, K.J. (1998) *Experience Marketing: Strategies for the New Millennium*, State College: Venture Publishing.

Pine, B. and Gilmore, J. (1999) *The Experience Economy: Work is Theatre & Every Business a Stage*, Boston, MA: Harvard Business School Press.

Prentice, R. (1996) 'Managing Implosion: The Facilitation of Insight Through the Provision of Context', *Museum Management and Curatorship* 15(2): 169–85.

——(2001) 'Experiential Cultural Tourism: Museums and the Marketing of the New Romanticism of Evoked Authenticity', *Museum Management and Curatorship* 19(1): 5–26.

Quan, S. and Wang, N. (2004) 'Towards a Structural Model of the Tourist Experience: An Illustration from Food Experiences in Tourism', *Tourism Management* 25: 297–305.

Richards, G. (ed.) (2001) *Cultural Attractions and European Tourism*, Wallingford: CABI.

——(2011) 'Creativity and Tourism, the State of the Art', *Annals of Tourism Research* 38(4): 1225–53.

Rifkin, J. (2000) *L'era dell'accesso*, Milano: Mondadori.

Ritzer, G. (1999) *Enchanting a Disenchanted World*, Thousand Oaks: Pine Forge Press.

——(2005) *Enchanting a Disenchanted World: Revolutionizing the Means of Consumption*, second edn, Thousand Oaks, CA: Pine Forge Press.

Simonsen, J., Baerenholdt, J.O. and Buscher, M. (2010) *Design Research: Synergies from Interdisciplinary Perspectives*, Abingdon: Taylor & Francis.

Smith, M.K. (2009) *Issues in Cultural Tourism Studies*, New York: Routledge.

Sundbo, J. and Darmer, P. (eds) (2008) *Creating Experiences in the Experience Economy*, Cheltenham: Edward Elgar.

Swarbrooke, J. (2000) 'Museums: Theme Parks of the Third Millennium?' in Robinson, M., Evans, N., Long, P., Sharpley, R. and Swarbrooke, J. (eds) *Tourism and Heritage Relationships: Global, National and Local Perspectives*, Sunderland: Business Education Publishers, 417–31.

Urry, J. (2002) *The Tourist Gaze*, second edn, London: Sage.

Vaughan, R. (2001) 'Images of a Museum', *Museum Management and Curatorship* 19(3): 253–68.

Xanthoudaki, M. (ed.) (2003) *Un luogo per scoprire: insegnare scienza e tecnologia con i musei*, Milano: SMEC.

Zorzi, Y. (2004) 'Sviluppo degli studi museali e crisi dell'identità dell'istituzione', Working paper 03/2004, Università della Svizzera Italiana – Istituto per la Comunicazione aziendale.

# 49

# Visitor experiences in cultural spaces

## *László Puczkó*

It may surprise some that most customers are not interested in museums, galleries or other forms of cultural establishments. Their primary interests are related to the benefits of visiting the cultural space or site. Any curator or manager should consider the question, 'why do our visitors want to visit us?' People have many reasons and motivations for becoming visitors. These can include a search for entertainment or social interaction, cultural interest, lifestyle preferences or simple curiosity. The factors behind cultural demand have already been analysed in great detail – especially considering some principal questions of interpretation (e.g. Goodey 1973; Field and Wagar 1976; Falk and Dierking 1992; Knudson *et al.* 1995; Knapp and Volk 1997; Beck and Cable 1998), experience creation (e.g. Prince 1982; Kaplan *et al.* 1998), and applied psychology (e.g. Loomis 1987; Ham 1994; Cassidy 1997). The number and variety of motivations for people to become customers are almost innumerable. All of the above-mentioned motivations could apply to any cultural space, meaning that different people with different backgrounds and needs are brought together at the same time.

Given this variation in motivation and reasons for being in a cultural space, the issue of interpretation becomes very important. The main objectives of interpretation in cultural context are:

- To involve customers through first-hand (personal) experience with different dimensions and elements of culture.
- To affect the behaviour and attitudes of the visitors towards and to communicate messages relating to the use of certain traditions, rituals, etc. that form the base of cultural services.
- To provide an enjoyable and meaningful experience.
- To ensure the visitors have fun.
- To increase the customer's understanding, awareness and the appreciation of various aspects of culture.

Interpretation, by definition, can or should have an impact on visitors in such a way that they react to the stimuli in the desired form (e.g. learning, enjoyment, appreciation or relaxation). It is anticipated, however – and this is one of the key reasons why interpretation is used – that the reactions of customers can be managed or at least influenced.

Visitors at a cultural space are basically purchasing experiences. These experiences, though, are co-created by the consumers themselves. Experience is or can be very subjective and specific to a person. In order to understand how these experiences are created and what factors can have an influence on them, it is necessary to understand the information-gathering and experience-building processes of human beings.

Ritchie and Hudson (2009) distinguished among the various levels of experiences that conceptually seemed to form an evolutionary trail of experience thinking. This trail involves the basic experience, the satisfactory experience, the quality experience, the extraordinary experience and the memorable experience. The framework of experiences has been described by Jennings *et al.* (2009) as organisational or business-based, individualistic, psychological and social in nature. Organisational-based frameworks focus on 'marketing, value and delivery'; individualistic framings relate to 'personal, affective, embodied and memory'; psychological framings were associated with 'feelings, memory, intellect and behaviour'; and social framings were noted as connected with 'lifestyle, and social contexts'.

One of the key principles of environmental psychology (Cassidy 1997) is that the reaction of people should not be taken out of context, but should be analysed in relation to it. This is the so-called person-in-context principle. According to this approach, the behaviour and experience of people can be understood within an interactional framework or described with the function $B = f(P,E)$, where B is behaviour, P is person and E is environment. It assumed that human beings, who presumably are always looking for a balanced environment, would somehow react to the stimuli stemming from the environment (i.e. cultural space) surrounding them.

We see that consumers want context-related, authentic experiences and seek a balance between control by the experience stager and self-determined activity with its spontaneity, freedom and self-expression (Binkhorst and Dekker 2009). Prahalad and Ramaswamy (2004) have called for a strategic approach based on shared values, allowing customers to co-create their own experiences in search for personal growth. Based on the co-creation experience perspective, if companies provide experience environments, where dialogue, transparency and access to information is optimal, these will allow the customers to co-create unique experience and value. The emphasis thus shifted in recent debates from narrow conceptions of staging or production to broader notions of experience co-creation, involving a wider range of agencies and processes (Sundbo 2008).

Developers, curators, designers or managers should not forget that environmental stimuli are categorised by customers, such as those causing extreme reactions and those that would not cause any undue reaction. Too much or too little of something, e.g. colours, noise, sound or too much complexity or not enough content can equally create unpleasant experiences, and can cause stress or fatigue. What is too much or too little? Visitors perceive environmental stimuli differently and depending on their attitude, previous experiences and knowledge, physical state, etc., they can react very differently. Some people like state-of-the-art design, while some prefer a more 'functional' atmosphere. Some people like to be surrounded by other people and prefer close interactions, while some would like to enjoy some privacy. For some environmental factors or stimuli, such as colour, both too much and too little would be inconvenient. To make the issue even more difficult, the preferred level of stimulus for the same person can also differ over time (e.g. in a large exhibition hall his or her favourite colour is very welcome, regardless of the fit or misfit of this colour with the exhibit itself, whereas the same colour could be very annoying in a crammed, dark room).

Thinking these psychology-related challenges through further, we should mention cognitive psychology (e.g. Alter and Ward 1994), which focuses on perceptions. It presumes that individuals relate themselves to the world they construct through experiences. Information or stimuli enter through the perceptual system of customers and are saved in the visual or sensual stores. The information (e.g. visual experience of an exhibit) is then transferred to short-term memory, in which it activates items (information, experiences, images, etc.) already being saved in long-term memory. These saved items can either be memories of previous visits, traces of what was learnt in family groups or absorbed through social norms, etc. Stored and new information then is linked and understood by the concept of 'chunking' (Ham 1994).

Understanding and storing information does not happen at the same time, but in chunks or clusters. Similar or somehow similar-looking information is synthesised and stored in the same clusters. Guides, for example, maybe without intention apply this chunking when they alter their service depending on if they are guiding individuals or groups. References a guide may use during the visit, for example, can affect the experience greatly from the customer's experience point of view (e.g. highlighting different aspects of the visit). If a guide relates a benefit or a person that has direct relevance to the customer, it is more likely that customers find the chunk that can make the experience beneficial.

Visitors do not intend to spend too much time with their visits or with trying to understand what is on offer (e.g. an exhibition). That leaves the experience creators with the option of trying to find elements in the service provision, and tools of the interpretive media, that can somehow relate to what visitors already know. With this approach, interpretation builds on existing and stored knowledge. This can then lead to the creation of new chunks or to the extension of old ones stored in long-term memory.

Applying these rules to cultural spaces and sites, there are creative ways in which cultural spaces can introduce new, exotic, fusion services, but the way in which this introduction takes place needs to be considered and then applied to the given facility using the principle of 'chunking'. This processing and chunking very much depend on the sense or senses through which the customer has actually received them. It is understood that customers can retain:

- some 10 per cent of what they hear;
- some 30 per cent of what they read;
- some 50 per cent of what they see; and
- some 90 per cent of what they do.

(Veverka 1994)

This leaves cultural spaces with the special challenge of the expected recollection rate, since cultural spaces tend to offer relatively limited options for visitor involvement – i.e. traditionally visitors tend to hear, read and see and only in a few places to actually do anything! We also know that people are primarily processing visual information, therefore messages structured around some simple visuals is a most efficient familiarising education medium. Managers and curators should not forget that customers are able to recognise up to 18 visual elements in a second (Goodey 1973)! They filter out most of the stimuli and will pay attention to only those that are somehow related to their existing knowledge, i.e. one or more chunks of their memory.

It is also interesting that their customers can think six-to-seven times faster than they can talk – i.e. most of the time we are talking to ourselves. This is why customers switch off so easily, especially if the information or more likely the interpretation is not relevant to their interests or previous experiences. This is what we call external-internal shift (Beck and Cable 1998).

It is often observed that cultural spaces (e.g. museums) were designed by interior designers, and not a team of experts and artists who would understand what visitor psychology has to say about cultural experiences. It needs to be stated here: interior design does not equal experience creation. Whereas interior design focuses on appearance and style, experience creation is a form of art and is rooted deeply in customer/visitor psychology. It is recommended, preferably as part of the development process or as preliminary of a service enhancement exercise, to apply the so-called experience mapping process (Puczkó and Rátz 2000). Experience mapping generates information and clues regarding the following major issues:

1  Way finding/orientation: the ways in which customers find the cultural space – information channels, information provided, etc.
2  Interpretation: the actual experience provided and consumed.
   - Customer flow: information provision, signs, colours, surfaces, etc.
   - Interpretation tools: written materials and visuals, user safety, length of stay at any stage of the visit, text readability, service protocols, atmosphere, waiting time management, web-based interpretation, etc.
   - Human resources: appearance, interpersonal capabilities, etc.
3  Performance monitoring: the ways in which guest experiences are monitored, both at customer and employee-end.
4  Additional services at/nearby the site and the relationship of the facility with the additional services: e.g. online services, packages, hotel, etc.

Experience mapping can make curators, developers and managers able to locate their cultural space in a grid. This experience grid gives a good indication of areas that need enhancement and improvement. The four key factors of the grid visually introduce how a spa, for example, performs from a visitor experience point of view:

- How beneficial: how complex the benefit structure is (e.g. one or more of the following likely benefits: learning, fun, relaxation, social interaction).
- How accessible: how do the customers find the facility itself (e.g. ambiance, safety).

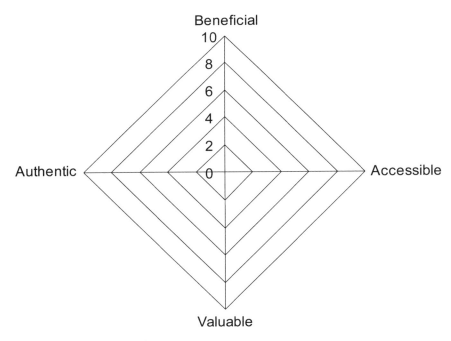

*Figure 49.1* The experience grid

- How valuable: how much and how wide is the associated value of the experience (and not individual services!) (e.g. value for money, how personal the service was, how much the customer was 'involved' in the creation of the experience).
- How authentic: how 'local' or how 'generic' was the experience (e.g. how much the service relates to the concept).

Experience mapping and planning can provide curators, developers and managers alike with tools, hints or solutions. The art of designing an interpretation programme lies in the ability to create authentic and valuable benefits.

---

## Box 49.1 Case study: visitor experience of Hungarian Museums

One of the authors (on behalf of Xellum Ltd) carried out a questionnaire-based survey in the county-level museums of Hungary between December 2007 and November 2008, with the support of the Hungarian Ministry of Education and Culture and the Klára Csilléry Centre for Museum Education and Training. This study was the largest research of its kind implemented among the visitors to Hungarian museums. Some 124 museums and similar organisations participated in the survey, yielding 12,722 completed questionnaires. The collection of data was carried out for 12 months for the sake of reliability, thus providing more balanced results and avoiding misleading conclusions due to seasonality. The survey was implemented through voluntarily completed, previously tested standard questionnaires (OKM 2009).

The key objectives of the survey were to collect information necessary for the segmentation of the visitors; to gather information on the activities in which visitors were involved during their visit; and last but not least, to analyse visitor experiences and satisfaction.

During the past 10 years several museum developments have been realised in Hungary, especially those funded by the Alfa Programme. The Alfa Programme (National Programme for Museum Development) was launched in 2004 and since then has been providing financial support redesigning outdated museum exhibitions and improving visitor-friendly provision (specifically in the countryside). These improvements were expected to be identified through the opinions of museum visitors.

The most important motivating factor of Hungarian museum visitors was to acquire new knowledge (85–89 per cent) and curiosity (86 per cent), as well as visiting a particular exhibition. On the other hand, several external motivational factors depending on certain situations, rather than the respondents themselves, were also important: recommendation from somebody (49 per cent); visiting as a member of a group (53 per cent); and visiting because of a companion's choice (38 per cent). Another important factor was when visitors just dropped by during their stay in the area (50 per cent), which referred to impulsive customers.

One of the aims of the survey was to find out what visitors actually do after they have entered the premises, as the activities that they undertake and the length of their stay are closely related with the understanding and internalising of the messages transmitted by the museum or the exhibition, as well as the behaviour that visitors thought to be acceptable in a museum. A fundamental presumption of the survey was that the flow of information and the communication between the museum and the visitors exist in order to transmit information, knowledge and data that are kept in the long-term memory of the visitors through the visitor experience. So far there

---

has been very little reliable information on the length of time visitors spend in museums in Hungary; however, it is as important as the reason why they go there, and the current survey also had limited methods to measure this information.

The data showed that most visitors claim to have seen all the exhibits. The average time spent in the museum was around one hour, which might mean that respondents were giving slightly misleading answers – that is, they were trying to meet the expectations but obviously they could not have seen all the exhibits within such a limited period of time. Typically, visitors spent their time looking at the exhibits (in fact, all of them); one-third of them took part in an event and also visited the museum shop or café where there was one. In museums participating in the Alfa Programme, visitors stayed longer on average, partly due to the new interpretation methods applied. The shortest time spent in the museum was recorded with student groups.

Some 64.5 per cent of respondents said that they had read labels and texts in the museum, and this percentage was slightly lower in Alfa Programme participants, while 38.5 per cent of the museums were said to have no interactive provision. Institutions using the Alfa funds made improvements to extend interactive facilities; however, visitors were not always able to detect them: 28.9 per cent of visitors did not use any of the available interactive devices, but those who did stayed longer in the museum on average. Most of the institutions offered group activities, although many visitors were not engaged in any of them. The survey found that people went on guided exhibition tours, but these were more popular in museums outside the Alfa Programme, and the same can be said of completing available worksheets. The percentage of local people was highest in terms of activity, involvement and utilising available devices, mostly because several new exhibitions were related to local topics, or local people were more informed about the achievements of the Alfa Programme, and also people from the local area could spare more time to visit.

The results showed that visitors were satisfied with the innovations and renewed exhibitions implemented under the Alfa Programme, and regardless of their age, several people evaluated the museum or the exhibition as 'youthful'. This youthfulness was mostly experienced by those who had internal motivation to come and learn, while people coming as group members or those having external motivation graded lower for novelty and youthfulness, which makes it highly improbable that they will become regular museum visitors.

Visitors were also asked to evaluate the exhibitions that they had seen, and the result was mostly positive in terms of being informative, interesting, impressive, rich in content, but they were more critical of youthfulness, innovations and entertainment.

One of the most important findings was that most of the visitors came to the museum for the first time. Second-time visitors were more typical in Alfa-supported museums, which is notable as visitors form their opinions based on their first impressions, and if museums want to keep them as regular visitors, they have to make improvements and innovations.

Respondents were also asked about the memories they would probably keep of their visits. Newly acquired knowledge and the exhibitions themselves were mentioned most often. Visitors to particular events were more inclined to mention the company that they were with than any other visitor segment. Most visitors found temporary exhibitions more informative.

## Conclusions

Customer or visitor experiences are crucial elements of a trip. This is what the travellers will remember, especially in the long run. Cultural spaces, such as events, festivals, museums or other attractions, need at least to consider the basic foundations of visitor psychology, experience creation models and new marketing concepts, such as co-creation. The case study gives an example of a state-funded programme that provided the necessary inputs expected by modern cultural consumers. Customer expectations are changing rapidly. Still, the managers and curators of cultural spaces are often reluctant to change or to consider new approaches or techniques. There is certainly a thin line between sheer entertainment and meaningful and authentic cultural experiences. Crossing it, however, is not impossible: it just needs a multi-disciplinary approach.

## References

Alter, P. and Ward, R. (1994) 'Exhibit Evaluation: Taking Account of Human Factors', in Hooper Greenhill, E. (ed.) *The Educational Role of Museums*, London: Routledge, 204–11.

Beck, L. and Cable, T. (1998) *Interpretation for the 21st Century, Fifteen Guiding Principles for Interpreting Nature and Culture*, Champaign, IL: Sagamore Publishing.

Binkhorst, E. and Den Dekker, T. (2009) 'Agenda for Co-Creation Tourism Experience Research', *Journal of Hospitality Marketing and Management* 18(2): 311–27.

Cassidy, T. (1997) *Environmental Psychology, Behaviour and Experience in Context*, Hove: Psychological Press.

Falk, J.H. and Dierking, L.D. (1992) *The Museum Experience*, Washington, DC: Whalesback Books.

Field, D.R. and Wagar, J.A. (1976) 'People and Interpretation', in Sharpe, G.W. (ed.) *Interpreting the Environment*, New York: John Wiley & Sons, 43–56.

Goodey, B. (1973) Perception of the Environment: An Introduction to the Literature, Centre for Urban and Regional Studies, University of Birmingham, Occasional Paper No.17.

Ham, S.H. (1994) 'Cognitive Psychology and Interpretation: Synthesis and Application', in Hooper-Greenhill, E. (ed.) *The Educational Role of Museums*, Routledge, London, 107–17.

Jennings, G., Lee, Y., Ayling, A., Lunny, B., Cater, C. and Ollenburg, C. (2009) 'Quality Tourism Experiences: Reviews, Reflections and Research Agendas', *Journal of Hospitality Marketing and Management* 18(2–3): 294–310.

Kaplan, R., Kaplan, S. and Ryan, R.L. (1998) *With People in Mind, Design and Management of Everyday Nature*, Washington, DC: Island Press.

Knapp, D. and Volk, T.L. (1997) 'The Identification of Empirically Derived Goals', *Journal of Environmental Education* 28(3): 24–35.

Knudson, D.M., Cable, T.T. and Beck, L. (1995) *Interpretation of Cultural and Natural Resources*, State College, PA: Venture Publishing.

Loomis, R.J. (1987) *Museum Visitor Evaluation: New Tool for Management*, Nashville, Tennessee: American Association for State and Local History.

OKM (2009) 'Hungarian Museum Research', *Múzeumi Közlemények*, 1 (Special Edition).

Prahalad, C.K. and Ramaswamy, V. (2004) *The Future of Competition: Co-creating Unique Value with Customers*, Boston, MA: Harvard Business School Press.

Prince, D.R. (1982) *Countryside Interpretation: A Cognitive Evaluation*, Birmingham: Centre for Environmental Interpretation, Occasional Papers: No.3.

Puczkó, L. and Rátz, T. (2000) *Az attrakciótól az élményig. A látogatómenedzsment módszerei*, Budapest: Geomédia Kiadó.

Ritchie, J.R.B. and Hudson, S. (2009) 'Understanding and Meeting the Challenges of Consumer/Tourist Experience Research', *International Journal of Tourism Research* 11: 111–26.

Sundbo, J. (2008) 'Innovation in the Experience Economy: A Taxonomy of Innovation Organization', *The Service Industries Journal* 29(3–4): 431–55.

Veverka, J.A. (1994) *Interpretive Master Planning*, Helena, MT: Falcon Press.

# 50

# Engaging with Generation Y at museums

*Anna Leask and Paul Barron*

## Introduction

Museums form a significant proportion of the cultural tourism offering in many destinations across the world. They 'serve the functions of collection, research and exhibition, as well as education and recreation' (Sheng and Chen 2011: 53) meaning that they have a broad range of objectives and measures of effectiveness (Leask 2010). Several authors have commented on the increasing focus on attendance numbers as museums are put under growing financial pressure (Madan 2011), in addition to the increased need to demonstrate value (Legget 2009; Semmell and Bittner 2009). As identified by Gilmore and Rentschler (2002: 745), 'in recent years museums have changed from being predominantly custodial institutions to becoming increasingly focused on audience attraction ... and the need to appeal to differentiated audiences has created new challenges for previously traditional, custodial directors'. Ames (1998: 151) states that in order to achieve growth in visitor numbers, museum managers need to know two primary sets of data: the 'age, education level, motivations and interests of the audience and, in order to attract the largest possible audience, the profiles of one's current and potential audience'. In a competitive leisure environment, achieving targeted visitor numbers may become a serious challenge (Burton *et al.* 2009), which is why many museums are now looking to engage with new markets. Generation Y (Gen Y) comprises around 11.5 million people in the UK (Office for National Statistics 2009), and this cohort offers great potential for current and future museum engagement. Recent interest in engaging with younger audiences, as researched by Gofman *et al.* (2011) and Benckendorff *et al.* (2010), has led to discussion about the characteristics and differing needs of this potential growth sector. As identified by Leask *et al.* (n.d.), Gen Y are often not the key audience in museums at present, although there is evidence that many museums have identified the potential of this market as an audience and are already offering opportunities for engagement in a variety of ways. This chapter will discuss the profile and characteristics of Gen Y consumers, some of the challenges faced by museums in attempting to attract this market, and discuss how museums are developing opportunities for greater engagement with Gen Y visitors.

## Generation Y as consumers

Gen Y is widely regarded as the next big generational cohort, with its own associated unique combination of needs, wants and expectations (Meredith and Schewe 1994; Schewe *et al.*

2000). Kupperschmidt (2000: 66) defines a generation as being 'an identifiable group of cohorts that share year, age location and significant life events'. Gen Y, like other generations before it, is a product of its time (Scott 2000). Mannheim (1952, cited in Scott 2000) proposes that individuals within a generation will be predisposed to adopt particular modes of thought and be shaped by experiences occurring within their particular generational timeframe. Different authors propose slight differences in the start and end years that define Generation Y (Wilkening and Chung 2009); however, for the purposes of this research the period from 1979 to 1994 inclusive is used to define the cohort (Neuborne and Kerwin 1999).

Moscardo and Benckendorff (2010: 22) highlight the differences in opinions amongst many researchers as to the exact nature and characteristics of Gen Y as a generation, but they also identify some level of agreement about the applicability and relevance of four particular themes, namely: that Gen Y is fairly unique in its particular approach to adopting and using digital media; it has very positive views on factors such as diversity, flexibility, social issues and its own future; it is strongly oriented towards family and social groups; and it has enjoyed an extension of adolescence.

It is widely recognised that Gen Ys have significant amounts of disposable income (Morton 2002) and that they prefer to spend this income on a variety of personal services and goods rather than to save some of it for a rainy day (Der Hovanesian 1999; Martin and Turley 2004). Moscardo and Benckendorff (2010) also found that Gen Ys tend to spend less on recreation and travel than do previous generations. The need to highlight value for money was also found to be imperative, though Williams and Soutar (2009) feel that value, in the tourism context at least, is actually a much more multi-dimensional concept. Indeed, it was found that additional aspects such as functional, emotional and novelty value combine with monetary value to create differing perceptions about what value actually means to each of them. Brand value is also an important driver for Gen Y consumers looking for association with what they consider to be like-minded brands.

Being highly socially oriented, Gen Ys respect the opinions and advice of their friends and family over that of advertisers (Shepardson 2000), and thus they are known to be much more responsive to word-of-mouth communications originating from within their immediate social circle (Gardyn 2002). Fields (2008) reports that Gen Ys' key considerations before purchasing a product or service are: the cost (preferably cheap or at least good value); quality (must be good); and level of service provided (should be fast). They also look to have all these aspects encapsulated in some sort of 'experience' rather than just engaging in a basic and rather mundane purchase transaction.

Gen Ys are acknowledged to be very technologically adept (Ashridge Business School 2008; Davidson 2008). Jennings et al. (2010) concluded that, given their overwhelming need to fit in, it is important for Gen Ys to feel part of a particular peer community, and within these communities members are interconnected via various forms of computing technology that employ essential Gen Y tools such as online social networking. The explosion of social media use has extended their community membership participation to virtual communities in addition to physical ones.

Bound et al. (2008) found that the night-time economy and an 'open all hours' culture are both important considerations for Gen Ys. Kubaki et al. (2007) found that there is significant potential for venues such as nightclubs to compete on the quality and variety of the complementary services they provide, for example music-based entertainment offerings, rather than relying on the usual core offerings of alcohol provision and promotions. There is also significant evidence that Gen Ys prefer to frequent events and activities that are specifically arranged for and targeted at them as a distinct audience group. This is supported by the general conclusions reached by Grove and Fisk (1997) and Lovelock and Wirtz (2007), indicating that leisure-related organisations need to manage their customer portfolios appropriately to ensure that all their customers get the type of leisure experience they are seeking. The tendency of Gen Ys to be hedonistic and to live for the moment does, however, mean that they can be rather fickle and are constantly on the lookout for 'the next big thing' (Nancarrow *et al.* 2002; Moss *et al.* 2009).

How to meet, or ideally exceed, the particular needs and expectations of such a large and potentially valuable audience segment as Gen Y is a particularly important consideration given their propensity to spread their opinions on products and services via both word of mouth (Godin 2003) and also, perhaps more importantly and worryingly, via 'word of mouse' (de Valck *et al.* 2009). Hill and White (2000) found that an organisation's website is more often than not the first point of reference for many people prior to them taking any decision to actually make a visit to a place. Semper and Spasojevic (2002) and Buhalis *et al.* (2006) recognise that the creative use of technology onsite combined with a well-designed web-based component (such as a website and perhaps also a social media presence) can extend the visit experience both before and after the actual visit has taken place. Galani and Chalmers (2002) recognise the importance of integrating a social aspect into any information communications technology (ICT)–based visit experience. Chatchaidamrong and Leelapanyalert (2009) concluded that the organisations most likely to be able to maximise the benefits they can realise from engaging with this audience segment are the ones that actively participate in virtual communities and social media themselves rather than standing timidly on the sidelines.

## Generation Y and the museum experience

Gen Ys are considered to be the consummate 'experience seekers', especially in their leisure time. Organisations in the tourism and leisure industry need to offer Gen Ys the types of entertainment-based experiences they seek if they are to attract this potentially very profitable audience segment to their business. To do this, however, museums need to recognise that experiences are much more than just services. Pine and Gilmore (1999) outline the fundamental differences between a service and an experience and discuss how different basic product and service offerings can be customised to create different types of experiences. An example of how museums such as the Victoria & Albert Museum in London and the Australia Museum in Sydney currently engage with Gen Y is through the development of 'Lates' events (www.lates. org). These usually involve the development of a themed event specifically targeting Gen Y via extended opening hours in the evening, a child-free environment, music performance, the provision of alcohol and food points, and experience-driven interactions with existing collections. Grewal *et al.* (2009) and Verhoef *et al.* (2009) recognise how past customer experiences can influence future customer experiences, and how those past experiences could create issues if they did not live up to customers' expectations, aspects to be considered in the programming of school and family visits too, given their potential influence on future visits.

Gen Ys place a strong emphasis on integration of technology within all aspects of their lives, thus creating a sense of expectation that technology will be a central part of their leisure, work and study experiences. It has been a commonly accepted assumption that Gen Ys are 'the Internet generation', consequently placing a heavy reliance on the Web for their information and communication needs. Park *et al.* (2010) concluded that the rapid proliferation of wi-fi technology and the rate at which Gen Y is embracing its use means that the attractions and tourism industries have to respond by providing access to their various products and services any time, any place and anywhere if they are to capitalise on this rather frenzied Gen Y enthusiasm. The opportunities afforded by using social media such as Facebook, Twitter and Flickr to communicate, engage and interact with Gen Y visitors are extensive and have been used to great effect for pre-, during and post-visit engagement. For example, the National Maritime Museum in London makes extensive use of such opportunities to engage with their audiences and build relationships through sites such as Twitter and Flickr. Likewise, the use of technology-based interpretation at museums is considered to be an important tool for managing visitors whilst also meeting (or preferably exceeding) their needs and expectations, as seen in the development of downloadable apps for interpretation of the Terracotta Warriors exhibition at the National Museum of Singapore and the Smithsonian.

Personalisation of products and services is known to make them more attractive to customers in general, and to Gen Ys in particular. The ability of ICT to personalise an interpretive experience is one of its major advantages, allowing visitor attractions to offer a range of experiences for different visitor segments, as currently occurs at the Tate Modern in London, where one of the three different mobile multimedia experiences offered was specifically designed to meet the needs and interests of core group Gen Ys (Wilson 2004). Hawkey (2004) and Hafner and Chase (2004) all agree that appropriate personalisation combined with mobility is the way forward in audience development for many, though perhaps not all, types of visitor attractions.

Chen and Chen (2010) discuss how the customer experience has now become the central consideration for attractions management with interpretive events and learning opportunities forming essential elements of the overall experience. Mintel Oxygen (2008) suggests that retaining a core sense of authenticity and offering a range of different levels of experience for different customer segments and age groups are key aspects in attracting new visitors and enhancing commercial opportunities. Benckendorff and Moscardo (2010) found that Gen Ys typically want to listen less and do more in their visit experiences – they show less interest in any educational or interpretive aspect of a visit, preferring instead to focus on getting real value from the physical engagement aspect. Jennings et al. (2010) support this finding, having established that having fun is an important aspect, if not the most important aspect, of a visit experience for Gen Ys. Jennings et al. (2010) go on to state that the interconnectivity of the entire visit experience, right through from pre- to post-visit, is highly important to Gen Ys, who are often more than willing to pay relatively high prices if they can be assured that they will get the truly memorable experiences they seek.

Leask et al. (n.d.) established that the provision of social space and opportunities for socialisation is important to Gen Y, all ideally within a child-free environment. While physical space for such activities was welcomed, this also included online opportunities for visitors to share their experiences at the point of delivery, most notably via social media.

---

### Box 50.1 Case study: Royal Bank of Scotland Museum Lates at the National Museum of Scotland (NMS)

The NMS re-launched in July 2011 following a £47.4 million refurbishment that offered the opportunity to consult widely, redesign, represent and develop the collections and space. The operating environment is competitive, with several new attractions opening and extending their offering nearby during 2011. The re-launch offered the NMS the opportunity to realise two objectives: to re-engage with existing visitor markets and members following the three-year period of refurbishment, and to connect with and engage potential new audiences such as Gen Y.

This case study is based on analysis of three informal interviews with managers responsible for the development of the Royal Bank of Scotland (RBS) Museum Lates events, the results of a front-end consultation for Late Events (NMS 2011a), observations gathered on the night of the first event, and the results of the visitor survey conducted at the first event (NMS 2011b).

The first RBS Museum Lates event, 'First Look Live', took place in November 2011. Development of the programme was based on the findings of research undertaken to identify the needs, wants and expectations of the 18–30 age group (NMS 2011a). This had identified a desire to visit after standard opening hours, the opportunity to interact with the exhibits in a child-free environment, to feel welcome and to enjoy specific events such as music sets. The aim of the first event was to try ideas out and undertake visitor research, to provide a quality and fun experience linked to the collections, and to animate the collections whilst including a light learning message. This resulted in an event product that included a red carpet welcome for visitors, silent disco, animal-handling opportunities, socialising space with games and activities, face painting, live music and DJ sets, photo opportunities, art online, goodie bags, and which culminated in a display of acrobats on silks.

Communicated via both traditional and digital marketing methods, the ticketed event sold out well in advance. Technology was used to engage with potential audiences via Facebook and Twitter, with online activities such as a competition to name a cocktail for the event and win tickets were used in the run up to the event.

Visitor feedback via Twitter and Facebook was very positive, with extensive use of each media before, during and after the event. Research undertaken by the NMS (2011b) indicates that 70 per cent of the survey respondents were female and that 88 per cent were 44 years old or below. A total of 55 per cent of the visitors came as part of a group and 84 per cent were from the Edinburgh area. Some 76 per cent had visited the museum previously. Local and national media publications and programmes all ran very positive reviews of the event.

The event achieved many of its aims, offering flexibility, variety and choice to the visitors. The event provided opportunities for visitors to have a different view of the space, to engage with that space and the collections at their own leisure and to experience some unexpected surprises. The variety of options regarding level of visitor engagement was also considered to be positive by visitors. Early concerns within the organisation about potential damage to the collections or inappropriate use of the space proved unfounded, although converting the space for the different use in a very short period of time between the museum closing time and the event start was a challenge.

As discussed earlier in the chapter, such events make use of the existing collections and space within a different social context and aim to appeal to satisfy the general characteristics of this Gen Y population – child-free environments, later opening hours, a variety of experiences that allow for flexibility and choice during the visit, and the provision of food and alcoholic drink. They successfully achieved these aims and plans for further events are underway.

## Conclusions

As this chapter has demonstrated, Gen Y is potentially an attractive market for museums to engage with further, because their characteristics and needs as consumers can be met by adapting the existing museum offering. As noted by Burton *et al.* (2009: 31) 'museums can respond to visitor demand by packaging and repackaging their core purpose of experience, education, and social activity to meet needs either as a single entity or in collaboration with other providers'. However, it is important for museums to determine whether or not they want to engage with

Gen Y or if resources can be better spent elsewhere. If it is a market of interest, then museum managers should involve their own Gen Y staff and teams to establish what resources, products and themes would be best suited for development and that appeal to the characteristics of Gen Y. Key features in encouraging engagement appear to be based on timing, child-free, innovative product offerings, appropriate branding, flexibility of visit choice, music and the use of social media to communicate – not all traditionally aspects of museum products, but it is certainly within their means to package existing resources into products that appeal to Gen Y.

## References

Ames, P. (1998) 'A Challenge to Modern Museum Management: Meshing Mission and Marketing', *International Journal of Museum Management and Curatorship* 7: 151–57.

Ashridge Business School (2008) Gen Y Research – Summary Report, Berkhamsted, Hertfordshire: Ashridge Business School, www.ashridge.org.uk/Website/Content.nsf/wFAR/Generation+Y+Research?opendocument (accessed 4 November 2009).

Benckendorff, P. and Moscardo, G. (2010) 'Understanding Generation-Y Tourists: Managing the Risk and Change Associated with a New Emerging Market', in Benckendorff, P., Moscardo, G. and Pendergast, D. (eds) *Tourism and Generation Y*, Wallingford: CABI, 38–46.

Bound, K., Beunderman, J. and Mean, M. (2008) *The Place Race: The Role of Place in Attracting and Retaining Talent in Scottish Cities*, Edinburgh: Scottish Enterprise.

Buhalis, D., Owen, R. and Pletinckx, D. (2006) 'Information Communication Technology Applications for World Heritage Site Management', in Leask, A. and Fyall, A. (eds) *Managing World Heritage Sites*, Oxford: Butterworth-Heinemann, 125–44.

Burton, C., Louviere, J. and Young, L. (2009) 'Retaining the Visitor, Enhancing the Experience: Identifying Attributes of Choice in Repeat Museum Visitation', *International Journal of Nonprofit and Voluntary Sector Marketing* 14: 21–34.

Chatchaidamrong, G. and Leelapanyalert, K. (2009) 'The Influence of Marketing Communication Mix on 18–34 Years-old International Tourists Travelling to Thailand', in Neal, M.W. and Jones, C.J. (eds) *3rd International Colloquium on Tourism and Leisure*, Bangkok, Thailand, Pathumthani: Asian Institute of Technology, 1–29.

Chen, C.-F. and Chen, F.-S. (2010) 'Experience Quality, Perceived Value, Satisfaction and Behavioral Intentions for Heritage Tourists', *Tourism Management* 31: 29–35.

Davidson, R. (2008) What Does Generation Y Want from Conferences and Incentive Programmes? Thatcham, Berkshire: VisitBritain, www.insights.org.uk/articleitem.aspx?title=What%20Does%20Generation%20Y%20want%20from%20Conferences%20and%20Incentive%20Programmes? (accessed 5 November 2009).

de Valck, K., van Bruggen, G.H. and Wierenga, B. (2009) Virtual Communities: A Marketing Perspective, *Decision Support Systems* 47: 185–203.

Der Hovanesian, M. (1999) 'Spending It, Investing It – Coming on Strong: The Children of the Baby Boomers are Affecting Spending and Investing as Significantly as Their Parents Did; The Similarity Ends There', *Wall Street Journal*, online.wsj.com/article/SB942785816835228037.html?mod=wsjcrmain (accessed 24 April 2012).

Fields, B. (2008) 'Marketing to Generation Y: What You Can't Afford Not to Know', Pehrson Web Group, www.ideamarketers.com/?Marketing_to_Generation_Y_What_You_Cant_Afford_Not_to_Knowandarticleid=399648 (accessed 5 November 2009).

Galani, A. and Chalmers, M. (2002) *Can You See Me? Exploring Co-visiting Between Physical and Virtual Visitors. Museums and the Web*, Denver, CO: Archives and Museum Informatics.

Gardyn, R. (2002) 'Educated Consumers', *American Demographics* 24: 18.

Gilmore, A. and Rentschler, R. (2002) 'Changes in Museum Management: A Custodial or Marketing Emphasis', *Journal of Management Development* 2: 745–60.

Godin, S. (2003) *Purple Cow: Transform Your Business By Being Remarkable*, New York: Portfolio.

Gofman, A., Moskowitz, H. and Mets, T. (2011) 'Marketing Museums and Exhibitions: What Drives the Interests of Young People?' *Journal of Hospitality Marketing and Management* 20(6): 601–18.

Grewal, D., Levy, M. and Kumar, V. (2009) 'Customer Experience Management in Retailing: An Organizing Framework', *Journal of Retailing* 85: 1–14.

Grove, S.J. and Fisk, R.P. (1997) 'The Impact of Other Customers on Service Experiences: A Critical Incident Examination of 'Getting Along', *Journal of Retailing* 73: 63–85.

Hafner, K. and Chase, K. (2004) At Museums, Computers Get Creative, *New York Times*, query.nytimes.com/gst/fullpage.html?res=940DE5DA1E3EF931A35751C1A9629C8B63andsec=andspon=andpagewanted=3 (accessed 23 November 2009).

Hawkey, R. (2004) *Learning with Digital Technologies in Museums, Science Centres and Galleries*. Nesta Futurelab Series, London: National Endowment for Science, Technology and the Arts.

Hill, L.N. and White, C. (2000) 'Public Relations Practitioners' Perception of the World Wide Web as a Communications Tool', *Public Relations Review* 26: 31–51.

Jennings, G., Cater, C., Lee, Y.-S., Ollenburg, C., Ayling, A. and Lunny, B. (2010) 'Generation Y: Perspectives of Quality in Youth Travel Experiences in an Australian Backpacker Context', in Benckendorff, P., Moscardo, G. and Pendergast, D. (eds) *Tourism and Generation Y*, Wallingford: CABI, 58–72.

Kubaki, K., Skinner, H., Parfitt, S. and Moss, G. (2007) 'Comparing Nightclub Customers' Preferences in Existing and Emerging Markets', *International Journal of Hospitality Management* 26: 957–73.

Kupperschmidt, B.R. (2000) 'Multigeneration Employees: Strategies for Effective Management', *Health Care Manager* 19: 65–76.

Leask, A. (2010) 'Progress in Visitor Attraction Research – Towards More Effective Management', *Tourism Management* 31(2): 155–66.

Leask, A., Fyall, A. and Barron, P. (n.d.) 'Gen Y – Market Opportunity or Marketing Challenge – Strategies to Engage Gen Y in the UK Attractions Sector', *Current Issues in Tourism*, DOI:10.1080/13683500.2011.642856, published online 2011, forthcoming.

Legget, J. (2009) 'Measuring What We Treasure or Treasuring What We Measure? Investigating Where Community Stakeholders Locate the Value in their Museum', *Museum Management and Curatorship* 24 (3): 213–32.

Lovelock, C.H. and Wirtz, J. (2007) *Services Marketing: People, Technology, Strategy*, Upper Saddle River, NJ: Pearson/Prentice Hall.

Madan, R. (2011) *Sustainable Museums: Strategies for the 21st Century*, Edinburgh: MuseumsEtc.

Martin, C.A. and Turley, L.W. (2004) 'Malls and Consumption Motivation: An Exploratory Examination of Older Generation Y Consumers', *International Journal of Retail and Distribution Management* 32: 464–75.

Meredith, G. and Schewe, C. (1994) 'The Power of Cohorts', *American Demographics* 16: 22–31.

Mintel Oxygen (2008) Historic and Cultural Visitor Attractions – UK, London: Mintel International Group Ltd, academic.mintel.com/sinatra/oxygen_academic/my_reports/display/id = 300250andanchor = atom#atom0 (accessed 27 January 2010).

Morton, L.P. (2002) 'Targeting Generation Y', *Public Relations Quarterly* 47: 46–48.

Moscardo, G. and Benckendorff, P. (2010) 'Mythbusting: Generation Y and Travel', in Benckendorff, P., Moscardo, G. and Pendergast, D. (eds) *Tourism and Generation Y*, Wallingford: CABI, 16–26.

Moss, G., Parfitt, S. and Skinner, H. (2009) 'Men and Women: Do They Value the Same Things in Mainstream Nightclubs and Bars?' *Tourism and Hospitality Research* 9: 61–79.

Nancarrow, C., Nancarrow, P. and Page, J. (2002) 'An Analysis of the Concept of Cool and its Marketing Implications', *Journal of Consumer Behaviour* 1: 311–22.

Neuborne, E. and Kerwin, K. (1999) Generation Y: Today's Teens – the Biggest Bulge Since the Boomers – May Force Marketers to Toss Their Old Tricks, www.businessweek.com/1999/99_07/b3616001.htm (accessed 3 November 2009).

NMS (2011a) *RBS Museums Late 1 Audience Research*, Edinburgh: National Museum of Scotland, unpublished report.

——(2011b) *National Museum of Scotland Late Events Front-end Consultation August 2011*, Edinburgh: National Museum of Scotland, unpublished report.

Office for National Statistics (2009) *Key Population and Vital Statistics*, Newport: Office for National Statistics, www.statistics.gov.uk/downloads/theme_population/KPVS34–2007/KPVS2007.pdf (accessed 30 July 2010).

Park, M., Jang, H., Lee, S. and Brayley, R. (2010) 'Tourism and the N Generation in a Dynamically Changing Society: The Case of South Korea', in Benckendorff, P., Moscardo, G. and Pendergast, D. (eds) *Tourism and Generation Y*, Wallingford: CABI, 85–97.

Pine, B.J., II, and Gilmore, J.H. (1999) *The Experience Economy: Work is Theatre and Every Business a Stage*, Boston, MA: Harvard Business School.

Schewe, C.D., Meredith, G.E. and Noble, S.M. (2000) 'Defining Moments: Segmenting by Cohorts', *Marketing Management* 9: 48–53.

Scott, J. (2000) 'Is it a Different World to When You Were Growing Up? Generational Effects on Social Representations and Child-rearing Values', *British Journal of Sociology* 51: 355–76.

Semmell, M. and Bittner, M. (2009) 'Demonstrating Museum Value: The Role of the Institute of Museums and Library Services', *Museum Management and Curatorship* 24(3): 271–88.

Semper, R. and Spasojevic, M. (2002) *The Electronic Guidebook: Using Portable Devices and a Wireless Web-based Network to Extend the Museum Experience*, Denver, CO: Archives and Museum Informatics, www.archimuse.com/mw2002/papers/galani/galani.html (accessed 11 November 2009).

Sheng, C. and Chen, M. (2011) 'A Study of Experience Expectations of Museum Visitors', *Tourism Management* 33(1): 53–60.

Shepardson, N. (2000) 'New Kids on the Lot', *American Demographics* 22(1): 44–47.

Verhoef, P.C., Lemon, K.N., Parasuraman, A., Roggeveen, A., Tsiros, M. and Schlesinger, L.A. (2009) 'Customer Experience Creation: Determinants, Dynamics and Management Strategies', *Journal of Retailing* 85: 31–41.

Wilkening, S. and Chung, J. (2009) *Life Stages of the Museum Visitor: Building Engagement over a Lifetime*, Washington, DC: American Association of Museums Press.

Williams, P. and Soutar, G.N. (2009) 'Value, Satisfaction and Behavioural Intentions in an Adventure Tourism Context', *Annals of Tourism Research* 36: 413–38.

Wilson, G. (2004) *Multimedia Tour Programme at Tate Modern*, Denver, CO: Archives and Museum Informatics, www.archimuse.com/mw2004/papers/wilson/wilson.html (accessed 11 November 2009).

## Further reading

Benckendorff, P., Moscardo, G. and Pendergast, D. (eds) (2010) *Tourism and Generation Y*, Wallingford: CABI.

# Conclusion

One of the main themes to have emerged from this publication is the notion that tourists have traditionally been over-directed in their experience of tourism. The tendency to rely on guides or guidebooks or prescribed routes of the past (i.e. the Grand Tour), has been something of an enduring legacy until relatively recently in the history of tourism. Even today, many tourists may experience a certain degree of *angst* if they are exposed to new and unfamiliar surroundings and encounters, as discussed by Mike Robinson in his chapter. Although some of the most enriching cross-cultural experiences come from spontaneous encounters, historically, most tourists have been socially and culturally conditioned to follow certain scripts. David Bruce discussed in comic detail the reliance of both aristocratic and middle-class tourists alike on guidebooks. Our experiences are also mediated by what Noel Salazar referred to as 'imaginaries', which includes our (over-)exposure to specific representations of places and experiences. On the other hand, Tony Seaton describes how many tourists seem to be keen to follow in the footsteps of famous or historically significant people in their travels. Clearly, not all tourists want to be entirely independent, and this includes highly educated and sophisticated cultural tourists.

However, there has been a recent surge of interest in the proactivity of tourists and their desires to subvert pre-determined scripts. For example, Kevin Meethan explored the notion of performativity and reflexivity in his chapter, suggesting that individuals can play a much more active role in their interpretation and appreciation of places, people and experiences. Kevin Hannam and Sujama Roy referred to the need for more emphasis on the personal and emotional geographies of tourism. The human component of tourism is emphasised in the context of landscapes and destinations, where Marjan Melkert and Wil Munsters note that there are very few truly 'authentic' landscapes that have not been in some way altered by human activity. Similarly, David Crouch shows how spaces are transformed into places through human experiences and interactions. The process of co-creation in tourism has become an increasingly important theme, which is noted by several authors, especially in the tourist and visitor experience section of this book. For example, Sonia Ferrari and Zsuzsanna Horváth both refer to this phenomenon in some detail. Visitors no longer wish to be passive in their experiences of cultural tourism. They want to engage fully in interactive and creative ways, using all five senses. Nikki MacLeod discussed how cultural products such as trails need to take into consideration the growing need for independent exploration and co-creation. In addition, it is important that cultural attractions designers and managers fully understand visitor psychology, as noted by László Puczkó. This is especially important for younger generations, such as Generation Y, as researched by Anna Leask and Paul Barron, and there will clearly be cultural variations according to nationality as well as age-based segments.

Fully engaging this new breed of cultural tourist can be relatively challenging. As noted by Gernot Wolfram and Clare Burnill, the term tourist has become increasingly pejorative for many people, who may prefer to be labelled differently. These so-called 'tactical tourists' want somehow to become a part of the destination and the everyday life of its people, especially those activities that take place in 'backstage' or fringe areas. Antonio Paolo Russo and Alan Quaglieri-Domínguez discuss how many bohemian or creative tourists have become almost indistinguishable from local populations in destinations like Barcelona. In the case of Erasmus students, who stay for a relatively long period of time in a destination and become fully immersed in the culture, they can even become 'ambassadors of cultural tourism', as discussed by Karolina Buczkowska.

However, in some cases, tourists may not be welcomed into the 'backstage' of locals' lives. For example, many residents of Barcelona have become unhappy with the over-development of tourism and the city is almost a victim of its own success. Simon Woodward explores the tensions that exist between academic communities and visiting tourists in university towns. This attitude can be even more prevalent amongst communities in remote areas. Many past cultural tourism publications placed considerable emphasis on the negative impacts of tourism on the lives and traditions of local communities. Jarkko Saarinen showed that there is still a tendency to misrepresent indigenous peoples in cultural tourism marketing with a skewed image of their exoticism or an emphasis on selective aspects of their culture. This is a phenomenon that Donald Macleod refers to as 'cultural configuration', where culture is interpreted and depicted selectively, often to exclude or enhance reality. On the other hand, Michael Ireland discusses how documentary films can be used to represent the lives and traditions of communities, which can result in a more 'authentic' and realistic representation of community life.

Other authors in this publication focus on 'adaptive' views of cultural tourism, for example, Xerado Pereiro. He discusses the various ways in which political self-determination and empowerment can improve the tourist experiences for both local people and tourists alike. Anna Thompson-Carr focuses on the relatively positive experiences of the Māori people in New Zealand. Philip Sloan, Willy Legrand and Claudia Simons-Kaufmann show how it is actually possible to transform the entire economic and social fabric of communities' lives through social entrepreneurship initiatives. However, it is not only indigenous and tribal communities in developing countries that need to be managed carefully and sensitively. Donald Macleod makes the point that anthropologists are becoming increasingly interested in non-tribal communities, which can include ethnic communities in cities as discussed by Anya Diekmann and Stephen Shaw. Both authors focus on the tendency to depict what is 'exotic' about ethnic quarters, often without sufficient understanding of the needs and wishes of the communities involved.

The theme of authenticity in the context of cultural tourism is still a major focus for many researchers in cultural tourism. Sean Beer discusses the philosophical difficulties of determining the true nature of authenticity. Marjan Melkert and Wil Munsters argue that there are few landscapes offering authenticity in a true sense. In many Asian destinations, the understanding of authentic culture and heritage may be very different from European interpretations, as noted by Joan Henderson, and Myriam Jansen-Verbeke, Yehong Sun and Qingwen Min. Decisions may need to be made about how far to preserve or conserve traditional areas – especially heritage buildings – and how far to build modern and contemporary ones. Authenticity may be much more closely connected to intangible traditions than to tangible heritage (e.g. buildings, architecture). Heather Skinner suggests that many nations are essentially presenting 'fakelore' with their inauthentic representations of place which are based more on what place marketeers want visitors to hear than what the visitors might actually want to hear. Michael Hitchcock suggests that authenticity can be a matter of choice for many communities, which can decide quite how far they adapt or even exaggerate their culture for tourists. It is still debatable as to how far tourists know or care about the authenticity of their experiences and the products they buy; however, it is usually assumed that cultural tourists are fairly educated and discerning in this respect.

Although it has been suggested that beauty in the context of tourism has been under-researched, there is an increasing shift towards emphasis on historical value instead (for example, industrial sites becoming World Heritage sites or regenerated cities becoming European Cultural Capitals). Most of the authors in this *Handbook* do not subscribe to the view that cultural tourism is purely about aesthetics; instead, there is a recognition that cultural tourists are interested in all aspects of human culture, including the darker side of existence. For example, Karel Werdler talked about dark tourism and especially perceptions of death and dying. The point is made that even difficult and uncomfortable subjects can be presented in an interesting and creative way, as long as it is done sensitively. Nevertheless, some domains of people's lives may need to remain sacred. For example, Erik Cohen discussed the intervention of the Thai government to prevent certain religious signs and symbols from being misused in tattoo art for foreigners.

Creativity is a central theme in this book. It has become a major element in regeneration strategies for cities that are competing for certain accolades like European Cultural Capital or for events like the Olympic Games. It is an essential part of museum, gallery and heritage site interpretation, especially as visitors become more discerning and experienced, and competition becomes greater. Without creativity, cultural tourism strategies can result in the homogenisation and standardisation of cities, as described by Clare Carruthers. Michael Hall also referred to the problems of serial reproduction, where cities copy each other's strategies and initiatives instead of attempting to be original or unique. Greg Richards discussed ways in which this could be overcome, for example through creative experiences that involve processes of co-creation.

Nevertheless, it should be noted that regeneration strategies tend to over-promise and culture can only do so much. It is a common tactic to use culture and cultural tourism as tools for economic development. The economists in this book such as Juan Gabriel Brida, Marta Meleddu and Manuela Pulina, Celeste Eusébio, Maria João Carneiro and Elisabeth Kastenholz, and Juan Ignacio Pulido Fernández and Marcelino Sánchez Rivero analyse the different ways of measuring economic impacts and visitor expenditure. The increasingly instrumental approach to cultural tourism development is discussed by Tereza Raabová, Petr Merta and Alena Tichá, who suggest that an obsession with money often overshadows interest in other impacts of cultural tourism. Unfortunately, it appears to be somewhat common to milk the cow without feeding it! Few of the financial benefits created by cultural developments (e.g. arts venues) are channelled back into culture or the arts, or even tourism. Multiplier effects may be created for the local or national economy, but the money is rarely re-invested in cultural tourism. Although authors in this book do not necessarily advocate a return to the 'art-for-art's-sake' movement, the point is made by Philip Long and Nigel Morpeth that creativity should sometimes be allowed to develop for its own sake, rather than as a vehicle for something else.

Many of the authors recommend different approaches to managing or planning cultural tourism. For example, Patrick Föhl and Yvonne Pröbstle emphasised the need for stakeholders to work together. Simon Woodward referred to the growing trend for destination management, which encourages stakeholders to collaborate. Can-Seng Ooi explored different models of managing destinations, for example top-down and bottom-up, also emphasising the importance of a balanced approach to stakeholder interests. James Kennell advocates grass-roots approaches to cultural tourism development, for example artist-led strategies in the context of regeneration. It is perhaps important to note that true consensus is difficult to achieve, especially as many destination management groups consist of numerous stakeholders. However, even the process of debate and conflict can be creative and eventually lead to some productive outcomes.

In some cases, politicians 'hijack' cultural celebrations as a means of nation building and branding and identity construction. Two examples of this are given by Monica Gilli and Maria Cândida Cadavez of Italy and Portugal, respectively. In some cases this can result in positive developments and the diversification of cultural image, but in others it could lead to greater nationalism. Heather Skinner notes that nationalist narratives can distort representations of place. Instead of fostering hostility through nationalism, increased mobility could be perceived and accommodated in more positive ways. David Picard and Tom Selwyn suggest that governments and other agencies responsible for the development of tourism would benefit from returning to the traditional understanding of hospitality. Arguably, all people can be educated and trained to provide hospitality, regardless of their cultural background.

The globalisation of cultural tourism is a theme that has been explored extensively over the past few years, and is revisited here by Yvette Reisinger. Along with Mike Robinson, she dispels the notion that the cultural tourism phenomenon is constructed according to binarisms like global-local, host-guest, work-play, etc. Instead, we see the emergence of a spectrum or a continuum and a blurring of boundaries. Post-modern cultural tourism products have been developed to incorporate elements of both traditional and contemporary culture. Lóránt Dávid, Bulcsú Remenyik and Béla Zsolt Gergely analysed the way in which niche or special interest cultural tourism products can be developed to place destinations on the map. Such products draw on both the past and present of the region and its people.

In conclusion we could return to the argument of Keith Hollinshead and Milka Ivanova that a trans-disciplinary approach to cultural tourism is needed – one which involves academics and industry, as well as communities and tourists. Few of the authors in this book entrenched their work firmly in one discipline, because the cultural tourism phenomenon has become too rich and complex to be so contained. This process of moving towards trans-disciplinarity means that dialogue between individuals, groups, agencies and sectors is being fostered. This leads to more diplomatic, flexible, spontaneous and creative ways of working. All of those involved in cultural tourism, including the tourists themselves, can be engaged in a constant process of co-creation. It has been recognised and accepted that cultures are alive and dynamic rather than static and fossilised. This means that we have to be constantly alert to change and fluctuation. We have to ask ourselves more pertinent questions about who cultural tourists are, to know them better and to react accordingly. This will become even more important in the future as new markets and segments emerge, sometimes from the most unlikely locations. The cultural tourist of the present will keep academics and industry practitioners on their toes, but as a result, more creative, unique and sustainable products are likely to develop.

## Future directions for cultural tourism research

What might a *Handbook of Cultural Tourism* look like in 10 or 20 years' time? Just as the focus of cultural tourism research has shifted significantly in the previous two decades, it is likely to do so in the coming years. It is impossible to forecast exactly what might happen in the field of cultural tourism scholarship, but the contributions to the current volume help to give some pointers as to emerging debates and concerns.

A number of authors have questioned the basis of tourism as currently formulated. Mike Robinson, and Kevin Hannam and Sujama Roy argue in their contributions to this volume that the focus of travel is shifting from a narrow focus on tourism to a wider view of mobility. One important implication of this is that the relationship between mobility and culture implies a more complex relationship with vaguer boundaries between 'local' and 'traveller', or between 'global' and 'local' culture. In the rapidly moving arena of tourism studies, whereas in the past the problem with cultural tourism lay mainly with the term 'culture', it now increasing also lies with the concept of 'tourism'.

As Karolina Buczkowska points out in this volume, cultural tourism is no longer driven just by norms of taste, but increasingly by the medium through which information about it is transmitted and received. This increasingly shifts the meaning of cultural tourism experiences into the arena of relational aesthetics. This change was already signalled in discussions that emerged from the Association for Tourism and Leisure Education (ATLAS) Cultural Tourism Research Group meeting in Barcelona in 2005 (later published in Richards 2007), where differing responses to terms such as 'authenticity' made it evident that the context, just as much as the content, was important in analysing cultural tourism experiences. This implies that more attention will need to be paid to the relational aspects of cultural tourism: not just what cultural tourists, but also where, how and with whom they do it. The performance of cultural tourism, as Gernot Wolfram and Claire Burnill-Maier suggest here, is also moving from more scripted forms towards notions of framing and self-organised ritual.

Cultural tourism in contemporary society can therefore be seen as a closely related network of practices that combine the context, content and process through which experiences are produced and consumed. If in the past most research attention has been focused on the content of their experiences (what they consume and why), in the future it is likely that more attention will need to shift towards context (the places, spaces and events in which culture is embedded), and process (the ways in which experiences are co-created and how narratives emerge around different cultural tourism experiences).

This implies that we will also need to change the way we view cultural tourists. At the moment there is still a tendency to think about cultural tourists as an externally defined group. However, research is increasingly showing that the policy- and research-driven labels, such as 'cultural tourist', are not so clearly recognised by the tourists themselves. In addition to developing new labels, we may also have to rethink the boxes into which we currently try and squeeze cultural tourists. There is a tendency to think about them as belonging to particular national cultures, or cultural consumption styles, or visitor types. Again, though, research is beginning to show that many people insist on consuming 'outside the box', and mixing cultural tourism experiences in more co-creative, omnivorous and less easily measurable ways.

As Esther Binkhorst et al. (2010) have argued elsewhere, the rise of co-creation in tourism is forcing us to pay more attention to the holistic nature of cultural tourism experiences, and the way in which these are formed by rapidly shifting engagements between tourists, producers, places, 'locals', images, sights, sounds, tastes, etc. These engagements start long before travel begins, and end long after returning home. This makes research all the more complicated, because the traditional sites of data collection (whether at home or during travel) capture only a small fraction of the totality of experience.

Much is likely to be gained from adopting a practice-based approach to the study of (cultural) tourism, which, for example, can place the individual as the intersection of a series of practices which can take place at 'home' or during travel, which can link 'global' and 'local' culture, and which include a wide array of different forms of 'culture'. From a practice perspective we are concerned about the understandings, procedures and contexts of these forms of behaviour, which become routinised through their repetition over time by groups of people. Although the individual forms the intersection for a number of different practices, it is the social group that sustains the practice and generates the 'emotional energy' that makes it worthwhile undertaking cultural tourism and other forms of experience (Collins 2004). Because the generation of emotional energy is a collective endeavour, this means that the links between cultural tourists and between the tourists and their hosts become a vital focus of research. How are cultural tourists 'recruited' into particular practices such as visiting museums or seeking out 'hidden' corners of everyday life? How is the emotional energy attached to these experiences generated before, during and after travel?

Answering such questions will arguably lead us towards new modes of enquiry. As Bargeman and van der Poel (2006) have shown in the case of the Netherlands, tourist behaviour is very often constrained by the practice chains formed by previous holiday taking and links with travelling companions and local hosts. To uncover the 'interaction ritual chains' (Collins 2004) of cultural tourism, we will need to know much more about the way in which practices are formed and sustained, and how new participants are recruited to the practice. Why do some people abandon the beach in favour of the museum, and once recruited as cultural tourists, why do certain people then become 'voracious' consumers of culture on holiday? It is difficult to answer these questions using traditional modes of enquiry, and we may increasingly need to turn to tools such as online consumer panels, which can allow us to trace changes in cultural tourism over time. By understanding how cultural tourism experiences 'fit' into an individual's network of practices as a whole, we can begin to separate the serial cultural tourist from their more 'serendipitous' cousins (McKercher and du Cros 2002) and to understand the role that culture plays within different forms of mobility.

We can then also begin to focus on the relationship between mobility and sedentary behaviour, between 'cultural' and non-cultural forms of experience, and how people shift between these different modes. If cultural tourists are often seeking change (or seeking to be changed, as Erik Cohen discusses in this volume), then change should become a more important focus of research. What changes do people seek? To what extent do cultural tourism experiences change people? What are the memorable experiences? What are the factors influencing the degree of change produced by an experience? Who are the 'experience brokers' who can transform 'transformations' into marketable commodities? To what extent will the commodification of the transformation process lead to a further colonisation of the lifeworld? These and many other key questions form just the tip of an iceberg of research work that remains to be done in the coming decades.

## References

Bargeman, B. and van der Poel, H.J.J. (2006) 'The Role of Routines in the Vacation Decision-Making Process of Dutch Vacationers', *Tourism Management* 27(4): 707–720.

Binkhorst, E., den Dekker, T. and Melkert, M. (2010) 'Blurring Boundaries in Cultural Tourism Research', in Richards, G. and Munsters, W. (eds) *Cultural Tourism Research Methods*, Wallingford: CABI, 41–51.

Collins, R. (2004) *Interaction Ritual Chains*, Princeton, NKJ: Princeton University Press.

McKercher, B. and du Cros, H. (2002) *Cultural Tourism: The Partnership Between Tourism and Cultural Heritage Management*, New York: Haworth Press.

Richards, G. (2007) *Cultural Tourism: Global and Local Perspectives*, New York: Haworth Press.

# Index